Y0-AWH-503

The Story of The

Political Philosophers

OTHER BOOKS *by* GEORGE CATLIN

POLITICAL PHILOSOPHY

The Science and Method of Politics
The Principles of Politics
J. S. Mill's Subjection of Women (ed. and introd.)
Thomas Hobbes
Thomas Jefferson (in *Great Democrats*)

SOCIOLOGY

Liquor Control
Durkheim's Rules of Sociological Method (ed. and introd.)

POPULAR WRITINGS

Preface to Action
New Trends in Socialism (ed.)
Studies in War and Democracy (ed. with E. F. M. Durbin)
Anglo-Saxony and Its Tradition

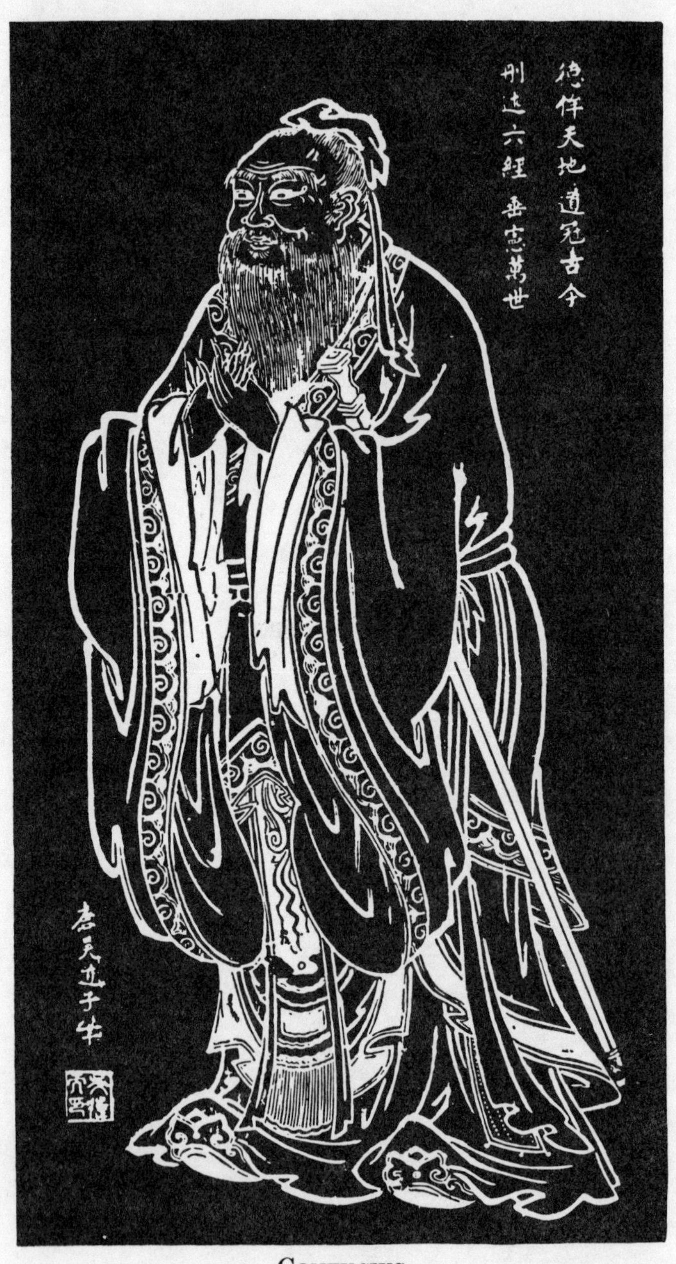
德侔天地道冠古今
刪述六經垂憲萬世
唐吳道子筆

CONFUCIUS
(551–479 B.C.)

The Story of The

Political Philosophers

by George Catlin

Author of *The Science and Method of Politics*,
The Principles of Politics, etc.

Volume 1

GORDON PRESS

NEW YORK
1976

JA
81
.C3
1976
vol. 1

GORDON PRESS—Publishers
P.O. Box 459
Bowling Green Station
New York, N.Y. 10004

Library of Congress Cataloging in Publication Data

Catlin, George Edward Gordon, Sir, 1896
The story of the political philosophers.

(Studies in political philosophy)
Reprint of the ed. published by Whittlesey House, New York.
Includes bibliographies and index.
1. Political science—History. I. Title.
JA81.C3 1976 320.9 75-44394
ISBN 0-87968-436-4

Printed in the United States of America

TO

H. G. W.

H. v. L.

encyclopaedists
humanists

Preface

IN THIS book I have endeavoured to provide a guide to political theory intelligible to the common reader, with quotations from the original sources sufficiently extensive to enable him to sample for himself the "taste" and "colour" of these writings. This history of theory has been placed against brief descriptions, as background, of the civilization of the times, as the reader passes down the avenues of thought from age to age.

The stress, however, is upon modern times and upon past thought and problems so far as they bear upon the rival philosophies of these times. The scholar will know that I have said nothing new—it is not my intention—but the student will, I hope, find the book sufficiently complete, even if it is a general public for which it is written, which requires some guidance in the adventure of living as citizens in these perilous, astounding and decisive days through which we are now passing.

I am well aware that too little attention is given here to, for example, Hooker and Burke, Coleridge and Kingsley, not to speak of Jurieu or Bayle or Condorcet, Southey or Disraeli. Reluctantly, from mere considerations of space, I have laid aside a manuscript chapter on Godwin, Shelley and Mary Wollstonecraft. They must wait for some other time. I have consoled myself with the thought that several of them will receive some attention in my *Anglo-Saxony and Its Tradition*, where I have tried to do in some slight manner for that tradition what M. Jacques Maritain has done so eminently for French Christian Humanism.

This present book is a history of political thought set against the background of the history of civilization. But that thought is also displayed in the setting of the characteristics and biographies of the thinkers, whose minds we search and whom we seek to know familiarly, however long ago gone to dust. Some light story about Plato tells us more of the prejudices of the philosopher, and, hence, of his own shaping of his own philosophy than a rotund and barbered phrase. The tale of Antisthenes walking with muddy feet on Plato's sumptuous carpets and remarking, "Thus do I trample on the pride of Plato," and of his interchange with Plato—"A horse [man] I see, but horsiness [humanity] I don't see." "That is because you have eyes but no intelligence"—tell me more than all of, for example, Cicero's dull, typical dictum, "Quid est enim civitas nisi iuris societas?" Moreover, although there is a dateless wisdom in the history of human thought, of recurrent validity, and although all is *not* relative and truth a fable, yet most thought is not so wise but that it is, not only conditioned, but even coloured by the time and place of the problem and the status and temperament of the thinker.

As I contemplate the work of my friend and late colleague, Professor Sabine of Cornell University; of Professors Cook and Coker and Dr. Joad—not to speak of Dunning and earlier writers ascending to Herder, as well as the great encyclopaedic works of Wells, Spengler and Van Loon—I am filled with humility about what I have rashly undertaken. Although, however, this book wears the fleece of a history of political philosophy, it is but fair that I should warn the reader that it is written as a philosophy of political history, a "tiger burning bright" at enmity with other current philosophies.

It discovers in the social history of mankind a certain agreement among rational men upon the objective good, upon the means of its expression in social life, and upon the arts of statesmanship and subterfuges of citizenship whereby this expression may be facilitated or frustrated. We discover, I have come to believe, a rational Grand Tradition of Culture and also (quite distinct) the beginnings of a Science of Politics. These may be our guides during these years of whirling confusion of values and of means, and of teachers pointing many ways. That philosophy I hope to develop more explicitly elsewhere. The first task, discussed in *The Principles of Politics*, has been one of method. The second, attempted here, has been to study the facts, including the facts of thought about the political acts. I have endeavoured to mount upon the bastion of three thousand years a searchlight that may project forward a ray for a few decades towards the horizon of the human future.

It should be added that the use of italics in material quoted in the text does not necessarily imply this use in the original. It is employed merely for the guidance of the eye. Readings are put at the end of some chapters, since they may be convenient to those who have the laudable intentions of reading the original texts. Other readers can ignore them. After hesitation, the system of recapitulation at the end of each chapter has not been adopted, as distracting to those whose interest is that of the general reader for pleasure.

Preface

Despite admonitions from my publishers, the spelling of proper names follows no special rule other than common usage where common usage seems to me to be decisive. Comments in square brackets are my own.

My debts are too numerous for specific acknowledgments. Some of them I have been able to note in the brief bibliographical lists, inserted for convenience rather than as a homage to learning, attached to the various chapters (in which books of especial interest to the common reader have been asterisked). Where books have gone through several editions, the date of publication is not inserted.

I am greatly indebted to Dr. C. H. McIlwain, Eaton Professor of the Science of Government, Harvard University; to Mr. R. H. S. Crossman, late Dean of New College, Oxford; to Mr. E. F. M. Durbin, of the London School of Economics; and to Dr. George Simpson, for most generously reading parts of the typescript of this book, for the faults of which they are, needless to say, in no wise responsible. I am also indebted to my indefatigable secretaries, Mrs. Katherine Nixon-Eckersall, for the preparation of the index, and Mrs. R. Drake, for checking the manuscript. Especially I wish to thank, for reading, for comments and for encouragement, my friend Professor H. H. Price, Wykeham Professor of Logic, University of Oxford, and, for my debts to him past and present, Dr. Ernest Barker, Burton Professor of Political Science, University of Cambridge. To my views and to my more extravagant endeavours to shake the shoulders of the common reader, they, of course, stand quite uncommitted. I hope, however, that I have not let the common reader off too lightly. One part of my task will have been fulfilled if I have held his interest, in what I humbly believe it to be to his interest to know.

George Gordon Catlin.

Acknowledgments

The author wishes to acknowledge the kindness of the following publishers and authors in permitting the use of quotations from material of which they control the copyrights.

Henry Holt and Company and Thornton Butterworth, Ltd.: J. L. Myres, *Dawn of History*.

G. P. Putnam's Sons and Constable & Company, Ltd.: F. A. Voigt, *Unto Caesar*.

Alfred A. Knopf, Inc., and Victor Gollancz, Ltd.: G. D. H. Cole, *What Marx Really Meant*.

Harper & Brothers and Faber & Faber, Ltd.: H. J. Laski, *Liberty in the Modern State*.

University of North Carolina Press and George Allen and Unwin, Ltd.: H. J. Laski, *Democracy in Crisis*.

Fabian Society: H. J. Laski, *Socialism and Freedom*.

Random House, Inc., and Victor Gollancz, Ltd.: John Strachey, *What Are We To Do?*

John Strachey and Modern Age Books, Inc.: John Strachey, *Hope in America*.

Ivor Nicholson & Watson, Ltd.: George Catlin, *Great Democrats*.

H. G. Wells and The Macmillan Co.: H. G. Wells, *Men Like Gods*.

The B. V. F.: Oswald Mosley, *Greater Britain*.

Harcourt, Brace & Company, Inc.: Morris R. Cohen, *Law and the Social Order*.

Golden Cockerel Press: Sappho poem by Poseidippus, from *The Greek Anthology*.

Contents

Preface ix

Acknowledgments xiii

List of Illustrations xvii

PART I

I. Introductory 3

II. Plato 35

III. Aristotle 72

IV. The Hellenistic Age and the Coming of Rome . . . 105

V. The Roman Law and the Christian Fathers 126

VI. The Middle Ages 146

VII. Renaissance and Reformation 187

VIII. Thomas Hobbes 221

PART II

IX. Locke and the Social Contract 259

X. The American and French Revolutions: Montesquieu, Jefferson, Burke and Paine 300

XI. The Early Utilitarians: Jeremy Bentham 342

XII. The Later Utilitarians: James and John Stuart Mill 381

XIII. Individualists and Anarchists 405

PART III

XIV. Jean Jacques Rousseau 435

XV. Georg Hegel 475

XVI. The Post-Hegelian Conservatives: Carlyle to Bosanquet 497

XVII. The Post-Hegelian Conservatives: Treitschke . . . 525

XVIII. Marx and His Predecessors 543

XIX. Kautsky, Lenin, Trotsky, Stalin 602

XX. Laski and Strachey 649

XXI. Internationalism and Fascism: Benito Mussolini, Adolf Hitler 700

PART IV

XXII. Conclusion and Prospect 745

Index 785

List of Illustrations

FACING PAGE

Confucius (551–479 B.C.) . . . . Frontispiece

Aristotle (384–322 B.C.). 74

Niccolò Machiavelli (1469–1527 A.D.). 192

John Locke (1632–1704) 282

Jeremy Bentham (1748–1832). 356

Speculum Mentis or Political Mirror. 404

Georg Wilhelm Friedrich Hegel (1770–1831). 480

Bertrand Arthur William Russell (1872–). 756

Part I

Chapter I

Introductory

1

If man's proper study is man, politics is especially his concern since it is the study of the control of man. Like chemistry and the natural sciences, but also like economics, politics is a study based on observation of the way things actually happen. It is a study also of how to gain control over these things. It is a study of power. But, like the humanities, it involves discussion and assessment of values. The first of these fields is that of political science. The second is that of political philosophy.

The two subjects together are Politics, which is the study of the control of creatures who have will and choice—or, more exactly, who have some energy of will and some range of choice, however limited by instinctive impulses, rational checks and material determinants. Politics, then, is something very much wider than the study of the State, which is a recent social form. It is the study of social relationships and of the human (and even non-human) social structure. It is nothing less. It is identical with Sociology.

In the Renaissance of the fifteenth century the interest of students, and of those mentally alive, centered upon the Humanities and upon the assessment of human values as touching the art and ends of living, as distinct from the logical proofs about these ends offered by those great reasoners, the Schoolmen. In the seventeenth and until the nineteenth century, men were preoccupied with their discoveries in Mathematics, the inorganic Physical Sciences and Biology. They were stimulated by the hope of effecting control of Nature. As in Ancient Greece, so in the Modern World, to the epic period, when man sang of his own life, had succeeded the age of the physicists, when men inquired into the world without. Moreover, the contemporary Despots were not always benevolent to those who pried into politics and secrets of state. Astronomy was much safer. With the twentieth century has come an overwhelming interest in the Social Sciences: in Economics or the study of the relation of man and material in the pursuit of wealth; in Genetics or the study of the relation of man and man in their generations in the pursuit of health; and in Politics or the study of will and will in the relationship of power.

Politics has become the overwhelming interest of our own generation, since it is becoming ever more acutely realized that man who has made such strides in the conquest of nature has, by reason of prejudice and passion, lingered behind in the conquest of man himself and his civilization; and that this weakness may have consequences fraught with catastrophe. A man may decide that he is uninterested in poetry and art or in chemistry and mathematics and no one may be the loser save himself nor will anyone trouble him. But, although a man may decide that he is uninterested in politics and may prefer to have the provincial mind, the practice of politics will not be uninterested in him, whether in peace or in war. If he will not pull his weight, he will most certainly be pulled.

The organization of our human life is perhaps a negligible matter, an idiotic gesture of self-importance, in the perspective of eternity. It is said that beyond the constellation of the Sculptor, a new group of stars has been discovered, estimated to be 250,000,000 light years away. The speed of light, however, is that of the ether wave. More tardy is that of a broadcast message which, dispatched at one instant, will yet circle this earth and be received again two-fifteenths of a second later. In such immensities of the universe, not only any individual among the 1,900,000,000 inhabitants of the earth, but the human race itself shrinks to less than the worm that is man, told of in the Bible. It is impossible to attach importance to a race, related in animal origins to the lemur and tree-creeping spectral tarsier; a descendant of one of several branches of speaking anthropoids who lived over 300,000 years ago; who emerges in the late Pleistocene Age, about 25,000 years ago, his fortune literally in his mobile hand and in that tongue attachment of the jaw; and whose 5,000 years of recorded history counts for only a few seconds in the day-clock of the history of this subsidiary planet. He descended from the trees or emerged, troglodyte, from the caves to which, in this last decade, in time of war he again returns. Or it would be impossible to attach importance, were not he who knew all this precisely an individual man, himself astronomer or archaeologist.

Before the majesty and the potential power involved in this knowledge, the dynastic wars of kings, the fights of Guelph and Ghibelline, of Montagu and Capulet, the party faction of Whig and Tory, even of Catholic and Protestant, even of Fascist and Marxist, seem to become fantastic squabbles of ill-tempered children. What alone seems, in this perspective, to matter is science, the limitless increase of the knowledge that is power, its significance for increasing the power of the human race and for improving its breed, the passionless mood of the man of science, in brief, the enlargement of Civilization, of which this knowledge is the seal like the signet of Solomon. Was Faust concerned with the politicians? Or Buddha or Christ with party membership? Were they "dividers of goods"? Is not civilization, progress, science itself endangered by these lethal factions? If there were a war, would it not be good for men of science to conspire to kill off the politicians? In the perspective of knowledge is not politics abysmally unimportant, on a level with incantations and witchcraft?

Throughout the millennia there is detectable a conflict between interest in Civilization and interest in Human Happiness or, again, between the interest of Society and the interest of justice for the Individual. In each case, the two are inseparable; but the stress is different. The trouble is that the advance of civilization, of the sciences and arts, has been due not only, or chiefly, to pure speculation or to disinterested love of beauty, but to motives of utility and to the desire for an effect upon the glory of some group or in furthering the ambition of some man. The humanist and philosopher could not, if he would, cut himself adrift from these passions and contest, nor does it help to call them battles of kites and crows. As Aristotle said: Intellect alone moves nothing.

The quarrel is not about who is to know, but about who is to enjoy. In this quarrel we all count among the ill-tempered children, seeking a material share-out favourable to ourselves or explaining that Civilization matters nothing to us if we are not to satisfy our own appetite by eating the fruits of its achievement, grown on the tree of knowledge. Good men in their own eyes feel themselves called upon to organize physical force to prevent bad men from attaining power—and rightly, for, as Plato pointed out, this is the only reason why a good man should engage in politics and seek power and dominion. Having, however, become preoccupied in strife, it may easily happen that the *clerici* and men of science forget their learning and that the torch of science is extinguished amid the animal conflicts of these risen apes that are men, as that torch for one thousand years in Europe was almost extinguished before, save in a few monasteries, during the last of those Dark Ages that appear periodically to descend on the world.

The appetites of man, the ape, on the one hand, and the non-attached pursuit of power over nature, through science, on the other hand, are not easily to be reconciled. As the clash between the claims of immediate Happiness and of Civilization, this constitutes the first problem of politics. It involves economic justice in the distribution of the fruits of a science fertile in applications, so that the health and power are increased of the race itself and so that there is not poverty in the midst of plenty.

The initiative, liberty and high hope, beyond conventions of good and evil, that fertilize science itself, on the one hand, and the discipline and morality that strengthen allegiance to a society and its culture, or to the concept of human civilization throughout the centuries, on the other hand, are not easily reconciled. As the clash between Liberty and Authority, this constitutes the second problem of politics.

The art and practice of politics have examples that can be gathered, like examples from business practice, over the five millennia of recorded history. *The science of politics*, on the other hand, like that of economics, is so immature as scarcely to be born. Politicians, like evil stepmothers, have stood at its cradle, ready to suffocate it, the saviour of our civilization. Nevertheless, the pace of history moves ever more rapidly. The nemesis of wilful ignorance comes. Biological time moves more quickly than geological time. Economic change may radically affect biological development; and economic change has its own time scale. That change may be controlled by human knowledge, but the Ancient World in large part fell to ruin in the Occident from lack of adequate economic knowledge alike in agriculture and in taxation. This control, however, is a concern, not only of the economists, but of the politicians who can frustrate the wisest experts. And who shall control the politicians? Who shall educate their masters? It is Bernard Shaw who says of political science that it is "the science by which alone civilization can be saved."

Lord Kelvin, the natural scientist, said, in describing the nature of scientific knowledge:

> When you can measure what you are speaking about, and express it in numbers, you know something about it; but when you cannot measure it, when you cannot express it in numbers, your knowledge is of a meagre and unsatisfactory kind: it may be the beginning of knowledge, but you have scarcely, in your own thoughts, advanced to the stage of *science*, whatever the matter may be.

Sir Arthur Thomson continues:

> It is very interesting that Clerk Maxwell should speak in one sentence of "those aspirations after accuracy in measurement, and justice in action, which we reckon among our noblest attributes in men!"

Professor A. North Whitehead states: "Science was becoming, and has remained, primarily quantitative. Search for measurable elements among your phenomena, and then search for relations between these measures of physical quantity." "The scientific man," writes Karl Pearson, "has to strive at self-elimination in his judgements." Nor shall we disagree when an eminent Marxist, Professor Levy, speaking of social matters, says: "The results of measurement will be entirely independent of any religious, ethical or social bias."

The art of politics throughout the ages provides instances of recurrent social behaviour and of the constancy of psychological reactions. Mass observations of social phenomena increasingly approximate to objectivity of judgement and to verifiable measurement. Sociology today perfects this technique. Nevertheless, there are those who will put aside this book with the unreasoned assertion that detached judgement of means in social matters is impossible; and others again who will, for their own reasons, deny that it is desirable. Political science is still embryonic, because its development has been too dangerous to the powers that be; and because man's indolence prefers habitual thought and rhetoric to technical thought that gives, not *belles-lettres*, but power and control.

Political philosophy, however, with its appraisals of social ends, has matured over two millennia. It may be said by the practical man of affairs that, in that time, it has made small advance. Neither have the human judgements on the beautiful and the good. It is yet no small matter to make a survey, through the ages, of the history of human society where it has been touched up to luminousness and self-consciousness in the greatest reflective minds of each epoch. Philosophy is a critical revision, ever going on, of tradition in the light of current experience. Thus we study history, not from the angle of heaped-up granules of fact, but from that of the evaluating intelligence. We view the drama, in each age, through the eyes of the greatest minds of that time. We shall, however, in this book forget neither the background, in the history of mass forces, nor the personal foibles that colour the views of these philosophers. We shall arrive at a conspectus of the history of civilization in terms of the thoughts of the men who thought about it. We shall cite their words. Thus far, at least, we shall reach objectivity, if in no other way. If their evaluations differ, we shall reflect that the essence of education lies, as Diderot said, in the stirring of doubt and of wonder.

In some cases these philosophies of social action, and of individual action in society, will be found to have arisen, reflectively and after the event, to justify action to reason and conscience. Such is the case of the social philosophy of John Locke in its relation to the English Revolution of 1688–1689. In other cases the philosophy provokes and shows the way to action. Such is the case with Locke's philosophy, through its influence on Jefferson, in its relation to the American Revolution. Writings of a philosopher, such as Locke, unsuited by their style and close reasoning to stir action, mediated by a man of letters, such as Voltaire, himself in turn publicized in his ideas by a journalist, such as Brissot, can have popular and revolutionary effect. We note the same thing in the influence of the writings of Aquinas upon Catholic conduct and of Marx upon Communist conduct.

The survey of the thought of these thinkers may be more than an educational enrichment, a leisured feast of reason. It may not only be itself a piece of civilization: it may have utility by enlarging civilization. We may be able, by the survey of the history of philosophy, to reinforce our philosophy of history and to strengthen political science. We may perhaps detect, among the opinions of the thinkers, certain recurrent themes and a leitmotiv. We may find traditions in thought, or a Grand Tradition of culture with variants. That may provide, not merely antique analogies and far-away critics, but a norm and canon whereby to judge new theories. We may recognize these novelties as indeed new explorations of old workings, which human experience has, with good cause, marked "no thoroughfare." Or we may find that hopeful experiments of the past, under modern conditions, have novel chances of success. Neither Communism nor Fascism will seem to us in all their characteristics entirely new. The advocacy, again, of the class war has been accepted and tried out before. But the Industrial or Mechanical Revolution, the Discovery of Electricity and the Control of Population introduce new differentiae with wide-spread, unprecedented effects.

This human philosophy and tradition are not to be traced only in literary exercises put together by fallible men. A valuable distinction can be made between Political Theory and Political Thought. *Political Theory* consists of such set treatises. But *Political Thought* is twofold and earlier. In part, it is a matter of the popular proverbs of the day. In this sense every man is a political thinker, even although he goes no further than to repeat the rhyme:

> When Adam delved and Eve span,
> Who was then the gentleman?

The common man cannot avoid having political thoughts. Untrained, however, there is no guaranty that his common-sense opinions may not be uncommon nonsense. Further, there is an even more primitive thought, less articulate and of which no record remains, but which we may legitimately conjecture from the institutions of a people of which we have record or the buildings that house those institutions which are their own record.

We may believe, with the philosopher Benedetto Croce, that "the chief meaning of history is the victory of freedom." Or we may have a different interpretation of this history of human thought about social action, which is political theory, in this dramatic and tragic age when we hesitate, about to enter the phase of the cycle of history which is analogous to the Empire of the Caesars—but still conscious of free will and of the right to create anew. The glory of the Renaissance was its explorers, stimulating an age to new thought by opening up vast vistas in geographic space and conjecturing the unknown from the known. The Columbus of today must stimulate adventure in ideas by surveying historic areas in time of economic and social organization; and so must move on, through record of revolution, to a prognostication and view and control of things to come.

2

The early historical, the proto-historical and pre-historical periods of the human race are epochs of what may be termed *Frozen Political Thought.* Man lived a social life—a social life more enveloping even than he was to live later. There is adequate evidence that he thought, reflectively, about this life and meditated upon its requirements and suppositions. But, in these days before social maxims were written down in Sacred Books or in Mosaic Ten Commandments, the political thought of a time must be conjectured from the analysis of the institutions of the age, of which we have either record or material remains in the institutional buildings. Into these institutions, as it were moulds, the thought of the time congealed. At least equally frequently, however, this thought is rather secreted by the friction in the functioning of the institutions.

The more primitive the society, the more completely are the institutions shaped by the hammer of the simplest vital needs for food beating upon the anvil of rock and land and geographic configuration determining economic supply. As Professor Myres says, in *The Dawn of History,* speaking of the pastoral phase of civilization when (in Aristotle's phrase) man "cultivated a migratory farm":

> Under these circumstances, industry can hardly pass beyond the replacement of things worn out or lost; and these are all things which anyone can

make and everyone does, if he cannot pass on the task to another: and as everyone can and does make everything as it is needed, exchange of products and specialization of skill are alike out of the question. The raw material is always to hand, so that there is no use in accumulating it in advance; and to manufacture in advance of demand is simply to cumber the baggage each time the camp is moved on. . . .

The institutions of pastoral peoples are of the simplest. Everywhere these societies have been observed to consist of small compact groups of actual relatives, each living as a single "patriarchal family" without other apparatus of government. The "patriarchal family" consists of a father, some mothers—the number of these depends principally on the supply—and some other animals and children.

This type of human society, with its state limited to a single family, its government vested in a single elderly man, and its conception of women and children as desirable kinds of highly domesticated animals, is simply man's ancient and habitual clothing, in a political sense, against a particular kind of weather. It will wear indefinitely and unchangeably as long as external conditions remain the same; and it will begin to wear out, and be discarded, in the event of any serious change.

In lands, however, suitable rather for hunting than for pasturage, the man, as hunter, goes off by himself, returning in due course to a particular spot. The children cannot keep up, and the family lives on roots or berries or, at a later time, on the cultivated "fruits of the earth." Cain's wife becomes the first agriculturalist; and agriculture, unlike hunting and shepherding, is a woman's job. At a later stage, the seed grain is scattered on the mud of rivers' banks and the river becomes the father of the land.

Certain societies, although not all, pass through an early so-called "matriarchal stage." In many cases this word is a misnomer, for the woman does not "rule." Merely, on the Roman law principle of *pater incertus*, the institution of marriage not yet being fully established, lineage traces through her. The man to whom the younger generation looks up is the maternal uncle. In the Malabar Coast a man mourns more ceremoniously for his maternal uncle than he does for his own father. Often the husband on marriage (Beena type) comes into the family of his wife. More rarely, as among the Iroquois Indians, who are huntsmen, the elder women as the guardians of the stable encampment, have become genuine matriarchs. They, not merely the maternal uncle, decide issues. The chief rules by their assent.

Sir Henry Maine, in his book *Ancient Law*, took his examples too exclusively from two areas, Europe, especially Rome with its "paternal power" (*patria potestas*), and India. Nevertheless, as agriculture spreads, a change takes place. The matriarchal type of family yields to the patriarchal. Rule increasingly is in the hands of the eldest "agnate" or male relative. In marriage (Baal type) the wife joins her husband's family. But social organization has spread beyond the family to the clan. The eldest male may be judge and priest and ruler, but he is not therefore always fitted to be war-lord. Moreover, matriarchy with its stable *hearth* has not merely yielded to the society typified by the *shepherd-king*. On the contrary, with the spread of agriculture and when the huntsman stays at home, it is the hearth that wins, as symbol of the unity of the clan and tribe, against the solitary hunter's individualism and the nomadism of pastoral peoples. The hearth, as de Coulanges shows in his *Cité Antique*, wins and its ritual. As clan replaces family, priest replaces mother; but the ritual remains as strong or stronger in its binding force. Survival requires "the brave," the leader of the war-expedition, the *dux* or *duce* or *duke*. But survival also requires cohesion and the *priest-king* of his people, "the sacred King."

In a small community, like that of which Sir James Fraser tells us around Italian Nemi, the priest-king rules until another comes to challenge, kill and replace him. The priest-kingship never grows old and dies; but each incarnation is sacrificed for the good of the people. So the lives of the early Pharaohs were overshadowed by this demand for their periodic human sacrifice, *because* divine and symbolic of the whole people, to appease the gods of the land. The sense of guilt and the need for ascetic discipline, *if* the tribe is to survive, grip the people. When, however, a large community grows up, as that which the Nile united into Egypt, an organized priesthood develops. Its members have no intention of being personally sacrificed, "lest the people perish." As in Aztec Mexico, slaves or foreigners could be found for that purpose or, as in Carthage, children. Nor need the dilemma any longer be faced of priest-king *or* war-lord. The war-lord or Pharaoh can be one of the priests, hereditary and one of the greatest but, nevertheless, powerless against the priestly institution.

The Divine Kingship is one of the earliest and one of the most persistent of institutions in human civilization. Sometimes, as with the high priests and the kings of Israel, the pontiffs and the consuls of Rome, the Popes and the kings of Europe, the priestly and royal offices divide (although seldom entirely). But in China the Emperor has always been the Son of Heaven; in Persia the kings were god-descended and even today are inspired directly by Allah; in the Babylonian cities reigned the priest-kings; in Egypt Pharaoh was god; the *rex* in Rome and the *basileus* in Athens held priestly office; in

Imperial Rome Caesar was god in death, divine Augustus; even the petty Gothic kings were descended from Odin; in Peru the Inca rulers were priests; to this day the Mikado is priest and god. These have been the symbols of community alone powerful and august enough to battle against the disruptive egoism of the human ape. They were symbols of conservative strength against disruptive scepticism and individual innovating initiative.

Priest-kingship was not an isolated institution. It was often part of a massive socialist organization of the community, although a socialism functional, pyramidical (not democratic-equalitarian) in structure, based on massed slave labour. In Peru, the Proto-Chimu culture from about 200 B.C. is succeeded by a dark age from A.D. 500–1100. Our records are inadequate about the social structure of this civilization; but of the succeeding Inca civilization we know that the socialistic-paternal form obtained, under which the labourer had security. In turn, however, he worked, if in part for himself, in part for the Inca ruler and for the gods. In Egypt the records are ample. Analogies between Egypt and Peru are hazardous and a quite inadequate basis for any assertion that human culture passes through a common cursus or cycle of civilization. But the temples of Egypt and Pharaoh are the great landowners; and, in this system of landownership, the peasant has assurance of tenure. Ships voyage from the Nile to Syrian Byblos carrying goods furnished by the Egyptian government in order to procure, in return, cedar-wood for the temples. The civilization massively endures, based upon cheap slave labour and forced labour. It is significant that the first great monument of human civilization is a grave, costing the death of thousands of slaves. It is a memorial connected with the death of a king, the Pharaoh Kheops, in ca. 3900 B.C., but asserting and assuring his immortality. It is the symbol, *aere perennius*, of the immortality of the community in which he was god-king.

Between 6000 and 3000 B.C. man has learned, in the area between Nile and Indus, in addition to the making of fire and clothes and cooked food and stone weapons, to harness the force of oxen and winds, to use the plough (with the male ploughman), the wheeled cart, the potter's wheel, and the sailing boat. Bricks were invented. By 3000 B.C. cotton is being grown in the Indus Valley and wool is used in Mesopotamia. Copper is being smelted in the East by about 4000 B.C. Perhaps in 4236 B.C. or perhaps in 2776 B.C. the Egyptian calendar, connected with the rising of Sirius, with all its implications for calculation of the Nile flood and Egyptian agriculture, begins. Priest-kings know the calendar. But along with these developments and the demand for a richer, more settled agricultural life, often involving concerted irrigation, goes the need for, and recognition of, a stronger cohesive authority.

Cities arise from India to the Nile. They do this, moreover, at about the same time and perhaps for reasons not disconnected. By 1500 B.C. learned men were travelling from Egypt to Mesopotamia, and employing one literary writing, a cuneiform script. The god of the city, for example in Babylonia, and his priest-king and priests, had a complex economy to supervise, involving accountancy. The god was the first saver or capitalist who could afford to go beyond subsistence to bedeck civilization with ornament and luxury. In Erech (Babylonia) before 3000 B.C. the first figures and writing on tablets are used to keep these temple accounts. Literacy has begun and the privileged position of the priestly scribe and *clericus*. In Egypt arises Thebes, as Homer says, "with mighty stores of wealth, a hundred gates."

A papyrus of the early New Kingdom in Egypt (ca. sixteenth century B.C.) contains the advice:

> I have seen the metal-worker at his task at the mouth of his furnace with fingers like a crocodile. He stank worse than fish-spawn. Every workman who holds a chisel suffers more than the men who hack the ground; wood is his field and the chisel his mattock. . . . Put writing in your heart that you may protect yourself from hard labour of any kind and be a magistrate of high repute. The scribe is released from manual tasks; it is he who commands.

It is a very early illustration of class snobbery for the most practical of reasons. It has its antithesis in a voice from a simpler civilization:

> Publish in the palaces in the land of Egypt . . . they know not to do right who store up violence and robbery in their palaces . . . that lie on beds of ivory and stretch themselves upon their couches. (*Amos*, 3: 6; ca. 760 B.C.)

The scientific inventions spring from the *practical* arts and from labour-saving devices. In such devices scribes able to employ forced labour—not machine labour but slave labour—had small interest. Rather their interest was to consolidate, even by keeping learning secret, their own power. Not the Egyptian priest, with his hieroglyphs (*sacred* script), but the Phoenician trader moved on to the invention and use of the alphabet.

The very binding force of the religious tradition in Egypt, hard-shelled and crustacean, while consolidating the community as homogeneous, suppressed invention and initiative and culture. Its effect was to check the adaptability of man and to stunt his cultured evolution even by the very magnificence and grandeur of its protective devices. It is perhaps for this reason that the private tombs of dynastic Egypt have a poetic interest that is lacking in the overwhelming size of the temples which annihilate man before their massiveness. The values of the sublime and immemorial confront the values of the beautiful and of the intelligent. Egypt used up inventions rather than renewed them. It gave a stagnant security to its workers. A static civilization, with its demands, stands over against all impulse to enlarge the happiness of the common mass by the routes of invention and of the devices that make for personal freedom.

Migration, commerce, conquest under warrior-kings involve a clash of cultures and serve to break up the cake of custom in the profoundly conservative, pious, ritualistic, socialistic, paternal, priest-ruled societies with their peculiar economic systems. The merchants are the innovators, where sheer economic need does not force invention on the pious timidity and natural indolence of man. After all, if the psychologists are right, the use of intelligence is not natural to man but very unnatural, due to pain and some breakdown in a happy, indolent social equilibrium. Mind itself is a painful, disease-like product of the struggle for survival—as Lord Balfour said, like the pig's snout, a food-finder.

In about 2525 B.C. Sargon of Akkad, as a military ruler, united Babylonia. Later the Assyrian and Hittite empires (as also the Persian and still later the Tatar and Turkish) are to be examples of primarily military, mechanical, non-organic empires, symbolized by the recruiting-sergeant and press-gang and by the tax-gatherer. Such empires, unlike the priestly kingdoms, were normally autocratic monarchies, whose rulers sprang from warlike folk in a more backward state of culture, living in lands where man had been less stimulated by the vagaries and wealth of nature to inventive resourcefulness. These military empires gave a peace of desolation; but there is little indication that they, when consolidated, any more than the priestly—indeed even less—advanced invention or new forms of material civilization (even when amassing a concentrated wealth), save in the art of war, or promoted more humane standards of conduct.

Where, however, the conquering peoples settle down in the land (as the Aryan invaders in India) and make it their own, they invoke religious sanctions to sanctify an authority founded on force. A new stable society of castes is, later, set up ranging from priest and warrior to slave, from pure Brahmin to outcast, in which the religious myth is that each performs a special function, in his station to which the gods have called him hereditarily, within the total society. The Caste Myth, like Priest-kingship, is one of the more firmly seated traditions of human history. It fuses mere force with specific social function and finds a sanction in the will of the gods, *i.e.*, in those very influences that make, *against violence*, for peace and stability. In a less marked form than in India the caste system appears in Egypt (but not in China). We shall later note the influence of its implicit "philosophy of function" on Plato.

It is not to be supposed that the priestly oligarchies remained unchallenged or were challenged only from without or by ambitious warrior-kings within. In some cases the reduction by law to writing is purely an affair of convenience. In these cases (as with the earliest Anglo-Saxon law codes) it is merely a matter of memoranda on the customary tariff of fines. So much to be paid for a broken head. . . . In other cases (as with the Hindu sacred Laws of Manu, ca. A.D. 500 or later) a priesthood may have sought to increase its own power by outlining in sacred writ—and writing itself is here a priestly, magic art—an ideal system. But in other cases there is reason to suppose opposition to the reduction to writing of the immemorial unwritten tradition; and it only takes place because a faction is challenging the current interpretation of the ritual tradition of the ancestors, "the silent ones," and is demanding the almost profane step of codification.

Another challenge may be made to priestly morality from a quarter that is less connected with sectional resentment and suspicion. A heretic king may arise, such as Amenhotep IV (Akhenaten) of Egypt. Prophets may denounce an empty ritual as did the Hebrew prophets, especially in ca. 800 B.C. Buddhism owes its origin to an Indian prince, Sakyamuni (560–480 B.C.), who carried one stage further the speculations, against the background of the Hindu Nature-religion, of the Brahmin metaphysicians and who led one of the greatest of all religious secessions. A route away from the oppressions and injustices in caste-organized society was found in the theme that, from individual contemplation of ultimate Being, the individual might, without social ritual, save himself. By study of "the noble, Aryan Path," and perception of the claim of inevitable cause and consequence, the way was found to disinterestedness or non-attachedness to pain-breeding, egoistic desire.

The Buddhist sage strove for neither power nor wealth—was a monk, pacifist, communist, mendicant. He was uninterested in war and in calls of "justice and honour" between nations. He was uninterested in money and in "social justice" as a matter of dividing wealth between men. He was uninterested in "liberty" and caste position or servitude or emancipation. He was uninterested even in the striving to perpetuate human life, whether of the individual or the species. Bliss was Nirvana, which is the recognition of the identity of ultimate Being with that which has no differential characteristics and is also Not-being. The Self discovers itself by its right to contemplate Reality and, thereby, has peace. And the Self, merging in Reality, ceases to seek to perpetuate the separated Self. The perfection of the goodwill is the end of striving. That was the practical message; nor was primitive Buddhism interested in any talk of gods or spirits, immortality or sacred writings, that had no bearing on this emancipation *in this life and in this world.*

The problem in civilization of how to preserve at once acceptance of authority, which binds men together, and the mood of liberty, curiosity and initiative, which is the matrix of material invention, is solved. Authority is indifferent to the saint who passively obeys; and material invention and lust for the tools of power are also interests without real importance. Buddhism is the beginning of individualism as against the Brahminical Nature-worship; but it is also its end, since the new consciousness of personal value leads out to no material consequences. It revolves within itself. Only the goodwill matters, liberated and non-attached. This doctrine, religious (although denying personal gods) and philosophical, of the monastic contemplative self, perpetually recurs as an undertone amid the chorus of the philosophies of Society and Tradition, of the gods of the land and of the divine kings of their people, whether worshipped in Tokyo or in Egyptian Thebes. It is as extreme and transcendental a doctrine of *soul liberty* as the unvarying worship of Pharaoh, the priest of his people, implies a doctrine of *social authority.*

The extremes omit the mean of mundane, material, orderly advance in the conquest of power for humanity. Neither in India nor in Egypt do thinkers concern themselves with the mundane, day-by-day conduct of human affairs in a fashion that is useful to the common mass and, because useful to man, perhaps obligatory on men. Under Buddhism civilization and social life are alike regarded as a seduction, an opulent veil of illusion. In Egypt moral obligation is to this agelong Civilization; and not to the contemporary Human Society. Where their interests clash Civilization comes first. The conception is essentially priestly. What matters is *not* human happiness at the time, but immortality with the gods in the unpassing glory of their temples. The first Utilitarians are to be found in China, whose classic thinkers based conduct upon useful ritual, and obligation upon that which preserved through the ages the life and fair name of each man's own family—father and mother and grandparents, with their shrine blessed by the spirits of the locality.

3

The civilization of China, using the ox, the plough and the potter's wheel, in the days of the Chou dynasty (1122–248 B.C.), centered on the Hoang-Ho or Yellow River. It is uncertain whether the Chinese reached these lands, including Shantung, by following the course of the great river from the West or from the South. Japan was unheard of or was rumoured as a land of dwarfs. Buddhism had not yet arrived from India. The lands on either side of the Yangtze were still areas of reed-covered swamp amid which barbarian tribes were beginning to set up some primitive government. A chief of the land of Chu, here, boasted that "I am only a barbarian savage and do not concern myself with Chinese titles"—but added that his ancestor had been suckled by a tigress. However, self-sufficient and proudly conscious of already over a thousand years of culture, the emperors of China held court in Loyang in Shantung. In the sixth century the policy of the Chou dynasty of extending their borders against primitive barbarism, by giving autonomous power to their nobility and even suffering the erection of castles, had issued in a feudal epoch. Fifty-two rulers, all in nominal and ceremonial allegiance to the Sacred Emperors, contended among themselves. It was not until 221 B.C. that the Emperor Chi Wang-ti endeavoured to inaugurate an improved civilization by his famous Burning of the Books. The force of tradition, however, prevailed against him.

CONFUCIUS (K'ung Fu-tze or Master Kung) was born, an ugly child with a wen on its head, in the feudal duchy of Lu, in Shantung, in 551 B.C. about the time that Nebuchadnezzar died in Nineveh. He was the son of a soldier, poor but of ancient lineage, by his second wife (the first wife having presented him with daughters only and a mistress with a cripple), espoused by him at the age of seventy. The earliest historians speak of the marriage as not a ceremonial one and, hence, of Confucius as illegitimate. The father dying, the boy was brought up by his widowed mother—a woman singularly free from beliefs in spirits and omens—and displayed in his earliest years a specialist's interest in ceremonial. Matter-of-fact outlook, absence of superstition concerning "the other world," punctilious concern with the art of living in this world were to remain the characteristics of the great teacher. China was a land of no Sacred Books. Confucius contributed only classical writings.

At the age of seventeen Confucius obtained employment in the baronial family of Chi, as an estate supervisor and tithe collector. He married and had a son from whom a numerous progeny traces to this day; but there is no reason to suppose that the marriage was a success and there is a tradition that tells of an early divorce. Of his parents, unusually enough in the case of the Chinese, he is recorded to have spoken scarcely at all; but he built them a tomb and, on that occasion, significantly enough declared, "I am a man who belongs equally to the north and the south, the east and the west. I must have something by which I can remember this place." His relatives abstained from becoming his disciples.

On his mother's death he decided to become a scholar, a *clerc*. His knowledge of ritual brought him to the attention of the ducal ministers. It was improved by a visit to the court at Loyang of the Chou emperors. And it moulded the teaching that he offered at the various feudal courts when he went into exile with his duke, and during the years of exile that followed. He found, however, in his wanderings that, oddly enough, despite knowledge, he was not loved by other scholars. Before all, Confucius was a political philosopher, his individual ethics and his views on religion being elaborations of his beliefs concerning the due conduct of society.

Unlike Lao-tze, "the Old Philosopher," the mystic and individualist, Confucius rejected the doctrines of non-resistance, non-interference and flight from the world, with their implications of a philosophic anarchism, trust in intuitive guidance and distrust of government, that have so pleased recent philosophers, such as Bertrand Russell, who have visited China. The godlike philosopher of Ritualism and of Morality *comme il faut*, all these years ago Confucius sought to refute the doctrine of the free, fantastic scamp which Mr. Lin Yutang has recently expounded so pleasantly.

Lao-tze, on the contrary, held that Power is the root of vice. "Only that government has value which is in accord with Nature or the *Tao* (or *logos*, Reason). All other civilization is corrupt error." A disciple of Lao-tze continued:

> In the days when natural instincts prevailed, men moved quietly and gazed steadily. . . . But when sages appeared, tripping people up over charity and fettering them with duty to one's neighbour, doubt found its way into the world. . . . Destruction of the natural integrity of things, in

order to produce articles of various kinds—this is the fault of the artisan. Annihilation of *Tao* [intuitive wisdom] in order to organize charity and duty to one's neighbour—that is the error of the Sage.

The animadversion is directed against Confucius; it is he who is "the Sage." The issue, basic in thought, to this day remains an unsettled enigma. To it we shall return.*

The corruption of contemporary politics was the pre-occupation of Confucius and the theme of his instructions to his disciples. On this matter he had practical experience since, after returning from his first exile, he had acted for a short while as governor of the town of Chung-tu. His régime, we are told, was one of strict sumptuary and funeral laws; and of enforcement of just standards, even including the prohibition of the manufacture of fake curios. The dying pious practice of suttee or human sacrifice was severely frowned on by the rationalist sage. Subsequently, but before the Duke of Lu's exile, he held positions as Minister of Public Works and of Police, which in fact made him chief minister of that duchy. Whatever his moral maxims, in this latter office the moralist sage did stern justice in a time of chaos and apparently held that most sins warranted the death penalty. He left Lu again for fourteen years, thanks to a court intrigue and to the preoccupation of the Duke with his women. He then resided in Wei where, perhaps to avoid future humiliation, he scandalized his followers by calling on the Duke of Wei's *maîtresse en titre*. It was to no purpose and, exclaiming "I have never known anyone who will work so hard on behalf of virtue as for a beautiful face," the philosopher temporarily left for the feudal state of Sung, where he took the occasion to lay down the principle that oaths made under duress have no binding force.

Confucius, a patriot concerned with the return of the cultural glories of the society which, as then known from the vantage point of the Yellow River, comprised the whole world, made like a merchant his tour of courts, seated on his dignified wheeled conveyance and offering his philosophic goods. "If there were any of the princes who would employ me, in the course of twelve months I would accomplish something considerable. In three years the government would be perfected." Lao-tze, however, had commented:

Those who know a great deal about practical affairs, and do things on a large scale, endanger their persons, for by their action and their knowledge they reveal the mistakes of mankind. He who is only the son of another has

* *Cf.* pp. 338, 476.

nothing for himself, for he owes all to his father; he who is only the official of another has nothing for himself, for he owes all to his superior.

Confucius, however, replied to the recluse who followed the precepts of Lao-tze and urged withdrawal, since none could control the flood of disorder:

If I do not associate with mankind, with whom shall I associate? If order and right principles prevailed throughout the world there would be no reason for me to change anything.

Nor was Confucius to be deterred by the statement that he was the man who kept on trying to accomplish what he knew to be impossible. Confucius, however, the First Political Philosopher, adds:

My doctrines make no headway. I will get on a raft and float about on the sea. . . . The sage suffers because he must leave the world with the conviction that after his death his name will not be mentioned. . . . Am I an empty gourd. Am I to be hung up out of the way of being eaten? . . . From these and many other examples it is definitely made known that whether or not a scholar has an opportunity to serve his ruler depends, not on himself alone, but on the time in which he lives. To be a gentleman one has only to be versed in learning and serious-minded in thought. . . . Before I was born there were many men of scholarship and virtue who were destined, as I may be, to live and die in obscurity.

Some of the maxims of Confucius show no marked difference from those of Lao-tze, the pacifist. Such are these:

Sir, in carrying on your government why should you kill anyone at all? Let your evinced desires and your example be for what is good and it will not be necessary to punish anyone.

To find *the central clue to our moral being which unites us to the universal order*, that indeed is the highest human attainment. People are seldom capable of it for long.

Among the means for the regeneration of mankind, those made with noise and show are the least important.

To fulfil the law of our being is what we call the moral law.

But Confucius, both in the book generally called *The Doctrine of the Mean* (or *The Common Sense of Right*), compiled by Kung Ki, his grandson, and elsewhere, says, with stress on family, heredity and society:

The moral law takes its rise in the relation between man and woman; in its utmost it reigns supreme over heaven and earth. . . . The moral sense is the characteristic attribute of man . . . the sense of justice is the recognition of what is right and proper. To honour those who are wealthier than ourselves is the highest expression of the sense of justice. . . . The relative degrees of natural affection we ought to feel for those who are nearly related to us and the relative grades of honour we ought to show to those worthier than ourselves; these are that which gives rise to the forms and distinctions in social life. *For unless social inequalities have a true and moral basis, government of the people is an impossibility.*

By nature men are nearly alike.

Intelligence, moral character and courage: these are the three universally recognized moral qualities of man. . . . Some exercise these moral qualities naturally and easily; some because they find it advantageous to do so; some with effort and difficulty. *But when the achievement is made it comes to one and the same thing.*

The moral law is not something away from the actuality of human life. *When men take up something away from the actuality of human life as being the moral law, that is not the moral law.*

There is in the world now really no moral social order at all.

Confucius, having returned to his native state, settled down to write the history of the duchy of Lu and to collect the ballads of ancient and feudal China, some dating from the Shung dynasty (1761–1122 B.C.). He did this with a strict eye for decorum and exercising the censorship of propriety. "The three hundred odes," he says himself, "may be summed up in one sentence: thought without depravity." Of the four remaining great Chinese classics, two containing the teaching of Confucius were written down by disciples and two contain the teaching of these disciples themselves. In the summer of the year 479 B.C., at the age of seventy-three, surrounded by his disciples but not his kin, and honoured by his duke, Confucius died.

The greatest of the disciples of Confucius was Meng (Latinized as Mencius, 372–288 B.C.), who lived in Shantung one hundred years later, an advocate of public education; of the public ownership of land with allocation of a certain acreage to each; and of pacifism save in self-defence or in destroying a domestic oppressor. "There has never been a good war, though some may be considered as being better than others." This pacifism of Confucianism has impregnated the whole culture of China so that perhaps in our own day it will be destroyed by Japan. However, this Empire is the oldest state on earth; and it already counts three thousand years among the yesterdays of its distinguished civilization.

Mencius' works are occupied with a balanced refutation of Mo-ti, who held that we should love all men, and of Yang Chu, who held that we should love only ourselves. Nevertheless, Mencius held that man was naturally good, but added, "*That whereby man differs from the lower animals is but small. The mass of people cast it away, while the superior men preserve it.*" Nor was Mencius, despite his belief in man's natural goodness, a critic like Lao-tze of civilization and an advocate of the return to nature. The manner of the working of things must be scientifically studied; and the handicraftsman and skilled artisan had their place beside the simple-life worker on the land.

The mystic anarchists believed in the doctrine of letting alone, of non-intervention, non-resistance and non-attachment, and of developing the Self according to Nature. Lao-tze said: "Requite hatred with goodness." His follower Chuang-tze commented, in derision of those who had the lust of power on which political action is built: "Therefore it is written, 'Who is bad? Who is good? He who succeeds is the head. He who does not succeed is the tail'. . . . A petty thief is put in jail. A great brigand becomes a ruler of a state. And among the retainers of the latter men of virtue will be found." The hit is at Confucius, the pilgrim salesman of political wisdom. Lao-tze and Chuang-tze esteemed only wisdom and spoke of the rest of the people as "the children." "Wisdom," however, would detect the spirit of the people and of their customs—the essential *nature* of the folk into which ordinance and ruler alike must fit and which would also shape them from *within*. The spirits of men as diverse as "Chou Kung and the monkey" could not, all alike, be shaped from *without* by the etiquette of morals and by the law and institutions of the country. Wisdom, however—*Tao*—could be shared, Lao-tze and Chuang-tze held, by all who willed, Emperor or hermit. These are doctrines that we shall find recurring throughout human history.*

Mencius, however, asserted (against this individualist preaching of the pure religion of equality and of the return to Nature) the importance, in civilization, of government and order, for the sake of the governed themselves.

> The destruction [he wrote] of the poor is their poverty. In such circumstances they only try to save themselves from death and are afraid they will not succeed. What opportunity have such to cultivate propriety and righteousness?
>
> Therefore an intelligent *ruler will regulate the livelihood of the people* so as to make sure that, first, they shall have sufficient to save their parents, and, second, sufficient wherewith to support their wives and children; that in good years they shall always be abundantly satisfied, and that in bad years they shall escape danger of perishing.

* *Cf.* p. 112.

However, Mencius added: "The superior man has three things in which he delights, and to be a ruler over the kingdom is not one of them." The superior man wills service, not dominion or will to power. In the words of the *Shu-King:*

> It was the lesson of our great ancestor:—
> The people should be cherished;
> They should not be downtrodden;
> The people are the root of the country;
> The root firm, the country is tranquil,
> When I look throughout the empire
> Of simple men and simple women,
> Anyone may surpass me.

The problems of political obligation in China are solved in terms of a system paternalistic but unmarked by a class status, ritualistic but utilitarian, pious but rationalistic and without religious revelation. Above all, it is solved in terms not of the Space-scale but of the Time-scale; of obligation not to contemporary humanity but to the generations; in terms not of the country-wide Empire but primarily of the particular family as the true Community. Like Egypt it tended to put the interests of Civilization in value before those of Contemporary Society (the current Human Majority) but, unlike Egypt, Confucius judged Civilization by its fruits not for the generations of the Few but for the lot through the decades, of simple men and simple women, the inventors of the useful, manual arts. China was a land of scholars, but not of a privileged class.

4

The traditional date of Homer is in the middle of the ninth century B.C. Four centuries later, in the days of Confucius in Shantung, Cyrus the Persian was occupied in the extension of his empire which, by the defeat of Croesus of Lydia in 546 B.C., he carried down to the Aegean Sea. In 539 B.C. Babylon fell to him. In 527, Cambyses the Persian, successor of Cyrus, occupied Egypt and terminated the twenty-sixth dynasty of the Pharaohs.

In about 1375 B.C., in the late Bronze Age, the grandeur of Knossos, in Crete, had ended in the days of Amenhotep III of Egypt. Mycenaean pottery is already to be found in El Amarna, the city of his successor, Akhenaten, the Heretic Pharaoh. The great age of Mycenae, at its height in the fourteenth century, follows that of Knossos. Probably in the twelfth century, on the verge of the Iron Age and the ascendancy of Doric Argos, occurs the Siege of Troy.

In Hellas, emerging from the Dark Ages that followed the heroic period of Mycenae and Troy, in the seventh century, we find the epoch of the Seven Sages, Thales, Pittakos, Bios, Solon the Athenian, Kleobulos, Cheilon and Periander of Corinth. Of these, Thales of Miletos, in Ionia (624–546 B.C.), Solon (640–558) and Periander (625–585), whom Plato excluded from the list, as a tyrant, are figures that stand out as more than names. Ionia, at this time, is the focus of Hellenic civilization. Towns such as Smyrna and Miletos had a population that was large and a commerce that was brisk. Merchants travelled between them and Tyre and Egypt, as they had done between Crete and Egypt in the days of the Shepherd-kings of Egypt one thousand years before. The arts and poetry flourished. Alkaeos and Sappho sang. As Poseidippos wrote:

> . . . the white page of Sappho lives on and lives for ever,
> Proclaiming your name also, your name thrice blest, the while
> That Naukratis shall remember while ships shall breast her river
> Standing in from seaward to the long lagoons of Nile.

This growing Hellenic civilization was moulded by certain determinant factors. Primarily it was a seaboard civilization and its people were fishermen and sailors. Further, especially in European Hellas, the configuration of the land, with inlets and mountains running down to the sea, shaped the life of the people into a series of relatively small communities, stamped by all the intensity of local life—an intensity confirmed by religious ritual. If, during certain seasons, the inhabitants were sailors, they were also agriculturalists. These communities were, from their nature, militarily weak and difficult to unite. Their characteristic form was the *Polis*, which it is permissible to translate as "City-state" or "Township," but which certainly must not, without risk of gross deception, be translated as "State."*

The Polis appears to be an almost universal form of human community at a certain state of human civilization. Families, having gathered into clans, are beginning to settle down on empty land and to acquire a certain level of stable civilization. It is a form that occurs from India to Spain. Peculiarly it is liable to take shape where the land is not plain-land, the natural home of large-scale military empires, or joined up by a river such as the Hoang-ho, Euphrates or Nile,

* We shall retain, throughout this work, the technical word Polis, without attempt at translation. From it, of course, the word "Politics" derives.

but is mountainous country where the community can gather for defence, in hill-towns, on some rise or *acropolis* (as at Athens, Corinth—and Dumbarton) or, as at Tyre, on some jutting rock. Granted that commerce is sea-born, a wealthy community can grow without any attempt (save at Carthage, founded on a hill in flat country) to develop an empire in the hinterland. Further, whereas advancing civilization and wealth terminate the nomad life of the tribe, mountainous country breaks up that tribe; confirms the clan-form (as in mediaeval Scotland); and prevents the shaping of a nation.

The Polis is neither a City nor a State, however translated "City-state." It is not a City, at least in European Hellas, because it is primarily an agricultural community, as indeed were, later, the Italian hill-towns. Emphatically, as we shall see, in its normal condition it is not a *metropolis* and repudiated the title. Nor was it a State, since it was at once less, in size, and more, in the sense that here civic life and government, in the modern usage of these terms, were bound up with kindred, with economic life and with religion. Rather it was an enlarged family—at once its normal development, and as we shall also see,* its rival. The whole problem-theme of Sophokles' play, *Antigone*, is whether the moral ties of the family or the regulations of the polis and its rulers are to take precedence. Because the structure of society tends to be a clan structure, it emerges in Hellas as aristocratic, a structure of the polis ruled by the family or clan (Greek, *phratry*) elders. (In ancient Italy its structure, *e.g.*, at Rome, is that of rule by the heads of the *gens*—the "gentlemen.") For the same reason, its law is customary; its customs are religious; and its religion the worship of the family hearth and ancestral spirits. *The origin of politics is in religion.* For the same reason, also, its manners are profoundly conservative and, even in Athens in the days of Pericles and after (as Aristophanes knew full well), so remained. This is not unexpected. What is unexpected is that a progressive civilization should have developed out of such ancestral custom and not merely a static civilization as in ancestor-worshipping China and in the Egypt of the priests.

The thought of Hellas takes its character from its distinctive, not its customary, conditions. Hellas is not European. It is a Euro-Asiatic bridgehead, a veritable Bosphorus ferry, a Levantine clearing-house. If, on the conservative side, the Greeks were agriculturalists, on the radical side they were sailors. They now produced for export; had a coinage; and money (*nomisma*) perturbed law (*nomos*) and upset all traditions—introduced new tyrannies and new philosophies. If Hesiod

* *Cf.* p. 60. *Cf.* also Aristotle, *Politics III*, ix.

can tell us of the life of the farm, with the man acquiring his house and his ox and his wife (in that order), Herodotus, the First Anthropologist, the Father of History, can tell us of far countries and ask the radical question: since men's religious customs differ so widely, which is right? Some men bury their parents and others think it more respectful to eat them. Strabo later, I regret to say, records that the Irish of his day were especially addicted to the latter practice as more pious. Is there anything "really right"? The farmers are conservatives, but the sailors are radicals—and they are often the same men. Discussion, then, over the wine is inaugurated. Geography gave to the Greek Freedom including Freedom of Thought.

> Thus speaks Hekataios of Miletus. I write all this in accordance with what seemed to me to be the truth; for the legends of the Greeks are, in my opinion, contradictory and ridiculous.

Moreover, the religion of the Greek was his family religion. There were indeed tribal gods of all the Greeks, remote and abstract on Mount Olympus, but the gods that touched his heart were the little family gods with their household rite and the shady gods of the underworld, Erinyes. They did not rule or try to rule his theories on Nature. Unlike India and Egypt, Babylon and Judaea, the Greeks had no Sacred Books, no revelation, save for the soothsayers at Delphi. Speculation, then, about Nature is secular speculation. Doubtless there are gods in things. But how? Whereas the Egyptian, who never left his country, did not let his thought stray beyond the immensely ancient, overwhelming, oppressive, sacred tradition of the Nile, the wandering Hellene had no such tradition but only tales of far lands, not only of wise Egypt but of wise Babylon. He developed, in his speculation on Nature, not a Theology but a Physics.

This, at least, is what Thales, astronomer and cosmologist, did, who may have learned a few things from the Babylonians by way of Lydian Sardis and some practical geometry from Egypt, but whose triumph was to get the world afloat in the universe instead of being the saucer-foundation of sky's inverted bowl. "All is water," said Thales—the earth a disk of frozen water afloat in ocean and in vapour (not yet "a globe of condensed and mould-covered dust, with a molten core, afloat in gaseous ether.") Thales, further, had thereby discovered or asserted the existence of a "single principle" in Nature or Reality. About that we shall hear much more.*

* *Cf.* pp. 114, 251, 618.

If thought was secular, not theological, scientific-experimental, not piously mythical, then profane men, not priests, could take a share. And government, the supreme mystery, might also be profaned and secularized. Government need not only be by "the silent ones." Those affected might put queries about what the silent ones in fact had said; insist that the tradition be written down in the early codes (like the Roman XII Tables); and even query the expediency of this or that application. Moreover, the seafaring life and the making of new wealth led to confusion of classes and to a direct challenge of the old, self-conscious clan aristocracy. Democracy itself became discussible as a principle of government—ceased to be an abominable profanity. In Hellas first it was launched on its course.

The importance of Hellenic thought is often affirmed. It is seldom grasped. It has this historic importance of being a pioneer. We shall see that it is not enough to say that it has the freshness of pioneer thought, just as early poetry has an unrecapturable beauty as "near the founts of song." What has been said once cannot be said with the same effect twice; and the old discussions are less encumbered with recent prejudice—more direct. However, mere past importance would be of little account in contemporary discussion, if for no other reason than because of the risk of false analogy. We no longer live in the Beginning of the Iron Age.

Hellenic thought, however, has moulded our own Western Tradition. First it has done this indirectly, conjointly with Judaism, through the Church Fathers and the Christian Church. Secondly, since the twelfth-century Resurgence and the fifteenth-century Renaissance—and still more since the early nineteenth century—it has done this directly through the influence of the original Greek authors, whose thought has been appropriated by modern thinkers. Moreover—peculiarly in politics—these authors have coined for us our technical terms, coloured and defined them.

Nevertheless, even this moulding influence of Hellas on Western Civilization, its legacy to us, is not the chief ground why this thought is important. To understand this third consideration we must accustom ourselves (as Copernicus did in visualizing the sun as having the earth go round it) to a strange correction in our normal perspective on the spiral of history. In the chronological history of events we see a movement on, century by century. And in the history of material civilization, although we may detect great recessions and may conclude that this march *on* is rather a spiral march *up* in which standards of well-being are found, lost and returned to at a higher, more opulent level, yet the conviction of progress is never shaken but is indeed confirmed. If we looked, indeed, at the *quality*, not extent and massiveness, of these achievements we might be less confident. In the fine arts, even in the useful handicrafts, from the point of view of taste is the advance so sure? When we have surveyed Western history we shall resurvey these considerations.* Enough now to note a strange phenomenon when we look to the history of thought.

The theatre of events in ancient Hellas (even in ancient Egypt) is so small, so miniature. But the miniature is very perfect, much simpler than our own theatre; and the thinkers were at least as capable of thought as ourselves. Hence Greek thought on these miniature problems is as it were microscopic, not telescopic, but astoundingly clear and, in specific details, *in advance of our own.* Let us phrase it that they were further round, saw further round, the bend of the spiral, at their level, than we are and do at ours.

Let us illustrate this point. What do the great Greek political philosophers discuss? Here is a list: Democracy, the freedom of writing and thought, censorship, the relation of democracy and the expert, feminism, eugenics, abortion, the problem of leisure, whether the prolongation of life by medicine cannot be carried to excess, nudism, psycho-analysis, revolution, the proletariat, the class war, what comes after popular dictatorship. Let us ask ourselves what meaning all this had to Mr. Mitford, the English historian of Greece, writing at the end of the eighteenth century, or even to Mr. Grote writing, as a good utilitarian Liberal, in the middle of the nineteenth. And have we ourselves yet settled whether Plato, who shaped political thought through Catholicism for two millennia, was a Communist (and in what sense) or a totalitarian National Socialist? Have we begun yet the discussion, in our political forum, of his problems of eugenics and of the subordination of the family to the race?

It is not merely the case that, if we bisect recorded history, we find Euripides and Plato nearer to us in time than they were to the Pyramid Builders. Euripides and Plato are our contemporaries and a bit more —more precisely, *our* grandchildren will, on the chart of civilization, be somewhere about *their* contemporaries.†

In the days of Heraclitus (Herakleitos, flourished in the early fifth century), of Ephesus, we see the beginnings of that democratic struggle

* *Cf.* Chap. XXII.

† I do not accept the strict cyclical theory of civilization; but this I have explained elsewhere. It does not interfere with my belief in the power of political science to predict and control as much as, but no more than, does economic science.

which we note in the Britain of C. J. Fox and the Duke of Wellington, in the France of Mirabeau and Louis XVI and in Spain, abortively, from Soult to our own day. An aristocrat of priestly family, founder of that Ionic school of vitality and Flux that held Fire as the primal principle and that "all things flow, one cannot step twice into the same river"—whirlwind king; and no stability even in the rule of Zeus the Law Giver and of eternal Reason—Heraclitus was a political, as well as a natural, philosopher. How can there be a Rule of Law? God, the Beginning, is beyond Good and Evil. Is it, then, the conclusion that the masses are to rule? No: they are incompetent.

> The Ephesians would do well to hang themselves, every grown man of them, and leave the city to beardless lads; for they have cast out Hermodoros, the best man among them, saying: "We will have none that is best among us; if there be any such, let him go elsewhere and among others." . . . What wisdom or sense have the masses, many are evil, few are good.

There is a *logos* or "wisdom"; but it is not that of peace and static law. It is this that, beneath dynamic tension, there exists an immortal reality, the fire or world-soul. But, superficially, all is tension of life and death, good and evil; and "war is the father of all things." The excellent, wise and strong should, then, rule. But what if, in war, the many have strength? Till Darwin, till Nietzsche, the question was to be set and set again. To this question the wisdom of Heraclitus gave no answer—how the excellent should be also the strong and whether might was not also right? Was man excellent, first, as a social animal, collectively strong, or excellent as the variety, the individual, the adaptable initiator? Should he seek to identify himself with the society of numbers in space or of generations in time?*

THE SOPHISTS, not physical philosophers or mathematicians like Pythagoras in Hellenic Italy, Magna Graecia, the New World America of those days, nor mystagogues like Heraclitus, were primarily educators. They performed in their day the great functions that, in the sixteenth to eighteenth centuries, the Jesuits performed. Like the Cynics, the Epicureans, the Jesuits themselves and the casuists, the name Sophists came to have a derogatory sense. Trainers in argument, having a commercial value among an argumentative, litigious people in a land of large juries and popular courts, they became the bagmen of learning, advertising that they would put a man wise for a few dollars. What, after all, could not be taught? They were the contemporary popular exponents of the craze for Mental Efficiency and of How to

* *Cf.* pp. 332, 529.

Begin Life at Forty. Logic was in its infancy. Disputers for any side of any question they became, by their "dialectic" (discussion, technically conducted by the rules), trainers of radicals. Above all they developed the issue (of which we shall hear so much) touched on by Heraclitus: the distinction between the Natural and the Conventional. Below custom and conventional peace lay—what? Perhaps the "war of all things," struggle, conflict.

What could not be taught? Did heredity, tradition, convention matter, when all depended on the right educational environment? Could character be taught? The very Greek word *typos*, "type" or [Hellenistic] *character*, both used as "impression of a seal," implied that it could. The Greeks ever tended to intellectualism and cleverness. Virtue was wisdom; and wisdom could be taught. Were yet, said the conservatives, the Sophists the men to teach it? They were empirics, pragmatists—but more, very nearly sceptics. Protagoras (ca. 480–ca. 411 B.C.), the early anticipator of pragmatism, had said, "of all things two views may be taken." Truth was relative. Was there yet not a fundamental Law, even in Nature itself, stable, resting on reason and instinct? (Centuries later the Papacy was to place its stress, as catholic legislator, just on these points: instinct and reason.)*

5

SOCRATES (Sokrates, 470–399 B.C.) was the greatest of the Sophists and their greatest enemy. Like them, he had turned his attention away from the natural philosophies and the mathematicians, students of the objective, and had sought, according to the Delphic maxim, to "know himself." He had made his interest man and the education of man by dialectic, the humanities and moralities.

A laudatory tradition has gathered round Socrates, largely due to the loyal work of his great disciple, Plato, and *his* disciple, Aristotle. To the early Christian Fathers he was a "Christian before Christ," the saint and martyr of philosophy. In their enthusiasm they, as it were, baptized him. His contemporaries viewed him with a different eye. The son of a sculptor and a professional midwife, ugly as a satyr with (as Aristophanes said) the waddling gait of a waterfowl, he was primarily a bore, even if a sincere one. Never at home looking after his family or his vocation (scandalmongers said he was a bigamist), he was, as it were, a frequenter of coffee-houses who boasted of seldom going into the country. A coffee-house politician, his habit was to buttonhole people, to whom he had scarcely been introduced, in the market place, and pertinaciously to ask them inconvenient and dis-

* *Cf.* p. 168.

courteous questions. Anyone, soldier, prostitute, priest was a fit subject for his inquisitive curiosity. A heavy drinker, he could be guaranteed to drink the rest of his boon friends under the table. A plebeian, although with private means, he was, to the conservative mind, doubtless an "original," but a pernicious one.

Socrates claimed the guidance of a "voice"; arrogated to himself a special message from the Delphic Oracle to give him local importance; gathered round himself a clique of disciples which included even some noblemen. Who were they? Flash, drinking, fast-living, perverted young men, such as Kritias, Charmides and Alkibiades (Alkibiades, for one, had in him the elements, speaking in terms of our own times, both of an Oscar Wilde and of a Winston Churchill), they were suitably found later mixed up with the Thirty Tyrants of Athens, along with their kinsman Plato. Not without probability the charge was made against Socrates of impiety towards the gods and of corrupting the youth—that is, of criminal immorality and seditious blasphemy. After all, his tutor and "friend," Archilaos, of Athens, who believed the earth to be a sphere, had been indicted and banished from that city for atheistic impiety. It is not at all surprising that a common jury of ordinary Athenian citizens condemned Socrates to death, as the associate of the reactionaries, by a substantial majority (281 to 220) in a popular court of over 500 members. The Roman Cato the Elder, a classic representative of the sound Roman virtues, after being persuaded to acquaint himself with the life and execution of Socrates—and not being at all the kind of man to be swayed by the views of a comic dramatist such as Aristophanes—passed the final comment: "He seems to have been a meddlesome fellow."

That is one side of the case; and it is formidable. It is not silenced by the fact that it all happened long ago and that there is "much truth" in Socrates' doctrines. Nor is his unblemished record as a soldier, his refusal to "break jail," and the voting of this friend of oligarchs against the popular judgement (which decided in its democratic anger to execute generals suspected of cowardice and treason) a sufficient answer. Nor is it satisfactory—although doubtless correct—to say that Truth often chooses very odd vessels through which to manifest itself. The contrary case really rests upon two things: the opinion of certain of his friends (all strong conservatives) that Socrates was a man of remarkable personality, a man of integrity and courage, sincerely and disinterestedly inquiring after truth; and the intrinsic value of some of the ideas that he, whether sage or disreputable reactionary, succeeded in starting running, including whether it be not better to be a great bad man than a small good one (*cf. Hippias Minor*, of Plato).

The picture indeed of the true Socrates is not easy to arrive at. It is made from a composite of the views of these friends, Xenophon, the bluff squire-soldier, Alkibiades, the flash aristocrat politician (for whose views we must yet rely on Plato) and Plato himself, the well-born young poet who later became the philosopher of genius. Socrates himself wrote nothing. All that we have of him is the views of his disciples. And, needless to say, these far from agree. In Plato's *Dialogues* we come across a character called Socrates. But, at least in the later dialogues, there is reason, from the character of the views expressed, to suppose that "Socrates" here is more particularly the mouthpiece of Plato himself. Moreover we tend to move in a circle, since the dating of the *Dialogues* is (if partly a matter of style) partly a matter of our opinion of whether the views are those of Plato, and the dialogue late, or those of Socrates—views which, *ex hypothesi*, we do not know and are trying to find out—and the dialogue early. The "Socrates" of Plato is a philosopher. The "Socrates" of Xenophon is another good-hearted Xenophon—but conceded to have been, in his early days, quite a good philosopher too, in the natural science tradition. The "Socrates" of Aristophanes, the comedian, is a sardonic, irreverent fellow, smart but gloomy, full of himself and of fantastic ideas and surrounding himself with a school of which the effect was disturbing even to Athenian morals.

Who then is the real Socrates? Perhaps it is too problematical to matter. We seem, however, to detect the head of a small school or group, that makes something of a scandal in the small-town life of Athens, the tiny metropolis, who had been interested, like all his predecessors, in physics but who is now primarily interested at getting to the root of things in ethics. He feels that he has a mission to do this—a mission which others regard as no more than warranting him to be regarded as a "character." He was a kind of Cyril Joad of those days. His inquiries and discussion, so far as we can judge from the early Platonic dialogues—the simpler ones—appear to have been almost entirely negative; and, if those whom he questioned were shocked, he seems to have taken a satiric, intellectual pleasure in that fact. In brief, he was often just naughty. The mock profession of ignorance, to lead the victim on, was the Socratic "irony." Thus hypocrisy, bombast, stupidity and even good-intentioned slow wits were exposed to make a feast for the group—those youths in whom Socrates delighted, who "tore arguments like young puppies."

Socrates did not regard himself as a reformer. His object was to destroy fallacy and to do it by the use of the most commonplace of instances. He is indeed the announced apostle of plain man's common sense. He finds it a means to upset, like Mr. Shaw, many a lofty apple-cart. But his object, in fairness, was not merely this. A core of constructive thought appears amid the negative wreckage. Nietzsche discovered in him the beginning of the Greek degeneration; and there is no reason to see in him a plaster-cast saint. His reaction against his early studies in the natural sciences (fortunately not able to counter the influence later of Aristotle) may be considered to be precisely reactionary. Men, under this influence, all too readily began to build up constructions of what ought to be, instead of painfully studying what is. But Socrates yet effectively turned men's attention to the proper study of man which is man. His very individual negativism produced in Plato a reaction towards stress on constructive society, its importance and virtues. There is then this, on the positive side, in Socrates that he provokes an inquiry, more systematic than any preceding Sophist, into social relations. He is the godfather of Western political philosophy, as well as the founder of speculative ethics.

Socrates, moreover, discovers the Self. The discovery indeed is not complete. The initiates of the Orphic mysteries had anticipated it, with their symbols of immortality. It does not become the basis of a coherent philosophy until the Stoics, although it had been anticipated by those Delphic gnomic maxims which were the household sayings of ancient Hellas. It has, however, been said that Hellenic civilization was still barbaric in the sense that it—the civilization of a traditional intense community unself-consciously worshipping its local gods had singularly little recognition of the value of the individual. In the famous declaration in the *Crito* (*Kriton*) Socrates declares, as a true Hellene, that a man has no right to break the laws of his polis or to seek to escape the penalties they impose. The Hellene is a profoundly communal being.

> Let me put it like this. Suppose we meant to run away—or whatever one ought to call it—and suppose the laws and the Polis were to come and stand over us and ask me, "Tell us, Socrates, what is it you mean to do? Nothing more nor less than to overthrow us by this attempt of yours—to overthrow the laws and the whole commonwealth so far as in you lies. Do you imagine that a city can stand and not be overthrown, when the decisions of the judges have no power, when they are made of no effect and destroyed by private persons. . . . Now that you have been born and brought up and educated, can you say that you are not ours—our child and our servant—you and your descendants? And, if this is so, do you think your rights can equal ours? . . . still we offer full liberty to any Athenian who likes, after he has seen and tested

us and all that is done in our city, *to take his goods, and leave us,* if we do not please him, and go wherever he would. *Only if he stays with us, after seeing how we judge our cases and how we rule our city, then we hold that he has pledged himself by his action to do our bidding.* If we mean to kill you because we think it just, must you do your best to kill us in your turn? Can you claim that you have a right to do this, you, the lover of virtue? . . . You act as the worst of slaves might act, preparing to run away, *breaking the contracts* (*tas synthekas*) —the pledge you gave to accept our government.

Plato, through the historical example of Socrates, preaches a stern doctrine of political obedience. No doubt is expressed whether the polis may not be an aggregate of warring economic groups or, again, whether (as later with the Stoics) some wider society may not transcend the polis. But it is asserted that it is *a free community that a man may quit at will;* and that it is based on the free consent of each of its citizens. Its law rests, not on force or blood and racial custom alone, but on the tacit social contract of these choosing selves.

Individualism, however conditioned by civic obligation, had clearly shown itself. The secular, intelligent, curiosity-governed democracy of Athens confronted the barbarous civilization of Persia, the mechanical empire. It defeated it. It confronted also, as type, the civilization of Egypt. The Athenian democracy, secular, grossly licentious, adaptable, unstable, a brilliant "variant" in human evolution, lasted from the fall of Hippias (511 B.C.) to the rise of the Thirty Tyrants (404 B.C.), that is, for a century. Its subsequent restoration scarcely gives ground for altering this judgement. The rule of the dynastic Pharaohs, priestly, traditional, stable, self-contained, largely an autarky or "closed economy," lasted for four and a half millennia. But radical Athens, in the century, contributed more, not necessarily to placid happiness in sloth, but to later human civilization than the wisdom of conservative Egypt in the five millennia. As in all biology, so in human biology the problem is that of the fit balance between variability and stability. In political terms, it is that of the balance between Liberty, as a social temper, and Law.

READING

J. L. Myres: *Dawn of History,* Chaps. I–IV.

BIBLIOGRAPHICAL NOTE

*W. J. Perry: *The Growth of Civilization,* 1924.
V. Gordon Childe: *Man Makes Himself,* 1936.
G. Catlin: *Science and Method of Politics,* 1927.
R. H. Lowic: *The Origin of the State,* 1928.

Chapter II

Plato

1

IN THE preceding chapter the peculiarly confusing character of the history of political thought was pointed out. The historian, starting his narrative with the dynastic Pharaohs, is able to record an advance, as judged by most tests, material and moral, when he reaches the history of our own times. The recession of the Dark Ages is but an interlude, almost an irrelevancy. The historian of political thought, finding his first Occidental texts in the full sunlight of Hellenic civilization, is in the odd position of reaching his most developed, his most mature and most "modern" thought at the beginning of his period. The reasons for this we have explained. The fact is startlingly exemplified in the case of Socrates' greatest pupil, Plato.

PLATO (428–348 B.C.), philosopher, politician, mathematician, poet, rich, broad of figure and weak of voice, cousin of Critias and kinsman of Solon, was brought up in a slave civilization and in an aristocratic household which yet, by marriage connections, was politically favourable to Pericles and to his democratic experiment. He was the most famous of Socrates' circle of pupils. It is, however, said that, on hearing Plato reading his dialogue *Lysis*, Socrates commented: "What a pack of lies this young man is telling about me"—a comment which bears out the remarks made earlier* about the difference between the actual and the "literary" Socrates.

Plato's letters, many of them almost certainly authentic, are preserved. Apart, however, from what we learn from them, much of his biography is conjectural. It is stated that, as a young man, he travelled in Cyrene, where he visited Theodorus, the mathematician, and later, (after Socrates' death) in Egypt. We know that in 388 B.C. he visited Sicilian Syracuse—the New York of its day—on the invitation of the ruler Dionysius I and of Dion, uncle of Dionysius II; and that he

* *Cf.* p. 32.

found the habits of these wealthy Greek colonials too luxurious for his approval.

> No one whose life is spent in gorging food twice a day and sharing his bed at night, and so on, can ever attain real wisdom.

Later Dionysius asked Plato, after their quarrel, to bear him no ill will; but received the terse reply that Plato had not the leisure to keep Dionysius in mind.

Some poems are preserved which are probably Plato's, about his mistress, Archianassa, and on germane topics.

> A kiss; and touch of lips; not strange my Soul should cling,
> Strive to cross, weep to turn, and starve with me, poor thing.

And,

> Star-gazing Aster, would I were the skies,
> To gaze upon thee with a thousand eyes.

There is not only "modernism" but an interesting sidelight in the inscribed lines:

> An apple am I, thrown by one who loves you.
> Nay, Xanthippe, give consent,
> For time is short and we too burn low.

We are told that he wrote more erotic poetry in his youth (which may well be, from the evidences of his *Dialogues*) but later thought better to burn it, as he did, a tragedy. Ausonius preserves a specimen or two—about the Cyprian and the Cnidian Venus. He, Plato, first popularized in Athens the light character sketches of Sophron. A copy, it is said, was found under his pillow.

We have Plato's letters. We have some of the comments of his contemporaries—of Alexis, the dramatist: "You don't know what you are talking about; run about with Plato, and you will know all about soap and onions." And from Kratinos, in dialogue:

> "Clear, you are a man and have a soul."
> "In Plato's words, I am not sure but suspect that I have."

In 387 he founded his school in Athens, in the Academy, because he was an Athenian rather than because he loved the Athenians—this was before his second and third visits to Sicily, and his attempts there to put into practice his philosophy, which nearly cost him his life. Plato died, at the advanced age of eighty-one, at a wedding feast. As he said truly of himself: "A man must first make a name, and then he will have no lack of memoirs." In his will, he left, among other things, a gold signet-ring and ear-ring, weighing together over four drachmas.

In the Academy, a gymnasium outside the walls of the city, in the olive grove of the hero Hekademos, his chief work was done. It was, as it were, a New School of Research. In accordance with the Pythagorean tradition, especial attention was given to mathematics. Here was to be found Thaeatetus, founder of solid geometry. A beginning was made with conic sections. At the entrance, it is said, was a warning that none should enter who had not mastered the mathematical elements. Jurisprudence also was a study there. Botany was not neglected. Plato's nephew and successor in his chair, Speusippus, was a classifying botanist such as Linnaeus was in modern times. Among his pupils were counted two women, Lastheneia of Mantinea and Axiothea of Phlius, of whom the latter is reported to have worn men's clothes. It throws a significant, if horrid, light on the limitations of the life of the times that Speusippus is said to have died boiling with lice.

The age was one dominated by the advances in the mathematical and natural sciences. Socrates had insisted upon turning attention to social studies and ethics. Pythagoras, however (he of the "Pythagorean Theorem"), and his followers whose names were famous in Hellenic thought, were quite accustomed to associate the notions of mathematics and politics. It was, then, no novelty for Plato. To put it briefly, if roughly, the early Pythagoreans were technocrats—although Archimedes (287–212 B.C.) had not yet been born to develop engineering; and slave labour discouraged its application beyond the stage of scientific toys or, at most, the technique of slave-owning Egypt. According to this technocrat tradition, rule should rest in the hands of the educated. It was a prejudice confirmed by the lapse into theology of the later Pythagoreans. The exact discipline of mathematics (not uncomplicated by a religious or astrological theory of numbers such as the Egyptians had) was the test of such education. It must never be forgotten that Greek civilization grew against the background of the priestly civilizations of Egypt and the East, with their respect for learning and their association of it with all the arts of government save those of the warrior. That philosophers should be kings was a theory not remote from the fact that kings were, as a bald matter of fact, temple priests.

The significance of Athenian slavery in its bearing on Athenian thought, must not be exaggerated. It does not invalidate the applicability of that thought to our own days. It was a slavery, in small industries or semi-domestic occupations, of men for the most part not deeply divided by race from their owners and sometimes Hellenes. The slaves, who never (before the fourth century) were a majority of the population, retained certain rights in law. The Athenian system was unpermeated by the terror under which the Spartan helot dwelt. Such occupations as that of seaman, agricultural worker in skilled crafts, or manual labourer were usually filled by free men. There was a free proletariat playing as extensive a role in Athenian democracy as the white proletariat plays in American democracy, while the position of the slave was midway between that of the American negro of the South today and of a century ago. The Athenian philosophers related themselves to problems of democracy not decisively dissimilar, in this respect, from those of today, especially in countries of negro population.

Actually, democracy in Hellas had been carried to a conclusion—by the equalitarian use of the lot in selection for executive offices (save those of military command)—with a more relentless logic than in any contemporary representative democracy. It was a "pure democracy." Citizens in the market place—although not resident aliens—took part (as in New England "town meetings" and in some Swiss cantons) directly in the work of government. Under a rota system every citizen might expect not only to serve on a jury (with judicial powers) but on the civic Council and even to be chairman. All were politically equal and "took it in turn to rule and be ruled."

Over against the democratic system, with its problems of over-population, demands for distribution of public moneys in payment for jury service and the like, equalitarianism, licence of morals, alleged inefficiency and demagogic devices, was the oligarchic system led by Sparta, ruled by kings and ephors, military, disciplined, but built on terrorization of the helot and semi-alien population. Without pressing any analogies with this policy of terrorization by secret police, it is worth note that the Spartan system presented specifically modern problems. It also was confronted with a population problem—that of under-population. It had a race theory and a eugenic problem. The issue of feminism was a live one alike in Athens (as the plays of Euripides shew) and in Sparta.

The conflict between the two systems led by the two cities related itself, in city after city among their respective allies, bound together for collective security, with an internal and embittered class war between wealth, landed and commercial, and the proletariat (in, *e.g.*, Corcyra, actively supported by the slaves). Long before Disraeli, it was Plato who referred to the two cities of the rich and the poor. In *Republic* IV, Plato says:

> For there are always in them [cities] two parties at war with each other, the poor and the rich . . . so long as the city in its increase continues to be one, so long it may be permitted to increase, but not beyond it.

And, in *Republic* III:

> But whenever they shall possess lands and houses and money in a private way, they shall become bailiffs and farmers instead of guardians, hateful lords instead of aids to the other citizens, hating and being hated, plotting and being plotted against, they will pass the whole of their life, oftener and more afraid of the enemies within than of those without—they and the rest of the city hastening speedily to destruction.

The situation in this small Greek city of Corcyra (Korkyra, Corfu) is described, in a memorable passage, by Thucydides.

> In war, with an alliance always at the command of either faction [those of the oligarchic or of the proletarian ideology] for the hurt of their adversaries and their own corresponding advantage, opportunities for bringing in the foreigner were never wanting to the revolutionary parties. The sufferings which revolution entailed upon the cities were many and terrible, such as have occurred and always must occur, as long as the nature of man remains the same; although in a severer or milder form, and varying in their symptoms, according to the variety of the particular cases. In peace and prosperity states and individuals have better sentiments. . . . Revolution thus ran its course from city to city, and the places which it arrived at last, from having heard what had been done before, carried to a still greater excess the refinement of their inventions [*cf.* Spain], as manifested in the cunning of their enterprises and the atrocity of their reprisals. Words had to change their ordinary meanings and to take on that which was now given to them. . . . Indeed it is generally the case that men are readier to call rogues clever than simpletons honest, and are as ashamed of being the second as they are proud of being the first. The cause of all these evils was the lust for power arising from greed and ambition; and from these passions proceeded the violence of the parties once engaged in contention. The leaders in the cities, each provided with the fairest professions, on the one side with the cry of political equality of the people, on the other side of a moderate aristocracy, sought prizes for themselves in those public interests which they pretended to cherish, and, recoiling from no means in their struggles for ascendency, engaged in the direst excesses. . . . Meanwhile the moderate part of the citizens perished between the two, either for not joining in the quarrel, or because envy would not suffer them to escape. Thus every form of iniquity took root in the Hellenic countries by reason of the troubles. The ancient simplicity, into which honour so largely entered, was laughed down and disappeared. . . . *In the confusion into which life was now thrown in the cities, human nature, always rebelling against the law and now its master, gladly shewed itself ungoverned in passion, above respect for justice, and*

the enemy of all superiority; since revenge would not have been set above religion, and gain above justice, had it not been for the fatal power of envy.

In another passage Aristotle provides us with the scanning oath taken by conspiring oligarchs: "I will be a foe of the commons and will devise whatsoever ill I may against them" [although, as Aristotle comments, an intelligent aristocrat should rather seek to be on the side of the commons].

The same attitude, in more complacent language, is to be found in the terse statement of the conservative author—known as "the old oligarch"—of the *Athenian Constitution*, falsely ascribed to Xenophon. "In every country the better class of people is adverse to a democracy" ("better class" meaning the traditional holders of power and the moneyed class).

From this problem of class war Plato is led on to the discussion of the technique of revolution and of communism of property and the revision of the family system, as a property system. Personal liberty and the right to freedom of speech and writing; the relation of theory and practice; the need for leadership and the problem of social discipline and education, including religious education—all are in turn discussed. So too are feminism, abortion, communism, psycho-analysis.

It was said above that Plato's discussion is "modern." That is an understatement. In no point is it more difficult to get the perspective of history than here. Plato and even the common-sense Aristotle have been bowed to, in recent centuries, as very great philosophers, but they were persistently regarded as "idealists," dreamers of utopias, who were scarcely imagined to have supposed, even themselves, that their prescriptions had practical bearings. Today we can begin to see that these men wrote from experience and that their suggestions, however drastic, were grimly practical, founded on an experience that was often bitter.

We may go further. Hellenic civilization is a kind of jewel microcosm of our own "great society" or macrocosm. In this little urban world, built up from barbaric and demi-feudal, Homeric antecedents, through priestly and monarchical ages, to the mature flower of its culture, we can see (and this without any mystic theory of history, but because social conditions are sufficiently similar) our own—not present—but future world foreshadowed. It is a tiny working model. Allowing for scale, the problems reproduce themselves of geography and trade; of population; of the relations of rich and poor under the play of the unaltering human instincts; of free speculation and religious decline. Before the re-establishment of satisfactory communications and transport, the growth of national populations, the urbanization of living, the termination of feudalism (just over a century ago in France, yesterday in Russia) and the decline of theological influence, no parallel to Hellenic conditions, on *any* scale, has been possible, just as it was not possible in the preceding millennia of Egyptian, Babylonish and Chinese civilization.

In so far as it is true that we can conjecture our own future from the history of Hellenic civilization, the conclusion is not exhilarating. The internal class wars and the rivalry of the two systems of government, oligarchic and proletarian, ended in the weakening of both sides and the establishment of an empire under Alexander, foreshadowing those of the Caesars and of Napoleon. The cycle of world history moves on into military dictatorship and declines into the luxury and decadence of the imperial courts. To Julius, the radical choice of the people, succeeds Augustus, the administrator; to Augustus succeeds Tiberius, the sullen autocrat; to Tiberius succeeds Caligula, who was merely mad; to Caligula succeeds Nero, who was both tyrant and mad. Utopia does not descend; the golden age does not return. The malignant Machiavelli counts up the grim record of the violent deaths of the emperors from Caesar to Maximinus (A.D. 235) and reaches his total of sixteen out of twenty-six.

The problems, then, which we have to confront have been confronted in a more advanced form by Plato. His thought has interest as that of one of the most brilliant of our younger contemporaries.

From the point of view of the student of political theory that thought can be studied in its clearest, if not in its most mature, form in *The Republic* or, as it is very significantly entitled in some of the early texts, the dialogue *On Justice*. The Greek word, however, has implications which would also permit the translation of the title as "On Righteousness." Along with this should be compared the discussion in the earlier dialogues, such as the *Gorgias*, and in the later *Statesman*. In the Platonic dialogues, as has been pointed out above in the case of Socrates, the characters appear to have been historical. Such men as Protagoras and Gorgias lived. Glaucon and Adeimantos were Plato's brothers. But the form of composition is purely literary. This style often involves digressions that are confusing and irritating to the reader today. The jocosity of the literary Socrates sometimes becomes intolerable. Like a train travelling on a subway or underground system, stations are reached of brilliant illumination followed by tunnels of obscurity not always explicable by the corruption of the text. Plato is emphatically a writer who requires to be read three times. He will be found to improve with keeping and on each tasting.

The *Dialogues* were not Plato's choicest contribution to knowledge. This was, it would seem, given orally to the inner circle of his school. They were merely brief literary compositions to interest the outside educated world. Of them only two—one of the middle period, before the second Syracusan venture, and one of the late period—*The Republic* or *On Justice* and *The Laws*, are of adequate length to be denominated books.

The specific background of Plato's writings must be borne in mind: the defeat of Athens in the Peloponnesian War; the death of Socrates; his own wanderings; his residence in Athens during the period of the Thirty Tyrants in Athens; the Peace of Antalkidas; the decline of the city-state and its strong traditional morality. He wrote during "depression years," not only for his country but for his civilization.

In his reaction to these circumstances, Plato, an aristocrat by birth, is more conservative and, therefore, in many ways, more a typical Greek than Socrates. His initial task, taken over from Socrates, may have been to discover the constitution of a commonwealth in which a reasonable man, such as Socrates, might live. He proceeded to draw up a scheme of a commonwealth in which a certain type of reasonable man should securely rule. These men were to be true aristocrats and the problem assumed the form: By what means, however radical, to conserve an aristocracy? It was a question Sparta had tried to solve and to Sparta, successful working model, Plato was inclined to look for clues.

Plato, also a true Greek, tends to identify those habits or *mores* which were *morals*, eternal values, and those *mores* which were social *customs* of the polis. He tends to identify his ethics and his politics. As a consequence—deplorably enough—he starts political science off along a road in which its study is, and is to remain for two millennia, thoroughly moralistic—he "ethicizes" his politics. As has been well said: "The Greeks wrote their political science in the imperative mood"—or, better, in the optative, not in the mood of observation. "Wishful thinking" besets it. The Delphic oracle had told Socrates to know himself—it was a command to the individual conscience. Socrates turned from natural science to the morality of the inner man. Plato turned again outwards and discovered that the man could only know himself fully in society (Plato added "his" society, his "city") and that this society is the individual consciousness writ large. The individualist scepticism of Socrates passes over into the magistral social dogmatism of Plato.

2

The Republic is an ethical treatise and, although an example of Socratic dialectic, is dogmatic in its conclusions, involves psychological investigations and contains an educational prospectus and a political constitution.

The ethical argument, on justice, runs true at the beginning to the customary Socratic form. What really is justice? It uses the customary gambits of current Sophistic discussion. The Nature versus Convention argument, anticipated by Heraclitus and the Sophists, is here clearly set out. It will accompany us throughout the development of political thought, down to our own days. Its statement was yet peculiarly appropriate when made by the Greeks—agriculturalists tied by every bond of habit and religion to a narrow clan morality and yet also seafaring men accustomed, as Herodotus sets forth, to meet strange people who regarded the manners of the Greek cities as outlandish and whose own moral code was, for Greeks, barbarous. Briefly the argument amounts to this: Does morals (*mores*, customs) mean "the customary," which cements by its tradition a particular society—the Conventional, the Etiquette *comme il faut* of Confucius? Or does it mean that which is really valuable in all times and places and whenever human nature is confronted with the problem of what it ought to do and what is its true or rational self—the Natural? (Even the Instinctive and Intuitive, of Lao-tze?) It involves two different ways of answering the question: Why *should* I be moral?

The moral is just or righteous. But what *is* the just? Those who answer that the just or moral is what tradition from age-old time declares to be so, so that the memory of man runs not to the contrary, have actually a good argument at their disposal—the moral *is* the habitual, that which long practice has shown to be to the advantage of a society in survival. There is no "reason" in it or about it. The issue is, however, rapidly (and unfairly) restated by Plato. Is the just that which is to the advantage of the stronger nation? Or, domestically, that of the stronger group or man? The "strong man" Thrasymachus, the anti-intellectual (probably sketched from Dionysius I, also used in Book IX),* is introduced into the dialogue in order to brush aside all moralizing refinements of philosophers and to state roundly, What is conventionally called justice is the advantage, here and now, of the stronger.

Socrates leads Thrasymachus on to the statement that he here means what is really to his advantage. What he merely capriciously

* However, Thrasymachus is an historical character.

wills may of course prevail—but, as touching systems of order, we are presumably to understand that to be "just" which the strong man, deliberately and not by mistake, decides to be to his advantage. We must not suppose the strong man a fool. What then is *real* advantage? Plato here skilfully steers away from what men actually hold to be to their advantage or good—away from some empiric definition of the just—on to a discussion of the real advantage or *ideal* good. Thrasymachus is delivered into his hands.

The case for the superman who wills his own pleasure and proposes to get it, against the guardians who would impose the shackles of duty, is stated more subtly in the *Gorgias*. Here Callicles does not argue that justice *is* the device of the strong. He reflects that a combination of the weak may often defeat the superman. The devil of it is that the superman is so often defeated. Callicles' argument is that justice *ought* to be this *fiat* of the superman. In the class war, the few ought to win.

What kind of few? asks "Socrates." The excellent—but in what sense? Apparently not just the men of brawn. Callicles is a radical—is even prepared to bring the proletariat to consciousness and to supply them with an enlightened dictatorship. But he is himself no proletarian. Does Callicles mean more than that those who ought to win ought to win? Callicles might answer that he meant to argue (like General Göring) for the survival of the fittest, *i.e.*, of the survival of those fittest to survive, *i.e.*, fittest to cause others not to survive—although why these not only will, but ought to, survive (since "ought to" would seem to mean only "succeeds in")* might not be so clear. But Callicles takes another route.

> I cannot say very much for [Polus'] wit when he conceded to you [Socrates] that to do is more dishonourable than to suffer injustice. . . . For the truth is, Socrates, that you, who pretend to be engaged in the pursuit of truth, are appealing now to the popular and vulgar notions of right, which are not natural, but only conventional. Convention and nature are generally at variance with one another. . . .
>
> For the suffering of injustice is the part, not of a man, but of a slave, who indeed had better die than live; since when he is wronged and trampled upon, he is unable to help himself, or any other about whom he cares. The reason, as I conceive, is that the makers of laws are the majority, who are weak; and that they make laws and distribute praises and censures with a view to themselves and to their own interests; and they terrify the stronger sort of men, and those who are able to get the better of them; and they say, that dishonesty is shameful and unjust; meaning, by the word injustice, the desire of a man to

* *Cf.* Spinoza's treatment of this issue, p. 252.

have more than his neighbours, for knowing their own inferiority, I suspect that they are only too glad of equality. And therefore the endeavour to have more than the many, is conventionally said to be shameful and unjust, and is called injustice, whereas nature herself intimates that *it is just for the better man to have more than the worse,* the powerful than the weaker; and in many ways she shows, among men as well as among animals, and indeed among whole cities and races, that justice consists in *the superior ruling over and having more than the inferior.* . . .

But if there were a man who had sufficient force, he would shake off and break through, and escape from all this; he would trample under foot all our formulas and spells and charms, and all our laws which are against nature: *the slave* [an unhappy choice of a word, that, for the Shackled Superman, this Prometheus on Caucasus] *would rise in rebellion and be lord over us, and the light of natural justice could shine forth.*

"Socrates" replies:

Of the frankness of your nature and freedom from modesty I am assured by yourself, and the assurance is confirmed by your last speech. Well, then, the inference in the present case clearly is, that if you agree with me in an argument on any point, that point will have been sufficiently tested by us. . . . Once more, then, tell me what you and Pindar mean by natural justice. . . . Are the superior and better and stronger the same or different? . . . The laws of the many are the laws of the superior? . . . And are not the many of opinion, as you were lately saying, that justice is equality? . . . Please to begin again, and tell me who the better are if they are not the stronger?

Then Callicles, like Thrasymachus, makes his fatal slip:

Most assuredly I do mean the wiser . . . that the better and wiser should rule and have more than the inferior.

In a moment, "Socrates" has pointed out that this involves "the superman" in a knowledge of true wisdom. All Platonism, all Catholicism and all Hegelianism follow from that admission. Whether *anyone* knows *true* wisdom, Plato (with a reservation to which I shall return*) does not inquire.

At least we have come near to the kernel of a vital argument. The "superior man," according, *e.g.*, to some biological standard, may be a valuable "variant" on the normal but far weaker than the normal or

* *Cf.* p. 57. Neither Socrates (so far as can be judged) nor Plato identifies true wisdom with *intellectual* ratiocination. Experience (*e.g.*, in moral wisdom, and of the good) is required. *Cf.* S. Anselm, p. 174. They are rationalists or not according to the interpretation of the word, but they are more mystics than intellectualists, either of the logical or of the utilitarian variety. Socrates, however, lacks a doctrine of moral *will.*

even sub-normal individuals collectively, if it comes to a contest of brute force. The route of superior survival value, in the short term, is pre-empted now by those who can take *collective* action, not by the *individual*. "Superior men" will have no chance unless either by a miracle they can so breed and multiply as to acquire superior collective might or they can, by persuasiveness and skill, win leadership of, or divide, the collective mass. Let us assume that this "variant" superiority is not *only* biological, but *also* aesthetic or touched by a sense for sublime values, and Plato's question of how by wisdom to control the mass becomes relevant and a genuine answer to Callicles. The argument reacquires relevance and has a force of gigantic significance in its contemporary applicability. It will be noted that both Callicles and "Socrates" are admitted *inequalitarians*.

3

The Republic is not only a treatise on justice. It is an exemplification of the dialectical method. It follows, in its dialogue, a particular method which exhibits, as illustrated above, the Socratic dialectic (or logical argumentation by cross-examination and the exposure of contradiction), lit up in many passages by the Socratic irony or profession of ignorance. It is, as we have seen, a negative method which reaches truth as the residue after the demolition of pretension and falsehood. To the physics of the earlier philosophers and the ethical stress of Socrates, Plato added the development of this Socratic dialectical method—and his own poetic dogmas in ethics. The dialectical demolition, however, was by no means always completely fair and often involved mental sleights-of-hand.

Plato's dialectical method is logical at a time when logic, as a science, was novel and fascinating and before even the first text-book on it had been written, by Aristotle. Thus, where Plato is discoursing on Communism, influences, *e.g.*, of competition, which might militate anti-civically, against communal interests, are excluded with logical precision. Aristotle later protests against this highly logical or mathematic concept of unity in society, replacing it by the more organic concept of self-sufficiency. Hence, perhaps, it is that the poets (despite Plato's own poetry) and the imaginative writers fare ill at Plato's hands. Even as a logical treatise, however, *The Republic* is incomplete, since sections of the working-out of the scheme, *e.g.*, the essential sections on the conditions of the classes other than the rulers, are often omitted on the ground, apparently, that they are not required in a literary demonstration.

This logical quality is both the strength and weakness of *The Republic* and of the other Platonic dialogues. It is questionable how far Plato hoped to see the practical fulfilment of his scheme. For reasons already indicated, it used to be customary to assume that he did not. As we shall later see, there are reasons to suppose that view entirely wrong. Plato himself explains that at least it is possible that his scheme should be realized in practice—but he does not propose to be deterred, by practical considerations of politics, in his logical pursuits in morals. "We must follow the argument whithersoever it may carry us." As a consequence the Platonic dialogues "date" singularly little. The problems Plato discusses are again with us today and his treatment, because logical and unencumbered by local "common sense," is fresh. The issue, "What is Justice?" so treated, has relevance for our age also.

The logical method, however, has the defect that, like theorems of geometry, it is static. Best has no better. This has certain consequences for Platonic doctrine to which we shall return.*

The dialectic is, moreover, thoroughly Sophistical, and that in the bad sense. Macaulay, for all his intellectual "Brummagem" and tinsel, was not entirely wrong when he accused Plato's "Socrates" of being chiefly anxious to get trophies after empty victories. Callicles has a case when he says, "Somehow or other your words, Socrates, always appear to me to be good words; and yet, like the rest of the world, I am not quite convinced by them." "Socrates'" opponents writhe in a trap; but too often it is only a trap. Thus, no sooner has Plato seized upon the practical notion of competition than he develops it, by ruthless but tricky *tour de force*, into the absurdly unreal notion of "a war of all against all," which is later to be a logical gambit (in the precisely opposite sense) for Hobbes.

Two thousand years later, Friedrich Nietzsche accused Socrates and Plato of being the fathers of the decadence in Hellenic culture. European culture, in brief, according to Nietzsche, had only just begun when these men infected it—with intellectualism and doubts of its native Homeric confidence, and with other-worldliness. Plato, twisting Callicles into the admission that it is better to suffer injustice than to commit it, is the kind of demi-pacifist whom Nietzsche especially disliked and against whom he restated Callicles' argument.†

It is at least true to say this that most of political thought since Plato has been concerned with exploring the truth of Plato's conclu-

* *Cf.* p. 58. There is no valuable liberty in the right to say that $2 \times 2 = 5$.
† *Cf.* p. 529.

sions and with reexamining those pleas raised by his opponents which his sophistic argument and ironic wit appeared to destroy. Above all it has been concerned with the fundamental problem raised by Callicles, quoting the poet Pindar:

> Law . . . makes might to be right, doing violence
> With highest hand, as the deeds of Heracles shew.

In proving Callicles wrong, Plato explicitly declared that he proved proletarian democracy and the common man at fault. (Callicles, it is to be noted, claimed to be of the "popular party" although a critic of "democracy," as much as Napoleon or any Fascist.) They displayed in general what Callicles displayed in particular, admiration for an intemperate, uncontrolled, irrational disposition, that of *l'homme moyen sensuel,* with a contempt for "mere speculation." Plato, the pope of philosophy, viewed them with ascetic distaste. His superior men must be priests of a disciplined church and commissars with a dogma. This means that there are problems of the modern temper—problems of emotion, imagination, initiative, personality and non-logical creative power—which it is difficult to hold that Plato has solved truly. If Callicles had not, in typical Hellenic fashion, admitted that by the stronger and better he meant "the wiser," and had contented himself with asserting that it was (biologically) good for the race that the strong and tough should rule, *i.e.*, that those who do rule ought to rule, his argument, as Hegel was later to see, would have been stronger, even if still a fallacious one. Instead he admits the Platonic moral dualism between *is* and *ought,* and ends in the absurdity of maintaining that the excellent strong "ought to be" strong but are not. There Thrasymachus, less subtle, makes a better running with his argument: the strong do make laws, define morality—and ought to do so. He trips by confessing that strength involves intelligence, that is, some absolute wisdom, instead of merely asserting that it involves practical, Machiavellian cunning. Neither Callicles nor Thrasymachus would probably have been right had they taken the other route—but their argument would have been more formidable.

4

The Republic, however, is not only a dialectical treatise on ethics. It is a dogmatic treatise. It embodies a teaching and conclusions. And this teaching involves a system upon which much of the philosophic structure and hence (why "hence" we will show later*) much of the

* *Cf.* p. 135.

social structure of Western civilization is to rest. Plato, like an artist, strikes out an idea which embodies itself and expresses itself in the material world. As he declared of his 'philosopher' (*Republic* VI,) "I am a painter of republics." Why does Plato's idea, in answer to the question, "What is Justice?" assume this social form, this form of a dogma seeking to mould, not only the individual, but whole societies? Let us go further: Why is it precisely true to say that if Plato had not been, Europe—Occidental civilization as a cultural unity—would not have been?

Let us look back a stage. Thrasymachus should perhaps have argued that what is is what ought to be; and that the strong man does, will, must and should rule, if not by force then by cunning. Thrasymachus tripped up. But does Plato give an answer, in replying to Thrasymachus, to the more substantial argument? Briefly (anticipating a little), we may say that his answer is the end of *laissez faire.* The answer is that cunning is an individualist quality, fitted for saving the individual. What, however, ultimately makes strength—if mere strength be the test—is union, that is, co-operation which involves moral qualities, including harmony and social justice, among those who co-operate. Co-operation then is the principle of power; cunning exploitation is the principle of division, egoism, anarchy and ruin. Assuming a static world, it is a good answer.

But it will be noted that Plato nowhere argues that co-operation should be maintained "for the good of the race." Otherwise "races" or "nations" would, as final entities, be entitled to engage in Machiavellian cunning against each other; and would be entitled, with Thrasymachus, to call this good or, with Callicles, to call the success of the winner, as long only as he is "the right sort" of winner, good. Plato argues that co-operation is produced by, but is also required by, justice—justice being the principle of harmony—and that social harmony or peace is a value in itself, an idea which the individual knows to be a value, which gives peace of soul *to that individual* and which civilization acquires in turn value and beauty by serving. There is no evidence that Plato is concerned with the survival either of the individual or of the race; but there is evidence that he is concerned with the beauty of civilization and with the peace of soul of *the individual* who grasps for himself that humane ideal or divine beauty. If, beyond the Happiness of the Many, is Civilization, beyond Civilization are the rational Eternal Values. "The Divine Plato" is the greatest of Humanists (save on one point only, his dogmatism) and, at least, the best of Theologians. Out beyond the notion of co-operation as (against the

Thrasymachi) the guaranty of force, is the notion of the moral (or good) as the harmonious (or true); and of the harmonious as the beautiful, grasped as such by the masters, which beauty is absolute value, irrelevant to all temporal interests, even of this globe itself.

5

The Republic is a psychological treatise. Over against co-operation, as logical alternative, Plato puts the *bellum omnium contra omnes*—"war of all against all." Sometimes men may admit a boxing ring-master—the law—and permit unbridled competition only within that ring. But the fundamental question yet remains, Why obey the law? Society will be chaotic with unbridled competition, but why, if I am thieving, trouble about society? And so Plato passes behind logic to psychological experience. Society is the individual writ large. But, conversely, the individual is society writ small. If society is chaotic, diseased, unhappy, so will the individual be. The soul of an Ishmael is an unhappy soul. And here the genius of Plato introduces a prophetically modern touch. (It will be found at the beginning of Book IX of *The Republic.*) The Ishmael may brazen it out in his conscious life. Even the successful Ishmael, the tyrant, "all his life long he is beset with fear and is full of convulsions and distractions." Is he happy when alone? Sodden with fear, his inner life also suffers from that chaos which his outer life promotes. Here is the real ground for not being seduced by the temptations of Gyges, the man who could become invisible, and whom no society or law could control. In sleep he betrays himself and the vices which make him Ishmael and fear-sodden. Appetites of the tiger and ape, which he refuses to check in life, however much he may excuse them, show their true shape in sleep when man re-enters the jungle from which he came.

> I mean those appetites which are awake when the reasoning and human and ruling power is asleep; then the wild beast within us, gorged with meat and drink, starts up and having shaken off sleep goes forth to satisfy his desires; and there is no conceivable folly or crime—not excepting incest or any unnatural union, or parricide, or cannibalism—which at such a time, when he has parted company with all shame and sense, a man may not be ready to commit.

Let us examine this formidable argument of Plato's against undisciplined vitality, irrational initiative and criminal excess. To anticipate a later term, emphatically Plato is a believer in Original Sin. The appetites, although perhaps in essence neutral, unchecked by discipline are evil.

It is popular today to call Plato a forerunner of Fascism. On the contrary, he is a forerunner of Catholicism. Belief in individual immortality, whether fact or myth, is cardinal for him.* It will be noted that (with a reservation later to be remarked†) he is, in the very core of his philosophy, a rationalist. He is the prophet of Reason by which, together with an educated will, the passions may be controlled. Although "Platonic love" is wrongly so called and, in a world where (as in the Orient and in some military communities) perversion was rife and fashionable, Plato only counselled against excess, nevertheless the Platonic philosophy is definitely one of discipline, if not of asceticism. Plato viewed the customs of the wealthy Sicilians, innovators, the Americans of his day, with fascinated disapproval. He could not keep away from Sicily; but he went to rebuke. In so far as clinical psychology may show that these natural impulses, "animals of the jungle," are good animals, as animals, and require to be understood and tamed rather than repressed, the Platonic teaching (which tended to ignore and treat as not really existent, if not to repress, "evil impulses") will be found to have a weakness. It is necessary, however, to be clear that Platonism, involving discipline, is not Puritanism. Its watchword is temperance, social, sexual, personal. Its repeated analogy is that of the instincts to racehorses which are needed to draw the chariot of life, but require to be reined in, and even whipped, as well as spurred. Platonism is grandly sane as perhaps no subsequent philosophy has ever been.

If weakness there be, it shows itself in Plato's distrust—we noted the same in Confucius—of a morality built up from within outwards, save in the case of a few demigods and philosophers of a rational insight. He distrusts the unredeemed, common, unenlightened "inner man." Morality is and must be determined by environment and by education through environment. Men, to be good, must be brought up in "a good pasture." Hence the attention to literature and music, to city life and even geographic position. Plato has little interest in "the beautiful soul" and "the sacred conscience" as individualistic expressions—certainly as individualistic expressions apart from a self-imposed but rational discipline. Who then should mould this environment and control it? Man. But man guided, not by his spiritual private conscience or caprices, but by Reason. Now Reason, for Plato,

*But *cf.* p. 66. Also p. 137, 721.

† *Cf.* p. 57.

like mathematics is "outward," objective, real apart from Smith or Jones. We hear, in the later dialogues, little of the "voices" and "demons" of Socrates.* And, against Reason, there are *no* natural rights. Plato is the antithesis of an anarchist. Profoundly, he is an authoritarian. Ethic—*ethos*, *i.e.*, the total ethical system in practice—is imprinted. The very (late) Greek word "*charactēr*" implies it: "a seal-mark."

This objectivity, non-subjectivity, is carried further and makes yet more plain its great historical defect, its one defect. Excellence, for Plato, as an idea is something capable of being grasped by reason, demonstrated and taught. The idea once rationally grasped, it cannot be surpassed. Progress consists solely in realizing it in practice. But, if the reasoning is once correct, there is no reason to suppose through all the ages improvement in the conception of the idea. Change is utterly contrary to its nature. Through all the centuries two times two equals four, and will so remain. The excellent cannot, from mere lapse of time, be replaced by the more excellent, since time is irrelevant and the ideas do not change. Either I grasp the idea or do not; but there is no more reason why John Dewey, after twenty centuries, should grasp it than Plato. Plato is an opponent of Heraclitus who "made whirlwind king." There is no conception of Progress in Plato because there is none, substantially, of Time. Time is not Real, but of the very nature of the incidental. Human Nature is real—and the values it apprehends, true, beautiful and good.

Hence Plato is uninterested in progressive individuals—in challenge, new moral insights, rebellion and initiative for their own sake. Once the truth is grasped by timeless logic, he who differs from it is merely wrong—a fool and perhaps an obstinate one. Better educate him if humble and punish him if proud—good Catholic doctrine. There is, for Plato, no sacred liberty to be wrong. Human morality has always tended to be retrospective, like that of the "wisdom of Egypt," not progressive. Plato stands in a middle position. The realization of the idea *can* be progressive. But the idea is transcendent to the time-process and, as it were, latently was "in the beginning before all worlds." Plato has no spark of sympathy for a character such as Ibsen's "Brand," the idealist rebel, or for Henry James, with his passion for freedom even from the cloy of Brook Farm Utopia—with this reservation, that, in the *Hippias Minor*,† Plato states that he prefers a great evil man, capable of achievement for good, to a little good man ca-

* But *cf.* p. 57.

† I am presuming that this Dialogue is genuine.

pable of nothing. But, for the rest, man in opposition, with his "freeman's worship," is for Plato neither happy nor good. Plato's thought here has dominated classical Christianity—we shall later see how.* Plato, the great conservative, has not taken account within his ideal world of the real significance of error, that is, of expanding experience.

Certain reservations, dubious but of immense potential importance, must be made. We have said that Plato in the *Hippias Minor* finds a place in his moral scheme (as, long after, sociologists such as Durkheim will do) for the criminal. The problem of the life and death of Socrates, the criminal, is, after all, the start of Plato's own thinking. Perhaps beginning as Socrates' dedicated vindicator, the true conclusion of Platonism is agreement with the jury: Socrates died justly. (Did he not himself say that he owed filial obedience? Pity that the jury was not wiser—but the executioner did his duty.) Further, in the *Letters*, in certain places Plato the dogmatist seems to hint at a basic scepticism whether man can know that he knows truth. And it will be noted that his assessment of ultimate value is no logical assessment (despite the so-called Cambridge Platonists of the eighteenth century) but an agreement among those whom we agree to be masters concerning what the beautiful may be. It is then arguable (we cannot here argue it) that there is a core of probabilism, of scepticism in Plato, which would make him transcend the dogmatists and father also the other major tradition in human thought, the empiric. Merely Plato thinks fit to be (almost) silent about it as "dangerous thoughts."

The Republic is one of the world's greatest political treatises, both by right of seniority and also by inherent value. Its only serious rival is Aristotle's *Politics*. Rousseau's *Social Contract* is too tenuous and uneducated, and Hobbes' *Leviathan* and Marx's *Capital* are both too specific to come within the same category. The socio-political treatment is a consequence of Plato's social conception of ethics and is, therefore, for him a necessary aspect of any discussion of justice. Justice is more than a balancing of contracts between individuals. It has implicit in it the principle of a social scheme.

6

Plato has shown himself a great Co-operator in his opposition to the principle of pursuing self-interest; a great Socialist in his opposition to all private interests that distract attention from putting society

* *Cf.* pp. 64, 143, 182.

first. His society is the city and his ethics are civics. Let us turn to his social plan.

Plato, the Social Rationalizer, in outlining his social plan, turns again to his psychological divisions. In the *psyche* or soul, Reason is like a charioteer controlling and driving the Instincts, both the spiritual instinct or will power, the *Élan vital,* and the bodily instinct of Lust, which horses show their true shapes in untamed dreams when the charioteer, the censor Reason, sleeps. Metaphor and dreams apart, there are three great psychological principles in man: Reason; Spirit, *Esprit,* principle of will and emotion; and the Appetites or Passions, corresponding to the digestive faculties in physiology, as the others do to heart and brain. Those guided by these last, businessmen and the like, are merely the mob, even if *ὁ τῶν πλούτων πλῆθος* (ho tōn ploutōn plēthos)—"the mob of the wealthy." There is a splendid arrogance about Plato's *aristocratisme.*

Corresponding, then, to these three psychological functions are three sociological types: those who love the best for itself, those who love the best for its personal glamour and glory, and those who love the best for what materially it will get us—those apart who do not love the best at all, perverted types.

Corresponding, again, to those three sociological types, according to which constitutes the governing class, are three political constitutions, the aristocratic, the timocratic (*timē*—"honour:" the military principle) and the oligarchic (merchant class). Where, however, the object of the ruling class is merely to maintain and increase their profits and spoils, and no ideal principle is involved, a degeneration sets in in which each pushes against each for these spoils and swag. In that competition the spirit of disciplined aristocracy, with its honour, is broken and mere force triumphs. The many, if led, have this force; and democracy, *i.e.*, sharing out the spoils, succeeds as a constitution. But what the many—still without any principle apart from gain, which (negatively put) is greed and envy—lack is continuous leadership. This popular leadership they must have if they are to maintain their gains. Demagogues are not enough: "the leader" must have the will to power, as well as a popular capacity to please.

Hence arises tyranny, which may be benevolent—most Greek tyrants (it is highly important to note) were. However, it knows no law save its own will—the will of "the leader," or chief "comrade," as prophet, being above formal law—and hence is irrationalist and the subversion of Reason, the assassination of the charioteer. Plato, as we have seen, is not only a logician but a rationalist. Monarchy is either regulated by constitutional law or hereditary. Tyranny is the rule of one man, using illusion or force. Plato, however, it must be noted, does *not* exclude a *Führer-princip* ('principle of leadership') where one man arises of supreme and *disinterested* rational intuition.

Later, in *The Statesman*, Plato provides us with a neat division of constitutions into categories, taken over by Aristotle and itself derived from Herodotus, divided by number of the rulers and by principle of government. The unperverted are three—by the one (Royalty), few (Aristocracy), many (True Democracy), and the perverted, unrestrained on principle by law, are three, by the one (Tyranny), the few (Oligarchy), and the many (False Democracy). The change is immaterial save that it places Democracy among the possible sound forms and heads the list with rule by the supremely wise one man, if he can be found. Hence Plato outlines a philosophic justification for Papacy.

What has all this to do with Justice? The answer is that the well-educated or temperate man is a man in whom reason is permitted to rule. To each faculty of the psyche—Mind, Spirit and Senses—is allowed its equitable function. In a sound human existence the principle that is equitable in the psyche is also equitable in society. Only if it exists in society, and is acquiesced in, can the individual be trained in sound principles himself and be happy. On this principle, discovered by introspection (and by logic) to be sound in our own souls, must be cast a society which will reimpress it, as a "character," upon the souls of future citizens. In this social order everyman must mind his own function or business, which he is fitted to do well. To observe this harmonious order is justice by one's neighbour, who is *doing his job.* Social justice then is each man minding his own business. Two millennia later we shall hear of it in the form of "My Station and Its Duties" and, yet earlier, in the Pauline injunction, "Ye are all members of one body." Plato even, in *The Laws*, XII, (and he is the first in the West) uses the organic analogy, speaking of the "trunk" of the body politic and of the guardians as the "head."

The Republic is a treatise on the art (which also involves a science) of Government. In the Just Society who shall be the ruling class?—for, in a differentiated, organic society, men apprenticed in the science of rule there will be. Clearly, the Rational, the Wise. Who are these? Plato sagely observed that they are few. That is the nature and limit of excellence. How are we to detect them? By ability. Plato is quite clear that his ruling class is *not* a caste and is not *necessarily* hereditary. The "golden-born" need not always—certainly until eugenic arrangements were improved—be of gold in parentage. Here we mark a great historic advance from the major political systems which had hitherto obtained and which had acquired a philosophy (implicit in theological writing) in Egypt and in India. His system deeply resembles these Theocracies when compared with modern government; but his system is not the same.

Ability, however, is not to be found full grown and created spontaneously and haphazard. It is not a substance, like a pound of tea, but a quality of plastic human nature moulded by environment. Plato fully recognizes the duty to provide *every* citizen with such material well-being as will enable him, by nurture, to develop to their rational perfection the powers latent in his nature. That falls within the Platonic notion of justice. Human nature, however, is not entirely plastic. "The golden-born" may have "silver-born" children, who should be deposed or "demoted" and the "silver-born" may have "golden-born" children who must be promoted. Especially is this likely to happen in a haphazard society. But in a just society appropriate stock will be selected. And it will be eugenically bred, thanks to a full sense of the grave public responsibility to humanity involved.

A good inherited nature must be improved by a good formal education, physical and intellectual. But formal education is not enough. The significant education which a man receives is that from the society in which he grows up. If, then, we seek just-minded citizens, not men made criminal by their environment, those who have the power have also the responsibility to mould a just society. Men do not finish their education with school, or always cease to be children on reaching adolescence. All one can say is that the power of education to change and correct, but not to preserve and guide, grows smaller. Plato is a paternalist in his plan of government.

How then is the climate of environment to be maintained at the temperature appropriate for justice? The answer is to be found in the outline of a gigantic anticipation of the Catholic Church. As Professor Ernest Barker says, speaking as a Protestant, of one side of Platonism and Catholicism: "All evil clericalism is to be found in germ in Plato." The connection, however, as we shall see later, between Plato and Catholicism is nothing miraculous; but the consequence, in part, of direct influence and, in part, of common tradition. It is true that *The Republic,* save by rumour and scattered reference, was a lost book from Proclus (fifth century) to Pico della Mirandola (fifteenth century). Only the *Timaeus* was preserved for reference in the early Middle Ages. The Early Fathers, however, of the Christian Church, not least St. Augustine (despite his imperfect acquaintance with Greek writers), were steeped in late Platonism. In order to fill in adequately the details of the plan we shall here also draw on *The Laws*, the later and less radical treatise, written by Plato in his late period after his second visit to Syracuse and unfinished at his death.

The Republic and *The Laws* are in effect, if the paradox may be pardoned, tractates in defence of the Catholic hierarchy. As we have seen, the best form of government obtainable is by the *basilikotatos aner*—"the most kingly man"—the wisest of the wise, the Platonic Pope. Truth, in the last resort, is not (we learn in *The Laws; cf.* also Letter VII) to be discovered by logic and syllogism but by mystic revelation, the appreciation of it being by an Areopagus of wise men, "required to meet daily between the hour of dawn and the rising of the sun," consisting "in the first place of the priests who have obtained the rewards of virtue." These are those who

> know these two principles—that the soul is the eldest of all things which are born, and is immortal and rules over all bodies; moreover . . . . have contemplated the mood of nature which is said to exist in the stars, and gone through the previous training, and seen the connexion of *music* with these things, and harmonized them all with laws and institutions . . . . able to give a reason of all things that have reason. (*The Laws,* XII, 967.)

Truth, however, is no subjective vision. Its touchstone is the agreement (as in music among masters) of those adjudged competent to judge. It is to be grasped not by logic (which only exposes falsehood) but yet by those grounded in metaphysics—one almost adds (in the most philosophic sense) theology. The final council is that of the Elders—those who know why they know. We may compare this with the ecclesiastical *presbyteroi,* "elders" (Presbyters, Priests). But the general work of government rests with a select body of rulers or governors. This is the class or function of society that corresponds with Reason in the individual: it is the trained group of rational men. These are the Platonic Governors. We may compare this with the *clerōtoi,* "selected" (clergy)—those in Holy Orders—in contrast with the *laicoi,* "populace" (laity).

In addition to the Governors or Clergy, Plato has two other Orders corresponding to the physiological and psychological functions in man of heart or *esprit,* and of digestion or appetite. These are the Warriors and the Workers for Profit. We may compare them with the Chivalry of the Middle Ages (Crusader Knights, Orders of the Temple and St. John) and the Merchants, Farmers and the rest. Plato, however, is preoccupied with the education of his Governors or Spiritual Directors and spares little space in outlining any detailed scheme for the flock of followers.

There may, however, be rebels against the rational rule of the directors—obstinate heretics who do not understand true metaphysics. They are to be reasoned with—we compare the Holy Inquisition—in a place ingeniously called a Sophronisterion or place-for-making-men-wiser, *i.e.*, a concentration camp. If they relapse, they may be dealt with vigorously by those who know how to use force—the secular arm—lest the public order be disturbed. This does not apparently violate, in his own eyes, Plato's priestly principle that it is better to suffer injustice than to inflict it. It is not injustice.

Literature also may poison the climate of the good state. There will certainly be no "free press." On the contrary, literature will be censored. We may compare the Papal Index.

7

The Republic was maintained, by Rousseau in his *Émile*, to be the finest treatise extant on education. Rousseau was himself something of a Platonist,* and had read Plato—perhaps to his own disadvantage—in a translation. Whether Rousseau was right each must form his own opinion. But certainly Plato, as an educationalist, is thorough with the courage of his convictions. Where he is perhaps most valuable is in his escape (easier in his day of private tutors for the few) from the conception that education means little boys going to school.

The Greeks used the word *mousikē* in a much wider sense than our "music." It was everything to do with the Muses—including even, odd though it may seem to scholars today, History. Briefly, it embraced all culture. And, by inquisition and index and spiritual directors, it was culture that Plato proposed to mould. A weakness in Plato to which we have already called attention—his disrespect for the imagination and its work, dynamic, demonic—here comes to the front. According to his own lights Plato, with his distrust of poets (as we must distrust Mr. Shaw today) and condemnation of the liar Homer, was right. The imaginative genius is extra-rational, too often in alliance with unchecked emotion, undisciplined, non-ascetic, dangerous. Solemnly the ex-poet, Plato, examines the poets and the musicians. The ancient equivalents of Shaw and Schnitzler are utterly banned—although Shaw might be allowed to possess a serious intent corrupted by an unphilosophic early training and an individualistic demagogic tendency to play *largo di basso* or big bassoon to everybody else's fiddle.

* *Cf.* p. 444.

The Lydian equivalent of immemorial African jazz was utterly taboo as stimulating the lower passions. To be frank, humour and suffering buffoons patiently were not Plato's forte. Unlike David, he thought it bad theology to dance before the Ark.* Degenerate art, inspired by dangerous ideas, poisoned education, defeated propaganda, weakened the salutary myth. He proposed to stamp it out.

8

The Republic and *The Laws* are Communist tractates. Plato—apart from the Egyptian priests, and the Hindu Brahmins and the Peruvian pre-Incas and many primitive peoples—is the first Communist. Unlike the priests, with their demand to be sustained in common wealth by the alms of the labouring, competing merchants and masses, he is a highly articulate Communist, although it must be noted that his communism also is only for the few, the spiritual directors, and apparently in some less precise measure for the military men. He takes the entirely common-sense point of view, later adopted by the Church, that those who want power must pay for it (and avert envy) by asceticism and frugality; but that the mass of men prefer money and their material share-out, whole product of their labour, to power. Granted a just modicum of security, they can only be driven to effort by hope of lucrative gain. Such a pursuit, is perhaps (as Dr. Johnson said) harmless—but harmless as long as such men are not permitted to pretend that gains, irrelevant to moral quality, constitute a social claim to power.

Plato is not—it is highly important to point out—a Marxian Communist. There has been, obviously, much Communism before Marx, and no little Communism since Marx is also non-Marxian. Plato is not, even by anticipation, a Marxian Communist for other reasons than that his communism is neither universal nor international. It is also not founded, as its rock basis, on the Economic Interpretation of History. It culminates in the Classless Society in the economic sense. But it certainly does not aim at the functionally undifferentiated society. (Perhaps neither does Marxism; but to that we shall return.†) Above all, it rests on the antithesis of the Class War and nowhere supposes that the establishment of Social Justice presupposes victory in the Class War. The defect of Plato's position, it must be pointed out, is that his Republic (but *not* the Communist Benedictine monasteries) remained unestablished and "utopian"—in brief, does not exist.

* Metaphorically. Actual dancing Plato regarded as a high form of art.

† *Cf.* p. 643.

In order to evoke the satisfactory environment for social justice it is not enough to regulate culture. Plato freely admits that one must regulate civilization, social and economic institutions, and technological and material conditions. The art and science of government is emphatically a whole-time job. It, therefore, requires leisure from industrial employment. Hellenes anyhow ought not to be used as cogs in a slave technology—animated tools; but many freemen engaged in *banausikai*, *i.e.*, mechanical, occupations were not suited to share in rule. Indeed the pursuit of any other occupation must necessarily exclude a man from political *expertise*. There must be no "part-timing." How, then shall a man get this leisure? He cannot get it by earning it. Can he get it by inherited private wealth? No, replies Plato. The self-made man will be occupied with profit and the heir with defending a private wealth not necessarily connected with ability and social service. Both will have their eye on their main chance, their pile—at least must defend it from inroads—and will be preoccupied, if not competitive. If the common wealth is to come before private wealth, at least for the directing group the two must be the same. Sparta, in its better days, with its property reallocations and common regimental messes, had shown the way. There must be thorough communism of property as touching everything that was likely to create rivalry or to distract attention from the public aim—not, of course, in clothes, wine glasses and the like, but in everything that might divide comrades. "To friends," Plato quotes a saw, "all things are common." The Spartans, in large part, did it; the Cretans did it; and it had succeeded in more than Prussian fashion—and this although a Spartan was taught in childhood, as part of his military training, how to steal and get away with it.

How about community of wives? The issue, Plato recognizes, through the ironic mouth of "Socrates," cannot be shirked. Whether or not monogamy, supplemented by concubinage, is or is not substantially an extension of the private property system, at least here in the family was the especial centre of those interests and affections, nobler than love of pelf, which a man might put in front of the public weal. As the French proverb (and the French are experienced) later ran: "Ces pères de famille sont capables de tout."* Discipline here might check even the military men—if the necessity of philosophic training did not—from aspiring to be governors when they had no ambitious wives before whom to display their personal glory and dignities.

* "These family men are capable of anything."

Plato, moreover, like Euripides, had faced the problem of feminism. Hellas had seen the emancipated Aspasia and the yet more emancipated Sappho—neither inglorious. (Sappho's poems were later destroyed by the horrified Byzantine bishops—whereas Plato had destroyed his own.) Plato saw no reason why women of ability, even if usually not quite so good as the men, should be precluded from sharing in that public work and research of truth which alone gave significance to life, just because of their sex, any more than because of colour of hair or skin. It mattered more that they should be men (the Greek word has no sex implications like the more barbaric Gothic)—fully conscious "humans"—not mere mob members. For the domestic joys and virtues which the dissolute Rousseau praised, Plato, when the art of controlling civilization was at issue, had no more sympathy than a naval officer on duty or the General of the Jesuits. It was very admirable for the lower orders. The population question, it should be added, was never far, at this time, from the Greek mind.

If, however, sex was not to matter, then this issue must be taken seriously. Women could not have it both ways and jealously maintain private property in their husbands. There was to be one big community in which public and scientific pursuits were to count first, but where eugenic considerations dictated the maintenance of a population of high ability and where, among competitors in a friendly way, the bold were to deserve the fair. It is clear that Plato, without encouraging his bugbear "appetite," does not disapprove of such cohabitation as must remove the edge from competitive rivalry, provided that there is no offspring or that the offspring is eugenically fit. The phrase "community of children" is correct, but the phrase "community of wives" applied to Plato may be misleading. He seems to have thought of parenthood, as distinct from cohabitation, as being by one selected man with one selected woman. But, apart from stress on eugenic selection, the text is not clear. Where children are involved, he is a rigid moralist about the obligation of the individual to respect his biological obligations towards race and *polis*. This apart, Plato is "temperate."

The Catholic Church did not balk at facing rigorously the same problems. For its priesthood—not the lay vulgar—it ordained poverty and, as touching monastic communities (often wealthy corporately), community of goods. The Order came first. As touching wives, inflamed by a Syrian tradition which regarded sex as intimately related to *the* original sin by which Eve tempted Adam, the Catholic Church found another solution of the problem: not to marry at all—unless, as Paul grudgingly says, the alternative were sexual mania. The early Christians believed that the end of the world would come before they had gone around the cities of Judah. The population question, therefore, did not trouble them anyway. Later, the principle of celibacy was made rigorous for the monastic orders only and, in the Western Church from the twelfth century, for the two senior orders of the clergy (out of seven).

The obvious objection to the Catholic solution of this problem (apart from human lapses of which Protestant critics made the most) is that stocks of ability became self-exterminating. It is, however, arguable that Plato's prescription would produce too grave racial difference between one class and another (even greater than today exists owing to the inadequate nourishment of the poor) and would end in a species of Huxleian Brave New World with its World Controllers or Sacred College. The Catholic supposition is the more democratic one: that high quality stock is very generally distributed and that as good children can be produced from the priest's brother, or from a pious layman, as from the priest or bishop. There is indeed no reason why the Platonic policy of eugenics should not be applied to all occupational groups in society. It must be admitted that the chances are greater that it will be begun in a limited number of groups—Commissars and Stakhanov workers, let us say. A Russian Soviet scientist has recently (1936) gone so far as to state that masses of men are, biologically speaking, slaves. This, however, seems to be an unproved dogma natural to totalitarianism.

The Catholic argument, however, for the biological extinction of the ablest, in the present stage of society, is not an easy one. On the other hand, it is clearly undesirable that women of ability should be left, as in the modern, secular world, with children stigmatized as illegitimate. According to Plato's system the community becomes responsible for all children desirable for the community. It is not necessary to call up before the mind a Russian system of communal crêches, communal nursery schools and communal eating places. Human parents, not a State Corporation without body or soul, could be responsible in human relations. But jealousy and private proprietary rivalry are excluded, to the point that parents will not claim, because they will not know, their own children—Plato is here being Shavian or thinking of a Reichsführer-schule—and the community countenances and finances the children which it requires. The system envisaged by Plato is apparently, not so much the *mari complaisant*, as something comparable to Noyes's Oneida Community in New York State (suppressed by the Baptist denomination, influencing a hesitant legislature). Malinowski, the anthropologist, insists that it is a natural enough form of living for primitive man, justified by the "law of Nature and Nations"—*ius naturale et gentium.*

Anyhow Plato is here discussing problems well ahead of our present stage of public opinion and requiring for their solution cultural controls that even Occidental civilization does not now command. Plato's argument is usually read with a shudder or followed by a hasty endeavour to explain that he did not quite mean what he said or was building a Cloud Cuckoo Land. However, through our numerous and increasing public institutional provisions for children, we have moved immeasurably far in his direction since the early Education Acts of the last century. The Catholic solution remains with us but, in Protestant countries, as an unintelligible religious idiosyncrasy, the legacy of a past age. The Protestant solution is an obscure compromise between Catholic asceticism (for which Plato provides an intelligible explanation), Syrian sex fear and Judaic patriarchalism. The feminist movement, of which Plato visualized one outcome, has as yet only begun, in the modern world, to reveal its serious moral and social—as distinct from its merely symbolical and vote-hunting—implications.

Plato, in the second-best community which he outlined in the *Laws,* was prepared to make certain concessions:

> The first and highest form of the state and of the government and of the law is that in which there prevails most widely the ancient saying, that "Friends have all things in common." Whether there is anywhere now, or will ever be, this communion of women and children and of property, in which the private and the individual is altogether banished from life. . . . I say that no man, acting upon any other principle, will ever constitute a state which will be truer or better or more exalted in virtue. Whether such a state is governed by Gods or sons of Gods, one, or more than one, happy are the men who, living after this manner, dwell there. . . . The *polis* which we have now in hand, when created, will be nearest to immortality and the only one which takes the second place.

Plato insisted on community of goods among the aristocracy. There is a certain ambiguity about this in the case of a suggestion from the Thebans that he should act as legislator for Megalopolis. Pamphila, writer of Memoirs, says in her twenty-fifth book (the statement is given by Diogenes Laertius, at the beginning of the third century A.D.) that Plato, when he discovered that they were opposed to equality of possessions, refused to act. However, on the evidence of his own writings, Plato seems to have had no objection to competition and profit-making among the bourgeois and proletarian orders. For him, therefore, the great problem of maintaining private initiative under any thorough socialist system among common men swayed by the profit motive and piece-rate wages does not apply. To each according to his needs and from each according to his ability applies to party-members only—the Platonic clergy, governors, or what Mr. Wells calls Samurai. The Catholic Church similarly insisted on poverty for the religious by vocation, specifically those in Monastic Orders.

Plato and the Catholic Church alike insist on unconditional obedience. The Catholic Church indeed admits the moral obligation to follow a bona fide conscience, even if erroneous. Plato is not so sure. But both are sure that there is on principle no liberty to err. *Extra ecclesiam nulla salus.* Outside the community there is no safety. Socrates, in one of his most certainly authentic utterances—he, the great Pioneer of Private Conscience—had himself insisted on this at his death. As much as Aristotle later, Plato believes that morals depend upon the way one is brought up. In the dialogue, *The Statesman,* Plato says that the politician, who is also politicist or political scientist, is like the physician, who is a physiologist, and his prescription must be followed—nor does it matter to the public weal "whether he cures us against or with our will." In the later words of Cromwell: "It is not what they want but what is good for them—that is the question." In the words of Mr. Bernard Shaw: "It is a simple historical fact that cultural institutions have to be imposed on the masses by rulers or private patrons enlightened enough to know that such institutions are neither luxuries nor mere amusements but necessities of civilized life." Hence Plato's stress on education and on "music."

Obedience was not only to be an act of duty: it was to be induced by the very air one breathed. Plato's communism is not materialist, but monastic (care is needed about the word "materialist:" we shall revert to it*—and the Marxists are also in practice monastic or disciplined in a hierarchy and "commissaristic"). Plato's sexual morality is not lax, but eugenic. He is not a sensualist, although sensually temperate or indifferentist, but idealist—and an idealist who knows that he knows the ideal and is entitled to demand obedience to it.

Such obedience involved—as in a monastic community—homogeneity in society. Plato decisively accepts this condition. He will

* *Cf.* pp. 573, 620, 630.

exclude aliens and race mixture. He will regulate population. He will limit its size to that of a small Swiss canton or less—or of Weimar or Rousseau's Geneva or a lesser Florence or Rome in its earliest republican days. The polis was to be of 5,040 landowning citizens (*Laws*)—let us say a total population of 30,000—*i.e.*, the smallest number (and here, as history was to prove, was the unknown variable) suitable for competent defence.

Plato goes further. He is not only an exponent of the Fascist closed economy. Although he would permit a certain number of trusted delegates, almost elder statesmen, to tour abroad and report on ideas and curiosities in the world without, nevertheless Plato—remembering the corrupting effect of the Sophists, the anthropologists like Herodotus, even the seafaring men, restless tellers of tales—would have the young men at home taught that no country was finer than their own country. Here Plato was the complete moral jingo—as it were, Italia finest and Mussolini always right; Russia unexcelled and Stalin right; "Deutschland über alles" and Hitler right; and Britannia ruling the waves. Plato, the mathematician, is drawing out swiftly the consequences of "known" and absolute truth, in unquestioning obedience and in the compromise of lesser truths, by the needs of practice, in myth. The very fruit of the original dogma betrays the need for scepticism.

9

How was the Platonic polis to be brought into being? And how maintained? The first, best by a demigod—a Divine Revelation. Doubtless the Revealer, perfectly just, would suffer and be put to death. Failing this, frankly, by capturing a tame dictator and hypodermically injecting philosophic notions. Hence the visits (in 388) to Dionysius I and (in 367 and 361–360) to Dionysius II of Syracuse.† How to maintain? It is here that we get the core of Platonism. The Myth is the Executive Clause of the Platonic Plan. It is the doctrine of the *gennaion pseudos*—the "genuine lie" or ideological Myth, to which mankind is found by experience to take kindly. This is how the wise man, the superior men, will conquer the empty masses whose might they require. Here are Plato's *Capital* and *Mein Kampf*.

Plato had turned the poets out of doors as liars. But that was because they might interfere with his own lie or propaganda. They were bad, black liars; he, white. Art and Science must be the servants of Theology, and of the Communist Commonwealth—not their masters.*

* *Cf.* pp. 174, 182.

† Or perhaps by a Commission on Constitutional Law.

> Truth embodied in a tale
> Shall enter in at lowly doors.

Plato, like Fletcher of Saltoun, proposed to provide the tales. It was a high moral imperative that the masses should sacrifice themselves to the community, to civilization and to its ideals, understood, of course, by the orthodox spiritual directors, Plato's communist philosophers. That meant, indeed, sacrifice of individual liberties, interests, ambitions in this life. What could persuade men to this sacrifice? Only the belief that, if not entirely happy here, in a totalitarian community, they would be elsewhere, in the Next World or after the Five-year Plan or the Four-year Plan—if they behaved themselves. Of course, the philosophers would understand what all this really meant—the truth. But the rest could be persuaded that they were individually immortal. This is the Myth of Er the Pamphylian. Not that they would just wake up in Heaven or Hell. On the contrary, they would be reincarnated on earth—moreover, they had had, as the Hindus also thought, many previous incarnations. That Myth would teach them to observe, contentedly or in God-fearing, the principles of Social Justice. A few could be trusted to be guided by their own altruism, sense of duty and grasp of metaphysical truth. Plato was among them.

How did Plato's scheme work in practice? We are not, I think, at all entitled to say that it was some More's *Utopia*, some dream never expected to work in practice. On the contrary he visited Sicily in 367 B.C., when nearly sixty, at no small risk to himself in order to put his plan into action.

Twenty years before, in 388 B.C., he had visited what was, for the Greek colonists, the America of those days and its Manhattan, Syracuse—largest city of the Western world.

> I was [he writes] by no means content with the "blissful life" which I found there, consisting, as it did, of incessant debaucheries . . . The human constitution cannot stand the strain of that sort of life for long. Nor would he ever be likely to learn self-control or any other virtue. What is more, no Polis, however good its laws, can retain any stability if its citizens believe in mad extravagance and exert themselves only in the pursuit of eating and drinking and in the vigorous pursuit of their amours. Inevitably in such a state there is a constant succession of tyrannies, oligarchies, and democracies; and the politicians cannot endure the mention of *just government or equality before the law.*

The last clause is an interesting stroke. It must never be forgotten that Plato, aristocrat, came of a pro-democrat family. Disgusted with his kinsmen among the oligarchic Thirty Tyrants he would even have favoured the democrats, for their moderation, had it not been their voices that condemned Socrates. His major charge against democracy is yet precisely that it is too tolerant; allows "even the asses to walk on the footpath"; has no standards of value; produces a piebald civilization, very varied; and denounces with fury as anti-proletarian, through the mouths of mere unself-conscious workers, those who insist on the new, disciplined, communist, vanguard puritanism; boasts of its sovereign power.

"Above all men the law" was with him a prime maxim. The law itself was Reason (not necessarily the Constitution). Nevertheless, it was precisely in opulent, vital Syracuse that Plato—partly from personal reasons and from friendship with Dion, son-in-law of the local boss or autocrat, Dionysius I—decided to make his experiment. After all, up north in Tarentum, they were accustomed to Pythagorean scientifico-political, as it were "freemason," technocrat experiments.

10

To Syracuse Plato, therefore, returned to "run," in collaboration with the able but puritanical Dion, the young man, Dionysius II, open to ideas, dilettante, *doré*, who had succeeded to the reins of government. The attempt was a failure—conspicuously so in the further venture of 361–360. The natural cue of the Platonists has been to blame the immoral weaknesses of the young man of thirty, not the political weaknesses of the sexagenarian sage. The matter, however, is not so simple. Dion, the puritan, although a man of ability, displayed the major error of an intellectual, the inability to conceal his own offensive cleverness. The chief fault of Dionysius appears to have been that of taking to philosophy as a young man about town takes to Buchmanism. To his credit be it said that he continued his studies of philosophy and mathematics (science and engineering, if one will) after Plato had, for the second time (361 B.C.) been sent about his business. What Plato and his friends did not grasp was that the Socialist commonwealth, as any other state, is conditioned in how it lives by what the neighbours will permit. Reforms, admirable in themselves, that provoke opposition and faction are only feasible, when the enemy is at the gate, if carried through with singular skill. They require caution unless their certain effect is to increase, not diminish, military force. And for the Sicilian Greeks, the Carthaginian was always at the gates. Philistos and the anti-Dion faction had the simplest patriotic argument at their command for opposing the alien visitor Plato.

Plato, who had carefully considered the menace of *stasis*—faction—within a closed economy, had failed to consider the bearing of faction upon the positions of rival states. His politics is singularly innocent of consideration of the power problems of state relations; of all adequate consideration of the meaning of foreign alliances; and even of such internationalism as existed in the Hellenic world. This is the more odd since Plato visited Sicily and legislated for Syracuse precisely owing to the reality of an Hellenic internationalism which he ignored. Moreover, a prescription for bringing the Just Commonwealth to birth through an Aristocracy that could command the support of neither proletarian Left nor oligarchic Right, but rested on the will of a reformed and inspired tyrant—in brief a Caesarean or Napoleonic or Mussolinian prescription for Communism—although not ridiculous, was scarcely satisfactory.

In 357 B.C., Plato was asked by Dion, who proposed himself to play the Cromwell, to set sail yet a fourth time. Dion's plan was ostensibly for a council of Elder Statesmen. Plato, nearly seventy, declined; some of his pupils, including Herakleides, went. Again it was discovered that politics is power and that the ideal requires power for its vehicle. The ideal, which was to be realized, became lost in mismanaged faction. One thing Dion did *not* do: to institute communism among the wealthy ruling Thirty-Five and to spread property more evenly among the proletariat. One thing he did do: to put his hand to approval of the assassination of Herakleides, the pro-democrat. In 353, Dion was murdered, at his own dinner-table, by the democrats led by Kalippos, the Athenian.

Plato was seventy-five. And suddenly the image of "the Divine Plato," writer of *The Republic*, fades and we see a bearded old man, with gold ear-rings, living in a pre-Christian age in a country where human sacrifice was not unknown, remote from us in time and place, garb and manner, excusing himself. He looks out towards the dictatorship of Rome and to the Dark Ages. The Golden Age of Greece is behind him, Athens a beaten state. Nevertheless, we still have the authentic letters—read, after two millennia, the lines from Plato's hand. The court, he writes, of Dionysius the Elder was sodden with suspicion. Not much could be done with Dionysius the Younger—and he had dared to put out a book which was an unforgivable travesty of Plato's own philosophy. "In my struggle with the slanderers I was worsted." The Athenians could not be blamed for Dion's murder; Kalippos was a nobody. He, Plato, gave advice only when asked. He was a humanist, concerned with ultimate truths—and a pacifist,

"Better to suffer unrighteousness than to practice it." No man ought "to apply violence to his fatherland in the form of a political revolution, whenever it is impossible to establish the best kind of polity without banishing and slaughtering citizens, but rather he ought to keep quiet and pray for what is good both for himself and for the Polis."

Not that he is any complete Pacifist. If Dion's policy had been followed, *after* reform, Syracuse—he is quite confident—would have been in a position, as in the days of Gelon, to throw back and reduce the Carthaginians. But "chance, stronger than man," had been against. The Sicilian experience had been bad enough; certainly he, Plato, had been "enraged"; but what really rankled was that book. Serious men impart wisdom orally, but do not put down, in vulgar writing, the real secrets of their philosophy—play to the vulgar, as it were, by commonplace intelligibility. Why did Dionysius treat "the leading authority on the subject with such disrespect. . . . Does he regard my doctrines as worthless? . . . If so, he will be in conflict with many, vastly more competent than he, who maintain the opposite."

Plato, who once had regarded democratic politics as cheap, now tends to regard all politics as contemptible compared with speculation about eternal, other-worldly truth. It is an interesting comment that his followers became sceptics. Here, indeed, was what Nietzsche called the degeneration. Perhaps Plato misconceived the nature of his own Academy. Existing to broaden exact knowledge, when current politics failed to fit the Academy's prescriptions, Plato turned away in disgust from objective experience itself. However, Speusippos, the botanist, succeeded him.

11

The old man is dead, twenty-two centuries ago, and, unlike the Pharaohs, we do not know where he is buried. But an odd thing has happened. Human nature does not die and precisely his love of abstract truth about that nature has saved him. The old problems have all come round again. The old answers are still true. Eugenics, nudism, abortion, feminism, communism, proletarian democracy, division of labour, class war, scientific *expertise*—all the problems are here. The Platonic vision grows again—some will think, far from pleasant, too like a Brave New World. But it insists again, as in the old days, on our answer to its Socratic queries. . . . "The Divine Plato"—Fascist, Communist . . . what?

The differences are, of course, great. It goes without saying. The world, in the beginning, was theological; and Plato also is a theologian—whereas the sense for theology, perhaps thanks to lack of attention to the meaning of ideas, the thinking of thought, has departed from us. Or perhaps our theologies are now "practical" and political, our demigods are boss politicians. (If so, the same thing happened in Rome—Marius, Sulla, Catiline, Julius and the rest—not so long after Plato died.) Plato obstinately tried to solve the problems of politics in terms of the small, intensive polis, not the cosmopolis. Even the internationalism that he knew, he ignored; and foreign affairs he overlooked to his cost.

He is the Philosopher of the Intensive Community—a completed society in which there is "community of pleasures and pains." It is precisely the functions of the intensive community which today, nationalists or cosmopolitan-minded, we ignore at a cost to our culture and happiness. In brief, let us be careful lest our criticism of Plato does not amount to this, that he is more modern and civilized than ourselves—that, in the grand cycle of history, we have not yet caught up with him, even if we be materially on the spiral ring above him. At least he has left us, as a challenge, with his scheme plainly set forth of the Just Society. Social Justice—on which individual justice depends—seems to require functionalization and authority; authority in turn demands discipline and obedience; willing obedience demands cultural and social homogeneity—which excludes universality and internationalism. A wrong solution, perhaps. But where?

Is it perhaps that the task of philosophy and science is not to provide cultural homogeneity, quickly through myths, to small communities, but by exploring facts to provide it slowly for a whole world—to create an international culture centred on assured, non-mythical knowledge? The task may be to invite all to understand, rich or poor, who will. Is this the New Academy that can save our civilization from the contemporary anarchy and civil war that Plato would have pointed out to us? Did Plato ever create anything that more truly expressed himself than his Academy—and do we not better find him here, questing for mathematico-political truth, than in Syracuse, fusing theory and Sicilian practice? Is there any such institution functioning today? Perhaps my friend Dr. Flexner's Institute of Advanced Studies, aided by a great mathematician, Einstein, alone can make a claim. I should think the responsibility of feeling that the world pivots on him must well-nigh crush him. At least this, I suggest, emerges: that if Plato was at all right, then we too must have, in order to focus and integrate our civilization (a civilization of more than the polis; cosmopolitan), an Academy—a World Academy.

The genius of Plato, the technocrat, has been such that men have preferred to treat him as a god—to assert that no letter of his can be genuine unless it reads like one of the Pauline Epistles—in order not to admit the applicability to themselves of his queries. But still the Socratic voice is urgent—has become, after Dark and Middle and Liberal Ages, again urgent. And, first, why not an Academy? (It is a theme to which Comte* reverts.)

At least, until the tale of human civilization is made up, as Meleager, of Gadara, wrote (A.D. 60):

> The Golden Bough of Plato, in all ways Divine,
> [Is] guide through the Universe for Good and Wise,
> Light that by its own virtue cannot cease to shine.

Perhaps not so good or wise. On that it may be that the assessment of two millennia will enable us to form a judgement.

READING

Plato: *The Republic* (ed. Jowett), Books IV–V, 441–473.

BIBLIOGRAPHICAL NOTE

*Ernest Barker: *Greek Political Theory, Plato and His Predecessors,* 1918.
J. Burnet: *The Greek Philosophers, Thales to Plato,* 1914.

* *Cf.* p. 746.

Chapter III

Aristotle

1

TEN years after the death of Plato, in 347 B.C., Philip of Macedon, at Chaeronea, defeated the Athenians. An epoch of international empire was to begin which differed from its Chinese, Assyrian and Persian predecessors in this, that it included, within its sweep, the history of a vital part of Europe. The vision of internationalism, of the world-empire, was never again to fade from the scene until 1815 when Napoleon Bonaparte, would-be Caesar and once crowned Emperor in the presence of the oecumenical Pope, sailed for St. Helena. Our own days have seen its revival.

The Macedonians, occupying the fringes of what is today Bulgaria, were not promising paladins of a world-culture. Greeks by dialect, still living in the Homeric age in their manners, no man sat down at their feasts until he had killed a boar, or removed the cord he wore round his waist until *il a tué son homme*—he had killed his man. Assassination, it should be added, was almost a normal incident of the Macedonian court. However, the courtiers were conscious of the deficiencies in manners of their countrymen. The Macedonian kings, flattered to be admitted within the ambit of Greek affairs, were striving hard after culture. Euripides paid them the tribute of dying in their capital city. They took professional advisers from Hellas proper. Such was a Hellene from the small island of Stagira, the court physician to Amyntas II, King of Macedon, Philip's father. The physician's son, Aristotle, became tutor to Philip's heir.

Philip's son was Alexander, whose reputed sarcophagus can still be seen in the Constantinople Museum, but whose dust, as Shakespeare says, may stop a bung-hole. As a pupil he had the disadvantage that he believed himself to be directly descended (like the Mikado) from a god—in this case, Hercules or Herakles. Also, his decision to murder the rightful heir, in order to assume for himself the succession, does not argue docility. A world-conqueror is not an easy pupil—even if, in Alexander's case, the flag probably followed the trade.

Aristotle

ARISTOTLE, the Stagirite (384–322 B.C.), pupil of Plato in Athens from about his seventeenth to his thirty-seventh year, had then no lighter problem with his pupil than Plato had with the Younger Dionysius. Aristotle, having left Athens on Plato's death and spent three years teaching in Assos, on the Asia Minor coast, must have been about forty-one when he left for Macedonia to take on this work. His success, however, was greater perhaps because his method was less exacting. After Confucius, Aristotle is the supreme apostle of Common Sense and of the Golden Mean. Even virtue, even culture, might be excessive. Living in the post-Peloponnesian War age as it slips from class war into dictatorship, enthusiasm is for Aristotle an ill, a plague, to which men of balance will not succumb.

Aristotle went his way, analyzing the theory of the only culture that seemed to him to matter, that of the polis—even if the Age of the Polis was over and the Athenian polity a museum specimen. He left to Alexander without censure the job of becoming Lord of the World, *i.e.*, of the barbarians, as no concern of a cultured man. Not that he was without interest. His late treatise, *On Colonies*, suggests to Alexander the dangers of promiscuous race-mixture; opposes Alexander's attempts at race-equalization; and maintains the theory that Greeks should be governed by constitutional measures, but that non-Greeks may perhaps be best ruled, as they are accustomed, despotically as lesser breeds. Chiefly, however, he occupied himself in collecting together all available scientific information. He preferred the truth that could be stabilized by a fact. The chair of Plato he, Plato's greatest pupil, left to others; and, after a sojourn in Assos and in Macedon, he founded his own rival school, the Lyceum, in Athens, where he and his followers—the Peripatetics—walked and talked. However, there is authority for the statement that Aristotle was the only one of Plato's pupils pertinaciously to sit out the public readings, by the master, of the *Phaedo*.

The Peripatetics were practical men. The scientific life, Aristotle taught, was better than that of its only serious rival, the life of practical politics. But speculation must not turn its back on or lose touch with practice. Aristotle's whole career and his missions for his friend Hermias, ruler of Atarneus on the coast of Asia Minor, to Macedon illustrate his attitude. Incidentally, then, Aristotle was a practising politician. Shocking although it may seem to the scholarly mind, Aristotle clearly entertained the ambition of exercising practical political influence. He was not an academic hack who, "being unable to do, taught." The psychological character studies, however, of his pupil, Theophrastus and his *History of Plants*, the 158 histories of *Constitutions*, of which Aristotle himself had set the model in his *Constitution of Athens*—these were what mattered.

Plato, if a technocrat, was also by temperament no little of a theologian; Aristotle, in his later years, not at all. Later critics said that he was a materialist. Anyhow his First Cause had the quality of the necessary limit of an argument, more than of an Almighty Creator. The cardinal Aristotelian doctrine of the eternity of the universe rather perhaps argues that universe's deification, "the great and visible God," subject to the supreme, transcendent form, the Unmoved Mover, and supplemented by those strange Aristotelian beings, the souls of the stars. The history of Aristotle's development, alike in Ethics and in Metaphysics, is one of movement towards empiricism and objective study and away from the ideal, a priori theological view of his early years in the Platonic Academy. In the end, Persian or Magian star-worship is one of the few residues left over, now that the transcendental Platonic real harmonies or Pythagorean mystic numbers, the mathematical "essences"—the ideas—have been criticized out of existence . . . this, and worship of the remote Unmoved Mover, beyond the furthest empyrean, or perhaps the worship of not *one* but *many* "movers of the spheres." In the final phase of his development even the star-souls became detached from his system of physics; and Aristotle stands out as an entire empiric and complete non-theologian. The relapse into theology, on his death, with the Stoics is almost immediate.

Greek philosophy is no native or autochthonous growth. Aristotle, like his master, Plato, is an admitted admirer of Egyptian wisdom—Egypt with which Hellas was in constant commercial contact. Aristotle's second successor, Strato, the physicist, established touch with Alexandria, of which the great Museum became the intellectual capital of the Western World. Aristotle, further, aided by Philip of Opus, was a keen student of the Babylonish or Magian science, and his tendency to star-worship as well as many of his theories in physics may well derive directly therefrom.

Finally, the wisdom of Zoroaster (Zarathustra, ca. 660–583 B.C.), the Persian, with his dualistic doctrine of the two fighting principles of Good and Evil, Light and Darkness, is specifically referred to by Plato in the *Laws*. He is generously placed by Aristotle 6,000 years before Plato; influences Plato's doctrine of good and bad world-souls; and determines Aristotle's doctrine of historical cycles, ending in physical catastrophe. It is no exaggeration to say that, for a while, in the Academy Zoroastrianism was the vogue—the new discovery.

Aristotle
(384–322 B.C.)

(Facing p. 74)

The self-hypnotizing theory of periods of ruin of civilization and of degeneration (later redeveloped, in a small way, by Spengler) comes from this quarter; and the thesis that truth is found, lost and is found again. It is perhaps of no small importance that Europe thus early tended to accept (although this tendency was intensified by Christianity) the fighting dualist, moralist tradition, emphasized also by the Old Testament, and not the pacifist, pantheist, monistic tradition of India and of Buddhism.

Greek thought at this time was as intoxicated by the results of astronomical discoveries (due to Babylonian data) as, two millennia later, European thought was by the mathematical discoveries of Descartes and by the physical discoveries of Newton. It is important to bear in mind this preoccupation of the great Greeks with the wisdom of the East. Human culture is continuous. The grain of our minds today still tends to be set by the hypotheses of the Persian Zoroaster and of the Babylonish priests.

Aristotle was the greatest of the Encyclopaedists of learning—and the first. Astronomy, natural history, obstetrics, metaphysics, economics, ethics, politics, rhetoric and the fine arts, the first text-book on logic—nothing came amiss. What he did not do with his own hand, he allocated to his school. Such allocated works probably were the little treatise on economics, and many of the studies of constitutions. Research workers gathered these from Corinth and Sparta, even from Carthage and from Byzantium. The master was the organizer of research. Occasionally Alexander the conqueror, in India or the Middle East, would remember to send a rock or a mineral to add to the natural history collection. In return treatises were prepared for him, as a gift, *On Monarchy*, after his accession, and *On Colonies*. Alexander, however, had also other uses. Aristotle, born in small Stagira, with *entrée* to the Macedonian court, resident in the cultural centre of Hellas, Athens, was in a happy position for a many-angled, detached scientific outlook in politics. But practical politics are never detached. The Athenians, for good reason, did not love the Macedonians, And he, whom Dante later called "the Master of Them That Know"—he who was, throughout the Middle Ages, *tout court* "the Philosopher," depended for his secure residence in Athens upon the influence of Alexander and of his viceroy, Antipater. The master was also the *protégé*. Alexander dead, Aristotle, suspect in Athens as a member of the Macedonian faction, the "internationalists," ended his life as an exile.

We have a few letters attributed to Aristotle. We have a few fragments of poems—one beginning, "Daughter of a mother blessed with fair offspring." On his own telling, he was no lover of the sea and no traveller like Plato. Vain, concerned with the arrangement of his hair, tending to baldness, lisping, spindle-legged and fond of wearing rings is the description of him by one biographer. But it is difficult to resist the belief that, like writers of lesser works, when Aristotle wishes to sketch his hero he is not innocent of a side-glance at himself. And there is no reason to suppose irony when he sketches his *megalopsuchos aner*—his "man of personality"—in the lectures on *Ethics* dedicated to (or, better, edited by) his illegitimate son, Nichomachos.

> Moreover, he is not a man to incur little risk, nor does he court danger, because there are but few things he has a value for; but he will incur great dangers, and when he does venture he is prodigal of his life as knowing that there are terms on which it is not worth his while to live. He is the sort of man to do kindnesses but he is ashamed to receive them. . . . Further, it is characteristic of the large minded man to ask favours not at all, or very reluctantly, but to do a service very readily; and to bear himself loftily towards the great or fortunate, but towards people of middle station affably; . . . And again, not to put himself in the way of honour, nor to go where others are the chief men; and to be remiss and dilatory, except in the case of some great honour or work; and to be concerned in few things, and these great and famous. It is a property of him also to be open, both in his dislikes and likings, because concealment is a consequence of fear. Likewise to be careful for reality rather than appearance, and talk and act openly (for his contempt for others makes him a bold man, for which same reason he is apt to speak the truth, except when the principle of reserve comes in), but to be reserved towards the generality of men. And to be unable to live with reference to any other but a friend; because doing so is servile, as may be seen in that all flatterers are low and men in low estate are flatterers. Neither is his admiration easily excited . . . nor does he bear malice, since remembering anything, and especially wrongs, is no part of large mindedness, but rather overlooking them; nor does he talk of other men; in fact he will not speak either of himself or of any other; he neither cares to be praised himself nor to have others blamed; nor does he praise freely, and for this reason he is not apt to speak ill even of his enemies except to show contempt. . . . Also slow motion, deep voice and deliberate style of speech are thought to be characteristic of the large minded. For he who is in earnest about few things is not likely to be in a hurry nor he who esteems nothing great to be very intent. And sharp tones and quickness are the result of these.

It appears to be a prescription for an extraordinarily unpopular character and, therefore (it might be argued), for a bad citizen. At best, it is a description of a hero in one of Disraeli's novels. This type of aristocratic dandy has marked characteristics that are qualities of Renaissance man. Tact is obviously a quality heavily at a discount—

almost immoral. Aristotle, however, apparently admired this type; and one of the most famous men that the human species has hitherto produced is presumably entitled to his own moral judgement, especially when he writes as a professional moralist. If, of course, he is right, most of modern civilization, with its democratic standards, is servile and wrong. How admiration for this T. E. Lawrence-Lindbergh type fits in with his general notions on civilization we shall see later.

Diogenes Laertius reports a rumour that Plato said, "Aristotle spurns me, as colts kick out at the mother who bore them." About his bitter difference with other students of the Academy, antiquity had no doubt. The feud lasted for three centuries in endless malicious gossip among the learned. However, towards Plato himself, Aristotle seems to have entertained a respect not inconsistent with increasing intellectual disagreement. After the master's death, this amounts to conscious opposition and the revision of Aristotle's work takes place in this spirit. However, "Socrates'" discoveries are referred to as always exhibiting "grace, originality and thought." In brief, Plato's work was poetry. In a votive offering dedicated to Eudemus, Aristotle describes Plato.

> He piously set up an altar of holy Friendship
> For the man whom it is not lawful for bad men even to praise,
> Who alone or first of mortals clearly revealed,
> By his own life and by the methods of his words,
> How a man becomes good and happy at the same time,
> Now no one can ever attain to these things again.

Apart from the pessimism of the disjunction of goodness and happiness, and the tribute to the divine Plato, the inscription is also interesting for the line about "the bad men." One suspects (as does his recent commentator, Werner Jaeger) that these were Aristotle's critics, the other Platonists. Still the *odium academicum*—academic jealousy—burned on, even in the tribute. What is also interesting is the length of Aristotle's period of tutelage to Plato and the lateness of the great philosopher's own development.

2

The writings of Aristotle, as we have them, are in a sharply different category from those of Plato. The elder philosopher appears to have sufficiently shared the ancient hieratic or priestly attitude to have objected to reducing to writing the inner core of his doctrine. He speaks of writing, if at all, in riddles. We shall find the same attitude in the Gospels, with their dark sayings and private instruction to the disciples. Hence what we have of Plato's are his literary writings and no lecture notes have come down to us. The tradition of the Academy was exclusive. On the contrary, at the Lyceum, outside the gate of Diochares, under Mount Lycabettus, Aristotle seems to have taught freely, for thirteen years, to all who would be "peripatetic" with him.

From early catalogues, we know that Aristotle published writings in dialogue form. But none is preserved entire, although sufficient fragments, especially of the dialogue *On Philosophy*, have been discovered to enable us to judge the character of this early work while Aristotle was still under the influence of Platonic idealism and theologism. What we have are, not so much his lecture notes by students (although in the versions of the *Ethics* and in perhaps the *Metaphysics* this may be the case), but his own revision of his notes. The *Politics*, which belongs to Aristotle's middle period (Books II, III, VII, VIII in about 345 B.C.; IV–VI later, after the study of constitutions; Book I added last, as introduction) is of this type. These were not published at the time and, hence, did not exercise their influence until it was too late for them to be effective in the ancient world. The editor was Andronicus, in the first century B.C.

Taken, however, as a whole, few writings in the world have probably had quite such great influence. In part the reasons for this are accidental. The number of scientists who can be so happily born as to come of age just when a science is in its first stages—not to speak of several sciences—must be few. There the Greeks, and above all Aristotle, had the advantage of us. The very terminology that we use in many of these fields—for example, in politics, the terms democracy, aristocracy and the like, as well as politics itself—is Greek. And the definitions that we recall are Aristotle's. Much of Aristotle's work reads familiarly for precisely the same reason that Shakespeare's writings are, as the old lady complained about *Hamlet*, "full of quotations." Moreover—a point we shall stress later—Aristotle, the physician's son, approached the social sciences in the same mood as he approached the natural sciences and gave to their treatment thoroughly empiric characteristics, even if not unsuffused by the Hellenic teleologism.

Further, Aristotle has been a favourite of history. Through translation of his writings, Western Europe in the Middle Ages became reacquainted with Hellenic thought. Emphatically a Greek, although attached to the court of a "semi-barbarian," he had for the unqualified barbarians of the Middle Ages an exotic fascination. From "the

Philosopher" they learned, not only metaphysics, but the beginnings of the civic and secular, as distinct from the churchly attitude in politics. Even on that remote front of time, the Later Middle Ages, Aristotle challenged the Platonists—and defeated them.

The writings have, however, intrinsic and not merely accidental importance of the first order. No Platonist, it has been said, can properly understand an Aristotelian. During his lifetime Aristotle was charged with being disrespectful to his old tutor, Plato. It is not, therefore, astonishing when we find Professor A. E. Taylor saying that "No Aristotelian book is quite so commonplace in its handling of a vast subject as the *Politics*." Professor Taylor is, of course, an eminent metaphysician and his opinion about politics is not a professional one. Anyhow it is almost certainly wrong (unless he gives much higher comparative ranking to other Aristotelian books than is general). It is, however, worth noting that the *Politics* may be argued to fall into two sections, one of four books (II, III, VII, VIII [traditional numbering, followed by Jowett]) belonging to the earlier Platonic period and occupied with discussions of the ideal state; and the other, more mature, section of three books (IV–VI) comprising the results of the empiric labour of the last period on the actual historical Constitutions, concerned with methods and disregarding discussion of ultimates.

The greatest single influence upon political thought—certainly academically and, in derivative fashion, popularly—during the last century and a half has been the revival of Hellenism, with its socialist implications. It permeated Hegel and, through Hegel, both Marx and Fascism. Of this influence a good half was Aristotelian, since it could make a contact with the Protestant individualist tradition which Platonism could not. Ruskin's and Green's belief that the Polis or the State "remains in being for the sake of the *good* life," the basis of much nineteenth-century Social Reform, is Aristotle's explicit teaching.

Aristotle is the greatest of Plato's critics. Nevertheless, both being Greeks, both have common assumptions, socialist in character—and in Plato's case carried to the point of opposing the private ownership of property—that would be challenged by a modern individualist. Aristotle's criticism of Plato is more limited in scope than criticism would be today. And it is captious almost to the point of deliberate misunderstanding.

Probably well before his second stay in Athens (ca. 335–323 B.C.) and even before he became tutor of Alexander (342), in his lost dialogue *On Philosophy*, Aristotle began that repudiation of the Platonic doctrine of pre-existent or real Ideas (*i.e.*, Mind as ultimate reality) and asserted the eternity of Matter (*materia prima*). In his *Physics* Aristotle develops the notion of substrata or substances, contrary manifestations differing in respect of the substrata by excess or deficiency. Aristotle, however, apparently differs from the later doctrine of Spinoza* by asserting the permanent plurality of substances. Moreover, it is matter that individualizes beings. The significance of this, so far as it concerns us in its connection with the doctrine of the common-sense "middle way" and in its connection with political individualism, we shall see later.†

Rightly or wrongly, Aristotle accused the transcendentalist Plato of asserting ideas or universals to be (*e.g.*, in Mind, here opposed to Matter) entities apart from the particulars which they specify. These points are not negligible, even practically, since the acceptance of Plato's supposed thesis has certain theocratic associations from which Aristotle's empiricism is free. Plato is an idealist to the point of being a priestly mystagogue in politics. Aristotle, as time passes, becomes even less of an idealist, even in political philosophy, and more of a believer in the value of the empirical and instrumental, not the utopian, dogmatic study of the field.

Into Aristotle's peculiar dualism of Form (active structural plan or creative energy—which *might* exist pure) and of Matter ("dead" matter, never discoverable "in the abstract," pure, apart from form) and into the question of whether his notion of the final substrata makes Aristotle really a dualist, a pantheistic materialist (eternity of *materia prima*) or a creative evolutionist by anticipation (immanent form as essence, subject to final cause), it is not our task here to enter. The issue has been considered thus far because Plato thought it important to Politics. Therefore, Aristotle's refutation of this theory is important. We are entitled to suppose cohesion between the metaphysics and the practical doctrine of any first-class philosopher. And, indeed, we are here seeing, in some not insignificant fashion, the antithesis between transcendentalism and immanentism, theology and natural science, papal ecclesiasticism and secular empiricism, dogma and experience, so far as they concern us in politics. These terms will become clearer later.‡ Let us merely say that there is more individualism implicit in

* *Cf.* p. 251.

† *Cf.* p. 286.

‡ In this paragraph I have been compelled to use technical terms which the student of philosophy will recognize but which it would overburden this chapter to explain fully. The reader who is unacquainted with them will find them all in every good dictionary or text-book of philosophy.

Aristotle's philosophy than perhaps even Aristotle himself, being a Hellene, recognized. Towards the end, when the emancipation was complete, it tended to be almost entirely the individual, *the superior individual,* who mattered.

Aristotle's criticism of *The Republic* is detailed and not very important. As might be expected, he fastens on the least "common-sense" portions of Plato's work: his communism of property and children. Apart from detecting in Plato's system some remote risks of incest and other practices religiously objectionable, his substantial criticism is that what is everybody's interest is nobody's interest. To which the answer must be: all depends upon the circumstances. Whereas the vulgar criticism of Plato's family communism is that it would mean an orgy of dissipation, Aristotle raises the interesting objection that, whereas the whole responsibility of government is left to be borne on the shoulders of a few, these few are allowed no adequate personal happiness to tempt them, whether as men of property or as family men. For the rest—and here Aristotle strikes nearer the mark—Plato is substituting mathematical uniformity for organic unity. He is, Aristotle asserts, omitting to allow for a variety in life which enriches it. (An old plea for private wealth—enriches whom?) In brief, Plato has carried his plan for an homogeneous society to logical, monastic extremes; and Aristotle turns back to the contemplation of normal, heterogeneous, varied secular society as he finds it.

3

Aristotle, in his *Politics,* is the Philosopher of Middle-class Common Sense. The prejudice in favour of this class is hereditary. By middle class is here meant, not the small trader, but that of the middling man of property, the peasant proprietor and the professional man. That class is best—a doctrine to find echo in the nineteenth century and, again, in German National Socialism. It was Aristotle's own class, as the son of a medical practitioner—Aristotle who, incidentally, had married the daughter of a freed slave who had become a local prince. Every polis without exception, he asserts, has in it the very rich, the very poor and the intermediate. He quotes Phokulides:

> The middle clan within the State
>   Fares best, I ween;
> May I be neither low nor great
>   But e'en between.

Further, the prejudice fitted in with Aristotle's entire philosophy, and with his famous ethical doctrine, reminiscent of the civil servant, Confucius, of the Golden Mean—"nothing in excess." Such expressions themselves seem to imply a personal, temperamental preference, rationalized into a system. Moreover, it appealed to Aristotle's shrewdness about the practical. This government of a Middle Class, equal and similar, not too low for good culture or too proud for co-operation, could be made to work. It reminds one strikingly of the consistent Aristotle's preference for Hellas as a place to live in, neither too hot and effeminate nor too cold and barbarous—therefore, capable of being demonstrated to be the world's best country.

Aristotle is not laying down rules, he points out, for creatures *e therion e theos*—either beast or god—but for ordinary men. And within this middle group the rule of equity for freemen—"neither to rule nor be ruled"—would be practicable, by the simple expedient of alternative rule, every man having an expectation of being a city councillor in due turn.

The practical Aristotle, confident that Hellas is "over all," does not look beyond the bounds of his own world. As much as Plato, he is the philosopher of the polis. His scientific curiosity leads him to inquire into the constitution of Carthage and to allude to Babylon. But his only discovery there is that Babylon, the great "metropolis," its outer walls 42 miles round,* its population so vast that Cyrus held its walls three days before some of its inhabitants knew, is patently not a "polis"—and, therefore, is merely inferior. As with his contemporary and rival Isocrates, so with Aristotle, it is not to be dreamed that any culture is higher than that of the polis. His pupil, Alexander, did not impress him. Heir of the civilization of a few centuries—no more than that of the United States—he confronted the majestic civilizations of Egypt and Babylon, already in their fifth millennium. And with glorious insolence, from his New World of Athens (or was it Stagira?), he decided that the political doings of the barbarous were, philosophically speaking, of no importance. Incidentally he was right. He gives a passing word of favourable notice to the distinction between the military and agricultural classes in Egypt; and to the institution of common meals by kings in Italy. What alone really mattered in these lands were the notions on physics of the priests and the Pythagoreans.

(*a*) Aristotle is a *conservative*, in the typical Hellenic fashion in which Plato is a conservative. Character depends upon the way in which a man is brought up; morals upon the social *mores*. Hence the

* The inner walls, however, only demarcate a city with diameter of about 2½ miles.

attention which Aristotle, like Plato, gives to education. What should give form to these social *mores* is the tradition of the country, sacred legal traditions or constitutions, unwritten laws (*nomoi*), not subject to change as are the mere regulations or popular votes (*psephismata*) passed in some citizen assembly on the impetus and general will of the moment. Here then lies the interpretation of the great phrase that there must be a rule of laws rather than of men. It is neither constitutional, in the American sense, nor anthropological in Montesquieu's sense—as we shall later see*—but traditional and almost religious, familial and ritualistic. Socrates' old faith holds true also for Aristotle, that the citizen is the child of his fatherland, owing reverence and eschewing all impious radical change of the basic, sacred laws of the forefathers.

The philosopher is not only a conservative but the member of a slave-owning civilization, himself a slave-owner. The comparison between classical slavery—where the slaves were usually Mediterranean peoples and sometimes Hellenes, war-captives—and negro slavery, to the advantage of the former, has often been made. It is not especially convincing—least of all where principles are concerned. The clauses of Aristotle's will governing the treatment of his slaves, and the emancipation of some of them, show him to have been a peculiarly humane man; and his alliance with a concubine or mistress after the death of his wife, of whom he is said to have been excessively fond, is not such as to indicate class prejudice. Aristotle, however, having very properly begun his *Politics* by an excursus in anthropology, displays no doubt that slavery is not only an immemorial custom of the human race but that it is an entirely justifiable one.

In his justification of slavery he uses the now familiar functional argument, already used by Plato. Brawn must serve brain. (Oddly enough, Aristotle does not apply this maxim when discussing the relations of men and women, where he is far more conventional than Plato.) Mere brawn is no more than "an animated instrument," a "hand," that is, a human machine.

The habits of Greek philosophic thought, especially Platonic (and the early Aristotle), with its talk of "ideas," "forms" and "species," tended to obscure the question, "brain for what?" I do not think, however, that Aristotle's answer even to this question is obscure. I have already mentioned the Soviet biologist who, at the time of the Stakhanovist movement, asserted that masses of men, *Lumpenproletariat*, were, biologically speaking, followers and slaves by nature and would so remain. Aldous Huxley has indicated (if not agreed with)

* *Cf.* p. 302.

the same argument, although the characters in his tale are preoccupied with how to condition the slaves to their chains and to make a follower prefer to be a follower. There is nothing in Aristotle to indicate that he would have viewed with disapproval either argument. "These persons are natural slaves and for them as truly as for the body or for animals a life of subjection is advantageous." The only thing that troubles him is that there are slaves in law as well as slaves by nature and that some who are slaves in law are not such by nature. Aristotle here is a progressive, an abolitionist. He notices the argument that superior force implies some strong (= good) quality (comforting doctrine: that the slaves or poor are really vicious); but he yet concludes that slavery, unjustified by nature, has no superior claim to respect than mere force. It leaves him with a residue of embarrassment from which he is unable to free himself.

Aristotle, indeed, vacillates between the treatment of the polis as the theatre of a play of social forces and as the matrix of the good life, between politics as a matter of purpose (as in the earlier books) and as a matter of anthropology and of historical means (as in the later books). This issue between the politics of the ideal and the politics of power, unsolved by Aristotle, save in terms of tension, remains unsolved to this day. Historically, the Greeks found their solution in flight from actual civic life, with its problems of power and whether the good man could always be a good citizen or every man in a harmoniously working polis be a "superior man." Men found refuge in flight, into the personal good life, in increased self-consciousness, in the route of individualistic philosophy, in the morality of the good will; and, then, in the individualist approach to a salvation which, during the Catholic period, still retained community sense and, during the Protestant period, did not. It is a route from which Western civilization is now in reaction, vainly trying to forget self-consciousness in totalitarianism.

In another direction, however, Aristotle proposes to go disconcertingly further than the slave-owners. Some men are quite servile, "only so far a rational being as to be able to understand reason, without himself possessing it"; others are still only partly cultured. And—as is to happen in later ages—Aristotle proposes to make distinctions of degrees of freedom. Many even of those who may be free and not slaves, have yet not the leisure or culture to be full citizens. Aristotle, therefore, briskly lumps in, for certain purposes, with the classical equivalent of the negroes, all traders, shopkeepers and small business men. "The fact is that we cannot regard all who are indispensable to the existence of the State as being citizens." The *hauteur* with which this friend of the drinking, fighting Lord of the World deals with his fellow mortals takes one's breath away. His theme substantially is one that we shall meet again, with the decline of Christianity, *e.g.*, in George Bernard Shaw—that what matters is civilization, not men; culture, not humanity.

It is interesting to speculate what his judgement would have been upon a world in which, on high matters of public policy, the press headlines the opinions of film stars and singers. That this is the final self-exposure of the pretensions of democracy, in a degeneration heralding tyranny, would probably have been the comment. It is yet arguable that a civilization is impoverished that cannot accommodate a Chaplin or a Toscanini, and that these are entitled, as artists, to take the headlines, even in their opinions on morals and politics about which their public is interested—not to wait for the verdict of an Areopagus of Aristotles. The public, of course, feels that it knows intimately a Robert Taylor and naturally wants, as a matter of "human interest," his opinion on peace, war and philosophy of life rather than that of John Dewey. Moreover, in the present position of philosophy, the odds are that other philosophers would hold Dewey wrong anyway. The public might as well, therefore, listen to Coughlin or Taylor. Like all Greeks Aristotle overestimates the importance of intelligence—especially technical intelligence in politics as against the opinion of the empty amateurs who command publicity. The contemporary moral is that the expert must command publicity: the Philosopher who would be a King must first get a Goebbels and be a pressman. Aristotle draws the opposite conclusion: that the amateur and advertiser must be suppressed. Plato recommended a concentration camp.

It is neither frivolous nor trivial to point out that no one has yet worked out a philosophy of the press; and that, in so far as the great Greeks make any contribution in this matter, it is, almost entirely, implicitly hostile to the freedom of the press as a matter of commercial enterprise. The publicity men, as the crossing sweeps of popular tyranny, would be put down into a very humble place. In that, I suggest, the great Greeks were not only undemocratic, but unimaginative and wrong. Their good taste got in their way, and their arrogance. As Hobbes later was to comment, "learning is small power"—but publicity is an instrument of power, which those who will the end must use as means. The public can only grasp a certain number of ideas and personalities at once. The booking list for immortality in the reserved stalls of history is already longer than most men can carry in their heads.

The successful business man, especially by speculation, is Aristotle's bête noire. Here he anticipates the French eighteenth-century school of Physiocrats.* The dutiful farmer who grows crops genuinely increases the country's wealth. The man who gets money in return for industry has earned it. Even when got in return for disposing in the market of the bounty of nature, it corresponds to real wealth. But money made of loaning other money at interest is artificial wealth—the owner is richer by speculation; but nothing has been put into the world that can be touched or seen, in return for these riches. The alleged social function of stock exchange and "curb exchange," even in the embryonic form in which they were then known as the money-lender, is disregarded. Also, since money is fluid, unlike land or industries, such a man has no stake in the country. Aristotle tends to regard him as potentially a bad citizen. Speculation is an artificial and unhealthy activity which should be checked (as Social Credit writers hold today) by criminal law. That "unseen services" may be rendered in connection with the organization of exchange, Aristotle ignores. His theory on speculation or usury had immense influence because it became the basis of the regulation of interest and capitalism embodied—and still embodied—in the Canon Law of the Catholic Church.

If Aristotle had been confronted with the theory of the function of exchanges, presumably his reply would have been that the free exchange is not indispensable and in a conservative, rural society may not even be desirable, since it may interfere with the economic symmetry of the local society; and, further, that much speculation in fact finds no justification in terms of even this social function.

(*b*) Aristotle is a *democrat.* The statement is challenging after what has been said. It has appeared that Aristotle's major and temperamental fault is the possession of far too low an opinion of the intelligence of man as man, negro as well as white, barbarian as well as Greek. When, however, we make allowance for Aristotle's prejudice against all who live by working for profit and we exclude from the politically active workers what Marx was later to call the *Lumpenproletariat,* we cannot fairly deny to Aristotle this title—although he, for reasons of terminology which we shall discuss later, would have repudiated it himself. He is not a proletarian or majority democrat or a believer in the *functionless,* as distinct from the *classless,* society. But he is a liberal democrat as against any dictatorship, even of the proletariat. He is a bitter enemy of all stress on the division of the community into classes pursuing primarily their class interest. He is

* *Cf.* p. 370.

yet quite free from Plato's hieratic and hierarchic tendencies. He would give every peasant owner full citizenship. And if (unlike Plato) he excludes women, so does the great, progressive French Republic which is usually, although technically falsely, called a democracy.

Far from distrusting the judgement of the "common man," within an electorate thus drastically but not capriciously limited, Aristotle constitutes himself his defender.

> It is possible that the Many, of which each individual is not a man of talent, are still collectively superior to the few best persons. . . . As the total number is large, it is possible that each has a fractional share of virtue and prudence. . . . It is thus that the Public is a better judge than the critics even of musical and poetical compositions; for some judge one part, some another, and all of them collectively the whole. . . . According to this [opponent's] theory then it is inadvisable to entrust the masses with final authority either in electing officers of State or in holding them responsible. It is probable, however, that there is some mistake in this mode of argument, partly—unless the character of the masses is absolutely slavish—for the reason already alleged, that, although individually they are worse judges than the experts, yet in their collective capacity they are better or at least as good, and partly because there are some subjects on which the artist himself is not the sole or best judge, *viz.*, all subjects in which the results produced are open to the legitimate criticism of persons who are not masters of the art. Thus it is not the builder alone whose function it is to criticize the merits of a house; the person who uses it, *i.e.*, the householder, is actually a better judge, and similarly a pilot is a better judge of a helm than a carpenter or one of the company of a dinner than the cook (*Politics* III, xi.)

Aristotle here is open to the academic criticism that he appears to think that many bad judgements and tastes added together make a good judgement and taste. But, as is his custom, he has safeguarded himself by excluding those below a certain standard of culture. And he is not discussing the Executive Council. With common sense he allows for the eccentricity and departmentalism of experts—and his argument comes to be an embroidery on the old theme that he who wears the shoe can best tell where it pinches.

Sound judgement, however, is not divorceable from practical experience. It is clear that Aristotle attaches the highest importance to this direct experience of the responsibility of rule:

> The virtue of a citizen may be defined as a practical acquaintance, both as ruler and subject, with the rule characteristic of a free community.

To put it in other words, everybody who is competent to vote ought to have a chance in life of being a town councillor and learning what government means. Similarly every tax-imposer should be a tax-payer.

(*c*) Aristotle is a *socialist.** He was this as was every Greek brought up in the strong civic tradition of the polis whose claims invaded every field of life, religion, business and family. Socialism is, of course, not inconsistent with the deepest, even feudal, conservatism. In the economic field we have already commented on Aristotle's bias in favour of the regulation of wealth and suppression by law of capitalist (*i.e.*, interest-taking) developments. But he was a socialist whose socialism was heavily modified by aristocracy and by an ethical individualism whose implications he scarcely perceived himself. Marx, as will become apparent, would have met with his vigorous disapproval as an apostle of political perversion. The extent, however, and limitations of Aristotle's socialism will become apparent when we inspect his actual scheme of political and social organization.

Characteristically he discusses types of polity, not necessarily best absolutely and in theory, but practically and under the circumstances. And his discussion turns not on the type of society that illustrates Social Justice but upon the type of society calculated actually to conduce to Man's Happiness. Aristotle, the moralist, is unable to divorce his discussion of politics from the prior issue: What does man want of life? "It is plain that the best polity is necessarily the system under which everybody can do best and live happily." Even in his later, empiric years, when he revises his thesis in politics (or his notes), he is content to leave this earlier treatment untampered with.

If the answer be happiness, what do we mean by happiness? Here Aristotle has the courage to admit that one constituent of the conditions of happiness is Chance, *i.e.*, the accidental presence of external goods. It was a conclusion from which, as we shall see—and it was of the first importance for civilization—most of his successors revolted with unhappy results. Happiness, however, is not only or chiefly my material happiness here and now with a good (material) standard of living. Aristotle tends to ignore the extent to which this material standard for the masses is the pre-condition of their spiritual independence and personality—nor indeed, as a Hellene, is he too fond of abstract independence. The concept rather is artistic [*cf.* Goethe] —and there are authorities, he reminds readers, on taste. Happiness is "an energy of spirit well directed" ("according to virtue") "in a complete life." "The best life, whether for each individual separately or for the Polis collectively, is one which possesses virtue, furnished

* The terms Socialist, Communist, etc., are more precisely defined on pp. 557–558.

with external advantages to such a degree as to be capable of actions according to virtue." This theory of "virtue," as well as happiness, depending upon certain external conditions has somewhat sinister implications which we shall consider later.*

Happiness, however, also depends upon nature, habit and reason. Habit and the use of reason depend, again, upon education. Accidental animal happiness is . . . animal. Education, properly considered, involves the entire environment and nurture of the man as individual, social being and citizen—and, hence, the constitution of the Polis in which he lives. In all this Aristotle's answer is characteristically Greek, and the approach is that which Plato had taken before him. Let us first consider the political organization which Aristotle regards as desirable.

4

Political constitutions Aristotle, following a precedent set in one place by Plato, holds can be placed in categories according to the two principles of number and of quality.

All governments may be divided according to whether they are by the one, the few or the many. They may be cross-divided by whether they are government "for the benefit of the community" or "for the benefit of the governing class." The latter group is stigmatized as perverted. We thus get the classification: Sound forms—Monarchy, Aristocracy, Polity; Perverted forms—Tyranny, Oligarchy, Democracy. The hall-mark of Aristocracy is virtue; of Oligarchy, wealth; of Democracy, freedom. The Democrat believes that "persons, if equal in any respect, are equal absolutely"; the Oligarch believes that "persons, if unequal to others in a single respect, are wholly unequal." It is this issue that is the chief single cause of revolution. Mass numbers are the strength of a Democracy; discipline of an Aristocracy. Whereas Plato, with his theocratic leanings, is clear that Monarchy—government by the one best, if discoverable—is theoretically the most desirable and Tyranny the *corruptio optimae pessima*, the worst form, Aristotle is not sure that a monarchic form, which excludes "subjects" or "flock" from a share in the responsibilities of supreme rulership, is politically masculine or healthy.

Of more importance are Aristotle's views on Democracy and Tyranny. It will be noted that Democracy is listed among the perverted forms of constitution. The question-begging name of Polity or Constitutionalism is selected for the sound form, where the many

* *Cf.* p. 99.

exercise sovereignty for the benefit of the whole, *i.e.*, democracy as generally understood today, but in a mixed constitution which allows for degrees of quality. It is not, however, obvious that the actual will of the majority—Rousseau tended to assume this—must be the general or real will of the whole. Here is that issue of the morality of Minority Rights that is to vex us for two millennia. It is worth while to repeat that Aristotle, like Plato, lived his life against a background of conscious class war. The Marxist school today would deny that there was any *one* community and would assert that difference of class was substantively deeper than unity of country. As against a superficial bourgeois concept of democracy, it would assert the claim of a proletarian democracy which, in order to attain the true community of a classless society, must pass through the phase of the dictatorship of the proletariat during which non-proletarian sections, resisting assimilation, must be liquidated. Aristotle, in his age, was faced with democratic [Athenian] and oligarchic [Spartan] "fronts," each with their foreign alliances. Democratic government, in the sense in which he condemns it as "perverted," is specifically government *by* the free proletariat *for* the proletariat.

Is there not a flaw in Aristotle's assumptions? Are we not entitled to say that the majority is empowered to settle what is the good of the community? Therefore, when the majority governs according to its *own* will and for its *own* good it governs in accordance with the will and for the good of the community—since it itself is alone competent to decide that will and good. There will of course always be minorities dissentient against the law: such men are criminals. Aristotle's response would appear to be that it is dishonest to confound a minority, protesting against iniquity by natural standards, with criminals who have offended against law, not only conventional, voted as *psephismata* [popularly voted regulations], but *nomoi* [constitutional laws] fundamental, traditional and even natural. And, although Aristotle shifts his interpretation of "natural" from his early one as the rational type to his later one of the empiric norm, this does not affect his attitude, as a scientist, to temporary "sovereign" decisions. Further, it is *not* the case that the majority is competent alone to decide upon the will and good of the community, since it may well be that the more intelligent—by any natural, impartial criterion—and more rational are part of the minority. In that case, rationally the minority, and not the majority, would have the better right in equity to decide upon the good of the community. And it is cardinal to the argument that Aristotle asserts the historical existence of a real community as well as postulating its ideal need. Equality is an equitable principle. But, then, what does equality mean?

> Equality is to render equal things to the equal and unequal things to the unequal.

A Labour Party may then rule, truly constitutionally, for the rational benefit of the whole community. Or it may rule as a group dictatorship for the benefit of, *e.g.*, weekly wage-earners, and without consideration of those who have small investments or plots of land. If so, as a proletarian democracy, it is a perverted form. *Supposing* that men have a *rational* right to small investments or to their own plot of land, then it is unequal to refuse to render them their share in the community goods or to liquidate them—as it is patently unfair for oligarchs or tyrants to do the same at the expense of the sections *they* exclude. This rational equality may of course be overruled by force. But mere force does not always reside with democrats any more than always with oligarchs.

But what reply can be made if it be asserted that no one can be impartial about the "reasonable" or rational rights of others, and that the issue is merely one of which section of society will be better organized for fighting the issue out? It is not enough to comment that a rational man can have no moral interest in the issue of such a fight. An active, ethical thesis is here maintained: that what matters is the power to apply force. That thesis Aristotle is still Platonist enough to repudiate. The fight itself—the class war or *stasis*—Aristotle unequivocably condemns as a damage to the community and to good morality. About the moral damnability of gratuitous stirrers up of *stasis* Aristotle and Plato are entirely at one. But how then shall the democrats stir their followers to adequate fighting resentment against the oligarchs? How shall they resist them, without class consciousness?

Is, then, Aristotle not in fact an oligarch or a plutocrat or—to use, in a loose sense,* modern terminology—like Plato, just a Fascist? Does he not speak of nobility as ancestral wealth and virtue, and add that virtue is rare? In view, however, of his expressed and high-handed attitude to the claims of private wealth, the charge of being a plutocrat may be dismissed. That of being a friend of rule by a traditional, middle class is far more serious. In objecting to *stasis* is not Aristotle objecting to those changes that can only come by force? And if so is he not a conservative, an oligarch, ready in fact (whatever the theory) to accept the oligarchic interpretation—the "upper-class"

* *Cf.*, however, p. 51.

interpretation—of what "the good of the community" is? Or a Fascist? Does his stress on the unity of the polis amount to more than this? Or is he discussing an ideal polis, and have the relations between the ideal and the actual (with its consequences for the theory of unconditional political obedience) never been satisfactorily settled by him? Probably not.

In an unsatisfactory criticism of the *Laws*, Aristotle complains that Plato here finds his "second-best" constitution in something between democracy and oligarchy. Aristotle, against this, desires some aristocratic form after the Lacedaemonian or Spartan mòdel. To be frank, Sparta—although both complain of its militarism—had a fatal fascination for both philosophers. So far the charge would seem to be proven, and even the charge of Fascism is tenable. Certainly it is no great reservation to point out that Aristotle recognized that the relation between Spartiate and helot, with its Terror, was a source of weakness, and even military weakness, in that constitution. Here surely was an oligarchy at its worst morally, if not at its most corrupt—suffering perpetually from the evil of class war or *stasis*, which the Athenians set out to exploit for their own political ends. We are left with the passages, which are perhaps the crux of the whole matter, where Aristotle asks (but does not answer) the question whether, in some corrupt community, it is possible for a "good citizen," *i.e.*, law-abiding, to be a good man. It is the old issue, restated, of Sophocles' *Antigone*.* It is Aristotle's weakness that he did *not* radically answer this.

Aristotle's own treatment is academic and unhelpful; and turns on his belief that a "virtuous man" (*n.b.*, the Greek *aretē*, like Italian *virtù* = "virtue" *or* "talent") is a "superior man," whereas not all citizens can be superior men.

> It is clearly possible to be a virtuous citizen without possessing the virtue characteristic of a virtuous man. . . . The functions proper to people of this description [servile work] are not such as should be learned by any good man. . . . The fact is that we cannot regard all who are indispensable to the existence of the State as being [full and active] citizens . . . the subject may be compared to a flute-maker and the ruler to a flute-player who uses the instrument.†

Not until the coming of Christianity and monasticism, following the Cynics and Stoics, was dignity assigned to manual (menial) labour, and

* *Cf.* p. 25.
† *Cf.* p. 720.

the distinction denied between those necessary to culture and those who shared in it.* Aristotle's discussion "dates." It is that of a writer of the slave age, not of the machine age. Its relevance lies only in the doubt whether third-class minds, in *any* economic strata, can share directively in a first-class culture—a doubt to which Aristotle, as also Plato, had an answer. The answer was "no." The wealthy, added Plato, frequently had third-class minds.

Discussion whether Plato, the Communist, and Aristotle can intelligibly be called Fascists is best deferred until we have analyzed Fascism.† Crude comparisons easily lead to false analogies. This much, however, can now be said, that Aristotle is a vigorous exponent of the doctrine of the dominance of constitutional law and of the judiciary and an opponent of the methods of force and *coup d'état.* And he is no friend of dictatorship. Also, he is a *minimalist* in legislation (*i.e.*, a believer in custom as the bond of society, suspicious of all self-conscious lawmaking and increase of statutory regulation), relying upon the levers of education and of voluntary co-operation within a customary social scheme.

Tyranny is the usual term for one of Aristotle's constitutional divisions (*turannis*). But it is a misleading one. It carried, to Greek ears, no necessary implication of misrule. We are dealing with technical terms about which it is essential to be clear, since only so can Greek thought and conclusions be brought to bear on modern conditions. A Benevolent Despot could be, for Aristotle, a Tyrant *save that "despot"* for a Greek meant a master of subjects or slaves and was a term applicable to, *e.g.*, a King of Persia, *and that* the eighteenth-century dynastic Benevolent Despot or Autocrat, as hereditary and recognized by law and custom, was what Aristotle would have called a "dynast."

A *Dictator* technically (*i.e.*, for the Romans, who invented the term) was a strictly constitutional ruler, entirely constitutionally invested with extraordinary powers during a limited period. In this sense alone —and then only by stretching of terms—could Mr. Roosevelt be described, as he was once by the pro-Communist press in New York, and later in other quarters, as a "dictator." Any notion of *coup d'état,* despite the cases of Sulla and Julius, was rather excluded than included. Today a dictator, making his own "constitution" (*psephismata,* not *nomoi*), may well be such by *coup d'état.* What he relies upon is that he is there, or declares that he is there—as Napoleon I and III de-

* *Cf.* pp. 137, 143.

† *Cf.* pp. 722, 743.

clared—by popular will. He is not usually an hereditary Dynastic Autocrat. He is an autocrat by popular choice, unlike those claiming to be such (as Czar and Mikado) by divine will alone. He may be benevolent; but he is precisely a popular Tyrant.

It is important to note that Peisistratos of Athens and Periander of Corinth were both great and even benevolent rulers, and that Peisistratos was largely responsible for great public works which were among the glories of Athens. It is important, also, to note that the *popular origins* of tyranny are especially stressed by Aristotle—an Ivan the Terrible, a Henry VIII, a Nero or Caligula are *not* typical tyrants in the technical Greek sense of this word, but rather bad dynastic autocrats. Tyranny was reached when democracy had passed over into a demand for government by "the people's choice"—"popular government" (which is sharply distinct from "democracy"). Everything that Aristotle said, twenty-two centuries ago, as a political scientist, about the historical conditions of the arising of tyranny, as a *popular* form of government, has (to the horror of Liberals) in our own days been astonishingly shown to be true. The tyrant, unlike the autocrat, is a species of the demagogue, relying on plebiscite or vote but without *organized* opposition or permitted alternative.

> It usually happened in ancient times, whenever the functions of demagogue and general were united in the same person, that Democracies were revolutionized into Tyrannies. *The great majority of ancient tyrants had been demagogues. . . . They were able to do so in all cases by possessing the confidence of the commons, the ground of this confidence being their detestation of the wealthy classes.*

Aristotle continues, referring to Elective Dictatorship (Aesymnetic) and to Despots, such as the Persian:

> No doubt there are certain points of difference between these two forms; but they both approximate to Monarchy in their constitutional character and the voluntary obedience of the subjects, while they resemble a Tyranny in the despotic and autocratic nature of the rule. There is a *third* species of Tyranny which may be regarded as Tyranny in the strictest sense, being the counterpart of absolute Monarchy. A Tyranny of this kind is necessarily realized in the form of Monarchy which is an irresponsible exercise of rule over subjects, all of whom are the equals or superiors of the ruler, for the personal advantage of the ruler and not of the subjects. And hence the obedience is in this case involuntary; for no free person submits willingly to such rule. . . . For Tyranny is one-man rule for the good of the one man; Oligarchy of the few for the good of the wealthy; and Democracy of the many for the good of the poor; none of them subserves the interest of the community

at large. . . . Kings are guarded by the citizenry in arms; tyrants by a professional force [or police].

In this description, Aristotle becomes vague again in his definitions.

Is it, then, equitable to describe the rule of Peisistratos and Periander, as Aristotle does, as tyrannies, since these men doubtless benefited their communities? They got things done. They were brought to power as democrats. *Were* they only ruling for the good of themselves? The answer seems to be that they were interested primarily in maintaining the prestige of their own régimes. "The good of themselves" does not necessarily mean graft and corruption. There was no constitutional method of replacing them if they were not wanted. There was no constitutional opposition; only one party was tolerated, their own.

If, then, we ask the question, of high practical importance, whether in technical terminology the régimes of Hitler, Mussolini and Stalin, or of the Caesars, should be classed as Tyrannies, it certainly does not mean that we are discussing these rulers as political Al Capones. We may indeed chop scholarly straws by asking whether the Dictators do not more nearly correspond to what Aristotle calls Heroic Rule, popularly acclaimed. Here, however, Aristotle means no more than the family, traditional leadership, especially in war, of the Homeric Kings.

Perhaps, it may be argued, the comparison is closer with what Aristotle calls *Pambasileia*. But this closely corresponds with Plato's theocratic supreme Kingship or (better) Papacy or Mikadoate. Where there is genius, Aristotle indicates, it is improper that it should be subordinate. Here is the "Leader-principle." Aristotle, however, points out that this supreme talent is not hereditary. Aristotle concludes, in normal circumstances, against this monarchic form, however voluntary in its basis, and in favour of the rule of law, as intelligence without passion, and of the "constitutional" system of popular share in the responsibilities of rule. Aristotle, then, speaking with the impartial authority of that distant, experienced age is our support as constitutional democrats [bourgeois democrats].

Does Aristotle favour the Leader-principle? The individual statesman, he maintains, is never free from bias; may well fall into the hands of a clique, with vested interests of its own and more capable of corruption than the electorate; and has, after all, only a human and limited capacity. With none of the spectacular imagination of a Plato in his day or the demigod back-slapping, coruscating, mentally cavorting qualities of a Bernard Shaw in ours—not to speak of the crossing-sweepers of dictatorship—nowhere does Aristotle better display the essential sobriety of his judgement than here. Like most sound judgements, it unhappily is emotionally flat and tends to dullness.

Aristotle, however, is not free from the charge of being more than a little oligarchic in his own bias. One would have liked to see his examination of the constitution of Venice. Oligarchy, however, he verbally maintains without qualification, is a *bad* form of government, corrupted by respect for money making, and defending its own privileges. He is merciless on the men of business enterprise. He has a weakness (explicable in terms of his times) for agriculturalists—like Herr Hitler. He states his preference for a mixture of aristocracy with constitutional democracy (*politeia*), with its rule of law and popular share in responsibilities, in language that anticipates Harrington.*

> The legislator in his political system ought always to secure the support of the middle class . . . *it is only when the numbers of the middle class preponderate either over both the extremes or over only one of them that there is a possibility of a permanent polity. For there is no danger of a conspiracy of the rich and the poor against the middle class,* as neither rich nor poor will consent to a condition of slavery, and if they try to find a polity which is more in the nature of a compromise, they will not discover any other than this.

Aristotle, then, visualizes the permanence of unequal wage rates and savings, and a kind of pragmatic balance of social power. He is not pro-capitalist; but (indeed like Marx later†) he is non-equalitarian. It is not the case that his judgements are valueless because he could only think of a slave civilization, and not of a machine civilization, since most of his remarks are directed to the free population. Nor is it true that he ignores the economic aspects of social life. It is not the case that he condemns *stasis* because he is an obstructionist to all change. The reasons for this moral condemnation, and the significance of the part he expects his aristocratic element to play, are indicated when we turn to his scheme of social organization.

5

(*a*) Social organization is one factor in educational practice. It is a factor in the education of character that is essential for the happy life, which is a life social and energetic. The Greeks had a habit of taking

* *Cf.* p. 300.
† *Cf.*, however, p. 642.

their politics seriously. To control that all-important factor Aristotle was prepared to go to remarkable lengths. The control of the size of the territory and of the population is accepted with a matter-of-factness that is astonishing. Such schemes would arouse against any modern democratic statesman insuperable objections. Here, however, Plato and Aristotle are in entire agreement. As has been indicated earlier, the relation of "the master of them that know" and the "divine" Plato was not a happy one. The charge that Aristotle makes against Plato here is only that the size of the population suitable for the Polis, suggested by Plato, in the *Laws*—a modest 5,000 citizens (or, say, 30,000 total, including slaves)—is ridiculously *large*. The same consideration governs Aristotle's suggestions for *limiting*—not enlarging—the size of the population and his suggestions on matrimonial arrangements. Memories of food shortage apart in sparsely cultivated Hellas, the dominant consideration is the typical one of homogeneity, and manageability of the community. The polis is to be *eusunoptos*——"all easily to be seen at one view." Its citizen democrats should all be capable of being addressed at one time in one meeting (a problem now easily overcome by modern technical inventions). About this social homogeneity—which has no little cultural similarity to a doctrine of race purity—Aristotle appears to feel passionately because this is the very basis of his social ethics—of that unifying sentiment which excludes *stasis* and class war. Legislation can be applicable "to none but those of the same race." Indeed it must be stated that the modern German doctrine of racial purge and cultural *gleichanschaltung* or homogeneity is consonant enough with the ethical belief of the great Greeks. To this day it is unsettled whether democracy means decision of the majority of adult inhabitants (as in Czechoslovakia) or of voters (as in France) or of blood-nationals.

What is here meant by ethics? In the Christian era, and especially in Protestant countries, the question "What is ethical?" raises associations of problems for the individual and his conscience. Although there are some anticipations of this attitude in Socrates, for the Greeks—and not least for Plato and Aristotle—the association called up is that of *ēthē*, like the Latin *mores*—"social customs"—and especially of *ēthos*—the system or integration of customary morality. In brief, the immediate reference is social. Put in another way, the great Greek teachers, at this epoch, took it almost for granted that an *ethos* involved a community, a Polis. To be more precise, just because the notion was coming under challenge with the break-down of the family system and with incipient individualism, they affirmed it the more vigorously.

The object of civil society is no maintenance of a contract of individuals (Plato discusses this theory in order specifically to reject it, and Aristotle, in set phrase, concurs), but a social condition under which it may be possible for the citizen "to live happily and well." It is moreover a socialistic condition—religion, matrimony, family life and, of course, business life, trade and interest-taking: all lie under its paternal surveillance. With Plato the scheme is socialistic in the full economico-political sense. In Aristotle's case (as later in Proudhon's*) it is socialistic in a distributivist sense, and by virtue of its rigorous regulation of wealth. Even Socrates did not challenge the need for this.

Let us mark well Aristotle's significant words: "*The Polis comes into being for the sake of life; it remains in being for the sake of the good life.*" It is "a community for the sake of good life . . . for the sake of the perfect and *self-sufficient* life." Briefly, Plato and—despite all talk of "variety"—Aristotle are fairly complete totalitarians, with affiliations of thought with modern Communism and Fascism. Of the two, Aristotle, with his empiricism and stress in variety, is a far better democrat than the communist Plato. We shall later see that there is a direct connection between these modern movements, the decline of the influence of the Christian churches, and the revival of Hellenic, non-churchly thought. The Polis—frequently, if most incorrectly, today translated "State"—was for the Hellene his all. Thus Aristotle concludes (here in thoroughly Platonic fashion):

> As the end of the state as a whole is one, it is clear that the education of all the citizens must be *one and the same,* and the superintendence of it a public matter rather than in private hands as it is now.

The Greeks assert that the individual finds his moral life in the community. It is therefore very important to note the exact nature of this community. Examination will show it to be very distinctive: quite unlike the modern state. Aristotle insists with reiteration that the Polis must be small and homogeneous. The historical examples of which he approves were such. Such a metropolis as Babylon was not a polis. Today if Aristotle had been confronted with the National Socialist expulsion of the Jews from Germany or with the liquidation of the non-proletarian classes in Russia, he would have faced a dilemma. In the first case, we may logically conjecture that he would have praised the Hitlerian concept of cultural homogeneity but he might, I think, have condemned the *stasis* involved in Hitler's methods. In

* *Cf.* p. 554 *ff*.

the second case, he would certainly have condemned the *stasis* incited in the native Russian population, but he would have had reluctantly to admit an unsolved problem in his own philosophy. Aristotle visualizes cultural education as the great check on class war. Himself a "resident alien," he nowhere inquires whether the need for cultural homogeneity as the basis of moral education justifies the elimination of non-assimilable classes or national groups or whether his condemnation of *stasis* is to be carried to the point of admitting permanent cultural heterogeneity. In brief, the communist liquidator, on this point, may be a better Aristotelian than Aristotle. The probable answer is that Aristotle held to the faith that a unified, rational, middle-class culture could be caused to permeate, voluntarily, the entire free population across economic divisions. This voluntary permeation, however, would have been actively assisted by the censors of "good morals." Plato had, of course, another technique of dealing with these divisions—the total divorce of wealth and power, and the priestly technique of "the myth."

(*b*) The worst of Aristotle, the slave-owner, appears at this point. Because he is a great man, it appears in a form so deceptively attractive that it has had followers throughout history. There is, implies Aristotle, a "good culture" or *ethos* which some people *know* and which they are entitled to inculcate. Inculcation is not a mere matter of schooling but of the regulation of the whole social (and the selection even of the physical) environment. Thus such immoral disturbing proletarian elements as seafaring men are to be kept at a distance; and the community is to be small, homogeneous and governed by profound respect for traditional, constitutional law. Even, however, granted law as a norm, social morality must embody itself in certain persons as examples and leaders. Here, for Aristotle, is the function of an aristocracy and that aristocracy is a middle, leisured class.

It is here that Aristotle shows himself a stupendous snob, although an intellectual snob. Unlike Plato, he is not a natural dogmatist. The ethos is *known*, but not in some final, syllogistic or mystic fashion. It is a matter of sense and taste: of probability as well as of truth. But the sense and taste of whom? Here Aristotle reverts to the famous maxim of the Sophists that virtue can be taught. Virtue, let us remember, means much more than the condition of a clear conscience. It is an active condition of exercised talent and developed culture. This takes time—virtue takes time; culture takes time. "Banausic," *i.e.*, trading and industrially employed, men have no time for more than a tincture of culture. The uneducated are damned in their sins. Only the leisured are virtuous—*Kaloikagathoi,* "beautiful and good." It is the antithesis of the Christian belief, which is individualistic, resting on the "immortal soul," eternally individual—but it is not, therefore, negligible. If virtue is *social* (as Aristotle and many writers today have said) then either the virtuous condition is that of brotherly commonplaceness or it is an excellence of the few. If so, then the moral society will differ from Plato's hierarchical ordering only in degree.

Aristotle elaborates his position with reference to the arts. His social philosophy—as we saw in the case of "the man of personality"—is a "gentleman philosophy" and that in the bad, arrogant sense. And a gentleman must not occupy himself in servile, manual works. He must not even occupy himself too much with study of the technique of the arts—be a scribbler or a school "dominie" or a man in an orchestra—or carry the practice of that technique beyond the point necessary for forming a competent artistic judgement. In his sharp division between gentlemanly knowledge of theory and vulgar practice, the spindle-legged Aristotle of the many rings is, as an educationalist, merely wrong. The product would be dilettante. Such a man as Michelangelo, the craftsman, knew better.

There is, however, just enough truth in this arrogant master-attitude—so long as it is the individualistic corrective of that inquisitorial collectivism that Plato praises—to make Aristotle, the democrat, one of the subtlest foes of democracy. It may be that science will show that only the man in health, of a good stock and nature, nurtured on a good diet physical and emotional, free from anxiety and with his natural confidence unbroken—the *natural* aristocrat—is capable of the highest excellence, mental and spiritual, and of raising the level of civilization itself. The answer, nevertheless, to Aristotle surely is threefold. There is no such divorce feasible between pure, dignified speculation and impure, vulgar practice. Moral knowledge, again, is *not* the static perquisite of the selected leaders of society; but is something growing and experimentally attainable, in which every individual's contribution matters. The contrary is the old error of Plato—and of Egypt; *its correction is the chief glory of the Anglo-Saxon Tradition.* Further, natural aristocracy is no perquisite of plutocracy and even if—as Aristotle resolutely asserts—full powers, as a civilized man, depend upon material goods, *i.e.*, the virtuous are the moderately rich, there is no reason in distributive justice why, in an ever wealthier civilization, all men or most should not have their quota of these material requisites of the cultured life. Here Plato had shown the way. Here Aristotle, from precisely the same premise, about the economic conditioning of the valuable life, reaches (wrongly*) the opposite conclusion from Marx.

Let us, however, observe—since no question in all politics is more critical—that this answer is not so clearly decisive, but that most of the world's history has not been constructed upon the dogmatic (and here Aristotle is dogmatic and Platonic) hypothesis. The curse of social experimentalism, as Plato and Aristotle insisted, is ethical nihilism, criminal anarchy, democratic vulgarity in its motley, inefficiency and low standards. In brief, liberty and variety have to be paid for—but the payment is perhaps the price of progress. However, we do well to recall that Aristotle is a very dubious basis, if *uncorrected*, for public education in a modern democracy. He poisons the wells with a slave doctrine before youth has begun on its journey. This stricture does not mean agreement with his contemporaries, Timon and Theokritos of Chios, who called him "futile" and "the empty-headed Aristotle"—*kenophrōn Aristotelēs*. Precisely the contrary. If Plato is (which I doubt) "the Christian before Christ," Aristotle is the great pagan, superb in his mercilessness to common clay. Also there is reason to suppose that, in his later years, Aristotle—once the dogmatic disciple of Plato—had changed to an experimentalist (even social), himself.

6

Aristotle, son of a physician, is a scientist. It is when we turn to this field that we perceive the real grandeur of "The Philosopher." Science for the Greek—slowly struggling to get loose from theology and ethics before Socrates—is, since Socrates, unfortunately permeated with a priori ethical conceptions. The theory that nature is rational—a theory often fusing with pantheism—forms a bridge. Aristotle, exponent of the doctrine of so-called "final cause," views all physical nature in his observations, in the perspective of "purpose." This holds true despite the fact that his concept of "the natural" changes from the Platonic "typical" to the scientist's statistical "normal," in the course of his own development as a natural philosopher. His treatment of physics is teleological, looking to the shaping of the final "form" or "*gestalt*" of the genus or species, its alleged "end" or "perfection." So is his treatment of politics and social phenomena—neither more so nor less. We must disentangle, in his social science, this prejudice from the rest of his work. It is that remainder which deserves attention. The important thing to note is that as Aristotle grew older, and rewrote

* *Cf.* p. 773; also pp. 552, 599.

his lecture notes in the light of increased experience, his idealism dropped more and more away; scientific precedence is assigned to empirical research, although this might discover from amid the multifarious a norm; and he himself became ever more the political scientist, not the moralist—and the father of political science.

The study of political—or, to be more precise, social—principles, is based upon observation. First, Aristotle notes the physical environment, the geographic position, its economic potentialities, the climate as ultimate background of human social life and politics. The historical evolution of the Polis from family and village is discussed. Comment on developed constitutions is based on study of over 158 from Byzantium to Carthage, of which the *Constitution of Athens* we still have, from Aristotle's own hand. These studies are concrete enough and Aristotle, as a politicist, is careful to distinguish between ideal constitutions (*haplōs aristē);* constitutions best for the mass of cities (*pasais tais polesin harmottousa);* and the best constitutions practicable under the actual circumstances (*ek tou hupokeimenou*) and under hypothetical circumstances (*ex hupotheseōs*). He fully recognizes that the good constitution lies within the intersection of the good surveyed by ethics and the psychologically viable surveyed by political science.

As a politicist, and not only a political philosopher, he has the courage to survey with dispassionate interest constitutions that, as a philosopher, he condemns as perversions and even, in Book VI, to note the technique by which they may be maintained. This may be termed mere study of the art of politics. But the description, in Book VIII, of the causes of revolutions and that of the metamorphoses of constitutions, although entirely undisfigured by the historical mysticism which we shall later find in the Stoics and still later in Spengler, makes the fundamental scientific assumption of such a constancy in human affairs that a science of social conduct based upon these psychological permanencies becomes conceivable.

It is important to note that his word "Politics" has an exact, and not the vulgar current, sense. It is the study of the community—a scientific sociology. It has no reference to the State, which indeed, in the modern sense, did not exist. It is in the light of this that we must understand Aristotle's famous remark "man is *politicon zōon*, a political animal." He elsewhere explains that man, among all animals, is one of the most evil and difficult to control. It is interesting to note that he assigns, as the causes of revolutions, mixture of race (a remark that would please the Germans), disproportionate increase of one class and—a favourite stroke—weakness of the middle class. With the exception perhaps of this last, Aristotle's methodical observations are undisturbed by "wishful thinking." Non-evolutionary, despite his anthropological studies of human origin, there is yet an astringent Darwinianism in his treatment of the human fauna.

Aristotle's *Politics*, if a companion study to his *Ethics* (much more definitely separated in later versions, although never divorced), is also an appendix to his *Historia Animalium.* He points us, across a gulf of two millennia of half-civilized history, on to the establishment of a science of man and society, thanks to which man may study himself objectively and thereby master the art of control of his own civilization and self.

It is possible to discuss Aristotle as a great bourgeois, the apotheosis of the bourgeois. Such intelligence, however, knows no class. His common-sense philosophy provides a compass to sanity for the human race. His scientific approach (incomplete although it necessarily was on the quantitative side) is the only hopeful one if we are to understand human social nature, although it is an approach that, after him, will hear no footfall on its path of inquiry until two thousand years have gone by.

His belief that there can be "no culture without kitchen maids" may be monstrous error, but we have not yet worked out an equalitarian remedy. Mr. Aldous Huxley suggests a college of cardinals (or world-controllers), and biological conditioning to contentment with the lot suitable for an ability scientifically assessed. It is an answer not so remote from the facts of modern Russia. Is this the true answer or is the answer a Lincolnian (and rural) individualist democracy? Aristotle's aristocratic challenge to proletarian democracy cannot be ignored. Perhaps an empirical, hit-or-miss democracy alone suits the large, heterogeneous cosmopolitan order of society. Aristocracy may be only appropriate (as Aristotle himself confessed and insisted) for the small homogeneous polis or community. This will be a clue worth watching as we study the centuries to come until our own day. Perhaps we must seek a return to that Polis, and shall have to conduct a new scrutiny of what today we mean by "the community"—is it State, Church, Commonwealth, World-league, Village, or Party?

Aristotle had no interest in, or theory of, cosmopolis. An admission of the common culture of Hellas was as far as this Philosopher of the Polis got to a theory of civilization. But, as the Founder of Political Science, he has laid down for us the earliest rules showing how we can develop such a theory for ourselves when we have the patience and talent.

These matter perhaps more than the common-sense political utopias of a lonely man. In one of his letters, preserved for our eyes by the commentators, we read, "The more solitary and isolated I am, the more I have come to love myths." Perhaps there might be something to be said for the star-souls . . .

In 322 B.C., at the age of sixty-two, Aristotle died, an exile alike from the home of his birth and of his adoption, immortal for all time as "the Philosopher," "the master of them that know." Some say he died by his own hand as a suicide, by drinking aconite, others—less strikingly but not inconsistently—from an intestinal complaint. In his will he makes provision for his concubine, whose affection for him he puts on record; for his children; and for the manumission of his slaves. Of his epigrams some sufficiently reveal the man to be worth putting on record. To a chatterer who asked whether he bored him, Aristotle replied: "No; for I was not attending to you." To the question, how we should behave to our friends, "As we should wish them to behave to us." Distinguishing the educated and the uneducated, he declared that they differed "as much as the living from the dead." Beauty he declared, with unexpected humour and humanity, to be a greater recommendation than any letter of introduction. Asked what advantage he had ever gained from his philosophy, he replied, "This, that I do without being ordered, what some are constrained to do by their fear of the law." The epigram characteristically omits to mention the issue that obsessed him, as it had troubled Plato: whether the good *man* might not be driven *not* to do, thanks to his philosophy, what the good *citizen* did in obedience to law, so that the good was *not* the happy. Had he not declared, in his epitaph on Plato, that no one again should be both "good and happy at the same time"? And, adds his biographer, asked "What is it that soon grows old?" he replied, "Gratitude."

READING

Aristotle: *Politics* (ed. Jowett) Book I, i–x; Book VII, i–v. (order of books varies in different editions).

BIBLIOGRAPHICAL NOTE

A. Zimmern: *The Greek Commonwealth*, 1911.
Werner Jaeger: *Aristotle*, 1923, trans. Robinson, 1934.

Chapter IV

The Hellenistic Age and the Coming of Rome

1

ALEXANDER the Great, Aristotle's pupil, built up the widest flung empire the world has seen, stretching from Adriatic to Ganges, until Britain built her Commonwealth and the United States linked two oceans. The master was uninterested. Although we do not know the full contents of the tractates Aristotle presented to Alexander, Aristotle seems to have regarded this Empire as barbaric in culture, inferior in spiritual value, mechanical in its principles of administration, not to be compared in significance with Sparta and Athens. It must be confessed that Aristotle had his excuses. His kinsman, Kallisthenes, whom he recommended to Alexander, fell under suspicion of sedition, perhaps owing to a frankness excessive in the presence of leaders who were persuaded that they were demigods. Suspicion was enough. He was promptly put in an iron cage and forgotten there for so long that he became neglected in his person, lousy and verminous. In this unappetizing condition he was turned out of his cage by Alexander's orders and thrown to the pet lions who habitually accompanied that monarch to solace him on his travels.

This lack of interest was, nevertheless, a strange distortion of perspective due to the ethical disregard of quantity in the name of quality. The history of the next fifteen hundred years, after this epoch of *intensive* Greek culture, is to be an improvisation on the theme of *extension*. It is for this very reason that, from this time forward, until a century ago, so much Greek political thought appeared irrelevant. The mechanical theory of government succeeds to the cultural. To the polis-society succeeds the police-society.*

The rule of Alexander is followed by that of the Diadochoi ("leaders" in the succession after Alexander) in the kingdoms of Macedon, Syria

* The etymology of polis and police is, of course, the same, although the implications of the ideas are so different.

and Egypt under the Antigonids, Seleucids and Ptolemies. This is the Hellenistic Age, with its culture centered in Alexandria, Antioch and Athens. Aristotle was right in thinking that Alexander's empire was mechanical, without organic life. But the system suited the epoch. Already civilization, after its Hellenic bloom, is moving down to the Great Recession. The finest age is in the past. To the perfidious intrigues and assassinations of the Seleucids in Antioch succeeded the corrupt, extortionate rule of the Roman proconsuls of the Republic. In the Alexandria of the Ptolemies the old system lasted on, royal brother marrying royal sister and continuing the succession of the godlike Pharaohs.

The social scene of Pericles and Plato has passed away. The intensive culture of the polis, with its quota of 5,000 fully armed troops or maybe twice that number, is defenceless in a world where imperial armies are on the march. The polis is, militarily speaking, obsolete. The world moves forward into a period of military grandeur where force is the test. Concurrently, the almost family life of the polis is broken up by the new trade developments. A cosmopolitan culture replaces the intensely civic life. Against this world background an individualism and (as ever, with it) an internationalism appear which know no local roots. The current political philosophy takes colour from the social facts.

Within three centuries this new Great Society of the Mediterranean and the Middle East receives its appropriate organization, not in the Empire built by the personal genius of the erratic Alexander, but in the solid mass of the Roman Caesardom.

Rome, even in the imperial days, remained head of a confederation of City-states. The Roman Empire was urban. Until the late Byzantine period (ninth century) the classical world did not depart from its city-state (or poli-tical) form. For these thickly populated lands of the hill-towns, with their farming and small trading population, the civic form was as natural as the form of a realm, national or tribal, was appropriate in the almost unexplored forests of the barbaric North or a military despotism in the open plains of the torrid Middle East, with their effects of unlimited space. Rome preserved this small-scale civilization as the unit in its own vast agglomeration. It became effective, unlike the kingdoms of Seleucus and Mithridates in Syria and Asia Minor, because it was able to weld these units together.

The Roman Empire, however, was an agglomerate of City-states under a Military Government. Literally and etymologically, its Emperors were *imperatores*, *duces*, field marshals—who had the additional advantage of having learned in the East to be divine. According to Aristotle's classification, at least after Octavian, they were benevolent tyrants, since they were not constitutionally removable and were primarily concerned to maintain their own regime. The fatal weakness, however, of the moralistic element in Aristotle's classification here shows, since it would be as difficult to show that Aurelius did rule for the good of himself, not the whole, as that Nero did not. The Emperor is concerned to maintain *his personal regime*, and the succession, unlike that in a dynastic monarchy, is seldom certain—and yet it can well be argued that his concern is to maintain the imperial *system*, with its selection of rulers by ability (including ability to survive). In terms of Roman political theory, the Emperors were the successors of the entirely constitutional dictators, deliberately appointed for a time for the better safety of the commonwealth. Their power was partly tribunician (*i.e.*, popular) and partly military, and either way constitutional. Octavian, above all, stickled on these constitutional points. At least the Emperors were as constitutional as the absolute Benevolent Despots of the eighteenth century whom generically they resembled. And, even if the system of the Roman Empire were unconstitutional, unstable, dying, assuredly it took longer dying than any known system in the world, save the Chinese, has taken to live.

The Roman Empire had such powers of endurance because it was a system capable of giving Peace and Law. Often the so-called peace given by the Roman legions was, as Tacitus said, a desolation. But it did not remain such. The Empire, although soulless compared with the life of Athens and Sparta, is not merely mechanical. It is organic—organized on the principle of Law. The Law, based on prescription and on natural justice, does not have to take cognizance of persons, localities and sentiments. It centres itself round no traditional, ancestral altars, like the Greek Ethos. It is merely the expression of the impartial will of the armed empire for its subjects and citizens. It is formal Authority. But for these citizens it is nevertheless equitable. Later, it will be found that impersonal impartiality, the abstract form of authority, is not enough to satisfy the human spirit—or even, as personification of that authority, the worship of field marshals. A search begins again for intensiveness, intimacy, a personal religion that is not detached form or abstract civic duty. The civic religion of the polis is now dead. The Empire becomes the world-vehicle for carrying to triumph world-religions, Mithraism and others, but chief among them Christianity.

The nature of the civilization and culture of Rome must be grasped before we can comprehend the impact of the political philosophies of Hellenistic and later Imperial periods upon the minds of the hearers. The new civilization was cosmopolitan, in the limited sense of the whole area, European, Asiatic, African, laved by the Mediterranean Sea. Its two great languages, Latin and Hellenistic Greek, never national, had ceased to be merely local and had become the languages of a supra-national culture.

The new civilization was, moreover, proletarian. I do not merely mean that occasionally slaves such as Epictetus, and frequently freedmen, in the Roman civil service—men of Aryan or Levantine extraction—played an important part in moulding its culture. Whereas the thought of Plato and Aristotle was through and through aristocratic, the Roman Empire placed, in dazzling eminence, the Emperor, frequently himself an uneducated soldier, and, on the other side, the flat, equal mass of the citizenry which, after the Emperor Caracalla (A.D. 211–217), meant the entire body of adult male freemen, *i.e.*, citizenship had ceased to mean much. It was an equalitarianism against which the historian Tacitus, speaking for the patricians, protested passionately but in vain. It was confirmed by the appointment of freedmen to high places and was deliberately encouraged by the emperors as a matter of jealousy and policy. The stream was not reversed until the late Byzantine days, with their counts and marquesses. Local magnates abounded; but even here taxation was so directed as to grind down the *curiales* to the general level. Caesar, the embodiment of the Empire, and his soldiers, officials, bureaucrats, all appointees at will, alone stood out.

The economy of the empire was, so far as it suited the bureaucrats (for purposes of taxation) and the equality-loving, jealous Emperors, a "planned economy," in which the propertied *curiales* could not change status and escape from their obligation to hold office and be taxed, and the peasants and old soldiers, settled on the land, for the better convenience of administration and civic services became "tied to the soil," *glebae ascripti*, and entered into that relationship, technically known as emphyteutic, which was the beginning of feudalism and of the class system of the modern world. Commercially, however, it was a free-trade empire.

2

The Hellenistic culture that corresponded to this social scheme is, on the whole, well tinged with pessimism. The optimism of Herodotus, standing at the threshold of the Age of Exploration, is no longer characteristic. Religious certainty and even the stability given by the established *ethos* of the Polis have gone.

The old religion of the farmer republic of Rome, with its agricultural rites and temples that resembled butchers' slaughter-houses, no longer had power in a more sophisticated and cosmopolitan world.

The tendency towards a new heroic, patriotic faith, deriving its force from the habits of the idolatrous East and the bureaucrat's uneasy feeling that some sentiment must cement the Empire, gathered momentum. The Roman populace had saluted, in a sudden burst of passion, dead Caesar as a demigod. Octavianus Augustus had to consent to sacrifices being offered to his genius—but that staid citizen made the reservation that it should only be outside Italy, in Pola. The conquest of Egypt involved the introduction of Egyptian manners. Caesar, as the godlike Pharaohs before him and the Mikado today, was saluted as "prince of princes, elect of Ptah and Nun the father of the gods, king of Upper and Lower Egypt, lord of the two lands, autocrat, son of the sun, lord of diadems, Kaiser, ever living, beloved of Ptah and Isis." It is a far cry from the prose of Aristotle to this salutation of the Roman *duces*. Vespasian, dry sceptic, dying accepts in duty his official fate. "Vae, puto deus fio," he exclaims. "Bah! I see I'm becoming a god." Diocletian takes the appellation Jovius—"of Jove"—and Maximian that of Herculius. Aurelian, in the third century, states the matter bluntly in his title: "Aurelian, lord and god." The political consequences of this Egyptian doctrine of the divinity of kings, at the time and for two thousand years, are incalculable.

The new official religion of Rome, however, could have little more sway over men's hearts than the old. A tolerant polytheism—and polytheism, unlike monotheism, could afford to be tolerant—was adorned, like a pillar with decorated capital, by the worship of Rome itself and the "divine Augustus." This official religion of the Empire was supposed to replace in men's hearts the fire of affection for local gods and the local patriotism. The religious cults could flourish, as a private matter, for all any Roman magistrate cared, luxuriantly or rankly, provided the public imperial rites were maintained. But, as Professor Gilbert Murray says, it was spiritually unsatisfactory to deify only emperors and millionaires. Nero was unimpressive as an incarnation of Apollo.

The disgust of the aristocrats at this orientalization of manners in place of the Roman puritanism can be found souring the pages of Tacitus and Juvenal. The "greedy Greeks" had come, and strange worships of the barking Anubis and of Cybele, wherein piety and morality varied in inverse proportions. "Into Tiber," writes the indignant Juvenal, "now flows the Syrian Orontes." All citizen *ethos* and sober morals had gone amid this welter of cults. Uneconomic taxation, political exclusion from office by imperial jealousy, spiritual orientalization and moral degeneration, partly from the old luxury, partly from the new loss of self-respect, resulted in what the German historian, Otto von Seeck, has called the "rotting away of the best." Cosmopolitan, proletarian Rome, for Tacitus, with its "spawn of Romulus," clamouring for bread and circuses, has become "the sink of the world." What the proletarians thought of Tacitus or of the drinking aristocrats and their new plutocratic rivals, gorging Trimalchio and the rest, is not recorded. The common citizenry, descendants of farmers who (under the new economics) could no longer run their farms for profit, held that they too had a right to be fed; and politicians, for the sake of the vote or to prevent revolt, were prepared to throw in the butter of circuses and races to add to the bread, which belonged to a true Roman citizen by civic right. Before we accept Tacitus at face value, let us remember that his (first-century) reference to Christianity is as "a lethal superstition which broke out not only throughout Judaea, the origin of the evil, but through the city (Rome) where flow all atrocious and shameful things." For Tacitus Rome is scarlet with the sins of Apostolic Christianity.

If we ask, apart from Tacitus with his Rembrandt colours, what reasonable men made of the culture of their age and how they looked upon this imperial cult, we shall find help in the rationalizations of an Emperor, Marcus Aurelius, who may have been, as his enemies said, "*philosophica anicula*"—"a philosophizing old woman"—but who undeniably had a sincerity superior to sham. For him the official Roman religion was a religion of patriotism which had the singular merit of being a religion of polytheistic tolerance, except to the intolerant, and of being a religion of patriotism of a singularly enlightened, world-wide kind. The old Greeks had clung to their local altars and found in their cities the stuff of their moral life. Marcus Aurelius felt himself a citizen of the world, not to speak of being its Emperor. He would have been happy in modern Geneva. "The poet has said, Dear City of Kekrops [Athens]. Shall I not say, Dear City of God?" The Emperor was the high instrument of the Divine Reason ordering the world, a *nomos empsuchos*—"incarnation of law." Such was the theory. Every man had a claim to respect for his *individual personality* as a citizen of that supernal city. The plain man too often—

the proletarian—failed to discover that this philosophizing was a religion at all. He asked for assurance, revelation, sacred books such as the East and the Egyptians had, and the already ubiquitous Jews. Too late and in vain the Emperor Julian, in the fourth century A.D.—"the Apostate"—sought to revive the human quality of the old religion and, casting around to find a sacred text, discovered it—in Homer. It was too late. *Tu vicisti, Galilaee.**

The old religion had been one of fears and terrors, panics sent by the Nature-god, Pan. The great Lucretius (98–55 B.C.) wrote one of the finest philosophic poems in human literature, *De Rerum Natura,* to rid men of this fear of death, this superstition which wrought so great ill—and died a suicide. The Greek had faced death with the pathos of resignation without hope—accepting fate without even the consolation of the myth of the Egyptians, those great tomb-builders. "Here his father Philip has laid his twelve year old, his very high hope, Nikoteles." It is an Hellenic inscription of centuries before our era. To the undying simplicity of this epitaph, worthy of David's lament over Absalom, succeeds the more sophisticated, half-humorous pessimism of Hadrian, poet and emperor of the world.

Animula vagula blandula,
Hospes comesque corporis,
Quae nunc abibis in loca
Pallidula, rigida, nudula
Nec, ut soles, dabis jocos.†

The mood was one of philosophic doubt. The old Roman *ethos* had gone and the age was too cultured to be moral. The background of the new manners was social confusion and, to this again was added, after Marcus Aurelius, not "dictatorial efficiency" but the violence of the legions and the murders of the empurpled dictators, their chiefs.

3

Against this background let us observe the fate of such of the so-called "Ten Schools of Philosophy" as here concern us. The Academic and Peripatetic Schools we have already discussed in terms of

* "Thou hast conquered, o Galilaean."

†Humane little soul, little wanderer,
Guest and friend of the body,
Now shalt thou depart forth into places
Pallid and stark and bare,
Nor ever again reply, as thou wast wont,
With some merry joke.

their founders, Plato and Aristotle. The Cynic School was founded by Antisthenes the Athenian, contemporary and admirer of Socrates, rival of "the conceited Plato." It deserves attention because of its influence on Stoicism. The Cynics were the "simple-lifers" of their day—"dog-men," as the etymology signifies: my brother, the dog*—like Antisthenes' pupil Diogenes, the banker's son, preferring (metaphorically speaking) to live in a kennel. The comment is worth recalling of Socrates on Antisthenes, studiously displaying the hole in his cloak: "I see your love of fame peeping through." The Cynics were, by anticipation, the Rousseauites, protesting in the name of honest virtue, against the vices of a sophisticated, over-elaborated Athenian civilization. More, they were the Salvation Army men of their day, bluffly buttonholing their acquaintances and asking the *jeunesse dorée* whether it had been saved. Salvation was by plain virtue. Virtue, however—in characteristic Hellenic fashion—was by wisdom, the sagacity of the sage. Only the sage was saved. But wisdom is an individual characteristic which is no privilege of the rich (let the leisure-class, conspicuous-consumptionist Aristotle say what he liked). Any plain man could attain the wisdom of virtue which was the true virtue of wisdom.

Classes and rulers are conventions contrary to nature. By nature man is an individual, "a man for a' that," and individuals by nature are equal in their chances of pursuit of virtue. The Cynics were universalists, not men of any parish; progressives; anti-ritualists; even nudists; levellers. They have, then, two political claims to fame: as the first philosophic equalitarians and (connected therewith) as the first, not excluding Socrates, to substitute an individual morality of virtue and self-development, "liberty," for a civic morality of duty to the free polis and *its* liberty.

The Cyrenaic School, founded by Aristippos of Cyrene, also a pupil of Socrates, is at the opposite pole to the Cynics, asserting that moral life is an art† and refurbishing the Aristotelian argument that the artist requires materials for his art, even precious metals. Aristippos' retort to the censure of Diogenes, washing vegetables—"If you had learnt to make these your diet, you would not have paid court to kings"—if not logically consummate, yet sufficiently indicates the outlook. "And if you knew how to associate with men, you would not be washing vegetables." One suspects Aristippos of snobbery: the Cyrenaics, it may be, liked to talk about frugality at the tables of the rich—naturally going first, as has been also seen in modern times, to

* However, the name comes from the place of teaching, the gymnasium of Cynosarges.

† *Cf.* p. 19.

those most in need of the preaching. The attitude yet earned for Aristippos the praise of the princely Plato: "You alone are endowed with the gift to flaunt in robes or go in rags." It was expressed in Aristippos' own dictum that what he had gained from philosophy was "the ability to feel at ease in any society." It is the philosophy which we shall much later find, less adequately, in the eighteenth-century writings of Shaftesbury. There is a pleasant modesty in its claims. As the Cynics form a bridge of thought to the Stoics, so do the Cyrenaics deserve note as making a bridge to the Epicureans.

The two philosophic schools that dominated the thought of the early Roman Empire were those of Zeno of Citium and of Epicurus, of the Porch and the Garden, the Stoics and the Epicureans. Both asked themselves questions, not put in pre-Socratic philosophy, novel even in post-Socratic: What is the Way of Life?

The pre-Socratic philosophers, Ionian or (like Pythagoras) Greek-Italian, had been concerned with nature, mathematics and the objective world—What is the nature of Nature? Even when Socrates had forced to the fore the question, What is Ethics? the answer about the Good Life had been given by Academic and Peripatetic alike, by Plato and Aristotle, in social and civic, not in individual terms. Plato had glanced at the social contract of individuals and thrown it aside. The individual mattered—but as the servant of social and supra-social, eternal values. In the beginning, said Aristotle, was the Polis. Society, temporally, logically and morally, was prior to the Individual. Now the Polis is broken up; the internationalist Empires have replaced it; and men are asking themselves, How shall a man act in the World? Dean Inge has called the resulting philosophies the "Don't Care Philosophies."

As the cloud of pessimism and trouble descended on the ancient world, not unnaturally men became preoccupied with the question: How should a man live and die with dignity in the midst of it all? It is interesting to note the preoccupation with death in a world of cultivation unfurnished with adequate medical or any anaesthetic facilities and where old age must have been painfully miserable. No wonder there is shadow amidst the lights of the poet Horace. Nevertheless, "don't care" is an inadequate description. These men cared very much about the right life, which had become a matter not of god-given tradition but of individual choice. It is, however, true that these philosophies are "escapist" and, for that very reason, have in them the seeds of subjectivism and defeatism. And, for all the southern delight in life, the outstanding men had little doubt that it was a vale of trouble, tyranny, corruption and violence, in which it was necessary to fortify the heart.

The Stoic School owes its foundation to Zeno of Citium, in Cyprus, (270 B.C.) who taught in the Painted Porch or Stoa of the market place at Athens, a man, we are told, flabby, thick-legged and fond of basking in the sun. This gossiping description, inspired by native Athenian malice, of Zeno, "the Phoenician," like Antisthenes no pure Athenian but of Asiatic ancestry, probably Semite, is interesting since his teaching as it has come down to us has some of the quality of a Hebrew prophet. We are told that he harangued, clenching his fist, maintaining that when a man has the real intuition of the truth it seizes him as it were by the hair of his head and drags him with conviction so that he cannot escape. Timon's description appears less than just: "A Phoenician too I saw, a pampered old woman ensconced in gloomy pride, longing for all things: but the meshes of her subtle web have finished and she had no more intelligence than a banjo." The Greeks, being Greeks, had no particular kindliness for their neighbours, even if philosophers.

The watchword of the Stoic School was *apathia*—which cannot be translated "apathy," but "non-suffering." Whatever may have been the character of Zeno, who seems to have added Greek vices to Levantine passion, the School laid stress rather on conviction and *character* than on that metaphysical and epistemological *speculation* which was ending, in the Middle Academy, in scepticism. It took over some of that tradition earlier identified in Hellas with Sparta and thus prepared the way for its own acceptability in Sparta-admiring Rome. Stoicism was a training school of the firm upper lip and discipline under pain, not because it sought woodenness as its ideal or denied the existence of pain, but because it asserted as central in its philosophy that Man, as autonomous in his Will, was master of his soul and hence captain of his fate. The right to suicide—in the final need, the right to turn the keys of the portals of death—was at once a theoretical concession and a practical corollary. Not stupid tolerance of pain, but the resolve to do nothing save on one's own moral choice and at one's own will, was the core of the philosophy.

It will be noted that such a philosophy of the mighty human atom maintaining its freeman's worship is highly individualistic. It followed that it was cosmopolitan—man related himself to no city, county or little platoon but to humanity and to the world of which he was a citizen. Zeno, it is significant, comes after Alexander the Great and is an immigrant to Athens. The Stoic tended, like the Quaker later, to detach himself from public life lest he lose spiritual self-mastery. Seneca, squeezing his millions by speculation, serving Nero and yet posing as the Stoic, found before his suicide that the moral problem of public life under the dictator Caesars was a very real one. Unlike Plato and Aristotle, the true Greeks, Zeno and his Stoics had not the citizen ideal. Their work was explicitly directed against the Platonic civic ideal as narrow and "conventional."

Like the Cynics and later the Puritans, the Stoics were at once equalitarians and aristocrats, profound spiritual snobs, as is shown by the excesses of the slave-philosopher Epictetus and by the priggery which disfigures the practical outlook of that admirable, worthy man, cursed with a criminal wife, the Emperor Marcus Aurelius. Slave and Emperor, they rejected unphilosophic, artificial, conventional distinctions of class. They were equalitarian on this worldly plane. It was blasphemy to assert—and the point, against "empty-headed" Aristotle, is important—that any man, granted a will, *could not* be virtuous. Salvation by Will was open to all. They were, however, both profoundly convinced—which comforted the proud teaching slave in his slavery and the humble self-conscious Emperor amid his business routine—that they belonged to a select spiritual, international aristocracy of those who grasped the identity of wisdom and virtue. No longer, however, do we draw the humdrum, if potentially revolutionary, conclusion that social virtue can be taught by dialectic; but rather the conclusion that wisdom—moral wisdom—is reached by conversion of morals. Meanwhile the dangerous, individualistic, moralistic but anti-political tenet is permitted, as a sign of ethical "high-souledness" that worldly status "does not matter"—a tenet of which Plato and Aristotle would never have been guilty, a tenet that bears the marks of world-flight and "escapism."

The Stoics, individualists, cosmopolitans, and social equalitarians, are not anarchists. Members of a school Greek in origin they accepted that identification of Nature and Reason—Divine Reason: the Moulding Mind of Anaxagoras—which was natural for a pantheistic people that believed that the gods were to be found amid, and even in, the forces of Nature. They were pre-eminently natural philosophers impressed almost mystically by the consideration, common ever since Pythagoras, that the *abstract* conclusions of mathematics correspond *necessarily with natural fact.* Predominantly the Stoic philosophy was pantheist and (like Heraclitus) monistic, unifying, with this interesting consequence that Nature, put into opposition to passing convention, was a rational Cosmos or Order. Law was its principle. This Law was above men and—for the Stoics, unlike Platonists—above and separate from the local sacred tradition, finding its only adequate expression in the world and in world-wide society, a convenient theory for the Roman Empire. History was rational and ever repeated itself in "grand cycles" of civilization, epochs of culture. Despite its moral discipline for the individual in *apathia*, Stoicism, thanks to this identification of the course of civilization with reason, is liberal and optimistic about history. The gods guide everywhere. The Stoic view is memorably expressed in the hymn to Zeus of Kleanthes (331–232 B.C.):

> Supreme of gods, by titles manifold
> Invoked, O thou who over all dost hold
> Eternal dominance, Nature's author, Zeus,
> Guiding a universe by Law controlled,
>
> Whereby thou guid'st the universal force,
> Reason, through all things interfused, whose course
> Commingles with the great and lesser lights—
> Thyself of all the sovereign and the source.

Later we shall have to concern ourselves with the doctrine of Natural Law which took its rise from this Stoic School. Here it is important to notice that, despite all its ethical quality, this Order of the Universe was (as ever since the days of early Ionian philosophers) identified with the law of physics. The common term, linking both, is mathematico-logical necessity. Sound ethics was, for the Stoics, demonstrable like geometry because it sprang in first principles from the very (rational and divine) nature of things. Over against the natural was—our old friend of the Sophists—"the conventional." Seneca, the Spaniard statesman Stoic (3 B.C.–A.D. 65), was prepared to call human government an artificial thing and to look back upon a golden, heroic age of primitive innocence. Later, with the Christian writers, we shall hear much of this Garden of Eden, before Original Sin came into the world. The Stoics, unlike their forerunners, the Cynics, were prepared to put the feasibility of the "simple life" into the past.

It is difficult to exaggerate the importance of the influence of Stoicism on human thought. I am not here concerned with whether it is right. There is no proven connection between truth and influence: the assertion of it is an act of faith. But Stoicism had the luck of history on its side. *Its background is the break-down of the Polis and the rise of Empire.* It was the dominant philosophy at a time when two of the greatest instruments in the control of civilization were being forged: the Roman Law and Christianity. And it stamped both of them with the impression of its own ultimate optimism, rationalism, asceticism, internationalism, equalitarianism. It offered a stern but hopeful alternative to the relaxed pessimism of the Roman Imperial age. It was too stern to be Liberal and too optimist to be Puritan; but (through Aquinas and through Augustine) it was the remote mother of both. It should be added, in warning, that its strong moral quality had its drawbacks. If ethics was like geometry, alas! geometry was too like ethics. Typically enough, it was Kleanthes the Stoic who, with that singular intellectual arrogance which besets good men conscious that they know the good, demanded that Aristarchos should be prosecuted—because he impiously suggested that the earth on an inclined axis moved round the sun. We cannot imagine the colder blooded Aristotle demanding any such prosecution—he had been the victim of a prosecution for impiety himself.

The great rival School is that of Epicurus (341–270), the schoolmaster's son, typically enough called "the School of the Garden," where Epicurus taught at Athens. In this garden purchased for eighty minae ($1,320 or £260) Epicurus lived with his group—"content with half a pint of thin wine and were, for the rest, thoroughgoing water-drinkers." His life, even from the accounts of his detractors, seems to have been no more immoral and somewhat less perverted than that of his opponents. In a later age Epicureanism tended to be the intellectual refuge of every sensual scoundrel. Its disciple, Horace, gives it in jest no good name by referring to *porci Epicuri*—"the pigs of Epicurus." The division is thin from Trimalchio and suchlike vulgarians mirrored for us in the *Satyricon* of Petronius. So difficult is the Aristotelian road of Temperance. Actually, however, alike by prescription and practice, the early Epicureans were not epicures. A better comparison is with a body of Cathedral canons living lives placid, scholarly, respectable, harmless. Like the Stoics, the Epicureans asked the question: What is the key to rational living? But, instead of the Stoic slogan *apathia*, they gave their followers the maxim *ataraxia*—contented "undisturbedness," "untroubledness."

The answer clearly involved far more of wish and contingency, less of a discipline competent to meet all emergencies. The Epicurean was not so much a pleasure-lover as a pain-fleer. Temperance was the route. Not even pleasures too much. From the Cyrenaics they had learned stress on the Art of Living. But, for that, much depended upon human forbearance. Just as Zeno was an immigrant, so Epicurus had been an exile, living with a band of fellow exiles in Colophon. In surroundings where the ethical *background of the Polis was no longer to be found*, what mattered was the friendly attitude of individual to individual. It was something that, later, the ordinary Roman official moving from place to place, mixing with a cultured cosmopolitan society drawn from all known lands, himself in fear of the caprice of imperial displeasure, could well understand. Joy-pursuing, Epicureanism yet had a sober notion of what joys were obtainable and ultimately it was tinged with pessimism. Epicurus, the school-teacher's son, is author of the salutary epigram: "Hoist all sail, my dear boy, and steer clear of all 'culture'" (*paideian*—"school-teaching"). It offered, as Way of Life, not a faith, even Stoic, but a cultivated man's philosophic resignation. All depended on the civilized temperance of the individual.

Epicureanism yet had its own humane theory of society. Going back on Plato, it discovered the basis of the social order in a kind of contract—*synthēkē tis*—a mutual give-and-take, doing as one would be done by (the phrase is Aristotle's as a maxim among friends) and forbearing as one would be the recipient of forbearance.

The poetic pessimism of Epicureanism, its diffidence about the right way of life, the contingency of its own suggestions, its basing of the social order, not on reason or social organism, but on the chancy wills of individuals working in some kind of gentleman's agreement for a tolerable life in the interest of all, its liberalism, has its background in an ultimate metaphysic. That philosophy was not one of rationalism, determinism, incipient Stoic Calvinism, necessity—still less of the Platonic idealism or of the early Eleatic School with its stress on space and stability—but of free will, probability, chance and of the School of Heraclitus with its stress, that Plato hated, on time and flux. Demokritos, the physicist, with his dance of the atoms, was its forerunner and apostle. Chaos might be king. But man had to live by the temperate common sense of considering probabilities. Here then are the beginnings—thoroughly individualistic, be it noted—of the later famous doctrine of Social Contract. (There is, however, no direct lineage, although Hobbes is, in much, an unconscious Epicurean.) If, however, the Epicurean had a modest philosophy of life, he had also one of death. It is expressed in the words of Dionysius of Oenanda (flourished A.D. 200) "God is not to be *feared*. Death is easy. The good we need is easily obtainable. The evil is easy to be borne." The pleasure philosophy in the end had to lose its phantasies and hopes in wishful thinking. Nevertheless, it had the confidence that Nature, if too much were not expected of her, was not to be feared and guided by instinct all her creatures in the search towards pleasure—Nature whom Lucretius, the Epicurean and humanist, saluted:

> Aeneadum Genetrix, hominum divomque voluptas.*

Platonism had become a memory. However, at the very beginning of the Roman imperial era, a strange conglomerate of philosophy, Platonic, Stoic, Neo-Pythagorean, with apologies to Polybius, was brought to literary expression by Cicero, successful lawyer, self-made country gentleman, admirer (in the best circles) of the new culture just coming over from Greece.

4

Polybius (204–122 B.C.), hostage to Rome for the Achaean League, had taken the opportunity of his Italian sojourn to praise his hosts. In the Sixth Book of his *Universal History,* he links the classification of the Greek political theorists, Plato and Aristotle, with the actual constitutional system of Rome. He elaborates the Aristotelian theory of revolutions, as part of a process that ends in the dying off of civilizations. The normal process of change and decay could, however, be slowed by a corrective mixture of constitutions. This happy mixture of the monarchic, aristocratic and democratic constitutions, occurred, remarked the ingratiating Polybius, in Republican Rome, like Sparta of old, with its consuls, senate and comitia. Polybius, in short, first enunciates the doctrine of the constitutional balance of power; and, it will be noted, he does this in the interest of that conservative stability which was Rome's excellence. A little later, it may be noted, Titus Livy (59 B.C.–A.D. 17), in his *Histories,* set forth that parable of Menenius Agrippa which compared the bodies physical and political.

Marcus Tullius Cicero (106–43 B.C.) exploring, as a liberal constitutionalist—as Liberal as a Roman could be—the way to maintain the Roman republican system between the impassioned forces of optimate or rich man's dictatorship, under a Sulla or Pompeius, and proletarian dictatorship, under a Gracchus, Marius or Julius Caesar, reverted to Polybius' defence of it as a mixed constitution, and therefore one of the best that had yet been seen. This defence was the task of his dialogue *De Republica.* Here, however, and in the *De Legibus,* we find certain definitions and theories of society and law which are not to be without subsequent influence on the Roman jurists. Indeed

* "Mother of us, Aeneas' children, joy of gods and men."

Cicero's treatment of the social order is from the standpoint—not Greek—of a theory of law. "What is a *civitas* except a society under law?" ("Quid est enim civitas nisi iuris societas?")

Society or a people (*populus*) is not a mere aggregate. It is "a gathering associated by a common sense of right (*iuris consensu*) and by community of utility (*communione utilitatis.*)" The commonwealth is a *natural* congregation of men. Following Aristotle, Cicero affirms that the human race is not one of solitaries or lone wanderers. This naturalness of civic life is important for Cicero since he agrees with the Stoics that our moral duty is to live according to nature (*ex natura vivere summum bonum*), *i.e.*, by the rational precepts of healthy human psychology. What then is law? Basically law is this rational rule discoverable by observation of nature, and a sound jurisprudence is to be drawn from this observation (*ex intima hominis natura haurenda est juris disciplina*).* I suppose that this is the profoundest thing that Cicero ever wrote; and we shall see later its implications. In a moment of cynical resignation Cicero, the Roman, remarks that no government would be such a fool as not to prefer to rule unjustly rather than serve justly; but he does not doubt that what ties a society together into a commonwealth is precisely its sense, and respect, for law. But (the whole thought is Stoic) "true law is right reason consonant with nature, diffused among men, constant, eternal." Local statute law is law only by courtesy, and when it infringes the basic, objective moral law, it is intrinsically void juristically—mere force. No one was less of an anarchist than Cicero. It is necessary, then, when we meet what is superficially a mere confusion of law with subjective morality, to bear in mind this Stoic belief that the rational law of human nature is as certain, objective, indisputable as that of gravitation.

Every rational being is entitled to his own moral choices, is so entitled as of right—hence all have rights, Cicero holds, before the law. Note, please, the resting of equality before the law on this quality of reason and of the rational being's moral judgement. Reason, of course, is regarded not as subjective, but as something objective, written in the heavens, apprehensible by the individual. Cicero's argument will collapse if the Cosmic Reason is reduced to a subjective rationality admitting of degrees. Here he is a Stoic—or Platonist—not an Aristotelian. Further, he maintains that all men do not differ among themselves under given circumstances as much as each man differs from himself at different times. Cicero's equalitarianism is

* "The discipline of law is drawn from the innermost nature of man." *Cf.* Lao-tze, p. 18.

partly—like most equalitarianism—environmentalist; partly due to positing a general human nature. Men are equal *in se*—whatever that may mean. Unlike both Plato and Aristotle he—the self-made man—minimizes heredity. Probably he is right. At least his position and that of his masters, the Stoics, is corrective of that of the earlier philosophers of the leisure class. If slightly muddle-headed, he urgently recommends, as a good liberal, the virtues of reasonableness. He adds: "No species of society is more deformed than that in which the wealthiest are thought to be the best. . . . One thing ought to be aimed at by all men; that the interest of each individually, and of all collectively, should be the same; for if each should grasp at his individual interest, all human society will be dissolved." Cicero omits to notice that, in this last passage, he states a problem rather than solves it. However, it was a gallant ethical protest against the actual political conditions of the corrupt Republic.

Professor Dunning, the commentator, writes: "The circumstances under which the great orator lost his life surround with an air of pathos his efforts to find the elements of rational perfections in the moribund institutions of the Republic." The institutions of Tiberius, Caligula, and Nero, not to speak of gloomier tyrants, were obviously, for Professor Dunning, to be preferred. The fate of beheaded Cicero may well be that, mankind being what it is, of constitutional Liberals today caught in the political game of *Rouge et Noir* between the Fasces and the Hammer, Red and Black. It is a warning.

5

The later Roman Empire saw a change of scene as the gilded age of the Adoptionist Emperors, Trajan, Hadrian and the Antonines, did not return. As the times grow darker, Epicureanism, with its suppositions about the cultivated life, disappears and even Stoicism, with its aristocratic appeal, loses influence. Men desire, not discipline but salvation, not apathy but sympathy. Platonism takes a new lease of life; but in the very different and theologically preoccupied form of Neo-Platonism. Plotinus (ca. A.D. 203–262), the Egyptian, enunciates his ultra-individualist, spiritual-ascetic, but reason dominated doctrine of the "flight of the alone to the Alone"—the Absolute or Mind that rises above the "emanations" and "creations," and star-souls, partly divine, partly natural, proceeding from the Absolute and governing "the spheres" and all material things. The issue no longer becomes that of finding a Rational Way of the Happy Life in the World but of finding a poppy Way, an opiate Way, from the Evil World to Eternal Life.

Even Indian Brahmin influences may have been at work. That route, under the guidance of the philosophers, Porphyry, the Syrian (A.D. 233–305), author of a lost or destroyed criticism of Christianity, and Iamblichus, also of Syria, (died ca. A.D. 333), becomes almost as complicated as that along which the soul is piloted in the Egyptian Book of the Dead.

Meanwhile, from a congeries of conflicting cults, those of Isis, Mithras, Serapis, Christianity arises into prominence—flowing by Syrian trade routes from Jewish colony to Jewish colony, falsely confounded by Roman governors with Judaism. The early comments are by members of the governing class. Tacitus' words I have already cited. The younger Pliny takes note of the cult—"a depraved, immoderate superstition. . . . I did not doubt that, whatever their precise creed, a pertinacious and inflexible obstinacy [against authority] ought to be punished." It is *they* who were intolerant, so it seemed . . . of the imperial worship—although in Egypt strange things took place, mixings of the worship of Christ and pagan Serapis. Marcus Aurelius holds up to respect those who have an undramatic faith, "not in a sheerly obstinate manner like the Christians." A century later, Celsus (whose works the Christians thought it unnecessary in the cause of literature to preserve) attacks the Early Church as unpatriotic, while Rutilius Namatianus finds the epithet, "the root of folly." Briefly, the early Christians were fanatics and, in the eyes of the governing classes, uncultivated fanatics who might, for example, if they saw a statue of one of the gods, smash it. Most of them were Oriental slaves although a few, systematic pacifists, were to be found in Caesar's household, such as Flavius Clemens, a cousin of Domitian. Although not (until the days of Julian) physical-force men, they were, so to speak, the Communists of those days. Not until later was it discovered that systematic thinking had been done, almost from the first, in these proletarian quarters. The Emperor Aurelius—however, as a Stoic, he held the thesis of human equality—did not socially know St. Justin Martyr.

Jesus ben Miriam, the Nazarene, of the stock of David, did not long remain the spiritual rebel, peasant preacher, centre of stories of miracles, mastering hearers by his personality, preaching a doctrine of absolute pacifism for those who had ears to hear and who, unlike Herod's soldiers, sought the Way of Eternal Life through the purification of abnegation of wealth and of ambition and of self. By the time of the Fourth Gospel the influence of Philo and the Platonists shows itself. The Idea has taken charge of the man. In Egyptian Alexandria a school is at work well accustomed to speculating on demigods and absolutes. "*Aut deus aut non bonus*" is soon the cry.* The entirely good man is the perfect man, typal and archetypal—the true Reality or essence of Man, the "Idea" of Man, and the idea of man proceeding from the mind of the final reality, the Absolute Idea.

As Prince Sakyamuni became Buddha, the Enlightened, so Jesus became Christ, the Anointed. The great drama of the Trinitarian Procession of the Godhead was developed. The Absolute Godhead displayed its three facets, of Power, Wisdom and Love. Was Christ, the Jewish Messiah, of one nature, and that less than divine? That was the Arian heresy. Was he of one nature and that only divine? This was the Docetic and again the Monophysite heresy. The Church affirmed the truth only by denying the false, as Communism does today. Duophysite, Duothelite, the Christ was Perfect Man and Perfect God, perhaps the one because the other, but not less the one than the other. "Light of Light, very God of very God," existing before all worlds, of one substance with the godhead; and He, the Logos or Reason, proceeding as Creative Idea from the Godhead. Also, revealing Himself really and truly under the chosen symbols of Bread and Wine. This is a greater thing than any local Hebrew prophet. It is the Drama of the Second Person of the everlasting Godhead—an unveiling of Reality through a new mystery—a drama with all the weight of Greek philosophy, as well as of Hebrew prophecy, behind it.

How little of Christian theology is intelligible save against the background of Neo-Platonic philosophy. To the Judaean revival Hellenic philosophy gave an explanation cosmic, not physical but metaphysical. The time, in the third century, had come to brush away tepid common sense and liberal, epicurean moderation—tasting as secular as the worldly maxims of Aristotle. The times demanded an idealism more drastic, Messianic, total—as some think we do today.

The Christian Religion was other-worldly. The revolutionary cataclysm would soon come; and it profited little to make plans and acquire worldly science about what should happen after that Judgement. Cultivated admonitions to avoidance of sensual excess had seeped down, in society, into excuses for sensuality and were now checked by the more than Platonic myth of hell-fire. The Christian religion sprang from, and understood, the proletariat. It placed, like any Cynic, the morality of the Ten Commandments before refinement. Its gospel was for those convinced of weakness and sin, and asking for redemption of will. But the route to salvation for the spiritually

* "Either god or not good"—because claiming the impossible.

elect was, not by revolution and the sword, but by passive-resistance. The treasure was within.

St. Paul of Tarsus (died ca. A.D. 64–69) declares that the ruler, therefore, "bears not the sword in vain" against the non-elect, as a correction for evil-doers. And to the ruler *in his own public realm*, although here alone, passive obedience was due. As St. Paul says, in Romans 13:

> Wherefore ye must needs be in subjection, not only because of the wrath, but also for conscience sake. . . . Let every soul be subject unto the higher power. For there is no power but of God: the powers that be are ordained of God. Whosoever, therefore, resisteth the power, resisteth the ordinance of God: and they that resist shall receive to themselves damnation.

It cannot be said that the lead which St. Paul gave to Christianity in the matter of slavery, witches, women and the advancement of science was, morally speaking, a fortunate one. Happily, religion is greater than St. Paul. But the political guidance of St. Paul and St. Peter alike cannot be accused of ambiguity. Obedience to legitimate power, since temporal life was of little moment, is counselled without reservation and in a fashion far more than pacifist because passivist. "Honour the King." And "render to Caesar the things that are Caesar's." Pay tribute to Caesar in respect of those things of minor moment that Caesar controls. Also slaves obey your masters, and wives your husbands. As St. Peter says (I Peter, 2):

> Submit yourself to every ordinance of man for the Lord's sake: whether it be to the King as supreme, or unto governors, as unto them that are sent by him for the punishment of evildoers, and for the praise of them that do well. For so is the will of God, that with well doing ye may put to silence the ignorance of foolish men: as free, and not using your liberty for a cloak of maliciousness, but as the servants of God. Honour all men. Love the brotherhood. Fear God. Honour the King. Servants (slaves) be subject to your masters with all fear; not only to the good and gentle, but also the froward. For this is thankworthy, if a man for conscience towards God endure grief, suffering wrongfully."

It is difficult to over-estimate the political effect of these words.

Wisdom is virtue and alone matters. And wisdom is this: that the elect live in love among themselves, well content to be an example of the good life but imposing their ways on no man not of the free brotherhood, disinterested in the noisy, superficial strife about liberty and power and the just or unjust sharing of worldly goods which matter nothing. And that the elect show their light to the world by displaying charity in principle towards their enemies as a new technique of conquest of this world and its evil, in order to enjoy true goods of the soul in the immortal society of the elect. The citizenry of Faith and the fraternity of the Future succeed to the old citizenry of Polis and Empire and to the patriotism (not unriven by class war) of the mundane community. For the first time in the West *individualism* is born as a popular force, with the notion of the incalculable value of my soul—"The treasure is within"—although its expression is otherworldly *and* it is emphatically held in leash by the obstinate Judaeo-Hellenic insistence upon salvation being *in the community*. St. John had no tolerance for the heretic Cerinthus bent on irrationally finding the way of Life in his own fashion. Moreover, the background of the Roman Empire, guaranteeing Peace and Law, tends to be presumed. An adequate Christian political theory has to wait until the Church can no longer presume this as given, but has regretfully herself to confront these problems of the *social order* fit for the run of common, unregenerate men and not only for the elect and the religious.

BIBLIOGRAPHICAL NOTE

E. Bevan: *Stoics and Sceptics*, 1913.

The Legacy of Rome, intro. by Henry Asquith, 1923.

Cicero: *On the Commonwealth*, trans. and intro. by George H. Sabine and Stanley Barney Smith, 1929.

Chapter V

The Roman Law and the Christian Fathers

1

THE Roman Empire maintained the World Peace. If it was dying, it was an unconscionable time a-dying. The years between Romulus and Julius were more than doubled in the period between Julius and its formal demise in the days of Constantine XIII. In the East, it remained until the Fall of Constantinople in 1453, the names of Rome and Caesar being perpetuated in the Sultanate of Rum, in Rumania and in the Czars. In the West a Kaiserdom that claimed direct succession from the Caesars did not lay down its nominal claim to be Holy and Roman—"the Holy Roman Empire of the German People"—until 1806. In 1938 Adolf Hitler revived in imperial Vienna the Third Empire of the German People. Charlemagne was crowned in Aachen as sixty-seventh Augustus since Octavian. The Hofburg in Vienna is still decorated with statues of German Kaisers, with the pedestals inscribed "Caesar, semper Augustus." Both the Napoleons and the Italian Duce of our own day have sought to revive not only the Roman Empire's glory but its name.

If it endured through time, it extended through space. If a man walked from Rome West, he could go on walking round the Mediterranean until he returned to Rome from the East and, if he would but take a ferry over the Bosphorus, he would not have left the Empire of the Caesars. If he walked from York to Damascus, he need not leave the protection of the Roman eagles. In the words of the poet Claudian (flourished A.D. 400),

> "The ages shall see no limit to Roman rule"*

—which "provides the human race with a common name."

* "Nec terminus nunquam Romanae ditionis erit."

The Roman Empire *was* civilization—standing in awful, in awe-inspiring isolation. Outside its boundaries to the North was the forest barbarian and to the South the desert nomad. Far to the East indeed lay the yet more august civilizations of China and India—scarcely more ancient, since Egypt gave its diadem to the Caesars. Every second week, indeed, a boat left the Red Sea ports for India. The Emperor Huang Ti at Loyang dispatched a trade embassy, we learn from Chinese records, to the Emperor Antun (Antoninus) of Ta Tsin. But between the Euphrates and the Roman Empire, walled on the North, on the one side, and the Yang-tze Kiang and the Chinese Empire, walled on the North, on the other, was interposed, not only India, but a Parthian Empire whose notion of Greek culture was to enliven the tragedies of Euripides by bowling the decapitated heads of conquered Roman foes into the midst of the theatre stage.

The Roman Empire was not sustained by the citizens of the city of Rome, *proles Romuli.* Even the Emperors for the most part, after the Julian line had expired, did not come from there. It was sustained by provincial legionaries serving in distant parts—provincial levies seldom trusted, as a matter of policy, in their own provinces. Racially cosmopolitan—with its Spanish, Dalmatian, Arabian, Thracian Emperors; Syrians brought up in Gaul; Constantine born in York of a British barmaid*—without colour consciousness or any seditious talk about purity of blood or even class consciousness—the Roman Empire was mentally cosmopolitan. It was indeed itself the cosmos ("order"); and it was natural enough that the writers of the New Testament should refer to Augustus as ruler of the world. "And Augustus Caesar sent out an order that all the world should be taxed."

The field marshals gave Peace. Rome was a proletarian, equalitarian, cosmopolitan Empire, ruled by these field marshals under apologies for democratic forms. It was precisely a popular government. But like the old Empires of Assyria and Persia and Lydia, as later of Turkey, it was a mechanical affair of the tax-gatherer and the recruiting-sergeant. It represented, against Hellas with its intensive, qualitative culture, the triumph of the essentially barbaric idea of the external, extensive, quantitative force of the military organization. Essentially it stood, not with Hellas, for the Community, but for Government—not Polis, but Police. Nevertheless, it thereby gave stretching space for the individual. If the characteristic of Hellas was organic inequality, that of Rome was mechanical equality. Rome had no soul—and uneasily knew it (as its anxiety about its official religion indicates)—but it had a mind. That mind lay behind its law.

* According to a not undisputed tradition.

2

The Roman Law was Rome's greatest gift to humanity after the Roman Peace. The Law Code typically begins by stating that the Roman Emperor holds his power by the dual claims of war and of law. The Roman Law was, as it were, the mental and articulate expression, the conscious spirit, of the Roman Empire. The Roman Law, however, as we customarily refer to it, was not so much the working system of the Empire in its heyday as a last will and testament to humanity, embodying principles that were rather a guiding hope than a daily fact. By the time that the compilation or Codex was complete, the dominating notion of the military Empire, the divinity of Rome and Augustus—*Roma et divus Augustus*—had been modified, so far as the legal system was concerned, by a Stoicism familiar with Greek jurisprudence and by Christianity.

The Roman Law begins, like most ancient tribal law, as the religious prerogative of born clansmen, citizens of the city, Quirites. It is the Quiritanian law which, at first no plebeian, and later no non-citizen is entitled, without sacrilege, to claim for himself. It was the perquisite of those who shared the patriotic religious rites of the *urbs* or polis. Rome, however, spiritually isolated from surrounding gentiles and self-sufficient, had perforce economic relations with the neighbouring Latin and Tyrrhenian world. It had even at Ostia a flourishing port. It was on the north-south trade route where it crossed the Tiber.

It was, then, the duty of the appropriate police magistrate, the Praetor for aliens or Praetor Peregrinus, to lay down publicly, in an edict, the principles by which he would administer justice to those traders who were not *gentiles* (gentlemen, men of the *gens*) or in suits between citizen and alien. Inter-nation law ever grows out of the needs for commercial law. And, although the Praetor might be guided in his decisions by private judgement and none could say him nay, elementary considerations of reciprocity led to the finding of those principles in the common customs of the trading peoples of the Western Mediterranean basin—the *jus gentium* ("right of nations," or, equally, "law of peoples") of those trading with Rome. Common convenience, again, and private alike decided that, although not bound, he should follow the principles embodied in the edicts of his predecessors. As Rome grew, those who fell within the jurisdiction of the Praetor increased in number and importance, and proportionately the importance of the Quiritanian Law, modified in popular *comitia* or assembly, decreased. The last *lex* of the *comitia* was passed at the end of the first century A.D. in the days of the Emperor Nerva, Trajan's predecessor. The Praetorian Edict has become an established core of law, by the days of the Emperor Hadrian, Trajan's successor, as the Perpetual Edict. The *Edictum Perpetuum* has become the Roman Law, supplemented by new edicts of the Emperors, "novels" or *novellae* (up to the days of Charles V, of Hapsburg, and beyond) exercising their police or praetorian power.

Rome, however, was no less lawyer-minded than police-minded. The imperial edicts, as "statute law," were supplemented by a peculiar species of case law, the legal opinions of eminent counsel, the *responsa jurisprudentium*. The point here was not that the court had decided, since appeal or edict could override it and the co-ordination of decisions was incomplete, but that "masters" of wide experience, relying upon their own reputation alone, ventured opinions on difficult issues—opinions not always of detail but often of guiding principle—which the courts were prepared to accept as pointers and the codifying emperors to authorize as having the weight of case-law. Since learned counsel were sometimes learned men, from this source an immense amount of philosophy, especially Stoic, was injected into the Roman law and jurisprudence. The soldierly Romans became practising philosophers, although their philosophy was Greek and second-hand.

Various codifications, or reductions to system, of this body of law took place, for example under the Emperor Theodosius II (408–450) and under the Emperor Basil (867–886). The most famous and the earliest complete codification is the *Codex Justinianus* or Codex of the Emperor Justinian, completed in A.D. 592 by a group of Jurists headed by Trebonian. Nothing so monumental has been produced since, until the *Code Napoleon*, drawn up under the directions of the jurist Cambacères. Here, in the Codex, the Perpetual Edict and subsequent edicts of the Emperors were co-ordinated and condensed. Supplementing the Codex were the Pandects or Digest of the *Responsa Jurisprudentium*, including Greek material of as much as 1,300 years earlier—106 volumes condensed into five and a half—and the Institutes. The latter was an introduction or manual for law students in four books, largely based on the earlier work of the eminent jurisprudent Gaius, at the close of the second century A.D.

Peculiarly in the Pandects and Institutes can be detected the influence of Stoicism with its Cynic equalitarianism. Here is to be found the famous maxim, as basic to just law: "*Quoad ius naturale omnes homines aequales sunt*" (Ulpian)—"So far as natural law pertains, all men are equal." The old Sophist distinction between Nature and Convention has come through to legal recognition. It is worth noting that Roman *Civil Law* (being the law of the *civis* or citizen, and so emphasized not in contrast to "criminal law," which it includes, but to Ecclesiastical or *Canon Law*) is distinctive from the great rival legal system, Anglo-Saxon *Common Law,* in that it is only too anxious to repose law, not on mere competent authority or established precedent about *what actually is,* but upon philosophic or moral first principles of *what ought to be.* The distinction dear to lawyers of the school of Austin, which we shall discuss,* between law and morals is, in essence, inapplicable to the Roman Law system and its derivatives today, the codes of the Latin countries, of Scotland, South Africa and, in part, of Germany. This adds to the difficulty, in language, of distinguishing "right" (*ius*) moral and legal; or German *Recht* and French *droit* as law and as moral right. The *responsa,* moreover, of academic authorities, as much philosophers as lawyers, sometimes carried a weight in the courts under the Roman system quite unlikely to obtain in courts swayed by the spirit of the Common Law. The effect is important upon the discipline of jurisprudence and upon later discussions.

Jus gentium has already been referred to. Alongside it, in the Imperial epoch, and in writings of earlier students, such as Cicero, of Greek jurisprudence, occurs the phrase *Jus Naturale,* "law of nature." The essentially practical Roman lawyer had proceeded by a method basically anthropological, in compassing his practical difficulty of administering justice to aliens. He sought to discover the highest common factor among local customs and then declared that he recognized in this a non-local, universal law common to peoples (*scil.* of the Mediterranean). The abstract-minded Greek looked within and by introspection discovered psychological principles which, as permanent to human nature, he put in contrast to the curious customs of barbarous tribes recorded by Herodotus. These basic principles, such, *e.g.*, as parental affection, rationally formulated, the Stoics had acclaimed as Nature's own law in accordance with which it was the moral man's duty to live—"*secundum naturam vivere.*"

Gaius, in the second century, identified the universal Law of Nations (common to peoples; *not* International Law or mere Treaty Law *between* peoples) with the rational Law of Nature. Substantially this identification, thanks to Roman practical sense and Greek philosophy, continues, from this time on, to hold good. The positive *lex*

* *Cf.* p. 246.

(law), in so far as justifiable in jurisprudence, derives from this basic *ius* in the double moral and legal sense. Subsidiary variations, however, occur. Thus, in the third century, the lawyer Ulpian brings the *ius naturale* back to its psychological origins; and asserts that the test of the *ius naturale* is the approval of instinct; whereas the *ius gentium* is mere general human custom, as distinct from local custom, and no more necessarily rational or truly natural than cannibalism or slavery. But even the animals recognize Natural Law. We have here an answer to the issue "Does human nature change?" or "Does human nature not change?" St. Isidore of Seville, the encyclopaedist (seventh century), and later writers will follow Ulpian here.

In view of the fierce later discussions on this issue and the tremendous influence, from the pre-Socratic Sophists right through to our own day, exercised by this concept of Natural Law, it is well to recall the intimate connection for the Stoics that existed between Natural Law for men—or, phrased differently, the Laws of Human Nature—and Natural Physical Law. Galen, the great physician, in the days of Marcus Aurelius explained that God's law was not arbitrary, but revealed through Nature—adding, "in this matter our view . . . differs from that of Moses." Physics, Psychology, Jurisprudence, in this order form a continuum for those necessitarian, monistic schools of the Greeks, such as the Stoic (not Aristotelian), in which *one* principle was seen as underlying the universe. The same rules govern all. This is exceedingly important in view of later moralistic attempts, under ascetic, anti-materialist, dualist and free-will influence (with *two* contrasted principles, *e.g.*, Light and Darkness, Mind and Matter, underlying the universe), to assert that law and politics cannot be approached by the methods of the natural sciences because social man is somehow supernatural. It is also necessary to note—in view of the professional objection that so-called "natural law" is not, technically speaking, real law, but a mere misleading analogy—that etymologically "real," *i.e.*, positive law, is a concept derivative from natural, physical law. This last is the older, basic notion. The gods, in nature, "found" true law before capricious, curious-customed man made the attempt. Later, we shall have to note the transition to the identification of Natural Law, via the concept of "the rational," with Divine Law. Thus the (? tenth century) legal *Fragmentum Pragense* (*i.e.*, "Fragment of Prague") declares that Natural Law "is nothing other than God." And Pope Gregory IX, in the thirteenth century says, more precisely, that breach by whomsoever (positive legislator or otherwise) of the fundamental Natural Law "risks the imperilling of the transgressor's salvation," *i.e.*, is mortal sin—an interesting basing of ethics on a Reason also underlying physics. To these points we shall return later.*

It is necessary here to note that the concept of Natural Law has a double edge. On the one side, it is an instrument of conservatism. It asserts that there are certain fundamental principles holding true of all human beings in all times and in all places. Any attempt to violate these principles is as sure of nemesis as any attempt to violate those of physiology and sound health—they *are* indeed the principles of psychology and of the rational psyche. They abide permanent throughout the ages. All sound politics is a therapeutics of the body politic designed to bring it *back* to health by those principles. All chatter of reform and revolution contrary to them is mere fever; and the so-called doctors who talk in this way must themselves be regarded as gravely ill patients, if not lunatics. On the other hand, the doctrine of Natural Law is the very river that waters, across the map of history, the gardens of Radicalism. Any legislation that flies in the face of this law is merely noise, entirely fatuous and without claim to respect from law-abiding men. Much positive law, therefore, by legislators of low "intelligence quotient," is inherently mere error and ethically void. To the double consequences of this profound doctrine, accepted by implication in the massive Roman Law, we shall also return later.

The Roman Law, be it added, was not incapable of contradictions which, affirming the pre-eminence of natural law, also (apparently subordinately) affirmed the dictatorial principle: "*Quod principi placuit legis habet vigorem*"—"What pleases the *princeps* (prince, chief, *capo del stato*) has the force of law." The two positions were reconciled by reference to the so-called *lex regia*, that is, to the theoretical derivation of the absolute imperial power, especially as based on the old power of the tribunes, from the vote or plebiscite of the Roman popular *comitia*. It thus sought to reconcile the "*Führer*-principle" with constitutionalism based on law.

Whatever its philosophic inconsistencies (and they are few), the codified Roman Civil Law presented a logical system infinitely more coherent than any of the systems—if such they could be called—of customary law of the barbarian tribes that were destroying the old, and perforce building the new, Europe. Even where it was not the law of the land, it was—when the educational stage had been reached, with the coming of the universities—the discipline of the lawyers, moulding their concepts of jurisprudence. Outside the lands of the Eastern

* *Cf.* p. 167.

Roman Empire and the Latin lands, it was "received" in the German Reich in the early sixteenth century. It was a major element in shaping, from Gratian in the eleventh century onwards, the Canon Law of the Catholic Church which was actually administered in church courts—the so-called Courts Christian—throughout Western Europe.

3

Catholicism itself—whether universal or (in years of schism) of the Latin or the Greek Orthodox variety—supplied the spirit to this vast bulk of the Roman Empire. It was strictly its other-worldly, spiritual counterpart. The Roman Empire of the Caesars was a mechanism providing Equality before the Law and under Caesar, and Liberty collectively from the barbarian, but in obedience to the Law, the "powers that be" and the Genius of Caesar. It was so jealous of those small, voluntary organizations that were the heart-blood of Greek cultural life, that Trajan viewed with suspicion even fire brigades; and the early Christians had to register their churches as burial clubs. Fraternity it was left for Christianity to supply—a fraternity based on neither blood nor land (although Judaism illustrated the influence of both, and in Armenia there was a perceptible tendency for the headship of the Church to come into the hands of those claiming descent from the brothers of Christ), but based on an ideal principle, on "the Word." This emphasis upon fraternity, not unparallelled in earlier religions such as Mithraism and the Orphic mysteries, was something inconspicuous, if not new, in the teaching of the recognized philosophies.

The Roman Empire, failing in its attempt to maintain respect for the imperial religion, official, desiccated, heartless and without affection, compromised under the Emperor Constantine (279–337) with Christianity for its own advantage. The Emperor saw to it that he did not lose gravely by the bargain. The Emperor ceased to be god but, even although unbaptized until on his deathbed, he became "bishop in externals"—and the universal Church, still undivided between East and West, became loyal. The Roman Empire drew—or imagined that it drew—the life-blood of sentiment which it required to hold its fleshly bulk from corruption. Soon the Emperor had reachieved official position as "Isapostalos"—"equal of the apostles." Elsewhere the ruler was to become "Most Catholic," "Most Christian," "Most Religious." The days were over when the churchman Tertullian could say: "What have we to do with the Empire?" The Church Council of Chalcedon (A.D. 451) saluted the Emperor with the words: "Thou art at once priest and emperor, conqueror in war and doctor of the faith." We have returned to the old creed, in a form merely decently veiled, of the Caesars, the Pharaohs and the Mikados—the theory of the divine King or, at the least, of the King by divine right. It was one of the merits of the Papacy that it was to end by breaking this tyranny. In the days of Justinian, an eminent churchman could enunciate the doctrine: "God has need of none, the Emperor only of God." Heresies, then, were acts, not only of rebellion against the Church, but of sedition against the Emperor. And, in practice, they were frequently the cloak of local discontent or, for example, in Egypt, of national separatism. The spirit of the Empire was one that insisted upon the political importance of religious uniformity. The Emperor, "shining image of the Most High," took on, as All-highest, some of the attributes of God. Still more dangerous, God took on the attributes of the Roman Emperor, autocrat, absolute, alone, administering hell-fire for sin as the Roman Law administered earthly fire for parricide.

The Catholic Church, like the Roman Empire, was universal, unique, outside it no security—*nulla salus*. The Catholic Church, like the Roman Empire, was everlasting. Voltaire might say, of the still existent Roman Empire of his day, that it was neither Holy nor Roman. Goethe might exclaim: "The dear old Roman Empire, How does it hold together." But still it went on, to get itself lost in the entanglements of the rise and fall of Napoleon. Nevertheless, it was written in the Book of the Prophet Daniel that the Fifth Empire shall last until the Last Judgement and the end of the world. Even when bereaved of its mundane, secular sister, the immemorial Catholic Church, *semper eadem*—"ever the same"—like some ancient woman when her elder house-mate dies, fails to recognize to this day the demise. In the Catholic Missal, in the Good Friday service, still occurs the prayer:

> Let us pray also for our most Christian emperor, that God and our Lord may render all barbarous nations subject to him, for our perpetual peace. Almighty and everlasting God, in whose hands are the powers and rights of all governments; look favourably on the Roman Empire; that the nations which trust to their own fierce might may be overcome by the hand of Thy power.

The Catholic Church, however, was much more than the Empire's chaplain. It was the organization of Roman citizens through baptism in the Christian community. No less cosmopolitan than the Empire, it did not limit its frontiers with the Empire. If it questioned whether the heretic, in a Christian Empire, could enjoy full citizenship, the historian Orosius, pupil of St. Augustine, could declare that the Christian Goth, outside the imperial limits, was also a comrade and a brother. Both Empire and Church were theoretically unique, universal—but perhaps with different frontiers penetrating into black barbarous space.

The Church, moreover, like the preceding philosophies, asked and answered the question: What is the Way of Life? The gospel of the developed Church came from Semitic Judaea, but its organization came from Rome, bishops being mitred prefects—and its philosophy came from Hellas. The Stoa supplied the systematic moral theory which reached expression in St. Ambrose of Milan (ca. 340–397).* Plato supplied the theory of the community. The Neo-Platonics supplied the systematizing ideas for the theology.† The Church moved on, enriched by the treasures of the ages, not even forgetting titles and phrases and festivals that recalled Isis, and the gods of Egypt. Briefly, the way of life was salvation by rational faith. The ancient Church, however, was truer to the classical mood than it is easy now to recognize. Its thought, Platonic, was essentially *social.* Salvation was in and through the community, with its sacraments, and accompanied by social works. The love of the brotherhood was to be more than a good intention or a gift of grace unfructified in deeds.

It fought for Orthodoxy, and was intolerant, precisely because the social bond mattered and, therefore, heresy as revolt against that social bond of the common faith was a treason against the community in and through which men prepared themselves for the final community or communion of Saints. Like Cynic and Stoic and even Epicurean, it contemned (less wise than Aristotle?) worldly circumstance, goods and respect of persons. It campaigned against neither war, slavery nor private wealth.

Its primitive spirit was Pacifist and Communist. Ananias and Sapphira had been blasted by Peter, spiritually electrocuted, for giving only part of their possessions to the common stock. In the early days, the Church in the Holy Land had all things in common, as had the disciples of the Lord. Slowly "the great Church" (= Lord's House, *Kuriou oikos;* or *Ecclesia,* the "called-out" and "chosen") had made precise its belief in these matters. The elect, the fully religious, those of vocation, must not bear arms. A monk of St. Basil, who served in the army, before he could return to his Order, must do protracted penance. The clergy (clerōtoi—"elect") must not fight. And, as we have seen,

* *Cf.* p. 139.
† *Cf.* p. 121.

an Orosius could insist that even the enemies of Rome were brothers as being also Christians.

A restricted Communism was maintained. If Clement of Alexandria could make his appeal to the rich, St. Ambrose could declare that "he, who having a superfluity, leaves his brother in want is a thief." The doctrine was evolved that wealth is a trust. But matters were carried further. The fully religious, of vocation, accepted the life of poverty. This Communism certainly was not Marxist—and no worse service to clarity of thought has been rendered than by the assumption that Marxism and Communism are synonymous. But the voluntary Benedictine monastic communities were the most successful working experiments of Communism in history until the coming of coercive Marxist Russia. Later, we shall discuss the attempt of the Popes to regulate more precisely the Church's authoritative attitude to community of property. Briefly, the Church dealt with these issues by making a clear distinction between those especially chosen, by vocation, to live the ideal life of religion—and incidentally to act as spiritual directors to the rest—"regulars" who practised pacifism and communism, and the bulk of the *massa peccatrix*, "the sinful mass" of humanity, which could only be expected to keep the letter of the minimal moral law and who might fight out their quarrels and quest after gold. The distinction is startlingly Platonic.

The Greek, especially the Peripatetic, was fully conscious that men were animals, and frequently unpleasant animals. Civilization was an entity, in which most must serve as tools and instruments in order that the glorious social structure of culture might be raised to its peaks. The mass was negligible mess: matter that did not matter. The proletarian Church could adopt no such attitude. That was its innovation. All were "members of one body"; and the least of the faithful, no less than the proudest, served to the greater glory—not of luxurious pomp—but of Him, the Eternal Maker. To all salvation was freely offered, although not all had grace to answer. But, for the animal nature, the Church substituted Original Sin—and never forgot to remember its part in human affairs. As much as Plato (with certain reservations) the Church was social-minded. And, as much as Plato, the Church was aristocratic—but *neither* by birth *nor* ability in success, but by talent and grace to serve. So the Pope took his title: "*Servus servorum Domini*"—"Servant of the servants of God"—but of them only.

The Way of Life was that of Sympathy, not Apathia. The outstanding contribution of the Church, despite all its socialism, was its equalizing individualism. The point is important. Socialism for Aristotle was inequalitarian: the mass were animated instruments of society and morally, because socially, bound to be such. If we like to put it so (I have already shown the grave limitations of such a phrase*) Aristotle was a Fascist. Society (*not* the State) was Leviathan. The individual *as such* (especially in Aristotle's early Platonizing period) had no claim, but only in terms of his immediate power to contribute to the social good here and now. The object indeed of the polis is the life of the citizens; but their best life (the "best" determined by independent values, not caprice or "votes") *in* that polis. The epoch-making, if not novel, contribution of the Church was the assertion—so much wider than in the case of Socrates—of the immortality of the soul, *i.e.*, the incalculable value of the *individual*. And this it asserted, however superficially fantastically, against pantheism and "fusionist" theories—"fusing all the skirts of self again, should fall remerging in the general soul." He was immortal *in* the community but, nevertheless, immortal *as* an individual. He was an individual living member of the Brotherhood; not a cog in a society. In his own right he was entitled to co-suffering, sym-pathy, sympathy. He had a natural, moral right to this as a human soul. Hence, under all its Platonic hierarchic order, the Church remained profoundly equalitarian, as being in the logic of respect for *human dignity* (as distinct from civic or national glory)—the dignity of *all* human beings as such.

Whereas, again, Plato had too often spoken as if he presumed that justice is *social* (and had thereby made it "static"), the humble man having no right save to mind his business in his actual humble job, the Christian idea found its essence in its doctrine of salvation. It saw each man for what he potentially might be. It insisted that the true, divine justice is *individual*, rendering in earth or heaven, now or ultimately, to each man severally and alike, honour according to what he had the will to be, even if crushed down in circumstance. It found in immortality the myth—not of course so un-Platonic—against which it could set forth the central doctrine of the right before God of each man alike, lowly or of high degree, to justice as a "dynamic" soul of incalculable value, entitled to respect even from rulers and commonwealths. The Communism of the Church was vocational, like indeed Plato's, not bureaucratic and shaped like Leviathan, as is the Webbs'.† Its doctrine of equality, however, was central, individualistic, revolutionary, "dynamic."

* *Cf.* p. 91.
† *Cf.* p. 652.

The Church was equalitarian because it was a brotherhood, but even in a brotherhood there are diversities of gifts. More profoundly it was equalitarian because it moved the focus of observation of value from this world, with its civic utilities, to the next and to the eye of God. In His eyes all were sons; all immortal; all individuals; all having value enough to merit the supreme redemptive act. They had sonship by sacrifice. This equalitarianism was then thoroughly other-worldly, unconnected with and apart from convenient, conventional rank—not even equality by nature, but by ideal grace or spiritual potentiality (*i.e.*, supernatural, transcendental). The Platonic "natural" (*rational*) becomes the Christian supernatural (*non-material*) way of life. The doctrine was connected with repudiation of this world as unimportant. It was ascetic. It was deplorably bound up with hostility to this world and to the body. But it understood the meaning of discipline (*askesis*).

The Church, defending its equal, proletarian community against the "cultured" argument of Aristotle, pledged itself to fight against the world, the flesh and the devil—public business life, the body's demands and intellectual pride. Briefly, more cynical than the Cynics, it damned the Hellenic idea of civilization from its foundations; and arrayed spirituality against that civilization and its works. The Church alone met Aristotle by a total repudiation of his common-sense assumptions. "*Credo quia absurdum,*" said Tertullian: "I believe because absurd." Despite all claims of reasoners and dead culture, the Church knew that she had spiritual power to move history. The faith worked. And respect was claimed for the simple man against the proud as being more than all Aristotle could see in his knowledge, more than an *organon empsuchon*—"an animated instrument."

During the early centuries the Church so far had the mentality of a persecuted body and again was so far chiliastic—that is, believing that "at the end of the thousand years'" cycle, the Second Coming was now at hand—as to give little serious attention to a political and social theory of this world. The serious thought of the theologians only slowly overtakes the literalistic, Messianic revivalism of the masses. Slowly the School of Alexandria, led by St. Clemens Alexandrinus, constructs its elaborate neo-Platonic theology over against the more factual School of Antioch. It is not, however, until after the conversion of the Emperor Constantine that the Church begins to elaborate a theory of the relation of Church and Empire. Gradually the Church had begun to accommodate itself to the notion of remaining on the earth indefinitely, having mundane responsibilities and therefore having obligations, as the supreme supernatural community, of exercising mundane control. Instead of enthusiastic discussion about what Christ did, we have reasoned dogma of what the Church taught.

4

St. Augustine (Aurelius Augustinus, died 430), Bishop of Hippo, in what is now called Tunisia, old Carthaginian territory, a Numidian born in Thagaste of North African parents, was the man who provided the Western Church, along with many volumes of theology and the memorable *Confessions*, with this needed political theory of a Church now recognized by the Empire.

Augustine had especial qualifications for the task. The son of a country gentleman accustomed to responsibilities, with no little of the resentment of a passionate provincial against the alien metropolis, Rome, he yet owed, if not his conversion, at least his early religious instruction to the great Ambrose, aristocrat, Roman Governor of Liguria, who had been made, almost under compulsion, Bishop of Milan, the Northern Imperial residence. In the *Confessions*, Augustine tells of his early attempts to gain the intimacy of the great bishop.

> Often when we had comc (for no one was forbidden to enter nor was it his custom that any callers should be announced), we saw him reading to himself, and never otherwise. And having long sat silent (for who would dare intrude on anyone so intent?) we had to leave, thinking that, in the small interval which he obtained from the turmoil of business to refresh his mind, he was in no mood to be taken off.

Rebecca West may be right in asserting that "a fundamental determination to take and not to give explains why [Augustine] never performed any action during his seventy-six years which could possibly be held up as a pattern for ethical imitation." He was yet a genius who contrived to impress his personality, after being in turn pagan, Manichee heretic and Catholic, upon the faith of his last adoption.

Perhaps this determination to take, and dependence upon his dominating mother, may explain alike the intensity of his quest, among competing faiths, for spiritual security and the moral irresponsibility with which he permitted this lady to send packing his mistress of fourteen years' association, the mother of his son, when, as it seems on such evidence as is available, a promising financial match was in the offing. He explains that "his heart was wounded, yea, and blood drawn from it"; but took no further action. Later he came to reflect that she had been an impediment attaching him to the world. It is, however, a commentary on the odd incoherence of Augustine's attitude that he elsewhere states that prostitutes are necessary in these times lest "everything be disturbed by lust."

The Church, for Augustine, is something apart from "the World"—primarily an invisible Church of the true saints, although not lacking a visible organization, with disciplinary power, in this world. It fights against "the World"—"this age," with its secular ambitions and sensual pleasures. Augustine, artist, full of the African passionate immoderation, is preoccupied with this contest. His views find expression in what, it must be confessed, is a somewhat dull book, *De Civitate Dei*—"Concerning the City of God"—which nevertheless had not only a wide, but a prolonged and profound, influence and was used as a bed-book by the semi-literate Emperor Charlemagne.

Primarily, the *De Civitate Dei* is a devotional book as much as seventeenth-century Richard Baxter's *Saints' Everlasting Rest*. But, secondarily, it carries on the old controversy which one finds earlier in the pages of the works of St. Cyprian, Bishop of Carthage, concerning whether the pacifist Christians were the cause of the decay of the civic spirit and military vigour of the Romans. Actually the historian Gibbon, with his allegation that bishops and barbarians destroyed Rome, may be partially right, but only partially, in this matter—the Christian *non-civisme* was only a symptom of a condition due to the mechanical nature of the Roman Empire. In it men were bureaucratically regimented, from the wealthy *curiales* or gentry down to the peasant increasingly regarded as tied to the land, in their place and function (from which after the days of the Emperor Diocletian there was increasingly small prospect of escape), in a mercilessly planned and totalitarian society, Socialist in the worst possible sense, a veritable nightmare of Bernard Shaw's. The citizen was tailored to fit the taxative system and the need for metropolitan doles, and not conversely. Not unnaturally, Christians—Cyprian and Augustine among them—were highly sensitive, even if African provincials from the region of Carthage, to this charge of anti-patriotism—as sensitive as any German Lutheran pastor or Catholic priest today.

Augustine's reply to the gentile writers is that it is justice alone which holds a society ethically together—a good Platonic reply—and that justice is not possible when men are only seeking paltry interests and have no grasp upon eternal values (still Platonic) and the true, Christian faith. Hence Christianity, far from destroying any Roman commonwealth worth preserving, offers the only principle upon which a sympathetic and organic community, as distinct from mere crass, exploitative imperialism, can be founded. It is an attractive piece of theorizing—nor could bishops gallantly substituting for Roman officials, and leading the military defence of their flock against the barbarians, be accused of failing, albeit at a late hour, to put their civic principles into practice. We shall later note* how Augustine is among the first clearly to abandon pacifism and to begin the development of the Christian theory of "the just war." Also Augustine is one of the first to hold that the Church could recommend (of course, for civil reasons) to the Emperors the persecution of obdurate heretics as a public menace.

In the third place, however, Augustine had to produce a positive theory of his own. This he does, although it occupies only a small portion of this one among his many books. It is a theory, however, which will be dominant for a millennium. It starts out from a quite non-Hellenic dualism between the secular and the spiritual communities. This dualism, however, it should be noted, certainly does not mean that Augustine and his successors contemplated a schism between the political and the ethical aspects of life. All Catholic thought forbids that conclusion, even if Protestant thought occasionally gives colour to it.

There was indeed, for St. Augustine, in the phrase of Marcus Aurelius, a "dear City of God." It was universal, in space extending beyond the Roman Empire, and also in time, eternal. It had, for Augustine, two aspects: the City Triumphant of those who had gone beyond and were now known to be of the communion of saints and those, in the City of Pilgrim, the Church in this present vale of tears, whose salvation by grace was yet under probation. And ever against these two spiritual cities was the city of this world. Like Plato, Augustine—last of the Romans but also introvert, "first modern"—turns to psycho-analysis. The Cities Triumphant and Pilgrim are held together by a common living principle; they are one *voluntary* City of Other Love. And—this is what is crucial—it is patent that the principle of the first City, of Other Love, is more sublime and valuable than the principle of the second City, of Self-love and of This World. Allegiance to the first city takes precedence of all allegiance to this second worldly city. Here is indeed the new philosophic world-citizenship of the Stoics with a vengeance recoiling on the old, local citizenship of Aristotle with his civic pagan gods of Acropolis and hearth.

The City Triumphant is alone satisfying to the immortal individual soul, merely temporarily resident here, but heaven-bent on salvation. "There are two loves"; and love of it and its brotherhood in

* *Cf.* p. 701.

Christ is the true love. What then is Rome? From the context it clearly appears that pagan Rome, guided by its ambitions and lust, without true faith, is the City of Other Love. It can indeed maintain a kind of fist-right order—but only like a brigand gang under its chief. "Justice being removed, what is a commonwealth but a great robber's nest," with its taxation and recruitings. And Augustine enunciates principles conspicuously similar to those of the early Messianism. "The earthly power will not be eternal. . . . It has its good here, which it enjoys so far as that kind of thing can be enjoyed." But this competitive, capitalist, military world is yet damned. "The first founder of the mundane commonwealth was a fratricide," Cain.

Can this fratricidal system of force and property be saved? It can. Although without an eternal principle in itself and bearing the coercive sword only because man, steeped in original sin, needs the discipline of force to check him—a discipline based on sin and existing because of it—nevertheless the Commonwealth can be saved if it accepted (as Cicero himself had said) the principle of justice as its guiding principle: a justice informed by grace of the faith, and that the True Faith. Briefly, the Empire was saved when it obeyed the spiritual directives of the true Church. Otherwise, it was a mere association of selfish, aggressive men to defend their own forcible acquisitions, and was damned in its sins. Those may note who care the similarity—and the difference—between Augustine, one of the eight Doctors of the Universal Church, and Marx. At least in this they agree, that some day the imperialist State will wither away like a scroll in the fire.

St. Benedict of Nursia (died 543), in Italy, another Father of the Church, deserves our attention not so much for what he wrote as for the political thought frozen into what he did. A century later, St. Isidore of Seville, the encyclopaedist, was to write that, "by natural law all possession is common." Benedict it was who gave practical realization to Platonism—was the first practising Communist in the West after that style of Communism of Noyes and Brook Farm, in nineteenth-century America, which we find set out in the pages of Nordhoff's *Communistic Societies of the United States*. But Benedict, not without precedent in the money fleeing hermits of the Egyptian Thebaid and in St. Basil in the East, established his settlements on the basis of religious zeal. The wandering individualistic hermit and solitary monk hc regarded with suspicion. In his *Rule* he lays down for his monks—the world-famous Black Monks of St. Benedict, carriers of civilization over barbarian Europe—three principles: conversion, obedience, stability in one place, the basis of community life. For him the community came first, took charge, was the necessary environment for the fully religious life. His monasteries were to be "workshops of (and for) souls." In the Benedictine community, small, centring round its church and its abbot (*abba*—"father,") with religious culture of jewel-like intensity, the Platonic Republic came to life in a shape that made it capable, amidst the ruins of a dying Roman civilization, of confronting the oncoming Dark Ages.

5

"The world itself," wrote St. Cyprian of Carthage, in the third century, "announces its approaching end by its failing powers." Africa, granary of the Mediterranean, was becoming desiccated—and the practical Romans were no agricultural chemists, neither were the Christians. "*In occasu saeculi sumus,*" wrote the great Ambrose—"We are in the decline of the age"—the end of the "great cycle" of which, Spengler-wise, the Stoics had written. Nevertheless, the moral world has conspicuously changed for the better. In Christian circles asceticism by reaction has replaced the erotic orgies of Syrian ritual and the homosexual vices that were the commonplace of ancient Hellas and, not least, of its Puritan city, regimental Sparta. Even in non-Christian circles a new, more exacting standard of manners has replaced the old violent luxury—a preparation for the meticulous, mandarin scholarship of the Byzantine epoch, incredibly erudite if entirely unoriginal.

The late fourth-century nobles of Rome, still pagan, piqued themselves on their better morals; visited each other; constituted a cultured society; spent quiet hours in a library. A mild Romanticism was in the air. Symmachus, pro-pagan Governor of Rome, writes from the country, "now we rusticate here at our ease and in a thousand ways enjoy the autumn." He will not even be severe about the Christians. They moved in quite good social circles and included even the Emperor (although reported to be what these Christians called "a heretic") in their ranks. Symmachus was tolerant. "It is not possible to arrive at so great a secret by exploring one way only." Another great magistrate and landowner, a Dalmatian, St. Paulinus of Nola, declares, "I have sought much and far but found nothing better to believe than in Christ." Maybe the best were dying out, as Tacitus had foretold. Maybe the world, with new manners and a more mildly cultured aristocracy, was moving on to Byzantine placidity. St. Augustine reflects that "to abstain from all assent to faith is to abstain from all action." One must have the will to believe. There must be a unity of theory and action. But, for all that, he will be a reasonable man and a (neo-) Platonist. "The clear and luminous face of Plato has shone forth, free of the mists of error which had hidden it, most clearly in Plotinus." "I feel sure that I shall find among the Platonists all the truth that can be attained by the subtlest reason and then I shall follow *so long* as their teaching does not conflict with our religion." There is a wistfulness in the common tone. As has been written of the pagan philosopher, poet, huntsman, later Bishop of African Cyrene, Synesius—"the man's hope flickers upwards towards the last and most adorable figure in his pantheon," the Risen Lord.

O Christ, Son of God Most High, have mercy on thy servant, a miserable sinner who wrote these hymns. Release me from the sins which have grown up in my heart, which are implanted in my polluted soul. O Saviour Jesus, grant that I may hereafter behold Thy Divine Glory.

The barbarians were coming. Orosius could look over the frontiers and salute them also as brothers. Were not many of them being drawn, and that for many a year, into the Roman mercenary army? As we today, so the Roman provincial then, was optimist. Had not the eminent and cultured Sidonius dined with Theoderic II, the Goth, and found him not so intolerable? The barbarians were flattered to converse at dinner with a Roman. There was talk of establishing a school of studies at Bordeaux with salaried professors.

On New Year's Day, 406, the Vandals, announced foes of Caesar, not mercenaries, crossed from the East the frozen Rhine, moved South through Gaul and Spain, leaving their vandal track, and on into Africa. In 410 Alaric, the Visigoth, sacked Rome. In Alexandria Theon the mathematician had died—Alexandria of the Museum and the Library, Athens' heir. The fanatic, dirty monks murdered Hypatia, pagan Theon's daughter. The light of science became extinct and, apart from kindling in infidel Bagdad and Cordova, mathematics did not blaze forth again until twelve centuries had nearly run their course. In his city of Hippo, besieged, surrounded by the Vandals, in 430, died Augustine, its bishop, saint and doctor of the Church. In 476, Romulus Augustulus, the little Augustus named after Rome's first king, fled Rome to offer his diadem to Zeno, co-emperor in Constantine's great city on the Bosphorus. For the while, the Western Roman Empire had fallen. As the deacon Salvian said, early in the fifth century, "the Roman world was laughing when it died." Half a century and a Gallic bishop writes, as one might write today of Spain and China: "All Gaul is one vast funeral pyre."

BIBLIOGRAPHICAL NOTE

J. N. Figgis: *S. Augustine's City of God,* 1921.

G. Ferrero: *The Ruin of Ancient Civilization and the Triumph of Christianity,* trans. Whitehead, 1921.

P. Vinogradoff: *Roman Law,* 1909.

Chapter VI

The Middle Ages

1

The Middle Ages were not merely a gigantic irrelevance interposed into the course of history. Classical civilization, broken, was like a precious box of spikenard of which the contents were now spread abroad. Civilization, in the West, ceased to be Mediterranean and became European. Exception made of the separate Chinese sphere of influence and, in part, of India, all humanity outside Africa, south of the Sahara, was now brought under the Romano-Hellenic sway. Arabian civilization acknowledged the debt. The price paid for this involuntary diffusion of the civilization of the Walled Empires was six centuries of barbarism. When the process had been completed, with the Christianization of the Slavs and the rule in Russia of the successors of Rurik, there was no longer in the globe a barbarian outside the gates. Civilization finally ceased to be merely a matter of river bank and seaboard strips. The Dark Ages represent an advance, just as perhaps our own coming Dark Ages will do in building a World Sovereign.

The Middle Ages roughly falls into two periods, which may be termed the Dark Ages and the Resurgence of Learning. As long as it is clearly understood that all attempt at precision in dividing into periods—since man does not live by periods like school text-book writers—is misleading, then we may say that the Dark Ages is the six centuries from the mid-fifth to the mid-eleventh, and the Resurgence is the following three passing on into the High Renaissance.

The distinctive mark of these Dark Ages—we may also speak of earlier Dark Ages before 3000 B.C. in Egypt, as Spengler does, or after Agamemnon in Greece—is ruralization. The outstanding phenomenon is the break-down of communications. The courier no longer ran from York to Rome. The Roman roads were overgrown with bush and their passage no longer safe. The Greek and the Italian and the Phoenician had been town dwellers. The German and the Slav, like neolithic man, were hamlet or farmstead dwellers—their township was not a city (*civitas*) but a village (*villa*—farm). When the Greek had gone out as a trader and colonist, typically he had established himself on new land and built up his commonwealth round some acropolis or hill-town. The relation of the aristocratic Spartan to the Messenian stock is an interesting exception. Even the Celtic Remi around Rheims and the Parisii around Paris had, with increasing civilization, tended to assume that city-state life which appears natural to humanity from Cadiz to the Indus.

Why, then, is Northern Europe not a land of the city-state? Because the Teutonic invader found (save in his native Germany with *its* hill-towns or fortified places) a Roman provincial population already in possession of higher civilization than himself. Least in the case of the Anglo-Saxon; more in that of Frank, Burgundian, Visigoth; especially in that of the Norman, they tended to spread themselves thin over the land as a stratum of conquerors, protected against attack by forming a military upper class, furnished with privileges for better self-defence. We get, not a city-state society, with its typical political problems, but a class society based, not on capital, but on race and the sword.

To the coming of the Barbarians we have already referred—for example, to the Vandals who entered Gaul in 406 and whose name to this day is a byword. No less notorious are the Mongolian Huns, strange emissaries from that other sphere of civilization where China dominated, defeated by the Chinese Emperor Wu-ti, "the Chinese Trajan," who appear on the horizon, on the Volga, about 374 and, despite their employment as mercenaries and, later, defeat, in 451, by Aëtius and the Visigoths on the Mauriac Plain near Troyes, remained a menace until the death of Attila (453). The Mongolian inroads, indeed, continued (excluding the mongoloid Turks) until the days of Genghis Khan, who raided west to the Crimea and who, eastwards, took Peking in 1215, establishing that Mongolian dynasty of which Kublai Khan was the most outstanding Emperor. It is, however, unnecessary to search further than the German tribes for manners strange and peculiar which give lurid significance to the "barbarian." Thus Alboin, the Longbeard (Langobard), conquered Lombardy from his barbarian predecessor, married his daughter, Rosamund, made a drinking cup out of his skull, and invited his bride in the friendliest fashion to drink from it. Perhaps Sidonius had been mistaken in his charitable opinion about the barbarians. It is not surprising that, a few centuries later, scourged by the Viking raids of the Northmen, the French monks added a new clause to their litany:

"*A furore Normannorum libera nos, Domine.*"*

* "From the fury of the Northmen (Normans), deliver us, O Lord."

In the Emperor's city, indeed, Constantinople, as in Damascus, Bagdad and Cordova, all was different. These were Manhattans of those days—Babylons. Luxury unheard of by the barbarian stirred the occasional wanderer from Northern lands to awe and greed. Here was the last refuge of the Romans—Greek-speaking now—the subtle men, the Niebelungen, whose learning was magic. But as Professor Bury says, by the middle of the sixth century, the Eastern Empire was "touched with the dispiritedness of the Middle Ages." Men occasionally shivered with the cold of the approaching shadows. "A conviction that the limits of human knowledge had already been reached began to prevail universally." The Eastern Empire was crustacean; even contented; very scholarly and marvellously erudite, bejewelled, full of craftsmanship—but it had lost its nerve. Rumour spread that the great Emperor, Justinian, walked his palace in ghostly form. For the outside Norsemen, to whom tales of it came, Constantinople was "the Great City," Mickelgarth, the magic city where the Roman Emperor, King of the Niebelungen, reigned.

Along with physical ruralization went mental rustication. The barbarians were "pagans" in a precise sense, for the word "pagan" means men of the tribe (*pagus*, or countryman). Just as Catholicism in Protestant England, so paganism lasted on in portions of the country, in a Europe slowly becoming Christianized during the period of the great seventh-century missions. The process of Christianization itself was patchy, making necessary concessions to rural obstinacy and to the rough sensuality of primitive warriors. On the one side the Church, fighting against the rural superstition of the village, of goblins and wishing wells, took over these wells as saints' wells; identified Christmas with the Druid Yuletide feast; only drew the line when the villagers took to worshipping the bones of the saint-dog Gellert—then with bishop and bell and candle would exhume the bones. On the other hand, it fought desperately against those more sophisticated, dangerous gods—those of the Roman upper classes, by no means "pagan" country-rustics. The Church might use statues of Jupiter as statues of Peter, statues of Apollo and the Wolf as statues of the Shepherd and the Lamb, but Apollo himself became the demon Apollyon, and all these gods—not unreal, but very real—devils.

The literature of "pagan" antiquity was soaked with these references to the false gods, these devils of the heathen. How then could a Christian read Virgil? As the Dark Ages drew on and men became less sure of themselves, increasingly they suffered from bad conscience. They dreamed of the books of the heathen transforming themselves into pots of vipers. Even the great scholar, St. Jerome (346–420), who translated the Bible into Latin, as the Vulgate, dreamed of being refused by the irate Peter access into Heaven. "Thou art not a Christian. Thou art a Ciceronian." Illiteracy increases. Virgil becomes pre-eminently a great magician. The Emperor Charlemagne, in the ninth century, Frankish barbarian that he was, could only just sign his own name. In the eleventh century a more literate Emperor played a prank on one of his bishops by obliterating from the prayer-book the "fa," where the bishop was to pray for all God's manservants and maidservants—"*pro famulis et famulabus.*" The bishop accordingly prayed for the "he-mules and she-mules."

Authoritatively, the attitude and fears of the Church are expressed, in the sixth century, by St. Gregory of Tours: "Let us shun the lying fables of the poets and forego the wisdom of the sages at enmity with God, lest we incur the doom of endless death by sentence of our Lord." And, in the same century, a great Roman, acclaimed as "the last"—an educated man of high birth—Pope St. Gregory I, the Great, said:

> The place of prepositions and the cases of nouns I utterly despise, since I deem it unfit to confine the words of the Celestial Oracle within the rules of Donatus [the grammarian]. . . . Let us, therefore, with all our soul scorn this present world as already brought to nought. Let us close our yearnings for this world at the least, at the very end of the world's existence.

The Pope may have had a sense of humour. But his contemporaries did not take him so.

The age is obsessed with the idea of death. Not life and hygiene; but death and salvation matter. The Way of Life towards eternal salvation lies through death, the vale of tears and judgement. It is an ascetic path. Happy, it has been said, is the age that has no history; but this can scarcely be said of the Dark Ages. They had a history; but men were for the most part too busy slaughtering each other to record it. In the country men tilled the fields of Northern Europe in their one-piece shirt as their only garment. In the towns, when at last superstitious fears of town life and Roman-haunted ruins were overcome, the refuse gathered in the stinking streets. Plagues swept the land. Death came early. Only in the monasteries and in the Church civilization kept alight its torch—save in the East and in the paynim lands of the Arab and Moor. On weather-beaten, wind-swept isles, Celtic monks gathered to their prayers and illuminated their missals. Sometimes a warrior, converted from violence, would join them in the ascetic life and win God's peace.

Ipse post militiae cursum temporalis,
Illustratus gratia doni spiritualis,
Esse Christi cupiens miles specialis,
In hac domo monachus factus est claustralis.
Ultra modum placidus, dulcis et benignus
Ob aetatis senium candidus ut cignus.*

The mood of the age found late expression, but in supreme form, in the thirteenth-century hymn, *Dies Irae.*

Dies irae, dies illa
Solvet saeclum in favilla
Teste David cum Sibylla.
Quantus tremor est futurus
Quando iudex est venturus
Cuncta stricte discussurus.†

Of this Mediaeval period in Western Europe there are, politically speaking, three key-notes: Feudalism, Romanism and Catholicism.

2

Feudalism is not so much a theory about a system as a chaotic fact, not uncustomary in the world's history, not without parallel in ancient Egypt, not unanticipated (as emphyteutic tenure) in the Later Roman Empire, but stamped distinctively by the institution of "knight-service," *i.e.*, the tenure of land from a feudal lord in return for military services rendered or due. If, however, no man of letters worked feudalism up into a political theory, the lawyers in a litigious age did not fail to give to the current system a theoretical and legal coherency. If the theory by no means always corresponded to the facts,

*He, after his temporal warrior's course,
Illumined by the grace of spiritual gifts,
Desiring to be the especial soldier of Christ,
Became an enclosed monk of this house,
Entirely placid, gentle and benign,
His hair by age as white as a swan.

†O Day of wrath, O dreadful day
When this age shall pass away,
Witness David and the Sybil.
How great the trembling will there be
When He, the Judge, shall present be,
All things then to settle strictly.

Note the reference to Hebrew David and pagan Roman Sybil—here regarded, not as devilish but as magically inspired.

that is no more than is to be expected of a romantic age. It corresponds almost precisely with the character of Romanticism, in contrast to the defined and limited Classical assurance.

Feudalism, no more than the Middle Ages, is an irrelevancy, although it is the very negation of the later *Stato* or State, and of the former *Imperium*. It is conditional anarchy, in which a congeries of baronies and free cities are lightly tied together, which has almost lost the very remembrance of the Caesarean totalitarianism and of the Greek *civisme*. But it is not a disease. It nurses a cooperative individualism. It is an institution which admirably corresponds with the economic situation and military needs of the period. That situation, as we have mentioned, is the break-down of communications, ruralization, the agricultural self-sufficiency of the village and its farm lands or manor.

However, no more than the old Greek polis—even less, since not every manor has its fortified hill—is the village militarily self-sufficient. It has its keep or church-tower as the first point of defence against a barbarian raid; but it needs to have the right to call in outside assistance from the county, the duchy, even from the realm. On the other hand, the first defence must be local—locally organized and locally supported. The duke cannot, conditions being what they are, arrive for five days and the king for twenty. By that time the marauders will have vanished. And there is certainly no money to sustain a standing army nor any indication that it would be more efficient under the current conditions of material decentralization, when, moreover, the men of Northumberland, as late as the fifteenth century, were to claim that they admitted no king but a Percy.

Exchange of Services is of the essence of the feudal institution. According to a theory in many ways admirable, all land was held in return for work done. The symbol of the feudal system is a three-sided pyramid. On the side of craftsmanship the lowest tier is the apprentice, rising to journeymen, master craftsmen, worshipful masters of craft guilds, worshipful mayors. But this is the face upon which the sun of feudal glory shines least.

The knightly or military face is of those who held land, lords who were land-lords. Below the knight (*Knecht*) ranked the peasants who hold "by the plough" (*per carucam*), being free peasants; free peasants holding by servile tenure; serfs; even a few slaves (in England freed by the eleventh century). Above the knight, holding his land "by the spear" (*per hastam*) range barons, earls, dukes, culminating in the king of the realm and—for the real feudal visionary—above the king in Christendom, ranged against the Paynim, the Emperor himself. This then was the earthly face.

There was also the unearthly face of those who hold "by prayers" (*per preces*). And if they too became lax and ceased to serve, there could be a writ for ejectment—its ground, that they had "ceased to sing:" the writ *de cantare non cessando* ("concerning not ceasing from singing"). Here in the lowest tier is the laity which merely is bound to fulfil the moral law. Above them the lofty structure rises—those having vocation, spiritual directors. First, the five minor orders; then the two major orders of deacons and priests. Then bishops, archbishops, metropolitans, patriarchs. Finally the top stone is the Holy Father, Pope, Patriarch of the West, Metropolitan of Italy, Archbishop of Latium, Bishop of Rome. Whether he also was coping stone of the whole pyramid as Vicegerent of God, or whether the structure, with Pope and Emperor, here soared to Heaven itself, was, as we shall later see, one of the prime political conundrums of the Middle Ages.

Contract, not Dominion, is consequently also of the essence of feudalism. Although the logic broke down when the landlord had to deal with his serf, over whom he exercised a measure of dominion, as between "fully free" men no one had any claim to services who did not render them. It will, however, be noted that (unlike the nineteenth century), despite all talk of contract, feudalism yet *also* talks in terms of *status* and of contract between *corporative groups* associated by mutual *customary* obligations. The constitution, as the historian Maitland says, was an appendix to the law of real property. And under this law (with certain minor reservations to which we shall return) there is a relation of suzerainty and vassals but not of sovereignty and subjects. The baron is *baro*, etymologically *homo*, just "a man"—the first human who is "a man," because he is entirely, Homerically, anarchically free, save under his own voluntary contract. One recalls Homer's phrase about the slave who is only half a man. When, therefore, Robert of Gloucester rebels against his liege, King Stephen of England, the contemporary complaint is not so much against his rebellion as against the fact that he rebelled without going through the solemn form of *diffidatio*, or "casting off of faith." In brief, he was not a gentleman. A Count of Flanders, invited by Henry II of England as Duke of Normandy, to rebel against his liege, Philip Augustus of France, explains that he owes to the king feudal service in so many horse and this sworn duty he will duly perform. But the rest of his forces he may send to the assistance of the other side. A century earlier a Sieur de Puiset may, on ground of some grievance, obstruct successfully the passage of the King of France from Paris to his country estates until later the Sieur de Puiset chooses to go on Crusade. Two centuries later, a German baron will declare private war on the City of Cologne because his niece has been insulted at a city dance. But in Germany private war, like the duel, is a habit.

The formula of the feudal contract is phrased by Bracton [or Bratton], Archdeacon of Barnstaple (died 1268), in his *Concerning the Laws and Customs of England*, a work written under the influence of the Civilian, Azo of Bologna, and being the earliest attempt at the systematization of the Common Law of England (*i.e.*, legal custom—"*sola Anglia usa est . . . non scripto*"—"in England alone use . . . not written"), common to all parts of the realm (or most of them), save for the treatise *On the Laws of England*, ascribed, perhaps wrongly, to Ranulf Glanvill, chief justiciar of England from 1180 to 1189. "There is," says Bracton, "such a connection established by homage between lord and tenant that the lord owes as much to his tenant as the tenant to his lord, saving only reverence" ("*quod tantum debit dominus tenenti quantum tenens domino praeter solam reverentiam*"). Bracton has his own way of dealing with the absolutist dicta of Roman law. The ruler's will may have the force of law, but this is to be interpreted in the light of the conclusion that we are not rashly to presume what is the king's will but to understand it in the light of his intention to do justice. However, the dictum has value because, as Glanvill points out, it gets over the difficulty whether English common law can rightly be considered such, not being written. The answer is affirmative because, unlike mere custom, it is sustained by the will of the king. Bracton, however, has a way of dealing with tyrants and is clear that the king, although under no man, is

> . . . under God and under the law because the law makes the king. For there is no king where arbitrary will rules and not the law.

The Crusading Kingdom of Jerusalem was the finest example in structure of a feudal kingdom. More developed than the mere marauding band of a German chieftain and his companions, it is yet an affair of warrior ventures of which the king is little more, save in reverence, than first among equals. Like William the Conqueror and his very mixed company of Normans, French and Flemings, the crusading kings were presidents of a joint-stock company—and none too sure of their position at that. In England, by Roman law dictum, "all land is the king's," but it is thought best to supplement this abstract maxim by an original contract. By the oath of Salisbury, in 1086, William assured himself that all his tenants in chief, and even their tenants, admitted their contractual obligation of service in return for royal protection.

In the East, where the king even more obviously depended upon the support of his nobility, not native to the land but there on conditions and by their own choice, a yet more elegant expression of the prevailing theory is possible—although, as is often the case with political theory, it comes late and in the works of a jurist writing after the Lusignan dynasty of kings of Jerusalem had left that city for Cyprus.

JEAN D'IBELIN, in his *Assize of Jerusalem*, at the end of the thirteenth century, writing in Cyprus, again lays down the feudal principles which were later to develop as those of governmental contract, constitutional checks and balances, and constitutional monarchy. "*L'ome deit tant plus au seignor par la fei que il li est tenus que le seignor à l'ome, que l'ome deit entre un ostage par son seignor*," etc. The tenant owes just this much more to the lord, than conversely, that the tenant must be prepared to act as hostage for his lord, to give him his own horse in battle and to act as security for his lord's debts. On the other hand, if the lord or king breaks faith, the high court may take action by process of law even against the king, for "lady or lord is seigneur only by reason of right." And if he will not submit to justice, allegiance is at an end.

More striking but more dubious is the oath stated to have been administered in Spain to the King of Aragon before coronation by his nobles. "We, who are of as much worth as you, and have more power than you, choose you king upon these and these conditions, and there is one between you and us [the Justiciar of Aragon] who commands over you." Certainly the very existence of a Coronation Oath implies a contract between the king and those entitled to administer the oath. And even the Germanic Roman Emperor, elected to the headship of the Holy Roman Empire, when crowned in Aachen (Aix-la-Chapelle), was asked by the ministering prelate, the Prince Archbishop Elector of Cologne, "if he will maintain the Church, if he will distribute justice, if he will defend the Empire, and protect widows, orphans and all others worthy of compassion;" and so takes oath. Legal checks fade away into moral—but not without the stern sanction of licensed rebellion to give them force.

The principle of licensed rebellion or conditional anarchy is enshrined in the Great Charter of Andreas of Hungary, 1222. It is enshrined in the earlier Great Charter or Magna Carta of John of England, 1215.

If we shall not have corrected our abuse within forty days . . . those twenty-five barons, with the whole commonwealth of the realm, shall distrain and press us in any fashion that they care.

It is, however, interesting to note that this licensed feudal anarchy—this conditional anarchy—so scandalous to the modern lawyer, is never merely such. The contractual obligation or feudal covenant is between men who, whether individually in their consciences or by a specific relationship on oath, are already under law, the prime, natural moral law of God and reason. This law of God, moreover, is not something only subjectively determined by private conscience. There is a rational law, of which the consensus of men and the moral judgement of the Church is interpreter. The very notion of contract comes from God's law, positively expressed in the Old Covenant. In Chap. IX of the Book of Genesis we read of the Covenant made by God with Noah, as sign of which He set His rainbow in the sky, and again in Chap. XVII, of the compact of God with Abraham for the benefit of the Chosen People. Joshua made a covenant with the people. Saul also was rejected from the kingship of Israel because of disobedience (in not massacring Agag) and David was anointed in his place by Samuel, the priest.

This notion of a basic covenant, back of the temporary feudal covenant, between God and man is a commonplace of the period. It is, however, worked up into striking theoretical form, in the midst of the controversy between Pope and Emperor, by the eleventh-century German ecclesiastical writer, Manegold of Lautenbach. Here the Emperor, as supreme secular ruler, is agreeably compared with a swineherd. Sound contractual theory, indeed, is to some extent departed from by the implication that the governed are the swine. But the contract in which the ruler is involved is clearly brought out. If the swineherd does not tend the pigs but maltreats or kills them, then the owner "*a porcis pascendis cum contumelia illum amoveret*"—will remove him from pig-feeding with contumely. "It is one thing to reign, another to exercise tyranny in the kingdom . . . for in the greatest empire is least licence." The metaphor is mixed, since it is not clear whether God, the superior, shall remove this swineherd or the swine themselves shall dismiss him. This at least is clear that the pact to obey a ruler, when he abuses his office, becomes null—and this precisely because of the ethical dignity of that office by reason of which the pact has obligatory force. Actually the Papal See and the Synod of

Rome declared the Emperor Henry IV deposed; but this was merely for the court to proclaim the pre-existing fact that Henry, by his own abusive action, had released his subjects from that pact of allegiance which, like all pacts, was two-sided.

William Wyclif (died 1386), Master of Balliol College, Oxford, so far as his political theory is concerned is almost unintelligible except in terms of this feudal background which indeed, to the student of political theory, he is chiefly important as illustrating. Perhaps no writer, from Plato to today, with whom we shall have to concern ourselves is more remote from the modern outlook than Wyclif. For that very reason he is an arresting and angular example of a past world-view, a genuine primitive. It is interesting to note that Wyclif was condemned for his ecclesiastical views in 1377, five years before the condemnation of his doctrinal, sacramental views. Whereas the citizens of London backed their bishop and lampooned John of Gaunt, Gaunt and his aristocratic faction, including Joan of Kent, were backing Wyclif for the benefit which these astute politicians imagined might be derived from a priest who could irritate the bishops. An extra chaplain or two were cheap at the price when the game was, not evangelic truth, but fourteenth-century politics.

Wyclif is a very learned man, which perhaps explains the tortuousness of his thought, who derives his ideas from three major sources. Wyclif is an Augustinian in the sense that, like the later Calvinists, he follows St. Augustine in placing stress on the evangelical notion of Election by Grace. In a moment we shall see the part played in Wyclif's thought by the notion of an "elect" or society of saints—the perpetually recurrent notion of a spiritual aristocracy. Wyclif, also, in his earlier days, was profoundly under Franciscan influence and especially of what we may call the Franciscan Left, with its extreme stress upon the spiritual value of material poverty. Further, Wyclif was under the influence of the new philosophic School of Occam, which was not only Nominalist (*i.e.*, atomizing and individualizing) but also anti-curialist, *i.e.*, critical of the part played by the Papal Court or *curia*. To these elements—and unlike the imperialist or internationalist Occam—Wyclif adds a peculiar nationalism of his own, entirely politically acceptable to Gaunt and to Richard II against Catholic, internationalizing bishops. The work for which he will be remembered, the new translation of the Bible into English (it has been done before), just as St. Jerome had translated it from Greek into the "vulgar" Latin (Vulgate), fits in alike with his nationalism, if in the fourteenth century one may begin to use such a phrase, and with his genuine concern for the lay folk of the non-possessing classes. Although he did not commit himself deeply (any more than Luther later), he is part of that social movement which also threw up such fruits as John Ball, the preacher of the days of the Peasant's Revolt in England. The Franciscan friars, later his enemies, also looked for the influence of their preaching to the same quarters.

The clue to Wyclif's peculiar doctrine is his theory of "Dominion," in which indeed he is not so much original as the follower, fairly closely, of FitzRalph, Archbishop of Armagh (died 1360), author of *The Poverty of the Saviour* and himself a critic of the Franciscans. Dominion is of two kinds, "by grace" and "civil." In what follows it is necessary to bear in mind that Wyclif was an academic and a Schoolman, that is, someone brought up in the philosophic schools of the time with all their peculiar qualities, for good or evil, of abstraction and logical nicety. Dominion by Grace is, says Wyclif, the only "true" dominion. It is the dominion or rule which God Himself exercises through his elect or saints. Theirs is the vineyard of the earth. The Church Fathers had held that dominion of one man over another, like slavery and private property, is only "conventional" and not "by natural law." This notion Wyclif develops. The only "true" priority is that of righteousness. The rest is not natural, but usurped. As the eleventh-century pro-imperial *Vork Tractate* had said: "The reprobate and sons of the Devil of whom the number is greater, are not members of the body of Christ. . . . Thus there are two Roman Churches, one of Satan, the other of Christ."

Do not then the unrighteous bear rule? They do apparently—but *false et pretensum:* "a false and pretended rule." Nay more: that the wicked, ripe for damnation and hell, had a free use of God's vineyard to profit by it and bear rule in it, that they had this of right and could enforce the right, might be law but it was the law of the Prince of This World and of Darkness. It was a diabolic law. Here then the radical consequences of natural law doctrine appear again, which are later to wash up Jean Jacques Rousseau. Wyclif's doctrine, however, is extreme to the point of anarchy. There is no reason why non-moral rulers should be obeyed. Only the saints were entitled to reverence—and presumably Poor Priests like Wyclif's. At the same time, a principle of rulership does remain. The Roman Curia, full of lawyers and corrupt men, cannot decide who the saints are. That is determined by Predestination and Grace. But, nevertheless, the earth is quite literally the Lord's and his rulership as real as any feudal baron's. There is in

Wyclif a strong vein of what can only be described as Seventh Day Adventism. (One recalls other Churches of Latter Day Saints, who marched to find a land where they could live by a pure rule.) It is not remarkable that the doctrine made some secular rulers raise their eyebrows, not least when it moved over to Czech Bohemia (native country of Richard II's queen) and came under the leadership of John Hus.

There is, however, also a *Dominium Civile*—a Civil Dominion. Wyclif, the evangelist, has gotten himself into difficulties. But Wyclif, the Schoolman, will pull him out. The Virgin Mary obeyed Augustus Caesar. Nay, more (the illustration is Wyclif's), did not God Himself obey the Devil?—by being crucified? Wyclif hastily swings back into line with received ecclesiastical political theory. Sin is in the world which is sodden with it from its origin. And the secular rule, with its coercive sword, is by reason of sin—and must so remain. Wicked Roman Emperors are tolerated of God—not of course of right but of sufferance—to chastise the more wicked. If the Civil Law of Rome pretends more than this (the Emperor's alien law, not good English law) then the Civil Law is wrong. For what is it, after all, but "paynim mannes law"—a law of Roman pagans, damned in their sins. Nor is the Pope's Canon Law much better, since it is irrelevant to grace.

How then are sinful men to be ruled, since ruled they must be? . . . and even the saints must tolerate this sad necessity whereby sinners chastise sinners. The answer is to look at the Bible, the [written] Word. The country must be governed by the Bible. Now, the Bible is not very favourable to earthly kings. As we learn from the holy Samuel, it prefers oligarchs or Judges. Who shall interpret the Bible? Lawyers? Clearly not—but theologians, who alone are competent to interpret the Word of God. The country then must be governed, under God as recognized Overlord in Chief, whose earth and land this world is (and all land is the heavenly King's), by Judges—that is, by saint-befriending noblemen (such as John of Gaunt) guided by Biblical-minded theologians (such as Wyclif)—and governed straight from the Bible itself.

Feudalism, lawyers apart, did not lend itself, even in a logical age, to strict and systematic exposition. It was too much the product of circumstances. Wyclif's doctrine, which was to have great influence among the Bohemians, with their dislike of Emperor and Germans, was a mixed brew of feudalism and theology. William Stubbs, the historian, was not, however, entirely paradoxical when he insisted that the Middle Age was the period alike of liberty and of ethical right (before the Machiavellian power-politics took the stage again).

Slightly differently, it was the epoch of rights rather than right, privileges rather than *leges*, liberties rather than liberty. Its doctrine of the rights, against the ruler (scarcely, yet, "Government"), of the *baro*, the freeman—vassal but not subject, against suzerain but not sovereign—fitted in practically with the wider but less tangible Churchly claim of the individual worth and immortality of every soul, whether that of King Robert of Sicily or of his jester. "*Deposuit potentes de sede*"—"He hath put down the mighty from their seat"—declared the Church in *Magnificat*. "We being as good as you," declared to their king the privileged barons, descendants of free German and Norse barbarians, free by their sword.

Like the Roman Empire with its Code of Law, so Feudalism reaches its fullest theoretical expression after its own effective demise in Europe. Actually it lasts as a system longer in confederate Germany, where dukes have become autonomous kings, than in centralized England and France where the New Monarchies have made dukes into subjects. And it is in the German free town of Emden that we get the last flower of this theory. In order to make clear the connection, tenuous but genuine, between feudal thought and modern, we shall therefore take two steps, of centuries, forward to modern times. It is perhaps permissible, in this fashion, to emphasize that the story of political philosophy is not a mere chronological matter of a list of dates but one of following out those skeins of human tradition in thought that bind together the ages and assure us that no century or epoch is entirely "dead" and irrelevant to our own.

JOHANN ALTHAUS (Latinized as Althusius, 1557–1638), magistrate of the city of Emden, wrote there his *Systematic Politics* (1603). It is intelligible against the background of a Germany where the *theory* of feudalism, with its counties, free knights and free cities, is passing over into the theory of federalism. Some alternative was ever more urgently needed, as the *facts* of feudalism recede, to that centralization of the empire as conceived by the Roman lawyers, which was yet still utterly unacceptable, at that time, to the German mind.

Supreme power, says Althusius, is merely a matter of brute *de facto* dominion or even something capriciously constituted; any government. Power, however, deserving allegiance, *true constitutional* power, is power to fulfil the *purpose* of the commonwealth. This constitutional power is a form of *law* (*ius regni*—"law of the realm"—or *ius majestatis*) established by "the whole associated body"—*universatis consociatio symbiotica*. Thus feudalism, including the group corporative notion in feudalism, passes over into constitutionalism. The commonwealth itself is a federation, *communitas communitatum* ("a community of communities"), made up of associations ascending in pyramidical form from the basic unit up. This basic unit (as Aristotle indeed had said) is the family. The whole is a co-operative commonwealth of which the virtue is work done God-fearingly and of which the blessing is material prosperity. Althusius is a Protestant, a strong Calvinist, reinforcing his argument in the fashion of that post-Reformation age by no less than two thousand texts from Inspired Writ. The incentive to this co-operation among sinful men is the fear of damnation.

Kings are not unrestricted landlords, exercising absolute dominion, but functional agents exercising sovereign power on behalf of the whole. This ultimate power, being used for the purpose of the commonwealth, inheres in the entire people which it is designed to serve. It should be added that Althusius enunciates certain general principles of politics which will be discussed in their proper place.*

It cannot be asserted that Althusius' theory was of any immediate or profound interest. His *Systematic Politics* would today be a mere literary curiosity had it not been for the great revival of interest in Mediaeval History which characterized the nineteenth century, partly under the influence of the Romantic revival, partly under the mistaken notion that the charters of Teutonic liberalism were to be found behind the Saxon stockades at Hastings or in the heart of the German forests. Further, the nineteenth century saw a revival of the agelong lawyers' fight between the exponents of Civil Law principles and the defenders of Common Law or native German custom. In the process of that very practical fight, Professor Otto von Gierke, a "Germanist" and author of *The German Theory of Association Law* (1881), published a small tractate entitled *Althusius*. The subsequent struggle, and the influence of Gierke upon English thought owing to the work of Professor F. W. Maitland, with his *Theories of the Middle Ages* (1900), translated from Gierke, and of Professor Ernest Barker, with his further translation from Gierke, are matters appertaining to the history of our own times. It is enough to note that Althusius, even as a "bottle-neck" connecting the Mediaeval with the Modern age, had played his part. It is absurd to dismiss Mediaeval Feudalism as an irrelevancy when one of the most important movements in contemporary politics—Pluralism and Guild Socialism in its various forms†—derives from it. It would be truer to say that it is only irrele-

* *Cf.* p. 653.

† *Cf.* p. 653.

vant to the Hellenic tradition. It indeed colours the dominant Western European tradition until the revival of Hellenism, in the political field at the close of the eighteenth, and especially during the nineteenth, century. All Federalism and much Constitutionalism and Individualism look back upon it for their roots.

3

Catholicism, whether the Eastern and Western Churches were in union or schism, was now dominant, moulding the history of the Middle Ages. But it moulds those Ages, as it were, externally; it is in them, but not of them. When the Emperor Gratian (375–383) removed the "pagan" Altar of Victory from the Senate House in Rome as offensive to the Christian faith, Catholicism had become established and was no longer the tolerated religion which it was under the Edict of Milan (313) of Constantine the Great. It soon even lost the character of a purely voluntary, if no longer persecuted, society. By the time of the Emperor Theodosius II (408–450), heresy became so far identified with civil sedition as to earn civil prosecution. Catholicism became, in one aspect, the sustaining vehicle of the Roman idea.

The Dark Ages and the centuries following are penetrated, as it were, by two great tunnels that convey, as aqueducts through barren mountains, the purest waters of classicism into our own age. Whereas feudalism is genuinely characteristic of the post-barbaric age—a form of society natural for the free fighting man, *Knecht* and Knight, *comes* and count, after he has become a conqueror—the Roman Empire and the Roman Church remain witnesses of a totally different, non-romantic but Roman, civilization. Hence we get the phenomenon of theory being discussed in the Middle Ages, only capable of explanation by tradition and only related to the historical conditions of the day in the connection of moulding transcendent idea and brute material. Whether the etymology be or be not sound, the Roman Pontiffs (*ponti-fices: ? pontis factores*) were "bridge-builders" in the most precise sense from an immemorial past into the present.

The Holy See, at least from the days of Pope St. Leo the Great (440–461) had been rapidly consolidating its position, which by the second century had acquired recognized pre-eminence, as appears from the testimony of St. Irenaeus. In a Mediaeval World of nobility by blood, the Chair of the Fisherman could alone among thrones be occupied by a man of humble birth, a student living by alms such as the English Breakspear, Pope Hadrian IV, or a carpenter's son, such as Hildebrand, St. Gregory VII, as much as by any Orsini or Colonna or

Medici. The custom has lasted to this day, when the brother of Pius X could continue to go his postman's rounds in Milan. Nevertheless, as we have said, the Pope constitutionally was very much Plato's philosopher king and the Cardinals of the Sacred College his Areopagus. He was head of a community that regarded itself as complete to itself—*communitas perfecta*—at least in every sense in which Plato's Guardians constituted a complete community. The controversy of the eleventh and twelfth centuries about Lay Investiture turned upon the issue whether bishops were to be primarily territorial lords, the nominees of those who gave them land and who expected in return feudal dues and the performance of civil offices, or the elected servants of the Church. The issue was complicated by the claim, set forth by St. Augustine, of the eternal Church-society (which perhaps also was the visible Church) to a superior allegiance, unless Caesar were to be placed before God.

The Church, as a community of all Christians, naturalized to this citizenship by baptism, had then, in the Clergy, its own officers. It had its own law in the Canon Law. It had, in excommunication and penance, its own penalties. In annates, Peter's pence, tithe and the like, it had its own direct taxes imposed on the faithful. In the crusaders it had its own armies, and in the Military Orders of the Temple and the Hospital. As its Canon Law was infinitely preferable in system and enlightenment to most current common law, so its civil service at the Papal Court stood head and shoulders in efficiency above anything of the kind to be found elsewhere west of Constantinople. In the Papal legates it had, before any modern nation, its own diplomatic corps. The universities of Europe were primarily schools for the clergy (I except medical Salerno and legal Bologna, after Irnerius, with its Civil as well as Canon Law) and the educational system was the Church's. As Lord Morley, no partial witness, stated, the Mediaeval clergy might be ignorant and but little ahead of their flock, but that little meant all the difference between stagnation and leadership in progress.

The Papal Church had three problems to solve, one of domestic and one of external relations, and also one of its own guiding law. Dr. Poole, the mediaeval historian, says: "The history of the Middle Ages is the history of the Latin Church." Dr. Harnack, the great German historian of Christian dogma, adds: "The history of monasticism is the history of Latin Christianity."

The first problem of statesmanship was to harness Monasticism to Papalism within the Catholic Church—to harness a waterfall of spiritual energy so that it should do useful work in the control of men in this world. Dr. Troeltsch, the eminent German historian, puts the matter neatly: "World-flight in the service of the world-dominating Church: world-domination in the service of world-renunciation—that was the problem and the ideal of the Middle Ages." God might indeed serve the Devil but it was a voluntary act, not contemplated as a permanent relationship. Obedience was due to the Powers that Be, but God did not design that these should remain pagan but accept the yoke of Christ. Thereby, his Church, as spiritual director, also became one of the Powers. As such it had to deal with sinful men and their secular princes. The monk, on the other hand, exclusively dedicated to the religious life, was in flight from the world.

How, then, to use these reservoirs of spiritual energy in the monasteries to keep the Church clean from the contaminations of secular life and responsibility? The answer is the history of the regular orders, the monks and canons, and of the friars, from SS. Augustine and Benedict, through the Monastic Revivals and the work of SS. Francis and Dominic and their friars, on to St. Ignatius Loyola and the Society of Jesus. Thanks to these movements, the Church retained a measure of spiritual integrity, even in years when the Papal Curia had become almost entirely secularized in outlook, preoccupied as it was, not with sentiment and enthusiasm, but with the concrete problems of law and of government. The result was the majestic institution which is the Catholic Church, that is, a realized Platonism.

The character, however, of the ecclesiastical hierarchy must not be associated with mere secularism: it represented realism, responsibility and even charity. The vice of the monk and the elect was exclusiveness. It is a significant piece of symbolism that, today in Belgium, crucifixes made under the puritan Jansenist influence, have the body drooping and the arms half closed, Y-shaped, whereas the more orthodox crucifixes have the arms wide open, the Church insisting that she is more than a congregation of "religious" or known "elect," and is catholic, offering salvation to all.

The second problem was the agelong one of the relation of Church and State. Indubitably there was an *imperium in imperio*—"an empire in an empire." The Church has its claim to final allegiance. The real issue of the Middle Ages and even later was, which empire enclosed which. Did a barbarous kingdom, emerging from tribalism, enclose the Catholic Church, whose Pontiff drew his title from the priests who functioned from the very foundation of Rome, and from the High Priests of Israel; or did the Catholic Church include these petty, recently civilized kingdoms of Saxon and Frank and Visigoth? As Dr. Troeltsch says, the Middle Ages had "no feeling" for the State—and not unnaturally, since the State, in the modern sense, did not yet exist. The reality was feudalism and the king as first baron among his peers—*primus inter pares*. To represent, however, the relationship of Pope and Empire (or Pope and Kingdoms) as one of perpetual conflict is misleading. Apart from a brief period during the reign of the Emperor Charles V, the only gap in the good relations between Papacy and Empire from the ninth to the nineteenth century was between the late eleventh and early fourteenth century. The relations were good when neither was stimulated by the ambition for power to push legal logic too far. It was the lust for power—later degenerating into the lust for local power, first of the Kings of France issuing in the Great Schism, and then of other national Kings—that broke up the reality, such as it had, of the Platonic Christian Republic. Let us examine the orthodox theory of representative and moderate men on this issue.

The Christian Republic, *Respublica Christiana, Civitas Dei*, was the prime object of every Christian man's allegiance, on peril of his eternal salvation. *This* was the society, and no other, in which that salvation had to be worked out: this was the "dear City of God" on earth. The implications of this allegiance had been developed by St. Augustine, and later writers were less hesitant about clear identification with the visible Church, although it was admitted that many of the tares of Satan were to be found as well as the wheat of the "true Church," and that in the highest places, in Rome or Avignon. Society, then, *tout court*, was the Church. As the chaplain and biographer of the Emperor Frederick I, the Red-bearded (Barbarossa), Bishop Otto of Freising, of the twelfth century—no partial Papalist—put it: "History is not of two cities, but of *one only Church*, instituted of two elements, divine and human." In the same century, the canonist, Stephen of Tournai, in the Low Countries, writes in the same vein:

> The commonwealth is the Church. The King of the commonwealth is Christ. There are two orders in the Church . . . two lives . . . two principles . . . a double jurisdiction. . . . If each has its due rendered to it, the whole will fit together.

The specific relation of Church and Empire ("State" is still an anachronism) is amply dealt with in the pamphleteering of the Age of the Investiture Controversy (eleventh–twelfth centuries). The orthodox position is classically defined in the famous formula of Pope

Gelasius I (died 496). There is "one body with two aspects. . . . The Christian Emperors need the Pontiffs for their eternal salvation; [for outside the Church Society there is no assurance of salvation—it is the old Platonic argument] and the Pontiffs use the Imperial administration for the oversight of temporal things." However, the Emperor, at least in internal matters, is flock, not shepherd. Caesar is "*non praesul sed filius*"—"not governor but son"—in the Church. (This throws an interesting light upon the demand of Henry VIII of England to be Head of the Church of England.) The Pope, in his coronation ceremony, was told by him who administered the oath: "Remember that thou art set to be the Father of Kings and Princes, Lord of the World, Vicar of Christ." But it was orthodox to recognize that if the Pope had his especial spiritual function, involving final direction in society for salvation, the Emperor also had his legitimate secular function in the coercive regulation of sinners for the protection of well-doers.

Pope St. Gregory the Great (died 604) had no more doubt than his predecessors that "coercive government has been made necessary through sin." If, that is, all men would come to grace and be converted from their sins, these Emperors, Kings and their henchmen would all be rolled away—but Pope and Bishops, pacifist overseers in the saintly flock and wiser than the rest, would remain. The temporal power was also a temporary power. The substantial thought is very Marxian.

Pope St. Gregory VII (1073–1087), that striver after righteousness who declared on his deathbed, "I have loved justice and hated iniquity, therefore I die in exile," makes that comparison even more forcible. In the famous letter to Bishop Herman of Metz, he writes (1081):

> Who does not know that kings and duces derive their origin from those who, ignoring God, have striven in blind lust and intolerable presumption, to dominate over their equals, that is, other human beings, by pride, rapine, perfidy, homicide, and indeed by almost all kinds of crime, being stirred up by the prince of this world, the devil?

Such indignant outbursts, however, must be put in the context of Gregory's remarks elsewhere that the ecclesiastical and temporal powers were, if in agreement, like two eyes and the general clerical doctrine that they were like sun and moon—the moon indeed being the lesser light used in our dark sojourn here and deriving its light from the greater.

There were indeed two swords, spiritual and temporal. No one denied the customary delegation of the temporal sword to princes to exercise coercive justice. But was the temporal sword delegated by the spiritual power?—or both swords by Christ alone and *not* by his Vicar or Vicegerent? There lay the issue. It was the merit of the Patristic and Churchly theory that, for it—as much as for any Anarchist later (and there is something of the anarchist in the early Fathers)—*the temporal authority is essentially coercive and, for that very reason, non-ideal or incompletely ideal.* Innocent III, in writing to one of the German Elector Archbishops, is frank enough to confess that he personally prefers the same man, a bishop, to exercise both powers—but that it was a matter of local arrangement.

Difficulties are reached only when the dependence of the temporal upon the spiritual, international power is emphasized and, by a logical mind, carried to its conclusion. When so carried, as by Pope Boniface VIII, in the Bull *Unam Sanctam* ("One Holy"), 1302, the result is an early enunciation of the cardinal political doctrine of Sovereignty. It will, then, be noted that this doctrine was first enunciated by the Church. The Church, Boniface VIII asserted, must have one head—*non duo quasi monstrum*—"not two as if a monster." Hobbes himself could not have put the matter better. A theory of sovereignty emerges inevitably from applied Platonism.

John of Salisbury (died 1180), less well known as John Small, illustrates well enough in his writings, such as the *Policraticus*, the attitude of the ordinary "high" churchman. John of Salisbury, secretary of St. Thomas à Becket and later Bishop of Chartres, was one of the Humanists or pre-Humanists living during that early period of the resurgence of learning, prior to the great Schoolmen, and connected with the names of Abelard and Anselm and the founding of the Universities of Paris and Oxford. It is an age not without dignity. The letter in which Peter the Venerable, Abbot of Cluny, announces the death of Abelard to the Abbess Heloïse is one of the most beautiful in all literature. Apart from pleasant literary excursions that show a mind not yet broken to the logic of the Schoolmen, John is preoccupied with such age-old questions as the relation of "free will" to the nature of God. His political views—apart from a significant little tractate *Concerning the End of Tyrants*—appear as asides. The prince, he says, in words worthy of bishops of the Eastern Church, is an image of the Divine Majesty on earth. But, if such an image, then he must behave in a fashion worthy of it. If not, he may be distinguished as a tyrant and the moral source of his authority has gone. And this also is true of law. "Vain is the authority of all law unless it bears the image of the divine law: and unless it is conformable to the decrees of the Church."

In the *Policraticus* John of Salisbury writes:

> This [temporal] sword, then, the prince receives from the hand of the Church, although she herself in some sense holds the sword of blood. She, nevertheless, possesses this sword but she uses it by the hand of the prince on whom she confers the coercive power over the body, reserving the authority over spiritual things for herself in the pontiffs. The prince, therefore, is in a sense the minister of the priestly office, and one who performs that part of the sacred functions which seems unworthy of the hands of the priesthood. For every office concerned with the sacred laws is religious and holy, yet this is a lower office because it consists in the punishment of crimes, and seems to bear something of the character of the executioner.

It is interesting to set beside this the authoritative statement of Pope Innocent III (1198–1216) to Philip Augustus of France:

> No one of sane mind is ignorant that it pertains to our office to snatch every Christian from mortal sin; and, if he despises correction, then to coerce him by ecclesiastical censure.

Here lay the bases of the powers of excommunication, interdict, dispensation from allegiance, and deposition. They followed from the premises like a demonstration in Euclid.

It is worth pointing out here, by anticipation, that this view of the relations of Church and State is in no fashion substantially different from that later adopted by that logical-minded Frenchman, the Reformer, John Calvin (died 1564), of Geneva. Although Calvin substituted a black-gowned papacy at Geneva for that at Rome, and his system was (his own position apart) rather oligarchic and consistorial than monarchic, he did not deflect from the traditional notion that the Temporal Power sanctified itself by subserving the higher purposes of the Spiritual Power.

The Development of Natural Law is the third political issue—besides the internal and external relations of the Church—of this epoch. It is the issue of the rule—of what shall be the norm—under which the Church itself is to grow as the dominant society of baptized humankind. Natural Law, in the condition in which it was taken over by the Church Fathers from the Stoics, we have already discussed. It was, in the beginning, indistinguishable from physical law—it was the Law of Nature and Human Nature—but much rationalized and, nevertheless, confounded by the Roman, with the anthropological principle of "universal" human custom. It now, resting upon an a priori, non-experimental basis, undergoes a phase (lasting to this day) of being heavily moralized. We have already quoted the passages from the *Fragment of Prague* and from Pope Gregory IX which identify it with the moral law of God. As such it was self-evidently superior alike to royal decrees and to local custom. It was not, of course, a code of statute law any more than the laws of psychology are a code of positive law. (Later some Canonists—and, emphatically, the Calvinists—were to develop the notion of this moral law as "command." However, all attempts to divorce law commanded by faith from the law of Reason have been damned, as late as the last century, by the Papacy as heresy.)

Although the Canonists were not free from citing the Ten Commandments as a concrete example of Natural Law, it was indeed rather thought of as a set of Maxims of Jurisprudence, such as was to be found alike in the Institutes and the Digest of Roman Law. But it exercised a dominant influence in moulding the positive Canon Law which had been growing up, since the days of the [probably] Jewish monk, Gratian, in the eleventh century, from a mixture of Bible, Church Council decrees, Papal rescripts and Roman Civil Law. This Canon Law, of course, required interpretation; but the Church had at its disposal the finest body of lawyers of the age. Indeed most lawyers of the day were clergy; but the best lawyers were not only clergy but canonists. And, from the point of view of the Church, the Natural Law and the derived Canon Law had the supreme merit that they had a final interpreter and arbiter in the Pope. It will be noted that the assumption of this final law is that it could not be overruled by any subsequent statute law, clerical or lay. Unlike the secular "sovereignty" systems, which we shall discuss later, in a very genuine fashion (and by direct connection with Greek thought), for the Canonist, above all men was the law.

Azo of Bologna (died 1230), himself a Civilian (*i.e.*, professor of the Civil Law), makes the interesting and, from him, significant assertion that the imperial rescripts, or edicts, if contrary to Natural Law, are void. This law itself—and here Azo hedges, but entirely in traditional fashion—is based upon instinct and upon reason. It is a rational psychological law. It will be noted, therefore, that a doctrine of conditional obedience as touching positive law is (unlike some Protestant and some modern Pluralist doctrine) in no sense basically anarchist, since this norm of Natural Law and reason is fully admitted. It is *only* by the test of that norm that the positive law is declared void. However, for the most complete expression of orthodox Catholic doctrine we must turn elsewhere.

St. Thomas Aquinas (1225–1274), Neapolitan nobleman, Dominican friar, Doctor Angelicus, fifth doctor of the Western Church, having written his *Summa Theologiae* in eight volumes, his *Summa Contra Gentiles*, his *Commentaries on the Politics of Aristotle* and various minor works, about seventy in all—written, it will be recalled, in manuscript —as well as various poems of eminence, the whole entitling him to be placed alongside Aristotle, died at the age of forty-eight. These incredible labours sprang from a single-hearted devotion to his vocation which produced irritation rather than praise in his family. His brother, Arnalfo, the poet, even adopted the crude expedient, in order to confound the young student's equanimity, of intruding a lady of scant dress and less virtue into his castle apartment; but, the biographer records, plucking a brand from the burning, the Dominican saint drove her therewith fierily forth shrieking. So poet and philosopher (as through all time), emotion and reason, confronted each other. Such trifling, edifying, pre-Boccaccioan stories, with their quaint, antique flavour, must not allow us to deflect attention from the rigour of thought and timeless value of the man. His work covers the fields of logic, theology, metaphysics, ethics, economics, politics, and law. The method adopted is the strict scholastic one, magnificent in its accuracy although unreadable to a discursive-minded and "literary" age—first the question, the arguments *pro* and *contra*, with authorities cited; then the conclusion; then the refutation of the arguments rejected, all done concisely and marching as from question to question, from part to part, *pars prima secundae* ("first of the second"), *pars secunda secundae* ("second of the second"), through the compact whole of the eight-volume *Summa*. If the work of Aristotle, as later of Diderot (a mere editor), is more encyclopaedic, perhaps no work of man is more systematic. It has remained the intellectual backbone of all subsequent Catholicism, although reset in some vertebrae by the Jesuits.

That Aquinas is merely Aristotle rewarmed was a statement fashionable in many liberal circles of the last century. It is a statement misleading and grotesque. The attempt (and even, for his time, the achievement) of St. Thomas was to fuse what without exaggeration may be termed the two great traditions of human thought. The one is idealist, transcendentalist, dogmatic, dramatic, static, authoritarian. The other is common-sense, pluralist, empirical, utilitarian, scientific, stressing initiative, dynamic, libertarian. With many grave reservations we may say that the first finds its early expression in Plato, the second in Aristotle. (For clarity, I am greatly simplifying the position.) Later, we shall find that this struggle goes on to our own day. Hegel and Marx represent, by and large (and subject to reservations later explained), the first tradition against what is termed the Empirio-criticism of the Anglo-Saxon philosophic tradition, which has kinship with Aristotle.

St. Thomas, as a Churchman, was brought up in a Patristic school of doctrine compounded of two elements, neither friendly to Aristotle, *viz.*, the Bible and Platonism (including Neo-Platonism). The Church had always suspected the worldling Aristotle, "the Philosopher." Thomas, however, had the advantage (it was about the only advantage yielded by the Fourth Crusade, which took Constantinople) of living in an age when "Frankish" scholars, sometimes residing as Bishops in the new Crusaders' Empire of the East, were able to study the Greek text which hitherto had only percolated through in Latin translations from the Hebrew (in Toulouse), from the Arabic (in Spain), from the Greek. Thomas counted among his friends such a scholar, as William of Moerbeke (died 1286), Archbishop of Corinth and translator (on Thomas' instigation) of Aristotle. To reconcile the truth in "the Philosopher" with the Patristic tradition was Thomas' self-appointed task, in the midst of the other works of this energetic man in organizing Dominican studies, a college in Naples, another in Rome, and in attending Councils at the summons of the Pope.

Plato had insisted that the final sanction of the social order must be found in a philosophic myth. The Church, led by instinct and philosophy, had found that truth in the Word, both living and written as Holy Writ. That writ Thomas had perforce to accept (as much as any Protestant later) as inspired by Divine Wisdom or Reason itself, the Incarnate Logos, and as, therefore, final. He could not challenge the Sacred Book, unlike the Greeks who had none but who (*e.g.*, Plato) only said that one had to be invented. But he could—and did—interpret this Writ. And, in that interpretation of doctrine (to the no small scandal of later Reformers), "the Philosopher," who had already established his own position firmly as a great logician in the universities, counted for Thomas almost as much in weight, and fully as much by the test of frequency of quotation, as the Church Fathers themselves. It was a bold thing to do, and shows the amazing rationalism and unsentimentality of the best Scholastic tradition.

Unfortunately the theistic element of metaphysics so preoccupies Thomas that his observations on law and politics, always in the context of ethics, become little more than asides. Moreover, of one of his chief tractates on politics, *Concerning the Rule of Princes*, most of the second (after II, iv) and remaining books are not his but by a student hand—probably that of Ptolemy of Lucca. It is interesting to compare in the work of Thomas those elements that are part of the Greek tradition with those that are novel, or specifically ecclesiastical, in their character.

St. Thomas makes the extremely important admission that man is naturally "political," *i.e., society* is natural. (This does not, as we shall see, mean that the Temporal Power or State is natural.) Monarchy is best and tyranny the worst form of government. Tyrants may be overthrown. The *civitas* or commonwealth is best when small. Education is an essential task of government. The object of government is to assure the good life (a piece of straight Hellenism, almost verbally Aristotle). There is nothing new in all this: any Hellene might have said the same. Merely it is whimsically unreal against the background of the England of Henry III and even the France of St. Louis IX.

There are, however, new elements which one finds neither in Plato nor in Aristotle. Man is depraved and, therefore, requires a coercive *temporal power*, which is only so far natural as sin is natural but which, as man attains spiritual gifts, will disappear; and the order regulative of spiritual matters is superior to this temporal, criminal-catching order. There is no division between ethics and politics, but an ethical control of politics through specific social institutions. Kings are indeed the images of God; but the hierarchy is higher as the supreme authority in faith which is the linchpin of all society. *Tyranny, monarchy, democracy and the like are mere forms; what matters is the purpose of society in seeking to achieve unity and peace.* If tyrants are to be overthrown it must be, not by private revolt against the Powers that Be (every man his own judge), but by the public authorities or magistrates. And, that these may be able to proceed constitutionally, an Elective Monarchy (like the Holy Roman Empire) is best. The small commonwealth is good because there is therein a desirable moral community in society of manners and customs. But, for the same reason, nationality and national realms have value and should be respected. (A dangerous doctrine this, as we shall see, for an upholder of the universal Papacy.) It is the concern of authority that there shall be education; but also that none shall suffer want—a specifically Christian, non-Greek, equalitarian and "fraternal" addendum. Finally, *authority must not only assure the good life, but the good life as defined in terms of its object,* i.e., *to secure salvation and man's lasting blessedness, not mere passing happiness.*

> It pertains to the office of a king *so* to procure the good life of the many as is congruous with their attaining eternal beatitude.

Therefore, the Pope may excommunicate princes from the final society of the faithful, of which he is Vicar, who pervert the purposes of temporal, subordinate government.

In brief, the Church knows (as Plato knew that he knew) what is the good life. It knows it on the basis of Revelation by the *Logos* (or Divine Reason), sacred tradition (*nomoi*, Aristotle would say) and continuing inspiration, final in faith and morals. It is not *a* Church but is *the* Church, speaking without diversity of voices since it has one head and arbiter. It is true (and Thomas' concession is significant) that it is a voluntary society; those outside it through "invincible ignorance" may perhaps be pardoned; and each individual is under obligation to obey his own conscience, *sive errans sive non errans*—"errant or not errant" (*Summa* I, 2, *q.* 19, *art.* 5). What, however, precisely does Thomas mean by conscience? We are told that it is "not a special power higher than reason, but a certain natural habit in matters of action as intellect is in matters of speculation." The obligation then to obey the habit of conscience is an obligation derivative from our duty to obey reason, which we must seek and which is expressed in Natural and Divine Law. And we are *only* under an obligation to obey an erroneous conscience, *i.e.*, erroneous reason, when involuntary ignorance excuses us from knowing the true reason. Thus in the *Summa, Prima Secundae, Quaestio* 94, *Articulus* 1, *o. ad* 2, Thomas says,

> Conscience is called the law of our intellect just in so far as it is a habit containing the precepts of natural law which are the first principles of human activity [in pursuing good and avoiding evil].

Also (*q.* 96, *art.* 4, *concl.*)

> *Just human laws oblige men by conscience, by reason of the eternal law from which they derive.*

This doctrine of political obligation we shall do well to remember when we come to later discussions, including those of our own days. The frequent change of law, he adds, is not to the advantage of public security, and change should only be made by reason of evident necessity or *maxima reipublicae utilitas* (the maximum *utility* of the commonwealth). Hence custom, if not abusive, may have the force of law. Thomas' distinctions between laws eternal, natural (*i.e.*, applied to man), human (positive) and divine (revealed) are of no great significance; and his introduction of the concept of "will" into the definition of law—the Natural Law being the command of a very personal God, a super-Caesar—is unfortunate. The early concept of law as primarily physical law bearing its own sanction is being forgotten. The consequences, in *Real-politik*, will soon be apparent in the irrationalism about ultimate ends of the Scotists, of the Calvinists and of Machiavelli. There is, however, another more valuable aspect in Thomas' teaching. Natural law, Thomas still maintains (as orthodoxy since has maintained), although the rule of ethical actions, is itself no matter of custom or of capricious moral intuitions, but is the law of reason. And (here we revert to the basic Stoic concept) this law of reason itself is but part of that eternal law that governs the universe, as law for the physical and ideal worlds and, indeed, for all reality.

Natural law is a derivative of eternal law, and the impression of the divine light on the rational creature, whereby he is inclined to fit acts and purposes.

Apart from his work as an organizer, St. Thomas is the author of about thirty-eight works (of which the *Summa* is one) and, in addition, about forty tractates. Yet at the beginning and the end of a life so methodical, we find signs of a man of emotions. They are to be seen in the young man, already displaying a prodigious memory, who preferred to suffer imprisonment at the hands of his family than abandon his intention of joining the new Dominican friar movement, although this involved a vow of poverty. And it shows in the strange year and a half at the end, before his final journey towards Lyons, to the Council of Gregory X, during which he died. During these last months he wrote nothing; replied to questioners that "all he had written was no more than straw." He appears to have been seized, perhaps from very exhaustion, by the sense of some concept incapable of translation into terms of scholastic logic—we get hints of the same problem in Plato, where he discusses ultimate truth in the metaphors of music. For the interpretation of this last phase in St. Thomas Aquinas we must turn to the poems, and especially to the immortal hymn before the Host, *Adoro te devote.**

*Adoro te devote, latens Deitas,
Quae sub his figuris vere patitas,
Tibi se cor meum totum subjicit,
Quia te contemplans totum deficit.

Credo quidquid dixit Dei Filius:
Nil hoc verbo veritatis verius.
In cruce latebat sola Deitas:
At hic latet simul et humanitas.

Jesu, quem velatum nunc aspicio,
Oro fiat illud quod tam sitio;
Ut te revelata cernens facie
Visu sim beatus tuae gloriae.

Hidden God, devoutly I adore Thee,
Truly present underneath these veils:
All my heart subdues itself before Thee,
Since it all before Thee faints and fails—

I believe it, for God the Son hath said it,
Word of Truth that ever shall endure,
On the cross was veiled Thy Godhead's splendour
Here Thy manhood lieth hidden too.

Contemplating, Lord, Thy hidden presence,
Grant me what I thirst for and implore,
In the revelation of Thine essence,
To behold Thy glory evermore.

If St. Thomas built with straw, it yet made bricks of a pyramid higher in human civilization and thought than any yet raised by a single man since Aristotle and than any, or almost any, have raised since. It was indeed a pyramid based on Revelation and upon the Neoplatonic theology of the Nicene Creed. It had no meaning unless Jesus was very God and the Bread and Wine the veils of a Reality that was immanent Deity. Upon that pyx and that belief the Platonic-Catholic concept of politics pivoted. The Reason was not abstract but incarnate, and yet did truly govern all nature and creation. Reality was rational. The Neoplatonic theology perhaps had its ample justification if it could produce so great a vision. It could even, at least within the fold of that voluntary society which was the Church, be forgiven its dogmatic conviction that it knew, and could infallibly teach, the final truth beyond all experiment.

It may be that the cardinal error was that the leaders of the age held, with St. Bernard of Clairvaux, that "faith is not an opinion, but a certainty"—a suspect variant of the experimental truth enunciated by St. Anselm of Canterbury, that we must first experience before we can profitably reason and discuss: "we must first know belief in the profundities of the Christian faith before we can presume to argue about them by reason." Nevertheless, here, in the succession of Plato, we have the supreme answer to date—clericalist as Plato was clericalist—to the problem how society should be ordered, given along the positive lines of command, exhortation and vision (static *because* vision, as Plato's vision was static) and not along the negative lines of striving, resistance, pressure groups and dynamic energy pushing liberally all ways.

With the fifteenth century the feud of Papacy and Empire had reached an accommodation. Each might have united Europe, but the trouble was how both might. It is felt that the logic of Boniface VIII had been carried too far. Pope Nicholas V (1447–1455) on the threshold of the High Renaissance, declares that, if each power would mind its own function, peace could be ketter kept. There is a tendency to return after a thousand years to the Gelasian Compromise with, if not the Emperor, then the new kings in a rather better position than a millennium before. The Temporal Power is there to stay. Political dualism is now the social basis. The only question is: What shape shall the Temporal Power take?

4

The days of the great Julius, brisk pro-proletarian aristocrat, dictating to four secretaries at once, were long since past. But his system, grown crustacean, vast, hypnotizing, continued on. . . .

The Roman Empire remained. Across all the Middle Ages it cast a gigantic shadow, unsubstantial but even more immense than its mighty self. In the East, despite a consummate strategic system of defense, the "Roman" legions were being forced back behind the walls of Anastasius and behind the battlements of Constantinople. In the West, the Germanic Kaisers periodically descended like a hurricane through the valleys of the Alps, cantered down on Rome, received the imperial crown and a hasty blessing from the Pope and, bidden good riddance, departed with the Roman plague at their Teuton heels. With sparse intervals, not until Hapsburg Charles V in the sixteenth century was the Imperial power in Italy a reality, save for the half-Sicilian Frederick II von Hohenstauffen, "Marvel of the World," with his anti-clerical, blaspheming court, his Arabian science, and his curious habit of cutting up the bellies of criminals to see how the digestive system worked. Even twelfth-century Frederick I, the Red-bearded, the Popes had successfully kept in check.

Theoretically the Roman Empire is still one; the Emperors of the East and West, Greek and Frankish, are partners. There are times, as under Frederick I, when this is uneasily recognized. National Kings are told bluntly that they are mere "Kinglets." The Roman Law is still being elaborated by such "civilians" as Bartolus of Sassoferrato (died 1357), with their subtle distinctions between imperial proprietorship and private possession. Normally, the Popes are in the happy position of being one (whatever schismatics might say) while the Emperors were two and their Empires regarded, each by each, as usurpations. The Pope, however, although he might protect himself from the hug of too intimate a relation with the Kaiser, patently could not temporally rule and unite Italy. Who was to do so? Still less could he bring temporal peace to the world. Who was to do this? And there were still Italian patriots to be found who replied: the Roman Emperor.

DANTE ALIGHIERI (1265–1321) is one of these. Son of a notary, inscribed (but not practising) in the medical guild, a magistrate or prior of his native city of Florence, caught in the fierce feuds of Guelphs and Ghibellines and of "Blacks" and "Whites" into which the former were subdivided, driven from Florence in 1300, his goods confiscated and he, absent, condemned to death by burning, he spent his life as an exile, finding in most Italian cities a similar prevalence of sadistic, fanatical feuds. No wonder he laid high stress on world order and on the Empire as an instrument of peace. Amid his wanderings, at one time there seemed hope of a return to Florence in the train of the Emperor Henry VII, of Luxemburg; but the expedition was as luckless as many of its predecessors.

For Henry VII, however, Dante's tractate *De Monarchia* (1310–?), is intended. Dante is, of course, primarily the poet. Like the Chinese scholar today, Hu Shih, who is departing from the tradition that poems must only be written in mandarin Chinese and who is writing them in the language of the people, so Dante first finds fame as the pioneer who explores the use of the "vulgar speech," Italian, as a literary language, instead of Latin. This fame, however, is overshadowed by that of the author of *The Divine Comedy,* the dramatization in poetry of that which St. Thomas, his master, had taught in the syllogistic theology of the schools, the greatest didactic poem since Lucretius and indeed of all history, not excluding Milton's great work.

The argument of the *De Monarchia* is essentially scholastic, and is an elegant example of the style's strength and defects. It is complicated by a distinctively mediaeval confusion. The Empire had not always brought peace. For by what title did the German Kaisers now bear rule? As the successors of those Romans who had conquered all their predecessors in *ordeal of battle.* "It is manifest that the Roman people prevailed over all competitors for the rule of the world; therefore they prevailed by divine judgement and consequently obtained it of right." Dante, however, desires to draw a very different conclusion from that of the universal rule of fist-right.

"*Maxime unum est maxime bonum*"—"what is most one is most good," he starts off with as his premises, sufficiently abstract. He reinforces it with the entirely sound argument that the purpose of human civilization is the fullest development of man's powers of thinking and acting, and that this work of civilization demands peace. Civil power exists, then, to procure peace—which is best effected by the elimination of a factious plurality, and the substitution of unity. "When many things are ordained to one end, they are best ruled by one authority." In brief, if the object of the state is peace, plurality defeats that object and is an imperfection in the state. Therefore the perfect state is one, universal and, in fact, the Roman Empire. Does then this imperial authority depend upon God or upon his Vicar? Unlikely though it may seem, the *Nicomachean Ethics* of Aristotle are brought in to prove that it is from God alone, for so the imperial power has unity in its own species . . . there is no interference. Each is "type" in his own province. It is contrary to nature, and unwilled by God, that the Church and Pope should have direction in temporals.

> The quality of controlling the kingdom of our mortality is contrary to the nature of the Church, and therefore is not among the number of its qualities. . . . For man needs a double direction to his twofold end, to wit, the Supreme Pontiff who leads the human race to eternal life by Revelation; and the Emperor who directs the human race to temporal felicity by the counsels of the secular philosophers.

The division between the mundane and the eternal, always acute in Christianity, is being carried to the point where the Church is propelled upwards into a purely supernatural and miraculous sphere, soon to become artificial, unnatural and impotent. Unfortunately, as Dante found, there was still nothing there to fill the vacuum. The restored Roman Empire of Henry VII vanished in summer miasma. Dante, disillusioned, turned back to the sublimation of his love for the lady he had met, before his unhappily married wife, when he was nine and the lady was eight and who had died sixteen years later (when the poet was twenty-six)—*la gloriosa donna della mia mente,* "the glorious lady of my mind," the divine Beatrice Portinari. Nevertheless, in this brief excursus into the theory of politics, the great poet had not only written the epilogue of the Roman Empire; he had by mixed logic and insight arrived at writing the prologue of the League of Nations, if not of the Third Reich of Adolf Hitler and the Rome-Berlin axis. He had supplied the Genevan League with its most cogent argument: that a state, to fulfil the prime function of a state completely, that is, to keep peace, must be a world-state.

Pierre Dubois, *avocat* at Norman Coutances, at the turn of the thirteenth century, in the days of Philip the Beautiful of France, is a very different character, one of the early pamphleteers and publicity men for the policy of that unpleasant monarch against the Papacy and its agents, the friars, who commanded the prime organ of contemporary publicity, the pulpits. There is something significant of a new age in this conflict of pamphlet versus pulpit; in the fact that Dubois (like Dante, for that matter) is no *clericus* but a layman, and moreover a lay lawyer; and in the fact that (so unlike Dante) it is on behalf of a national king, and not of the Holy Roman Emperor, that he writes. In his tractate *Concerning the Recovery of the Holy Land*, a traditional crusading theme appears. One yet notes that it is the *French* who are again to lead a united Europe against the Turk; and the fact that the kings of France, rather than the Emperors, had taken the lead against the infidel shows that the French, rather than the Germans, are the true imperial race. The king will, of course, reasonably enough, expect some slight recompense for the pains of France in the service of Civilization. These are still days when the "natural frontier" of France is the Rhone; but Dubois suggests the addition of Provence (not yet in France), Savoy, Lombardy and up to the Left Bank of the Rhine as a modest guerdon. Hereby Dubois shows himself to have foresight.

Dubois, with tact, dedicated the book to Edward I of England, who had his own difficulties with the Papacy and an interest in crusading. Dubois suggested that the Pope might be suitably and adequately occupied in saying his prayers, preaching and inviting Christian peoples to appeasement. In order to sustain him in this office he might be put on the civil list of the Most Christian King. It should be added that Philip le Bel's outstanding contribution to the cause was the suppression of the chief Military Order (of the Temple) which bore the Christian white man's burden under the Syrian sun and the burning alive of its Grand Master. In conclusion, it may be pointed out that Dubois notices the influence of climate on politics. There is no reason to suppose that, except among recent antiquarians, Dubois has had himself great influence.

Marsiglio (Marsilius, died 1343?) of Padua, physician, Rector of Paris University, who quit that post some say because of the persecution of the clergy and others say because of his creditors, in order to offer his pen to true religion and the Emperor, was a far more influential figure. His *Defensor Pacis* ("Defender of the Peace"), of which it may be that Jean of Jandun shares the authorship, was written under the influence of that great English Schoolman, the Franciscan William of Occam, in Surrey, also one of the "antagonists of the Papacy." The *Defensor*, however, was far more lucid than the involved work of Marsiglio's master.*

William of Occam, whose general writing technique was to conceal his own opinion behind that of weighty but opposite opinions, became involved in the affair of the famous "Ugly Duchess," Margaret Maultasch, as part of his defence (*a*) of the sacred poverty of the Franciscans, and (*b*) of the Emperor Ludwig IV, the Bavarian, then his protector (for his own purposes). The Emperor proposed personally to arrange for the divorce and remarriage of this lady, his feudatory, for reasons connected with her estates; but found the Papacy uncomplaisant. Occam, thereupon, proceeded to supply a learned argument in effect in favour of civil divorce. This general line of argument, hesitantly advanced by the devout Occam, is carried much further by the secularist Marsiglio.

Marsiglio flatly maintains the doctrine of secular supremacy in secular things, not excluding matrimonial causes. As he caustically remarks, "to trade, steal and murder are not spiritual offices," and, if a cleric engages in them (the old issue with Thomas à Becket), the case should come before the secular court. Again the Papacy might claim that it did not interfere in secular matters of government "by reason of the fief but because of sin." But, on these grounds, to tell the Electors of the Emperor that they must not elect a heretic to be temporal head of Christendom was like saying to a man, "I will not injure you," and then knocking his eye out. The task of the temporal ruler was (*cf.* Dante, but also Augustine†) to keep the peace. This required coercive power. And the ruler must not be interfered with in exercising it. "The ruler" for Marsiglio, Italian-born Rector of Paris residing at a German court, was the Emperor. But Marsiglio, a genuine secularist, is far more anti-Papal than pro-Imperial. The essence of Marsiglio is that he does not accept the Catholic "myth" or "ideology." In modern terms, he is a *saboteur*.

Who then shall control the Emperor, if not the Vicar of Christ? Marsiglio here shows the influence of Occam, spokesman of the

* The famous phrase, however, is Occam's: "Domine Imperator, defende me gladio et ego te defendam calamo"—"Lord Emperor, defend me with the sword and I will defend you with the pen."

† *Cf.* p. 142. It is an argument recurrent with the imperialist writers during the Investiture Controversy.

democratic Franciscans, who is maintaining the pure Congregationalist theory that Church officials should be elected by all the Christian people, male and female—Occam, the first feminist since Plato. Marsiglio, however, boggles at this. The ruler is a "regent," not absolute. He bears power as the instrument of the whole people or, he adds cautiously, of the *valentior pars* (the weightier or more significant part—a traditional mediaeval phrase for recognizing distinction of quality). But shall then Christendom be ruled by the appointees of unfaithful men and heretics? Marsiglio, the first secularist, shrinks from the logic of his own secular argument. Those who choose are to be "the faithful people." How shall we know who are faithful? A knotty point, to which he vouches no answer.

What then of the Church and its authority as arbiter? The Church must be poor and pray. Its clergy should not be arrogant directors. They should be elected—by the faithful (no: not women—that is going too far). It must be a Church humble—and, in fact, impotent.

Has not, however, the Church its own law and discipline for its flock? It may have, but should only apply its penalties in the confessional. It has no right to impose civil penalties. Nor should the civil magistrates at its behest. What then about Christian uniformity in the society of the faithful? There must be toleration. The Court of Heaven in Kingdom-come will doubtless see to a man's intentions. A secular court below must not be presumptuous and is only concerned with concrete disturbances of the civil peace. The very core of the Imperialist argument is always that civil *order* matters more than all other goods or values—even the ideals for "the better standard" of the Churchmen. Civil Society exists not to give the "good"—still less the "happy"—life to devotee or to worker, but to give *peace and order as by law established*—an argument against Utopian fanaticisms from that day to our own.

Further, it will be noted that probably no more straightforward argument for secularism has been penned since, than this by Marsiglio. The demand for a "faithful legislator" (*legislator fidelis, i.e.*, orthodox), even if sincerely put forward, is but a thin veil.

Almost more important, at least in immediate influence, is the bringing back to life of the influence of Aristotle's *Politics*. The *Logic* had been influential for a couple of centuries, and the *Metaphysics* since St. Thomas. But, although St. Thomas had commented on the *Politics*, and Aristotelianism had shown itself in the able work of St. Thomas' successor, Aegidius Romanus, the very development of a papal doctrine of sovereignty by the latter shows the limits of its claim to be political Aristotelianism. It is now that Aristotle's non-ecclesiastical or pre-ecclesiastical thought begins to show its full implications in the justification of a purely civil commonwealth, perhaps Roman but not Papal, and to show them by the pen of Marsiglio, citizen of the city-state of Padua, exponent of mixed imperial and city-state philosophy, almost Greek. The process now begins—while eviscerating the State of that ethical content with which Aristotle had endowed the Polis—of making for it all the ethical claims on the individual which the great Greeks presumed for their own intimate and cultural community.

5

We are now nearing the end of the period which may be termed that of the Christian Social Dominance. Patently this does not mean that after the fifteenth century Christianity is no longer the dominant religion in Europe. It is—and its only rival in the Mediterranean, Islam, recedes. But what is true is that the Platonic, disciplinary system of the Church is from this time broken. It is impossible to build up a social system, international and overruling particular kingdoms and states, upon three hundred or more different views of what that social system should be. And unity of discipline was of the essence of the scheme.

What had happened? The laymen no longer believed, as in what has been called "the Ages of Faith," that the priest *knew*—the Platonic governor was no longer respected by warrior or trader. The farmer distrusted his parish priest—perhaps had his own views on the Bible. The farm labourer distrusted the mendicant friar; paid money for pardons; but was not quite sure that what he or his wife got in return for the cash was worth while. In brief, the Myth had broken down. Its haloed glory had departed. The prince distrusted the Pope's legate—at least, had no intention of subordinating the interests of his trans-Alpine kingdom or Italian tyranny to some prince like himself, for all His Holiness' scheme of being international Vicar of Christ and lord of the world. The monarch was clear that if his subjects were to be members of an earthly society, it was to be one of which *he*, not the Pope, was top.

What weapons should the Pope use to restore a respect that was fast being lost ever since the Avignonese Captivity and after Philip le Bel had shown at Anagni that even Popes were mortal? Heretic rebels could, in the past, be suppressed. When the Bohemian Hussites discovered, *inter alia*, in the jealousy between Czech and German, that it was really essential for their salvation to take the sacrament in two kinds, and not only in one, they could be suppressed after bloody wars. The Church properly insisted that what it was interested in was obedience, discipline, and that on the trifles of ceremonies it was willing enough to compromise. But the time was now coming when the secular powers would, *for their own ends*, support, not suppress, heretics. This danger from lust of power Plato himself had foreseen. So the vision—presuming on dogmatic knowledge, inconsistent with the new freedom as men understood freedom, inconsistent with lay initiative in moral experimenting, inconsistent with the Faustian spirit,

> Ist es der Sinn, der alles wirkt und schafft?
> Es sollte stehn: Im Anfang war die Kraft*—

so this vision faded of the Platonic World-community. To Faith succeeded Life; and to the cult of virtue, excellence and stability, the enjoyment of vice, progress and change.

Clericalism had become obnoxious. And clericalism is the natural form (however concealed by other names) of any society in which a limited group, Catholic or Jacobin, Fascist or Communist, claims—as Plato urged they *must* patently claim—to *know* truth and securely to judge values. The human frailty of priests and the human obstinacy of princes is only a very partial explanation of why this remarkable system of Christ's Kingdom on Earth had broken down. Let us enumerate other factors. The issue is of grave current interest, since this system was the most successful totalitarian scheme (with certain reservations to be made later†) that history has seen—certainly since the end of the priestly traditional system of Pharaonic Egypt. The Church was compulsive. Beginning as a *voluntary* society, for those who sought salvation, in the days of Augustine it admitted the coercion of heretics by the secular arm lest the Christian *social order* (which must involve law and rule) be disturbed in education and morals. The Church was secularized. And this even through the very titanic attempt, not

* Does the mind work, create and with life dower?
It ought to stand: "In the beginning was the Power."
—Goethe: *Faust*, I.

† *Cf.* p. 615. *But* let me add three sharp distinctions between Catholic Platonism and modern Totalitarianism: stress on personality; rationality as against force; moral choice of the voluntary society. *Cf.* J. Maritain's *True Hamanism* (1939).

solely to withdraw from, but to control the world and the empire. Legalism grew as the Church had to confront practical problems of control and of conflict of rights, and declined to take refuge in vague sentimental generalities about first principles. Clericalism, in the bad sense, of the exclusive *esprit* of a privileged body, haunted the Church as much as bureaucracy haunts the modern state. Above all, it was, upon its very suppositions of Revelation, static. Human performance might improve. The vision might grow clearer in the quest of the Sang Real—the "Grail." But the Myth did not change.

An economic explanation of the change has been given—the lust of the lords for the lands of the Church. This may competently serve to explain why these lords finally declined to co-operate with the Churchmen in suppressing the heretics. Behind Protestant defiance the lord saw hedges broken down that protected, for monastery and abbey, broad acres richer far, thanks to good husbandry, than that warrior's own lands. The explanation, however, is inadequate in giving a reason —not for Protestant victory, but for the existence of the original Protestants at all. Strange, revivalist sects were, of course, no novelty with views on baptism or even on nudity. Here, however, a movement triumphed thanks to a circumambient anti-clericalism, explaining Reformation and Renaissance alike, which itself needs explanation.

A material explanation may carry us further than the narrowly economic. Sewerage was being disposed of. Plagues were decreasing. The death rate was falling. Life was becoming more enjoyable; men more pleasure-loving. Break-down of communications was at an end. Communications were being established and commerce opened up. An urban civilization, centred in great trading cities, was resuming its sway. Living was more opulent. Men were ever less tolerant of ascetic checks. Fear, as the leitmotiv of life, was less natural. The Day of Wrath seemed remote, with the barbarians themselves good bourgeois. Religion had become again rather an aspect than a background of life. God Himself, whose miraculous hand had been seen in everything, was now becoming (as Gierke says) philosophic *causa remota* ("remote cause"). The growing education of the lay wealthy was inclining them to ask strange questions and to challenge their masters. Man felt himself good. "Jeshurun waxed fat, and kicked."

Spiritually, stirrings of education and science increasingly resented a clerical curb. The plain man asked what the clergy made out of their rule, and why. The religious enthusiast demanded a direct way to voluntarily chosen, "free" salvation, past a worldly, cynical priesthood, blocking the road with its monopoly, that was admittedly the agent of the current social order—an order which, because historical, was, by that fact, obviously imperfect. The ideal reconfronted the actual as it had done in the early days of Christianity itself. But this time it was a private ideal, although evangelic in mode, with its background in the feudal individualism of the free, fighting, obstinate barbarian, not in the social piety of the servile, cosmopolitan, classical world.

Christianity, as a prophetic mood (distinct from the classical world and from Catholicism in form so far as the latter had been injected with the communal spirit of the earlier classical world), encouraged individualism—although distinctly evangelic and other-worldly. Feudalism, as distinct from Roman Imperialism and its law, encouraged individualism checked by custom. Neither force, however, had been strong enough, hitherto, to turn the scales against the allied spirits of Rome and of Catholicism. Now localism, assuming a less mean form as "the loyalty of the realm" (scarcely yet "nationalism"—but hatred of the foreigner), came to the support and overthrew universalism; it began the liberation of the sectional interest and, later, of the individual and of his individual pursuit of happiness as legitimate aim, as distinct from the greater glory of civilization, God and the Emperor as integrally united. The process was rendered possible by the concurrent subordination of feudal sectionalism to the social demands of the realm, which now became the appropriate organ of law and order.

Further, increasing education, presupposing peace and opulence, had brought an entire new civilization into ken—a culture the more seductive because it did not reject, but merely ignored, Christian and Papal claims, knew nothing of them. The Christian Fathers were not fools when they called the gods of the heathen devils, for they had power. As objects of lovely verse and of august rhetoric, as beautiful statues, alluringly they came back in the wake of the New Learning. "Alas, the gods of the heathen," might exclaim the sixteenth-century Pope Hadrian VI as he went through the Vatican Museum. But the gods were back—merely, of course, as models of good taste. Asceticism and monkery were in disfavour. The Popes themselves were seduced, leading the new heathenism, called Enlightenment. Aristotle, too, the Philosopher, was back, under the very best auspices, making some very strange suggestions, not at all consistent with prime allegiance to a Universal Church.

The change of intellectual climate shows in the poetry early and late in our period. From the early period, the time of the Romances of the Rose, of Parsifal, of King Arthur, of the cathedrals of Salisbury (thirteenth century) and of Chartres (thirteenth century), let us select two hymns. The first is by twelfth-century Bernard of Cluny:

The hour is late; the times are evil; we await.
Lo! he comes, he comes in wrath, the Judge Avenger.

. . . .

He removes the rough, the crushing weights from the loaded mind,
Rewards the prudent, punishes the evil, both alike justly.*

And, again, a little earlier, a hymn by King Robert of France:

O best consolation,
Sweet host of the mind,
Sweet calm.
In labour quiet,
In heat coolness,
In woe solace.

O most blessed light
Fill the intimate places of the heart
Of thy faithful.
Without thy divinity
In man is mere inanity,
In man is only evil.†

But even by the thirteenth century, in the romance of *Aucassin and Nicolette*, we get another note:

For none go to Paradise but I will tell you who. Your old priests and your old cripples who are down on their knees day and night, who cling to the

*Hora novissima, tempora pessima sunt, vigilemus.
Ecce minaciter imminet Arbiter Ille Supremus.

. . . .

Auferat aspera, duraque pondera mentis inustae,
Sobria munerat, improba puniat, utraque iuste.

(Even the reader who "has no Latin" may still be interested in the music of this majestic verse.)

†Consolator optime,
Dulcis hospes animae,
Dulce refrigerium.
In labore requies,
In aestu temperies,
In fletu solatium.

O lux beatissima,
Reple cordis intima
Tuorum fidelium.
Sine tuo numine
Nihil est in homine,
Nihil est innoxium.

altar stairs, and in old crypts; those also who wear mangy old cloaks, or go in rags and tatters, shivering and shoeless . . . and who die of hunger and want and misery. Such are they who go to Paradise; and what have I to do with them? Hell is the place for me. For to Hell go the fine churchmen and the fine knights, killed in the tourney or in some grand war, the brave soldiers and the gallant gentlemen. With them will I go. There also go the fair, gracious ladies who have lovers two or three besides their lord. There go the gold and silver, the sables and the ermines. There go the harpers and minstrels and the kings of the earth. With them will I go so that I have Nicolette, my most sweet friend, with me.

The same note echoes in the song of the troubadour of the same century, or minnesinger, Walther von der Vogelweide, perhaps crusader, certainly German anti-papalist poet:

Most blessed God, how seldom dost thou hear me praying.
Lord, Son and Father, let thy spirit give my heart correction.
How should I ever love a man who treats me ill?
To him who's kind I needs must bear a better will.
Forgive my other sins!—in this I'll keep the same mind still.

We now come to this poem of a ruler, by no means lacking in piety, the fifteenth-century Florentine, Lorenzo the Magnificent:

How beautiful is youth,
Which flies so swift away.
Let him who will be glad.
Who knows tomorrow?*

The Speculum Mentis, the single mirror in which all experience is focussed with spiritual unity, this magic mirror of Shallott, has been shivered into fragments. What matters is not the mystic society of the one Catholic Church, but what is relative to the creative individual. What matters is not eternity, which dwarfs man, but "the now" which he enjoys or curses—not eternity but time, not spiritual authority but personal power. We are in the midst of the Renaissance.

BIBLIOGRAPHICAL NOTE

* Osborne Taylor: *The Mediaeval Mind*, 2 Vols. 1911.

* C. H. McIlwain: *Growth of Political Thought in the West*, 1932.

A. W. and A. J. Carlyle: *History of Mediaeval Political Theory in the West*, 1903 (a classic in several volumes).

O. Gierke: *Political Theories of the Middle Age, trans.* F. W. Maitland, 1922.

*Quant'è bella giovenezza
Chi si fugge tuttavia.
Chi vuol esser lieta, sia;
Di doman non c'è certezza.

Chapter VII

Renaissance and Reformation

1

THE first characteristic of the Renaissance is opulence—an opulence relative to the standards of the times and limited to the merchant and noble classes, but marked by contrast with the centuries that had preceded it. With that opulence go higher standards of demand; improvement in polite manners; technological improvements; developments of invention; new and unabashed curiosity; in brief, Progress.

It was an unoriginal epoch. Such a statement needs justification. More precisely, then, despite all its vitality, there is something disappointing about it. As Professor A. North Whitehead says: "In the year 1500 Europe knew less than Archimedes, who died in 212 B.C." When Mediaeval man entered upon the Renaissance of classical culture, he did so as a child overawed by the ancient models to which he was learning to give attention. He had not discovered that the way to imitate the Greeks was not to imitate those who themselves imitated nobody. Hence he was most successful in those fields, such as painting, in which those models were irrecoverable. In literature, freedom of expression was increasingly hampered, as the decades went by and the original vitality died down, by a willingness to become "an ape of Cicero." Actually, the Renaissance was definitely rather of Latin culture, with which Italy had common bonds (even Constantinople was the Eastern Rome), than of Greek.

The Renaissance even represented, it may plausibly be argued, a mental relaxation or retrogression. Certainly we may suppose that it was felt to be such by the great Universities, Bologna, Paris, Oxford, which were dogged opponents of the New Learning. And not without reason. Instead of the strict scholastic logic, which it regarded as *démodé*, worthy of a Dunce (otherwise of Duns Scotus, the "Subtle Doctor"), it substituted an admiration for *belles-lettres* which, at heart, was a relaxation from excess of theology. Instead of this "divine science" was put literature. For the exact study of Aristotle's metaphysics was substituted the imaginative mixture of Plato and the Jewish Cabala, by Pico della Mirandola. And the age was not untouched by a recrudescence of superstition and magic, such as St. Thomas had solidly condemned.

For the discipline of asceticism it offered in substitute the cult of aestheticism. The daughters of Poggio, the humanist, might enter a convent, but monkery is out of fashion. The fashionable world reverted to Cyrenaic or Epicurean standards and not always to the most rigorous and genuinely Epicurean at that.

The Renaissance leaders were romantic about the Classical epoch of the ancient world, especially the Roman epoch which alone they understood. The Mediaeval Church had been massively classical and self-sufficient in its rule of the romantic mediaeval world of aspiring barbarians. Nevertheless, the leaders of the New Learning aspired to the apparent self-sufficiency in living of the old pagan masters. The interest in the "next world," or eternity, as predominant factor in one's scheme for living, declined. The Renaissance, typically, was non-salvationist.

The Renaissance, however, adds to its cult of the ancient world one note of its own: the cult of the individual. The feudal individualism of the Middle Ages had been held in check by Churchly morality. The Renaissance emancipated man from those checks. Even an Alkibiades or a Themistokles in Hellas was curbed by his sense for the City and for the traditional morality of the Polis. The Middle Ages had little sense (a remark to be qualified in Italy and especially in such Hellenizing writers as Marsiglio the Paduan) for *civic* virtue. The residuum, after Renaissance man has finished with the criticism of Mediaevalism, is the individual, the superman universal in his talents, the *universale uomo*, complete and balanced as a work of art, uninhibited by Churchly or Socratic conscience. For the old anthropocentricism of the pious, that was shocked by Copernicus' discovery that man's earth was not the centre of the Universe, the Renaissance substituted a narcissistic anthropocentricism of its own, not undermined until Darwin.

There is no known connection between the Ages of Progress and those of Morality. The golden age of Hellas was not one of conventional morality, any more than that of today's America. We shall later discuss the sociological connection between crime and progress.* Perhaps for this reason, every age of progress is very short-lived. The Renaissance was a non-moral and non-theological age. Its predecessors

* *Cf.* p. 774.

being times of theological morality, it was non-moral because it was non-theological—but also because the wine of opulent success and the strong waters of aggressive individualism had gone to its head. The age was no longer interested in the fight against the world, the flesh and intellectual pride which had interested its predecessors (although Dr. Coulton of Cambridge has made it a labour of piety to show that these Christians were not so moral as has been generally supposed). The new age was on excellent terms with all three. The sadistic pleasure of ascetic idealism had no longer attraction. The old morality appeared "anti-this-world" and anti-vital. The new emancipation released vitality. That vitality issued in progress, material and intellectual.

Megalomania was released as well as vitality. The antithesis of the Churchly fear of God was to be found in Alberti's dictum: "Men can do all things if they will." A more fantastic expression of the same spirit is to be found in the case of the tyrant of an Italian town who, having entertained together Pope and Emperor and taken them up on to his tower, died with one regret on his conscience: that he had not won immortality by throwing both of them down to death with his own hands. An inferiority feeling in relation to the ancient Romans was compensated by moral licence; by the cult of notoriety and individual eccentricity; and by the belief that scrupulosity was not merely no virtue but a contemptible vice. The Age of the Italian Renaissance, following that of Catholic orthodoxy, is of peculiar interest to us since it is so like our own, when the vigour of Protestant orthodoxy has spent itself—especially like our own in America, which can only be fitly judged by Renaissance standards.

King Ferrante of Naples exemplifies the macabre eccentricity of the time—King Ferrante who, after dinner, would take his guests through his private museum where he had on show, stuffed but in excellent preservation, the corpses of his enemies. These were days when men took their own wine and drinking glasses when they went to dine with the dangerously great—as being safer. Nor could the Holy See, itself taking a lead in progressive culture, offer any moral bulwark against this flood in the days of Innocent VIII and Alexander VI. On the walls of Rome the citizens, going to morning work, found an inscription lampooning the Pope. "He hath sold the priesthood, he hath sold the bishoprics *et Corpus Domini*—and the body of the Lord. And rightly, for he bought them." In 1476, Galeazzo Maria Sforza, Duke of Milan, was assassinated in the church of San Stefano. In 1478 the Archbishop of Florence became involved in a conspiracy against the Medici rulers, Giuliano and Lorenzo the Magnificent. Giuliano Medici was assassinated; but the Archbishop was hanged in his robes. Earlier Giovanni Maria (died 1412), Duke of Milan, had forbidden the priests to say in the mass, "give us peace"—*dona nobis pacem*—but they must substitute "tranquillity" instead. A criminal passion for the colossal pervaded all—criminal but splendid, a kind of Satanism.

The Renaissance must be clearly distinguished from the period I have differentiated as the Resurgence of Learning—the period of John of Salisbury and Abelard, of the growth of the Universities and Teaching Orders, of St. Thomas and of Dante, of the building of the Scholastic Philosophy against the background of Catholic Faith. The Renaissance is a period of reaction against the raking over of the ponderous, wordy volumes of the Patristic writers (the Church Fathers) and of the definitions of Aristotle with his Logic and Metaphysics. It is a period of reaction to Imagination, Art, Plato (misunderstood—rather Neo-platonism) and what Plato loathed but practised—fine literature. The writings of Plato, such as *The Republic*, just before the days of Pico della Mirandola, are being circulated again. It is the age of Polizian (1454–1494), Titian (1477–1576), Aretino (1492–1557), Cellini (1500–1571).

In 1464 Schweinheim set up the first printing establishment in Italy. The brisk, mechanical work of the printing press replaces the painstaking, artistic care of the monastic scribe and the illuminator. Learning itself has become secularized, a matter of wheels and machinery.

Sure advance, moreover, was made in the field of the sciences. In 1543, dying, Nicholas Koppernigk (Copernicus), Canon of the cathedral of Frauenberg, in Old Prussia, brought himself to publish his *De Revolutionibus Orbium Coelestium*, dedicated to Pope Paul III. He readvanced the old Pythagorean theory, not heard of since Aristippus, that not the earth, but the sun, is the centre of the planetary universe. Adam fell from his place of being centrė of creation. Man began again to conceive, since Socrates led them astray, of some other proper study for man besides man and his salvation in an anthropocentric world. The placing of the sun in the centre, itself one among the "fixed" stars, was far more than a discovery in astronomy. Meanwhile the pilgrimage to Jerusalem became provincial as the discoveries of Columbus widened the boundaries of the world both of geography and (still more) of imagination and avarice. In the same year, 1543, Vesalius, the physician, published his revolutionary work on anatomy.

Definitely the centre of gravity in culture had shifted from the next world to this; and from theology to politics. The increasing prosperity was not only cause but consequence of strong government—except in Germany, which had neither the one nor the other. It gave protection to the merchant and even could afford (and happily, unlike today, regarded it as an adornment to its glory to afford) patronage to scholars and to talent. In adjudging strong government, upon which the new progress as against the feudal anarchy depended, accomplishments, not intentions, entered into the reckoning. Aggressive individualism, adventure, strong government at home, meant an ambitious policy abroad. *Il faut grandir.* State, like individual, must magnify itself. No longer is there question of the Mediaeval ethical rule derived from the law of cosmopolitan, universal Rome, itself impregnated with an equalitarian philosophy: *jus suum cuique reddere*—"to give to each man his due." The due of the lion is not that of the sheep; the lion and fox will take what they can. A new Natural Law: Survival is Nature's law. Already we are in the age, not only of the New Monarchies of France, England and Spain, but also of an incipient New Nationalism, however still disguised by local spirit or personal loyalism to a monarch.

It is possible to divide the history of political thought into epochs that, for convenience, may be called, perhaps not too frivolously, "hard-boiled" and "soft-shell" periods—or, in William James's terms: "tough-minded" and "tender-minded." The thought of Hellas had been permeated with the notion of *well-being:* that of Rome with the notion of will, force and law—what it is now fashionable to call (if trivially and misleadingly), *power-politics.** The thought—not necessarily the practice—of the Middle Ages was again permeated with the ethical notion of what conduct *ought* to be and of spiritual well-being. The following age, that of Machiavelli, is the most "hard" and "tough" in its opinions of any that had reached literary expression yet.

2

Niccolò Machiavelli (1469–1527) was, in 1492, Secretary of the Second Chancery of the Florentine Republic and Secretary of the Council of Ten. A nobleman by birth and a republican by conviction, he was Ambassador of his native city-state to the court of France.

* The term is justifiable if we mean a *macht-politik* that seeks to solve political problems chiefly in the relationship of dominion and subjection. It is misleading if it obscures recognition that *all* politics is a study and practice of power-relations, even if by the route of co-ordination. The only person entitled to question this is a systematic anarchist—who believes only in power to follow his own will.

In 1512 took place the Medici *coup d'état* and the restoration of that ruling house. In 1513, Machiavelli found himself in prison on suspicion of conspiracy. His release was procured by the aid of Cardinal Julian de'Medici. Machiavelli rewarded this patron of scholars and prince of the church in a fashion very typical of the Renaissance. He sat down and wrote for private circulation a book, which was *The Prince*, which contains a useful little chapter entitled "Concerning the Secretaries of Princes." And he dedicated the book to a member of the ruling Medici family, Lorenzo the Younger. Prudence, however, delayed its general publication until 1532, after the author's death. As Professor Hearnshaw says, "Those who read it should realize that they were not meant to do so."

The Prince was followed, in 1516–1519, by Machiavelli's *Discourses on the First Decade of Livy*. In 1525, the *Florentine History* was dedicated to the Medici Pope, Clement VII, who apparently decided that Machiavelli was more suited to be a man of learning and letters than a practical man in the harsh world of politics. However, in 1526 Machiavelli was employed by Clement in making a report on the fortifications of Florence. He has also to his credit some plays, including *Mandragola*, a farce brilliant but obscene, written doubtless with a moral purpose, and some poems. His style was improved in freshness by his fortunate ignorance of the works of his predecessors: like Hobbes, he made no profession of being a schoolmaster of bookish information.

Machiavelli is a definite Renaissance type. He, living in the native land of the *condottiere*, has the Renaissance admiration for the man of poise and of varied talents, the "adventurer" in every sense, the *universale uomo*. *Virtù*, for Machiavelli, is a word used as in English the word "virtue" is used when speaking of a medicine or herb. It is a quality that makes it "good for something." It is "talent in use." Machiavelli's respect is for the man who can "deliver the goods." But these goods have little to do with moral value, everything to do with success for the purpose in hand.

Thus Machiavelli's contempt is reserved for Pietro Soderini who, holding public office, was too scrupulous a man to take those legally dubious methods which would have frustrated the Medici *coup*—Soderini being (in the words of the Anglo-Saxon Chronicle, about King Stephen) "a good man and weak, who did no justice." His admiration, equally naturally, is reserved for that amazing soldier of fortune, Cesare Borgia, Duke of Valentino, son of the Pope, Alexander VI (the progressive Renaissance Papacy having discovered, as against

NICCOLÒ MACHIAVELLI
(1469–1527 A.D.)

(*Facing p. 192*)

the obscurantist monks, that, since St. Peter was married, so could the Popes be). The only disadvantage here, from the standpoint of Machiavelli's political success cult, was that Machiavelli was backing the wrong horse. Instead of ending the Papacy (what Wyclif called "Anti-Christ") by establishing a hereditary Papal State or a decent Roman princedom, Cesare Borgia died unsung from a wound received when besieging a city in that Spain from which his unpleasant family had sprung. As Machiavelli wistfully remarks, the Duke had allowed for everything save that he should be ill when his father, the Pope, died —doubtless owing to an Act of God.

Machiavelli has his justification in protesting against an indulgent good nature or a legalistic scrupulosity (such as that of George III, of Britain, in refusing to sign an act for Catholic Emancipation as contrary to his coronation oath) which subordinates concentrated and ruthless attention to the public good to its own caprice of formal friendships. A man may be a bad citizen because a good man or a personally pleasant man.* It is not, however, clear that Machiavelli is always thinking in terms of public duty. Perhaps, living under a regime which was not his choice, he found it convenient rather to treat the issue as one of incompetent scrupulosity in antithesis to that master spirit that demands personal obedience. Living in an age of the personal tyrannies in the Italian states, it is not the abstract concepts of Commonwealth or State, but the concrete notions of Prince or People, that dominate his thinking. It may be that the prosperity of the State is the (true) interest of the Prince, as was argued until the days of Charles II of England and of the Treaty of Dover. But Machiavelli's prime concern, at least in *The Prince*, is the technique of success in personal rule.

Sharply Machiavelli distinguishes between politics and religious principles. More precisely, he treats religious institutions as the instruments of the politician for giving sentimental support to the stability and bravery of the State. He is a secularist but, unlike the foolish, pedantic secularists, he does not boggle to recognize the influence of religion. "The rulers of kingdoms and commonwealths . . . should countenance and further whatsoever tells in favour of religion, even should they think it untrue; and the wiser they are, and the better they are acquainted with natural causes, the more ought they to do so." In these comments on religion, thoroughly Erastian in tone (as we shall later explain),† it is perhaps not fantastic to detect the note

* *Cf.* p. 92.
† *Cf.* p. 204.

of the disappointed idealist. He adds, "To the Church, therefore, and to the priests, we Italians owe this first debt, that through them we have become wicked and irreligious." The divorce, however, between the principles of religion and those of politics, in the writings of the secularist Machiavelli, is more apparent than real. The truth is that, in the background of his mind, what he disapproves of is not religion (*e.g.*, that of the Polis), but the cosmopolitan Christian religion.

> Our religion places [the highest good] in humility, lowliness and contempt for the things of this world; or if it ever calls upon us to be brave, it is that we should be brave to suffer rather than to do. This manner of life . . . seems to have made the world feeble, and to have given it over as a prey to wicked men to deal with as they please; since the mass of mankind, in the hope of being received into Paradise, think more how to bear injuries than how to avenge them.

It is the anti-Pacifist argument that will later be used by J. J. Rousseau.* For these reasons Machiavelli's own name has gathered round it a lurid legend. Nicholas may convey associations of the devil, but of the associations of Machiavellianism there has been no doubt. The early sixteenth-century Popes, over-cultivated Renaissance gentlemen, were deprecatingly compelled to disclaim his *Prince* and its dedication. Among Protestants his works were a cause of horror to the pious and hence were early commented upon and denounced, *e.g.*, by Gentillet in his *Antimachiavel*, 1576. Several early translations were made, into French (1553) and Latin (1560), to gratify the malice of realistic thinkers.

Machiavelli's reputation is, in large part, misleading. It is true that he gives critics a handle against him by his startling literary manner. Thus we find one literary piece headed, *Description of the Methods Adopted by the Duke Valentino When Murdering Vitellozzo Vitelli, Oliverotto da Fermo, the Signor Pagolo, and the Duke di Gravina Orsini.* It is the kind of thing to make those brought up on the political theory of Thomas Aquinas open their eyes. Again, one chapter of *The Prince* is inventoried as being *Concerning the Way in Which Princes Should Keep Faith.*

> A wise lord cannot, nor ought he to, keep faith when such observance may be turned against him, and when the reasons that caused him to pledge it exist no longer. If men were entirely good this precept would not hold, but because they are bad, and will not keep faith with you, you too are not bound to observe it with them. Nor will there ever be wanting to a prince legitimate

* *Cf.* p. 459.

reasons for this non-observance. . . . Therefore it is unnecessary for a prince to have all the good qualities I have enumerated, but it is very necessary to appear to have them. And I shall dare to say this also, that to have them and always to observe them is injurious, and that to appear to have them is useful. . . . Let a prince have the credit of conquering and holding his state, the means will always be considered honest, and he will be praised by everybody; because the vulgar are always taken by what a thing seems to be and by what comes of it; and in the world there are only the vulgar, for the few find a place there only when the many have no ground to rest on. One prince of the present time, whom it is not well to name, never preaches anything else but peace and good faith, and to both he is most hostile, and either, if he had kept it, would have deprived him of reputation and kingdom many a time.

Qui nescit dissimulare, nescit regnare—"who knows not how to dissimulate, knows not how to reign"—is the maxim, later quoted by Cromwell. In brief, a politician is a quick-change artist, who frequently has to appear resplendent in religion and loving-kindness—but it is highly inconvenient if this garment happens to be his skin. The point that Machiavelli, not having lived in modern times, appears to have overlooked is the superior efficiency of self-deception to dissimulation.

Machiavelli is a patriot. Not unnaturally Benito Mussolini, that great actor and realist, has written an essay on Niccolò Machiavelli, which was his doctoral thesis on the occasion when he, once vagrant, honoured the University of Bologna by accepting from it a Doctorate of Law.* Mussolini shows Machiavelli in this light as the great—and perhaps the first—Italian patriot. An examination of the *Discorsi*, written under less trying personal conditions than *Il Principe* and perhaps more just to his actual views, reveals him rather as a democrat than as a supporter of autocracy. His opinion is caustic rather than high of the great Julius. The details of his career display him as definitely a republican. These points will be discovered by the student who goes behind sensationalism and prejudice; and who studies the first politicist since Aristotle with the attention that he deserves.

Machiavelli is the first political scientist. To an extent that Aristotle, his great predecessor, emphatically does not, Machiavelli makes a distinction between ethics and political science. By the same token he makes a distinction between religion (which the Schoolmen had, quite rightly, bound up with ethics) and political science. Machiavelli was able to force home these distinctions (which, although obvious, had been piously overlooked by preceding centuries which insisted on

* *Cf.* p. 718.

keeping eyes fixed on political "ultimate" *ends*) owing to the flagrant discrepancies, characteristic of the Renaissance, between religio-ethical professions and human political practice—and this even in Papal Rome itself. The great Greeks had ignored this distinction because, for philosophic reasons, they wished to do so—since by education they wished to ethicize politics just as they also ethicized natural history and physics itself as the manifestation of immanent reason. It is Machiavelli's merit that he brings his readers back from a moralo-philosophical discussion, long become formal and empty, upon how men *ought* to behave to a sociological study, aided by history ancient and contemporary, of how they *do* behave, persistently and despite all fine exhortations, universally approved, to the contrary. He brings them back from man's maxims to man's nature. This is the significance of his interest in history; and of his commentary on *Discourses on the First Decade of Livy* and of his *Florentine History*. Machiavelli gives us that reverse of the ethical medal of the Schoolmen which is necessary for the complete understanding of the subject.

Machiavelli is a political scientist, not a political philosopher. That is, he is a student of *means*, not *ends;* of efficiency where the objective is assumed, not of the value of the objective itself. Even *The Prince* (and, certainly, the more solid, if less sensational, *Discourses*) cannot be dismissed as some mere "manual for diplomats." It is, moreover, *not* only a study of the "art" of politics. And Machiavelli himself tells us this. He tells us that his task has been (*Prince*, Chap. XV) "to go through to the effectual truth of the matter"—the efficient causes. Elsewhere (*Discourses*, I, Chap. XVI) he explains that he has made his study from the point of view of the governors, because the rest only ask passively for security. *The politically conscious groups are the determinant forces in the social order.*

Machiavelli does not, of course, entirely live up to his professions. He is not so detached as he professes to be. That, in view of the novelty and pioneer nature of his position, is not surprising. Indeed, like that oddly discrepant personality, Dante, he is an idealist, but a disappointed one. Mussolini is not entirely wrong in seeing in him the Italian patriot who looks for a strong man to unite torn Italy against the foreigner, and who is not interested whether that strong man has the morals of a Borgia or the temperance of a Rechabite. Let us recall that *The Prince* concludes:

This opportunity, therefore, ought not to be allowed to pass for letting Italy at last see her liberator appear. Nor can one express the love with which he would be received in all those provinces which have suffered so much from these foreign scourings, with what thirst for revenge, with what stubborn faith, with what devotion, with what tears. What door would be closed to him? Who would refuse obedience to him? What envy would hinder him? What Italian would refuse him homage? To all of us this barbarous dominion stinks. Let, therefore, your illustrious house (the Medici) take up this charge with that courage and hope with which all just enterprises are undertaken, so that under its standard our native country may be ennobled, and under its auspices may be verified that saying of Petrarch:—

> "Virtue will take arms against the Fury
> And will battle him:
> For the antique valour of Italian
> Hearts yet burns alive."

Once again the City-state, even in the most glorious days of Florence, Urbino, Venice, Genoa, demonstrated its fatal incapacity, although a gemlike microcosm of intensive culture, to keep out foreign foes commanding the strength of nation states, French, Spanish, German. Machiavelli is the harbinger of nationalism and, especially, of the national state. With him the fifteenth-century word *Stato* ("the State," the con-*stitu*tion, the static, the *esta*blished order, that which "stays put") comes into authoritative use. The State is with us.

Machiavelli has other prepossessions, typical of his time, which, even if unvoiced, yet intrude into his discussions of means certain tacit assumptions about ends. He respects the "universal man," the man of talent, who is entitled to his gratification in power. The study of those qualifications, and the means to them, is Machiavelli's especial subject. Machiavelli does, however, apparently admit a moral rule overriding individual egoism. He takes it as unchallenged that "the safety of the people is the supreme law" (*salus populi suprema lex*)—it is a good old Roman maxim. Actually he interprets it often in a Renaissance fashion by identifying it with the grandeur and strength of the prince, as a *person*, from whom flows popular security. But negatively, he throughout adheres to it, whether it be prince or republic that he is admonishing. This safety is never to be sacrificed to other ideals. In brief, the wisdom of Machiavelli's "realism" comes to this: the welfare of humanity, for a Florentine, must be morally subordinate to the local interests of the municipality of the Florentines. This is the "new learning" as against the old Catholic universal morality and Roman cosmopolitanism. Machiavelli tacitly takes this as self-evident and as not calling for discussion. It is an object on which all would agree; and the only task is to discuss the means. Perhaps not Florentines, but Italians. That would be the only question.

After all, men do think and behave like this—not by the mathematical law of moral logic. Everywhere what matters, as a basis of loyalty and morals, is the "we-group." What is the "we-group" men take from tradition.

As political scientist Machiavelli's importance is twofold. He is the theorist of force. And he is the student of methodology—of the science and method of politics.

The power-theory of politics is not new. We must, however, scrupulously distinguish between it as the theory of what does happen and as the theory of what should happen. As the latter it had been vigorously stated by "Callicles," eighteen hundred years earlier. "Callicles" reply to "Socrates" is, once again, in this "hard-boiled" age, coming to the fore.* The statesman has no right to conduct himself as a private individual or to be swayed from attention to the major public interest by minor concessions of generosity, mercy or even by desire for show, in response to the appeals of private persons to his affection or benevolence. So much had been established by the example of the consul Brutus at the beginning of the Roman Republic. Are we, however, to assume that Roman virtue and standards of honour (as in the case of the return of the hostage Atilius Regulus) govern the conduct of the State itself? Or govern the conduct of a great man or *duce* who thinks he alone can save the State?—save it, for example, from the "unnatural" rule of weak men? Or is the strong man, who ought to rule, to make up his own moral rule about how he shall deal with weak pretenders?

In a passage compact of truth and falsehood, Machiavelli writes (*Discourses*, III, Chap. XLI):

> When the entire safety of our country is at stake, no consideration of what is just or unjust, merciful or cruel, praiseworthy or shameful, must intervene. On the contrary, every other consideration being set aside, that course alone must be taken which preserves the existence of the country and maintains its liberty. And this course we find followed by the people of France, both in their words and in their actions, with the view of supporting the dignity of their king and the integrity of their kingdom; for there is no remark they listen to with more impatience than that this or the other course is disgraceful to the king. For their king, they say, can incur no disgrace by any resolve he may take, whether it turn out well or ill; and whether it succeed or fail, all maintain that he has acted as a king should.

* *Cf.* p. 44.

When Catherine de' Medici became Queen of France and adviser to her royal sons, and in the "thorough" days of the Bartholomew Massacre, the French may have had more strain put upon their alleged belief that there was nothing disgraceful that a king could do. At least the Italians did not lose the opportunity to comment on French honour. We see abundant examples of the same mood today.

In brief, the issue that Machiavelli presents is the very old one that troubled Aristotle and, in different fashion, the Christians: How can a good man in a bad world be other than a bad citizen? To put the matter differently: Morality is based upon co-operation. If a good citizen owes ultimate allegiance to his own state in a world where there are many competing or warring states, how can a good citizen be other than a bad man? Machiavelli's answer is: A good citizen *ought* to be a bad man—or (phrased differently) there is no such thing as a moral law but only patriotism; or, again, patriotism is the final moral law and patriotism means applauding the leader, *i.e.*, the leader is the incarnate moral law. The issue is one that has not been solved from that day to this. Christian morality, with its pacifist presuppositions, postulates universal brotherhood. The State postulates the perpetual potentiality of war. Dante had foreshadowed the only solution—not fantastic in the days of the Roman Empire. That solution was the world-state or the international federation. With the rise, during the Renaissance, of the national sovereign State, pledged by implication to the methods Machiavelli so logically exposed, that solution faded from the field of practical politics.

Machiavelli's work is the more impressive since he is not to be understood as a mere defender of despotism to save his own skin, or an ironic glorifier of force and fraud. He is bitterly opposed to mercenary troops as sapping the military vigour of the nation that employs them. "It is not gold, as is vulgarly supposed, that is the sinews of war, but good soldiers." He gives warning that mere additions of territory, far from spelling real additions of strength to a country, may in fact weaken it. Without illusions about the fickle populace—*chi fondà in sul popolo fondà in sul fango:* "who builds on the people builds on mud"—he was no lover of the nobles who lived in their castles, engaged in feuds and sapped the strength of the city.

One cannot by fair dealing, and without injury to others, satisfy the nobles, but you can satisfy the people, for their object is more righteous than that of the nobles, the latter wishing to oppress, whilst the former only desire not to be oppressed. It is to be added that a prince can never secure himself against a hostile people, because of their being too many, whilst from the nobles he can secure himself as they are few in number. (*Prince*, Chap. IX.)

Nor has Machiavelli more use for the wealthy, with their privileged and special interest:

To make it plain what I mean when I speak of gentlemen, I say that those are so to be styled who live in opulence and idleness on the revenues of their estates, without concerning themselves with the cultivation of their estates, or incurring any other fatigue for their support. Such persons are very mischievous in every republic or country. . . . It follows that he who would found a commonwealth in a country where there are many gentlemen, cannot do so unless he first gets rid of them. (*Discourses*, I, Chap. IV.)

—one of the most outspoken arguments that I know for class liquidation.

Elsewhere I have shown that no ordinance is of such advantage to the commonwealth, as one which enforces poverty on its citizens. And although it does not appear what particular law it was that had this operation in Rome (especially since we know the agrarian law to have been stubbornly resisted) we find, as a fact, that four hundred years after the city was founded, great frugality still prevailed there; and may assume that nothing helped so much to produce this result as the knowledge that the path to honour and preferment was closed to none, and that merit was sought after wheresoever it was to be found; for this manner of conferring honours made riches the less courted.

Machiavelli's ideal emerges as the Aristotelian one of a middle-class oligarchy or (since wealth is specifically subordinated) aristocracy—although in particular circumstances the dictatorship of some able man, competent to take the helm, is welcomed. A chapter of *The Prince* is entitled *Concerning Principalities Which Are Acquired by One's Own Arms and Ability*. A chapter of the *Discourses* (I, Chap. lviii), however, is entitled *That a People Is Wiser and More Constant Than a Prince*. And later (II, ii) we get a comment on personal government, striking from Machiavelli, even if not entirely accurate. It is doubtless stimulated by the thought that the so-called Roman Empire in fact achieved *most of its expansion under, not the Empire, but the Republic.*

It is easy to understand whence this love of liberty arises among nations, for we know by experience that States have never signally increased, either as to dominion or wealth, except where they lived under a free government. And truly it is strange to think to what a pitch of greatness Athens came during the hundred years after she freed herself from the despotism of Peisistratus; and far stranger to contemplate the marvellous growth which Rome made after freeing herself from her kings. The cause, however, is not far to seek, since it is the well-being, not of individuals, but of the community which makes a State great, and, without question, this universal well-being is nowhere secured save in a republic. . . .

The rule of a people is better than the rule of a prince. . . . Nor let anyone finding Caesar celebrated by a crowd of writers, be misled by his glory; for those who praise him have been corrupted by his good fortune, and overawed by the greatness of that empire which, being governed in his name, would not suffer any *to speak their minds openly* concerning him.

One may welcome Machiavelli among the Liberals in this Fascist age.

Machiavelli is not only no *enragé* defender of personal leadership. He is not even a defender of fraud except within well-defined limits. The chapters of his works have lurid captions: "That promises made on compulsion are not to be observed"; "How women are a cause of the ruin of states"; "That we are not to offend a man, and then send him to fill an important office or command"; "That fraud is fair in war"; "Why it is that changes from freedom to servitude, and from servitude to freedom, are sometimes made without bloodshed, but at other times reek with blood." On the last point he makes the observation, relevant to contemporary revolution, that it all depends upon whether the government thus challenged, itself began in violence and revolution. Machiavelli, however, having observed (I, Chap. lix): "As to engagements broken on the pretext that they have not been observed by the other side, I say nothing, since that is a matter of everyday occurrence," yet continues:

This, however, I desire to say, that I would not have it understood that any fraud is glorious which leads you to break your plighted word, or to depart from covenants to which you have agreed; for though to do so may sometimes gain you territory and power, it can never, as I have said elsewhere, gain you glory. The fraud, then, which I here speak of is that employed against an enemy who places no trust in you, and is wholly directed to military operations.

Machiavelli had not advanced so far as the contemporary theory concerning the negligibility of bourgeois morality.

Machiavelli's fame, however, for the student of Political Science must rest finally upon the fact that he is the first modern master of this subject. In his eyes, human nature throughout the ages does not significantly change—and, what men have done, they are, on equal provocation, liable to do again. No talk of religion or ideals alters this fact, since both alike rest on this same human nature. "Men seldom know how to be wholly good or wholly bad." The ideal for the politician moves within the field of the practicable for human nature. And what is permanently practicable, because in accordance with this nature, is not to be discovered by observing winds of doctrine and thunderings of ideology, but is open for all to study in history as in an open book.

> Men are born, and live, and die, always in accordance with the same rules. . . . Anyone comparing the present with the past will soon perceive that in all cities and in all nations there prevail the same desires and passions as always have prevailed; for which reason it should be an easy matter for him who carefully examines past events, to foresee those which are about to happen in any republic, and to apply such remedies as the ancients have used in like cases.

Machiavelli held (in the words of Dr. Arnold of Rugby) that "the history of Greece and of Rome is not an idle inquiry about remote ages and forgotten institutions, but a living picture of things present, fitted not so much for the curiosity of the scholar, as for the instruction of the statesman and the citizen."

Two things will be noted. Machiavelli is not saying that "history repeats itself" or that what happened in ancient Rome will happen again, in just the same way, in modern Italy. There is, for example, no antique parallel to Italian nationalism. Nor (we shall return to this*) was he committing himself, like Vico later, to some mystic doctrine of recurrence or cycles in history. All he is saying is that human "desires and passions" remaining the same, where the incidents of life are comparable, humanity will tend to find the same remedies and repeat the same conduct. There will be recurrent behaviour patterns upon which (so long as it is always recalled that the incidents must be comparable) a social science can be founded, alike by economist and politicist. Machiavelli's entire *Discourses on the First Decade* is a labour to this end. Its incomparable importance and the rarity of the genius that attempted it, we shall perceive later, when we come to discuss the later development of this science. Today statues are erected to Machiavelli the patriot. Some day, they may be unveiled to Machiavelli the scientist, disinterested, so little the plotting egoist that at the end of his life he was poorer than at the beginning.

3

The period after Machiavelli is marked by an intellectual relapse into unoriginality. The Renaissance when it crosses the Alps, having

* *Cf.* p. 467.

no longer the same basis of urban economic prosperity, has lost its bloom. The glories of the court of Lorenzo de' Medici in Florence are replaced by the intrigues of the court of Catherine de' Medici, Queen Mother of France. Responsible for the massacre of the Protestants on St. Bartholomew's day (1572), acquiescent in the assassination of the Catholic Guises, accused by the Protestants of being a woman of blood, one of those who maintained "a Monstrous Regiment" ("regimen"—Knox's phrase), and by the Catholics of being pro-Huguenot, in her day practical "Machiavellianism," as a technique of domestic government, attained its fine, ill-scented flower. The comment upon her of Henry IV of France, Henry of Navarre, is interesting: "What could the poor woman do with five little children in her arms, after the death of her husband, and two families in France, ours and the Guises, attempting to encroach on the Crown? Was she not forced to play strange parts to deceive the one and the other and yet, as she did, to protect her children, who reigned in succession by the wisdom of a woman so able? I wonder that she did not do worse!"

"Machiavellianism," which had sprung up as a policy in countering the envenomed feuds of Italian city-states, was carried over, North of the Alps, to cope with the dying throes of feudal selfishness and with the fanaticism, not of class but of religion, which led the Pope, good man, to illuminate St. Peter in the ecstatic belief (false) that the Massacre of St. Bartholomew was piously premeditated; which led Knox to bless with the authority of his unpleasant, primitive, Hebrew prophets, the assassination of Cardinal Beaton; and which converted first France and then Germany into a shambles and a desolation.

Nous sommes las, became the watchword in France—"tired of it all." Henry IV found the taking of Paris and the unification of his kingdom well worth a Mass. It would have been well if the heavy Germans could have learned the same lesson. The Popes, reformed, religious and fanatical—these are the days of Pope St. Pius V (1566–1572)—placed Machiavelli's works among the first upon the Index of prohibited books, instituted in 1557, and resolutely kept them there. "Machiavellianism" had become a legend of horrors, perhaps to be practised, but never to be mentioned. The charge against Catherine was that she had taught her children "*surtout des traictz de cet athée Machiavel*"—"especially the writings of that atheist, Machiavel." But it was left for a prince of the Church, Cardinal de Richelieu, to support the Protestants in Germany in order to defeat the encirclement of France by the Habsburgs—as though Il Duce today might support Stalin in order to retain his hold on the Italo-German Tyrol or Adolf Hitler support Stalin in order to beat the French. The intricacies of these distressed times produced two major political developments, the Doctrine of Religious Toleration and a new Theory of the State.

The Doctrine of Toleration, which ended the Christian Catholic domination, anticipated by Marsiglio and mothered by the Catholic Catherine de' Medici in 1562, was confirmed by the ex-Protestant Henry IV in 1598 by the Edict of Nantes. It marks the end of that epoch of domination of politics by Religion which can appropriately be said to begin with the Emperor Constantine's Edict of Milan, of 313. It was essentially a political doctrine springing from the lassitude and disillusion which ever follow uncontrolled idealism and unleashed fanaticism when Pope and Reformer alike were ready to advocate the assassination of opponents. It sprang from such a mood of reluctant compromise under pressure of facts as were later to dictate the Declaration of Indulgence (1687) of the Catholic James II. Toleration for conscience' sake, when not advocated by a persecuted minority, comes later—unless we see its foreshadowings in the secularism of Marsiglio and (with reservations) of Machiavelli.

Erastus (died 1583), the Rhineland Calvinist, had done no more than advocate that civil magistrates should concern themselves only with civil, not religious, offences and differences. He was only one more Protester against Lutheran persecution. Erastianism, although deriving its name from him, is a very different matter. It is indeed the theory which governed the famous formula of the Peace of Augsburg, of 1555—*cuius regio, eius religio:* the lord of each territory will settle the religion of the land where he is landlord. In case of dispute, it is for the civil authority, *concerned with the public peace*, to intervene, decide and regulate. It is little more than the theory of the pro-Imperialists in the Investiture Controversy and Marsiglio's theory applied to circumstances where the issue had become morbid and inflamed.

The group known as the *Politiques*, in France, maintained an intimately related position. Outstanding in the group is the Sieur Michel de l'Hôpital, chancellor of Charles IX. Their task was to explain to men of one Christian sect why they should obey a monarch belonging to another—why, in brief, inside Christianity, it was no longer true, as Augustine had said, that the brotherhood of faith had the first claim to allegiance. We shall return to an explanation of the individualizing and atomizing of religion and of this supernatural brotherhood.*

* *Cf.* p. 218.

All that here requires note is that it was the task of the *Politiques* to reintroduce, to the Modern World, the supreme allegiance of the State, if not yet the religion of the State. That last was to come later. At the moment all that was asserted was that the State, new born in the days of Louis XI of France, Henry VII of England, and Ferdinand and Isabella of Spain, was not to be ruined for the sake of any religion, however divine. Loyalty, for the first time since the Emperor Theodosius II (408–450), has become disjoined from orthodoxy.

Men ceased to be interested in Platonically saving (if necessary by burning) the soul of the heretic in this world lest he should burn in the next. The days, at least North of the Pyrennees, of good sincere men like the Inquisitor Torquemada (1388–1468) were over. (It may be added that the records of execution after due process by, *e.g.*, the Inquisition of Toulouse, compare very favourably, as touching numbers, with those of illicit negro lynchings in America. It cost about $150 to burn a heretic. The numbers were economical.) The distinction between the position of the *Politiques* and that of the signators at Augsburg is that now, instead of inter-national toleration, *i.e.*, diversity within the total *respublica Christiana*, which is a fading concept, there is to be intra-national toleration and diversity within the secular realm. As J. N. Figgis has put it: "Dissent is put in the category of unrecognized but permitted vice." Protestant "temples" are, as it were, "*maisons tolérées*." It is worth while to note that essentially the *Politiques* (one is reminded of Pierre Dubois) are a group of lawyers, and those lawyers "civilians."

The development of a new Theory of the State is well illustrated in the works of another of the *Politiques*.

Jean Bodin (Latinized as Bodinus, died 1596), Councillor of State, attached to the court of Henry III of France, at one time a Huguenot, as early as 1572 a defender of toleration, is from the point of view of political theory the most outstanding of the group. In his *Heptaplomeres*, with its discussion between representatives of seven creeds, there is a foreshadowing, apparently, of that religious agnosticism which we find in that Legend of the Three Rings which recurs from Boccaccio to Lessing's *Nathan the Wise*. As a consequence Bodin was attacked by all partisans alike. His *De la Républlique* (1576)—ten years later (and this in itself is highly significant of the break-down of clerical internationalism) translated into Latin as *De Republica Libri Sex*—lacks, with its conventional, legalistic preoccupations, the fresh originality of Machiavelli. It is the book of a lawyer, not of a politician.

It was, therefore, naturally enough, used as a text-book within a generation in the universities (*e.g.*, Cambridge, England), whereas Machiavelli's book was put on the Index. And, although Bodin is the first to use the words "Political Science," and declares that Machiavelli "*n'a jamais sondé le gué de la science politique*," it is in fact Machiavelli who refounds it after Aristotle. The *De Republica* is confused by its traditionalism and its conservation of the idea of an earlier, more liberal, less despotic age which is so different from the new "conservative realism." Bodin is concerned with Legitimacy and Sovereignty; Machiavelli with Power. The secularist theory, of the State or Empire, of Marsiglio, continued by Machiavelli with a difference, is carried further by Bodin, with a difference.

The traditional elements in Bodin appear in his theme that the family is the basic social unit; provides a natural basis for authority; and that this authority is a natural (*i.e.*, instinctive and rational) right. In the line of traditional Scholasticism is the position assigned to reason, which discovers the purpose of the State, and regulates it in the light of that rational purpose. Bodin will even admit—and the admission is, of course, conservative and traditional—that the "republic" or "commonwealth" (there is [*n.b.*] no Latin word for "state" —*imperium* could not be used by any loyal Frenchman: the days of the imperialist writers are over) is subject to the restraint of law. It is restrained by laws revealed, natural and universal—"*divinae, naturales et gentium*." Thus "to keep a contract" is demanded by natural law. The whole doctrine, however, of Natural Law is in a condition of degeneration. Thanks to the rapid development of physics, Nature is beginning to resume a material quality but without the Stoic implication of immanent rationality. It is matter of which the uses, under Providence, are to be explored by laboratory experiment. "Nature" is not God but a laboratory specimen. On the other hand, although Bodin, as a "civilian," retains the notion of the rationality of law, this Natural Law is becoming merely moral and disconnected from the Scholastic notion of a rational law actually observed in the universe. It is becoming the Law that the God of the Bible wills, or would like, to be observed and for breach of which He will send men to hell; not the Law which they are predestined to observe. There is now a clear dualism of Ideal and Real which characterizes the age. And what practically matters is the real. Similarly Bodin renders formal homage to a *Respublica mundana*, the old *Respublica Christiana*—but the homage is without political significance.

The real argument of Bodin is to be found in the novelties which he tries, lawyerwise, to pretend are not novelties and to square with a tradition that he is too timid to reject. These novelties are not so valuable as the older values of the Hellenic and Scholastic tradition. But for the next three centuries the political thought of the West will be preoccupied with these ideas, with a new theory of the State and with the concept of Sovereignty.

The State, for example, Bodin maintains (and Gregory VII had maintained it, in his wrath, before him), is characterized by coercion and conquest. Civil associates, guilds, cities and the like, are associations at will so that a man is free to come and go as he chooses. Bodin avoids the thorny question whether churches and families are also such associations at will, although he advocates a new freedom of divorce.

The State stands above all ranks of society and all individuals. The notion of the feudal pyramid and of the contractual relation of classes has gone, and one of legal dominion, more congenial to the Roman law, has superseded it. Bodin, it will be noted, has here made the decisive transition—he has definitely begun the identification (however hedged around) of superiority in the social order with superiority of force, which is the precise ground upon which St. Augustine had allocated to the Temporal Power or City of Self-love inferiority in the social order, *i.e.*, imperfection, remoteness from the ideal order and absence of moral claim to ultimate allegiance. It is a typical *politique* attitude. The Renaissance "toughness" has done its work. The local State, which is of this world, is *en route* to take effective precedence of the Church, which is an eternal society of all men past, present and future (since even the infidel is also, willynilly, in Christ's flock and potentially under His shepherd). And this is done without reference to the Empire. As Richard II of England had claimed, every ruler is *entier empereur* within his own dominions. Bodin's notions are theoretically monstrous but they will prove dominant for several centuries. Like feudalism, state sovereignty has its evolutionary significance. In the new age of "the realm," while sowing war abroad, these notions do, in fact, make for peace and stability at home—even more than the shadow of the Roman Empire, which is alone theoretically satisfactory.

Sovereignty replaces suzerainty. The sovereignty is not deduced from the Roman notion of universal law but from the notion of civil peace and hence the need for a final authority within a given area or realm (not yet nation or people). The problem, faced by Dante, of the civil peace between areas is ignored, or rather sovereignty reverses itself and becomes the right to inter-national anarchy (always, Bodin, the traditionalist, would add, under Natural Law).

The Greeks had a strong sense of the priority of society, of the community or Polis. Like Machiavelli later, they had the notion of personal power. This is expressed in the speeches at Melos of the Athenian delegates. But there is here no notion of state sovereignty—on the contrary we have the exact opposite notion of the priority of immemorial law, not subject to human sovereignty. That is the theme of Sophocles' *Antigone* and of Aristotle. The Roman law, with its doctrine of *imperium* and of "the will of the prince" comes nearer to the concept. But although we have here a strong doctrine of centralized authority, the will of the prince is still subject to universal law, and there is no developed notion of sovereign relations with external states. For Rome there is no claim to a right to its own will within civilization, since it identifies itself with civilization and indeed is in the primitive stage of admitting no law but its own (after its absorption of Greek law). It is yet thanks to Rome's own universality that countries deriving from Rome admit the validity of each other's domestic law, as resting on a common traditional basis in jurisprudence.

Feudalism, as was later to be pointed out, is the negation of the concept alike of State and Sovereignty. Since, however, the Church is far the most highly developed political body in early Western civilization, it is to it that we must look for the forms of all those political ideas which later develop in the field of that more recent and upstart organization, the State. Here, then, there are anticipations. Attention has already been called* to the doctrine of the unity of authority in the encyclical of Boniface VIII, *Unam Sanctam*. Earlier, in the thirteenth century, the great canonist who was later Pope Innocent IV had developed the doctrine, of which we shall hear more, of the *persona ficta* or "personality in law."† Some personalities, natural and corporate (legal), were "real" personalities. Such was the Church. Others, like guilds and chapters, were personalities at law, but only by the pretence and mandatory will of the "real" societies or persons. By the time of Marsiglio the Empire or State ("a state") is to be that "real person," although no one yet dares to suggest that the Church ("a church") is only *persona ficta*. Marsiglio refers to a civil authority "*superiore carens*"—"lacking any superior."

* *Cf.* p. 166.

† *Cf.* pp. 653, 712.

Briefly, the State (or "the Modern State,") was begotten of the New Monarchies and conceived by Bodin. In *De la République* occurs the decisive word, *souveraineté*. In the Latin version we get the definition: *maiestas est summa in cives ac subditos legibusque soluta potestas*—"majesty (*souveraineté*) is the supreme power, not bound by the laws, over citizens and subjects." Greek and Roman lawyer and Schoolman alike would have repudiated, horrified, any notion of a power "not bound by the laws." St. Thomas talks of this claim to self-sufficient power as "the insolent claim of that Nicanor," the Greek tyrant who boasted of his powers against the Almighty—a claim patently blasphemous. Bodin himself is half afraid of his own temerity—explains that of course all authority is subject to natural and divine law. But he continues (ostensibly about municipal or domestic positive law but by implication about all law recognized in the courts), "law depends upon the will of him who holds supreme power in the state."

Absolute monarchy replaces feudal kingship *inter pares* or "among the peers (equals)." The majesty and sovereignty of the State (the word still used is the classical one: "Commonwealth," used by Queen Elizabeth, *respublica, république*) are represented through the government—Marsiglio's "regent." And this authority of government may reside in a monarch. Moreover the monarch is no less a sovereign if he is a tyrant. Bodin, in an age when the problem of tyranny was being widely discussed and when Henry III of France was soon to fall a victim to an assassin, could not entirely avoid the issue of what relief a country might expect from tyranny. He introduces the amusingly conservative and legalistic suggestion (so contrary to his own doctrine of sovereignty, so reminiscent of the older *respublica mundana*) that a tyrant might be put down by his peers, the neighbouring princes. Bodin, after all, is a legitimist, not a Machiavelli.

The notion of the citizen as it existed in the antique world, at least North of the Alps and outside a few free towns, is dead. The notion of the vassal, of the Mediaeval world, is being replaced by that of the "subject." The difference is not one in words only. There is a fall in stature from the proud *civis Romanus* to the rank of one of the conquered people under Rome. The notion of the rights of the national by blood as against his ruler has not yet appeared, while that of the king as feudal father is fading. The "subject" is the mere lay figure of civil administration. The Chinese philosopher, Mencius, in the beginning of civilization, put his finger-nail on the kernel of fallacy in this lawyers' doctrine by his maxim: "If the ruler considers the people as blades of grass, then the people will consider their ruler as a robber or enemy." Bodin does not visualize this subject as participating in government as the Greek and even Roman citizen had actually or theoretically participated, or as holding feudally by his oath and equal contract. Dominion has replaced compact. The subject is distinguished from the slave by the fact that he is juristically free.

Democracy, Bodin holds (and looks far away, South of the Alps, to Florence) is unstable. What matters is Government. And he stops to extinguish a dangerous heresy (not unsupported by St. Thomas). What if somebody says that the king is head of a race or a nation or that his realm should embrace only those of one style of culture, customs, institutions? On the contrary, is the King of France not to rule in Provence, Brittany and Navarre? The State may embrace all kinds and conditions and recks nothing of cultures. The State is Administration. Must then the State not be universal Administration—the Empire? (Always an inconvenient question to a Frenchman.) Bodin, demi-realist, turns back to the facts. France is. The Empire, save in name, is not. The main thing is that *men must be governed* and disturbing influences put down. Religion indeed had got out of hand and therefore Bodin, anti-fanatic, recommends toleration—not because he likes it but because he hopes that fanaticism, ignored by the State and by patriots, will wither.

4

The thought of Bodin is overshadowed by the conflict of ideas and of men in the Age of the Reformation and the Counter-reformation. The clear, harsh light of the Renaissance has given way to smoke. Shocked by the immorality of a progressive age, men are assassinating each other to the glory of God in the intervals of seeking a new way to salvation by grace. It is an age, not of Faith constructing a society, but of passionate faiths, too often burning to destroy each other—of multiple denominations and hydra sects. If this had its fruit in toleration, such toleration was no part of the intention of the dogmatic leaders. It has been said, by Professor Becker, that St. Thomas wrote twenty volumes, to reassure a world on the verge of doubt, to say that it was really right that things should be wrong, God only knew why. The Reformers did not see the reason for the twenty volumes—since they had the Bible and their primitive consciences to guide them.

The relation to the Renaissance of the Reformation—in part trans-Alpine, provincial continuation, in part anti-Italian, obscurantist reaction—is not a simple one to understand. In two centuries a German, contemporary of Goethe, Wieland, looking back on the wreckage of all Erasmus has stood for, commented: "The Reformation was an evil and retarded the progress of philosophy for centuries. Luther ruined everything by making the populace a party to what ought to have been left to the scholars. Had he not come forward with his furious knock-down attacks on the Church and excited a succession of horrible wars in Europe, liberty, science and humanity would have slowly made their way. Melanchthon and Erasmus were on the right road, but the violence of the age triumphed." Wieland forgot that the mass of mankind prefers fighting to reason, as showing greater moral indignation. As Professor Whitehead says, "The Reformation and the scientific were two aspects of the historical revolt which was the dominant intellectual movement of the later Renaissance." He continues, "It is a great mistake to conceive this historical revolt as an appeal to reason. On the contrary, it was through and through an anti-intellectual movement."

The Schoolmen (granted their presuppositions) were thorough rationalists, a-priorists—"School-Divinity, which, in all difficulties, useth reason," as its exponents stated. The experimentalists in the sciences of matter and the Reformers were not a-priori rationalists. (About the Counter-reformers we shall be able to judge when we come to the Jesuits.) The stress of the Reformers is, not on the Reason (the *Logos*), but upon the inscrutable Will of God as the sustainer of man's destination and salvation by grace or damnation to hell. The Reformers, moreover, introduce a new stress upon Sacred Books, infallible beyond all challenge of human reason and not aided by the logical disputations of the Schoolmen. The matter is further complicated by the cross-current between the religious reformers and the experimental scientists whom the former readily consigned to perdition as materialists and atheists.

Martin Luther (1483–1546), damning Galileo for presuming to declare, contrary to Holy Writ, that the earth moves round the sun, illustrates, by his act, the charge of Erasmus: "Where is Luther, there is noise." Luther's reply was characteristic of his attitude: "Erasmus, an enemy of all religions and especially hostile to that of Christ." It was only after four generations of religious (*i.e.*, idealistic) wars, envenomed by sectarianism, that Goethe's circle could then declare, in the Germany of the Enlightenment, that the Reformation in the fields of culture had spelled reaction. An exhausted Europe, bled white and in a hot-bed for looting criminals, awoke from its illusions of idealism and discovered how little Catholic oppression, human nature being ever the same in the mass, differed from Protestant oppression. The charge of Goethe and Wieland, as we shall later see,* is, however, only partly true.

The sectarianism which Luther had unleashed he had unleashed unwittingly. When he declared "I can no other" and appealed to his own conscience (without Socrates' reservations of filial, pious obedience or the Schoolman's confidence in the logical reason), he had yet a profound belief that conscience and Word alike led back to one, more certain, no less objective authority—that of the primitive Church. It was Luther's misfortune and historical illusion that, as Dean Inge says, he sought for the primitive Church, not in the socialistical-minded, even communistic, sacrament-habituated Hellenistic world, but "in the forests of primaeval Germany." Later, when enthusiasts arose holding strange views on Baptism, anarchists recovering the true primitive communism, Jan van Leyden ruling and persecuting (by revelation) in Münster, peasants declaring that "Christ has freed us all"—each man holding that the unmistakable Bible was on his side—Luther, terrified for the success of his own sect, could only range himself with the secular powers, fulminating, exhorting "stab, kill them like dogs." The world, he added, had reached such a pass that a man might win most grace thereby.

Augustinian canon, masterful and pugnacious fighter of the priests, obsessed with the sense of his own morbid sin, seeking salvation from predestined damnation through Christ's liberal grace, denouncer of the secular Renaissance culture, husband of a nun advising carnal intercourse three times a week (Frau Luther complained that, as the years passed, grace did not advance), evangelic hymnwright, his great (if uncontemplated) work was that, by freeing the Christian from the discipline of the priest and his Church, he emancipated immortal man from temporary society. Socrates had contemplated the work but with Hellenic piety had turned back. Later Protestant bodies, especially the Quakers, guided by their inner light, were to carry the matter further. Luther, like Machiavelli but so differently, gave us the individual. The secular Renaissance gives us the secular egoistic individual, *universale uomo;* the Reformation gave the spiritual individual, with an emphasis of which the judicious Erasmus was incapable. What stirs the world, in the short run, is not truth, but truth publicized in tickling slogans—not the sober truth of philosophers and scholars, but truth made gaudy and tricked out with highly coloured, hell-fire doctrine

* *Cf.* p. 220.

and appeals to animal emotion. Later we shall have to assess the value of the gift.

Luther himself, a spiritual Henry VIII, contributes no coherent political theory. His *dicta* vary with the occasion. As touching the Church hierarchy, he was the last man to preach the moral sublimity of passive obedience. But in order to attack that Church he had to win over the secular princes. He generously made a present of passive obedience to them. For a consistent theory we must turn to Luther's colleague, the scholar Schwartzerd (Hellenized as Melanchthon). The Lutheran Reformation might proclaim the emancipation of the individual from that ordered society which was the hierarchic church. It might denounce the corruption and put a check on the cynical abuses of that hierarchy. But the concrete condition of its own success was the support of the lords and princes who had their own quarrel with that wealthy, interfering body. If then the soul is to be emancipated, expedience requires that the body shall be bound.

We may conveniently divide the Protestant Reformers into two groups: the civil-minded and the ecclesiastical-minded. The Lutherans and the divines of the Established Churches of England and Sweden belong to the former group. The Calvinists and (in a sharply different sense) the Brownists or Independents [Congregationalists] and the Quakers, to the second.

The phrase "civil-minded" is misleading if it be understood as implying that Luther or Melanchthon has "a sense for the state," any more than Augustine. Merely their temporal circumstances were different. The counter-balance of spiritual emancipation, in order to reassure the secular power, was the doctrine of Passive Obedience. In entire despite of their intentions, the Lutherans replaced—as much as did Machiavelli—the dominant Church by the dominant State. The excuse was that temporal matters so little concerned a spiritual man that he was happy to be entirely passive in these trivial regulations—an entirely non-civil, if not anti-civil, doctrine.

> The temporal regiment has laws that reach no further [writes Luther] than body and goods and what mere things of earth there are besides. For over souls God neither can nor will allow that anyone rule but Himself only. . . . For no man can kill a soul or give it life or send it to Heaven or to hell.

The doctrine of Passive Obedience was already maintained in its most emphatic form by the early Reformer and translator of the Bible, Tyndale (died 1536). In his *Obedience of a Christian Man and how Christen rulers ought to govern, wherein also (if thou mark diligently) thou shalt fynde eyes to perceave crafty conveyance of all jugglers* (1528), Tyndale wrote, in a fashion characterized by the most offensive form of pacifism or passivism:

> He that judgeth the king judgeth God; and he that resisteth the king resisteth God and damneth God's law and ordinance. . . . The king is, in this world, without law, and may at his lust do right or wrong and shall give accounts but to God only . . . though he be the greatest tyrant in the world yet is he unto thee a great benefit of God. . . . The greater number of men are and always will be unchristian, whether they be baptized or not. . . . It is God, not man, who hangs and breaks on the wheel, decapitates and flogs: it is God who wages war.

Philip Melanchthon (1497–1560), professor of Greek at Wittenberg at twenty-one, educationalist, colleague and adviser of Luther, holds, as much as St. Thomas, that the object of government is that the multitude may look, "*non ad quaerenda et fruenda ventris bona*" ("not to seek and enjoy the goods of the stomach,"—as Marx wanted), but the goods of life everlasting, here understood as "Kingdom-come." Sound government rests on the Jewish Decalogue or Ten Commandments and on certain principles declared to common sense. The right to property follows from the commandment against stealing, but does not preclude confiscation of monastic properties. Nor does the right to freedom preclude slavery. The prince must be obeyed, although restricted in his own conscience by the law of God. The prince indeed had duties such as the extirpation of heresy, especially, the mild Melanchthon insists, when this amounts to overt blasphemy and gross scandals such as masses for the dead and the celibacy of the popish clergy. But if the princes misconducted themselves—as indeed the German princes frequently did, tearing Germany apart so that almost the rule of the old bishops was to be preferred—it was the duty of a Christian man to obey and, at the most, practise passive resistance.

Pacifism, indeed, emphasizing passive obedience but not excluding passive resistance, appears to have been the creed of both Luther and Melanchthon, in their more philosophic moments, and of many of the Protestants, as of the early Church. Two points, however, have to be noted. If these men are pacifists, Luther regarding force as futile in all matters of grace, their pacifism, and even their passive resistance (about which they are liable to make the most amazing *volte-faces*), is not a technique in civil society but is merely non-civil, and the consequence of a desire to withdraw from an order which did not concern Christians under grace anyhow. (The position here is so similar to Wyclif's that Melanchthon goes to great pains to refute him.) It recalls early Christian Chiliasm. It is the kind of irresponsible non-civility which, as we shall see, it has taken Europe three centuries to grow out of. Further, where these men were precluded from escaping into the non-political and had to face civil obligations, they took, with however many lookings-back, precisely the road that St. Augustine more resolutely took, of countenancing persecution as a check on public scandal and as a corollary of the moral function of the prince or ruler. In this fashion, partisans in a time of transition, they betrayed alike the causes of authority and of liberty.

The doctrine of the Godly Prince formed a convenient bridge. The prince or ruler was entitled to be obeyed also because, if a Protestant prince, he was under a gospel obligation to be an example to his people as David (save for some minor homicidal and adulterous aberrations) had been. Luther was even in doubt whether the Old Testament did not authorize the godly prince to commit bigamy. It is this prepossession of the age with the godly David which explains such an oddity as the frontispiece of the "King's Bible," of Henry VIII of England, when a large, crowned Henry in the foreground receives from a less conspicuous Almighty and Dove above, a Bible handed to His Majesty, which His Majesty hands on to the attendant bishops, and lords, to give to the swinish but expectant multitude.

The Divine Right of Kings was a corollary. It was not, of course, in any sense a new doctrine. All kings, even ungodly princes, ruled, not absolutely, but by God's will, as Paul had said, since God willed other corrupt men, in a vale of tears, to be ruled. That was a commonplace since Paul's *Epistles*. What was new was the stress: kings seemed more to rule by Right Divine since Popes had been repudiated. The specific doctrine of the Divine Right of Kings (as once of Emperors—and Melanchthon wistfully becomes convinced that there must be none of this, the Emperor being an obstinate Catholic) is the reply to the Divine Right of Popes.

The Duty of a Godly Prince, however, put—as it had done ever since the days of John of Salisbury—a limit on his right. Divine Right and Absolute Right were not synonymous nor did Luther ever think them so. The ruler had the obligation to be pious. He was not a secular, profane prince, after the style of Machiavelli. He had the obligation to persecute, if at all, *because* he was moral and a minister also of God's Word. Religious Acts of Uniformity were a plain deduction from the certainty of that Word.

The ecclesiastical-minded Reformers, such men as Calvin and Beza, did not here differ. They merely were indignant with Melanchthon's backsliding moderation in dealing with the counterparts in those days of Anarchists and Trotskyites today.

JOHN CALVIN (1509–1564), as was pointed out in the last chapter,* continues the scholastic Catholic tradition with only this major change, that for Rome must be read Geneva, and for a "Pelagian" Romish doctrine of works and free will must be read grace and predestination, even to damnation. If Luther is the Danton of the Reformation, Calvin is its Robespierre. He represents Augustinianism, in theology, carried to its final and cruel limit. God was not Reason (or the Reason was inscrutable) but was Will. The logic of this Frenchman, who adopted Geneva as his home, had a clarity such as the German Luther never attained. *The Institutes of the Christian Religion* is marked by all the clear-cut dogmatism of the man, aged twenty-eight, who wrote it.

Unlike those of Luther, Calvin's political principles emerge clear. The first is the aversion of the great disciplinarian, pessimist about sinful human nature, from anarchy. More emphatically than the Church Fathers, he maintains that there must be rule—coercive rule and secular rule. The Fathers were doubtful whether private property or slavery or even dominion of man over man was "according to nature." But if the original nature of man is evil the difficulty is removed. The correction of sin is not incidental but natural to human life. Paradise was finally Lost long ago. There must be government.

There are (and here Calvin displays himself a strict traditionalist) two separate powers—spiritual, seeking its ultimate ends in salvation and imposing spiritual penalties; and secular. Salvation is not membership by sacraments of the society of the Church and communion of saints past, present and to come. It is a more miraculous result of special divine interposition by grace with the individual, inscrutable, not to be prognosticated or controlled, issuing in life, not only of eternal value but of everlasting duration. Of these two powers the Church, as Augustine said, is superior. After the flunkeyism of the minor, civil-minded reformers and even after the pathetic tragedy of Luther, it is refreshing to turn back to this masterful doctrine with its still nervous determination to control the world. The business of the State is to protect religion—Calvin asserts it as strongly as any Papalist—and to enforce Christian morality.

As touching this civil order Calvin, even more than Melanchthon, is a natural oligarch (or aristocrat), not intolerant of an admixture of democracy although close to sedition, and looking to the city-states

* *Cf.* p. 167.

(Geneva, Basle, Strasbourg) for his model. Monarchy, however, least pleasing to mere men, has the commendation of God. Against democratic anarchy, Calvin insists on the duty of passive obedience—to the princes in their various realms, whatever the character of those princes. He includes in his condemnation religious anarchists with an "inner light." "Persons," he writes, "who, abandoning the Scripture, imagine to themselves some other way of approaching God, must be considered as not so much misled by error as actuated by frenzy." The unaided reason of man would have only produced carnal and foolish things. Princedoms exist because God so wills it. The servile quality of primitive Christianity reappears.

> It is a vain occupation of private men to dispute about the best kind of constitution . . . *spiritual liberty may very well consist with civil servitude.* . . . Since the insolence of the wicked is so great, and their iniquity so obstinate that it can scarcely be restrained by all the severity of the laws, what may we expect they would do, if they found themselves at liberty to perpetrate crimes with impunity, whose outrages even the arm of power cannot altogether prevent. . . . *To hurt* and *to destroy* are incompatible with the character of the faithful: but to avenge the afflictions of the righteous at the command of God, is neither to hurt nor to destroy. . . . How did David, who discovered such humanity all his life-time, in his last moments bequeath such a cruel injunction to his son respecting Joab; "Let not his hoary head go down to the grave in peace:" and respecting Shimei; "His hoar head bring down to the grave with blood." But Moses and David, in executing the vengeance committed to them by God, in this severity *sanctified their hands,* which had been defiled by their former lenity.

The native cruelty of idealism again displays itself. Calvin's "God" is the Chief Pardoner exempting men from the dictates of the moral law of their own unbaptized and unsophisticated natures. Calvin continues:

> Wherefore, if we are cruelly vexed by an inhuman Prince or robbed and plundered by one prodigal or avaricious or despised and left without protection by one negligent: or even if we are afflicted for the Name of God by one sacrilegious and unbelieving, let us first of all remember those our own offences against God which doubtless are chastised by these plagues. And secondly let us consider that it is not for us to remedy these evils; for us it remains only to implore the aid of God, in whose hands are the hearts of kings and charges of kingdoms.

God sometimes aided by a plague himself, as of Pharaoh, or by a foreign war.

However, as against the unrighteous, Calvin is not to be supposed to mean that non-resistance to a prince is the same as obedience to ungodly demands. In Geneva itself under Calvin, after 1542—and in a fashion somewhat inconsistent with Calvin's own separation of the powers—the ecclesiastical Venerable Company (composed of professors of theology and ministers) and the Consistory, which united powers ecclesiastical and temporal, dominated the secular councils. Whereas the Catholic Church had offered a centralized discipline, Calvinism or Presbyterianism (the "invisible Church" apart) could only offer an aggregate of churches and presbyteries within the respective cities and states. The Church was atomized. Nevertheless Geneva under Calvin's own rule constituted a model. The true faith was upheld and, to that end, the heretic Calvin, with his doctrine of justification, not by faith *also, caritate formata* ("formed by charity,") but by faith *alone*, by personal intervention procured the burning of the Unitarian heretic Servetus, in 1553, to the greater damnation of heresy. A monastic discipline was enforced on the model republic so that Calvin's own daughter was disciplined for immorality. Blasphemy was punishable by burning. The styles of clothes and the details of cohabitation in matrimony were alike regulated. Pinchbeck Geneva claimed all the authoritarianism of Rome in order to impose the rigid regulation of a Carthusian priory upon the common laymen.

Outside Geneva and its Model Church of the Saints, Calvin's writ could run in no such fashion. But it was still true that ungodly commands were not to be obeyed, although active resistance to a prince was resistance to God until God removed him (as was resistance to a husband by a wife). There could be no question of a conditional contract limiting obedience. Who argues thus, *il argueroit perversement*—"he would argue perversely."

> But to the obedience which we have shown to be due to the authority of governors, it is always necessary to make one exception, and this is entitled to our first attention, that it do not seduce us from obedience to Him, to Whose will the desires of all kings ought to be subject, to Whose decrees all their commands ought to yield. And indeed how preposterous it would be for us, with a view to satisfy men, to incur the displeasure of Him on Whose account we yield obedience to men.

We must suffer rather than deviate from piety. What then shall determine when a law is unrighteous? The Word of God. And who shall interpret it? It is always clear, and it is damnable to deny this. (The point is important. Servetus died for a Left-wing deviation about this.) Who then knows what is its clear meaning? Briefly, the Calvinist professors of theology. Calvin knew personally all about the Will and

Word. Like Chillingworth, later, Calvin was prepared to assert that "the Bible is the only religion of Protestants"; and, like a humble follower, one Gabriel Powel, that their doctrines are "the only word of God."

The superiority of the Kirk to the king has conclusions, despite all talk of non-resistance, not dissimilar from those in the Catholic Church, when the professors of theology felt themselves strong enough. Not unnaturally James VI of Scotland left for England, as James I, never to return, after the unmannerly treatment from the ministers of the Kirk, as for example from Andrew Melville, with his comment to his king—"Ye are but God's silly vassal." New presbyter was but old priest writ large.

Should then a Catholic magistrate (or Mary Stuart) persecute for his or her true faith? Certainly not, says Calvin.

> God does not command us to maintain any religion, but that only which He hath ordained with His own mouth. . . . He condemns the presumption of all those who go about to defend with fire and bloodshed a religion framed to fit the appetites of men.

Shall then Protestants not persecute? God forbid. A Scottish observer to the Long Parliament writes back home: "They have here a strange monster called toleration." In the Scottish Solemn League and Covenant (1638) it is declared:

> That we shall in like manner . . . endeavour the extirpation of Popery, prelacy, superstition, heresy . . . lest we partake in other men's sins, and thereby be in danger to receive of their plagues; and that the Lord may be one and His name one in the three kingdoms.

At least on one matter, ecclesiastical-minded and civil-minded reformers could agree—the future of the heathen (*e.g.*, Plato and Aristotle):

> Works done before the grace of Christ, and the inspiration of his Spirit, are not pleasant to God . . . yea rather, for that they are not done as God hath willed and commanded them to be done, we doubt not but that they have the nature of sin. (Article XIII of the Church of England.)

The obsessive meditation on death which overshadowed the Dark Ages had lifted with the Renaissance. It descends again as a religious pall with the renewed emphasis on Original Sin and man's utter corruption.

Protestantism has come to stay and to play a role of importance for three centuries. If it is scarcely a dominant role, this is because the ideological crusade—*either* Protestant *or* Catholic: Geneva black or cardinal red—is seldom permitted to take sole charge of the draughtboard of history. Statesmen trained in the *Politique* tradition cut across it. Elizabeth gives assistance to a Catholic France; Cromwell refuses it to a Protestant Holland. Above all, Cardinal de Richelieu supports the German Protestants in order to check the encirclement of France by the House of Habsburg.

The effect of the specifically Protestant doctrine of Justification by Faith, condemned as heresy like that of Arius by the sixteenth-century Catholic General Council of Trent (1545–1563), we shall be able to judge when we come to the origins of European Liberalism. Basically, like the original Pauline doctrine, it was extra-rational and deeply anti-rationalist. The Council maintained that the saved "grew in righteousness, *cooperante fide bonis operibus* (faith co-operating with good works) and are in a greater degree justified." In brief, Catholicism held fast to the social notion. Like Luther and like Augustine, pursued remorselessly by a haunting sense of sin and only hoping to escape from the Just Judge by grace, the Protestants were religious individualists. The elect were aristocrats, not partners of any worldly society or even of an earthly, centralized Church. They were saved by, as it were, a gift or talent (not theirs by work or merit) capriciously bestowed by Divine Grace transcending society and vindicating the Elect. God held private intercourse with each several, immortalized individual—immortal in his own right, and not by right of society. The Individual, needing no priest, was sanctified. The Roman-Hellenic idea of the priority of society to the actual individual, secularly ended by Feudalism, was spiritually ended by Protestantism. The Ego has come into its own.

READING

N. Machiavelli: *The Prince*, trans. W. K. Marriott, Chaps. VIII, XV–XIX, XXVI.

BIBLIOGRAPHICAL NOTE

*N. Machiavelli: *Discourses on the First Decade of T. Livius*, trans. Thomson, 1883.
J. W. Allen: *Political Thought in the Sixteenth Century*, 1928.
*J. Burckhardt: *The Civilization of the Renaissance in Italy*, trans. Middlemore, *n.d.*

Chapter VIII

Thomas Hobbes

1

IN THE Bodleian Library, the University library, at Oxford, hang two pictures of the Restoration period, at first glance almost indistinguishable. They are pictures of Charles I of England, and of Christ. Such a comparison did not shock the Cavalier mind any more than it would have shocked the mind of a Byzantine churchman. As has been explained, the scholasticism of St. Thomas shared much of the rationalism of the earlier Greek philosophy. Duns Scotus had emphasized the element of will—inscrutable will in a God transcending human intelligence. The Reformers, by the doctrine of grace without pretence of human merit, had tended to stress the same notion—of the Will of a Personal God, monarch of the universe, who had revealed this final and unchangeable will in Sacred Texts. It was but a short step to assert—and there was an established Patristic tradition for asserting—that kings were like God. Calvin quoted the text "I have said, Ye are gods" (*Ps.* lxxxii, 6, *cf. Exod.* xxii, 28) to that effect—although it rests on a play on the Hebrew word *elohim* which may be "gods" or "judges." Even if kings in their morals scarcely resembled God, nevertheless "all authority is from on high"; and they ruled by right divine. Nor would the civil-minded churchmen accept the restrictions of Isidore and Bracton and of the Papalists' corollary that what was by the Church declared *not* to be from on High was *not* authority.

Even Luther's Passive Resistance was too strong meat for some ecclesiastical stomachs. Passive Obedience would alone suffice. Some such as Mainwaring, the Caroline divine, carried the exaltation of monarchy to a point that earned rebuke from a Parliament still conscious of its mediaeval rights and of liberties dating from that age of Feudalism that had preceded the New Monarchies. Clearer even than such theorists of the fusion of national State and Church (anticipators of Dr. Arnold of Rugby) as Archbishop Laud in his claims for kings, as partners in the alliance of Church and State, bishop and "godly prince," is a writer who has the advantage of being a king himself.

James I, of England, and VI, of Scotland (1566–1625) wrote, while still in Scotland, his *Trew Law of Free Monarchy or the Reciprock and Mutuall dutie betwixt a free king and his natural subjects*. Long ago, in the days of the Emperor Nerva, it had been observed that it was better to have a ruler who permitted nothing than one who permitted everything. This is the thesis of James when dealing with the argument that subjects must have some recourse against tyranny. He recedes from the liberal attitude of St. Thomas on the ground that anything is better than anarchy. It must be recalled that James Stuart wrote from bitter experience, not only of the murderous, nation-weakening feuds of the Scottish clans, but of the treatment of his mother, Mary, Queen of Scots, and of his own bondage to the Presbyterian divines and nobles—not least his tutor, George Buchanan. If there were a contract between ruler and ruled, not one party to the case but (no, not the Pope—for Protestants) God in Heaven alone could be the umpire. Paul himself had said that all authority was from above. Briefly, the True Law was that only monarchs were free. The "Reciprock Dutie" of king and subject was for the one to wield godly rule and for the other to obey.

The *Basilikon Doron*, or "Kingly Gift" intended for his elder son, Henry (who died before accession), shows yet more clearly, because in a fashion less hampered by argumentation, the views of the pompous monarch of whom the witty Henry IV, of France and Navarre, observed that he was "the wisest fool in Christendom." It will be found among his works, along with studies on "Demonologie" and on the Vice of Tobacco, which shocked his moral conscience. It begins with a brief poem to his heir, composed by the royal hand (the Stuarts ran to the arts):

> God gives not kings the stile of Gods in vaine
> For on his Throne his Sceptre do they swey.

James gives various pieces of personal advice to Henry: the duty of training his talent (*ingenium*) or—as James puts it—"to exercise his engine." The duty of being fitly clothed:

> Be also moderate in your raiment, neither over superfluous, like a deboshed waster; nor yet ever base, like a miserable wretch . . . not over lightly like a candie soldier [chocolate soldier] or a vain young courtier, nor over gravely like a minister. . . . [Yet] a king is not mere *laicus*.

In selecting his wife, he will consider well before he picks on wealth or beauty; "what can all these worldly respects avail, when a man shall find himself coupled with a devil to be one flesh with him."

Most significant, however, is his political advice about the estates of his realm. He has no high opinion of any of them. The Scottish merchants "buy for us the worst wares and sell them at the dearest prices." The nobility were moved by a "fectlesse arrogant conceit of their greatness and power; drinking in with their very nourish-milke that their honor stood in committing three points of iniquitie, to thrall by oppression, the meaner sort that dwelleth neare them, to their service and following, although they hold nothing of them;" and "maintenance" in courts of justice; "and (without respect to God, king or commonweale) to bang it out bravely, hee and all his kinne against him and all his."

Above all, he warns him about the Presbyterian ministers:

> Some of them would sometimes snapper out well grossly with the trewth of their intentions, informing the people that all kings and princes were natural enemies to the libertie of the Church. . . . Take heade therefore (my sonne) to such Puritans, verie Pests in the Church and Common-weale, whom no deserts can oblige, neither oathes nor promises bind, breathing nothing but sedition and calumnies, aspiring without measure, railing without reason, and making their oune imaginations (without any warrant of the Word) the square of their conscience.

It was of a piece with this that James should declare, at the Hampton Court Anglican Conference, in 1604: "No bishop, no king"; and, in 1616, "It is atheism and blasphemy to dispute what God can do . . . so it is presumption and high contempt in a subject to dispute what a king can do, or say that a king cannot do this or that." Subjects "rest in that which is the king's revealed will in his law." "Kings," James said to Parliament in 1610,

> are also compared to fathers of families: for a king is truly *parens patriae,* the politic father of his people. And, lastly, *kings are compared to the head of this microcosm of the body of man* . . . do not meddle with the main points of government: that is my craft: *tractent fabrilia fabri;* to meddle with that, were to lesson me.

James further compares himself to an old stork, and his subjects to the pious young in the nest.

The view of the metaphysical James was that which Shakespeare ascribes rightly enough, to Richard II, son-in-law of the Roman Emperor, Wenceslaus of Bohemia [then in the Reich]. Richard's head was full of imperial notions.

> Not all the water in the rough rude sea
> Can wash the balm from an anointed king;
> The breath of worldly men cannot depose
> The deputy elected by the Lord.

It is desirable here to call attention to a book of no especial importance at the time, published in 1680, after the author's death, but made famous as the object of that attack by Locke which established the power of Whiggery and of Liberalism—the *Patriarcha* of Sir Robert Filmer (died 1653). His *Observations Concerning the Originall of Government*, less well known, is abler. Filmer, with his fantastic comments on Adam the first father and Nimrod the first king, can be spitted on the sword of Locke's argument, on the ground that he traces the divine right to rule of James I by primogeniture from Adam and his elder son. Actually all that the encumbered Filmer is seeking to do is to assert that from the beginning, men were not equal, but the elder ruled the younger. Filmer has, moreover, the singular merit for his time of being, as it were, an anthropologist, although born out of due season. He asserts that human society like animal is natural, but naturally unequal; that authority originates from the family relation; that rule is customary; and that traditional custom, not deliberate and rational consent, is the basis of rule; that *authority always has lain and should lie in the hands of less than all, and here, among those in control, a majority can make out no better claim than a few.* "If it be tyranny for one man to govern arbitrarily, why should it not be far greater tyranny for a multitude of men [*e.g.*, a 'sovereign' Parliament] to govern without being accountable or bound by [traditional or constitutional] laws?" The pardoning power and equity are proofs that men—the executive—are and should be above laws. Filmer, although more inclined to use "natural reason" and slightly less heavily armed with proof texts than his sectarian contemporaries, yet actually has significance by his attempt, in vain, to turn the thought of the age from abstract principles to observation of human history, although in a less cynical fashion than the Italian school.

It is scarcely possible to cap a doctrine of kingship so high as that of James I. However, it was attempted in France, as she emerged from the wars of the Ligue and Fronde. Fénélon was to instruct the young Louis XIV, by his *Télémaque* (1699) in those moral checks on absolutism dear to the Catholic tradition; but the Gallican bishops, led by

Bossuet of Meaux, piled adjective on adjective in praise of the sacred character of the Most Christian Kings, if not precisely of their flagrant moral lapses. (After all, Louis XV was not guilty of the offence of marrying Mmes. de Pompadour or du Barry.) The general view, however, is adequately expressed earlier (in 1625) by the then Bishop of Chartres:

> Kings are ordained by God, and not only they are so ordained, but also they are gods themselves . . . not in essence but by participation, not by nature but by grace.

In the following century, in 1770, Louis XV of France was to declare: "We hold our crown of God alone: the right to make laws appertains to us without dependence upon or share with another." Yet a century later the theme that crowns were held by inheritance and divine right was maintained by the Kaiser William II in a speech at Königsberg. It will be noted that the Continental doctrine of divine right, subject to certain traditional restrictions of Catholic theory, tends to pass over to Absolutism in a fashion that is not, for historical reasons, true of English theory.

As touching British theory a caution, of some subtlety but some importance, is required. We have stressed the later scholastic and Protestant notion of super- or ir-rational, inscrutable Divine Will. But the more orthodox Catholic doctrine, which passed over into Anglicanism, emphasized the notion of rational Law. We thus find the Caroline writers following the tradition of John of Salisbury who had clearly subordinated the "divine right" of rulers to the divine law of a rational God. There is a division in their minds, not clear but firm, between rule by divine right and arbitrary rule—which was indeed its perversion or antithesis. "I was never such a fool," declares Laud, Archbishop of Canterbury, "as to embrace arbitrary government." What their doctrine did exclude is a human contractual theory of authority.

More difficult is it to say (and what emerges is that the thought of these writers before the English Civil War was *not* clear) whether the *rational and natural law* of which Bishop Andrews talked included the allegedly historical, but vague, "*fundamental constitutional law*" of England. If not—and Laud asked, against Coke, whether such a law, superior to the King, existed—then was this undoubted subordination to law to be understood as a subordination of the King's divine right to the *actual laws* and legislature of England? The King, argued Sir Robert Berkeley in the Hampden case (1637–1638), has *iura summae* *majestatis* ("sovereign rights"), but his government is to be *secundum leges regni*—"according to the laws of the realm." (These transient laws, however, *e.g.*, Field held, must be "profitable and beneficial to the society of men to whom they are presented.") This subordination Filmer denied; but it is noteworthy that a practical statesman such as Laud, in the context of English local constitutional custom, did not deny it. At the most an emergency power is claimed for the king as ruler. So far the Parliamentarian fiction of an English parliamentary constitution established in the fifteenth century, in the style sketched by Fortescue, was not challenged, at least by Laud, on Tudor precedents. The real ground, however, of the quarrel with Laud, the High Churchman, was a different one. As much as John Robinson, the Congregationalist, Laud would have agreed that there are no things indifferent or irrelevant for religion. Laud drew the conclusion that "the Commonwealth can have no blessed and happy being but by the Church"—*i.e.*, the totalitarian conclusion of the need for national, cultural homogeneity which is the issue in our own days.*

Francis Bacon (1561–1626), Lord Verulam, Lord Chancellor of England, expelled from that post for taking bribes, philosopher and essayist, found it expedient to support the claims of King James I. The king's judges, he declared, were lions but lions under the throne. He probably excused himself in the name of an efficiency which counselled support of a central authority, against the popular relics of mediaeval confusion. The justice, for example, of the Star Chamber was quick and cheap. His comment on tyrants by *coup d'état* was certainly caustic enough: "He doth like the ape that, the higher he clymbes, the more he shewes," etc. Perhaps Bacon had studied Machiavelli not wisely but too well—of whom he records, "We render thanks to Machiavelli and writers of that sort, who openly and without hypocrisy declare how men are accustomed to act, not merely how they ought to act." It is true, as Bacon confesses, that the sciences are "far from being equal to the complexity of human affairs." It is presumably from Machiavelli that he learned the maxim, which he says was wrongly condemned by "some of the Schoole-men," that "there is no Question but a just Fear of an Imminent danger, though there be no Blow given, is a lawfull Cause of a Warre." The greatest protagonist, however (since his namesake, thirteenth-century Roger

* Nevertheless Laud's conclusion, like Hooker's, is rather churchly [*vide* p. 164] than secular-totalitarian, although like its rival in stressing cultural homogeneity. *Cf.* Richard Hooker: "with us *one society is both Church and commonwealth*"—and note the order of priority.

Bacon), of the empirical method firmly directs our attention to the objective study of political phenomena, and away from the theological bombast and incantations which tended to serve as the political principles of his age. It is, however, his contemporary, Thomas Fitzherbert, in 1606, who specifically deplores as avoidable, "the imperfection of all *political science*"—not that Fitzherbert, with his plea for true religion, is any politicist or social scientist.

In passing, Bacon's comment, which aligns him not only with Aristotle and the Canonists but also with Machiavelli against a nascent capitalist individualism, is worth note:

> Above all things good policy is to be used, that the treasures and monies in a State be not gathered into few hands. For otherwise a State may have a great stock and yet starve; and money is like muck, not good except it be spread.

2

THOMAS HOBBES (1588–1679), of Malmesbury, was Francis Bacon's secretary. From that position he passed on to be tutor to the member of the Cavendish family who later became second Earl of Devonshire. He enjoyed the patronage of these Earls until his death. He was, for a while, mathematical tutor to Charles II, when in Paris, and perhaps encouraged in that intelligent monarch interests that resulted in the foundation of the Royal Society.

The son of the Reformed parson of Westport, in Wiltshire, whose chief reputation was for "ignorance and clownery" and who subsequently disappeared under a cloud, Thomas Hobbes proceeded to Oxford University, a stagnant institution, where no little of his time in those days of the Explorers, not spent in bird catching, was occupied in "gaping on mappes." A little later, a friend of Ben Jonson's, he was "much addicted to musique and practised on the base-violl." However, it was not until 1610 that he first saw the great world when he went on Continental tour with his pupil. These tours—there were several—brought him into touch with the best minds in Paris and even with Galileo, in Florence. That, however, of 1640 had another incentive than learning. His "little treatise" of 1640, *Elements of Law Natural and Politic*, had raised a storm; the Long Parliament was about to assemble; and, the circumstances well considered, Hobbes (in the words of his own verse autobiography),

> Stocked with five hundred pounds of Coin,
> Did desert or leave [his] native shore.

He was, however, also one of the first of those to come back, in 1651, since demonstrably the principles of *Leviathan* (1650–1651) were not inconsistent in any fashion with the dictatorship of Oliver Cromwell. He could even pride himself on having retained "a thousand gentlemen in conscientious loyalty to the government of the day." Before he left Paris his "realistic" views had already made him intensely unpopular with the legitimist and church-minded Cavaliers. As he remarks, "then I began to ruminate on Dorislaus' and Ascham's fate"—the assassinated ambassadors of the Protectorate. Having ruminated, he quit Paris. The graver problem arose when the Restoration came. His great book, *Leviathan*, presented to Charles II, after his return from the battle of Worcester, by his old tutor, could be squared with the Protectorate. But how to square himself with the Restoration? Hobbes had no option but to write a new book, *Behemoth*, attacking the Long Parliament. Charles II forbade (until 1679) its publication. Hobbes' defence of Monarchy was all too embarrassing. The tolerance, however, of that monarch availed more. Hobbes, after publishing, in 1662, *Considerations on the Reputation, Loyalty, Manners and Religion of Mr. Thomas Hobbes*, and engaging in mathematical controversy, solaced his declining years with translations, including one of Homer. He played a game of tennis at the age of seventy-five; was accustomed to sing aloud for his health's sake; and died, in full possession of all his faculties, aged eighty-nine. Aubrey, the biographer, tells us that in the later years, he was bald and his greatest trouble was to "keepe off the flies from pitching on the baldnes." He adds that Thomas Hobbes "had a good eie"; and that, when stirred by discourse, "their shone as it were a bright live-coale within it."

Among his earliest work had been a translation of Thucydides, of whom he gleefully (if falsely) writes:

> He says democracy's a foolish thing,
> Than a Republic better is one king.

Hobbes was perhaps not a poet, although not from lack of perspiration since he translated Euripides' *Medea* into Latin verse at the age of fourteen; but he was one of the greatest of English stylists. It is his misfortune as a philosopher and has led to much misunderstanding and speculation among learned and literal-minded, rather than literary-minded, commentators. It is a matter for reflection that Hobbes and Plato are the only philosophers who have been lucid and good stylists—the rest have preferred to approximate to the symbols and letters of algebra, in their passion for accuracy, rather than to *belles-lettres* in any pursuit after a popular and aphrodisiac lucidity. Rational philosophy is the sworn enemy of pleasant imagination as is sacred love the enemy of profane.

During these later years he was able to attack his *bêtes noires*, the Puritans, the Churchmen, the Jesuits, the universities and the Common lawyers. All these men were sowers of anarchy, each in his several way challenging the final authority of the sovereign. The Puritans believed themselves to be guided by a private revelation which took precedence of man-made law. Even Cromwell's son-in-law, General Ireton, had been tried when he found individuals who had private revelations about which way the army should march or whether taxes should be paid or not. Hobbes complains that "every boy or wench thought he spoke with God Almighty." Hobbes himself had been near death from illness (and had then insisted that Bishop Cosin, of Durham, should pray over him strictly according to the formula as by law established, exclaiming to officious clerics, "let me alone or else I will detect all your cheates from Aaron to yourselves"). He notes an instance of prophecy by a pious Puritan. "Nor do I much wonder that a young woman of clear memory, hourely expecting death, should bee more devout than at other times. 'T was my own case."

The Churchmen forget that "neither is a clergy essential to a commonwealth. . . . There is no nation in the world whose religion is not established and receives its authority from the laws of that nation. . . . If he, that commands me to do that which is sin, is right lord over me, I sin not." (The priesthood, it should be added, must be more scrupulous, and is, indeed, paid to undergo martyrdom.) As for the Calvinists and the Jesuits, they both brew sedition with their pretence of a Church above the [State's] law. "Calvin looketh asquint in the same fashion that Bellarmin doeth."

The universities, resurrecting the writings of the Greeks and Romans that praise tyrannicide, introduce the wooden horse of Troy and hatch treason. There may be a case for a rival institution in London. "Mr. Hobbes will instruct the young men of Gresham College [London] in mechanics, if they will ask him," and deal civilly with him. "In the meantime Divinity may go on at Oxford and Cambridge to furnish the pulpit with men to cry down the civil power."

The Common Law men, however, the very priests as they should be of the temporal power, are the chief stone of offence, with their talk of above all men, *i.e.*, the sovereign, being the law. And, above all, Coke. Who should interpret this law, if not men? And, if men, why the judges and not the sovereign? In the *Dialogue on the Common*

Laws (1667, pub. 1681), Hobbes remarks of Sir Edward Coke's *Institutes:* "Truly I never read weaker reasoning." Proof texts from inspired Writ were the order of the day; but the irrelevances of the proof texts nauseate Hobbes, for Coke "meant none of this but intended (his hand being in) to shew his reading or his chaplain's in the Bible." "But you know that in other places [Coke] makes the common law and the law of reason to be all one; as indeed they are. Why, by it is meant the king's reason." Coke, on the other hand, regarded himself as based on the "fundamental law" of Magna Carta, of whom a wit has remarked that he was, by his interpretations, "the inventor."

Hobbes's method as a political thinker merits attention. It is not to be inferred that his writings are mere *livres de circonstance.* His philosophy is expounded in a series of works (issuing from the *First Principles* of ?1630) that fit into a strictly logical order, although Hobbes himself deplores, in his letters, that he was compelled to publish them in the reverse chronological order. He excuses himself on the ground that the basic political principles are, anyhow, sufficiently well known from direct experience—as Burton, in his *Anatomy of Melancholy* (1621), also held. There are "two maxims of human nature"—the "concupiscible part, which desires to appropriate to itself the use of those things in which all others have a joint interest; The other proceeding from the rational, which teaches every man to fly a contra-natural dissolution [fear of death] as the greatest mischief that can arrive to nature." These writings of Hobbes are the *De Cive* (1642: or *Philosophical Rudiments Concerning Government,* 1651, the English version); *De Homine* (1658: or *Human Nature,* 1650); and *De Corpore* (1655). The first two are anticipated in the *Elements of Law* of 1640.

The temper of the age was mathematical. Just as the fifteenth century had been dedicated to the humanities, so the seventeenth century was overwhelmed by a sense of the significance of mathematics as an instrument of discovery and invention. Tycho Brahe (died 1601) had completed his great work on astronomy. It was the age of Galileo (died 1643), Torricelli, Harvey and Gassendi. Descartes (died 1650) was developing that legacy of Arabian civilization, algebra. Symbolic logic, Mathematics, in this age played the role that syllogistic logic had played in the thirteenth century. Hobbes records his coming across his first book of geometry almost as though it had been a religious conversion. "By God, is it possible?" he exclaimed of the Forty-seventh Proposition—and found it was not only possible but certain. There seemed to be nothing that, by aid of mathematic precision, could not be reduced to rule and reason. Here then, although equally concerned with *things*, Hobbes departs from the empiricism and "psychologism" of his master, Bacon. As political scientist, he maintained that what he wrote he "demonstrated." The influence of Bacon, however, must not be underrated. Dogma about human "moral characteristics," in the style of Theophrastus and Bacon and Burton, makes a basis for the hypotheses of Hobbes's science. In so far as Hobbes falls into the line of the English tradition in philosophy, he owes this to the influence of Bacon.

> Weighing the justice of these things you are about, not by the persuasion and advice of private men, but by the laws of the realm, you will no longer suffer ambitious men through the streams of your blood to wade to their own power; that you will esteem it better to enjoy yourselves in the present state, though not perhaps the best, than *by waging war endeavour to procure a reformation for other men in another age*, yourselves in the meantime either killed or consumed by age. . . . For though I have endeavoured, by arguments in my tenth chapter [*Concerning Government*], to gain a belief in men, that monarchy is the most commodious government; which *one thing alone I confess in this whole book not to be demonstrated*, but only probably stated; yet everywhere I expressly say, that in all kind of government whatsoever there ought to be a supreme and equal power . . . they are not so much spoken for the maintenance of parties as the establishment of peace, and by one whose just grief for the present calamities of his country may very charitably be allowed some liberty.

Elsewhere, Hobbes produces the important observation that political science

> consisteth in certain rules, as doth Arithmetique and Geometry, not (as Tennis-play) in practice only. . . .
>
> From the principal parts of Nature, Reason and Passion, have proceeded two kinds of learning, mathematical and dogmatical. . . . *To reduce this* [political] *doctrine to the rules and infallibility of reason, there is no way, but, first, put such principles down for a foundation, as passion, not mistrusting, may not seek to displace;* and afterwards to build thereon the truth of cases in the law of nature (which hitherto hath been built in the air) by degrees, till the whole have been impregnable.

It will be noted that Hobbes's method is placed by himself in direct antithesis to what he calls the "dogmatic." "The immediate cause . . . of indocility, is prejudice; and of prejudice, false opinion of our knowledge." He goes so far as to out-Jefferson Jefferson and out-Jackson Jackson with the radical assertion that aristocrats cannot claim to rule from superiority of knowledge concerning social values, since "*right reason is non-existent.*" It will be noted that his radical scepticism, on which he bases in part his equalitarianism, attempts to torpedo the whole Hellenic aristocratic tradition of the right to rule of the more enlightened, a philosopher caste—and is not followed by Milton or indeed by Locke. It is not a necessary hypothesis of the Liberal tradition. Actually he is guilty of no more than of the a priori argumentation of the Schoolmen whom he criticized, and of substituting a tidy logical system of materialism for that empirical use of hypothesis which is the instrument of scientific illumination.

Hobbes was a psychologist, perhaps the first observational psychologist. Very properly and significantly he bases his politics on his psychology. But his psychological theory is permeated with the passionate controversies of the times. His misfortune is that he becomes the dogmatist—the counsel for the defence—of his own psychologico-moral hypotheses, instead of regarding them with detachment. And they happen to be crude, inadequate and misleading. In the issue of free will and determinism, he is a militant determinist, thinking of the "motions of the mind," after the plan of the mechanics of Descartes, as rather like balls on a billiard table striking each other on impulse from a cue. In his famous controversy with Bishop Bramhall, later Archbishop of Armagh, he writes (with select malice):

> He the Schools followed, I made use of sense,
> Whether at God's or our own choice we will.

Human liberty "doth not consist in determining itself but in doing what the will is determined unto . . . no man can determine his own will, for the will is appetite."

Hobbes revives the atomic materialism of Democritus and, in a crude form, the moral philosophy of Epicurus, discussing the latter and Lucretius by name, although cautiously. (For Luther, any rationalist, and even Erasmus, had been an Epicurean.) Hobbes, for obvious reasons, was naturally concerned to deny for himself the damning charge of materialism, as atheistic, although he maintains ambiguously that God has "the being of a spirit, not a spright, an infinitely fine spirit and withal intelligent," corporeal, extended—and comparable, as Hobbes says, to a mineral water that can change ordinary water to white where no whiteness was before.

Hobbes was a "sensationalist," who had hypotheses about the fundamental springs of human action. These are the axioms of his psychological mechanics. The fundamental sensations are pain that repels and pleasure that attracts. More permanently, in memory, the basic sensations are fear and desire for power (including power to obtain particular pleasures, sensual and non-sensual). As the devil said in the Book of Job, "skin for skin, yea, all that a man hath will he give for his life." Stated yet again, they are fear of violent death (which is the sobering and rational guide, leading men to attend to *facts*) and vanity or "vaine-glory" (which puffs men up with wishful thinking and *imagination*). Or it is the claim to life and limb against the claim to triumph over all comers—to boast.

> The object of man's desire is . . . to assure for ever the way of his future desire. . . . So that in the first place, I put for a generall inclination of all mankind, a perpetuall and restless desire of Power after power, that ceaseth onely in Death. (*Leviathan*, xi.)
>
> Good is to everything that which hath power to attract it . . . agrees well with Aristotle who defines Good to be that to which all things are moved, which hath been metaphorically taken but is properly true. (*First Principles.*)

Hobbes's doctrine of law, crime and punishment directly depends upon his atomism and mechanistic theory of the nervous system. Men may be deterred from those acts of crime to which their determined impulses force them if greater weights of punishment be, as it were, hung on the other side as deterrents. The law must have the sanction of a sovereign and absolute power capable of imposing decisive and unquestionable deterrents. "The cause of appetite and fear is the cause also of our will: but the propounding of rewards and punishments is the cause of our appetite."

Hobbes necessarily, on the assumptions of his psychology of self-defence and self-assertion, is an individualist. Rightly, he bases politics on psychology—but much of his bad political philosophy is due to his bad psychology (an error in which, as we shall see, he is not alone among political philosophers). It is necessary to bear in mind how fundamental is this individualism, since in the *Leviathan* (and indeed in the very title) Hobbes uses for his own ends the metaphors of a body politic and of the political organism—already in use in pamphlets of the period (and, *e.g.*, in the writings of Hooker and James I) and deriving from the Church Fathers and St. Paul or from Livy's fable of Menenius Agrippa. Indeed, the famous frontispiece of the *Leviathan* displays the body politic, compounded of human beings as corpuscles, wielding in either hand sceptre and bishop's crook and crowned with the head of (in later editions) Charles II. Hobbes, as we shall see later, is always clever at using any argument that tells in his favour.

Hobbes's method, then, is logical, aspiring to mathematical precision, deliberately schematic, and with an argument which bases his sociology on psychology, his psychology on physics, and his physics on metaphysics. We must not, however, overlook the pressure of historical factors on his political theory—and this not only in the sense of an opportunism which made him keep an eye in writing on his personal career. (Not that Hobbes can be accused of being a time-server; he was all too liable to offend his own party for that.) But his political theory is biased by a double experience of the break-down of order, in the England of the Civil War and in the France of the Fronde (1648–1652), as well as by experience of such outstanding men as Richelieu, Mazarin and Cromwell. And, as touching his later writings, they have background in the reflection that the best comment upon the Puritan Revolution was the demand for the Restoration.

3

Hobbes's political science—and with him, as with Machiavelli, we are entitled to use this term since his concern is with means, not values—is built up, however crassly, in an endeavor to answer a simple question. How shall man, being selfish, be saved from anarchy? Aristotle had said that man, of all animals, had the greatest capacity for evil. Hobbes is prepared to work on the basis of the great Stagirite—of man as a subject of natural history. Sir Robert Filmer had stumbled, half unwittingly, on considerations of anthropology and psychology that could have eased Hobbes's task. But he chooses to discard these props.

Hobbes accepts (for which he is severely chided by Filmer) the religious thesis, also expressed by the Levellers, of the natural equality of man—not, however, on any religious basis, but just because brawn plus wit in all men about balanced out as equal, or at least as of unpredictable inequality, when it came to a fight, man to man, with knives in hand. "I know that Aristotle . . . for a foundation of his philosophy maketh men by nature, some more worthy to command, meaning the wiser sort such as he thought himself to be for his philosophy; others to serve." But Hobbes had a low opinion of Aristotle. In a state of nature, he asserts (wrongly—Cicero could have put him right), the condition of man is "solitary, short, brutish and nasty." It is a condition wherein *homo homini lupus*—"man is to man a wolf." A Lord Shaftesbury was not yet forthcoming to point out that even wolves have a herd instinct. After all, urges Hobbes with astounding cogency, are not States still in a condition of nature to each other—

"in the posture of gladiators?" Hobbes, indeed, has seized the whole of a half-truth. How, from such disorder, to produce order? There is the heroic problem.

Authority is the child of fear. Progress emerges from men's terrors. The state of nature is intolerable in which a man must watch all night against his enemies. He, therefore, is driven and bludgeoned into a bargain: he will surrender some of his chances of getting the better of his fellow—his "fist-rights" or, if one will, natural rights—if his fellow will do the same and join with him in mutual defence.

The social contract, as collective security, emerges from men's fears. The sanction of this contract is terror—"the arrow that flies by day." Hobbes, here, with characteristic effrontery, again takes for his own use a weapon of his opponents—for Contract, as we shall see,* is a choice weapon of the opponents of absolute monarchy. The contract is, moreover, irrevocable. A new order of civil society has emerged and, if a man would quit it, he relapses into the condition of a wolf who may be killed at sight. There is no question here of moral obligation but of patent private advantage. It will be better to kill him since then the advantage will be obvious even to the most selfish. The Social Contract, we must carefully note, is a contract of each man with each—*not* with the ruler or government. Later we shall have occasion to point out that Hugo Grotius, the Dutch internationalist lawyer, in 1625, also bases civil rights on *stare pactis*—"standing by one's pact"—and an "obligation from consent"; but will only admit that private utility reinforces Natural Law.† This last, Grotius contends—as against Hobbes—springs from a human nature which is blessed with *societatis appetitu excellente* ("an excellent appetite for society": the Aristotelian thesis).‡

What advantage, however, can it be to a man to pledge himself to fight and die as a soldier? Hobbes faces the issue and replies blandly: None. A man is under no civil obligation when he is sure, by giving evidence against himself or awaiting execution or being a conscript or obeying a king in a losing cause, that the fate of him and his will be

* *Cf.* p. 275.

† *Cf.* p. 702.

‡ *Cf.* p. 102; and Aristotle's *Eudemian Ethics,* 1242a: "Man is not a lonely being, but has a tendency to partnership with those to whom he is by nature akin." And contrast Cicero's *De Republica,* III, 13: "But since one fears another, and no one dares trust to himself, a sort of compact is made between the people and the powerful men, and it is from this that exists that form of united state which Scipio was praising." Cicero as usual endeavours to have a foot in both positions.

worse, if he obeys, than if he looks after the integrity of his own skin. In view, however, of the onrush of anarchy, Hobbes points out that these occasions will be rare. Normally, of course a man will wish to keep in well with public opinion. "There can be no greater argument to a man of his own power, than to find himself not only able to accomplish his own desires but also to assist other men in theirs."

What advantage (if we follow the argument of Hobbes as contrasted with that of Grotius) can any State, being in a condition of nature in relation to its neighbour, have in collective commitments if thereby it is liable to suffer in a war more than by disentanglement? Some states, in such collective obligation, may have the satisfaction of playing a dominant role. But social obligation must always be proportionate to proximity of threat, not absolute. Men will keep their social and treaty obligations when they fear not to do so.

Natural Law is the law of reason. Reason dictates, not categorically but prudentially, that we consult our own good. "Everyone calls that good which he desires and evil which he eschews." The Sermon on the Mount or the Decalogue is natural law so far as intelligent. It will be noted by the student that it is, according to Hobbes, especially difficult to carry out the rational Natural Law in an anarchic State of Nature. Civil Society permits a better observance—save so far as the Law of Nature reduces itself to the simple principle: "To seek peace when we may have it and when not to defend ourselves." Natural Right—or claim; the unalterable claim of our human nature—precedes the rational regulation of Natural Law. The latter is law miscalled, as Hobbes is among the first to assert with his customary impiety. "Law, and Right, differ as much as Obligation, and Liberty." It is important to note that Hobbes, the only begetter of the high sovereignty theory of the lawyers, is the very man who insists that law depends on my right (= natural claim, prior to laws, moral or social), *not* my right on law. Hobbes is a master of paradox; but here, granted his definitions, paradox involves no contradiction. Almost Hobbes is a Liberal!—because certainly he is an individualist, although one that believes in Original Sin. He is the father of utilitarianism.

How then shall men, having seen the convenience of foregoing some measure of their natural fist-right, and having entered into a social compact for collective security, be induced to maintain their contract or undertaking? By terror of anarchy. But what if anarchy, however disadvantageous to most, be to the advantage of particular persons, natural or corporate?

Here Hobbes develops his peculiar doctrine of the sovereign. Not for a minute can men be trusted to maintain their undertakings against their own interests. Therefore, simultaneously with the resignation of the full "right of self-defence" (or offence) a power is set up competent to hold *in terrorem* those who are tempted to abuse that resignation. It must be a power that is competent to make the life of the seceder or criminal much less pleasant than his life would be if he yielded obedience to the universal authority—to break him. It holds the sword of blood. There are obviously no legal rights against it. It is bound by *no* Contract, natural or social or governmental. There are no natural "rights" against it save the right to secede and take the consequences. There being no rights against it, what it does is by definition just. Hobbes has taken over Bodin's notion, without his reservations.

The sovereign is final, supreme and loose from restraint of the laws, itself being the source of laws. The Executive is not there (as Aristotle thought) to execute the decisions of the Judiciary declaring immemorial common law or custom. The Judiciary is there to apply acts of a legislature which is itself but one aspect of the Will of the Executive.

The only way to erect such a Common Power, as may be able to defend them from the invasion of Forraigners, and the injuries of one another, and thereby to secure them in such sort, as by their owne industrie, and by the fruits of the Earth, they may nourish themselves and live contentedly; is, to conferre all their power and strength upon one Man, or upon one Assembly of men, that may reduce all their Wills, by plurality of voices, unto one Will: which is as much as to say, to appoint one Man, or Assembly of men, to bear their Person. . . .

This is more than Consent, or Concord; it is a reall Unitie of them all, in one and the same Person, made by Covenant of every man with every man, in such a manner, as if every man should say to every man, I authorise and give up my Right of Governing my selfe, to this Man, or to this Assembly of men, on this condition, that thou give up thy Right to him, and Authorise all his Actions in like manner. This done, the Multitude so united in one Person, is called a Common-wealth, in Latine *civitas*. This is the generation of that great Leviathan, or rather (to speak more reverently) of that Mortall God, to which wee owe under the Immortall God, our peace and defence. . . .

And he that carryeth this Person, is called Soveraigne, and said to have Soveraigne Power; and every one besides, his Subject. . . .

Every one, as well he that Voted for it, as he that Voted against it, shall authorise all the Actions and Judgements, of that Man, or Assembly of men, in the same manner, as if they were his own, to the end, to live peaceable amongst themselves, and to be protected against other men.

It will be noted that Hobbes's sovereign is not necessarily an individual, although he expresses his preference for monarchy or dictatorship—autocracy—as providing unity of natural will. Nor can Hobbes be taxed with leaving unsolved the problem of the man who, entering a community without choice by birth, declines to subscribe to the original Contract which lies at the origins of immemorial society. Hobbes in effect does not base authority merely on Consent. Authority is based on a consent compelled by Fear, not by conscientious or fastidious choice. The individual has the full natural right of resuming his place in the state of nature as a wolf and of being lynched. As Tom Paine later observed, it is hard to argue against the old rascal. And yet even in sovereignty by Conquest or Acquisition (the alternative to Contract) there is a measure of contract—"obey me and I promise to spare your lives."

His paradox of power is produced by ignoring those emollient forces of custom, sociability and general community feeling upon which Aristotle and Grotius build their theories, assuming man to be instinctively a social animal. The experiences, however, of Hobbes's own time, in Britain and France, with its revelation of the contempt for co-operation and of the latent hostility between province and province, group and group, sect and sect, class and class, even man and man, declared Hobbes rather than Aristotle the practical man. Not the class war, but the war of each impersonal human atom against each, in competition, is the basis of his thinking. He saw before him societies tending to relapse into "the state of nature." Aristotle deplored *stasis*. Hobbes accepted it as part of his problem. Not unnaturally the result was a philosophy of the Terror and of Tyranny, eminently applicable to the *stasis* of our own days. Incidentally, the logic of Hobbes's argument issues in the most powerful justification yet of a new, universal Roman Emperor, a new Charlemagne or Napoleon, or of a mail-fisted League Council of Geneva, smashing down by armed force those who dare to secede or even to stay out. This interesting speculation, however, is one upon which Hobbes, for obvious reasons, lays no stress. *Leviathan* is, for him, a beast that swallows all only in home waters. The radical contradiction in Hobbes's theory of security, collective at home but not abroad, is hushed up. Grotius alone here opens up a line of thought, to which we shall return.*

Must Sovereignty be indivisible? Hobbes's answer is brief and to the point. If we admit of disputes without a sovereign arbiter, "then

* *Cf.* p. 702.

the private sword has place again." If we admit of two arbiters or authorities both claiming sovereignty, we must reflect that

> If two men ride on an horse, then one must ride in front.

But must not the People be sovereign? If so, like the old Athenian democracy, they must govern themselves directly, by referendum or plebiscite. In the alternative, we do but "stir up the multitude against the people." When a multitude has chosen its government (or found it or had it imposed on it), then "the democracy is annihilated and covenants made unto them void." And no loss, for what is called democracy is but "an aristocracy of orators." This is all mere anti-parliamentary invective. The kernel of the theory is rather to be found in the remark: "In a monarchy, the subjects are the multitude and (however it may seem a paradox) the king is the people." This is an early and more cautious variant of a modern theory that could be phrased: The subjects are the multitude and the Leader is the voice of the State (or the Nation).

Hobbes cannot be dismissed as an apostle of tyranny. It is true that he refuses (as was convenient in the days of Oliver) to distinguish *de jure* ("by right") and *de facto* ("in fact") rule, and declares bluntly that by tyranny men merely mean a strong monarchy or dictatorship that they dislike. His theory could (although wrongly, as shown) even be defended as organic or as a theory of a corporative state. For corporations themselves, however, as for all groups or sects or unions or guilds that might be nuclei of dissidence, he displays a profound distaste. Vividly he describes them as "worms in the body politic." As for the notion of a Spiritual Church organized over against and above the State (even claiming that men have a higher interest than civil peace and self-preservation):

> Their whole Hierarchy, or Kingdome of Darknesse, may be compared not unfitly to the Kingdome of the Fairies. . . . The Ecclesiastiques are Spiritually men and Ghostley fathers. The Fairies are Spirits and Ghosts. Fairies and Ghosts inhabite Darknesse, Solitudes and Graves. The Ecclesiastiques walke in Obscurity of Doctrine, in Monasteries, Churches and Church-yards. . . .
>
> When the Fairies are displeased with anybody, they are said to send their Elves, to pinch them. The Ecclesiastiques, when they are displeased with any Civill State, make also their Elves, that is, Superstitious, Enchanted Subjects, to pinch their Princes, by preaching Sedition; or one Prince enchanted with promises, to pinch another. The Fairies marry not; but there be among them Incubi, that have copulation with flesh and bloud. The Priests also marry not.

The Ecclesiastiques take the Cream of the Land, by Donations of ignorant men, that stand in aw of them, and by Tythes: So also it is in the Fable of Fairies, that they enter into the Dairies, and Feast upon the Cream, which they skim from the Milk. . . .

For it is not the Romane Clergy onely ["the Papacy . . . the Ghost of the deceased Romane Empire, sitting crowned upon the grave thereof"] that pretends the Kingdom of God to be of this World, and thereby to have a Power therein, distinct from that of the Civill State.

The Sovereign is the source of law, as of all authority, and has authority over the law to interpret it, since neither law nor Holy Writ interprets itself. The sovereign is "the public conscience"—*i.e.*, Charles II is the public conscience, as "God's lieutenant." Charles II was to interpret the Bible and, as it were, to decide whether the world had been created in seven days or not; and whether Elijah had behaved respectfully to Jezebel. "For when Christian men take not their Christian sovereign for God's prophet, they must either take their own dreams . . . or be led away by some foreign prince or a fellow subject," *i.e.*, Pope or Prelate. Although, however, there is no unjust law, Hobbes, as will be seen, does not tyrannously multiply laws. He believes in Liberty.

Hobbes, by implication, denies the existence of a Moral Law. Law for him emanates as the expression of the sovereign will of a Body Politic or Leviathan. He does not choose to consider whether such a competent Body Politic can be smaller than a universal World Commonwealth (as Kant will later argue) or, at least (as Dante argued), than the Roman Empire. He dismisses (Marsiglio had given a lead) Catholicism as an Elfin Kingdom, incompetent to check civil disorder. The moral law then reduces itself to the patriotic maxim of Machiavelli: *salus populi suprema lex.** And the *populus* reduces itself to the Sovereign individual or assembly that "bears its person" and executes its judgement. *Jus est quod jussum est.* "That," precisely, "is right which is commanded."

In order to leave no doubt upon the issue, Hobbes enumerates the six diseases of a Commonwealth. These are (1) that a ruler, to obtain a kingdom (*e.g.*, Henry IV of England) is sometimes content with less than absolute power; (2) "that every private man is Judge of Good and Evill actions"; (3) "that whatsoever a man does against his Conscience is Sinne† . . . for a man's Conscience and his Judgement

* "The safety of the people is the supreme law."

† *Cf.* p. 170.

is the same thing; and as the Judgement, so also the Conscience may be erroneous . . . the Law is the publique Conscience"; and "that Faith and Sanctity, are not to be attained by Study and Reason, but by supernaturall Inspiration, or Infusion"; (4) "that he that hath the soveraign-Power, is subject to the Civill Lawes"; (5) "that every private man has an absolute Propriety in his goods; such, as excludeth the Right of the Soveraign"; (6) "that the Soveraign Power may be divided." Also, "the constitution of man's nature, is of it selfe subject to desire of novelty"; and in this men are much encouraged by reading about the policies (*cf.* the Girondins of the French Revolution) of the Greeks and Romans. Also, the setting up of a spiritual Supremacy against Sovereignty; Canons against civil Laws; and Ghostly Authority against Civil—a problem of the totalitarians, Nazi and Marxist, today.

Hobbes, however, admits of reservations to despotism. As he is an entirely consistent theorist, these reservations acquire importance. First, the law is never wrong—but there is no wisdom in multiplying vexations and restrictions. "Laws are for dykes," not dams. The sovereign legislator is never "wrong," but he may be foolish. Second, there is a Natural Law of reason, which counsels the legislator not to be foolish. There are Natural Rights, indicated by reason, such as the right to life. Are we not then entitled to protest against law, as immoral, in the light of Nature and her rights? Not at all, replies Hobbes: we always have the right to choose Nature rather than a foolish sovereign. We have our alternative—and must not complain. But Nature gives no more "right" than that to die fighting unless we have the wit to escape. Thirdly, we have no obligation to obey a sovereign who is not so *de facto* (a dangerous admission at a Stuart exile court, although convenient in the England of the Protectorate) and whose protection of us is mere pretence. For we obey him because he protects us. We need not obey if he can neither protect—nor punish.

Hobbes, fourthly, favours toleration in thought and religion. "An oath is but a gesture of the tongue." No civil power can bind the mind; and it is futile to try. But we must not build too much on this thesis. The old atheist naturally preferred religious toleration because persecution about matters negligible seemed to him a waste of civic energy. For the rest, the defence of toleration, apart from personal temperament, only rests on the preceding (third) argument that a sovereign is limited by his power.

Fifthly, Hobbes remains, not a worshipper of despots, but an individualist to the core. His doctrine of monarchy (although designed to inculcate obedience, not show wit) is not so far different from that of his friend and contemporary, the lawyer Selden, who maintained that kings, like cooks, are "a thing men have made for their own sake, and for quietness' sake." For the rest, said Selden, Sovereignty is but the civil version of Papal Infallibility. "The Pope is infallible, where he hath power to command, that is, where he must be obeyed; so is every supreme power and prince." For the rest, if any talk of infallibility in Church Councils, as Selden said: "the odd man at the count is the Holy Ghost." Hobbes and Selden are the first Utilitarians.

4

Hobbes's theories, scarcely ingratiating with any party, as was natural, met with such bitter criticism in his own day as almost effectively to discredit him in his homeland. He was the Bernard Shaw of his day—but the English of his day were less tolerant than now. John Locke, it will be noted later, chose the incomparably less profound but more representative Filmer as his easier and especial target of attack. He leaves Hobbes to suffocate in his own unpopularity, after a pompous reference to "Hobbes and Spinoza, those justly censured names."

Aubrey, the biographer, records "that in Parliament, not long after the king was settled, [in fact it was 1667,] some of the bishops had a notion to have the good old gentleman burned for a heretique." The explanation appears to be that respectable people were looking round for the causes of God's wrath as displayed in the Plague and Great Fire of London, and none better occurred than the alleged atheism of Mr. Hobbes. So a committee was appointed and Hobbes had quickly to write a book *Concerning Heresy* (1667, pub. 1680) to prove that he could not legally be burned. Even so he had the courage to begin by a quotation from Lucretius about superstitions, no more to be dreaded than what boys fear in the dark—but found it expedient to attend daily divine service in the Devonshires' private chapel. He would not, however, stay on for the sermons, because he knew the contents. The Bible, a Hobbist informs us, he believed to be written "by a sort of innocent, harmless men." The Bishops he did not view in the same light and, although the issue was uncertain, Hobbes demonstrated that the day had dawned when he could bait them (under Charles II) and not they, with their faggots, him.

Tenison, later Archbishop, provides a summary of the Hobbist creed:

I believe that God is Almighty matter; . . . that it is to be decided by the Civil Power whether He created all things else; . . . that the prime law of Nature in the Soul of Man is temporal Self-love; . . . that whatsoever is within in these books [of Scripture] may lawfully be denied even upon Oath (after the laudable doctrine of the Gnosticks) in times of Persecution.

A contemporary writer describes the matter more luridly in the very title of his pamphlet: *The true effigies of the Monster of Malmesbury: or T. Hobbes in his popular colours (Mr. Cowley's verses in praise of Mr. Hobbes oppos'd). By a lover of truth and virtue* (1680). The philosophers were not much kinder. Descartes had written as far back as 1643, with that light gesture of patronage touched by malice which marks a watchful senior colleague, "his whole purpose is to write in favour of monarchy, which could have been done more adventageously and more solidly than he does, by taking more tenable and virtuous maxims." Leibnitz, in a letter of 1670, accused Hobbes of licensing men to do what they pleased, "which is only possible in a Utopia of atheists." Nevertheless, to Leibnitz he was "a prince of the new philosophic age." Bishop Burnett summarized the matter, as touching *Leviathan*, in his *History of My Own Time:* "A very wicked book with a very strange title."

Lord Chancellor Clarendon, in the days of Charles II, passed beyond invective to the central criticism: "the doctrine of self-interest is the seed of sedition." The trouble was that Hobbes and his friends were much too clever, as well as truculent. Hobbes indeed had nowhere shown why any individual (or state) should obey who, by interest or temperament, was inspired to be a gunman or Capone. Neither indeed had Machiavelli nor perhaps Bodin—which the former would have admitted, and the latter not. Hobbes attempts to disguise the issue by much semi-dishonest talk about a social contract or promise; monarchs "bearing the person" of all; and membership of the body politic. Hobbes, however, is essentially too honest a thinker not to admit frankly, between times, that these matters are mere trimmings of his individualistic argument, which is always one of conditional anarchy. He gets his effects by a dramatic reinforcement of the passion of fear—terror of aggression. Here, surely, the moral would seem to be, *sauve qui peut*. Make treaties, yes—as Machiavelli said—but don't keep them when inconvenient. Plato, long ago, saw this route, from which the spirit of cooperation is remote and sectional interest all; and discarded it as mothering *stasis*. Has Hobbes really any reply?

Let us summarize the complicated argument. For Aristotle, let us recall, the self-interest of the majority as a basis of a constitution, as much as of a minority, issues in perversion. There is no right divine or utilitarian of either minorities *or* majorities. The rational interest of the whole was the sole legitimate basis. Who, however, is to decide this rational interest—an interested few or an interested many? Plato replies: "Neither; but the wise." Who, however, shall decide on the wise or (if we reply, "eminent men of knowledge"), give them power? Marsiglio says: "The majority *or* weightier part." Hobbes says: "Those who have power by conquest or acquisition"—not necessarily (or, with Hobbes, even desirably) the majority but the power-holders. Has not, then, the majority a *moral* right? Plato and Hobbes, for opposite reasons, would agree in replying, "None." Has not, then, the majority an *expedient* or utilitarian right to select its wise leaders? Is not the peace and progress of a society best advanced on the basis of give and take? (Plato would agree, with reservations, if we mean, not compromise, but co-operation.) And does not give and take mean compromise, in which it is simpler for the many minorities to yield to the one majority? That is true if we admit (as Aristotle, in his more democratic moments, comes near to admitting) that every thinking man has about an equal claim, so far as we can ascertain the truth, to a judgement on ends and values, or—more precisely—that we have no philosophical ground for excluding any sane man (adequately informed) from essaying a judgement that may be as good as the Pope's own. The Pope's judgement, Aquinas would admit, is only final in faith and morals because a churchman voluntarily admits as his own choice, for the sake of the weal of the Church, the argument from reason and revelation upon which this finality rests. Similarly, Hobbes argues about the finality of the Sovereign, for the sake of the order of the State. It is, however, only true that it is expedient for the majority to decide in so far as the majority also *expediently compromises or co-operates, in give and take, with the minority—since the moral bond is not assurance of the public interest* (*a matter for the few wise*) *but merely the utilitarian one of keeping the public peace.*

Compromise, then, by *all* sections is the principle of any social order which does not *either* believe that it can first select and then follow an aristocracy of final knowledge (such as was visualized in the Platonic and Catholic schemes) *or* else is not content to admit the tyranny of force and to find a justification for it. This last Hobbes—with whatever hedgings—does. Tyranny, briefly, however unwise and atrocious, is still better than anarchy. Hobbes's argument is the only possible one for those who base the "right" to rule on the vindication of group self-interest, whether plutocratic or proletarian, and discard alike utilitarian and co-operative compromise and co-operation based upon a reasoned scheme of social justice. Thus far Hobbes anticipates Marx's theory of the state as an instrument for the suppression of certain classes by dictatorial force.

Clarendon is, then, right in pointing out that *no* ground for civil obedience can be found in self-interest alone, once the edge of fear is removed, or unless that self-interest be reinforced by considerations of some rational scheme or of respect for the judgement of others, strength apart. The nearest that Hobbes comes to this last position is when he bases contract upon the supposed equality of individual man with individual man, in physical strength and in wits taken conjointly. This supposition is palpably false; and is only used to show that no man is *so* superior as to be fearless and able with impunity to dispense with the contract. Hobbes, however, the pre-Utilitarian, is more illuminating than the traditional moralist and High Churchman, Clarendon, in the issue how to *compel* the mood of *compromise*—a neat and knotty political antinomy or paradox.

No significant advance will be made, beyond this discussion excited by Hobbes, until we reach the Utilitarian school, which will raise the question whether (even granted that they both be tyrannies of group-interest) a proletarian is not preferable to a plutocratic tyranny; and whether it is not for the majority to decide what is the true or good or best-working social system and to enforce it. Of the Utilitarian philosophy, Hobbes, we shall later see,* is an historical pioneer. We shall also discover that Utilitarianism does not end by adding to the three choices in social order: the Philosophic (or Scientific) Good; Empirical Compromise, with federal implications; the Force or Tyranny of the Many or Few, according to *de facto* capacity to organize, plot and use this force. Hobbes's system in the final analysis is not merely (we have discussed, above, the reservations), but is substantially, a defence of Tyranny—not in the opprobrious sense, but in that of a Despotism that may find it prudent to be Benevolent. His cult is that of the Efficiency That Gets Things Done. Its worship is that of the Strong Individual or Class.

The Doctrine of Sovereignty, it should be added, of which we have seen the ecclesiastical foreshadowings in the rulings of Gregory IX and Boniface VIII, taking shape in the writings of Marsiglio and Bodin, reaches full expression in those of Thomas Hobbes, so that this doctrine itself sometimes is called by his name.

* *Cf.* p. 349.

It will, however, be noted that Hobbes's doctrine, although one of an Absolute Sovereign, is not (contrary to common belief) necessarily one of an absolute monarch. Hobbes, with such states as Venice in mind, carefully makes the reservation that the sovereign may be "an assembly of men." Hence this adaptable theory could suit not only the rule of Charles I and the protectorship of Cromwell. When James II fled, it could suit the rising power of Parliament. It was a theory of power for those who actually held it—whether king or king-in-parliament. Hobbes expresses his private preferences for autocracy, but this does not affect his formula.

Hence, as we shall see,* the Swiss historian De Lolme was able to apply this theory of absolute power, in the most uncompromising terms, to the British parliament; and the great eighteenth-century jurist Blackstone, while making, like Bodin, conventional reservations about Natural Law, was able to make a statement about parliamentary power directly consonant with Hobbes's statement. Elaborated by Bentham, the theory received its final shaping at the hands of the nineteenth-century jurist John Austin and, hence, in contemporary discussion is usually referred to as the Austinian theory of sovereignty.

The statement by Austin (1790–1859), professor of jurisprudence in the University of London, where he defines sovereignty—a statement almost verbally identical with one by Bentham—is so far classical as to merit quotation:

> If a determinate human superior, not in a habit of obedience to a like superior, receive habitual obedience from the bulk of a given society, that determinate superior is sovereign in that society, and the society (including the superior) is a society political and independent.

The danger of this famous *Austinian Doctrine of Sovereignty* is two-fold: (a) that it provides a definition of a 'society political,' in terms of the Modern State, which previous ages (as Maitland was to show) would not have recognized; and (b) it made no inquisition into the limits of "habitual obedience," but substituted a lawyer's fiction of absolute authority for a sociological observation of conditional authority, to the extent of overshadowing the moral limits of actual obedience by a juristic abstraction about theoretical power. It put government, in effect, in front of law and denied, in the name of ephemeral sovereignty, the reality of Natural Law as formula of social fact. It is permissible to cite the warning of the Chinese Zenni philosopher, of the

* *Cf.* p. 305.

ninth century, A.D., who said: "Pray never substantialize that which does not exist."

We shall further see in due course* that the Fathers of the American Constitution, following Locke (who never uses the word "sovereign"), rejected so far as in them lay *any* theory of sovereignty, and substituted for it the doctrine of the Division of Powers. So far as the word "sovereign" was used, it was used in a non-Hobbesian sense and in the face of Hobbesian logic. Thus a sovereignty was asserted to inhere *both* in the United States *and* in New York State, each (phrase reminiscent of the old ecclesiastical or Gelasian doctrine) within its own sphere. Professor H. A. Smith goes so far as to say:

> Since the Declaration of Independence, the theory of parliamentary sovereignty has never found a place in American political thought, and it is universally held that neither a legislature nor any other agency of government is a complete expression of the sovereignty of the people. . . . The people of the United States are *a greater sovereign* than are the people of any particular State, and they claim the right, through their judicial organs, to determine all cases of conflict between the various agencies of government.

These words are necessarily to the Hobbesians as foolishness.

The heart of the trouble appears to be that Hobbes rightly affirmed that, within any given sphere of government, there must be an arbiter to settle disputes. Whereas, however, the sphere of this arbiter may be settled by a constitutional morality or custom, which is the ground for obedience, Hobbes typically assumed that it was settled by force. Hence he proceeded from the correct doctrine that in any given political society a final judicial arbiter is required for the adjudication of disputes under law, to the fictitious doctrine that in all political society there must be an executive authority with absolute physical power to make law, compel obedience and decide the sphere of control between one political society and another.

Since (short of a universal emperor) no executive authority exists competent to settle disputes between state and state, and yet each state, on Hobbes's assumption, must claim to determine for itself its own limit, Hobbes's theory, if not indeed an incitement to perpetual war, at least does nothing, in external affairs, to maintain that peace and order which is his avowed object. He falls into patent contradiction.† It is a doctrine of *internal* authority only; and even here unsatisfactory. Developed two centuries earlier it would have been a theory

* *Cf.* p. 310.

† *Cf.* p. 238; also 204.

justifying each baron as *souverain dans sa baronie.* A sister doctrine was used by the Popes to justify their infallibility. It merely happens to come to maturity at a time when it could serve as a justification of the New Monarchies and their States. It is definitely inferior, as theory, to the old Imperial Theory, which (as in principle universal) presented no such contradiction between internal and external authority.

Another line of argument, similar to that of Hobbes, is essayed at this time. There is this difference that, whereas Hobbes (as Thrasymachus of old) said that the strong do rule and we save our skins by obeying quietly, the new argument alleges (like Callicles) that the strong ought to rule because this is the nature of things. Unlike Callicles, however (and more forcibly), we take the step of asserting that we know who ought to rule by discovering who does. God and "the big battalions" are synonymous. This brings us to the study of a philosopher whom Hobbes applauds and describes as "going beyond him a bar's length"—whatever that may mean—adding that he [Hobbes] "Durst not write so boldly."

5

Baruch de Spinoza (Benedictus de Spinoza, 1632–1677), was a member of a family of Spanish Jews who escaped that persecution in Spain from which the Moslem Moors of Granada had abstained but in which the baptized Christians (being more morally totalitarian) indulged. It had settled in Amsterdam. A junior contemporary of Hobbes who yet predeceased him, Spinoza was a tradesman's son who made his living as an optician by polishing lenses, a man well acquainted with the mathematical and scientific thought of his day, a correspondent of the newly founded Royal Society of London, a non-Aryan who declined an invitation to the chair of philosophy in German Heidelberg on the ground that it would restrict his freedom of opinion.

Even as it was, the evil effects of persecution could be seen in Spinoza's life history. In tolerant Holland, the Calvinists were busy excommunicating the Arminian exponents of Free Will, putting an interdict on their worship and contriving the imprisoning or worse of the leading men of the faction. Inside Jewry, which had been taught the discipline of intolerance by persecution, Spinoza's views were found insufferable. "The heads of the Church Council have for some time been aware of Baruch de Espinoza's evil opinions and doings, they have tried by various methods and promises to withdraw him from his evil ways . . . they have decided, after full investigation, in the presence of the learned Rabbis and with their assent, to anathematize the said Espinoza and cut him off from the people of Israel. Herewith accordingly they place him under anathema"; and no one is to hold commerce with him by speech or pen, enter the same house or come within six foot of him, do him kindness or read his writings.

Expelled from the synagogue and drawn to the Arminians and to the Anabaptists or Baptists of the Mennonite section, Spinoza had the opportunity of observing the internecine persecutions of the Christians. Certainly philosophy did not escape. That of Descartes was especially obnoxious to the Calvinists and, although the Dutch presbyters could not touch the soldier-philosopher, who could snap his fingers at them from France, they could make life hot for academic followers who, in 1675, were deprived of their positions. Arminians and Cartesians alike found support in the leader of the oligarchic republican party of the wealthy burgher, Jan de Witt, in whom Spinoza felt that he had a protector and who, in fact, provided a pension. Even so, the *Ethics*, which might arouse persecuting tendencies, was held up by Spinoza from publication until his death and he did not scruple to publish, as a business matter, expositions of Descartes, without comment, which may have been faithful to Descartes but which Spinoza himself, with more dangerous doctrines, regarded as exploded. After all, the doctrine of "two truths" was a philosophic commonplace (if heretical) since the Middle Ages; and neither Plato nor the Gospels had hesitated to distinguish between the teaching for the disciples and the tales "for the multitude." Scepticism, indeed, about the intelligence of this last may have appeared to Spinoza justified when Jan and Cornelius de Witt were lynched and kicked to death, in 1672, by the anti-French patriot populace of the Hague. On this occasion, Spinoza contemplated affixing handbills of protest near the prison but was considerately locked in by his landlord. Later he seems to have been used as a go-between with the French by certain Dutch factions. He thus was drawn into the fringes of the life of an active politician—if being himself nearly lynched by the mob as a spy can be described as the fringes. Instead of the *Ethics* the great philosopher turned his attention to the *Tractatus Theologico-Politicus*, which was intended to have immediate bearing on the political fray, and promptly published this in 1670. It will be noted that neither Hobbes nor Spinoza—nor any of their predecessors—were philosophers of the chair and that both, not content to be overgrown and titled schoolmasters, deliberately chose to immix themselves in politics. Spinoza, solitary bachelor, pipe-smoking, liked (as Renan emphasized) by children, died at the age of forty-five, of consumption perhaps aggravated by under-nutrition. His work, in effect, was done at the age of thirty-eight. His sister Rebecca, who disapproved of his notions, put in a claim to his few chattels but withdrew when it seemed probable that the debts would exceed the assets. His desk, with his manuscripts locked in it, was sent to his bookseller. His *Tractatus Theologico-Politicus* was amiably described as "a wicked instrument forged in hell by a renegade Jew and the devil, and issued with the knowledge of Mr. Jan de Witt."

The doctrine of toleration, with Spinoza, comes out into the open. The basis, however, chosen for it, is a narrow one, already anticipated by Hobbes and by the *Politiques*. Indeed the philosopher Leibniz (1646–1726), who refers to Spinoza's *Tractatus Theologico-Politicus* as "an unbearably free-thinking book," also expresses the hope that Bodin's agnostic *Heptaplomeres*, which is now "flitting about from land to land," in manuscript, will "never be published." Spinoza declares that "the right of dominion is limited by power only." Here is the expedient basis of toleration. This, however, has a corollary, already seen in Hobbes. Where, from the nature of the case, there can be no power, as in the control of thoughts, there can be no rational dominion. The thinking of the *Politiques* was essentially legal, Roman and mechanical; and Spinoza here makes no advance. Plato's great problem of Education is not discussed. Inquisitorial methods, leading to hypocrisy, are merely brutish and stupid. Spinoza, however, also advances an ethical plea. It is the duty of man to worship God with true religion and to mind his own business. Books probably written under Spinoza's influence stress, as Marsiglio had done, the supremacy of the civil power and allow the clergy no rights of civil interference beyond those assigned to them by law. Religion, in brief, is a matter of the individual; and by Spinoza, as by Machiavelli, it is set forth with a clarity not discoverable elsewhere that the state is secular. The duty of the State, then, is to maintain the civil peace and put a check on the fanatical, peace-disturbing churches or sects (not, as of old, the Church to put check on the warring states or murdering factions).

Spinoza, however, in his *Tractatus Theologico-Politicus* advances to a much more remarkable position as its kernel. We are to think what we will, guided by reason, and to speak what we think because *reason will lead to order*. Truth will prevail. In brief, the recognition of a rational law in the universe is inconsistent, not with spiritual individualism, but with disorderly anarchy. "The loss of public peace and religion itself must necessarily follow were liberty of reasoning taken away." This position is not so profound as the early pacifist, Patristic one that truth will prevail *even* under, and because of, persecution, martyrdom and concentration camps. It is however, a practical argument, inspired by the customary optimism of rationalism. It will be noted, however, that Spinoza's plea for toleration does not depend upon sceptical indifferentism, but upon a doctrine of the ultimate self-evidence and harmonizing power of reason. Left alone, the rational will find its own level—the top. We are confronted by a species of metaphysical *laissez faire.*

Spinoza's *Ethics* raises the Theory of Power in a new form and one inadequately considered by Hobbes, the materialist. Spinoza here shows himself as a pantheist and a monist. God *is* because Reality *is;* "Reality" equals "God"; and Nature is but Extended Reality which is God. Dualism had hitherto been the order of the day in philosophy. Both Mind and Matter were real. Even Plato, who took over from the Heracliteans his theory of matter but treated it as, because in flux, therefore impermanent, trivial, nevertheless accepted its reality. So did Aristotle; and Aquinas. Even the Stoics, who affirmed the divine permeation of the Creation, and may be styled pantheists, did not fail to assert a distinction of Creator and created. The Democriteans, with their materialist theory of all as a conglomerate of atoms, came nearer to a pure materialism. This is not the place to discuss the difference between the "matter" of the Stoics and the "matter" (*quantitate signata*) of Descartes. With Spinoza, however, we have the affirmation of the unity, Reality, of which Mind and Matter are the aspects. This has an interesting ethical consequence, especially for a determinist such as Spinoza. No longer is it possible to place in convenient duality and disconnection what is and what ought to be. Either What Ought to Be is an empty phrase, or What Is is illusion, or What Is and What Ought to Be are identical. "The Law of nature," writes Spinoza, "is the power of nature." Nature is God—or at least, God is, in one aspect, Nature. The survival of those fittest to survive in Nature, is as it ought to be. Spinoza can prove it. Let us, therefore, "wait and see."

Spinoza is an optimist about the Logic or Dialectic of Nature.* It cannot be said that he is an optimist (or indeed had ground to be) about human individuals. About pretty-pretty morality he is refreshingly disconcerting. "Men are so much the more to be feared as they are more crafty and cunning than other animals. And because men are in the highest degree liable to *true* passions, therefore men are naturally

* *Cf.* p. 576.

enemies." Shape and vigour are given to Spinoza's thought by the fact that he makes no attempt, with Leibniz, to suppose any Pre-established Harmony in the best of all *possible* worlds. As with Hobbes, so by Spinoza, we are confronted with the stark conflict of human appetite for power, will against will.

The purpose of the State Spinoza, not unnaturally under the circumstances, finds (along with Dante, Marsiglio and Hobbes) in the maintenance of peace and security. What maintains this peace is *eo ipso* right. The right, *i.e.*, the right to decide what is right, is the will of the multitude *or* [*n.b.*] its stronger part. Consistency leads Spinoza on to the quite logical paradox: the citizen's right grows less as that of the commonwealth grows greater. There is no need and therefore justification in self-help where collective security, which can command so much greater power, is effective. "The more [? stronger] they are that combine together, the more right they possess." The same argument should be applicable to states; but Spinoza, in the Low Countries, (like Hobbes) shrinks from the old imperialist argument. States rather are natural enemies; they must each seek "the welfare of its own dominion"; and any statesman who is trapped by a treaty into action against his interest is a fool. On the contrary there is a natural right of each individual (and state) to the fulfillment of himself, that is, of that power which gives right.

Spinoza is essaying the famous *pons asinorum*—the bridge in politics which leads across from Might to Right. Both the teaching of Hobbes, whom he does not quote but whose *De Cive* he had clearly read with attention, and his own monistic philosophy compel him to cross this bridge. The clue is found in an analysis of the nature of Might. The more who cooperate the greater the might *and* right. Might then is not subversive of right. Might requires co-operation. Moreover the truer might is that which endures. True might is displayed by peace. But the real central term of the equation is to be found in reason. Might is based on reason (intelligent, planned might). Now reason is a principle of order, the unity that makes force, co-operation and peace. And reason is the basis of right. Might = Reason (which will prevail) = Right. Reality displays two facets, as the actual and the ideal.

Spinoza's motives for advocating toleration are patent enough. His reason for applauding "the stronger ruler" with totalitarian tendencies (especially as a Republican at a time when this spelled burgher oligarch opposition to the popular monarchical faction of the House of Orange) is not so clear. In part it is the logical product of a mystic mind reared on the teaching of the Jewish philosopher Maimonides, which teaching again connects, through Arabian thought, with the totalitarian monism of the East. In part, it may be due to the desire of the persecuted and weak to find somewhere a strong arm to avenge and vindicate; and to the cynicism about human sentimental goodness that persecution breeds.

Does Spinoza succeed in his attempt? Yes: in the sense that the Good must not be assumed to be merely abstract, an "horizon ideal," didactic, possible but not actual, detached from history, "in the mind" or "conscience." (Hegel later develops this argument). No: in the sense that—even granted that rational faith which some of us prefer—the present "irrational" often occupies (even for centuries) the historical foreground before it reveals its fallacies and yields to the permanently "rational." And no, quite clearly, if we reject this rational faith, since then the connecting link in Spinoza's equation is broken. There are many mights; and it is quite impossible to know what might will prove right until the end of history—just as Solon spoke of calling no man happy until he be dead. But it is not impossible to analyze what is rational, even if ultimately we must end, like Spinoza, "that God-intoxicated man," in a faith.

It is not clear, in surveying the history of thought, that even centuries of conquests by this or that people have seriously shifted our sense of values by which we judge these centuries. By those canons of value we judge Jamshid and Khaikhosru, Alexander and Julius—although applications once thought consistent may now seem inconsistent. This only we can say, that the strong man as efficient is rational as touching *means*, although it may be for others to judge ends; and the rational man is *pro tanto* strong. "Efficiency," obviously, answers no questions on *ends*.

Does Spinoza succeed in his synthesis of might and right as touching ends? Let us admit his assimilation of might, order, reason, and co-operation or harmony; and let us admit that harmony is *an* end of action. There are other ends. Truth might perhaps be identified with logical harmony and, in some remote Miltonic fashion, with power. It is not clear that the beautiful can be so identified. The realm of power *may* serve the realm of ends; but the realm of ends is *not* necessarily connected with the realm of human power—not even in the perspective of history. Spinoza, when he moves on the plane of human historic events, as do Hegel and Marx later, affronts my moral judgement. What matters is, as Plato said, social justice—and this cannot be equated anyhow with successful force, which is merely its empiric tool, good when properly used. The pomp of world-history, in the short run, is not world-justice; and, in the long run, is empty words. But beauty remains clear and luminous. And so do values tested, not by success in history, but by the consensus through history of men of genius, thus shaped into a Grand Tradition.

Spinoza gave much attention to method. On this ground alone his posthumously published *Tractatus Politicus* merits reading. Here is his triumph. In the *Ethics* he out-Hobbes Hobbes and, in that mathematical age, proceeds by the route of strict geometrical proof from axioms and definitions. He is an anti-Baconian who believes that, not experience teaches with certainty about the future, but only logic and deduction. Nevertheless, he has a balancing contempt for the plaster cast moral types of the Schoolmen and lesser theologians, removed from study of actuality. Machiavelli is "that most far-seeing man." As for those others,

> . . . such as persuade themselves that the multitude of men, distracted by politics, can ever be induced to live according to the bare dictate of [abstract] reason, must be dreaming of the poetic golden age, or of a stage play. . . .
>
> For they conceive of men, not as they are, but as they themselves would like them to be, whence it comes to pass that, instead of Ethics they have generally written satire, and that they have never conceived a theory of politics worth serious turning over.

Spinoza most rightly, with Machiavelli and Hobbes (and for that matter Bacon), prefers to base himself for axioms, on the observed principles of human nature and the verified constants detectable in the way in which men do actually behave. His psychological observations recall the manner of La Rochefoucauld. A contemporary anonymous pamphlet, *Homo Politicus* (1671), professedly supported and actually satirized the political theory of Hobbes and Spinoza. Spinoza contemplated an anonymous reply to this attack on his abstract method, explaining the unimportance of the gross pursuit of wealth and honours; but this pamphlet, which would have brought out the difference between his own position and that of the materialist sage of Malmesbury, Hobbes, was never written. The method, however, despite its excessive a priorism, and a tendency to confuse hypothesis with fact, makes Spinoza a significant contributor, after Machiavelli and Hobbes, to the building up of a Political Science.

READING

Thomas Hobbes: *Leviathan*, Chaps. XI–XVII, XXIX, XLVII.

BIBLIOGRAPHICAL NOTE

*J. N. Figgis: *The Divine Right of Kings*, 1896.
J. W. Allen: *English Political Thought*, 1603 *to* 1660, 1938.
C. H. McIlwain: *The Political Works of James I*, edit., 1918.
Leslie Stephen: *Hobbes*, 1904.
G. P. Gooch: *Political Thought from Bacon to Halifax*, 1914.
*G. P. Gooch: *English Democratic Ideas in the Seventeenth Century*, 1927.

Part II

Chapter IX

Locke and the Social Contract

1

St. Thomas Aquinas was the first Whig. In the alternative it has been suggested that the Devil was the first Whig. The first thesis, of St. Thomas as a radical, is maintained by Lord Acton in his famous essay on "Freedom in Christianity" in which, taking some liberties, he abridges the views of St. Thomas as follows:

> A king who is unfaithful to his duty forfeits his claim to obedience. It is not rebellion to depose him, for he is himself a rebel whom the nation has a right to put down. But it is better to curtail his power, that he may be unable to abuse it. For this purpose the whole nation ought to have a share in governing itself; the Constitution ought to combine a limited and elective monarchy, with an aristocracy of merit, and such an admixture of democracy as shall admit all classes to office, by popular election. No government has a right to levy taxes beyond the limit determined by the people. All political authority is derived from popular suffrage, and all laws must be made by the people or their representatives. There is no security for us as long as we depend on the will of another man.*

Like St. Thomas à Becket before him, he is a protagonist against secular absolutism and says (or his editor for him) of autocratic sovereignty that "nomen istud a supremo dominio fastuose et elate trahit originem, unde et ille superbus Nicanor," etc.†

Besides these constitutional doctrines of St. Thomas which, enunciated on behalf of the Pope as universal arbiter or supreme *judge*, were developed during succeeding centuries against the theory of the absolute sovereignty of kingly autocrats or *executives*, his theory on two other points on which the Christian Church held decisive views—war and pacifism: property and communism—merit attention. To

* *Cf.* also the discussion of the humanism arising from the position of St. Thomas in M. Jacques Maritain's *Freedom in the Modern World* and *True Humanism*, with the theme that variety of thought must needs be—*oportet haereses esse.*

† " . . . that name takes its origin pompously and loftily from supreme dominion [which is God's alone], wherefore also that proud Nicanor," etc.

the former of these, and to St. Thomas' delimitations of "the just war," we shall return later.* On the second point, property, St. Thomas adhered—while belonging to a friar Order which imposed the surrender of all private property whatsoever as a condition of entrance—to the Trustee Doctrine of wealth already outlined by St. Ambrose. Wealth, he points out, is not the purpose of economic activity; the purpose is well-being. Riches are the cause of ills of attachment, pride and anxiety avoided by poverty. Is poverty, then, a ground for absence of anxiety? Under certain circumstances, yes. Pride of life is renounced by obedience; sensuality by perpetual chastity; and wealth (an obvious evil) by poverty for those dedicated to the discipline of the religious life.

> Perfectioni religionis repugnat divitias vel facultates proprias habere, non autem eas in communi ad necessarios vitae usus possidere. (*Summa,* II, 2, q. clxxxviii, art. 7, *c.*)†

Nevertheless, it is possible to use well what also may be used ill, and to show a good disposition of liberality and charity as touching those things that Providence has sent our way. Generosity is not therefore a vice because those who have nothing cannot display it and vicious men can display it. This, then, is the interpretation put by Thomas, with his characteristically Catholic-Platonic distinction between those with vocation to act through discipline as spiritual guides and those without vocation, upon the statement by Gratian in that *Decretum* which is the basis of the Canon Law:

> The common use of all things which are in this world appertains to all men.

The Scholastic tradition is anti-trader and—following Plato, Aristotle and the Fathers—quite definitely anti-capitalist, in the sense of "anti-interest-taker." The *Decretum* declares:

> Whosoever buys a thing, not that he may sell it whole and unchanged, but that it may be a material for fashioning something, he is no merchant (usurer). But the man who buys it, in order that he may gain by selling it again unchanged and as he bought it, that man is of the buyers and sellers who are cast out from God's temple.

What then of the socially useful function of transporting and distributing goods? The answer is that the reward for this comes under the legitimate heading of wages for work done. The wages of management

* *Cf.* p. 701.

† It is repugnant to the complete religious life to have riches or private means, but not to possess such in common as are requisite for the needs of life.

are also legitimate. Annuities are permissible. The indication (not necessarily fixing) of fair or normative prices—"measuring rods"—is desirable. Nor does St. Thomas object to the legitimate wages of the importer and exporter,

> . . . when anyone enters on trade for the good of the community, that there may be no lack of what is necessary for a country, and seeks his gain not as an unconditional end but merely as the wages of labour.

What then of the interest on investment when there is grave risk for what is invested, *e.g.*, in a ship's cargo? Here the doctrine is developed of *damnum emergens:** he may take a fair rate to compensate him for probable loss. Also the doctrine of *lucrum cessans:*† money that might, *e.g.*, have been put into a farm, and had produce, may reasonably be compensated for, according to the measure of expectation, if loaned to another,

This is a large concession, but it still excludes two important categories of capitalist profit. (*a*) The taking of interest by legal bond where there is, therefore, no risk, but where there is no indication that the money could otherwise be employed at the same or a higher profit (*e.g.*, insistence on payment of debt by farmers at a rate fixed under other economic conditions and protest against reductions of this rate as confiscatory) is condemned as sin. (*b*) Speculation where the interest is not calculated upon any basis of probability of loss in a sound investment, but upon mere gambling hope of the maximum gain the market will yield, is sin. Either course involves the unnatural vice of attempting to live without labour. The money-lender was in effect, under the decrees of the Third Council of the Lateran (1175), Lyons (1274) and Vienne (1312), an outlaw. Positive institutions and law to the contrary are null. As St. Thomas says:

> Every law framed by man bears the character of a law to exactly that extent to which it is derived from the law of nature. But if on any point it is in conflict with the law of nature, it at once ceases to be a law; it is a mere perversion of law. (*Summa*, II, q. xcv, a. 2.)

It is that great Canonist, Innocent IV, who states (*De usuris*) that, if usury were general,

> men would not give thought to the cultivation of their land, except when they could do naught else, and thus there would be so great a famine that the poor would die of hunger; . . . the rich, for the sake both of profit and security,

* "Loss emerging."

† "Profit ceasing."

would put their money into usury rather than into smaller and more risky [but socially more desirable] investments.

In brief, the flow of investment solely in accordance with the play of the stock market and irrespective of more permanent social interests may result in unemployment, asymmetry in production and grave social damage to institutions vital to the life of a nation. St. Thomas lays down the rule that a man, in secular life, cannot be regarded as immoral if he charges such interest, as wages, for his services as enables him to maintain his secular status. (It will be noted that the clergy, like the Communist and Fascist parties today, had their own hierarchy which was unregulated by secular status and which treated their members, at least theoretically, and largely actually, without respect to wealth.) A fourteenth-century Schoolman, Henry of Langenstein (*De contractibus emptionis et venditionis**) continues:

> He who has enough to satisfy his wants and nevertheless ceaselessly labours to acquire riches, either in order to obtain a higher social position, or that subsequently he may have enough to live without labour, or that his sons may become men of wealth and importance—all such are incited by a damnable avarice, sensuality and pride.

A certain section, however, of the Franciscan Order of friars or Minorites—"Spirituals," Fraticelli, a "Left-wing"—sharing St. Francis' (1182–1226) emphasis on self-abnegation and *voluntary* poverty as a disciplinary virtue, traversed the position of the great Dominican, St. Thomas, and asserted that poverty was a moral obligation on *all* Christians who would go through that "eye of the needle" of salvation that leads to the Kingdom of Heaven.

The controversy, which started off from discussion on whether and in what fashion the Franciscans themselves might hold property, shook the Papacy and was a contributing cause of the Great Schism. For the first time, regular clergy were—on this issue of the obligation of poverty—prepared in an organized fashion, to challenge obedience to the Papacy. Pope John XXII (1316-1334) had to declare that the virtue of obedience of spirit took precedence of the virtues of poverty of goods and chastity of the flesh. He made the significant claim—on which the Friars Minor and Occam seized, as tinctured with heresy, to attack the Pope himself—that one Pope might withdraw the declarations delivered "by the key of science [knowledge]" of his predecessors. Nicholas III (1277–1280) in the Encyclical or Bull

* *Concerning Contracts of Purchase and Sale.*

Exiit qui seminat had declared that the Franciscans followed the example of Christ in having property neither collectively nor individually.

In 1323 John XXII, in the decretal *Cum inter non nullos*, declared that it was heretical to assert that Christ and his apostles could possess no private property jointly or severally and could not use this, to sell or give, as they chose. It was on this issue that Duns Scotus' great successor, the Schoolman William of Occam, offered the Emperor Ludwig IV the services of his pen against the Pope. The effect of the Decretal was to confirm the acceptance of the thesis that voluntary renunciation of private property (not inconsistent with communal possession by an Order) was an evangelic counsel and admirable as an example in the religious life; but that it was not so laid down by Christ as a moral obligation that the layman who declined to follow it was guilty of sin and the Church that owned corporate property was thereby corrupt.

It is not until the nineteenth century that confessors in the Catholic Church were instructed not to disturb the minds of penitents by questions, in accordance with the Canon Law, on the subject of the taking of interest.

Aegidius Colonna Romanus, Archbishop of Bourges, and the greatest of the immediate pupils of St. Thomas, published in 1301 his *De ecclesiastica potestate*, which it is relevant to mention here as an authoritative statement of another aspect of the Canonist's position on property. If private men only held property on *trust*, and the perfect example was of the *renunciation* to the common good of private property, who had a final title to property, not merely in use but in proprietary *right?* The argument is that somewhere a right, as distinct from the mere fact (such as any thief might have), to property must lie. It can lie only (we have already noted this argument pursued along more anarchistic lines in Wyclif) in God and those holding by right of obedience under him, *i.e., property rests on a basis of recognition within the framework of the moral scheme.* It is not an inherent indefeasible right of any man; but derives from the social order. That somebody has the happy accident of being somebody else's son sets up a mere casual and convenient claim; but establishes no ethical and social claim as such.

The right then inheres in that supreme and ideal community which is the universal Church (and here Aegidius develops a doctrine of sovereignty of the Pope as the Church's administrator). This does not interfere with the derivative enjoyment of possession by princes and proprietors, whose title is indeed improved once this moral basis is recognized. But it does mean that any prince or proprietor in rebellion against, or challenging, this moral order which is the Church, is thereby destitute of all *right* to property whatsoever. The book is patently, not only important but (as Professor McIlwain points out) profound; and marks the high-water level of the Catholic theory of the *respublica Christiana*, the Christian Commonwealth.

Sir John Fortescue (died ca. 1476), an eminent layman, Chief Justice of England in the days of Henry VI (although for the most part in exile as a Lancastrian), well illustrates the political liberalism of the great Dominican, St. Thomas, whose authority he is prepared to accept on issues of principle. The suggestion of Professor Ernest Barker is worth attention that the parliamentary constitution of England as shaped under Simon de Montfort may owe no little to the influence of the constitution of the Dominican Order.

The title of Fortescue's work of 1470, *De laudibus legum Angliae* ("Concerning the Praises of the Laws of England"), is itself significant. In his later book, *On the Governance of England*, at the very time when the absolutist New Monarchy was being built up in England by the adequately unscrupulous rulers of the Houses of York and Tudor, Fortescue drew a distinction between a *regimen politicum et regale*—a "government constitutional and monarchical"—and a *regimen tantum regale*—a "realm absolutely monarchical." France was the second; England the first. France, however (under Louis XI), had only recently passed into this absolutist phase—perhaps, the exile adds, from "lakke of hartes and corage wich no Ffrenchman hath like to an Englishman." The distinction is that, under the *dominium tantum regale*, the people are governed by a king, by "lawes as he makyth himself" and "imposicions such as he wol hymself, with owt thair assent." Fortescue did not foresee the success of the Tudor New Monarchy in utilizing the reaction against the Wars of the Roses to make the English "subjects" (a Roman term, *subiecti*)—a title which lawyers fantastically retain for the English to this day.

Fortescue rests positive law (very rightly) on the law of nature which is the law formulating the order of *all* created things, incidentally including human beings, and to which positive law is supplementary and elucidatory. It is a profound doctrine, involving none of the difficulties of Hobbes's arbitrary theory of government and law. Fortescue then quotes with approval St. Thomas' maxim (itself an adaptation of St. Isidore in the fifth century, and followed also by Bracton in England), "*Rex datur propter regnum, et non regnum propter regem*"—"The king is there for the sake of the realm and not the realm for the king." However, he admits that a king, guiltless of arbitrary exactions, must yet tax—a sore point in the Middle Ages when the baronage were inclined to regard the royal government as a private charge on the royal estate just as the gouvernance of their own estates was a charge on their own privy purse: "que notre seigneur le roy vive de soen"—"that our lord the king live on his own." Government "wol not be done with owt grete costes." However, Fortescue consoles himself. "Oure commons be riche."

2

Natural Law in the Middle Ages—despite the reservations of St. Thomas, who, with his keen logical mind, had insisted on the strict rational element in natural law, which rational element also permeated under Providence the objective world—had become ever more closely identified with some presumed "moral law." It lost its objective basis, and was no longer either the law of the rational physical order of the Stoics or the universal custom of the Romans: it became fairly closely identified with the moral system taught (and enforced) by the Church, based on the Jewish Decalogue. Men were beginning no longer to look at the order of the starry world above, which Cleanthes had apostrophized, and its Creator Logos, but at the heart within and its monitions. This unhappy and misleading identification with conventional ethics—in effect with the law of the Jewish Tribes—Natural Law (which began as the antithesis of Convention) from now on never loses.

Cardinal Nicholas of Cues (Cusanus, died 1464), who played a distinguished part at the General Church Council of Basle, Switzerland, in 1431–1433, produced in his *De concordantia catholica* a theory of originality and profundity which preserves relics of the older, more rationalist type of thought. Philosophically the thought of Cusanus in interesting ways, as we shall see,* anticipates Leibnitz; but it is suffused by mysticism. The thesis is that there is an order or pre-established harmony (organized rather than social-organic) in the universe, which is or "should"—physiologically speaking, *i.e.*, for its good health or normality—be reproduced in human Society, and especially in that society that is the *respublica Christiana.* This international commonwealth is, for Cusanus, still a reality. The Cardinal has what (if we may anticipate our own times) we may call essentially the "Genevan mind." His thought about society is not feudal, but also not Roman; it

* *Cf.* p. 704.

is federal. His notion of good government is, as is Fortescue's, not absolutist but constitutional. And, as ever in Western history, ecclesiastical thought anticipates secular, and the ecclesiastical struggles anticipate those in the more immature lay government.

The attempt of Cusanus and the Council men, the Conciliarists, was to substitute a federal, constitutional and oligarchic, *i.e.*, episcopal, or (with Cusanus as with Occam and the Franciscans) democratic theory for the demi-Hobbesian theory of sovereignty anticipated in the Papacy by Boniface VIII. The Papacy is merely allowed by Cusanus the position not of constitution-maker (as with John XXII) or law giver, but of federal executive or *cura praesidentialis*. As Dr. J. Neville Figgis says: they argued "from the idea of a society to its consequences"; their theory "decides upon the best form of government in general, and *lays down the lines which controversy took until Whiggism succumbed to the influence of Rousseau.*" They were indeed true churchly Whigs. It is significant that at this point the doctrine of *Natural Law*—of a universal objective Order; the order of the macrocosm—passes over into the doctrine of *Natural Right*, of a natural claim of the particular unit, federated in this harmonious order; of the individual microcosm. Still, however, a relation is presumed—certainly by Cusanus—between this claim of the microcosm on the one side, and God, the causer of law, and the order of this macrocosm, on the other side.

Protestant individualism—of which the rise is in no small measure due to the non-success of Conciliar federalism—gives new impetus to the tendency, found in St. Paul, towards a species of subjectivism in which man is not co-ordinated with the objective world, but in which there is an antithetical dualism between man, as immortal supernatural soul, and matter. The Patristic doctrine of Equality was based on the Christian doctrine of equal salvability, "without respect of persons," and ultimately, through the Stoics, on the Cynic doctrine of the capacity of *intelligent men, apart from all social status*, to grasp truth, which is wisdom, which is virtue. Cusanus, it is interesting to note, elevates this claim to equality into a natural *right*.

The Natural Rights to Equality of men, as monads in the universal concordance, and to Freedom, are the convenient bases for Cusanus' doctrine that government rests on consent; and are corroborated by his semi-mystic thesis that God works through the people—His voice theirs. This conveniently gets over the great stumbling block—the Pauline-Petrine excessively clear dogma that all power comes from above. The Holy Spirit of Reason works in the latent capacity of the mass, as on the day of Creation. The mass, the community, the whole—that is what counts. Consent, including the consent implied in custom, is the sole basis of political obligation. The magnates, however, may be representatives, having agency for the rest. The effect of this ecclesiastical doctrine, here systematized by Cusanus, upon subsequent secular thought, through Conciliarism and Protestantism, is too patent and startling to require labour in pointing it out.*

It is interesting to note that Cusanus become a supporter of the Papal See when the tendencies, not so much individualist as separatist and national separatist, of Conciliarism became apparent as also of that Czech Hussite movement which the Councils themselves condemned.† This was the logical issue of a theorist whose basic principle can perhaps best be called (in Professor W. Y. Elliott's phrase) "co-organic"—a belief in the combination of the federal with the organic and in that stress upon variety in unity, as against uniformity, upon which Aristotle had insisted in his criticism of Plato. The Platonic element itself in Cusanus is far too strong to permit him to encourage any atomizing tendencies in the Catholic Church or any of what, by anticipation, we may call "Balkanizing" tendencies in that German Roman Empire in which he still affirmed his belief.

With the Jesuits, we pass to a school of theorists of the Counter-Reformation that never at any time wavered in their allegiance to the Papacy; that constructed the first system since St. Thomas that was to have wide practical political influence at the time; and that deliberately worked out a doctrine of democracy for its own purposes. Once again ecclesiastical theory anticipated secular, but in this case the theory was not one—as with the Conciliarists—of the Church and *Society*, but of the *State*, developed by Churchmen. Whereas, however, the Thomist school was one of a victorious and established Church, universal and in possession, the new school stated the case of a Papal Church militant and fighting for its existence in a world divided between opposing fronts. The new school is that of the Society of Jesus, the Jesuits, whose founder was the sixteenth-century Spanish Knight, St. Ignatius Loyola (perhaps compensating for the sins of the Spanish Borgias), whose missionaries went from Paraguay to China with St. Francis Xavier, and whose educators taught Catholic Europe—including Voltaire—for the next two and a half centuries. The defeat of the Society and its (temporary) dissolution by Pope Clement XIV, in 1773, when the General of the Society declared "either it shall be as it is or

* *Cf.* pp. 269, 273, 278.

† *Cf.* p. 158.

not be," was perhaps chiefly due to its own efficiency in militancy for an order of things that no longer corresponded with the individualist secular ideology of the eighteenth century or the national-state secular ideology of the nineteenth century.

FRANCISCO SUAREZ (1548–1617), the flower of Jesuit theology, which in some quarters superseded Thomism in orthodox Catholic teaching, professor at Salamanca and Coimbra, Doctor Eximius, born in Granada, died in Lisbon. We are told that he was "laborious, modest and given to prayer." Colour is given to these monumental phrases by the praise he received from the Protestant unprejudiced Grotius: "one of the greatest of theologians and most profound of philosophers." His philosophic task was again to achieve the Thomist fusion of secular science and of faith. In politics his excursions stirred the world of thought and provoked to stuttering wrath the learned James of England and Scotland. His *Catholic Defence against the Errors of the Anglican Sect*, especially animadverting on the inquisitorial oath of allegiance demanded from all subjects by James in 1613, was burned in Britain by the common hangman and in the name of Protestant liberty its perusal was forbidden by their dread lord to the king's subjects under the severest penalties. James went further and appealed to the *esprit de corps* of his (Catholic) fellow monarchs against the book, including Philip III of Spain, on the ground that it contained doctrines contrary to the prerogative powers of sovereign princes. In 1614 the Parliament of Paris obligingly also prohibited the book. The reason for the stir is not far to seek in that odd circumstance that makes the Jesuits the avowed nursing fathers—like the Communist Party members today—of democracy.

In his doctrine of Natural Law, elaborated in his *De legibus ac Deo Legislatore* (1613), Suarez follows St. Thomas. Since the task of these theologians was to construct a system, and a system of law, they proceeded by the route customary with lawyers, *i.e.*, the appeal to authority, that is, precedent and common usage. Natural law is not only rational but is commanded. There is an imperative to follow reason lying in the nature of things as willed by Absolute Deity. Suarez is obviously here troubled by the notion that law to be truly such must involve command—a semi-error (philologically, an entire error) which we have already discussed when dealing with the Stoics.

Natural law, however—command apart—is drawn in its outlines, by reason and by instinct. As such it is immutable. Outlined by reason, *i.e.*, logic, its conclusions (as, for example, in the prohibition of fornication and of capitalists from taking interest on investments) may be too complicated for the untrained lay intellect immediately, and by the light of mere impulsive nature, to grasp. "*Ignorari possunt invincibiliter, praesertim a plebe*"—"it can be a matter of invincible ignorance, especially by the common folk."

Natural Law, then, is distinct from the merely expedient *ius gentium*, or general custom of peoples, under which alike slavery and private property are authorized. Community of goods and liberty of the person are "natural," not in the sense of being enjoined by natural moral law, but as normative. The natural law is indeed eternal, as logic and instinct are eternal, but . . . Suarez distinguishes between principles of jurisprudence and methods or applications of positive law. The Natural Law has a variable content, that is, as it passes over into the maxims guiding positive law, it properly is conditioned by the circumstances of the people, the time and the place.

There is, further, a *Natural Right* to do what *Natural Law* bids, even against positive enactment (which in this event is not just; and, therefore, by definition, not law); and positive law, even by the Pope, contrary to natural law is null. The question immediately arises: Who then is to decide when it is contrary and null?

The Pope, Supreme Pontiff, is this arbiter. In the spiritual realm of faith and morals, which presupposes choice of conscience, the authority accepted by the faithful is final. Its directive must be taken as final since there cannot be a multiplicity of patterns of salvation. This finality lies in the nature of revelation (or, as a Platonist—not, of course, Suarez—would say, of a single governing myth). The community of the faithful, or Church, wills this as necessary to salvation. In the secular community the depository of power lies in this community itself—not in any princes, claiming an independent divine right. The people may, as by the Roman *lex regia*, transfer their power and the transfer may be unreserved. But it is not, thereby, to be presumed that they have transferred any power to the ruler to demand obedience in sin. In the total Great Community, the Pope as judge of sin, *ratione peccati*, must act as arbiter, with power to release the several communities from their allegiance to rulers who break natural law.

The Jesuits are, along with Hobbes, the first Utilitarians. The appeal to *utilitas* is, of course, not new.* But, as much as John Selden, they treated secular authority as existing for the convenience and happiness of the masses—although not, needless to say, in a fashion inconsistent with orthodoxy and eternal values. Of these, however, the

* *Cf.* p. 172. *Cf.* also Cicero, p. 120.

Church was judge and guardian. For Suarez (following a sound Patristic tradition), *dominium* of man over man could not be claimed as natural; it was socially expedient. Princes were neither divine, as the Mikado, nor all-wise. Certainly they must not (in the words of the historian, Bishop William Stubbs, about the Tudors, including such a lecherous tyrant as Henry VIII) be permitted to regard themselves as "the Pope, the whole Pope and something more than the Pope." Secular rule was permitted by God and indeed justifiable; but it did not attain to the level of a spiritual or ideal principle. *Secular rule is a mundane utility.* Suarez, along with most writers from the sixteenth century on, assumes the mechanical division or dichotomy of society into ruler and people. But he retains the feudal notion of a ruler's contractual obligation to the people, "according to the pact or convention made between kingdom and king." Nor must the king exceed the "measure of the transfer or convention" or the limits set by custom. Against tyrants a just war must be waged.

The people then, it is reaffirmed (*cf. lex regia*), is the source of power, which people is a kingdom or indeed *unum corpus mysticum*—"one mystic body" (a Pauline phrase less misleading than the pseudo-exact "social organism")—thanks to the consent of the individuals who make the aggregate. It is constituted "from individual men by their own proper consent" ("*a singulis hominibus per proprium eorum consensum*"). The Jesuits, after the ineffective Occam, are the first democrats of the modern world. But they are this because they sought to bring in the people to redress the balance of the papacy against the kings. Of more profound importance for the future is Suarez' distinction, which is quite vital in political theory, between the ideal principles of the voluntary society seeking ultimate ends, values or goods and the utilitarian principles of the coercive society seeking immediate and mundane advantages or goods. This is almost the core of political wisdom.

Cardinal Robert Bellarmine (1542–1621), Jesuit, Hobbes's aversion, is not a writer of the same originality as Suarez. His comments on a mixed constitution, as being best owing to human corruption, are commonplaces of political thought since the days of Polybius. He was held by some to be guilty—a peculiar position for a Jesuit—of having unduly restricted the power of the Pope by explicitly denying him direct power in temporals, outside the estates of the Church. At the same time, Bellarmine had no doubt that the Pope had a universal jurisdiction over all governments where sin was involved, *i.e.*, as international guardian of morality. The interesting point in Cardinal

Bellarmine's theory is his further elaboration of the age-old doctrine of the separation of the spheres, spiritual and secular, and his assertion that the claim to obedience of a prince is not an absolute moral imperative, but is founded on the public convenience. Therefore (against Wyclif's doctrine) the prince did not lose authority *eo ipso* if his own morality was bad. The prince, as such, was not concerned with salvation.

This is a theory which would make a bridge across to the recognition, not only of infidel princes outside Christendom (nothing new), but of heretic princes within, and even to James II's Declaration of Indulgence in Britain. It re-emphasizes, however, as against, *e.g.*, Laud and, in certain aspects, the Lutherans, the Jesuit thesis of the non-ideal quality of secular, coercive power. It reaffirms against Hobbes the old Augustinian thesis that *the secular Leviathan or State had no ultimate, but only a derivative, secondary and expedient claim to obedience.* And Bellarmine brings in Democracy to confront the Divine Right of Kings. It was his odd fate to have his books burned—not that it would have troubled much the Jesuit prince of the Church—by the Anglican University of Oxford, in 1683, in the harlequin company of those of John Milton, Richard Baxter, John Knox and Thomas Hobbes.

3

The second re-dressing of Natural Law is when it appears, not as identified with scholastic and post-scholastic theories of the Moral Law, but as identified with the Law of Custom—not with the *ius gentium*, universal in space, but with tradition uncontroverted in time.

For example, in England, ever since the days of the reply of Henry I to the papal claim to temporal suzerainty, there was assumed to be a common law, distinct from the local peculiarities of districts and from the statute law, which common law was the formulation of the governing constitutional morality of the realm. So far as the barons of Magna Carta had a theory, this was their theory and that of Cardinal Stephen Langton. These were the "*libertates et liberas consuetudines*"—"liberties and free customs" of the realm. Far more influential, however, than the facts of Magna Carta in English History have been its fiction and myth. The myth of a fundamental custom of the realm, formulated by Magna Carta and kings as a contract, lasted on into the nineteenth century as a halo of the ark of English liberty. It was the theory of Bracton and Fortescue. There was a national constitutional law above ordinances. It was that to which Sir Thomas More appealed—although he also appealed to the custom of Christendom—as rendering unconstitutional the legislative and executive acts of Henry Tudor. It reappears in Coke's doctrine of a supreme law of which only the judges, and especially Coke, were the interpreters. And where natural law is referred to in the courts, it is usually this local constitutional morality. It was under this "natural law" that, as late as the early eighteenth century, as Professor McIlwain points out, positive statute law was occasionally voided by the Courts in England. Even Blackstone pays it formal homage. It throws a brilliant light upon the theory of the United States Constitution and the function of the Supreme Court. Few, nevertheless, went as far as Coke and asserted that "if any statute be made contrary to Magna Carta, it shall be holden for none." Even this obstinacy, however, showed an appreciation of the drift of the Hobbes-admiring Harrington's remark: "wherever the power of making the law is, there only is the power of interpreting the law so made"—a dictum definitely repudiated in United States constitutional law [*cf.* I Cranch 43, 51 (1815)].

This local lawyers' natural law, this fusion of *ius naturale* and *usus* ("use"), was not peculiar to the land of the Common Law and its spirit. The identification of *ius naturale* and *usus* is connected with the stress on national tradition by historians writing, not in the style of the monastic chroniclers, but polemically against the innovations of the New Monarchies. The study of history takes new life with the emergence of propaganda: the historians of modern Europe begin, it is well to remember, as propagandists.

In Scotland George Buchanan, the very other than well-beloved Presbyterian tutor of James VI (of Scotland) and I (of England), wrote his *Rerum Scoticarum historia*—"History of Scottish Affairs"—and then summarized his political and legal wisdom in his *De jure regni apud Scotos*—"The Right of the Kingdom among the Scots" or "Scottish Constitutional Law" (1579). In his *History*, Buchanan quotes the saying of the Regent Morton, in 1578, to the Scottish Parliament: "It is evident that government is nothing more than a mutual compact between the people and their kings." In the *De jure regni*, Buchanan makes the interesting (and un-Aristotelian) assumption of men living solitary and lawless, like Scottish crofters, in a primitive state. However, natural impulses and *utilitas communis* (the "common utility") lead them together. What, by anticipation, we may call a constitutional morality (already discussed in connection with Hobbes and sovereignty*) results; and a law takes shape. This law is prior to

* *Cf.* p. 247.

any king and the king derives his authority from the law. He is such on the *condition* that he obey the civil laws which are prior to him. We have here, in Buchanan's theory, the four notes of custom, priority of law, individualism and contract, the first and the last in an alliance (resting on feudal suppositions) which will later fall apart.

In Spain, a collection of kingdoms now being centralized under the New Monarchy of Ferdinand, Charles von Habsburg, the Emperor, and Philip II, Juan Mariana, of the Society of Jesus, wrote in 1592 his *History of Spanish Affairs*, which stressed the part played by the feudal Estates in the growth of the Spanish State—a part, especially in the case of Catalonia and Aragon, issuing in the vindication of liberties verging on conditional anarchy. In his *On Kingship and the Education of a King* (1599), dedicated to Philip III of Spain, Mariana drew together the conclusions of his reading. Like Suarez later, he holds that just war may be waged against a tyrant and, where constitutional assemblies are forbidden, assassination may be necessary. (He thoughtfully adds that it is undesirable by poisoning, because this involves constructive suicide if the victim gives himself the poisoned cup.) The doctrine is no new one. The Old Testament apart, with its fierce assassinating saviours such as Ehud, it will be found in the writings of John of Salisbury. But the Jesuits had to do a great deal of apologizing for this dictum of one of their number. The authority of the commonwealth in its people and estates, princes must learn, is greater than that of themselves; and this ultimate authority of the people, well based in Spanish history, justifies them in resistance. Civil society springs up thanks to human weakness—*not* merely crime—and incapacity for individual self-defence, which thus has its providential compensation; but, adds this typical Spaniard, laws may easily become far too many. What we must rather trust to is that "certain voice of nature speaking in our minds." Civil society then is grounded on the best of grounds: it satisfies self-interest—an item prophetic of later Utilitarian faith.

In France a book intrinsically less important, but more significant of a general trend during the disturbed years as the House of Valois drew to its end, was the Huguenot François Hot[o]man's *Franco-Gallia* (1573). Just as later, in England, a school of Whig historians developed the notion of Anglo-Saxon liberties suppressed by Norman privilege, so in France there is a theory of Gallic liberties suppressed by the Frankish (German) nobility. Hotoman's research convinced him that historically the monarchy in "Franco-Gallia" had always been constitutional and limited. He quotes with approval the feudal oath of

Aragon cited in a previous chapter.* An absolute monarchy is fit only for slaves or brutes; not for rational and free men. It will be noted that the absolute monarchy visualized is one in which rulers and ruled are in separate and opposed categories: not a "popular dictatorship" of the Octavian-Napoleon-Fascist model. Hotoman's answer then to the New Monarchy in France and to Bodin is a strictly conservative, although also liberal, one—France had never been an absolute monarchy and to make it one was an innovation. It is a line of argument later taken by the Parliamentarian constitutional lawyers of the school of Coke, in England.

The disadvantage of argument from custom and precedent was that it was common ground that some customs, even although richly ancient, might be bad. Who then should discriminate between good and bad custom? The great Jesuit school did not get itself involved in this Huguenot difficulty. It never asserted that individual consent was necessary for the maintenance‡ of secular government, but only general assent. It was not concerned to work out a theory of perfect moral obligation in the case of the State, which itself merely moved in the realm of the expedient. And as to the realm of perfect moral obligation, *i.e.*, the Church, the Pope as Voice of the Church not only had power of sovereign arbitration within it but the power of arbitration between it and other spheres, so that he could adjudicate when the primitive (feudal) contract between people and ruler was broken, being himself no party to the case. Protestant theorists, however, were in no position to take this route in the adjudication between executive sovereign and free people.

4

The theory of Natural Law, during the Protestant Reformation and post-Reformation period, progressively passes over into the theory of primary Natural Rights organized in civil society through a Contract. As has already been pointed out,† this doctrine of contract or covenant is as old as the Old Testament and corresponds with the facts of the Middle Ages—for example, the feudal oath taken by all tenants in chief to William the Conqueror at Salisbury, in 1086, and the Coronation Oath. As it develops it is a compound of the covenants of the Bible, itself the Old and New Covenant, with the Roman law-books' theory of contract, set against the historical background of the relation of the

* *Cf.* p. 154. Yet another version of Hotman's name is Hofman.

† *Cf.* p. 155.

‡ As distinct from the origin, *cf.* p. 279.

feudatories and of the estates of the realm. This last must be contrasted with the relation of subjects and State, which depends upon the Imperial notion in Roman law wherein the pleasure of the prince has the force of law. The harsh hard-boiled doctrine of Power and Sovereignty of Machiavelli, Bodin and Hobbes (especially the last two) provoked, as its counterpart, an equally harsh, angular doctrine of individualism—Rights of Freemen over *against* Government—of the school called by Barclay the Monarchomachi (Monarch-fighters). It was against these that Barclay wrote his book *De regno et regali potestate, adversus Buchananum, Brutum, Boucherium et reliquos Monarchomachos* (1600).

Whether the monarch-fighting writers were Protestant or Catholic depended upon whether, especially in France, the centre of the controversy, the monarch or legitimist claimant to be fought, was Catholic (Henry III) or Protestant (Henry IV). Opportunism at this stage entered deeply into theory. Persistently writers embarked upon an elaborate system, filling in details to choice, in order to prove something of which they were already convinced for other and more personal reasons. The function of reason was well exercised in its capacity of supplying rationalizations for those things of which the justice stated bluntly might not have so plausible and wide an appeal.

Governmental Contract, i.e., a covenant, compact, contract or quasi-contract, between ruled and ruled is the earlier form of the Contract Theory. Theodore Beza, John Calvin's immediate successor, who dominated Geneva after him, "refuter" of Castellion (one of the earliest advocates of toleration), is the probable author of a pamphlet (1550) declaring that ruler and ruled lived in a relation that was a "contracted obligation"—"conditions to which the ruler had sworn" and by breach of which he becomes a tyrant. Beza here, however, like Calvin, is only following the early High Catholic (*i.e.*, non-imperialist or ultramontane) tradition. Even King James I admitted a "Reciprock Duty." The question arises who was to decide upon its details and to proceed against him who broke it. The Catholics had an answer: they invoked the Pope—although Boucher and Mariana are also freer with other answers, besides invoking the Papacy, than the Huguenots. The Protestants waver and hesitate. George Buchanan, however, who has insisted that the king must function in accordance with the popular conception of justice embodied in the common law, gets almost as far as Mariana with a theory of deposition and, if necessary, assassination. A tyrant breaking the contract may be slain—although he discreetly cites the case of, not a king, but Cardinal Beaton, whose murder received Knox's approbation. The Calvinist minister, Lambert Daneau, writing his *Christian Politics* in Geneva in 1596, is also prepared to condone assassination. The outstanding Protestant instance, however, of due procedure in checking tyranny is that of the revolt of the Protestant Netherlands' magistrates and estates assembled against Philip II of Spain and the Low Countries. They declared, Motley quotes, that

> The contracts which the king has broken are no fantasies but laws planted by nature in the heart of mankind, and expressly acquiesced in by prince and people.

Vindiciae contra tyrannos (1579) is the most famous treatise during this phase of Contract Theory. The identity of the author, "Brutus," is in dispute; but it is almost certainly either Hubert Languet or Duplessis-Mornay, both Huguenots—and is probably Languet. The book summarizes the work of previous Huguenot pamphlets and can be taken as representative of them. It presupposes, rather than states, the existence of a governmental contract. But it leaves no doubt about the right to resist. It is, however, no more democratic than the writings of the Catholic Boucher and less so than at least the words of Mariana, Suarez and Bellarmine. In a style reminiscent of Luther, and anticipating Milton and Baxter, the *Vindiciae* dismisses the common mass as a "beast of many heads," apt to "run in a mutinous disorder."

In effect two covenants are involved. There is a covenant between God and man—both prince and people joining—the covenant of the rainbow. Religious anthropomorphism apart, such as disfigures the thought of this literalist Bibliolatrous period, what purpose is served by introducing this Covenant? A very specific one. It turns the front of the theory of the divine right of kings and, by providing a prior contract, and that divine, gives a prior moral ground for rebellion.

Further, there is implied (not verbally stated) a contract between king and people. This is broken by tyranny, since royalty is an institution for the benefit of the community. If the tyrant breaks what moral monition advises is the law of God and true religion, then there is a moral duty, not mere permission, to resist. How is this to be undertaken? The eyes of the writer turn to Elizabeth of England and to the German Protestant princes. He follows the line indicated by Calvin. The respectable magistrates and Estates—the magnates, not the multitude—may authorize resistance; and outside princes and republics may assist, correcting the tyrant in the sacred names of humanity and Christianity. We have here one of the last, but by now self-contradictory, appeals to the Christian Republic.

There were, however, difficulties in the way of Governmental Contract as a theory. First, what precisely constituted the contract? Was it the coronation oath? An historically correct answer could have referred to the elective origins of most European monarchies and to this oath, which in mediaeval days was most certainly taken seriously and constituted a ground, where the sin of perjury was alleged, for the deposing power of the Pope. Apparently, however, to this lay lawyers favouring a high theory of monarchy had an effective reply. The king was such before he was crowned. "The king is dead: long live the king." Secondly, who was to be judge of breach of the contract? Even King James I was prepared to accept the theory of Governmental Contract provided that he, *his* conscience and God alone remained judges of the breach. As he remarks, in his customary moralizing (and inconclusive) fashion:

> Whereas the proud and ambitious tyrant doth think his kingdom and people are only ordained for satisfaction of his desires and unreasonable appetites, the righteous and just king doth, on the contrary, acknowledge himself to be ordained for the procuring of the wealth and property of his people.

—a piece of pure Thomism. King James continues (1609):

> The king binds himself, by a double oath, to the observation of the fundamental laws of his kingdom—tacitly, as by being a king, and so bound to protect as well the people as the laws of his kingdom; and expressly by his oath at his coronation; so as every just king, in a settled kingdom, is bound to observe that paction made to his people, by his laws, in framing his government agreeable thereunto, according to that paction which God made with Noah after the deluge.

Thirdly, if this contract was to be taken as historical, then it was merely one historical way in which royal government had been established. Conquest was, as Hobbes said, another; and conquest was the more common. The only secure alternative was to allege that *all* government was contractual and so in its very basis and *by logical or "moral" necessity*—not by searching "in musty records." Fourthly, an objection could be raised that any contract required two or more persons, natural or corporate, with whom to contract. But how could any king of government contract with an unorganized multitude? Rather it was the government that paternally organized the multitude and made it into a people, nation or state.

5

The theory of *Social Contract* is developed in part to overcome these difficulties. Unlike Governmental Contract and the appeal to Use and Custom (with the drawback that admittedly there are bad customs), it does not necessarily make drafts upon the credit of history. It is questionable whether either Hobbes—who anyhow uses the theory dishonestly as a tour de force against his Puritan opponents—or Locke or Rousseau considered the state of nature and the entering upon the social contract to be historical conditions. Hobbes exemplified pre-contract man ably enough, by the contemporary analogy of the relation of sovereign states to each other. For the rest the state of nature was merely a primitive condition, sordid, brutal and reminiscent of the Homeric Cyclopean age. Locke freely admits that

> there are no instances to be found in story of a company of men, independent and equal one amongst another, that met together, and in this way began and set up a government.

Locke appeals to the absence of records of these pre-historic events; to the actual relations contemporarily of "a Swiss and an Indian in the woods of America"—and to reason. Rousseau, whose talent was that of a novelist, leaves his attitude towards the historicity of a state of nature more dubious. He could enter the plea that it had as much to be said in its favour as in that of the Biblical Garden of Eden. For both Locke and Rousseau the blight of Original Sin, in which the malignant Hobbes had rejoiced, flees away from the State of Nature which, if imperfect, is yet one of roseate innocence such as that of which Virgil and the pastoral poets had told.

The heart of the Social Contract doctrine is, against absolutism and the New Monarchies, that all civil order and *a fortiori* all government rests on consent. The relation of each with each in political or "civil" society is one of reciprocal duties and obligations, not of servile obedience and passive subservience even to the community or society—not to speak of any particular ruler—like an "animate tool" or cog. I refer to the pure doctrine, not violated by the tricky Hobbes. For Locke it was taken in conjunction with a species of governmental contract or (more precisely) fiduciary relation with the Government, for which trust, discharged by this Government, it provides a foundation by *incorporating the "people" as trustor*.

It will be noted that this Government is a subordinate, involved, as Professor Barker says, in a unilateral obligation to carry out the trust, "limited to the good of society." We may speak, with Sir Frederick Pollock, of a double contract in Locke—social and governmental—but, precisely, Locke, does not use the concept of Governmental Contract (with its conundrum: Who is the Arbitrator if the contract is broken?) but the safer one of Trusteeship. It is in Germany that we get the full formal elaboration, *e.g.*, in the early work of such a minor writer as Thomasius (1655–1728), professor of Leipzic and advocate of toleration, with his (*a*) social compact to settle the claims of dissentient minorities: "You came in"; (*b*) a *decretum* or constituent and constitutional law; (*c*) a governmental contract, under the constitution, of protection in return for obedience. Thomasius hopefully outlines this legal day-dream as a middle way—*media via inter Hobbesianos et Scholastico-Aristotelicos.* For Locke, it will be further noted, the trustee is the Legislature (really, of course, he means the British Parliament). As for the Executive, it is

> placed anywhere, but in a person that has also a share in the legislative is visibly subordinate and accountable to it

—so much for James II and his claims. For Rousseau, the Government is merely the delegate and functionary of the people, not even a swineherd but an office clerk. There is, in Rousseau, no Governmental Contract.

The phrase "Social Contract" is identified with the name of Rousseau, as the title of his famous book. Hobbes uses "Institution by Covenant." Locke, with many references to consent, speaks of an "original compact." In 1544, the Spaniard Marius Salamon, in a treatise dedicated to Pope Leo X, had referred to law as "*pactio quaedam*" among the citizens, but he is clearly following Augustine, who declares that there is "*generale quippe pactum societatis humanae obedire regibus suis.*"* Aegidius Colonna and Pope Pius II, a century earlier, had anticipated, as an historical suggestion of the origin of the state, the social as well as the governmental contract theory. The Jesuits, such as Suarez, psychologists with no illusions about human egoism and therefore strong authoritarians, had developed it—"by individual men through their own consent." The famous and judicious English divine, Richard Hooker, in his *Laws of Ecclesiastical Polity* (1594), had, like Colonna, bridged the Aristotelian and the *individualistic* Contract Theories:

* "As it were a general pact of human society to obey its kings"—it is not clear here whether a social pact is presupposed before the governmental. The phrase is one that Hobbes could have accepted. *Cf.* p. 235.

Two foundations there are which bear up public societies; the one, a natural inclination, whereby all men desire sociable life and fellowship; the other, an order expressly or secretly agreed upon, touching the manner of their union in living together.

In November, 1620, the Pilgrim Fathers, having landed in what was to be Massachusetts, declared:

We do solemnly and mutually, in the presence of God and one another, covenant and combine ourselves together into a civil body politic.

If there had never been a formal social contract before, there was historically one now. The foundation of the State of California by the pioneers offers highly interesting analogies of an original contract. Following the precedent, in the constitution of Massachusetts of 1780, it is declared:

The body politic is formed by a voluntary association of individuals; it is a social compact by which the whole people covenants with each citizen and each citizen with the whole people that all shall be governed by certain laws for the general good.

The connection with the democratic theory of government is made plain in the earlier (1776) constitution of New Jersey:

Whereas all the constitutional authority ever possessed by the kings of Great Britain over these colonies, or their other dominions was, by compact, derived from the people, and held of them for the common interest of the whole society; allegiance and protection are, in the nature of things reciprocal ties, each equally depending on the other, and liable to be dissolved by the others being refused or withdrawn.

In the English Civil War debates, a noticeably different theme is that of the Parliamentarian Ireton: Social contract is becoming a bolster, not of liberty, but of restraint and authority.

Here comes the foundation of all right that I understand to be betwixt men, as to the enjoying of one thing or not enjoying of it; we are *under a contract*, we are under an agreement . . . to that general authority which is agreed upon amongst us for the preserving of peace and for the supporting of this law.

Cromwell, at Putney, in 1647, gets as far as vigorous affirmation of Governmental Contract, the official Parliamentarian theory. "I think the king is king by contract." John Milton, in his *Tenure of Kings and*

Magistrates (1649), asserts that kings only hold office at popular will. For the rest, "men agreed by common league to bind each other from mutual injury, and jointly to defend themselves against any that give disturbance or opposition to such agreement." But the theory finds its clearest expression in the words of the Leveller, Wildman, at Putney:

> I conceive that's the undeniable maxim of government: that all government is in the free consent of the people. If so . . . there is no person that is under a just government . . . unless he by his own free consent be put under that government.

The very nerve of this theory of the *Voluntary Society* is exposed in remark, at the same time, of another Leveller, Rainborow:

> Really I think that the poorest he that is in England hath a life to live as the greatest he: and therefore truly, Sir, I think it's clear that every man that is to live under a government ought first by his own consent to put himself under that government: and I do think that the poorest man in England is not at all bound in a strict sense to that government that he hath not had a voice to put himself under.

It is the seventeenth-century re-expression of the Stoic Roman Law maxim, quoted at the beginning of Parliamentary history by Edward I of England: *quod omnes tangit ab omnibus debet approbari*—"What touches all ought to be approved by all"—to which Peter des Roches, Bishop of Winchester, had, in the previous reign, given such strict interpretation that he declined to be bound to pay a tax consented to in his personal absence and which, in Poland (as today in the League of Nations), had spelled the anarchistic doctrine of unanimous consent.

We shall have occasion later to trace the break-down of the Myth of Social Contract, just as in due course the Myth of Social Organism will break down in our children's days. It is a sobering reflection that good men are so seldom good thinkers because they substitute ideals for ideas—what they know they ought to think for what they ought to know they think. The extraordinary stir, however, over three centuries, almost unintelligible today, on this subject of Social Contract, may appear more intelligible if we reflect that what these men were taking so seriously is what today we, all collectivists nowadays, are taking too lightly: the moral basis of obedience to government by coercion. *Why* should *I* obey a government, bourgeois, Fascist, Communist, of which *I*, member of the minority, vigorously and conscientiously disapprove?

Locke and the Social Contract

6

John Locke (1632–1704), the man who justified by his philosophy Whigs in Revolution, was educated at Oxford, a fact that he regretted.

Whatever be the cause, Locke, like most great philosophers, was no stylist. The mane of hair brushed back, the high forehead, the wild eye betoken other graces. Perhaps the fault lay in himself and in his contempt for meretricious attractions.

> Montaigne [he writes] by a gentle kind of negligence, clothed in a peculiar sort of good language, persuades without reason . . . . he reasons not, but diverts himself, and pleases others; full of pride and vanity.

Locke's compensation is that, more than any other man, he fixed and determined the character of Anglo-Saxon thought in philosophy and culture, looking back on Bacon and Hooker and, ultimately, on the other Bacon—Roger Bacon—and on Scotus, and looking forward to Jefferson, Bentham, the Mills and William James.

A close student of medicine (like Aristotle, be it noted), Locke rejected alike that profession and the church, to become secretary to Sir Walter Vane, envoy to the Elector of Brandenburg, and later secretary to Lord Shaftesbury, the effective founder of the Whig Party. Having inherited from his father, a captain in the Parliamentary Army, independent means, he was able to reside in Holland in the years after he had been deprived of his university preferment at Christ Church by James II. He returned with King William and lived, an asthmatic, as the friend and guest of Sir Francis and Lady Masham, after a short period during which he held an office in the Board of Trade, until his death. As early as 1677 he is writing

> my health, which you are so kind to in your wishes, is the only mistress I have a long time courted, and is so coy a one, that I think it will take up the remainder of my days to obtain her good graces.

It is typical of the man that his most famous book, the *Essay Concerning Human Understanding*, was written in 1671 but not published until eighteen years later (1690), for which book he received from his publisher £30. Interesting as supplying an early key (1660) to his thinking is the title of his first work, the essay "Whether the civil magistrate may lawfully impose and determine the use of indifferent things in reference to Religious Worship." The answer, which anticipates his later (1685–1692) *Three Letters for Toleration*, is a negative. Locke writes in the preface:

John Locke
(1632–1704)

(*Facing p. 282*)

I would men would be persuaded to be so kind to their religion, their country, and themselves, as not to hazard them against the substantial blessings of peace and settlement, in an over-zealous contention about things which they themselves confess to be little, and at most are but indifferent. . . . I have not therefore the same apprehension of liberty that some have, or can think the benefits of it to consist in a liberty for men, at pleasure, to adopt themselves children of God, and from thence assume a title to inheritances here, and proclaim themselves heirs of the world, *nor a liberty for ambitious men to pull down well-framed constitutions, that out of the ruins they may build themselves fortunes.*

These are interesting words from the philosophical father of Liberalism, just after he had passed through the experience of the English Revolution.*

A new mental atmosphere prevails. Locke tells us, from Cleves in Germany, that "I have not met with any so good-natured people, or so civil, as the Catholic priests"; and, from Montpellier in France, that "the Protestant live not better than the Papist." We are on the road to the new Humanism of Goethe. The entry in the *Journal*, for May 16, 1681, is significant:

The three great things that govern mankind are Reason, Passion and Superstition; the first governs a few, the two last share the bulk of mankind, and possess them in their turns; but superstition is most powerful, and produces the greatest mischiefs.

Locke is one of the most eminent of the advocates of religious toleration. He does not advance so far as Spinoza, but this toleration is yet more integral, as we shall see, to his philosophy; and he advances far beyond such Huguenots as Jurieu.

John Milton, the poet of *Paradise Lost* and *Paradise Regained*, had already made his protest against censorship in the *Areopagitica* (1644). Books, writes Milton,

are not absolutely dead things, but do contain a potency of life in them to be as active as that soul was whose progeny they are; nay, they do preserve as in a vial the purest efficacy and extraction of that living intellect that bred them. I know they are as lively, and as vigorously productive, as those fabulous dragons' teeth; and being sown up and down, may chance to spring up armed men. And yet, on the other hand, unless wariness be used, as good almost kill a man as kill a good book. Who kills a man kills a reasonable creature, God's image; but he who destroys a good book, kills reason itself, kills the image of God, as it were in the eye.

* *Cf.* the remarks of another observer of revolution, Thomas Hobbes, p. 231.

Milton dismisses by name the supervisory system of Plato as well as of the Catholic Church.

> He that can apprehend and consider vice with all her baits and seeming pleasures, and yet abstain, and yet distinguish, and yet prefer that which is truly better, he is the true wayfaring Christian. I cannot praise a fugitive and cloistered virtue. . . .

Most of this is magnificent bombast. The obvious question is what is to happen with the man who *cannot* apprehend and abstain? Here the *aristocratisme* of Milton, to which we shall later refer, shows itself. It is a Puritan religious pride. "God sure esteems the growth and completing of one virtuous person more than the restraint of ten vicious." Why should we "deprive a wise man of any advantage to his wisdom, while we seek to restrain from a fool that which being restrained will be no hindrance to his folly?" We have here the germ (as usual, in the beginning ecclesiastical or religious) of laissez-faire and the doctrine of "the devil take the hindmost." The Platonic concept of the Polis as educator is not transferred—rightly indeed—to the Stuart State. "The State shall be my governors, but not my critics."

Milton passes from the individualistic moral argument to utilize the expedient and pragmatic. He quotes Francis Bacon. "The punishing of wits enhances their authority and a forbidden writing is thought to be a certain spark of truth that flies up in the faces of those who seek to tread it out." He adds that it is censorship that has "damped the glory of Italian wits." In that great battle between individual Intelligence and social Convention, Milton favours Intelligence and Plato Convention; and Milton is presumably (one wonders at this Puritan) prepared to pay the cost in Renaissance licentiousness and crime in lieu of Counter-Reformation morality. Civilization matters more than the masses—those whom Richard Baxter, the Puritan divine, denominated the "God-damn-me's." Milton and his friends will be guided by inner light. The same attitude shows itself in Milton's tractates advocating greater latitude of divorce. The issue is one of the most basic in human history: Superman versus Common-man.

> Give me the liberty to know, to utter, and to argue freely according to conscience, above all liberties. . . . Let (Truth) and Falsehood grapple; who ever knew Truth put to the worse, in a free and open encounter. . . . I fear yet this iron yoke of outward conformity hath left a slavish print upon our necks; the ghost of a linen decency yet haunts us.

This thesis Milton ably contrived to bind up with the tradition and pride of England as "the mansion house of liberty." In an age of commercialized publicity, of disbelief in objective truth and of a propaganda inspired by a rancour that puts the Inquisitors to shame, it is necessary to point out that Milton did *not* assert that "truth is great and will prevail" except on certain specific conditions of "free and open encounter." The freedom of commercial or party press proprietors and editors to suppress what they choose by no means follows from it, or their liberty to select only "what the public wants." What does follow is the mood of toleration, of experiment and of welcoming the new until it is found to be worse than the old.

Locke reinforces Milton's expressed belief in mental and cultural variety. As touching religion (which was quite rightly perceived to be the core of the whole moral matter), Locke asks the question, in his *Letters for Toleration:*

> You may say the magistrate is obliged by the law of nature to use force to promote the true religion; must he stand still and do nothing until he certainly know which is the true religion? If so, the commission is lost, and he can never do his duty, for to the certain knowledge of the true religion he can, in this world, never arrive.

Locke accepts the premise that man cannot here arrive at certain knowledge of truth in religion and morals, and concludes that the magistrate has no duty to enforce that about which he cannot be certain. From his famous philosophic *Essay concerning Human Understanding*, it appears, not that Locke denied the accessibility of truth, but that truth remained for human apprehension approximate, a matter of experiment and of increasing gradual apprehension. His contempt is reserved for a species not unknown today, those "who are sure because they are sure."

The profound philosophic difference between the two great traditions of thought that have dominated the human mind here shows itself. The Platonic-Thomist tradition, which we shall later see in new forms in Hegel and Marx, assumes that there is a truth, either capable of being reached by man or which may be dogmatically asserted to have been reached by man or through revelation, which truth is so final that those who deny can be confidently said to be in error. This truth exists in the field of morals and of the social order. Being one and final, the social order can be built up round it. Those in error, who persist in their ways which issue in evil-doing, it is a duty to punish or "liquidate." The rest must be educated according to the dogmatic standards of what is right—whether that the State is All or the Church infallible or whatever it may be. It is highly interesting, but is not immediately relevant, whether Plato, in putting forward his dogmatic teaching, did not do so against a background of personal scepticism, for the sake of social expediency, just as many eminent Catholics have done.

The opposite tradition, of which Bacon and Locke are the foster-parents, frankly accepts social expediency, and experiment as guide concerning what is expedient. It nevertheless is not basically sceptic but, on the contrary, reprobates dogma as obstructing the detached search for a clearer vision of truth. It is significant that Locke counts Robert Boyle, "the father of chemistry," among his intimates and refers to Sir Isaac, who deeply influenced him, as "the incomparable Mr. Newton." The movement is under the influence of believers in a rational order who are also great empirics and individualists. Whereas Platonism runs to Collectivism, communist or fascist, and a closed social order, Empiricism runs to Individualism and to belief in experiment, toleration, personal liberty and "an open world." Both traditions are rationalist, but both traditions are capable of alliance with irrationalism, the first from praise of mystic intuition, the second from distrust of abstract logic.

The position of Locke, which is of incomparable importance as the philosophic basis of the distinctive culture of the Anglo-Saxon world, can be summarized in a series of theses, not easily grasped by the inattentive mind, but highly important to understand. The emancipating effect of the first is obscure to the modern mind unless we recall the influence of the doctrine of Original Sin (or of the inherited Curse of Race), in which Augustine, Luther and Calvin passionately believed, and which—since, unlike modern race doctrines, it affected all humanity, without privilege of birth, save the redeemed saints—lay like a blight on the better minds of the age.

First, then, Locke maintained that men, not even entering into the consciousness of Adam, cannot be held answerable for the supposed sin of Adam; nor should men be counted cursed; since curse depends upon responsibility and responsibility is individual and for conscious acts (*cf. Essay concerning Human Understanding*, Book II, Chap. 27).

Secondly, Reason supplied with content by new individual experience, and not by innate, racial or divinely implanted intuition, is able to control the natural inclinations; and in that power of control lies the freedom of man.

Thirdly, the Emotions *should* be controlled by intellectual judgement, and it is the distinction and glory of man to be able so to control them. (The latent *aristocratisme* of this thesis, comparable to the position of Milton, is significant. Like the Stoics, also aristocrats, Locke, the Whig, believed in the potential salvability of all, and the actual superiority of some.)

Fourthly, Rational Judgement is founded on Probability, inferred from Experience, and not on Dogmatic Certitude; and that which arrogantly lays claim to Absolute Truth in empiric matters by that act shows itself probably False.

Fifthly, Human Judgement being of its nature approximate, unclear, but yet capable of assessing approximations to truth, it is unjust that any man, prince, president or pope, who desires freedom to announce his own supposed infallible conclusions should refuse like toleration to his neighbour.

Sixthly, man has a natural impulse to freedom; and a right, in an uncertain world, to liberty, in opinion and speech, to seek the truth in his own way.

Seventhly, every right of Civil Government over men depends upon a prior right conferred upon government by free men, unanimously constituting a civil society and, by majority, authorizing government to act in particulars. A government resting upon such consent is alone free, and all else is despotic.

It will be noted that Locke is not a sceptic about the reality of a truth which his very exploratory method presupposes. Scepticism is rather historically connected with the opposite dogmatic school of the Platonic New Academy, of Tertullian, of Pascal, of Newman—and of Trotsky—perhaps on the principle of the association of opposites. Locke goes well beyond Newman's "illative sense"; and affirms the capacity of the mind of man by reasoning—but about experience—to arrive at increasing approximation to truth. His treatment of his projected science of morals does not indicate that he recognizes, even to that extent which it has since become plain is necessary, the limitations of logical inquiry about ultimates.

It follows that a Liberalism that traces from Locke is not condemned to sceptical impotence. Liberalism is not the negation of doctrine but of coercive doctrine—it is an alternative doctrine which affirms only the duty to coerce the coercer. It is entitled to preach and organize society in accordance with its own truth, and to militate, even by force, against dogmatism and despotism, so long as it recalls that tolerance and experiment are part of that truth for the sake of which it undertakes to be militant and to use the implements of law, government and force. Whether we should tolerate the intolerant is an issue to which we shall return, but which Milton and Locke replied to with a clear, persecuting negative—although this on expedient, political grounds. The ultimate Liberal opinion was that the issue here—of the need to persecute the fanatics: Catholics, Fascists and Communists—depended upon the proximity of the danger to a peaceful and tolerant society. Many, of course, will disagree with this Liberal claim to a right to persecute and coerce on behalf of a liberal *status quo*. The issue must be studied in connection with the Whig-Liberal doctrine of physical rebellion.

7

In his *Two Treatises on Civil Government* (1689–1690) Locke sets forth his theory of government. The *First Treatise* is concerned with a detailed refutation of Sir Robert Filmer, in which John Locke follows much the lines already taken by Sir Algernon Sydney (or Sidney, executed 1683) in his *Discourses concerning Government*, published in 1688. Government, for Sydney, is something expedient, for the common good, resting on consent and to be tested by reason in its success, not something prescribed to subjects by a king as a father endeavours to prescribe for his children. It is capable of being examined by the critical judgement; and old prescription or habit is no bar to that examination. Sovereignty lies in the people; but power should be exercised through some constitution, not so much democratic, as of the old Roman Republican model. These classical examples, as Hobbes complained, since the learned Milton and even earlier, were entirely the fashion. Sydney writes:

> The base effeminate Asiatics and Africans, for being careless of their liberty, or unable to govern themselves, were by Aristotle and other wise men called "slaves by nature," and looked upon as little different from beasts . . . the whole fabric of tyranny will be much weakened, if we prove, that nations have a right to make their own laws, and constitute their own magistrates; and that such as are so constituted owe an account of their actions to those by whom, and for whom they were appointed . . . why did Caligula wish the people had but one neck, that he might strike it off at one blow, if their welfare was thus reciprocal . . . the liberty asserted is not a licentiousness of doing what is pleasing to everyone against the command of God, but an exemption from all human laws, to which they have not given their assent.

Locke's refutation of Filmer and his texts is, if possible, even more learned:

> Firstly, that this donation (*Gen.* 1, 28) gave Adam no power over men, will appear if we consider the words of it. For since all positive grants convey

no more than the express words they are made in will carry, let us see which of them will comprehend mankind or Adam's posterity; and those I imagine, if any, must be these—"every living thing that moveth"; the words in the Hebrew are *khăyyāh hāromeset, i.e., bestiam reptantem,* of which words the Scripture itself is the best interpreter. God having created the fishes and fowls the fifth day [etc.].

The *Second Treatise,* licensed for printing on August 23, 1689, is a very different matter from the *First Treatise.* Here we have that State of Nature, Natural Right and Social Contract which we have already discussed. Locke invents a State of Nature different from that of Hobbes and more reminiscent of Eden and the poetic Golden Age —a condition only defective by reason of a certain inefficiency and because men were not good enough to be trusted to be just judges in their own case. Out of a different hat from Hobbes, Locke produces a different rabbit. The practical utility of a State of Nature, for Locke, is that it provides as it were a cushion for revolutions, especially if moderate ones. Revolution might mean a temporary measure of anarchy, but this state of natural anarchy, as in Spain today, is not so intolerable—more tolerable than tyranny.

Political power is ordained "only for the public good"; and is better dissolved than used as an instrument of absolutism. As Jephtha says, "the Lord the Judge" is judge in the issue here who has broken the contract or exercised force without right; and we may "appeal to Heaven" on it, presumably by ordeal of battle. Whether I shall make that appeal, in a situation extra-legal or when positive law is contrary to its own basic principle of being for my preservation, "I myself can only be judge *in my own conscience,* as I will answer it at the great day to the Supreme Judge of all men." Indeed a ruler, *not* in a relation of contract or trusteeship with his people, is in a state of nature to them. Locke, however, makes it quite clear that this resort to arms only lies where there is no "common judge," constitutionally provided, or when the aggressor flouts this constitutional authority or when he takes the initiative in resorting to force in despite of that authority. These reservations from the great philosopher of the English Revolution require pondering. "Absolute monarchy," . . . however, "is indeed inconsistent with civil society," and by Hobbes's own principles might be destroyed.

The Arcadian State of Nature is one of equality—"men being by nature all free, equal and independent."

This equality of men by Nature, the judicious Hooker looks upon as so evident in itself, and beyond all question, that he makes it *the foundation of that obligation to mutual love amongst men on which he builds the duties they owe one another.*

It is "a state of liberty, yet not a state of license." With an eye on Hobbes, Locke adds that the State of Nature is as far different from being a state of war as one "of peace, good will, mutual assistance, and preservation" is from a state of enmity. In brief, it is an Anarchist's Paradise. It is a state regulated by the moral law or "Law of Nature which obliges everyone" and "which willeth the peace and preservation of all mankind." Under that moral law there are duties and rights—Natural Rights. Natural Rights are the moral claims of the individual, as a moral being, on his fellows—moral claims under the moral or Natural Law "which willeth the peace and preservation of all mankind"—the Law which is the rule of "reason and common equity." The State of Nature is a social condition.

The Social Contract does not inaugurate primitive society. It inaugurates a polity or civil society. Men address themselves to the need for government. In brief, it inaugurates government, not society. "I easily grant that civil government is the proper remedy for the inconveniences of the state of Nature." Not of course that this inconvenience is worse than absolute monarchy. On the contrary, men enter into the civil order for the sake of "an established, settled, known, law." "All men are naturally in that state [of nature], and remain so till, by their own consents, they make themselves members of some politic society." Then, having decided so to make themselves members, as a second step some particular Legislative is set up as trustee, with an Executive, whether monarch or otherwise. To Locke is due, in an early form, the famous doctrine of the Division of Governmental Powers. Chapter XII is "Of the Legislative, Executive and Federative [Treaty-making; Foreign Office] Power of the Commonwealth." "The legislative and executive power are in distinct hands . . . in all moderated monarchies and well-framed governments."

Conquest constitutes no title.

> It is plain that he that conquers in an unjust war can thereby have no title to the subjection and obedience of the conquered. . . . Paternal power is only where minority makes the child incapable to manage his property; political where men have property in their own disposal; and despotical over such as have no property at all.

Locke owes his popularity and reputation as a political thinker to the fact that he justified to their own consciences, after the event, the Whigs who had engaged in the Revolution of 1688. He showed them that James II, who could scarcely claim to rule by conquest as heir of William the Bastard, had broken his trust and was a civil official discredited and suitably dismissed. The almost bloodless "Glorious Revolution" of 1688–1689, unlike the Puritan Revolution and the Commonwealth, had no reaction and aftermath in a Restoration, despite Jacobite attempts. It was a good, unimpassioned revolution, not romantic. Further, Locke showed to the Parliamentarian yeomen, to the Puritan gentry of means, and to the Whig nobles—who had vague reminiscences that gathered round the myth of Magna Carta and of the feudal repudiation of *all* taxation save by almost individual consent; and who strongly objected to increased taxation—that the sacrosanctity of property was a natural right.

8

Locke is at his most unsatisfactory here, on this issue of property. Logically he should have stood for the natural right of all to property—a "three-acre and a cow" doctrine. This can legitimately and, indeed, alone consistently be drawn from his position. But indubitably the Whig lords understood him as meaning that each man's hereditary property was so sacrosanct; and Locke does not disillusion them.

> The great and chief end, therefore, of men uniting into commonwealth, and putting themselves under government, is the preservation of their property; to which in the state of Nature there are many things wanting.

The Whig-Liberal preoccupation with private property—alien to the Catholic and unmarked even with the Tory absolutist—dates from this time, although Mr. Tawney traces back the lineage to Calvin and the Reformed divines who took the multiplication of goods (like Abraham's sheep) as a visible sign of Divine favour and who, unlike the Catholic fathers of an earlier age, were not prepared to tempt Providence by scrutinizing too closely by what uncharitable means the money had been made. Indeed, there is this ambiguity, that Locke appears to assert that the natural right is, not of goods to each according to his needs, but to the whole product to each of his labour. It is in the course of this discussion that Locke makes use of what are later to become famous phrases, the corner-stones of even more famous doctrines, such as that "it is labour indeed that puts the difference of value on everything"; and that "whatsoever [a man] removes out of the state that Nature hath provided and left it in, he hath mixed his labour with it, and joined it to something that is his own, and thereby makes it his property." God "gave the world to men in common"; but he gave it for the benefit of those who would develop it, that is, "to the use of the industrious and rational (and labour was to be his title to it)."

Locke, as we have already pointed out in discussing his attitude to the first Puritan Revolution, was an apostle of toleration, moderation, free experiment. In settling the philosophy of the second, "Glorious" Revolution, he displays the same qualities. These perhaps made him the suitable draftsman of a constitution which he was requested to shape for the tolerant Carolina planters in America. Locke, in fact on the subject of property, speaks with a lucid obscurity befitting a philosopher faced with the difficulty of having to contradict himself. It is "very easy to conceive" of a time when "as a man had a right to all he could employ his labour upon, so he had no temptation to labour for more than he could make use of." But "it is plain that the consent of men have agreed to a disproportionate and unequal possession of the earth," thanks—an Aristotelian touch this—to the convention of recognizing the value of that which has small consumptive utility, silver and gold. There appears to be an oblique hit at usury here.

> I dare boldly affirm that the same rule of propriety—*viz.*, that every man should have as much as he could make use of, would still hold in the world, without straightening anybody, since there is land enough in the world to suffice double the inhabitants, had not the invention of money, and the tacit agreement of men to put a value on it, introduced (by consent) larger possessions and a right to them.

The clue is perhaps to be found in the rights of the "industrious and rational." All start, but all do not end, with an equal chance. Locke's conclusion appears to be a modified distributivism, conditioned by the rights of industry and intelligence.

> As much as any one can make use of to any advantage of life before it spoils, so much he may by his labour fix a property in. Whatever is beyond this is more than his share, and belongs to others. Nothing was made by God for man to spoil or destroy.

9

Locke, judiciously supporting himself on Hooker, proceeds to explain what he means by equality.

> I cannot be supposed to understand all sorts of "equality." Age or virtue may give men a just precedency. Excellency of parts and merit may place others above the common level.

What man has a natural right to is his "natural freedom, without being subjected to the will or authority of any other [individual] man." Man as such is governed by the "law of reason"; and *on his capacity to comprehend that reason his right to be considered equal depends.* "We are born free *as we are born rational;* not that we have actually the exercise of either; age that brings one, brings with it the other too." In brief, equality is the birthright of a potential rational being, so far as he matures as rational.

If this is equality, what then is freedom? The answer is markedly similar, and an anticipation, as we shall see, of that later given by Rousseau.

> There only is political society where every one of the members hath quitted this natural power, resigning it up into the hands of the community in all cases that exclude him not from appealing for protection *to the law* established by it. . . . Wherever, therefore, any number of men so unite into one society as to quit everyone his executive power of the law of Nature, and to resign it to the public, then and then only is a political or civil society. . . . No man in civil society can be exempted from the laws of it. . . . Though men when they enter into society give up the equality, liberty and executive power they had in the state of Nature into the hands of the society, to be so far disposed of by the legislative as the good of the society shall require, yet it being only with an intention in everyone the better to preserve himself, his liberty and property (for no rational creature can be supposed to change his condition with an intention to be worse), the power of the society or legislative constituted by them can never be supposed to extend farther than the common good.

Locke here quotes his great conservative counterpart, Richard Hooker, a man of moderation like himself. Hooker (1554–1600), in his *Ecclesiastical Polity,* writes:

> Civil law, being the act of the whole body politic, doth therefore overrule each several part of the same body [the social-organic analogy is noteworthy] . . . The public power of all society is above every soul contained in the same society, and the principal use of that power is to give laws to all that are under it, which laws in such cases we must obey, unless there be reason showed which may necessarily enforce that the law of reason or of God doth enjoin the contrary.

Locke concludes:

> Freedom of men under government is to have a standing rule to live by, common to everyone of that society, and made by the legislative power erected on it. A liberty to follow my own will in all things where that rule prescribes

not, not to be subject to the inconstant, uncertain, unknown arbitrary will of another man, as freedom of nature is to be under no other restraint but the law of Nature. *This freedom from absolute, arbitrary power is so necessary* to, and closely joined with, a man's preservation, that he cannot part with it but by what forfeits his preservation and life together.

The significance of Locke as a political philosopher lies in his stress —not on revolution and force, for his mood with its distrust and contempt of the "enthusiast" is not that of the temperamental revolutionary—but on personal liberty. It lies also in his work of raising men to fuller consciousness of the value of that liberty, both as the attribute of a being dignified by the power of moral choice and as the guaranty of toleration, initiative, experiment and progress in society and civilization.

This personal liberty is not that of a Robinson Crusoe (who anyhow owes his mental stock to his society), nor was it so thought of by Locke. The Social Contract is indeed rather a Political Contract conducting men from a simple but social life into one of organized civil society. The fiction is indeed a logical more than an historical one. And it corresponds to certain truths: that the social order rests, not on force, but on a consent (even if passive) which presumes the recognition of mutual obligations; that every law imposes new social duties and rights; and that, normally, each generation incurs new obligations unknown to the preceding generations and enters a more elaborate system of law compared with which that of its predecessors was almost an original, anarchic state of nature. Further, that it would be preferable by revolution to cast off these new obligations and to revert to the fashions of our forefathers, than to have these new obligations imposed by a tyranny itself unrestrained by established law or constitutional morality. These propositions are by no means nonsense, empty myth or exploded fallacy. They are of the first significance in our contemporary society.

10

Are there, then, Natural Rights? We shall see later* that this doctrine is attacked, *e.g.*, by T. H. Green, on the ground that either these rights are legal, in which case they presuppose and are not the basis of a system of positive law, or they are moral, in which case they still presuppose a society to which we have obligations as such, and do not precede it. This, however, appears to involve a misreading of

* *Cf.* p. 511.

Locke, especially perverse in the light of Locke's quotations from Hooker. Locke's State of Nature is *not* pre-social; and his Natural Rights are such under a moral law of man's being as a social animal, dictated by his inmost nature and formulated by reason. But these rights are prior, in logic and history, to any *particular* organized society and system of law and provide a norm of judgement whereby to test these. In brief, there is a touchstone, which Locke prefers to call Natural, rather than either rational or ideal, for the testing of every actual, historical and ephemeral social order.

Since Locke carefully associates Natural Rights with rational right, claimed by man as a rational being, he cannot be accused, it should be noted, of Anarchism (of the instinctive brand). His use of the term "Rights" is to be understood against the background of his use of Natural "Law"—a usage, later to be severely criticized, but (as we have seen) fully, scientifically and etymologically justifiable. Much of the criticism arises from an error of lawyers who presume that their own departmental definitions must be accepted in the face of the history of law, as it arises from custom, and in disregard of the perspective of philosophy which recognizes natural law as possessing a more basic and ancient meaning than any positive law as conceived of, *e.g.*, by Hobbes and Austin. Statute law is a late, minor and derivative thing. Any picture of law taken from it is utterly opposed, for example, to the Aristotelian and Stoic notion of basic law, or to Bracton's notion of common law. But Hobbes, Blackstone (in part) and Austin imposed on the lawyers their own peculiar philosophy.*

Locke's greatest difficulty is with the problem of the dissentient minority. If government rests upon consent, what about those who dissent? But they have agreed to accept the majority decision. But what if, at least on certain issues, they deny that they have agreed? An *Original* Contract may have virtue as indicating the force of tradition into which each child enters: society is not newly created every nineteen years. But I cannot yet be said to give free consent merely by the accident of being born. "*Salus populi suprema lex* is certainly so just and fundamental a rule, that he who sincerely follows it cannot dangerously err." But how far will Locke carry this principle much echoed by Machiavelli? Only to the point of insisting that government must be by majority legislative decision, unless a number larger than the majority is specifically stipulated. This follows from the intention of the Social Contract or "original compact." But how

* *Cf.* pp. 245*ff.*

are we to understand that a man enters into this compact? By a declaration express—or tacit. And what is the sign of tacit compact? The answer is residence; the compact lasting so long as does the residence. "He is at liberty to go and incorporate himself into any other commonwealth, or agree with others to begin a new one *in vacuis locis*."*

But is he? This was good enough in the days of the Pilgrim Fathers. But what reality has it today in Russia, Germany, Italy—or for the unemployed man elsewhere? Appreciating the difficulty, the philosopher Kant later introduced, logically enough, a "natural right" of emigration. The moral claim is by no means without significance, especially in issues of moral judgement. The only alternative seems to be the natural, moral right to go to jail—*and* to be treated as a political prisoner, not a criminal. (As distinct from Hobbes's thesis that such a one becomes a "wolf's head" or pariah.) It gives the moral right to protest. What ultimately is at stake is no less than this: the moral claim of the Private Conscience to judge the State—Socrates' old claim and Luther's (as touching the Universal Church). The better opinion is that that claim is beyond refutation when *rationally*, *i.e.*, *not* merely subjectively and capriciously, urged—although it may not always be expedient to give it civil recognition. The chief challenge to this comes from the Leviathan or Social-organic theory of the State, which we shall have occasion to discuss later when we come to the post-Hegelians. The right of a minority to resort to arms, except under aggression and when no protection is offered by due process of law, Locke certainly does *not* contemplate.

> *Whosoever uses force without right—as every one does in Society who does it without law*—puts himself into a state of war with those against whom he so uses it, and in that state all former ties are cancelled, all other rights cease, and everyone has a right to defend himself, and to resist the aggressor. . . .
>
> Whenever the legislators endeavour to take away and destroy the property of the people, or to reduce them to slavery under arbitrary power, they put themselves into a state of war with the people, who are thereupon absolved from any further obedience, and are left to the common refuge which God hath provided for all men against force and violence. Whensoever, therefore, *the legislative shall transgress this fundamental rule of society*, and either by ambition, fear, folly or corruption, endeavour to grasp themselves, or put into the hands of another, an absolute power over the lives, liberties and estates of the people, by this breach of trust they forfeit the powers the people had put into their hands for quite contrary ends, and it devolves to the people,

* "In the wide open spaces."

who have a right to renounce their original liberty. . . . *Thus to regulate candidates and electors, and new model the ways of election, what is it but to cut up the government by the roots, and poison the very fountains of public security?* . . .

People are not so easily got out of their old forms as some are apt to suggest.

Those in power are most tempted to abuse it and must most closely be watched. Magistrates may be resisted. It will be noted that, in Aristotelian style, Locke specifically contemplates the possibility of a democratic (or Parliamentarian) dictatorship and condemns alike it and (by implication) a Jacobin so-called "proletarian" dictatorship, *i.e.*, dictatorship by a group on behalf of the proletarian majority, as much as any Jacobite absolutism. The test which Locke uses is a very conservative one: the observance of the law and constitution. This constitution, however, is not mere use. It is that to which the people have assented. "*Wherever law ends, tyranny begins.* . . . I will not dispute now whether princes are exempt from the laws of their country but this I am sure, they owe subjection to the laws of God and Nature." Who is to be the judge? God is the judge, but each must be his own adviser whether he is justified in conscience in appealing to God by the ordeal of force. What touchstone shall guide conscience? "Force is to be opposed to nothing but unjust and unlawful force." Are we not here, with the words "unjust" and "unlawful" in an argument *in circulo?* Not quite. First, there must be *no force save against force.* (We have already seen this in our study of Locke's theory of toleration and of justifiable persecution.) Further, force is *then only legitimate where natural rights, indicated by reason, are violated.* And government is unjust which is contrary to the principles, recognizing natural rights, assented to "by the body of the people." Reason is corroborated by this assent of the body of the people; just as reason asks, "what is the interest of the body of the people?" "Those who set up force again in opposition to the laws, do *rebellare*—that is, bring back again the state of war," even though they be the legislators (abusing their trust) or the magistrates. Catholic Barclay says that tyranny even must be resisted with respect. But, sardonically comments Locke,

He that can reconcile blows and reverence may, for aught I know, deserve for his pains a civil, respectful, cudgelling wherever he can meet with it. . . .

How to resist force without striking again, or how to strike with reverence, will need some skill to make intelligible. . . . This is as ridiculous a way of resisting as Juvenal thought it of fighting: *Ubi tu pulsas, ego vapulo tantum.**

* "Where you strike, I merely get a flogging."

And the success of the combat will be unavoidably the same as he there describes it:

Libertas pauperis haec est;
Pulsatus rogat, et pugnis concisus, adorat
Ut liceat paucis cum dentibus inde reverti.*

Locke has been described as a second-rate political thinker. That is certainly not the case. His better thought, however, lies in connection with the wider presuppositions of politics and must be extracted (as indicated in the theses outlined above) from his *Essay concerning Human Understanding*. It will be noted that the old harsh dichotomy, Roman but without the Roman concept of citizenship, of the absolute Tory thinkers—Hobbes, rather than King James—the division between sovereign ruler and subject, which reappears inverted in the harsh Whig concept of a joint-stock company, with the individual shareholders watching the government as managing director for defalcations, is smoothed over by Locke. On the one side stands, not "the ruler," but the legislative as trustee; on the other, not the individual "ruled," but "the people" as testator.

What Locke does not satisfactorily clear up is what he means by "the interest of the body of the people." Here his reference is deplorably vague. He is not to be supposed to think (whatever he says) that it is decided by "law," often made by dead aristocracies. If the legislators are not competent to decide this interest, who is? Locke is clearly a minimalist in government, believing in the minimum of new legislation (as did Aristotle, oddly enough). "Freedom of men under government is to have a standing rule to live by." Is fundamental law, then, the measure for the protection of those natural rights modified, as agreed, under the social contract, which represents the basic interests of the body of the people? The answer, surely, is: Yes. And these rights are discovered by common assent, reason and the study of human nature. The individual, the rational individual, the scientific student, the political physician is judge. Locke is an exponent not of the revolutionary, but of the scientific, attitude in political science. He is the forerunner not so much of Marx—and certainly not of Rousseau—as of Bertrand Russell.

* "This is the poor man's freedom;
That beaten he begs, and struck with the fist, he prays
That he may be allowed to get away with a few teeth in his head."

Typically Locke is more backward than Juvenal in showing any full appreciation of this other aspect of property and its rights.

READING

John Milton: *Areopagitica.*

BIBLIOGRAPHICAL NOTE

J. W. Gough: *The Social Contract,* 1936.
Bede Jarrett: *Social Theories of the Middle Ages,* 1926.
H. J. Laski: *Political Thought from Locke to Bentham,* 1920.
H. J. Laski (ed.): *Vindiciae contra Tyrannos,* 1924.
*John Locke: *Second Treatise on Civil Government.*
R. H. Tawney: *Religion and the Rise of Capitalism,* 1926.

Chapter X

The American and French Revolutions: Montesquieu, Jefferson, Burke and Paine

1

IN 1656 James Harrington, Parliamentarian officer and allocated companion of Charles I during his captivity, a man regarded by his contemporaries as more brilliant in his views than weighty in his judgements, wrote *The Commonwealth of Oceana.* He deliberately bases himself on tradition in political science—the traditions of Aristotle and Machiavelli, "the only politician of later ages." From Aristotle he takes his first principle of government that it must be—as against the opposite thesis which he ascribes to Hobbes—"the empire of laws and not of men," what has irreverently been called the rule of "Judge & Co." It is, as we have seen, also the thesis of Locke; but Harrington is rather the would-be political scientist than the political philosopher and propagandist, and in the succession that passes on to Montesquieu rather than to Locke. His reference to the political scientist of Malmesbury is significant as coming from a practising Parliamentarian: "I believe that Mr. Hobbes is, and in future ages will be accounted, the best writer in this day in the world."

Writing after the Civil Wars and under Cromwell, it is both interesting and significant that Harrington selects stability, or permanence, as the test of a sound constitution. This is achieved—and here is Harrington's novelty, anticipating Locke's stress on property, Marx's economic determinism—where there is a direct *relation between economic and political power.* Absolute monarchy, mixed monarchy and commonwealth correspond to the holding of property mostly by the one, few or many. Tyranny, oligarchy and anarchy are perverted forms when, by violence, those try to rule who do not hold the balance of property, which is also "the balance of dominion."

This thesis might of course be used as an argument for a plutocracy holding both economic and political power. Actually Harrington does not use it so—any more than does Aristotle. He is a champion of the yeoman farmer, who is the beneficiary of this first economic interpretation of history. The distribution of property by the Tudors cut away the economic bases in England of both feudal aristocracy and absolutism (*cf.* the Stuart need for taxes). The future necessarily, therefore, lay with a commonwealth—a conclusion undoubtedly sound in the long run, and scientifically profound, but from which Harrington drew the theorist's conclusion that the monarchy would not be restored.

As much as Hobbes and Spinoza, Harrington sets himself the problem of how to adjust the diverse interests of man the egoist with his fellows. The answer given is aristocratic. The few, who are originators of ideas, must propose. The many will pass judgement. It is Aristotle's thesis. There is "*a natural aristocracy diffused by God throughout the whole body of mankind.*" These should correspond with constitutional bodies: a senate and a general council. These together with the magistracy, or executive, make up one of those triple divisions of powers of which we shall hear so much, not least from those Founding Fathers of the American Constitution, such as John Adams, who were students of Harrington's works.

To Charles Secondat, baron de Montesquieu (1689–1755) is due the classical formulation of the doctrine of checks and balances, and of the division of powers, although anticipated by John Locke. To his work as a sociologist we shall have occasion to revert later.* Montesquieu, a French provincial lawyer and nobleman, made his *début* in Paris society with his *Lettres persanes* (1721), one of the earliest of those essays in literary comparative anthropology, as a means of satirizing the home government and yet getting past the censor, which was fashionable at the time. In the *Lettres persanes* Montesquieu makes that oblique criticism upon contemporary manners and politics, as Voltaire did later in *Candide,* such as alone was possible in the age of Louis XV. It is a work characterized by a pretty wit which was less conspicuous in his subsequent and more famous *Esprit des Lois* (1748).

The comment upon the *Esprit des Lois* by Madame du Deffand, that it would more appropriately have been entitled "*De l'Esprit sur les Lois,*"† seems to do a somewhat dull and prolix production undue honour. Indeed, the *mot* seems rather to have been based upon his preceding reputation. The book is characterized by little of that cynical sagacity which made remarkable the work of his predecessor

* *Cf.* p. 751.

† "Wit on the laws," not "spirit of the laws." Perhaps Mme. du Deffand did not read the book.

and countryman, Montaigne. D'Alembert, the encyclopaedist, declared that Montesquieu occupied himself less with laws that have been made than with those that ought to be made—a comment more appropriate, however, to Montesquieu's polar opposite, Rousseau. Despite the moral enthusiasm with which Montesquieu's treatment of the subjects of slavery and civil liberty is endowed, the work on the whole rather deserves the criticism of Rousseau himself, that Montesquieu is concerned rather with how things happened than with asking why.

We have, indeed, here the beginning of the famous so-called "historical method." The anthropological discussion which had been introduced into the *Lettres persanes*, in order to provide a satire on French life in an age of censorship, here, in the *Esprit des Lois*, becomes a serious and scientific technique. Indeed, his definition of law itself, as the necessary relations sprung out of the nature of things has, not only a Natural Law background, but sociological implications that will be discussed when we come to the criticism of the writers of the Sociological school.

Montesquieu derives his political theory, as distinct from his large museum of political illustrations, from the writings of Locke and the theorists of the Roman constitution. *L'Esprit des Lois* appeared in 1748 and was preceded, in 1734, by his study entitled *The Grandeur and the Fall of the Romans*, an anticipation in title of Gibbon's great work. The British constitution appeared to Montesquieu to preserve a primitive spirit of liberty and, in words reminiscent of Tacitus, Montesquieu declares the British constitution was "found in the woods." His distinctive contribution, however, consists in his discussion of those qualities in this constitution which he, along with Voltaire, found peculiarly praiseworthy. Liberty is preserved by the balance between the parts of the constitution, of which he declares that "the one enchains the other and," he adds optimistically, "so the whole moves together." It would perhaps have occurred to him that it was rather a prescription for dead-lock if he, like Locke, had not been a convinced minimalist in legislation, believing that the least administered is best, with presuppositions about the work of the legislator better founded in civilized tradition than those of our own collectivist and maximalist (*i.e.*, law-multiplying) age, but entirely alien to these latter. "It is necessary," he continues, "from the very nature of things, that power should be a check to power." Montesquieu's discovery of the virtues of the British constitution achieved for him a reputation which, not unnaturally, was even larger in Britain than in France. His influence spread to the American colonies, where his interpretation, however unduly simple, was received as correct and had a profound influence upon the theory and practice of the Founding Fathers of the American constitution, whose prime object was to save the liberty of the citizen by reducing, if necessary, the mechanism of the government to a standstill.

Montesquieu, in developing his theory of governmental balance, formulates the classical doctrine of the triple division of constitutional powers. Locke has indeed referred to the legislative, federative (*i.e.*, treaty-making and foreign) and executive functions of government. Montesquieu takes over this terminology, but immediately changes it into that which has now become famous—legislative, executive and judicial. The preservation unimpaired of this distinction and balance, which guarantees personal liberty through a conservative and jealous suspicion of disreputable innovation by government, has been the chief object, through the last century and a half, of American constitutionalists. It explains the difficulties, not very long ago, of the President of the United States with the Supreme Court of Justice, and the grounds for the volume of conservative sentiment which lies behind the rulings, however inconvenient to the Executive, of those who have been called the Nine Old Men.

The doctrine also, for a brief period, had its influence in France—that is, so long as the Anglo-phile vogue lasted. The *Declaration of the Rights of Man*, of 1789, declared:

> Any society in which the guaranty of rights is not assured or the separation of powers is not determined does not have a constitution.

It is worth while also noting that in the establishment of the American Congress, the theory of checks between the constitutional powers, of Harrington, Locke and Montesquieu, was so far adhered to that a second balance was further contemplated between the Senate, representing the influence of wealth, seniority and locality, and the public House of Representatives. It was profoundly believed that, in the words of George Washington, "the spirit of encroachment tends to consolidate the powers of all departments in one and thus to create, whatever the form of government, a real despotism. . . . The concentration of powers in one hand is the essence of tyranny. . . . "

Montesquieu, it should be remarked, follows the thesis of Harrington in asserting that the distribution of the balance of power must be concurrent with, and will be dependent upon, the distribution of the balance of property. Only by this method has political power the means to give effect to its more fundamental decisions. As Locke had said, property is decisive.

Montesquieu, as sociologist, also advances the theory, reminiscent of Plato, that the form of constitution, whether republican, aristocratic, monarchist or despotic, depends upon those psychological characteristics which dominate in a given society. The characteristic in human nature dominating in a despotic state is fear, although Montesquieu does not make it clear whether this is causative or consequent. In a famous phrase, he asserts that the characteristic of a republican constitution, "the human passion which makes it act," is what he chooses to term virtue, defined as "love of country and of equality." With Aristotle, Montesquieu is tempted to conclude that virtue is rare, and, anyhow, that this love of equality is only a motive force in small communities and over limited areas. He thus maintains the theory generally accepted in the eighteenth century (and a serious obstacle, as we shall see, to those who undertook the task of constituting the United States in opposition to Tory Loyalists) that republics must necessarily be small in territory. He seeks, however, to overcome this difficulty by indicating the possibilities for them of a federal solution.

The general effect of Montesquieu's sociological and anthropological treatment of his subject—in which, despite imperfect anticipation by Machiavelli and Vico and the remote work of Aristotle, he was a pioneer—was to substitute a naturalistic treatment of politics for the ethical treatment which had been in vogue for over a millennium. The nature of constitutions, he maintains in a fashion that anticipates the theories of the later school of the economic interpretation of history, is contingent upon factors of climate and upon the physical structure of the country. The climatic theory has already made its appearance in the writings of Dubois, Bodin and others, but from now on becomes part of the received tradition of political theory. Montesquieu, however, besides occasional digressions of an ethical quality such as those on which D'Alembert comments, hesitates between a naturalistic theory of politics and a theory which explains social conduct from the character of the governmental constitution of a country. Thus, the political liberty (as distinct from that civil liberty which is the negation of chattel slavery) upon which he lays such stress, is held to be the consequence of, and to be preserved by, a particular mode of political constitution. That mode is one in which a government, owing to its interior divisions, is unlikely to set up a bureaucratic tyranny over the life of the individual. It is here that the full significance of Montesquieu's theory of the division of powers becomes apparent.

It is noteworthy that the eminent nineteenth-century historian of political theory, Sir Leslie Stephen, in commenting upon the work of a later writer of the same school, De Lolme, criticizes him for not observing that the balance between Parliament and Crown, *i.e.*, legislature and executive, upon which Montesquieu and De Lolme alike laid such great stress, was a balance that was being destroyed in De Lolme's own day. The supposition of Sir Leslie Stephen is that the power of the Crown is, under the British constitution, being progressively subordinated to those of the Legislature, and hence that the famous theory of division of powers, so far at least as Britain, as distinct from America, is concerned, is academic, hurtful and misleading. It is an interesting comment on the profundity of Montesquieu's insight that any writer on the British constitution today would almost certainly have to agree with him rather than with Sir Leslie Stephen. The outstanding fact of the present day in Britain is the swing-back of the pendulum, and the increase, in the perpetual balance between functions, of the importance of the executive, aided by its civil service and experts, at the expense of the parliamentary or congressional Legislature.

J. L. De Lolme (1740–1807) was a lawyer of Swiss extraction, a member of the Council of the Two Hundred in the Republic of Geneva, who possessed all Montesquieu's enthusiasm for the British constitution and who possibly expected to share in some measure that favour with which Montesquieu was received by the British nation. He therefore visited Britain, where he became a resident for several years, and in 1770 published in French, and five years later in English, his *Constitution of England.* If these were his hopes he was grievously disappointed, since, as he says, had he put the question to the English nation and its ministers that "he was preparing to boil [his] tea-kettle" with the manuscript, their answer, from all the contemporary notice that was taken, would apparently have been, "Boil it." From the accounts of the unhappy Swiss, the manners of the English were as rude in his day as they are today. Later, however, the author was rewarded by the appearance of several editions of his book in England and on the Continent.

De Lolme views the nature of any sound constitution as comparable to "a great ballet or dance in which, the same as in other ballets, everything depends on the disposition of the figures." Characteristically enough, he takes as the motto of his book the words of Ovid, "Balanced in its Weights"—"*Ponderibus librata suis.*" It will be observed that both of De Lolme's metaphors are artificial if not mechanical, and he nowhere penetrates beneath a static, mechanical theory of government to a comprehension, as did Montesquieu, of these dynamic and psychological forces. De Lolme's fame, in point of fact, rests not so much upon his theory of government, in which the ideal is the preservation of liberty through ever-present possibilities of governmental dead-lock, with a consequent minimalist theory of the duty of legislators, as upon an observation on the powers of the British Parliament which have quite other implications. When De Lolme produced the statement, in one of his panegyrics of the British constitution, that the British Parliament had such sovereign power that it could do everything save "turn a man into a woman or a woman into a man," he in fact produced a singularly striking exposition of that principle of the British Parliament's sovereignty which is the exact converse of any theory of checks and balances.

In the hands of some writers, however, the theory of checks and balances is presented not merely as one of a balance between the functions of a constitution or, again, the departments of government but, thirdly, as an equipoise of the constituent parts of society. In some cases this equipoise is regarded as established in the past and unalterable. In others, following the tradition of Harrington, a moving balance is to be sustained. Thus, in 1783, Mr. Justice Braxfield gave classical expression to the doctrine of a permanent order as basic when he said:

> The government in every country is just like a corporation and in this country it is made up of landed interest which alone has the right to be represented. . . . The British constitution is the best that ever was since the beginning of the world and it is not possible to make it better.

A more moderate expression of the belief in the perfection of the British constitution as striking a permanently satisfactory balance between social groups is to be found (as we shall see later in this chapter) in the writings of Edmund Burke—who, however, is prepared to admit that "a constitution made up of the balanced powers must ever be a critical thing."

2

If in Montesquieu and De Lolme the philosophy of Hooker, Milton and Locke found its Continental admirers, in America it had direct progeny.

John Cotton, leading light of Massachusetts, was as anxious as ever was Richard Hooker to refute Independency (Congregationalism or Brownism). His ideal was a Presbyterian theocracy.

> Democracy I do not conceive God ever did ordain as a fit government, either for Church or Commonwealth. If the People be governors, who shall be governed? . . . the meanest and worst form of all forms of government. . . . That is a civil law whatsoever concerneth the good of the city and the propulsing of the contrary. Now religion is the best good of the city, and therefore laws concerning religion are truly civil laws. . . . If the heretic persisted in his errors after admonition [*cf.* Plato], it would not be out of conscience. . . .

The antithesis, typical of the Modern State, of governors *versus* governed, persists.

In Connecticut a freer doctrine obtained. Here Thomas Hooker, in his *Survey of the Summe of Church Discipline* (1648), provided an early exposition of the theory of social contract as the basis of church government. It was, however, peculiarly in Rhode Island, where the statue of The Common Man to this day dominates the Capitol at Providence, that Independency found its leader in Roger Williams—"less light than fire," commented Cotton Mather—and the frontier forces of democracy surged over the aristocratic prejudices of Calvinist Puritanism.

"The form of government established in Providence Plantations is democratical; that is to say, a government held by free consent of all or the greater part of the free inhabitants." For the rest, as Roger Williams wrote to Sir Francis Vane: "We have drunk of the cup of as great liberties as any people we can hear of under heaven." This did not prevent an older Roger Williams, in 1656, twenty-five years after his arrival in America, finding it impossible to tolerate with any happiness the Quakers, some of whom were reported as guilty of nudism and whose founder Williams described as "a filthy sow." Others than Governor Spotswood of Virginia had ground to complain that "*the liberty of doing wrong is none of the least contended for here.*" It says much for Williams that he held by his principle that none should be excluded who did not disturb the civil peace. He held to his thesis in his *Bloudy Tene[n]t of Persecution for Cause of Conscience* (1644), against Cotton and the ministers. He had advanced so far towards individualism and the "inner light," as against the Platonic-Catholic concept, that he ventured to describe the Church as

> like unto a corporation, society or company of East India or Turkie merchants, or any other societie or companie in London which may . . . wholly break up and dissolve into pieces and nothing, and yet the peace of the citie not be in the least measure impaired or disturbed.

Such sentiments, when inspired by genuine piety and not by a Machiavellian or Erastian* statecraft, were still rare. They are the steps in the development of a sound doctrine of Community or Voluntary Society.

In Pennsylvania the Quakers, spiritual forerunners of the philosophic anarchists such as Kropotkin and Russell,† with their assertion that the only religion was that "of spirit and truth" and their denial that human nature was inherently corrupt, came into their own under William Penn. The early Quakers went among the common people and, like the later Salvationists, reclaimed them. Despite the free allegation of their enemies in England that they would "soon be ripe to cut throats," and that "some thought the Anabaptists and Quakers were coming to cut their throats," the Quakers, whatever their implicit anarchism, were, on principle, no antinomians or contemners of law. "Any such," declared the founder, Fox, "as cry, away with your laws, we will have none of your laws, are sons of Belial." It is to be feared, however, that some of the early Quaker enthusiasts—and this is Roger Williams' excuse—were precisely such, howbeit they considered themselves Second Adventists and, as it were, Latter-day Saints. Penn himself lays down a civic principle of the later soberer element that differed from the quaking Quaker as Baptist differed from Munster Anabaptist.‡

> They weakly err that think there is no other use of government than correction, which is the coarsest part of it.

The function of government is also, as Scripture says, to encourage those that do well. "Any government is free to the people under it . . . where the laws rule and the people are a party to those laws."

American political thought, with one or two exceptions, has been a matter of pamphlets and speeches, and has not expressed itself in systematic political theory. Benjamin Franklin (1706–1790), leading scientist of the eighteenth century, became a kind of Old Moore, embodying his political wisdom in an annual, called *Poor Richard's Almanack*. John Adams admitted the dependence of the colonies on the king, but declared that he was king in Massachusetts and denied the dependence of the colonial assemblies on the British Parliament —the post-war Dominion thesis expressed in the Statute of Westminster. "Taxation without representation is tyranny." That all

* *Cf.* p. 204.
† *Cf.* pp. 425, 431.
‡ *Cf.* p. 212.

should be consulted in what touches all was laid down as the Englishman's right. The British Parliamentarians, apart from Burke and those who shared his views, looked askance at independent bodies who might make grants to the king, just as their predecessors had looked askance at individual "gifts" in the fourteenth century. They —not only Tories but Whigs, obsessed by the issue between king and commons—saw the control of the king by the power of the purse weakened, and the sovereignty of the [British] Parliament, in the sense of Commons as distinct from King-in-Parliament, disappearing. It was "a great constitutional issue," and it was significant that it was Burke, founder of modern British Conservatism, who was most vocal in the pro-colonist minority. On the other hand, Stephen Hopkins put briefly the common-sense case for the colonists:

> There would be found very few people in the world, willing to leave their native country and go through fatigue and hardship of planting in a new and uncultivated one for the sake of losing their freedom.

As during the English Civil War, so during the American Revolution the first line of attack was constitutional, and turned on the relation of the colonial legislatures to the British Parliament and on the constitutional theory of representation and taxation. This argument, however, tended to become bogged in the learned arguments of the lawyers as the Parliamentarian argument itself had become bogged in the issue between Sir Edward Coke and his opponents.* Popular emotion demanded resort to a more lucid, forcible and "philosophical" second line—to those "primary principles" about which every layman has always felt himself entitled to argue, although usually found too difficult by philosophers who have devoted a lifetime to their consideration. Actually the statements offered by the colonists rested pretty solidly upon the philosophic foundations profoundly enough and deliberately offered by Locke.

Samuel Adams returned to the argument that kings and magistrates may be guilty of treason and rebellion against the rule of law, including natural law. American political theory throughout at this time was more "conservative," in the sense of representing an earlier phase of political and legal thought, than the contemporary English theory which had "advanced," in a Hobbesian direction, beyond the assumption of a distinction between natural law and sovereign positive law.

* *Cf.* p. 230.

It is true, as Professor McIlwain shows, that the thesis that a court could void statute law as contrary to natural law (now equated with a "constitutional" or immemorial common law) died out in Britain after decisions at the very close of the seventeenth century. But the notion was still alive in the mind of the colonists and was entirely consistent with Whig theory, if not with the practice of Whigs in office. It was to have a decisive influence on moulding the United States constitution; in the rejection of the British doctrine of Parliamentary Sovereignty; and in the assigning of legal priority to the constitutions as against legislative acts. These results are the legacy of Natural Law to America.

The practical Alexander Hamilton (1757–1804) went farther. He asserted:

> The sacred rights of mankind are not to be rummaged for among old parchments or musty records. They are written as with a sunbeam in the whole volume of human nature, by the hand of the Divinity itself and can never be erased or obscured by mortal power. . . . Civil liberty cannot possibly have any existence, when the society for whom laws are made have no share in making them.

Nothing can be a clearer admission of the importance of "theory" (unless we are to say "rhetoric") to a "practical" man. The significance of what today would be called the influence of propaganda upon public opinion by a rationalization of motives is shown, again, by Thomas Jefferson's resort to first principles in his appeal, in the Declaration of Independence, to a candid world. The revolutionary constitution of New Hampshire declared that the doctrine of nonresistance is "slavish, absurd, and destructive of the good and happiness of mankind."

The right to revolt—such was the influence of the Glorious Revolution of '88 and of Whig philosophy—as distinct from its expediency, was not usually challenged. When it was, the challenge took the shape of the argument of Jonathan Boucher, the loyalist, who deplored the irreverence of children in a modern day, the infidelity to the marriage relation, the attitude of the rich to the poor, democracy and the absurd supposition of universal individual consent to government, the theory of a parliamentary opposition and party government, the fallacy of human equality, the destruction of all motive to initiative in industry, the doctrine of rebellion begotten of Lucifer, and indeed any challenge to the doctrine that sovereign power comes, as Paul said, from on high. "A non-resisting spirit never made any man a bad subject."

The Revolution over and independence achieved, the tendency towards "normalcy" set in. The distance travelled is all the way from the landmark of the Declaration of Independence to that of the United States Constitution. The mood of the Constitution is best discovered, apart from the document itself, in the series of expository articles by men—Madison, Hamilton and Jay—who had no small share in framing it, published in *The Federalist*, these articles originally appearing in *The New York Packet*. Samuel Adams had declared, before the Revolution, of the British constitution:

> In none that I have ever met with is the power of the governors and the rights of the governed more nicely adjusted, or the power which is necessary in the very nature of government to be intrusted in the hands of some, by wiser checks prevented from growing exorbitant.

Mr. Justice Braxfield could scarcely have said handsomer. After the Revolution this temper again became in fashion, reinforced by the lessons of the dangers of merely confederate liberty as any basis for the necessary discipline of war. For its effect upon the constitution it was rewarded by the reciprocal compliment offered by Mr. Gladstone, the great Liberal Premier:

> As the British Constitution is the most subtle organism which has proceeded from the womb and long gestation of progressive history, so the American Constitution is, so far as I can see, the most wonderful work ever struck off at a given time by the brain and purpose of man.

The Federalist shows a slight tendency to depart from the doctrine, sacred since Aristotle, of the primacy of laws over men. The experience of war has done its work. Law comes first; but involves not only opinion, but a coercive power for its execution. As that Tory Revolutionary, George Washington, observed, "opinion is not government." As President Andrew Jackson was to remind Chief Justice Marshall, law to be effectual requires an effective Executive. If indeed "men were angels, no government would be necessary." Further, a representative *republic*, such because all its powers were derived "from the great body of the people" and because it was "administered by persons holding their office during pleasure, for a limited period or during good behaviour" (as against a *monarchy*), was, Madison held (*The Federalist*, no. 39), to be preferred to a pure *democracy*. Madison writes (no. 39):

> It is *essential* to such a government that it be derived from the great body of the society, not from an inconsiderable proportion or a favoured class of it. . . . It is *sufficient* for such a government that the persons administering it be

appointed, either directly or indirectly, by the people; and that they hold their appointments by either of the tenures just specified; otherwise every government in the United States, as well as every other popular government that has been or can be well organised or well executed, would be degraded from the republican character. . . . Could any further proof be required of the republican complexion of this system, the most decisive one might be found in its absolute prohibition of titles of nobility, both under the federal and the State governments; and its express guarantee of the republican form to each of the latter.

The electorate was to be the broadest yet known in any major state—far broader than in most states of the Union, many of which retained a property franchise. It was to be a universal white male adult franchise. But the representatives were to be chosen bearing in mind "the aim of every political constitution . . . first *to obtain for rulers men who possess most wisdom to discern, and most virtue to pursue the common good of the society.*" "The elective mode of obtaining rulers is the characteristic policy of republican government." Will, then, this electorate be corrupted?

This cannot be said, without maintaining that five or six thousand citizens are less capable of choosing a fit representative, or more liable to be corrupted by an unfit one, than five or six hundred.

Nor is the danger to the many from corruption real. Even in oligarchical Britain, "it cannot be said that the representatives of the nation have elevated the few on the ruins of the many."

A republic, moreover, as representative, *The Federalist* argued, overcame the difficulty raised by Montesquieu (and by Rousseau, although his influence was negligible) that democratic government postulated a small area or polis. The task was to persuade the suspicious colonists that to substitute one federal American government for thirteen separate legislatures, nominally dependent upon the King of England, was not to replace King Log by King Stork.

The answer lay in the acceptance of the Harrington-Locke-Montesquien doctrine of the division of powers; but stated in a cautious and moderate form. As George Washington had said: "The concentration of powers in one hand is the essence of tyranny." But the contributors to *The Federalist* are satisfied if they prevent that concentration; they abandon what may be called the "three jealous watch dogs" theory of the relations of Legislative, Executive and Judiciary. The danger to national strength lay, certainly in the opinion of Hamilton, in the rash presumption of the Legislatures; and the argument of *The Federalist* is weighed in favour of a competent Executive. Perpetual vigilance might be the price of liberty; but "liberty may be endangered by the abuses of liberty as well as by the abuses of power."

However useful jealousy may be in republics, yet when like bile in the natural, it abounds too much in the body politic, the eyes of both become very liable to be deceived by the delusive appearances which that malady casts on surrounding objects. (Jay, *Federalist* no. 64.)*

The writers trimmed carefully on the first issue in political theory: the just ratio of liberty and authority or, as F. W. Maitland put it, "finding a theory which will mediate between absolute dependence and absolute independence."

The writers of *The Federalist* introduce, further, a fourth constitutional balance, between federal and state rights. The balance here is weighted by the federal obligation of providing for defence—as Hobbes had shown, the first and overruling duty of any secular state. "Government . . . is only another word for political power and supremacy."

Is there not a manifest inconsistency in devolving upon the federal government the care of the general defence, and having in the State governments the effective power by which it is to be provided for. . . . A government, the constitution of which renders it unfit to be trusted with all the powers which a free people ought to delegate to any government, would be an unsafe and improper depositary of the national interests. [Hamilton, no. 23.] Assent and ratification is to be given by the people, not as individuals composing one entire nation, but as composing the distinct and independent States to which they respectively belong.

The third, or class, balance, however (already mentioned in our discussion, *cf.* p. 306), is contemplated, generally reminiscent of Harrington, to which we shall have occasion to recur in the discussion of Burke.

The idea of an actual representation of all classes of the people, by persons of each class, is altogether visionary. . . . Mechanics and manufacturers [artisans] will always be inclined, with few exceptions, to give their votes to merchants, in preference to persons of their own professions or trades. . . . They know that the merchant is the natural patron and friend. . . . They are sensible that their habits in life have not been such as to give them those acquired endowments, without which, in a deliberative assembly, the greatest natural abilities are for the most part useless. . . . With regard to the learned

* *Cf.* pp. 383, 471, 656.

professions, little need be observed; they truly form no distinct influence in society. . . . Nothing remains but the landed interest. . . . But where is the danger that the interests and feelings of the different classes of citizens will not be understood or attended to by these three descriptions of men? . . . Will not the man of the learned profession, who will feel a neutrality to the rivalships between the different branches of industry, be likely to prove an impartial arbiter between them, ready to promote either, so far as shall appear to him conducive to the general interests of society?

This is from the pen of Alexander Hamilton (no. 35). It is a thesis, foreshadowed by Aristotle, that we shall discover again in James Mill.* It is interesting to note how a practical man is so prepossessed by prejudice or theory as to state as actual, without further analysis, something that he merely wishes to be actual.

The Federalist, however, although it runs true to the doctrines of natural rights, social compact and division of powers, states these honoured revolutionary theses with great caution. There is "an original right of self-defence, which is paramount to all positive forms of government." Here and in the representative system are guaranties of liberty. "No political truth is certainly of greater intrinsic value" than that of the division of powers. But "parchment barriers against the encroaching spirit of power" (Madison, no. 48) are not enough. The two best specific guaranties are the *federal* nature of American government; and—as between the "different interests" that "necessarily exist in different classes of citizens," so that the rights of minorities become insecure—the *variety* of interests. We shall get the same thought in John Stuart Mill.† "In a free government the security for civil rights must be the same as for religious rights." The divine right of majorities is implicitly denied; and the division of powers developed as a bulwark against it.

John Adams, second president of the United States had, in his younger days, not hesitated to assent to Locke's maxim that all the principles of government could satisfactorily be reduced to one sheet of paper. He was guilty of the assertion (than which Aristotle, with his theme of democratic judgement and executive initiative, had long before shown a better way) that government is "a plain, simple, intelligible thing, founded in nature and reason, quite comprehensible by common sense." By 1787, Adams had revised his views in favour of checks and balances, and of aristocracy. His definition of aristocracy was liberal. "*There is a voice within us, which seems to intimate that*

* *Cf.* p. 384.
† *Cf.* p. 397.

real merit should govern the world, and that men ought to be respected only in proportion to their talents, virtues and services"—to realize this was the major constitutional problem. Adams' practice was conservative. As against John Adams, we find such men as John Taylor, of Caroline, arguing the old Aristotelian thesis in favour of rotation in office and against "the monopoly of experience."

Not less conservative in mood is James Wilson, of Philadelphia, signator of both the Declaration of Independence and of the Constitution, one of the most powerful advocates, up to the last moment, of colonial autonomy as distinct from independence. His conservatism is coloured by optimism—as when he declares: "I could never read some modish modern authors without being, for some time, out of humour with myself, and at everything about me. Their business is to depreciate human nature, and consider it under its worst appearances." It is interesting to note that Wilson, an Associate Justice of the Supreme Court, nevertheless maintains, in his lectures *On General Principles of Law and Obligation*, against Blackstone, a Whig doctrine of natural law of singular purity.

> Can there be *no* law without a [social or civil] superiour? Is it essential to law, that inferiority should be involved in the obligation to obey it? Are these distinctions at the root of *all* legislation?

Uncompromising assertions of the overriding force of Natural Law, as laying limits not only on statute law but on sovereign legislatures, are not uninteresting in the last decade of the eighteenth century.

3

Thomas Jefferson (1743–1826), third president of the United States, is the most eminent of the native-born sons of America who were systematic political theorists during the Revolutionary and post-Revolutionary period. If John Locke illustrates the function of political theory as justifiative after the event, providing rationalization for what men of action propose to do or have already done, Thomas Jefferson shows how that theory may influence the thought and, in turn, the action, of a new generation and determine the set of its problems and their solutions. He above all men is the legitimate heir of the English Revolution—the man in the midstream of the Anglo-Saxon Tradition.

The great Virginian, of Welsh descent, related to the Randolphs of Roanoke, began his political life at the age of twenty-two, when he heard Patrick Henry denounce Grenville's Stamp Act. In 1769, George Washington (another Virginian landowner), Henry, Jefferson and others met, in the Raleigh Tavern, Williamsburg, to discuss opposition to George Townshend's duties on colonial goods. Jefferson was one of the originators of the Committee of Correspondence which organized collective colonial action; he outlined, as a member of the Virginian Convocation, a "New Model Constitution of Virginia"; and became draftsman of the Declaration of Independence. His subsequent career is that of Governor of Virginia; ambassador of the new state to France; Secretary of State; third President; and founder of the University of Virginia. This last, the Declaration of Independence and the Virginia statute for Religious Toleration he regarded as his claims to fame. "By these as testimonials that I have lived, I wish most to be remembered."

Bertrand Russell speaks of Jefferson as "a democrat for the people, not of the people." There is indeed in him a happy and genuine combination of true democrat and great gentleman. It is a combination of radical love of liberty with appreciation of discipline so rare that Jefferson demands earnest attention in the history of political thought. He, more than any Englishman in England, is the fine flower of the Lockian philosophy. There is a pretty story that well illustrates Jefferson's conception of good manners. A negro bowed to the ex-President when he was out riding with his grandson, Thomas Jefferson Randolph. Mr. Jefferson returned the bow: the grandson did not. "Turning to me, he asked," records Randolph, "'Do you permit a negro to be more of a gentleman than yourself?'" Russell excellently describes the relations of Jefferson and Hamilton. "Jefferson, secure in his estates and among his cultivated friends, believed in the common man; Hamilton, who knew the common man, sought out the society of the socially prominent." It is an interesting comment on the Marxian *credo* of the class war.

In 1794, Jefferson expressed the hope that the French would "bring, at last, kings, nobles and priests, to the scaffolds which they have been so long deluging with human blood." His considered statement, however, in his autobiography, about his days as ambassador in the France of 1789 must be weighed against this. It is the voice of the American Revolution upon the French Revolution, by which we in our turn may judge the Russian Revolution.

> I was much acquainted with the leading Patriots of the Assembly. . . . I urged, most strenuously, an immediate compromise; to secure what the government was now ready to yield, and to trust to future occasions for what might still be wanting. They thought otherwise, however, and events have proved their lamentable error. For, after thirty years of war, foreign and

domestic, the loss of millions of lives, the frustration of private happiness, and the foreign subjugation of their own country for a time, they have obtained no more, or even that securely.

However,

> The appeal to the rights of man, which had been made in the United States, was taken up by France, first of all the European nations. From here, the spirit has spread over those of the south. The tyrants of the north have allied indeed against it; but it is irresistible. Their opposition will only multiply its millions of human victims; their own satellites will catch it, and the condition of man, through the civilized world, will be finally and greatly ameliorated.

"Ameliorated"—this is the essential Jeffersonianism.

His party, Jefferson declared at the end of his life, believed "that man was a rational animal, endowed by nature with rights, and with an innate sense of justice." In 1815, he declared to John Adams:

> The moral sense is as much a part of our constitution as that of feeling, seeing, or hearing, as a wise creator must have seen to be necessary in an animal destined to live in society. . . . Every mind feels pleasure in doing good to another. . . . The essence of virtue is in doing good to others.

The extent to which Jefferson and Adams, comrades in arms with such different prejudices, could in their old age reach agreement is a significant pointer in the philosophy of political thought. This may, however, be because in those days and that country of widening horizons, despite their Puritan ancestry (or, at least, Adams'), both had forgotten the doctrine of Original Sin, sapped by Locke's critique of innate qualities, but foundation of all reasoned doctrines of coercive authority. This optimism is the converse of General Ireton's dictum: "Men as men are corrupt and will be so." The advance made in amelioration during Jefferson's lifetime is clearly indicated by a comment of his biographer, Tucker. "There were probably twice or thrice as many four-horse carriages [in Virginia] before the revolution as there are at present; but the number of two-horse carriages may now be ten, or even twenty times as great as at the former period."

The practical and intuitive demand for "amelioration" in the lot of the common man, at the expense of traditional and vested interest, Jefferson regarded as a social imperative, resting upon the foundation of the natural rights of humanity, basic to law and morals. Those rights, which, in a fashion that any politician will appreciate, had all the revolutionary appeal of extremism but which in the greyer light of reflective thought appear unnecessarily doctrinaire—those "immortal principles" which today excite Fascist humour—Jefferson proclaimed in the well-remembered words of the Declaration of Independence:

We hold these truths to be self-evident: that all men are created equal, that they are endowed by their Creator with certain inalienable Rights, that among these are life, liberty, and the pursuit of happiness; that to secure these rights, governments are instituted among men, deriving their just powers from the consent of the governed; that whenever any form of government becomes destructive of these ends, it is the right of the people to alter or abolish it.

The full responsibility of Jefferson for that Declaration can be taken as established.* John Adams, one of the drafting committee, in his old age wrote,

The essence of it is contained in a pamphlet, voted and printed by the town of Boston, before the first Congress met, composed by James Otis, as I suppose in one of his lucid intervals, and pruned and polished by Samuel Adams.

To this charge Jefferson had the effective reply that he had never seen Otis' pamphlet. He added, in words that carry conviction: "I did not consider it as any part of my charge to invent new ideas altogether, and to offer no sentiment which had ever been expressed before." Jefferson's statement is that the Declaration was written without consulting books or pamphlets. His debt, however, in thought to Locke and Algernon Sidney, champions of "natural liberty," is obvious and acknowledged.

On the other hand, it is a popular error to suppose any debt to exist upon the part of the authors of the American Revolution to Rousseau or the Encyclopaedists. The debt is all the other way. This Lafayette symbolically acknowledged when he placed a copy of the Declaration of Independence conspicuously in his library, with a vacant space beside it for a comparable French Declaration. The debt of the "Patriot" group personally to Jefferson is indubitable.

Already in the *Summary View* of 1774, Jefferson had struck the distinctive note of the Declaration. The detailed and legalistic arguments of John Dickinson are abandoned. The right, admitted even by Washington, of the British Parliament to tax the colonies in specific cases, "with moderation," is no longer conceded. "The young," writes Edmund Randolph, "ascended with Mr. Jefferson to the sources of these rights." Jefferson substituted, for a temporary quarrel, eternal issues. That is his fame.

* The pages immediately following will be found in a more expanded version in my *Thomas Jefferson*, in *Great Democrats* (Ivor Nicolson & Watson, 1934).

King George, "as Chief Magistrate of the British Empire," is invited to hear "the united complaints of His Majesty's subjects in America." Deputies from "the other states in British America" were invited, in the *Summary View*, to concert in presenting an address. The jurisdiction of the British Parliament over these states is denied. The king rules in Virginia, by the same title, although in a different fashion, as he rules in Hanover. The union with Britain is a dynastic union and no more—but he is yet the king of free Englishmen who, exercising the natural right of free emigration, have brought with them to the shores of a new country those liberties that they had enjoyed since the days of their Saxon ancestors. The quarrel is with the British Parliament. But the king does not, in the *Summary View*, escape censure. "Open your breast, Sire, to a liberal and expanded thought. Let not the name of George the Third be a blot on the page of history."

When Jefferson came to write the Declaration of Independence he pursued, with more emphasis, the same policy. Fundamental claims are substituted for legal complaints. Again he "ascends to the source of rights." This source is no longer historical or traditional but a fount of truths esteemed to be self-evident. The complaint against the Parliament of Great Britain has been broadened into an indictment also against its king. The indictment, however, is framed, not in the legal and constitutional terms of a petition of right, but as an inevitable deduction from the first principles of all political philosophy. Rebellion cannot be supplied with a legal permit—nor would the French Ministry have been interested in a dispute that was to remain merely domestic and constitutional.

Jefferson framed an argument that could appeal to men of all nationalities in a candid world. It was not merely one that might have force with Englishmen trained in the free traditions, and acquainted with the legal principles, of their country. The Declaration is an international document in conception and appeal. Like the Germans with Lenin in 1917, so the French, in 1776, demanded a sweeping policy—which in the event, damaged the empire of Britain but demolished the social system of France; just as the plotters of the Wilhelmstrasse, with their "sealed train," destroyed the monarchy of Russia but swept away that of Germany.

There were many who were prepared to say, with such a Tory as John Lind, that Jefferson had "put the axe to the tree of all government." Charles James Fox could indeed claim that the Americans "had done no more than the English had done against James II." It was, however, clear that Congress had advanced, in fact even if reluctantly, to the enunciation under Jefferson's guidance of philosophical and practical principles much more far-reaching than those to which the Whig Revolution of 1688–1689 had committed itself. It was not for nothing that Condorcet exhorted the French to consider the principles of liberty and "to read them in the example of a great people" or that Mirabeau referred to the way in which the claims of the Declaration were "very generally applauded."

The Parliamentarians, in the days of James I and the early days of Charles I, had made humble pleas as subjects to their rightful sovereigns. The Whigs, in 1689, had effected a constitutional compromise with an executive magistrate who was also their liege lord. The Declaration placed, not only laws above men, but *irrefragable principles of society above positive laws*. It thereby prepared the way for the French Revolution that made magistrates the delegates and functionaries of the general will. But, of the two, the Declaration, by exalting the laws of human nature rather than the arbitrary will of a majority, adhered to the sounder principles.

Jonathan Mayhew, in 1766, wrote:

> Having been initiated, in youth, in the doctrines of civil liberty, as they were taught by such men as Plato, Demosthenes, Cicero, and other renowned persons among the ancients, and such as Sidney and Milton, Locke and Hoadly among the moderns, I liked them; they seemed rational.

Mayhew is representative enough of the average. There must have been many among those educated in the American colleges in the mid-eighteenth century, impressed by the radicalism of Locke and the rational system of Newton, who would have echoed Mayhew's judgement and approved his taste. Certainly Jefferson was among them. The writings of Cicero, Sidney, Locke, Montesquieu, Priestley and Malthus are all on the short list of books he later recommended to a grandson. Among these, Locke must count first in influence.

In his brilliant *Declaration of Independence*, Professor Carl Becker summarizes the attitude of Locke towards the problem of governmental authority. "Government ought to have the authority which reasonable men, living together in a community, considering the rational interests of each and all, might be disposed to submit to willingly." Primary among these rational interests are what the Lockians called men's "natural rights." Professor Becker happily quotes from the writings of William Ellery Channing, the great Unitarian and opponent of slavery, to show what the men of the generation after Jefferson understood to be the character of these natural rights that Hooker adumbrated, Locke enunciated and Jefferson proclaimed. "Man has rights by nature. . . . In the order of things they precede society, lie at its foundations, constitute man's capacity for it, and are the great objects of social institutions."

Today, when it is popular to describe both the theory of natural rights, preceding civil government, and the more mature theory of natural law as being discredited, we hear of the rights of women, urged on more than utilitarian grounds, and of the ordinary man's "right of continuous initiative" as the basis of a workers' democratic movement. Substantially these claims are not different from those urged by Jefferson on behalf of life, liberty and the pursuit of happiness.

The points in which Jefferson marks an advance upon Locke, in the history of thought, are that he discards any reference to an original social contract, and that he derives all "just powers" of government solely from the consent of the governed.

In the Lockian theory there is a double contract—the contract between members of society to conduct themselves as social and civil beings, and the trusteeship of a ruler or legislative for purposes of authoritative government. In the Jeffersonian theory no ruler stands out, over against the people, as an independent party to some contract, tacit or avowed. In the first draft of the Declaration man is described as being born "equal and independent." He is untied by any traditional or "original" social contract. The men of each generation maintain a government for its utility for themselves and their heirs, of which utility they are the judges. They recognize no obligation to any government that claims to derive its powers from a non-popular source or that endeavours to negotiate or enforce a contract, as a party independent of the people. They admit no vice-regent of God, or symbol of the eternal nation, or group claiming to rule others "for their good, as a moral obligation." Executive officers are functionaries entrusted with power by the people.

Jefferson, as is well known, carried this rejection of any tradition or "*original* contract" so far as to maintain that no generation was entitled to bind its successor. Statisticians assured him that a new generation arose every nineteen years. After each such period, therefore, he demanded a "revolution," an entire overhauling of the constitution, in order that it should again receive popular authorization. Force was given to this demand by the restriction imposed, in the American States, on the will of democratic legislatures by written constitutions. Such "revolutions," he held, like thunderstorms, cleared the air. "*A little rebellion, now and then, is a good thing.* . . .

The spirit of resistance to government is so valuable on certain occasions that I wish it to be always kept alive."

The objections to Jefferson's and Channing's theories of man's natural equality and independence are clear on the surface. "All men are born free? . . . No, not a single man," says Bentham, "not a single man that ever was, or is, or will be." In the days of the slavery issue in the United States, reverend gentlemen could point out that these were notions tainted by French infidelity, and that "a God-fearing people" would reject them. Today, every biologist, without calling in God's curse upon Ham, can riddle the argument about human equality. Every critic of Whiggery and Liberal individualism can point out the folly of regarding men as born, or as living, "independent." They are born as babies—and live as men—dependent and social beings.

The argument, however, dies hard—and properly so. The Cynics and the Stoics, who first elaborated the theory, did so as a protest against artificial and irrational inequalities, which had no basis in such values as sincere men could accept. It was on this basis that the theory was maintained by the Church as true "according to the law of nature." A rigid doctrine of predestination and of original corruption tended to undermine it. If all men were worms, it might well be that the more miserable worms had no ground of complaint against God's will which condemned them to servitude as children of damnation. It was the great work of Locke to free men from this bondage by declaring that the mind of each man at birth was *tabula rasa*, instead of bearing blazed upon it, with other innate ideas, the adverse decree of fate. Sensations, environment, enlightenment, education, would determine the future. Thomas Jefferson, no less than Robert Owen, was to draw the deductions. Men were to be assumed equal until it was known what a favourable environment could do to improve them, or an adverse environment had done to retard them. Equality, for Jefferson, was no herd-levelling, but an elaboration of the full meaning of liberty.

When he is discussing education, Jefferson states his principles in a form far less sweeping. It is highly important to note these reservations. In his proposals for elementary instruction in Virginia he writes:

> Of the boys thus sent in one year, trial is to be made at the grammar school for one or two years, and *the best genius of the whole selected, and continued six years, and the residue dismissed. By this means twenty of the best geniuses will be raked from the rubbish annually,* and be instructed at the public expense.

Repeatedly, however, Jefferson insists that the common man can be trusted: he "was not one of those who held fourteen out of every fifteen dishonest."

> The form of government which we have adopted [he writes in 1826 in perhaps his last letter] restores the free right to the unbounded exercise of reason and freedom of opinion. . . . The general spread of the light of science has already laid open to every view the palpable truth that the mass of mankind has not been born with saddles on their backs, nor a favoured few booted and spurred [Jefferson is quoting Rumbold's phrase from the days of the Civil Wars], ready to ride them legitimately, by the grace of God.

At the back of all Jefferson's metaphysic of inalienable rights, of which the only true grounding is to be found in the permanent qualities of human nature, lie a practical common sense and an anticipation of the importance for liberty of the right of experiment and of the danger of thrusting common men into class pigeon-holes, because they mischose their fathers, or at the arbitrary will of complacent, curmudgeon bureaucrats. It is a theory that protests against forejudgement of man by man. "Judge not . . . "

Jefferson's doctrine of equality, in brief, is one more protest against unjust equality, on behalf of a condition in which innate ability may be able to take its just place. There is, however, in the Jeffersonian doctrine little of the harsh ill manners of a society where the open career is being avidly seized upon by self-made men of talent. The social atmosphere desired is one that places the burden of proof upon the man who requires pre-eminence and unequal rights.

> What a satisfaction have we in contemplation of the benevolent effects of our efforts compared with those of the leaders of the other side, who have discountenanced all advances in science as dangerous innovations, have endeavoured to render philosophy and Republicanism terms of reproach, to persuade us that man cannot be governed but by the rod. . . . The room being hung around with a collection of the portraits of remarkable men, among them being those of Bacon, Newton, and Locke, Hamilton asks me who they were. I told him they were my trinity of the three greatest men the world had ever produced, naming them. He paused for some time. "The greatest man that ever lived was Julius Caesar," he said. Mr. Adams was honest as a politician, as well as a man; Hamilton was honest as a man, but, as a politician, believing in the necessity of either force or corruption to govern men.

The contrast of outlook and of personalities is age-long and ever-recurrent in politics.

Thomas Jefferson rode his horse until within three weeks of his death at the age of eighty-three. He died in the early morning hours of

July 4, 1826, having lived until the jubilee of the Declaration that he had fashioned and which had created the American nation. The admiration which all Englishmen must feel for him is an indication of the negligibility of political interests when balanced against the lasting values of civilization and humanity.

In Jeffersonianism the principles of social democracy were enunciated in their older and more individualistic form, appropriate for a republic of small farmers. Jeffersonian policy, as against the merchant interest bolstered by Hamilton, was prorural. It was the task of President Andrew Jackson (1767–1845), still inspired by the spirit of the frontier (but a frontier receding from respectable New England), to give to that social democracy further content. Jackson, like Lincoln, was a democrat for the people and of the people. Unfortunately, he proceeded to develop that error, excusable on the frontier but disastrous later, countenanced by Locke and of which John Adams had been guilty in his early days, of assuming the simplicity of the task of government. Politically it was a natural error when opposing those Benevolent Despots who claimed—in some cases, such as that of Frederick the Great, not without excuse: in others, such as Louis XV, most falsely—to be technicians in the art of government. Like Taylor of Caroline, Andrew Jackson asserted:

> There are, perhaps, few men who can for any great length of time enjoy office and power without being more or less under the influence of feelings unfavourable to the discharge of their public duties.

Power is poison; power corrupts. Jackson's aim was to "destroy the idea of property in office now so generally connected with official station."

> The duties of all public officers are, or at least admit of being made, so plain and simple that men of intelligence can readily qualify themselves for their performance; and I cannot but believe that more is lost by long continuance of men in office than is generally gained by their experience.

It is the defence of the amateur in politics. It is a case not without strength, but it contains latent within it, through undue simplification of the difficulties of political practice, the possibilities of error and of dangerous error. Its danger we shall have occasion to explore when we discuss the sentimental philosophy of Rousseau. The opposite range of truths from those enunciated by the libertarian individualism of Jefferson and Jackson, and the first serious break in the Anglo-Saxon political tradition from the classical statement by Locke, will be found in the pages of a great orator, the father of modern Conservatism, Edmund Burke, himself in his own opinion a loyal follower of Locke.

4

EDMUND BURKE (1728–1797), an enthusiastic Irishman, throughout most of his life in debt, began his political career relatively late, first in an Irish post and subsequently as secretary to Lord Rockingham. Of Lord Rockingham Burke declared that he found that "party was [for him] the depository of living principle." Burke is not without importance as one of the first men in English political life who was prepared openly to advocate the party system (condemned by De Lolme as encouraging rancour) on the principle that "when bad men combine, the good must associate." Burke's career arouses in his admirers an enthusiasm comparable to his own oratory which Lord Morley declared was one of unrestrained passion and decorated style. It is the essayist Hazlitt who says, "If there are greater prose writers than Burke, they lie out of my course of study or are beyond my sphere of comprehension." Matthew Arnold endorses this judgement. Sir Leslie Stephen says of Burke that "he was incomparably the greatest in intellectual power of all English politicians, as well as the life and soul of his party for some thirty years." The fact remains that Burke, although the prophet of political common sense against theory, was not in practice an especially good politician, partly owing to his impetuousness and partly because, in the words of Oliver Goldsmith,

> . . . he went on refining
> And thought of convincing when they thought of dining.

It is an interesting, but perhaps not entirely damning, comment upon the British electorate that, during the thirty years of the parliamentary life of the man whom Lord Morley described as "the largest master of civil liberty in our tongue," for only six did he sit for the great city of Bristol and, for the rest of the time, had to be content as the nominated member of a rotten borough. His views, although doubtless right, on Ireland, Catholic emancipation and America, together with his famous declaration that a Member of Parliament owed the electors "his unbiased opinion, his mature judgement, his enlightened conscience," not servile acquiescence in their opinions, were altogether too much for the free electors of Bristol.

Under the British constitution, in Burke's view,

> . . . the people, by their representatives and grandees were entrusted with a deliberative power of making laws; the king, with the control of his negative.

The king was entrusted with the deliberative choice and the election of office; the people had the negative in a parliamentary refusal to support.

For Burke, as much as for Polybius, the glory of a constitution was that it was mixed; and that this mixture corresponded to a certain balance in the compound of the society itself, a compound which yet was organic, not mechanical. According to Burke, the object of the Revolution of 1688 had been not to make a revolution but to prevent it. In brief, he attributes to the Whig nobility of the days of King William the same intention which Fascists today claim for themselves as against Communist policy. The object was to prevent dangerous innovation. Burke was no unmixed admirer of the monarchy as he found it. Henry VIII he described as "a levelling tyrant"; and he refers to "that series of sanguine tyrants, the Caesars." He was among that group which George III, in a famous message, described as "not the king's friends but his enemies"; and Burke did not hesitate to refer to what he called "the low and pimping politics" of the court and "the insect race of courtly falsehoods."

On the other hand, while protesting against those who "gave themselves under the lax and indeterminate idea of the honour of the Crown, a full licence for all manner of dissipation and all manner of corruption," Burke was a steady opponent of parliamentary reform and of the enlargement of the electorate. In all disputes between the people and their rulers, Burke held that the presumption was "at least upon a par in favour of the people." He quotes the words of Sully, the great minister of Henri IV; "Revolutions do not happen in great states by chance nor from popular caprice. . . . The populace does not revolt from any desire to attack but from impatience in its misery." It did not, however, follow that the people should be indulged. His belief was in *parliamentary sovereignty, not in popular sovereignty.* He held that owing to "the prostitute and daring voracity, the corruption of manners, and idleness and profligacy of the lower sort of voter, no prudent man would propose to increase such an evil if it be, as I fear it is, out of our power to administer to it any remedy." There was such a thing as a natural representative of the people. Those of tolerable leisure and of some means of information above "menial dependence"—in all about 400,000—were these natural representatives of the whole population.

This [declared Burke] is the British public and it is a public very numerous. The rest, when feeble, are the object of protection; when strong, the means of force. . . . When you separate the common sort of man from their proper chieftains so as to form them into an adverse army, I no longer know that venerable object called the people in such a disbanded race of deserters and vagabonds.

This last passage occurs in Burke's *Appeal from the New to the Old Whigs* (1791). Although we may be confident that the phrase does not come from Languet or Hobbes, the concept is reminiscent of them.

This *Appeal*, made under the influence of emotions due to the impact of the French Revolution, is, in effect, the initiation of modern Conservatism as distinct from the old loyalist and Jacobite Toryism of the preceding century. Along with William Pitt the younger, Burke can claim to be the father of the Conservative party, although he had begun his literary career by criticism of the cynicism of the past hope of the Tory party, the brilliant but unstable Bolingbroke. As much as Mr. Justice Braxfield, but expressing himself in a language incomparably richer in emotion and incomparably deeper in thought, Burke finds his ideal in the British constitution. "This constitution," he said, "in former days used to be the admiration and the envy of the world." In dealing with the problem of the revolted American colonies, he urges mediation on the grounds that conciliation was in accordance with the temper of that constitution. "I am sure that I shall not be misled when, in a case of constitutional difficulty, I consult the genius of the English constitution." The constitution for him is not a matter of laws or of governmental departments, but of a spirit almost personal and of a tradition. "We want," he continues, "no foreign examples to rekindle in us a flame of liberty; the example of our own ancestors is abundantly sufficient to maintain the spirit of freedom in its full vigour."

These statements about liberty, in the writings of Burke, are not mere rhetoric. His whole moral attitude, his conduct of investigations into corruption in India and into the administration of Warren Hastings and, above all, his attitude towards the American colonies demonstrate this fact. The liberty, however, in which Edmund Burke was interested was not an abstract and theoretic liberty, or even a liberty that involved profound social change in vindication of some natural rights of man, but a liberty, traditional, attested by legal documents and well-established customs and (it would be no exaggeration to represent Burke as feeling) tracing back, in Montesquieu's words, to those woods in which we found our constitution or, at the least, to the "iron barons" of King John and to Cardinal Langton.

His whole argument on American affairs has the very same basis. The American claims which were being challenged by Lord North were claims well established in the domestic history of Britain, of which the justice had especially been vindicated by the revolution—a revolution, not anarchical or some mass *émeute*, but solely corrective of the Stuart usurpation and innovation before 1688.

> The ablest pens . . . took infinite pains to inculcate, as a fundamental principle, that in all monarchies the people must, in effect themselves, mediately or immediately, possess the power of granting their own money, or no shadow of liberty could subsist. The colonies draw from you, as with their lifeblood, their ideas and principles. Their love of liberty, as with you, is fixed and attached on this specific point of taxing.

An Englishman, Burke held, was the unfittest person on earth to argue another Englishman into slavery and, he adds with effective force, "are not the people of America as much English as the Welsh?"

> In order to prove that the Americans have no right to their liberties, we are every day endeavouring to subvert the maxims which preserve the whole spirit of our own. To prove that the Americans ought not to be free, we are obliged to deprecate the value of freedom itself and we never seem to gain a paltry advantage over them in debate without attacking some of the principles or deriding some of those feelings for which our ancestors have shed their own blood.

England was then, for Burke, a nation which, in his own words, respected and formally adored her freedom. Alongside, however, the notion of freedom, Burke places the notion of duty. He anticipates almost in the same words the doctrine of the nineteenth-century Oxford School which spoke of "our station and its duties." He maintains that the Almighty, "having disposed and marshalled us by a divine tactic, *not* according to our will but according to His . . . virtually subjected us to act the part which belongs to the place assigned to us."

In his *Vindication of a Natural Society* (1756), which is a satire on the writings of Lord Bolingbroke written some years after Rousseau's *Discourse on the Arts and Sciences* (1751), Burke laid down that, in a state of nature, it was an invariable law that a man's acquisitions are in proportion to his labours.

> In a state of artificial society, it is a law as constant and invariable, that those who labour most enjoy the fewest things and that those who labour not at all have the greatest number of enjoyments. A condition of things this. strange and ridiculous beyond expression.

Burke, however, does not draw the conclusion that this condition of things should be altered, because he does not believe that it can be altered. To a high degree he had the conservative, religious mind: a century before he would have been temperamentally all for obedience. Burke draws the precisely opposite conclusion that the *civil* order can be impiously undermined by the same sceptical arguments of supercilious wit by which Bolingbroke had endeavoured to undermine current *religion* and theology. Hence the arguments, which proved too much, were false. The conclusion that Burke draws (in 1756) is not the need for a revolution in the social order, but the folly and impiety of Bolingbroke's argument for a revolution in orthodox religion. There is, throughout Burke's argument (as much as in that of Pascal and Newman), a profound pessimism, a deep belief in the original sinfulness of man. To flatter the poor and to tell them that they can greatly change their state is, in Burke's view, nothing less than fraud and wicked folly.

> I have some times been in a good deal more than doubt whether the Creator did ever really intend man for a state of happiness. He has mixed in His cup a number of natural evils (in spite of the boasts of stoicism they are evils), and every endeavour which the art and policy of mankind has used from the beginning of the world to this day, in order to alleviate or cure them, has only served to introduce new mischiefs or to aggravate and inflame the old.

Already the doctrine of Progress, with Priestley and Condorcet, has become the darling of the liberals. Reactionism against it, as a principle, can scarcely go farther.

The offenders, in Burke's view, who were guilty of perpetrating this confidence trick upon a pathetic toiling humanity were the abstract theorists, and especially the *philosophes* of France, forerunners of modern Marxists. It is a theme that he develops in his most famous work, his *Reflections on the French Revolution* (1790). He comments that these were men with "nothing but *douce humanité* in their mouth," but the conclusion of the argument was revolution and massacre. Men of science, with "their great lights about progress," were inspired by the philosophy of

> the geometricians and the chemists, bringing, the one from the dry bones of their diagrams, and the other from the soot of the furnace, dispositions that make them worse than indifferent about those feelings and habitudes which are the supports of the moral world. Ambition is come upon them suddenly . . . these philosophers consider men in their experiments no more than they do mice in an air-pump, or in a recipient of mephitic gas. Whatever His Grace [the reference is to the pro-Revolution Duke of Bedford] may think of himself, they look upon him and everything that belongs to him with no more regard than they do upon the whiskers of that little long-tailed animal that has been

the game of the grave, demure, insidious, spring-nailed, velvet-pawed, green-eyed philosopher, whether going upon two legs or upon four.

The substance of Burke's argument is the importance of experience as against abstract theory. He is tireless in his denunciation of the coxcombs of philosophy. As for their more serious teachers, he comments: "Nothing can be conceived more hard than the heart of a thoroughbred metaphysician. It comes nearer to the cold malignity of a wicked spirit than to the frailty and passion of a man."

Consistent with his pessimistic estimate of human nature and with his distrust of the "great lights" of illumination and progress, Burke is a minimalist in his theory of government, that is, he believed that the task of government is to interfere as little as possible with human nature as it displays itself in the day by day conduct of society. His attitude towards government is throughout empirical—the doctrine of passive obedience is a "dangerous exploded principle" (*i.e.*, contemporarily, ironically enough, it had the implications of Jacobite rebellion).

> What is government more than the management of the affairs of a nation? . . .
>
> The state ought to confine itself to what regards the state, or the creatures of the state, namely, the exterior establishment of its religion; its magistracy; its revenue . . . in a word, to everything that is truly and properly public, to the public peace, to the public safety, to the public order, to the public prosperity.

It will be noted that religion and morality, at least so far as they affect the outward order of society, are included by Burke within the proper function of state action, but apparently the regulation by legislation of the economic life of a people is not so included. The view is, of course, not novel. The expression, however, of this transitional error is striking.

It will further be noted that Burke's conservatism is, in his own eyes, bound up with defence of governmental non-interference—although not with individualism on moral principle. Burke and Jefferson here still shake hands on the practice of government.

The leading vice of the French monarchy, he holds, was "a restless desire of governing too much." A perfect democracy, in which the majority of the people is conscious of its own strength and admits of no limits to its power, is "the most shameless thing in the world."

> It is not necessary to teach men to thirst after power, but it is very expedient that by moral instruction they should be taught, and by their civil constitution they should be compelled, to put many restrictions on the immoder-

ate exercise of it and the inordinate desire. The best method of obtaining these two great points forms the important, but at the same time the difficult problem to the true statement.

It was inevitable that Burke, holding these views, should regard with abhorrence the French Revolution, which Charles James Fox was acclaiming when he spoke of the constitution of 1791 as "the most stupendous and glorious edifice of liberty which has been erected on the foundation of human integrity, in any time or country." Burke viewed it in a quite other light. The moderates who conducted it through its early stages he regarded as "men who would usurp the government of their country with decency and moderation." The French society that came into being in the later stages of the Revolution, he regarded as having the resemblance of

a den of outlaws upon a doubtful frontier; of a lewd tavern of revels and debauches, of banditti, assassins, bravos, smugglers and their more desparate paramours, mixed with bombastic players, the refuse and rejected offal of strolling theatres, puffing out ill-sorted verses about virtue, mixed with the licentious and blasphemous songs proper to the brutal and hardened course of lives belonging to that sort of wretches.

Jacobins were inspired by "determined hostility to the human race." The Revolution was a "hideous phantom; . . . One of the greatest calamities that has ever fallen upon mankind." Its authors were "the revolution harpies of France, sprung from night and hell"; its mood was "a drunken delirium from the hot spirit drawn from the alembic of Hell." There was a danger, he maintained, of Britain being led,

through an admiration of successful fraud and violence, to an imitation of the excesses of an irrational, unprincipled, proscribing, wasting, plundering, ferocious, bloody and tyrannical democracy. . . . *It is with an armed doctrine that we are at war.* It has, by its essence, a faction of opinion, and of interest, and of enthusiasm in every country. To us it is a Colossus which bestrides our Channel. It has one foot on a foreign shore; the other upon British soil. Thus advantaged, if it can exist at all, it must finally prevail. . . . England is not left out of the comprehensive scheme of their malignant charity.

For Burke, the inevitable conclusion urged through the pages of the *Letters on a Regicide Peace* (1796) was that Britain "must maintain her intervention," until the threat of this Jacobin International was destroyed.

His moral objections to the French Revolution, alike when specifically French and when international, and his economic anti-collectivism show Burke, as has been said, as the father of modern conservatism, although the doctrine of enlightened self-interest and the stress on liberties appear frequently enough to show the Whig in him. His *Reflections on the French Revolution*, although imbued by admiration for tradition and loyalty, do not display to equal advantage another of Burke's contributions to the enrichment of political thought. He is, however, although no compeer of Robertson or Hume as a professional historian, thanks to the mood he engendered, the co-founder of the Historical school. His entire treatment of political problems is suffused by an historical sense, if often a distorted one. Burke found in the immense slowness of history a corrective of radical ideas of individual Natural Rights, such as stimulated a revolutionary haste. His mood, in its faults and its virtues, was the precise opposite of that of Mr. Henry Ford. As with Bossuet, so with Burke, history displayed the decrees of God and, even better than the study of theology, checked an impious impatience. History was theology reduced to detail, a Book of Kings and Chronicles. If not the forerunner of Savigny and Gneist in Germany, and later of Maine and Stubbs in Britain, Burke, when not obsessed by rhetoric, at least did much to encourage a temper in Western civilization congenial to their labours.

5

If Burke was the great protagonist of the conservative protest against the French free-thinking Illumination and radical Revolution, there was no lack of antagonists, admirers of the French Revolution. Among these, who include the members of the London Corresponding Society and the Society of the Friends of the People (founded by Lord Grey and Erskine, the advocate) was Dr. Richard Price, minister, economist and author of a tractate famous in its time on the National Debt and Sinking Fund, and Dr. Joseph Priestley, Unitarian Minister and scientist. Price, moreover, was the object of Burke's attack by name in the *Reflections;* and a sermon of his, on the principles of the French Revolution, was the pretext for the writing of that pamphlet. The corner-stone of the offence of Dr. Price, whom Burke compares to Father John Ball, of the Peasants' Revolt, and to Dr. Hugh Peters, of the Commonwealth, was that, in a sermon at Old Jewry chapel, London, he said that George III was "almost the only lawful king in the world, because the only one who owes his crown to the choice of his people." Price's name, however, is chiefly connected with his pamphlets setting out the American case at the time of the War of Independence. The right of "Civil Liberty," as Price uses the term, is equivalent to a right of self-determination. He reverts, in his treatment, in his *Observations on the Nature of Civil Liberty* (1776), to the stock problem of Social Contract. The right to the observation of the contract "is a blessing which no one generation of men can give up for another; and which, when lost, a people have always a right to resume."

"If," Price continued, in order to preserve the unity of the British Empire, "one half of it must be enslaved to the other half, let it, in the name of God, want unity." Representation was the guaranty against imperialist enslavement. Every independent agent should have a share in government. "Here," in Britain, he adds somewhat naïvely, "it is impossible that the represented part should subject the unrepresented part to arbitrary power, without including themselves." In the colonies it was possible, and had been done. The people of America were no more the subjects of the people of Britain than those of Yorkshire were the subjects of the people of Middlesex. Price writes:

> Government is an institution for the benefit of the people governed, which they have power to model as they please; and to say that they can have too much of this power, is to say, that there ought to be a power in the state superior to that which gives it being, and from which all jurisdiction is derived. Licentiousness . . . is government by the will of rapacious individuals, in opposition to the will of the community, made known and declared in the laws. . . .
>
> All civil government is either the government of a whole by itself, or of a whole by a power extraneous to it, or of a whole by a part; the first alone is Liberty, and the two last are Tyranny.

Dr. Joseph Priestley, in his *Essay on the First Principles of Government* (1768), is concerned to draw a distinction between political and civil liberty, the first being the power of arriving at public office or voting, the second being power over their own actions which the members of the State reserve to themselves. Once again we are told that these civil liberties are rights, not to be resigned by any generation for and on behalf of its descendants, since

> it is manifestly contrary to the good of the whole that it should be so, but reassumed in virginal freshness by each generation as it attains years of discretion and rational maturity. . . . All people live in society for their mutual advantage; so that the goodness and happiness of the members, that is, the majority of the members of any state, is the great standard by which everything relating to that state must finally be determined.

As to those theologians who urged the words of St. Paul that the powers that be are ordained of God, "it is a sufficient answer to such an absurd quotation as this, that, for the same reason, *the powers which will be will be ordained of God also.*" The comment, in an agelong controversy, is an interesting and shrewd anticipation of later Hegelianism.

The idea of Progress, slowly developed since the Abbé de Saint Pierre (1658–1743), is beginning to take hold upon the human mind and is clearly expressed by Priestley.

> Were the best formed state in the world to be fixed in its present condition, I make no doubt but that, in a course of time, it would be the worst. History demonstrates this truth with respect to all the celebrated states of antiquity; and as all things (and particularly whatever depends upon science) have of late years been in a quicker progress towards perfection than ever; we may safely conclude the same with respect to any political state now in being.

In politics Priestley was a believer in personal liberty; in religion he believed in equal freedom (something more than toleration); in education he believed in experiment.

> From new, and seemingly irregular, methods of education, perhaps something extraordinary and uncommonly great may spring. . . . Pity it is then [wrote this Unitarian divine], that more and fairer experiments are not made; when, judging from what is past, the consequences of unbounded liberty in matters of religions promise to be so very favourable to the best interests of mankind. . . . Of all arts, these stand the fairest chance of being brought to perfection, in which there is opportunity of making the most experiments and trials.

Here we have a foreshadowing of John Stuart Mill's argument.

The forerunner of the Utilitarians lays down that riches are held for the good, not only of the individual but also of the state, which may demand their surrender. But he is typical of his century when he adds that "civil liberty has been greatly impaired by the abuse of the maxim that the joint understanding of all the members of a state, properly collected, must be preferable to that of individuals," whereas, in truth, the greater part of human actions are of such a nature that it is better to leave them to the arbitrary will of individuals than to regulation by society through law.

6

Among Burke's antagonists, however, Thomas Paine and William Godwin are outstanding.

THOMAS PAINE (1737–1809) was born at Thetford, England, the son of a Quaker stay-maker. Like the poet Burns, he found employment as an exciseman. He went to America on an introduction from Benjamin Franklin and first achieved fame in connection with his pamphlet published in January, 1776, entitled *Common Sense*, in which he advocated the separation of the colonies from Britain. After a stormy career, he returned to England and then proceeded to France. There he was elected a deputy of the National Convention but was imprisoned and under sentence of death during Robespierre's regime. Freed, he returned to America and died in New Rochelle, New York.

His chief claim to fame, however, is his book *The Rights of Man* (1791–1792), which was a vigorous criticism of Burke's *Reflections on the French Revolution*, written with that irreverence which was most calculated to be offensive to the rhetorical moralism of Burke. He quotes the passage where Burke says, "It looks to me as if I were in a great crisis, not of the affairs of France alone but of all Europe, perhaps of more than Europe. All the circumstances taken together, the French Revolution is the most astonishing that has hitherto happened in the world." Paine mordantly comments, "as wise men are astonished at foolish things, and other people at wise ones, I know not on which ground to account for Mr. Burke's astonishment; but certain it is that he does not understand the French Revolution." It is in denunciation of Burke's treatment of the Reverend Dr. Price that Paine writes a famous passage, commenting on Burke's declaration that the age of chivalry had departed.

> It is painful to behold a man employing his talents to corrupt himself. Nature has been kinder to Mr. Burke than he is to her. He is not affected by the reality of distress touching his heart, but by the showy resemblance of it striking his imagination. He pities the plumage but forgets the dying bird. Accustomed to kiss the aristocratical hand that hath purloined him from himself, he degenerates into a composition of art, and the genuine soul of nature forsakes him.

Burke the rhetorician had become, in Paine's eyes, merely one "mounted in the air like a balloon, . . . [a] genius at random." It was, in Paine's opinion, power and not principles that Burke venerated.

"My country is the world," declares Paine, "and my religion is to do good." He added, with truth and without false modesty, that he possessed more of what is called consequence in the world than anyone in Mr. Burke's catalogue of aristocrats. Burke's reverence for the British constitution was an affectation and a dangerous affectation.

Governments were of two kinds, either that springing up out of the people or that over the people. If of the latter kind, they partook of the nature of tyranny. Government arose from a compact of man with man, and not from any compact between men and governments, since there must have been a time before governments existed. Burke had "set up a sort of political Adam [*cf.* Filmer*] in whom all posterity are bound for ever; he must, therefore, prove that his Adam possessed such a power or such a right." Elsewhere Paine distinguishes governments under three heads; it is of priestcraft; it is of conquerors; or it is of reason. The first two, however, tend to enter into alliance. "The key of St. Peter and key of the Treasury become quartered on one another, and the wondering cheated multitude worshipped the invention." The prejudice, therefore, of Englishmen in favour of their own government by kings, lords and commons, arose as much or more, in Paine's opinion, "from national pride, than reason." As for the monarchy, it could trace its claim to no higher source than the power of the sword of William the Conqueror, "a French bastard landing with an armed banditti, and establishing himself King of England against the consent of the natives"—which was, "in plain terms, a very paltry, rascally original."

If, however, Paine had no high opinion of "the son of a prostitute and the plunderer of the English nation," his opinion was not much higher of "the House of Brunswick, one of the petty tribes of Germany." His *Rights of Man* was a protest against "the romantic and barbarous distinction of men into kings and subjects." Government had been too long "made up of mysteries," and he protested against Burke's "idol" which would be "as good a figure of monarchy with him as a man." Monarchy was "a silly, contemptible thing, . . . *the popery of government.*" As he had said earlier in his *Common Sense*, "virtue is not hereditary. . . . Through all the vocabulary of Adam there is not such an animal as a Duke or a Count."

If Paine protests against monarchy and hereditary aristocracy, he is not any believer in the sovereignty of parliament. These were the days when the demand for annual parliaments, ultimately to be made one of the points of the Chartists, was being formulated. Paine's whole argument is directed towards the effective establishment of the sovereignty of the People as against that of Parliament. "The continual use of the word Constitution in the English Parliament shows that there is none; and that the whole is merely a form of Government without a Constitution, and constituting itself with what powers it

* *Vide* p. 224.

pleases." On the other hand, Paine, somewhat inconsistently, maintained "the American Constitutions were to Liberty what a grammar is to language: they define its parts of speech and practically construct them into syntax."

Paine maintained that he was not a revolutionary by preference, or rather that he believed in producing *revolutions* "*by reason and accommodation rather than commit them to the issue of convulsions.*" It is true that his practice, in 1776, when he urged the colonists to declare their independence, was not entirely consistent with this maxim of moderation. Presumably, he was then confirmed by the opinion that he elsewhere expressed that, "when it becomes necessary to do a thing, the whole heart and soul should go into the measure, or not attempt it." Revolution, at least, was not worth while unless it was to be for some great national benefit, and then the danger would be for those who opposed. It was, he held, not difficult to perceive from the enlightened state of mankind that hereditary governments were verging to their decline, that revolutions on the broad basis of national sovereignty and government by representation were making their way. Nevertheless, he looked forward to a time, presumably subsequent to these revolutions, when "for what we can foresee, *all Europe may form but one great Republic, and man be free of the whole.*"

Paine's power to inspire his readers depended upon the vigour of his indignation against current abuses, the journalistic skill of his pen and the vividness of his vision of the future.

> Lay then the axe to the root, and teach Governments humanity. It is their sanguinary punishments which corrupt mankind. . . .
>
> *Man has no property in man* [nor, presumably, has a society composed of men] neither has any generation a property in the generations which are to follow. . . .
>
> There is a morning of reason rising upon man on the subject of Government that has not appeared before. . . .
>
> When it shall be said in any country in the world, my poor are happy; neither ignorance nor distress is to be found among them; my jails are empty of prisoners, my streets of beggars; the aged are not in want; the taxes are not oppressive; the rational world is my friend because I am the friend of its happiness: When these things can be said, then may that country boast its Constitution and its Government.

William Godwin (1756–1836) is too definitely an eccentric to be put among the builders of the Anglo-Saxon tradition. He provides, however, a corrective to Burke. Above all, the popularity of his *Political Justice* is an index of the vigour of the individualism in that tradition in the late eighteenth century. It is an ingredient of our tradition which it is easy, in the twentieth century, to overlook.

Godwin had read his Rousseau and Helvetius. Specifically he admits that these French writers have recognized, as Locke and Paine did not, the moulding effects of political institutions upon the minds of citizens. This temper of a constitution "insinuates itself into our personal dispositions, and insensibly communicates its own spirit to our private transactions." Having, however, made that admission, Godwin draws an unexpected conclusion—although one entirely consonant with the argument of Paine: it is imperative to reduce this influence. "Rousseau was the first to teach that the imperfections of government were the only permanent source of the vices of mankind; and this principle was adopted from him by Helvetius and others." But government, as Paine recognized, however reformed, "was little capable of affording solid benefit to mankind."

Godwin was little disposed to follow Rousseau into the realms of Book Four of the *Contrat Social.* Rousseau underestimated the rational obligation of social benevolence that rests on a good man. But he grossly over-estimates the part that can usefully be played, not only by government, but even by any particular society.

> Society is an ideal existence, and not on its own account entitled to the slightest regard.* The wealth, prosperity and glory of the whole are unintelligible chimeras. Set no value on anything, but in proportion as you are convinced of its tendency to make individual men happy and virtuous.†

It was a further complaint against Rousseau that his followers spent their time seeking to prove that men must be governed by something other than reason. The point is important and well-taken.

Godwin's views upon what he meant by reason are interesting but vacillating. There was, he asserted in various *obiter dicta*, an "immutable voice of reason and justice." There are matters on which we have "an irresistible persuasion." But Godwin is an enemy of the dogmatists. There is no infallible judge of controversies.

> To dragoon men into the adoption of what we think right, is an intolerable tyranny. . . . Every man thinks himself in the right; and, if such a proceeding were universally introduced, the destiny of mankind would be no longer

* *Cf.* J. Bentham: *Principles of Morals and Legislation*, ed. 1876, p. 3: "The community is a fictitious *body*, composed of the individual persons who are considered as constituting its *members*. The interest of the community then is, what?—the sum of the interests of the several members who compose it. It is in vain to talk of the interest of the community, without understanding what is the interest of the individual."

† *Cf.* pp. 349, 355, 547; and also Hobbs and Locke on happiness.

a question of argument, but of strength, presumption or intrigue. . . . He that speaks of [truth's] immutability, does nothing more than predict with greater or less probability . . . human science is attended with all degrees of certainty . . . but human beings are capable of apprehending and weighing all these degrees.

Men, moreover, who have been awakened to truth will not relapse.

Godwin's positive position appears to be a good Lockian one, that there are "laws of the universe" which we can approximately, but with growing clarity, apprehend. The laws of a determined human nature are among these general laws which a student of the Puritan theologian, Jonathan Edwards, is a priori prepared to accept. "*Politics is a science.* The general features of the nature of man are capable of being understood, and a mode may be delineated which, in itself considered, is best adapted to the condition of man in society." These basic rules are uniform to the whole human race. The duty to apprehend these laws is a check upon individual caprice. This, as against utility, is the element of truth in the obscure maxim that we should do good regardless of the consequences. "The universal exercise of private judgement is a doctrine unspeakably beautiful." But it is subject to this interior check. "Immutable reason is the true legislator."* Otherwise we have mere enthusiasm and fanaticism. "The most determined political assassins, Clement, Ravaillac, Damiens and Gerard, seem to have been deeply penetrated with anxiety for the eternal welfare of mankind. . . . The authors of the Gunpowder Treason were in general men remarkable for the sanctity of their lives and the austerity of their manners. . . . They were sincere enthusiasts; but had not recognized that there was a rational duty not to 'labour under prejudice.'"

The freedom of private judgement, illumined by reason, is a freedom in relation to external authority, especially government, and to all manifestations of the irrational brute fact of mass force. Is not, yet, the majority most likely to be right—to be rational? Of this Godwin is far from sure—and hence the quasi-anarchism of himself and his followers. "Truth cannot be made more true by the number of its votaries." "Truth disdains the alliance of marshalled numbers." On the contrary, all the great steps of human improvement have been the work of individuals—seeking alone after the apprehension of truths. Congregations of enthusiasts, heady Parliaments, proud of their numerical support, become insolent in their pretensions to power. "Gentlemen, you are not, as in the intoxication of power you have

* *Cf.* pp. 169, 268.

been led to imagine, omnipotent; there is an authority greater than yours, to which you are bound assiduously to conform yourselves."

"Nothing can be at once so unreasonable and hopeless as an attempt"—it is a remark to be echoed by the Economists—"by positive regulations to supersede the unalterable laws of the universe. . . . " Nothing can be more unquestionable than that the manners and opinions of mankind are of the utmost consequence to the general welfare. But it does not follow that government is the instrument by which they are to be fashioned." On the contrary, government is "the perpetual enemy" of rational and scientific change and innovation. Now innovation is good—adjustment in a moving civilization.

That Godwin should be a humanist, not a revolutionary, follows from his liberal premises. "If conviction of the understanding be the compass which is to direct our proceedings in the general affairs, we shall have many reforms, but no revolutions"—this conviction is making a "calm, incessant, rapid, and auspicious progress." There is no time-serving in his declaration that he "deprecated scenes of commotion and tumult."

> The legitimate instrument of effecting political reformation is truth . . . Let us not vainly endeavour by laws and regulations to anticipate the future dictates of the general mind, but calmly wait till the harvest of opinion is ripe . . . make men wise, and by that very operation you make them free.

In his praise of "innovation," in his declaration that, even if the mass of men is contented, he is "not contented for them," Godwin shows himself no temperamental conservative. On the contrary, he has a belief, highly progressive and well in advance of our own age, in what can be achieved under the guidance of a political science unobstructed by censorship and passionate prejudice.

What Godwin ignores, and Bentham later is to point out, is the importance of a pressure, calculated but constant and menacing, upon men in power, who are emotional and selfish as well as rational and benevolent beings. Bentham, moreover, was to point out, with insight, the "occupational disease" of philosophy, the vocation mostly of a sedentary kind of men, to wit, intellectualism. Godwin, nevertheless, has it to his credit, for good or ill, that he contributed by his influence, along with Wesley, to divert Britain from the course of revolution as followed in France and towards that of the Reform of 1832. The Parliamentary and Electoral reforms of 1832, a prescient Godwin could have claimed, were permanent; those of the French Revolution were not. The French paid an infinitely greater cost to win, in terms of bourgeois democracy, no greater prize. Humanism was justified of her children.

READING

Edmund Burke: *Address to the King*, 1777.

BIBLIOGRAPHICAL NOTE

C. L. Becker: *The Heavenly City of the Philosophers*, 1932.
*Edmund Burke: *Reflections on the Revolution in France.*
Alexander Hamilton, John Jay and James Madison: *The Federalist.*
James Truslow Adams: *The Living Jefferson*, 1936.
Kingsley Martin: *French Liberal Thought in the Eighteenth Century*, 1929.
*Thomas Paine: *Rights of Man.*
T. V. Smith: *The American Philosophy of Equality*, 1927.
Leslie Stephen: *English Thought in the Eighteenth Century*, 2 vols. 1876.

Chapter XI

The Early Utilitarians: Jeremy Bentham

1

THE END of the eighteenth century found Utilitarianism, if not as a philosophy then as an assumption, in the air in Britain. Rousseau's religion of enthusiasm made small headway, in that damp island, against the increasing and consolidated belief that utility was the proper test of policy. The mental climate was congenial to the belief. The Deists, the Unitarians and the demi-Unitarians, enemies of clericalism, had done their work in weakening the influence of a morality with supernatural sanctions. Sir Isaac Newton, strongly orthodox in religion, had thereby shown how piety could be allied with the most modern insight into an orderly world, rationally comprehensible. The fanaticism of the seventeenth century had been succeeded by respect for common sense. The classic calm of Addison and Pope was not congenial to "enthusiasm." The solid prosperity of the century in Britain, the improvement of conditions in France, led to a sophistication and relaxation of manners.

The "Glorious Revolution," of 1688, had inoculated the English, unlike the lands of benevolent despotism, against any desire for political excesses. The view, across the Channel, of the French Revolution was adequate to deprive them of such appetite as they might have. Wesleyanism confirmed their distaste and gave an alternative emotional outlet. The pro-Revolutionary London Corresponding Society, London Revolutionary Society of 1688 and Society of the Friends of the People—the first a workers' organization; the others patronized by the peerage—lived their brief career and collapsed, not without handing on their torch. The Tories came to power. The son of Chatham, that great Whig, became the Tory "young master." In reaction against Robespierre and Bonaparte came Burke and his practical disciples, the politicians Sidmouth and Castlereagh and Percival (Coleridge's "best and wisest statesman this country has possessed" since the

English Revolution). The Whig party of Fox and Lansdowne and Grey lay in hopeless eclipse. Men had to choose whether to side with Toryism, Church, State and Landlord or to work out some policy of progress uncontaminated by the Jacobins.

Meanwhile technology advanced. Watt and Arkwright took the place of Calvin's God. The effects of their inventions, even when deplored by squire and craftsman and admirer of the yeomanry of Merrie England, worked on to their predestined conclusions—acclaimed by the new men as providentially progressive—first in the British Isles, then in lands less blessed by the marriage of natural wealth and innovating wit. Britain became the workshop of the world—as Professor Clapham shows, not abruptly. There was no *der Tag* of the Industrial Revolution. Beginning well back in the eighteenth century, the factory system arose and made headway against the old guild restrictions, once the protection of the free worker, now the privilege of the "freeman" and liveryman of oligarchic companies. Between 1700 and 1801 the population of Britain grew from about 5,500,000 to 8,892,536; and to 12,000,236, in 1821. The cities grew. Children are thrust by parents, who want wages (from their human investments), not education and "ideas," into factories. An urban proletariat arises. This is the physical, technological and economic background of the New Epoch.

The manufacturers of Britain appreciate that this world is their oyster and that Free Trade is economic truth—and moral truth, too. The mills grind faster. No longer is there the unemployment that enraged the Luddite *saboteurs*, ignorant Luddites; but employment increases, as the Economists had said. The world is Britain's market. She has a mission to other nations: Trade and the Bible. No longer are the mills the poet Blake's "Satanic Mills," at least for the man making dividends. The factory wheels are going ever quicker introducing Jerusalem into a green and pleasant land, no longer rural England. Regrettable gin shops—but still a soberer nation than in the port wine and "Geneva gin" century. Nevertheless a compromise must be made with God, who had given the fatness and the increase.

Mr. Percival went to church; he was not a Jacobin. Paine and Godwin* of course did not go to church. Even Mr. Godwin, however, after hearing from Coleridge, thought better of it—at least, so the old Godwin said (his posthumous papers had rather another story). With Byron we have the mood of the Regency; but with Wordsworth, recovered from his ardours for the French Revolution, we have the

* Godwin, however, had begun as a Unitarian.

prophet of the coming Victorian period. We enter not only a new century but a new age.

In the 1830's, in England, the stage-coach still competed with the train. Travellers by coach were advised to take "a pair of pistol holsters covered with black fur and attached to the coach box" as defensive weapons. There was no harm in letting the landlord of any roadside inn at which one might stay see that one was armed. Not until the days of Sir Robert Peel was a regular police force established in London—"Bobbies" in silk top hats—and then only a small one. Sir Robert, when he assumed the premiership in 1834, took just the same time to return from Rome to London that the Emperor Constantine, fifteen centuries before, had taken to travel in the opposite direction. The London to Birmingham Railway was opened in 1838, following the Stockton and Darlington in 1825; the South Carolina Railroad was operated in 1829.

The "sanitary idea," largely due to the Utilitarians, was yet only just born. In about 1844, the average expectation of life for an infant of the manual working classes, in the great provincial cities, was no more than from twelve to fifteen years. In 1839 Dr. Southwood Smith reported of London:

> While systematic efforts on a large scale have been made to widen the streets, to remove obstructions to the circulation of free currents of air, to extend and perfect the drainage and sewerage, and to prevent the accumulation of putrifying vegetable and animal substances in the places where the wealthier classes reside, nothing whatever has been done to improve the condition of the districts inhabited by the poor.

Even so, in the mansions of the wealthy West-end cesspools "were regarded as equally sacred with the wine cellars." In the other areas,

> several families usually had to share a common privy, and empty it when and where they could . . . this fosters habits of the most abject degeneration and tends to the demoralization of large numbers of human beings, who subsist by means of what they find amid other noxious filth accumulated in neglected streets and bye places.

Homeless children flocking to outhouses to sleep were a common sight. The private-capital Water Companies took in water from a Thames contaminated by sewage. As late as 1853 and 1865, London had grave visitations of cholera. Nevertheless its condition was better than that of Hamburg.

In 1767 a Committee of the House of Commons reported:

> That taking the Children born in the Workhouse, or Parish Houses or received of or under Twelve Months old, in the year 1763, and following the same into 1764 and 1765, only seven in a Hundred appear to have survived this short Period.

The reports of the investigators prior to the passage of the Second Factory Act in Britain, of 1819—there was a Health and Morals of Apprentices Act in 1802 and a Society for the Suppression of Vice established in the same year—give no great ground for congratulation on the improvement over fifty years. As late as 1842 the report of the Royal Commission in Mines contained this statement of an underground mine worker, woman:

> I have a belt around my waist and a chain passing between my legs, and I go on my hands and feet. The water comes up to my clog tops, and I have seen it over my thighs. I have drawn till I have the skin off me. The belt and chain is worn when we are in the family way.

Children under five work in the darkness of the mines, alone. These things were the price of Victorian civilization.

The lot of the adult labourer was one hedged by restrictions such that Adam Smith declared that it was harder for a poor man to cross the boundaries of his parish—lest he become chargeable to parish relief elsewhere—than to cross a mountain ridge. "A violation of natural liberty and justice," free-trading Adam Smith called it. For a century before, pregnant women, when the children would have been illegitimate, were hounded from village to village, lest the child become chargeable on the parish. Over in America, Alexander Hamilton put a novel construction on freedom of contract, natural liberty and utility.

> Women and children [Hamilton wrote with complacency] are rendered more useful, and the latter more early useful, by manufacturing establishments, than they would otherwise be. Of the number of persons employed in the cotton manufactories of Great Britain, it is computed that four-sevenths, nearly, are women and children; of whom the greatest proportion are children, many of them of a tender age.

In 1816 only one Londoner in four could read. The poetical tract-writer, Hannah More, thought that the poor should be educated, although not enough to cause them to read the worthless works of Thomas Paine. Dr. Parr, D.D., agreed; but held that we must recall how "the Deity Himself had fixed a great gulph between them and the poor." Dr. Parr probably did not refer to that described in Holy Writ between the Rich Man in Hell (in the English Bible considerately still

Latinized as "Dives") and Lazarus in Heaven. Beggars abounded; drunkenness was rampant. There was a public house or saloon to every hundred inhabitants in London, in which city Patrick Colquhoun states, probably with exaggeration, that one woman in every six was living, directly or indirectly, on immoral earnings.

The legislators, alarmed by the excesses of the wretched population they regulated, had made with the passage of the centuries penalties more, not less, severe. Ignorant physicians, unable to diagnose the disease, they determined to suppress the symptoms. In May, 1833, a boy of nine, convicted of "breaking and entering" a dwelling house and stealing two pennyworth of goods, was by Mr. Justice Bosanquet sentenced to death. The judge had no choice. Again, although in practical abeyance, in law it was a capital offence to steal any material goods of over the value of five shillings. At the close of the eighteenth century in England there were two hundred capital offences. Gibbetting continued until 1832. In 1810, when a bill was laid before the House to abolish the capital penalty for stealing goods to the value of five shillings, or slightly over a dollar, not only the Chief Justice but the Archbishop of Canterbury and six bishops voted against it. Meanwhile the complexity of the law brought in money to the lawyers. Prisoners merely sentenced to deportation were sent to the penal settlements in plague-ridden hulks, but were aided on their way by libraries containing the works of Archdeacon Paley entitled *Moral and Political Philosophy*. Charles Dickens' *Household Words* was rejected because "the chaplain objects to it."

Attempts to ameliorate the law were almost as unpopular as attempts to improve education. The mobs which joined in the "No Popery" riots of Lord George Gordon (repeated by bigots in Edinburgh on a small scale within the last few years) and in the anti-Jacobin riots which sacked Dr. Priestley's Birmingham house, had as their natural descendants the mobs which pelted, in 1854, the Home Office messenger who carried from Palmerston a reprieve from hanging of a man of eighty-four—the lynch mob had been deprived of its show, the public execution. However, the condemned prisoner, in a world marked by the natural depravity of Cain's children, had his compensations. In 1840 the Rev. Mr. Carter, addressing a prisoner due for hanging, at Newgate, said:

> To you, my dear young friend and fellow sinner, it has now happened that for the last time you are here treading the courts of God's house of prayer. Before to-morrow's sun shall have set, your eyes will have closed on this world. But pray remember, my dear young friend, that, should you leave it

penitently (as I hope and believe you will) a choir of 10,000 angels will welcome you to the heavenly abode where you will then become a trophy of sovereign grace, and add yet one more jewel to the diadem of mercy.

It is impossible to understand the ferocity of Paine and even Bentham —or Marx—in their criticism of the customs of their times, except one first comprehends what was the mental attitude, normally engendered by this environment. Mr. Carter meant no harm—but it seems at least probable that Mr. Carter would not have voted, against his Archbishop, for abolishing the death penalty for children who stole five shillings.

There is a passage in a recent book of Professor W. Y. Elliott's which describes, briskly, the change which yet had taken place between the accession and the death of George III, seventeen years before the accession of Victoria.

> The old, old, old King had begun his reign in an Empire which passed loyal Addresses to the Throne in New York and Massachusetts, an Empire which had never seen a steam engine and scarcely a metalled road, before the great Enclosure Acts, before the Highway Acts. His accession was only fifteen years after the march of the Highland swordsmen to Derby, through an England of 7 million souls, when Lancashire was still the picturesque home of lost causes. This King died in 1820, when already twenty years had passed since the foundation of Tennant's Chemical Works and the fortunes of Margot Asquith.

The figure however who best symbolizes in his death the passing of the able, sceptical, morally latitudinarian, pre-industrial, aristocratic, conservative eighteenth century, is the Iron Duke, the Duke of Wellington. That funeral has been memorably described by Mr. Guedalla. The thud of the guns. The ranks at attention. "Duke of Wellington . . . Prince of Waterloo . . . Duke of Ciudad Rodrigo . . . Grandee of the First Class in Spain . . . Marshal of Russia . . . Knight of the Garter . . . Knight of the Sword of Sweden . . . of the Annunciado of Sardinia . . . Lord High Constable of England . . . Warden of the Cinque Ports." So the pomp passed.

> Bury the Great Duke
> with an empire's lamentation,
> Let us bury the Great Duke
> to the noise of the mourning of a mighty nation.

Till 1852, till within sight of Cecil Rhodes and Joseph Chamberlain, "Radical Chamberlain," he, the Great Duke, that shadow of Waterloo, the old man whose conversation shocked good Sir Robert Peel, had lasted on. The international age was over; the little family of crowned heads who made the politics of their peoples was being reduced; the curtain had fallen at Vienna on the agelong Roman Empire. The age of nationalism comes in; of industry and commerce, evangelicalism and prosperity; strike and revolution; war and dictatorship. The Victorian Age of Britain. The Gilded Era of America. And out beyond to Versailles. And beyond . . . Danton and the Corsican look forward. The Duke looks back. On Napoleon, his comment was, "the man was not even a gentleman." The Duke belonged to that epoch of which Talleyrand had said that no one who had not lived then could imagine how pleasant life could be—for the fortunate classes.

The philosophy which rendered these generations, at the turn of the century and into its middle, articulate to themselves was, in part, that of Coleridge and Southey—and John Wesley and the evangelist, Simeon. More, perhaps, than any other this conservative, evangelic pietism was representative of the thought of the age—if it did not lead it, much less change it. Later it was to acquire prophetic vision and come to vigorous life guided by the sage of Chelsea, Thomas Carlyle. In most respects antipodal, but not without unexpected agreements, were the Radicals *du sang pur*, lineal descendants of Paine, from William Cobbett (1762–1835), in his second phase, to the more intellectual and more shocking Bradlaugh (1833–1891). Forced by political fortune to share with these Radicals a couch but with garment unsoiled by the contact, were the Whigs and their brisk young Liberal allies, men to whom all things had been made clear and who remained undismayed by the revelation, such as Macaulay, who baldly maintained that "law was made for property alone." Whereas Coleridge at least attempted a philosophy, these men, well content with their own piecemeal observations and post-prandial complacencies, can scarcely be said to have felt the need for one. Fourth, and sharply distinct, are the "Philosophic Radicals," the Utilitarians. If not the most representative, this school (which retained the radicalism while rejecting the "natural rights" prejudices of the admirers of the French Revolution) was the most intellectually eminent. Moreover it moved in loose alliance with the rising school of the Economists.

The new industrial entrepreneurs required a philosophy to justify themselves—an economic philosophy. The holder of the Glasgow chair of Moral Philosophy, Adam Smith, with a contribution here and there from his French friends, came to their rescue. The hand of Providence points to the Division of Labour as the route of human advance to a well-pleasing condition—the Division of Labour between nations even—Free Trade: Britain to make the goods; other rustic peoples to buy them.

2

The remoter origins of the Utilitarian school we have already had occasion to indicate.* The school had four cardinal notes. The first was *utility*. If, however, one asked: Utility for what? the reply was, secondly, pleasure or *happiness*. Whose happiness? The third point: *the greatest number*. Why, however, should I consult the happiness of others? The pill, then, of egoism was coated with an instinct, *benevolence*, exercising a major influence in every breast.

Utility, first, was a concept familiar, as a moral key, to Dr. Samuel Johnson and to Archdeacon Paley, from whom for a century Anglican clerics drew moral wisdom—Paley, who jocularly remarked, apropos of the XXXIX Articles, that he "could not afford to keep a conscience." After Bentham's earlier publications utility was readily taken up by Godwin. It is central to the moral philosophy of David Hume.

Secondly, the Pleasure or Happiness principle—the achievement of an enduring balance of pleasure over pain—is the final legacy of Hobbes to his countrymen. The spiritual bones of the philosopher had long wandered in exile, especially among the congenial countrymen of La Rochefoucauld. Mandeville, of *The Fable of the Bees*, had merely shocked the eighteenth-century Englishman as Hobbes had shocked even the England of the Restoration. Lord Rochester had no need for cold systems and Lord Clarendon had no use for this one. In France the reception of Hobbes had been different: the influence on the Encyclopaedists, Helvetius and Condillac, was great. Through Helvetius and Bentham, the Hobbesian ethic, reclothed and sobered, but still the same, logical, militant, returned in triumph. As touching the charge of egoism it is interesting to note a remark—as significant of the temper of the age—of Hobbes's antithesis, the idealist philosopher, George Berkeley (1685–1753), Bishop of Cloyne. "Self-love being a principle of all others the most universal, and the most deeply engraved on our hearts, it is natural for us to regard things as they are fitted to augment or impair our own happiness; and accordingly we denominate them good or evil." Paley declared that, "virtue evidently consists in educing from the materials which the Creator has placed under our guidance the greatest sum of human happiness." Hobbes, however, unlike the Bishop of Cloyne and Archdeacon Paley, drew

* *Cf*. pp. 245, 272.

inconvenient conclusions. The solemn Utilitarians felt the need to socialize, baptize with the faith of progress, this heathen.

Thirdly, the sacred phrase, "the Greatest Happiness of the Greatest Number," Bentham, founder of the formal Utilitarian school, tells us he derived from Dr. Priestley. Priestley had, however, been anticipated by an academic exponent of the (later on, bitterly opposed) doctrine of "the moral sense," Francis Hutcheson (died 1747), Professor of Philosophy in Glasgow. The moral evil, he had said, of an action "is as the Degree of Misery, and the Number of Sufferers; so that, that Action is best, which accomplishes the Greatest Happiness of the Greatest Number." How precisely one was to count the greatest number—in what society in space and through how many generations in time—the Utilitarians, as we shall see, never answered. It was their great weakness.

Lastly, the principle of Benevolence will be found affirmed in the *Sermons* of the great and admirable Bishop Joseph Butler (1692–1752), son of a dissenting shopkeeper in a nation of shopkeepers, Rector of Stanhope, Bishop Palatine of Durham. Having lived the life of a conscientious parish priest, until promoted on the instigation of Queen Caroline—the queen to whom George II was so much attached that he proclaimed that after her death he would only have mistresses—and having written his famous *Analogy*, concluding with Sir Isaac Newton "a happy alliance between faith and philosophy," he died in his sixtieth year, and in the middle of the eighteenth century, amid the waters of Bath. "Pius, simplex, candidus, liberalis . . . mortui haud facile evanescet memoria," they truly wrote on his gravestone, "reverendi in Christo patris."* This good man is one of the ablest critics of Hobbes, and by implication of the Utilitarians; and, while providing these philosophers indirectly—they may never have read him—with one of their principles yet puts posers that, to the end of the days of the school's vogue, its disciples never answer, although poor John Stuart Mill tries his best.

> There is [says Butler] a natural principle of *benevolence* in man. . . . If, by a *sense* of *interest,* is meant a speculative conviction or belief that such and such indulgence would occasion them greater uneasiness, upon the whole, than satisfaction, it is contrary to present experience to say that this sense of interest is sufficient to restrain them from thus indulging themselves. And if, by a *sense* of *interest,* is meant a practical regard to what is, upon the whole, our happiness, this is not only coincident with the principle of virtue, or moral

* "Pious, simple, frank, liberal . . . the memory of this reverend father in Christ, although he is dead, will scarcely pass away."

rectitude, but is a part of the idea itself. And it is evident this reasonable self-love wants to be improved, as really as any principle in our nature. . . . So greatly are profligate men mistaken when they affirm they are wholly governed by interestedness and self-love; and so little cause is there for moralists to disclaim this principle. . . . We plainly consider compassion as itself an original, distinct, particular affection in human nature.

Maintaining the view of "plain common sense," without over-great refinements, Butler argues that the varied impulses of man are not so simple as all to be capable of reduction to one. Hitting at Hobbes, he continues:

> Could anyone be thoroughly satisfied that what is commonly called benevolence or good will was really the affection meant [by love of power], but only by being made to understand that this learned person had a general hypothesis, to which the appearance of good will could not otherwise be reconciled? . . . These are the absurdities which even men of capacity run into when they have occasion to belie their nature, and will perversely disclaim that image of God which was originally stamped upon it, the traces of which, however faint, are plainly discernible upon the mind of man.

Despite Berkeley and Hobbes and Helvetius, is "my interest" or "my pleasure" enough to explain moral obligation? Or shall we accept with Butler a plurality of "values" or "ends" to which (assessed by "conscience" or intuition) man is drawn? Before endeavouring to answer this question of political philosophy from the writings of the received Utilitarians, it is necessary to digress briefly in order to look at the work of their very nursing father, the Scottish philosopher-historian, David Hume. The famous sceptic is wholly a figure of the eighteenth century, an adornment of the glorious Enlightenment, meriting to be treated along with Jefferson and Franklin, D'Alembert and Diderot, and the great Frederick. Nevertheless his principles form a link with the nineteenth century perhaps even more—the fashions of thought being quicker in Europe—than did those of his junior, Thomas Jefferson, spiritual son of Locke.

3

David Hume (1711–1776) is the philosophic initiator, if not the popular founder, of Utilitarianism as a system. One of the most eminent philosophers that has adorned human civilization, and a judicious historian, his dull essay on a "Perfect Commonwealth" would have provided a theme to demonstrate that men of intellectual genius are inept as men of affairs. However, actual office in the British

Embassy at Paris showed him to be *capax imperii,* a shrewd and competent Scot (although not above lamenting the fact that he did not possess that apparent passport to success, "a true genuine natural impudence").

A bachelor, who had decided that a wife was "not indispensable," sustained by a trivial annuity, he produced at the age of twenty-five that *Treatise of Human Nature* which established his position among the immortals, achieved no significant sale as a book, and earned from the insolent conceit characteristic of anonymous young reviewers the comment that it was immature. His fame, however, spread, especially in France, and during his sojourn in Paris he was received by the whole *beau monde* and especially by the Dauphin. The last, with Gallic enthusiasm for intelligence, caused his sons, the future Louis XVI, Louis XVIII and Charles X, to recite verses in honour of this elder contemporary of Benjamin Franklin. It was not irrelevantly that Hume protested against colleges and the academic monopoly of the humanities, thanks to which "every part of what we call *belles lettres* became totally barbarous, being cultivated by men without any taste for life or manners." Indeed singularly few great men of intelligence have been well-read after adolescence.

Like the author of *The Decline and Fall,* Edward Gibbon, and equally typically of his era, Hume believed that bishops and barbarians were the prime enemies of humane culture. This otherwise great man suffers from the deplorable fashion of habitually referring to priests as bigots. He even goes further, and asserts that they have a vested, pecuniary interest that men should not inquire closely what precise and indispensable social function the clergy perform: they have an interest in the docile mind. Hume does not reflect that these often devoted men, did they but turn their energies to the cure of souls and become psycho-therapists and professional psychologists, would perform an admirable function in society.

One of Hume's chief claims to fame, as a political philosopher, is his flat assertion, in his *Essays,* that government rests, not on some Original Contract and the obligation *in vacuo* "to keep one's word," but on interest, on habit and on opinion—including even tyrannous government, as of a Henry VIII. Nevertheless he writes that liberty of the press "is attended with so few inconveniences, that it may be claimed as the common right of mankind, and ought to be indulged almost in every government except the ecclesiastical, to which, indeed, it would be fatal." In his defence it is perhaps worth observation that our current vital priesthoods, those of the Holy Trinity [Marx, Engels,

Lenin] of Moscow and of the Mahomets of Potsdam and Rome, do in fact place that great invention of the press under the control of their party bosses and "ward heelers," recognizing that orthodox religion is necessarily totalitarian in culture.

It is told that Hume, a mountain of a man, fell into a bog outside Edinburgh. Sinking like Peter, the philosopher begged a passing countrywoman to aid him. "My good woman, does not your religion teach you to do good, even to your enemies?" Representative of respectable opinion, suspicious of eminent deviators from the narrow road of Calvin, she replied: "That may be; but ye shallna get out of that till ye become a Christian yersell: and repeat the Lord's Prayer and the Belief"—by her Scottish simplicity and pious ignorance putting to shame alike the pride of philosophy and the lax flattery of the Most Christian King and his Court.

Hume, using Archbishop Tillotson—Tillotson famous as the writer on the Popish "Real Presence"—as a supporting peg, wrote his essay on *Miracles*, elegantly to show that only thanks to the happy interposition of Providence could man have been brought to believe so great absurdities. He demonstrated that the orthodox argument for the immortality of the soul was identical with "the hideous hypothesis of the famous atheist Spinoza." He wrote his essay *On Suicide*. "*Agimus Deo gratias, quod nemo in vita teneri potest,*" he quotes from Seneca.* And he died, with great fortitude and exemplary good humour, at the age of sixty-five, firmly disbelieving in individual immortality. With Hume the ghostly cloud of Predestination to Damnation that had overshadowed and haunted Cowper and the great soul of Johnson, and was even to fascinate Byron, began to lift over Northern Europe. David Hume, illumined by the dry daylight of his philosophy, had seen through all that.

It is intelligible that the attitude of this radical sceptic should have been intolerable, a maddening irritant, to a noble fanatic, a dogmatic atheist, of the cast of Lenin. Hume becomes posthumously of prime importance in political philosophy as a leader of that empiric, anti-dogmatic school which Lenin (necessarily, from his own point of view) selected for attack in his *Materialism and Empirio-Criticism*. To this issue we shall revert later.† Humane scepticism and dogmatic materialism cannot dwell together—or Hume's empiricism and the Hegelian theory of causes basic to the philosophy of Marx.

* "We give thanks to God that no one can be held in life (against his will)."

† *Cf.* p. 618.

Hume's philosophy, however, is something very other than the complacent rationalism of the Augustan Age of eighteenth-century letters. That type of intellectualism (although dominant, for example, in Godwin) commits suicide when tempted into rigorous logic by Hume and Kant. It is not the case that Hume is a sceptic *either* of reason as an instrument of inquiry *or* of the existence of causal laws. But, like Locke, he is a sceptic of the a priori way in which this instrument had been used, of the current interpretation of causation and of vasty intellectual constructions. He is the great empiric. Further, the stress with Hume is upon habit, interest and, oddly enough, emotion. Hume bridges the gulf in anthropology between Montesquieu and Buckle and, like most men with a respect for sociological fact, acquires a reputation for conservatism. "Obedience," he writes, "is a new duty which must be invented to support that of justice"—itself the basis of peace and order. To inculcate this obedience, to maintain a tolerably impartial order, is to the interest of rulers. "Habit soon consolidates what other principles of human nature had imperfectly founded." Actually Hume lays a very adequate stress on liberty; but he does not scruple to recognize its sociological inseparability from licentiousness and crime.

Hume perceives the tempting, if illusory, connection, which reappears from Pascal to Newman, between scepticism and respect for authority. He quotes, as Godwin might have quoted, with approval the apothegm on non-intervention of a certain Pope: "Let us divert ourselves, my friends; the world governs itself." In the eyes of a political scientist that maxim is precisely an entire half of the whole truth. However, Hume's Scottish sanity rescues his Scottish metaphysics and substitutes *the utility of interest*—not without a backward look upon the aesthetic judgement of values—for the refined scepticism of Catholic Modernism. Hobbes, throughout the eighteenth century, is a scarecrow for boys to beat the dust out of; but the robust cynicism of the old man reappears in Hume's phrases.

> Political writers have established it as a maxim, that, in contriving any system of government, and fixing the several checks and controls of the constitution, every man ought to be supposed a *knave*, and to have no other end, in all his actions, than private interest.

It is useful, because stable, so to base government as to allow for this principle. Hume (even in this last passage) is a Utilitarian in his positive philosophy, although he asks, as Bentham never would, "Why Utility pleases?"*

* *Cf.* pp. 369, 383.

Lastly, the imperturbable Hume is the philosopher of passion, so unlike in all else yet, in this, in touch with Rousseau, the philosopher of sentimentality. "Reason is and ought only to be the slave of the passions, and can never pretend to any other office than to serve and obey them." By this incendiary paradox Hume merely states the truth that the imagination of our desires determines our ends and that the speculative reason is limited to calculating means. Indeed, in his treatment of reason, that is, in the nominalism of his theory of general ideas, the basis of his limitation of rationalism, it may be asserted that Hume is, not only misusing good words, but merely wrong and in error. He is nearer the mark in his doctrine of the passions which are, for Hume, feelings capable of being placed in orderly and systematic perspective, in terms of ultimate values aesthetically appreciated in a fashion reminiscent of Shaftesbury. This direct unarguable judgement on morals supplies for Hume that datum from which reason must syllogize which Revelation provides for the Catholic Schoolman. Hume is no Rousseauite. He is a consistent enemy of "enthusiasm." He is the forerunner of the Utilitarians but, in terms of his theory of "ultimates," far wiser than any of Bentham's school.

It is said, Hume writes, that

> All morality is founded on the pain and pleasure which arises from the prospect of any loss or advantage that may result from our own characters or those of others. . . . [However], it is only when a character is considered in general, without reference to our particular interest, that it demonstrates such a feeling or sentiment as denominates it morally good or evil. It is true, these sentiments from interests or morals are apt to be confounded, and naturally run into one another. But this hinders not but that the sentiments are in themselves distinct, and a man of temper and judgement may preserve himself from these illusions. . . .
>
> To be endowed with a benevolent disposition and to love others, will almost infallibly procure love and esteem, which is the chief circumstance in life, and facilitates every enterprise and undertaking, besides the satisfaction which immediately results from it.

One further comment. Scepticism is frequently regarded as the peculiar manifestation of the detached philosophic temperament. Metaphysics and epistemology—how we know that we know what we know—are for Hume, as for Hobbes, only of interest as preparatory to the study of morals and politics, "the architectonic science." Like Plato, like Aristotle, Hume refuses to be a little blown-up schoolmaster, separating theory from practice. With this prince of philosophy there is no ivory tower, no academic chair, no contempt for the vulgarity of politics in contrast to pure thought. Hume in effect depreciates reason and the exact science of mathematics—his commentator, Mr. Lindsay, thinks Hume depreciates mistakenly—while crying up the social sciences. Like Machiavelli, Hobbes and Spinoza, Hume believes, as the title of one of his essays shows, "that politics may be reduced to a science." To this subject also we shall revert.* Enough to mention here that, like all the great writers on this subject, Hume seeks to found this science upon a constructive study of a "human nature" presumed psychologically observable and stable.

4

Jeremy Bentham (1748–1832), son of a lawyer, great-grandson of a pawnbroker, was the recognized founder of the Utilitarian School or (as it was, in its early days, somewhat misleadingly called) the school of Philosophical Radicals.

In manner and style of life Bentham, whether living like a recluse in Queen's Square, Westminster, or perambulating his garden at Ford Abbey, Somerset, face like Benjamin Franklin, straw hat on head, amid his cats, was certainly no stage radical. His most dangerous recreations were games of battledore and shuttlecock. At intervals of twenty years he indicated an inclination to propose to a lady who as regularly rejected him. Nevertheless he was, as he said, in a state of "perpetual and unruffled gaiety."

It is true that he showed—as did several of the Utilitarians—signs of being an infant prodigy. He wrote Latin at the tender age of five and three-quarters; and entered Queen's College, Oxford, at twelve, in which place of learning he profited no more than did Hobbes and Gibbon. His early literary exercises seem to have had no effect upon his tendency to write in a style progressively heavier as the years went by—a tendency shaped by his quest of accuracy. Unlike writers on politics today, he had the scientific courage to prefer the cultivation of precision even to *belles-lettres*, journalism and the distillation of literary aphrodisiacs. It was an insolence for Hazlitt, a man of microscopic intellectual proportions compared with Bentham, to adjudge that Bentham's works, translated into French, ought first to be translated into (Hazlitt's) English. There was, however (as we shall see later), perhaps point in Hazlitt's declaration that to the devil was left all the best tunes—"all the taste, sentiment and fancy of the thing to Mr. Burke's *Reflections on the French Revolution*."

Bentham spent his last years in placid and almost monastic calm, presiding over his teapot, called "Dick," or prescribing laws for

* *Cf.* p. 759.

JEREMY BENTHAM
(1748–1832)

(*Facing p. 356*)

Hindustan "as readily as for his own parish." Major Parry told Byron, the poet, a story—a source of great merriment in Byron's rakish circles—of how he, Parry, visited the philosopher for breakfast (at 3 P.M.) in order to satisfy his interest on the subject of war supplies for the Greek War of Independence. Before breakfast, the morning walk.

> Very much to my surprise, we had scarcely got into the Park, when he let go my arm, and set off trotting like a Highland messenger. The Park was crowded, and the people one and all seemed to stare at the old man; but, heedless of all this, he trotted on, his white locks floating in the wind, as if he were not seen by a single human being. As soon as I could recover from my surprise, I asked the young man, "Is Mr. Bentham flighty?" pointing to my head. "Oh no, it's his way," was the hurried answer; "he thinks it good for his health. But I must run after him;" and off set the youth in chase of the philosopher.
>
> Fortunately the chase did not continue long. Mr. Bentham hove to abreast of Carlisle's shop, and stood for a little time to admire the books and portraits hanging in the window. At length one of these arrested his attention more particularly. "Ah, ah," said he in a hurried indistinct tone, "there it is, there it is!" pointing to a portrait which I afterwards found was that of the illustrious Jeremy himself.

Normally, however, Bentham did not encourage promiscuous visitors and had little esteem for literary celebrities. Madame de Staël he declined to see and dismissed her as "a trumpery magpie."

Bentham gathered round him a band of disciples, the honest Swiss pastor, Dumont, abused as "a lazy fellow," the dour James Mill, Sir Samuel Romilly, the law reformer, John Austin, the jurisprudent, Bowring, even Brougham—even Sydney Smith. He offered his advice, through the Abbé Morellet, to Revolutionary France (in his sober *Political Tactics);* and, in 1792, was acclaimed by her National Assembly as a "citizen." He offered it to the United States, in the person of President Madison; and actually influenced, through Edward Livingston, the legal system of Louisiana. He offered it to the Spaniards; and George Borrow later found Spaniards treasuring the works of "the great Baintham" and comparing him to Plato and even to Lope de Vega. In 1822, he was asked by the Portuguese Cortes to give advice to Portugal. Among his works *Leading Principles of a Constitutional Code for Any State* jostles *On the Liberty of the Press, to the Spanish People, by Jeremy Bentham.*

He spent his time, in his own phrase "codefying like a dragon"—as his diplomatic visitor, Talleyrand, said: "pillé de tout le monde . . .

toujours riche." He died, at the ripe age of eighty-four, upon the breast of his faithful friend and editor, Bowring, having written nine large volumes and left behind him 148 boxes of manuscript, including (1830–1831) "a history of the war between Jeremy Bentham and George III." (The order is typical.) His mummified body, stuffing the clothing in which he walked and talked, can still be seen, a tutelary figure, in the library of University College, London.

Bentham, the *practical reformer*, had his share in effecting the mitigation of the Criminal Laws—his theory of punishment was singularly similar to that of Hobbes—and the abolition of Colonial Transportation; the repeal of the Usury Laws and of the Catholic Disability Acts; the systematization of the Poor Laws; and the Reform of the Parliamentary Representative system. He was the prophet of Free Trade, Women's Suffrage, the Secret Ballot, Sanitary Regulations, National Education and of International Peace through organization, including a World Court. Above all, he was an advocate of Publicity in all affairs called public. It is an impressive list.

Like many elderly men of placid lives, his tongue did not lack edge. It is reasonable to suppose that his formidable early education had produced in him the misproportions and the sensitiveness of the ungainly intellectual. In his early days he was content to criticize, for example, Blackstone whom, as a student of fifteen, he heard lecture at Oxford, immediately detecting Blackstone's "fallacy respecting natural rights." The patronage, however, later, of noble lords, such as "Malagrida" Shelbourne, Marquess of Lansdowne, both exalted and humiliated him—the first, because they listened to his theories; and the second, because they did not act on his suggestions. Bentham must be listed among the inferior-feeling people, although his is not a virulent case. The younger Pitt, we are told, was as frightened of him as he was frightened by the presence of the younger Pitt. Two incidents, however, revealed to him the array of what he called "the Sinister Interests," and made of Bentham a radical.

"I was," he writes, "a great reformist, but never suspected the 'people in power' were against reform. I supposed they only wanted to know what was good in order to be able to embrace it." The first shock came from a chance remark of Wedderburn, Lord Loughborough, and later Lord Chancellor. Wedderburn, consulted on Bentham's pet theory of "utility," had declared it "dangerous." How, argued Bentham, could *utility* be dangerous?—"The greatest happiness of the greatest number"—How? There could be only one reply: a Sinister Interest. . . .

Further, Bentham confronted, from official dilatoriness, continual disappointments in his scheme for prison reform, his "Panopticon" scheme. Under this scheme the convicts were to busy themselves in a building—"a mill to grind knaves honest"—where they could be employed in useful work under the all-seeing, panoptic eye of an overseer, which useful work could be sold, the whole concern being farmed out, without expense to the state, to an undertaker, *e.g.*, Mr. Bentham. The official commission, at long last, preferred to build Millbank Penitentiary on more orthodox lines. Moreover, Lord Shelbourne, with more wit than tact, suggested that the author of certain articles directed against this scheme was no other than George III. As a consequence that solid monarch became the object of Bentham's especial wariness and "the monarchy and its creatures" were detected as peculiar sources of corruption. The chief ramparts of injustice, however, were "the Church" and "the Law."

"The Church," Jeremy Bentham pointed out, did but mean "the churchmen." What then did the churchmen, and Church-of-Englandism, stand for? The Anglican churchmen were those who had perjured themselves by swearing to the Thirty-nine Articles—thirty-nine chains to bind intelligence and to hoist up insincerity. These were members of an immoral organization for promoting insincerity. Only those who kissed their chains could expect preferment.

> To a man thus circumstanced [it is to the Bishops in the House of Lords that Jeremy Bentham is referring] to talk reason would have something ungenerous in it and indecorous: it would be as if a man should set about talking indecently to his daughter or his wife. In vain would they answer, what has been so often answered, that neither Jesus nor his Apostles ever meant what they said—that everything is to be explained and explained away.

Bentham continues with an allegory:

> In virtue and knowledge—in every feature of felicity, the empire of Montezuma outshines, as everybody knows, all the surrounding states, even the commonwealth of Tlascala not excepted.
>
> Where (said an enquirer once, to the high priest of the temple of Vitzlipultzli), where is it that we are to look for the true cause of so glorious a preeminence? "Look for it!" answered the holy pontiff—"where should thou look for it, blind sceptic, but in the copiousness of the streams in which the sweet and precious blood of innocents flows daily down the altars of the great god."
>
> "Yes," answered in full convocation and full chorus the archbishops, bishops, deans, canons, and prebends of the religion of Vitzlipultzli: "Yes," answered in semi-chorus the vice-chancellor, with all the doctors, both the

proctors and masters regent and non-regent of the as yet uncatholicized university of Mexico:—"Yes, in the copiousness of the streams in which the sweet and precious blood of innocents flows daily down the altars of the great god."

Bentham attacked "Church-of-Englandism" for its sinecure offices, its wealthy bishops and starved curates, above all for its obstruction of the work of men like the Quaker Lancaster for national education. It was, he asserted, not the cause of the enlightenment and progress of the country: it was the champion of a self-interested and hypocritical conventionality that strangled the country's young vitality. Old vampire bats in lawn sleeves. There is a "class of persons who habitually exalt the past for the express purpose of depressing and discouraging the present generation."

> I am a priest (says a fifth), who having proved the pope to be anti-christ to the satisfaction of all orthodox divines whose piety prays for the cure of souls, or whose health has need of exoneration from the burthen of residence, and having read, in my edition of the Gospel, that the apostles lived in palaces, which innovation and anarchy would cut down to parsonage houses; though grown hoarse by screaming out, "No reading!" "No writing!" "No Lancaster!" and "No popery!"—for fear of coming change, am here to add what remains of my voice to the full chorus of "No Anarchy!" "No Innovation!"

Evil although the eighteenth-century Church in England was, it is doubtful whether, even when it did little or nothing to support slavery emancipation or used Bible texts to support the enslavement of the negro sons of Ham, it was quite as reactionary as Bentham asserted. A Church is from its nature committed to support the recognized *mores* —whether intolerance of witches (on the basis of the Old Testament) in the sixteenth century or tolerance of slavery (on the basis of St. Paul) in the eighteenth century or opposition to divorce law reform today. Bentham found a more justifiable object of attack in the Lawyers.

The corruption of the Law, in eighteenth-century Britain, was greater than the corruption of the Church. A traditional and highly complicated procedure (much of which survives in the United States, especially Massachusetts) served to enrich the lawyers with fees, while the multitude of sinecure offices, for which the litigants had ultimately to pay, were consolation prizes for their friends. In the words of Sir Samuel Romilly: "The state of the court of Chancery is such, that it is the disgrace of a civilized society." In 1798 the Keeper of His Majesty's Hanaper-in-chancery, the Earl of Northington, received for this important function £1,811. In 1808, he received £2,070.

> Why [writes Bentham, in his pamphlet *Truth v. Ashhurst*] is it that, in a court called a court of equity, they keep a man the whole of his life in hot water, while they are stripping him of his fortune? . . . "We will deny justice"—says King John—"we will sell justice to no man." This was the wicked King John. How does the good King George? He denies it to ninety-nine men out of a hundred, and sells it to the hundredth. . . . Under English law, not to speak of other systems, the sort of commodity called *justice*, is not only sold, but, being like gunpowder and spirits made of different degrees of strength, is sold at different prices, suited to the pockets of so many different classes of customers.

Despite Bentham, in England to this day one still buys the bar. A successful counsel makes £40,000 a year, and £1,200 on a two-weeks case. In America it is often not the bar that one buys. Even in Soviet Russia, competing Trust lawyers make fees considerable, if not astronomical—but, be it added, without burden on the private litigant.

To the attack on pecuniary abuses Bentham added an attack on the abuses of legal fictions, which conspired to the same end of the delay and denial of justice.

> When an action is brought against a man, how do you think they contrive to give him notice to defend himself? Sometimes he is told that he is in jail; sometimes that he is lurking up and down the country, in company with a vagabond of the name of Doe; though all the while he is sitting quietly by his own fireside: and this my Lord Justice sets his hand to. At other times they write to a man who lives in Cumberland or Cornwall, and tell him that if he does not appear in Westminister Hall on a certain day he forfeits one hundred pounds. When he comes, so far from having anything to say to him, they won't hear him: for all they want him for, is to grease their fingers.

It must be recalled that, at the period when Bentham was writing (and talking, not entirely jocosely, about the possibilities of the hangman's knife in his bowels), in 1801, a boy of twelve was hanged for stealing a spoon; while in 1786 one Phoebe Harris was burned alive for coining. Between 1810 and 1830 the consumption of spirits doubled. The Church encouraged education "to check the growth of popery" but, as Hannah More observed, education should not go so far as to enable the common folk to read Tom Paine. In 1819 a certain Carlile was sent to prison for three years and fined £1,500 for printing Paine's works.

The work of the early Utilitarians was especially a practical work. The activities of Bentham, Romilly and their circle were memorable as a successful achievement in that reform of the law, and above all of the procedure of the courts, which was even more required in their day than prison reform is required today. They began the work, which still has to be completed, of making justice accessible to the purses of all. The very word "codification," as also "international law," was of Bentham's invention.

5

The Utilitarians, however, as their name implies, were not mere experimental tinkerers and political artisans. They had an architectural idea of society, and achieved coherent notions through a philosophy, as well as being grounded on study of fact. The word "Utilitarian," used by John Stuart Mill for the society he founded in 1822, had been used by Bentham in 1781 and was proposed by him, with typical lack of smart advertisers' sense, as a substitute for "Benthamite," as a name for the school.

Bentham's *philosophy of society* was individualistic and, on the economic side, *laissez-faire*. "*Laissons nous faire*," or "be quiet," were terms, and theory, which he had taken over from Adam Smith. Taxes, for example, should not be used to compel men to labour, when they preferred to enjoy; or to labour for others. This would be unjust and adverse to human initiative. There is, indeed, Bentham maintained, a constant social pressure against initiative. "Common-place men have a common interest, which they understand but too well [could Bentham logically allow that anyone understood his interest too well? or was it only—one recalls Socrates' argument—an 'enlightened interest' that a man could not understand too well], it is that all should be common-place like themselves."

Laissez-faire, however, was not an absolute principle. It had to be tested and retested in its applications, from generation to generation and place to place, by the sovereign touchstone of "utility." It might be appropriate in Britain; inappropriate in Russia. One could only say that, the more opulent the community, the more could be left to private and voluntary enterprise. Of economic institutions, such as capitalism, and political institutions, such as the "matchless British constitution," he asks one question only: "What is the use of them?"

For Burke, with his defence of the unreformed House of Commons, Bentham has an unmeasured contempt. He is "the Rhetorician." "Erasmus wrote an eulogium on folly: but Erasmus was in jest:

Edmund Burke wrote an eulogium—he wrote this eulogium on peculation—and Edmund Burke was serious." He was, when he spoke of the French Revolution, "a madman . . . an incendiary, who contributed so much more than any other to light up the flame of that war." Bentham's *Book of Fallacies* (1810–1824) is a painfully painstaking attempt to oppose the principle of Utility to the fallacious appeals to, *e.g.*, Authority—from which fallacy the United States Congress suffered less than most—to Antiquity—"the virtue of barbarian ancestors"—and to Procrastination—"the hydrophobia of innovation."

Bentham, as leader of the Philosophical Radicals (and especially after the Wedderburn incident) insisted that Authority was usually but a cloak for the above-mentioned "sinister interests." Law must be obeyed—but it must be tested for signs of the fraudulent machinations of interested persons.

> In this, as in every country, the government has been as favourable to the interests of the ruling few, and thence as unfavourable to the general interests of the subject many—or, in a word, as *bad*—as the subjects—many have endured to see it—have persuaded themselves to suffer it to be. No abuse has, except under a sense of necessity, been parted with—*no remedy, except under the like pressure, applied.*

Bentham, however, conceded that the government of the United States was a felicitous exception to the general rule that government is conducted for the privy interest of the one or of the few. Here government was "better in every respect than in England"—it was a "radical" system of government which, nevertheless, had not subverted the rights of property in any respect. In Britain, especially, the Crown was the "fount of honour"—honours and corruption. Not unnaturally, Bentham was the recipient of complimentary references from President Andrew Jackson.

Bentham's doctrine of "Sinister Interests" is worth examination, in view of its *superficial similarity* to the more recent doctrine of "class war." Three distinctions stand out. Bentham holds that each man—not only those of a privileged class—places his own interests first. These are "sinister" from the angle of those who have other interests. Secondly, it is the characteristic of men in power, of the "ins," that they will always use their opportunity to extend their interest—not that of their "class," but of their "group," as powerholders and officials; and especially of themselves in that group. The story of the fight between Stalin and Trotsky provides an interesting commentary. Thirdly, this intent is only sinister from one angle. From another, it is for the *benefit* of humanity that each man should look after, and develop, his own interests. "Generally speaking, there is no one who knows what is for your interest, so well as yourself." The opposite thesis—always putting B's interest—which is little known—before A's, instead of A's—which is known—before B's, Bentham dismisses as "ridiculous in idea . . . disastrous and destructive in reality."

The pressure of interests is, then, historically speaking, beneficial, the spring of progress, and a "classless" (or, at least, group-interest-less or profession-interest-less) society hurtful. If Marx's psychology suffers from the fault of laying improper stress upon inevitable mutual aggressiveness and conflict, Bentham's has the same fault. But Bentham, unlike Marx, does not operate with the concept of a class; does not magnify the conflict into "inevitable" war; nor, as a political scientist, anticipate its ultimate utopian rolling away at a revolutionary "last judgement," ushering in society without group conflict. On the contrary, he lays bare what he believes to be characteristics, not of capitalism or socialism, but of human nature as such. And he finds the correction in the *power to press*, the right to discuss, choose and oppose. Here he provided the classic definition of democracy according to the Anglo-Saxon tradition—a definition never of more vital significance than today, amid totalitarian popular tyrannies, all claiming to be democratic:

> The characteristic, then, of an undespotic government—in a word, of every government that has any tenable claim to the appellation of a good government—is the allowing, and giving facility to, the communication [of opinion]; and this not only for instruction but for excitation—not only for instruction and excitation but also for correspondence; and this, again, for the purpose of affording and keeping on foot every facility for eventual resistance—for resistance to government, and thence, should necessity require, for change of government.*

* Recently several writers such as, for example, Leonard Barnes, and V. Gollancz have endeavored to stress Marx-Stalinism as "the *crowning* of individualism" and attacked the classification of it as totalitarian, as "muddle-headed stupidity" or worse. "Intellectual independence," indeed (not to speak of organized opposition) "*has* to be curbed, as a transitional method." It will, however, be noted that, if we depart from objective definitions about methods, to subjective definitions and claims about ideals ends, even Mussolini claims (*cf.* p. 721) that his regime is a democracy. If the test is to be neither form nor end but material achievement for the common man, then all these regimes have far to go before they are in a position to instruct the Western democracies. Certainly Russia's pathetic wage level warrants no position as instructress;

There is another side to Bentham's social philosophy besides that which reveals itself in the radicalism of the *Book of Fallacies* or in his wanderings around the social institutions of his time, rapping them with his stick and asking "What Use?" This other side appears clearly in the *Anarchical Fallacies* (1791) and the earlier and better known *Fragment on Government* (1776). The former is a meticulous analysis of the French Declaration of the Rights of Man; the latter a confutation of certain remarks of Sir William Blackstone, in his *Commentaries.* The American Declaration of Independence was "jargon"—a hodge-podge of confusion and well-intentioned nonsense. The French Declaration of Rights was much worse—full of "bawling on paper."

It is here that he criticizes decisively the doctrines of Original Contract and of Natural Rights, following Hume and Godwin. There was more to be said for Hobbes than was generally supposed; but as for Rousseau, "Let us leave geegaws to children. . . . I bid adieu to the original contract"—governments come not from contracts, but contracts from governments. "When society is once formed, government results of course, as necessary to preserve and keep that society in order" (*Fragment on Government*).* As to natural rights, "natural rights is simple nonsense: natural and imprescriptible rights, rhetorical nonsense—nonsense upon stilts."

With these hoary companions, then, of political theory of the schools through the ages, we now part company. In so far as they continue to live it is as revivified by Kant, but they never recover their old vitality from this time on. To the radical question: "On what does the right of Government to 'order' us rest save on consent?" Bentham answers, "Utility." The distinction is significant (although it is questionable whether Bentham fully recognized the implications of his own argument) when we have to consider minority rights and have to answer the question "Minority and majority of whom?"

As to those who arrogate to themselves a natural right to resist laws, because their conscience holds those laws to be unjust, of those

---

nor do the German and Russian popular beliefs that now it is *their* State-machine, their very own peculiar Moloch. In Russia, however, a measure of cooperative activity, not limited to members of the one Party (or "true Church"), upon local public committees, factory committees, etc., exists, and has been remarked by the Webbs, which is not equally conspicuous in Germany and which fits in with both the democratic and the Aristotelian concept of good government. It is perhaps a little similar to what Lenin called "democratic committeeism" (*cf.* pp. 634, 636). "Polity" is *not* majority rule (*cf.* p. 89).

* *Cf.* p. 237.

anarchists says Bentham (in his *Introduction to the Principles of Morals and Legislation*, 1789):

> The fairest and openest of them all is that sort of man who speaks out and says, I am of the number of the Elect: now God himself takes care to inform the Elect what is right; and that with such good effect, and let them strive ever so, they cannot help not only knowing it, but practising it. If, therefore, a man wants to know what is right and what is wrong, he has nothing to do but to come to me.

When we survey the thought of the early Utilitarians, three things stand out. To begin with, Bentham is not so much a political philosopher as a *political scientist*, in the succession of Hobbes, through d'Holbach and Helvetius. He and Godwin are among the first to use, in any precise sense, the actual name "*Political Science*." [Works, ed. Bowring, II, p. 400, ca. 1810; Godwin: *Political Justice*, Vol. I, p. 274, ca. 1793.]* His object, like that of Macchiavelli and Spinoza is to expound what he calls "a logic of the will." His treatment of social struggle is typical. This struggle is not a temporary misfortune, produced by evil intriguers, priests and capitalists and kings, to be messianically removed amidst the hosannas of the toiling masses. This struggle is a *permanent characteristic* of human nature, which the political scientist takes into account as a *datum*, a tendency always present.

Bentham (like his countryman of four centuries earlier, Occam) is, in scholastic terms, a nominalist. That is, where the Irishman, Edmund Burke, finding a collection of peers and landowners, soldiers and tallow chandlers, bakers and navvies, acclaims it as a mystic entity with a matchless constitution, and where Marx, the German Jew, found chosen classes, the Englishman, Jeremy Bentham, being confronted with words about Law, Church, Government, asks to what these practically amount, and discovers, hidden under these façades, tricky lawyers, fallible churchmen, ambitious "members of the governmental body."

Bentham's horror of abstract ideas let loose shows in his remarks on liberty and equality.

> Absolute equality is absolutely impossible. Absolute liberty is directly repugnant to the existence of every kind of government. . . . All men are born free? All men remain free? No, not a single man. . . . All men, to the contrary, are born in subjection.

* But *cf.* pp. 206, 227.

As much as Bacon or Locke, Bentham is an experimentalist. Like Hobbes, he is a student of the mechanics of society. The theory of social pressures is characteristic of this objective, positivist and pragmatic approach, which has been adopted again by contemporary politicists, especially of the Chicago School.* The political theory of the early Benthamites is pertinaciously objective.

The second note of the Benthamites is, of course, their stress on *Utility*. The stress is not new: it will be found (as has been said) in Samuel Johnson and in Hume. Bentham, a more honest character than Hobbes, uses his methods without reaching Hobbes's conclusions or sharing his prejudices. Despite his vehement suspicion of abstractions about equality and liberty, no man had a keener eye than Bentham for the menace of useless privilege or did more for practical reform and for the demolition of traditional restrictions on the legitimate conduct of individuals. This reform—as swift as but no swifter than the circumstances would allow—was to be undertaken in the name of utility. It was in the name of utility that the philosopher—or *philosophe*—rapped on the portals of august doors and asked what good their owners were to the world and who would be the worse if they were buried along with Kheops and Kephren.

What, however, precisely was meant by Utility? Let us admit, with Bentham, that no honest and disinterested man would oppose the "arguments of authority, antiquity and delay" to a genuine and convincing case based on social utility. We are yet entitled to ask: Useful for what? It is at this point that we pass beyond Benthamism as practical (and especially legal) reform, and beyond Benthamism as a social philosophy, to Benthamism as an *ethical philosophy* with its own psychology.

The third note of the Benthamites was that *Hedonism*, which Bentham derived from the *De l'Esprit* of Helvetius which he studied so avidly in his youth—and indirectly from Hobbes. It is unprofitable to discuss here Bentham's *Table of the Springs of Action* or his Hedonistic Calculus, with its cataloguing of pleasures by degrees of intensity, duration, certainty, propinquity, fecundity and purity (*i.e.*, unmixed quality: a mineralogical, rather than a sex-moralistic term). The psychology was neither sounder nor subtler than that of Hobbes. "Quantity of pleasure being equal," Bentham maintained, "pushpin is as good as poetry." This at a time when the House of Hanover expressed its preference of "bainting" to "boetry," and held (not unjustly in Mr. A. E. Housman's opinion) that Shakespeare was "terrible stuff." Pleasures were enjoyed in "lots"; and the greatest

* *Cf.* p. 753.

total of "lots" (intensity and other measurable factors allowed for) was the greatest pleasure. Of pleasure and pain men had direct experience; the rest was derivative. Happiness was pleasure of high duration. Unselfishness was the pleasure of benevolence; altruism usually the pleasure of good expectation. Asceticism and discipline were often the pleasures of cruelty or malignity, or the pleasure of knowing myself to be better than the Joneses. Men's actions, strictly speaking, were never disinterested—never could be, or they would lack motive. I will that which I wish, and wish that which I shall enjoy to have. As Professor John Dewey says: "Happiness was for them a matter . . . of industry guided by mathematical book-keeping." Not unnaturally Hazlitt, in his *Essays* commented that the Utilitarians "proceed by rule and compasses, by logical diagrams, and with none but demonstrable inclusions, and leave all the taste, sentiment, and fancy of the thing to Mr. Burke's *Reflections on the French Revolution*."

The "useful," then, in institutions and conduct, is that which makes for happiness. Whose happiness? Bentham has his answer ready, derived with acknowledgement from Priestley and anticipated by Hutcheson. The way had also been prepared by Hume, the third volume of whose *Treatise on Human Nature* had, in Bentham's words, caused "the scales to fall from my eyes." The answer is "*The greatest happiness of the greatest number*." Why not just the greatest happiness—of society? Because there must be distribution. Each had his claim on the general happiness; and "*each to count for one* and nobody for more than one." But why so? There is, in this phrase, something reminiscent of the much derided doctrine of Natural Rights. And yet Bentham had written: "I bid adieu to the original contract: and I left it to those to amuse themselves with this rattle, who could think they had need of it."

The answer is that, in the last analysis, Bentham is taking the other horn of the dilemma. He is not concerned about the happiness of some "real entity" called society. He is concerned with the claim—and observes in mankind the will to push the claim—of each individual. He is a democrat *because* he is an individualist—just as were Jefferson and the members of Natural Rights School before him. The legislator must allow for all individuals, without respect of persons. Hence "of the greatest number." If, however, we ask Bentham why *should* A subordinate his pleasure to that of B, C and D, he has no effective answer. He can only appeal, with Bishop Butler, to benevolence, or love of reputation, or say that A *will*, in fact, be punished if he does not subordinate his interest.

In the last analysis, Bentham does not genuinely believe that "each is to count for one" (and, hence, is indeed consistent in his opposition to Natural Rights in the abstract, equalitarian sense). He may—and does—cut out the words "of the greatest number"—not, however, in the interests of society, but of minorities. There is, in fact, *no* reason, no rational argument, why A should totally subordinate himself to B. No "tyranny of the majority." That subordination will often not lead to the greatest total of human happiness: better a share to each. Accommodation. Granted accommodation, however, it would still seem to follow that there is a natural "right" (not equalitarian)—or natural power—appertaining only to the stronger and abler. A beneficial power. It is the old Thrasymachean argument. Laissez-faire: society—in the long run—will be benefited if the strong man—or able man—uses his full power . . . accommodatingly and rationally. It is at this point that Bentham's philosophy tends to become bankrupt, since the meaning of "rational" is not developed. We are back where Plato began.

The legislator, certainly, must seek the greatest happiness of the greatest number. That is an affair of balancing and of social mechanics —one pressure against another. But the individual—*does* press, prudentially *should* press. Bentham does, and logically can, believe nothing else. Will then the greatest number find its greatest happiness in accommodation to the minorities' obstinacy, pertinacity and strength? We do not, it seems, subordinate ourselves to the happiness of the greatest number—that is not the pursuit of happiness. "Nature has placed mankind under the governance of two sovereign masters, pleasure and pain. It is for them to point out what we ought to do, as well as to determine what we shall do." If we can, we defy penalties and make the greatest number find their happiness in equilibrium with ours. These are awkward conclusions. They are the Neo-Darwinian conclusions that shocked J. S. Mill.

To the question, however, What is Utility? a precise answer can be given. Utility is *my* pleasure, duration, intensity and the like all duly, and enlightened-wise, considered.

Are there then no "higher" happinesses—pleasure of quality not distinguishable solely by duration, unmixedness and so forth; social pleasures—which *should* be pursued first? Are happinesses, or (as Carlyle said) "blessednesses," to be found chiefly in seeking "the good of society?" Hobbes and Helvetius said "no." That was the philosophic problem which was to haunt the later Utilitarians—but not until much of the practical benefits of "utilitarian" reform, advocated by Bentham, had already been garnered in. If their metaphysics were unsound—their resolute nominalism—the practical work of the early Utilitarians is definitely to be placed on the credit side, when the balance sheet of civilization is drawn up by laborious historians.

An understanding of the Utilitarians as social and moral philosophers involves also some understanding of the economic thinkers who formed their mental entourage and were often—as in the cases of Ricardo, McCulloch and Malthus—attached to what critics called their "sect." Conversely the effect of the Utilitarian leaders upon these so-called Classical Economists was profound, by providing them with a philosophic background and cohesion to their own ideas.

6

The Physiocrats, of France, were the spiritual parents of the British school of economists. Quesnay, the elder Mirabeau, Turgot, Mercier de la Rivière, Dupont de Nemours, were Free Traders, like Adam Smith, but with this difference that, in days of (as Voltaire said) a different system of law every time one changed one's stage-coach in France and with a local *douane* to every sizable town, they insisted upon free trade *inside* the Kingdom. They further demanded release both from feudal interference with commerce and from the antique and now obstructive regulations of the Guilds described by de Tocqueville, in his *Ancien Régime*. To effect these changes they looked frankly to the royal power and respected a benevolent despot as much as did Voltaire. "Give me a good government," declared Turgot (1727–1781) in the spirit of Hume, "and I will make good men." Reacting against the mercantilism of Colbert, they nevertheless proposed to use, in the cause of enlightenment, the methods of Colbert. Royalists, in the over-centralized France of the eighteenth century, it was yet Gournay, among them (the object of Turgot's *Eulogy*, 1760) who framed the famous watchword: *laissez faire, laissez passer*.

The Physiocrats were practical men, concerned especially with taxation and fiscal reform. They were single-taxers and the first article of their faith, which gave the name in agricultural France to their "nature rule" school, was that all wealth (and power) came from the land—a theory anticipated definitely enough by Locke and hinted at by Harrington. There was, as Mercier de la Rivière asserted in the title of his book, an *Ordre Naturel et Essentiel des Sociétés Politiques* (1767). The mood was not so remote from Rousseau and his "back-to-Nature" call. The very term which they used for their new "science," Political Economy (etymologically, Community Household Management), was significant. Very literally their concern was the farm management of the state. Their enemy was the spendthrift absentee landlord. But Quesnay, in *Le Droit Naturel* (1765), while developing a theory of exchange, was far from an adequate theory of value. Labour which did not assist Nature in producing for man the raw material, or did not, by its admixture, obviously modify its nature for consumption, was dismissed as "sterile." Agriculturists therefore, the natural lords of creation, hold an especially prominent value, with their increase of fruits four—or ten—or an hundred-fold. To agriculture and the farmer the Physiocrats gave—as did the farmers' friend, Arthur Young—an almost mystic prominence. It is a theory of which we shall hear more—with its over-simple disregard of "invisible" increments in value.

The "laissez-faire" principles, entertained by the Physiocrats in the economic field, more hesitatingly they applied in the political. As much as Godwin* they asserted that the basis of political wisdom was Justice. Now justice consists in respect for the rights of others: their personal rights—liberty—and their material or real rights—property. For this doctrine, suspicious of interference, they provided an important basis, by a revival and restatement, of quite cardinal importance, of the theory of Natural Law.

Natural Law appears reclad as Economic Law, but still guided on its way, as of yore, by the finger of Providence. Men do not *make* basic laws. They *find* them. Laws contrary to these natural laws—"*lois essentielles de l'ordre social*"—are void. As Dupont de Nemours says, in his *Origine et Progrès d'une Science Nouvelle*,

> Il y a donc un juge naturel et irrécusable des ordonnances mêmes des souverains et ce juge est l'évidence de leur conformité ou de leur opposition aux lois naturelles de l'ordre social.†

Public education was desirable—and religious tolerance—as giving men the freedom and ability to detect these eternal laws that described the frame of things.

7

Adam Smith (1723–1790) is the founder of Political Economy in Britain, although anticipated in researches by such students of social statistics as Sir William Petty. The cosmopolitanism of approach and

* *Cf.* p. 337.

† "There is a natural and final judge of the ordinances even of sovereigns, to wit the evidence of their conformity or opposition to the natural laws of the social order."

the individualism which he shares, for example, with Benjamin Franklin, make Economics a more appropriate title for his new science. A Britain which was already in the current of the Industrial Revolution and beginning, with the aid of sea power, to trade abroad, unlike France, was prepared to look with favour on Free Trade as a principle, not merely of local, but of international application. The pre-Adamite darkness ends, and Smith converted Pitt to the light. Moreover the objection to regulation of the Laissez-faire School—*pas trop gouverner*—wears, with Smith, the typically Anglo-Saxon suspicion of executive government as such.

With Adam Smith, Professor of Moral Science in the University of Glasgow, a quiet man of books little given to disputation or witty conversation, we are still in the mental climate of Bishop Butler. In his *Theory of Moral Sentiments* (1759), in the section entitled, "Of the Sense of Propriety," turning back from the chapter, "Of the Amiable and Respectable Virtues" and that headed, "Of the Pleasure of Mutual Sympathy," we find one that begins:

> How selfish soever man may be supposed, there are evidently some principles in his nature, which interest him in the fortune of others, and render their happiness necessary to him, though he derives nothing from it, except the pleasure of seeing it. . . . The greatest ruffian, the most hardened violator of the laws of society, is not altogether without it.

But a little chance, and Dr. Adam Smith would only have been known for this, at the time, much praised and, in general estimation, acute work, enlarging upon the themes of Locke, Hutcheson and Hume. However, the sociological influence of Hume ("by far the most illustrious philosophic historian of the present age"), in his *Essays*, and the fortunate circumstance that the young Duke of Buccleuch was wealthy enough and (encouraged by Hume) desirous enough of a tutor to induce Smith to resign his professorship and go on that great tour where he met Quesnay and Turgot, ensured (after ten years' cogitation in solitude with his old mother) the publication of *The Wealth of Nations* (1776). On this Hume wrote: "*Euge! Belle!* Dear Mr. Smith: I am much pleased with your performance. . . . It has depth and solidity and acuteness, and is so much illustrated by curious facts, that it must at least take the public attention."

Although popularly described as the founder of Economic Science, Adam Smith in fact rather took over the work of the Physiocrats, especially Turgot's *Reflections on the Formation and Distribution of Wealth;* added many illustrative, curious facts; and substituted for the all-too-brilliant logic of a tour de force a treatise where truth wrapped herself in the clouds of conditional clauses and circumambient detail. Not seldom, the wood is quite obscured by the trees. However, the result was truth, not fallacy; a more developed theory of value, which allowed for both intrinsic value and value in exchange; and an economics, still systematic, and adequately historic, based upon the analysis of the division of labour. There was, then, a natural law which expressed itself also in economic law; and a divine tactic which the reverent optimist could see in the consequences necessarily developing from this useful division and from "the natural effort of every individual to better his own condition." For Buckle, the historian of civilization, *The Wealth of Nations* was, briefly, "probably the most important book which has ever been written." Here, however, also we learn from Dr. Smith that the object of religious toleration is the production "of philosophical good temper and moderation with respect to every religious creed." For the rest, "the difference of natural talent in different men is, in reality, much less than we are aware of* . . . the effect of the division of labour . . . [and] the vanity of the philosophers."

When we come to the epigoni, abstract theory again takes the reins. There is, moreover, a remarriage between economics and philosophy, as there had been between the Physiocrat group and the Encyclopaedists. Utilitarianism provided a considered connection between the natural effort for self-betterment and benevolence. On the other hand, the economists kept the Utilitarians in touch with a natural right to increase property, and "every man to count for one" in laying claim to the produce of labour; and with a natural law—speedily becoming an evil, thin abstraction replacing observation—which, as touching the social order, could be formulated by the economists.

David Ricardo (1772–1823) was the son of a Dutch Jew who had settled in England. Having made a large fortune and bought an estate —whether or not, as Cobbett suggested of others, concerned to trace his descent from the Normans—he turned a brilliant intelligence to economic theory and political practice, and entered parliament. His friend James Mill, chief Apostle of the Utilitarians, persuaded him to publish, in 1817, his *Principles of Political Economy and Taxation.* Logic with Ricardo—as is the habit of logic—and a certain complacent

* *Cf.* Confucius' dictum: "By nature we nearly resemble one another; condition separates us very far."

love of paradox, brought out in his economic theory several somewhat unexpected conclusions.

Locke, a century and more before, had declared labour to be the source of wealth; and had stated that every man had a possessory right to that in which he had (solely?) admixed his labour. We have here the germs of the theory, alluded to by Godwin, of the right to "the whole product of labour." Adam Smith had gone farther, in his *Wealth of Nations:*

> Civil government, so far as it is instituted for the security of property, is in reality instituted for the defence of the rich against the poor, or of those who have some property against those who have none.

It is the converse statement to that of Rousseau that whoever appropriated to himself a plot of land, called it "mine" and found others fool enough to believe him, instituted private property. We shall revert to this theme in the controversy between James Mill and Macaulay, save that Macaulay will try to bind up the rich, who "have a stake in the country," with the cause of civilization.

Ricardo, however, enlarging on the Physiocrats, and turning bottom-up their argument, puts landlord's interest and that of the community in the most violent opposition. Writing with the absentee rich landlord and the mining royalty owner in his environment, if not before his mind's eye, Ricardo says: "the interest of the landlord is necessarily opposed to the interest of every other class in the community." The Classical Economy made paradox worse confounded when Ricardo subsequently added that this opposition, although necessary, was not permanent. Sir Leslie Stephen aptly comments that Ricardo's opponents could affirm that such a system as he described, if as he described it, was the embodiment of injustice and ought to be radically destroyed. Ricardo, in his paradox to arrest attention, outlined the case for class war. It is one of the issues which John Stuart Mill will be forced to confront, and upon which Marx built his theory and makes his observations. Actually, the Classical Economists can be fairly represented neither as oppressors of the poor nor (despite the gruffness of the Utilitarians) as conscious pioneers of revolution; but only as men trying to state the contemporary truth in systematic form and hesitating, no more than Hobbes, before a mordant definition.

It is necessary to point out that the Classical Economists assuredly did not belong to the school of Miss Hannah More, who wrote tracts to show that the poor should bear their inevitable afflictions patiently and, indeed, that they should be grateful since, properly considered, they really had none. Although Archbishop Whately is not free, in his economic popular writings, from advocating kissing the rod that strikes one, under the name of Economic Law willed by Providence, the economist Archbishop, nevertheless, is of the genuine and reasonable belief that a knowledge of these laws will encourage prudence, thrift and forethought.

Ricardo, it must be recalled, is making a debating point against Malthus and, in fact, is opposing the interest of the *agriculturalist* as against that of the free-trading *manufacturer*, as well as expounding the monopoly theory of rent, which is his distinctive contribution to Economics.

Actually Ricardo stated, in his correspondence with Malthus, in rebuttal of Say and in entire accord with the Utilitarian theory, that he regarded the low income groups, the majority, as "of far the most important class in society." He proposed that their status could and should be raised by good education—and by matrimonial prudence as a technique of population education. This may be counted among what J. S. Mill calls, "the superior lights of Ricardo." This did not prevent him from stating—at a time when (following excursions by Chadwick and others) attention was beginning to be given to the Poor Law; and following the indications of Locke and Turgot—what was later called the Iron Law of Wages. To this we shall revert.*

J. R. McCulloch, "whiskey-swilling McCulloch," Professor of Economics at the new University College, London, continued Ricardo's work; trimmed the edges; stressed the dogma. McCulloch, moreover, made an interesting statement about the theory of intrinsic value. It was, he maintained, a "fundamental Theorem" that the value of freely produced commodities depends upon the quantity of labour required for their production.

McCulloch could, with most of the school, argue in favour of public education, even compulsory, and could himself approve of the early Factory Acts. The general political outlook, however, of the school is adequately expressed by a phrase of Nassau Senior's: "*A state is nothing more than an aggregate of individuals . . . who inhabit a certain tract of country . . . whatever is most advantageous to them, is most advantageous to the state.*"

8

Thomas Robert Malthus (1766–1834), however, was the true *enfant terrible* of the Economists. This quiet, demure and even venerable clergyman, defended in writing by his Archbishop, was in his youth

* *Cf.* p. 581.

ninth mathematical wrangler of Cambridge University. He had appeared in the unexpected role of a rash optimist when Ricardo had accused him of treating rent as a gift of beneficent Providence—a natural bounty of the earth thrust into the pockets of the landlord—not the spoils of monopoly. Malthus, vicar of Albury, compensated for this generous lapse in his other work.

Since the days of the Abbé de Saint Pierre (1658–1743), in France, the doctrine of Human Progress had been developing. It had reached fine flower in the writings of the Abbé Raynal and of Condorcet and Godwin. The fruits of the earth more evenly shared, and limitlessly expansible, mankind would live in peace and prosperity, limitlessly perfectible. The malicious Hume, it is true, had put flies into the spikenard of Reason—had suggested doubts about Natural Rights, Original Contract and a rational world of cause and effect. Hartley (1705–1757), the psychological philosopher, had stuck together again, by "the Principle of Association," the world that Hume's critique of causation had laid or seemed to lay in philosophical tatters. Mind, Benjamin Franklin was briskly confident, was omnipotent over matter—he himself had invented a lightning conductor. He had made Jove's thunderbolt a bauble of science. Although Bentham with his lips denied natural rights and natural law, it was to the dogmatic moralists that he was in fact being offensive. Confidently Bentham affirmed, "each to count for one"—why, God and the theologians alone really knew. His friends the Classical Economists were most heartily assured that a natural sociological or economic law had merely to be found. Certainly the Utilitarians were not pessimists. But Ricardo had, as we have seen, reached some very strange conclusions. And now came Malthus.

The natural increase of the soil is, roughly speaking, by arithmetic progression. There is even a law of decreasing returns. But the human species, unchecked, increases by geometrical progression. Characteristically Godwin had asserted that there is some principle in human society by means of which "everything tends to find its own level and proceed in the most auspicious way, when least interfered with by the mode of regulation." But, for "the most auspicious way," there was no warranty save the assertion. The vicar of Albury watched his flock increase, the cottages become more numerous, the farm holdings creep up the hills opposite the vicarage—and wondered what would be the end of it all. He was not comforted by reading the tractate of the well-named Herr Süssmilch, *Göttliche Ordnung* (1761), which showed how Providence itself had taken care that the trees should not grow into the sky—although the illustration of how Providence caused the cork trees to grow to convenience the wine-drinkers is not his. Malthus had not met those who could demonstrate that, granted the wonders of science and peptonized, tabloid food, there was no inherent reason why population should not comfortably increase until, amid the beauties of the countryside, there was just space for each human mortal to turn round and breathe. Such demonstrations were left for later critics, a later generation of patriotic optimists. Merely he recorded,

> A man who is born into a world already possessed, if he cannot get subsistence from his parents on whom he has a just demand, and *if the society do not want his labour, has no claim of right* to the smallest portion of food and, in fact, has no business to be where he is. At Nature's mighty feast there is no vacant cover for him. She tells him to be gone and will quickly execute her own orders.

Malthus understated his case. In any social arrangements human, physiological and psychological need always sets up moral relations of duty and right, and these are the natural bases of law. But, with Malthus, we are back at the old basic argument of Aristotle, that in the good state there must be *limitation or regulation* of population. Briefly, there is a right and duty—it is the right of society and duty of the individual—that redundant population shall *not* be there. It is not only the case that no man has a right to subsistence which his labour will not purchase; he has no right to children whose labour will not be wanted. There is save, perhaps, in terms of the social regulation of population no *right* to labour, male or female, since it may amount to a right to deprive others of their union standard of living. Infanticide was the Greek cure. Mr. Malthus had other checks, discovered to be ordained by Nature and scarcely more pleasant. They were War, Famine, Vice.

The vicar—"parson Malthus," for Cobbett—later Professor of history and political economy at Haileybury College, did not precisely advocate vice or even war. He said, however, that under Providence they were Nature's cure for the improvident increase of population. Not so much shocked by his own conclusions, in his *Essay on Population* (first ed. 1798), as driven by a naturally inquiring mind, he travelled for three years through Europe gleaning statistics and then published a second edition (1803). In the first edition, it has been said, the paradoxes were striking, but the logic not watertight; in the second the logic was soundly grounded on fact, but truth converted to truism, by one noteworthy addition, was dull. The objection may be overdone. The effect of both editions was identical in pointing out that the future of natural progress was, not comfort for all, but penury all round and food scarce—*homo homini lupus*. Moreover, although benevolence was "the source of our most refined pleasures," the passion of self-love was "beyond expression stronger than the passion of benevolence" ("my family" being included in self-love).

Malthus made, however, (in his second edition) one concession to a disconcerted humanity—his addition. These horrors were the results of improvidence. But improvidence was not necessary. Malthus did not look forward to Bradlaugh and the Neo-Malthusian Societies or express agreement with the Stopesian conclusions of his defender against Godwin, the Utilitarian, Francis Place. When he said "moral," he meant it in the customary acceptation. There was then, he said (as an afterthought of this second edition), the Moral Check of intelligent forethought and self-control. But, as a friend of the Utilitarians if a Whig, Malthus attached no undue importance to a remote consideration unsupported by present pleasure. This Moral Check remained something that people *ought* to apply. As an economist he considered the sociological facts.

In these present days, when such authoritative bachelors as Sir William Beveridge are speaking of the instant importance of mothers producing more children (females: such as alone, demographically speaking, matter) lest the people—or the nation—perish, it is difficult to recover the perspective of Malthus' argument. Our alarm now is of the opposite order. Malthus urged it as a lethal *objection to Owenite communism that it would increase population.* Now the threat is that we, the Anglo-Saxons, or the Italians under Duce Mussolini or the Germans under Führer Hitler, will not be able to keep pace with the babies quick enough in the great baby war to populate the world faster than Communist Russia. Responsible Marriage Malthus had added to Private Property—both involving inequality—as a check on increase. The facts bear him out in the Soviet Union, where irresponsible marriage has actually been associated with the increase desiderated but not achieved in disciplined Germany and Italy. Even, in the period of reference, instruction on birth control, the relaxation of morals and the licensing of abortion seem to act almost as incentives (which will doubtless have to be considered by our population increasers) in the growth of the Soviet Union—now, moreover, emerging from agricultural penury into its industrial revolution. At least the more orthodox encouragements of Fascist governments—pursued contrary to Malthus—do not appear, pragmatically, equally successful.

The clergy, including Archbishops Sumner and Whately, heard Malthus unperturbed. His theory served to remind men that life here was, pending the Last Judgement, in a vale of tears, if not a den of damnation and chamber of horrors: a salutary warning. Some complacent contemporary writers were even prepared to accept infant mortality as a providential check.

What Malthus' doctrine upset was the utopia of the free-thinking optimists and of honest "Merrie England" radicals such as Cobbett. Even Franklin, in 1751, had pointed out the dangers of unrestricted human breeding—the tendency to breed to the limits of subsistence—and, in 1756, the elder Mirabeau had frankly used the illustration of rats in a barn. In his tempered second edition Malthus merely asserts a "tendency" of population to outstrip subsistence. With Free Trade (an attitude pleasing to the Utilitarians) even an increase of population might increase comfort—so long, of course, as population elsewhere did not also seek this comfort, outstrip subsistence and divert foodstuffs from export. Did not Malthus merely put off the evil day, as his opponents did by reference to wide-open spaces? Or did he underestimate what J. S. Mill, following Thomas Carlyle, was to call "the extraordinary pliability of human nature?" Did he do so less or more than our contemporary reverse Malthusians, with their prophesies, not of human rats in a barn, but of the last of the Nordics dying alone in a desert traversed by triumphant mulattoes?

Malthus, in conclusion, follows Archdeacons Tucker and Paley (1742–1805), quoting the latter.

> Human Passions [wrote Paley] are either necessary to human welfare, or capable of being made, and in a great majority of instances are in fact made, conducive to its happiness. . . . This account, while it shows us the principle of vice, shows us at the same time the province of reason and self-government.

Malthus comments,

> Our virtue, therefore, as reasonable beings, evidently consists in educing from the general materials, which the Creator has placed under our guidance, the greatest sum of human happiness; and as natural impulses are abstractly considered good, and only to be distinguished by their consequences, a strict attention to these *consequences* and the regulation of our conduct conformably to them, must be considered as our principal duty.

He repudiates Paley's notion of "a laborious frugal people ministering to the demands of an opulent luxurious nation," as uninviting and tending to privileged abuse. If a country, he comments, "*can only be rich by running a successful race for low wages, I should be disposed to say, Perish such riches.*" Poverty does but palsy virtue. And he concludes that an increase of population is indeed good if each parent had first made provision of subsistence for the children he proposed to bring into the world. As Sir Leslie Stephen remarks, with malicious exaggeration: Add to the Ten Commandments the new law, "Thou shalt not marry until there is a fair prospect of supporting six children." The conclusion is one counselling prudence, self-help, like that last of the old school, Mr. Samuel Smiles (1812–1904), individual advancement—man progressing through struggle; the improvident eliminated by Nature. Malthus brought the Perfectionists up against human biology. The cry, "bad government," of Paine and Godwin and even of Hume, was to be no alibi. In alliance with the Radical Perfectionists he smites the sentimental Tories such as Southey. Malthus is the precursor of Darwin; but a precursor who, in his lighter moods, assumed that every man who practised thrift and providence could discover the provision adequate to warrant him in increasing the world's population. "Hard as it may seem in individual instances, dependent poverty ought to be held disgraceful." How to discover this provision was a problem he bequeathed to trouble the later Utilitarians.

BIBLIOGRAPHICAL NOTE

Jeremy Bentham: *The Book of Fallacies.*
E. Halévy: *The Growth of Philosophical Radicalism*, 1928.
David Hume: *Essays.*
G. de Ruggiero: *The History of European Liberalism*, trans. Collingwood, 1927.
*Leslie Stephen: *The Utilitarians*, Vol. I, 1900.

Chapter XII

The Later Utilitarians: James and John Stuart Mill

1

FOR Jeremy Bentham, Utilitarianism was the dry evangel of a self-described "comical old man." For James Mill, it was a faith that could render a reason for itself such as might satisfy even a Scotsman. Contemptuously the elder Mill rejects the allegation that there was a "Benthamite school." The dispute recalls current controversy in America about a "Brain Trust." Perhaps the "school" never met; all were independent geniuses. The fact remains that James Mill, in his Encyclopaedia Britannica article on *Government*, wrote their political manual and testament.

JAMES MILL (1773–1836) was a Scot from Angus (*Anglicé*, Forfarshire), the son of a village shoemaker, also named James Mill before him, his mother a domestic servant of farming stock. Like many ambitious young Scotsmen he started in the Presbyterian Kirk, and was licensed to preach in 1798. Whether owing to some defect of manner or to a rebellious logic in disquisition, he received no "call"—came South of Tweed with his patron and countryman Sir John Stuart, and got work as a journalist. A temporary success as an editor was followed by years of stern frugality. Quite contrary to the principles of his future co-worker Malthus, he produced nine children, not too healthy. During these years, with the young John Stuart Mill at the other end of his desk being drilled in his lessons—"the man's hard and persevering labours to supply the wants of his child . . . his virtuous though painful course," says Mill, Sr., elsewhere in a discourse on social virtues—Mill wrote his *History of British India*.

By now the disciple, confidant and colleague of Bentham, he maintained in relation to his master, in these years wealthy, a manly independence. Self-help was rewarded, and James Mill ended his life most appropriately as chief Examiner of India Correspondence for the East India Company, full of useful official duties. By an influence characteristic of a laxer moral world, his son, John Stuart, was able, without any such apprenticeship of poverty, to begin life in the office of the "John Company," the old East India Company, which ruled an Empire as an after-thought to balancing its business accounts.

Besides the history of India, the elder Mill wrote an *Analysis of the Phenomena of the Human Mind* (1829), which is a milestone on the route between the formal and epistemological psychology of Kant or John Locke's *Essay* or David Hume's *Treatise of Human Nature*, and modern experimental psychology. The abstractness of the psychology, which is in accord with the style of the school, is perhaps fortunately, as Macaulay comments, not repeated in the history, where Mill displays a conservatism not infrequently resulting from the impact of India on British radicals and displayed also in the case of Mill's greater son. The writings of James Mill of significance most relevant to our purpose are his *Fragment on Mackintosh* (1835), and his article on *Government* (1814). His work, along with Bentham, in aiding in the foundation of London University, also deserves a place of honour in our memory.

Sir James Mackintosh was a Scotsman, a Member of Parliament, didactic, an eloquent historian and, at least in his own estimation, a philosopher, who rose to prominence as the author of *Vindiciae Gallicae* (1791), a defence on moral principles of the French Revolution against Tories. "The king of the men of talent," said Coleridge of him, meaning that he was not a genius like himself. A good Whig, like many another more eminent than he, when the Terror developed Sir James took fright and even communicated to the sage of Beaconsfield, Edmund Burke, a solemn retractation and apology. Mackintosh went so far as to declare that he lived to "wipe out the disgrace of having been once betrayed into that abominable conspiracy against God and man." The misguided man, however, was guilty of a yet worse offence. He ventured to criticize—nay, to treat with contempt—the systematic exposition of Utilitarianism by James Mill, and thus became the patent ally of Sinister Interests. He wrote: "They who have most inculcated the doctrine of utility have given another notable example of the very vulgar prejudice which treats the unseen as insignificant." Thomas Macaulay speaks of Sir James as having "a venerable countenance" and as showing in his writing, "the vivacity and the colouring of Southey." It availed nothing. James Mill dourly takes up his metaphysical dirk and rope and goes on the trail after this alien clansman, in the spirit of Knox against Beaton or the Campbells at Killiecrankie, with neither mercy nor quarter in his heart. He lassoes Sir James with the *Fragment on Mackintosh.*

Sir James had dared to take beauty, not utility, as the test in morals—mere feelings. He had criticized the Utilitarians for excessive stress on conscious motive, not intuition or habit. Habits were "the unseen." Was it not just the vulgar, says Mill, who were afrighted by—who stressed—the unseen? Are we to be told, as wisdom, that "a set of good habits is a very good thing?" Away with these "macaroni phrases" about "a heart converted to heaven." Mackintosh relies on Brown, the moralist. Mill writes:

> Brown was but poorly read on the doctrine of association. Had he known it better he would have easily answered himself. It is no rare thing, in the higher cases of complex association, for an ingredient, and a main ingredient, to be concealed by the closeness of its union with the compound. Nor does it follow that the general idea of utility is not present to the mind in moral approbation, because Dr. Brown was unable to trace it. Before the discovery of Berkeley, he would have been equally insensible of the presence of ideas of touch in the perception of figure and magnitude by the eye. . . . Sir James would have known the value of these things, had he read, as he pretended to have done, Mr. Mill's *Analysis*. . . . Acts are objects of importance to us, on account of their consequences, and nothing else. This constitutes a radical distinction between them and the things called beautiful. Acts are hurtful or beneficial, moral or immoral, virtuous or vicious. But it is only an abuse of language to call them beautiful or ugly.

The principle of Utility *is* the dictate of a well-informed conscience.

Behind, however, all this fine idealism, the "delicious feeling principle," there is a deeper flaw in Mackintosh. Like Hezekiah striking against the idol, James Mill strikes Mackintosh in fragments. He is one of those "who write for an aristocracy"—the Whigs. On the other hand—and the comment from the Radical Mill is highly significant—Sir James is capable of the contemptible act of seeking to curry favour with vulgar prejudice against the thinkers—naming as "very singular notions" that which, as Mill says, "differs from the common herd." What was his grievance against the Benthamites? That

> . . . they would not repose confidence in public men. That was the complaint. The not reposing confidence in public men, is another name for *requiring that their interests should be identified with the interests of those whom they govern.* And the confidence itself is another name for scope to misrule. The author of *Hudibras* said well; all that the knave stands in need of is to be trusted; after that, his business does itself. Sir James stood in the first rank

of those who called out for confidence in public men, and poured contumely on those who sought the identity of interest. The words on which Sir James has unfolded his sapience [etc.] . . .

Mill, incidentally, makes specific acknowledgement to Hobbes. Hobbes had grasped the principle of utility. Hobbes was, the Chief Examiner concludes, "a very unpretending writer; and Sir James one of the most offensively pretending that ever put pen to paper."

Another Scotsman came to the rescue of the distressed Mackintosh. Thomas Macaulay (1800–1859) had not yet reached the stage of fame as historian of the Glorious Whig Revolution or as Minister of War, darling of the young Whigs, in the Melbourne administration, nor had he been invited to Windsor Castle or sat up all night writing letters to his friends on Castle note paper. The speech on Confidence in the Ministry of Lord Melbourne, avowing preference for the secret ballot, repudiating universal male suffrage, enunciating the doctrine of "a stake in the country," glorying in the noble principles of Milton and Locke, was still unspoken. Macaulay was a young man still with his reputation to make—which he was fast accomplishing by articles in the *Edinburgh Review*. Here he wrote (1829) his criticism of Mill, "an Aristotelian of the fifteenth century, born out of due season." Braving "the reproach of sentimentality, a word which, in the sacred language of the Benthamites, is synonymous with idiocy," Macaulay continues:

> It must be owned that to do justice to any composition of Mr. Mill is not, in the opinion of his admirers, a very easy task. They do not, indeed, place him in the same rank with Mr. Bentham; but the terms in which they extol the disciple, though feeble when compared with the hyperboles of adoration employed by them in speaking of the master, are as strong as any sober man would allow himself to use concerning Locke or Bacon. The essay [on Government] before us is perhaps the most remarkable of the works to which Mr. Mill owes his fame. By the members of his sect, it is considered as perfect and unanswerable. Every part of it is an article of their faith; and the damnatory clauses, in which their creed abounds far beyond any theological symbol with which we are acquainted, are strong and full against all who reject any portion of what is so irrefragably established. . . . He seems to think that, if all despots, without exception, governed ill, it would be unnecessary to prove, by a synthetical argument, what would then be sufficiently clear from experience. But as some despots will be so perverse as to govern well, he finds himself compelled to prove the impossibility of their governing well by that synthetical argument which would have been superfluous had not the facts contradicted it.

So much for Mill's method. Mill argues for universal male suffrage, as alone a guaranty of "identity of interest" of rulers and ruled. But has he—*reductio ad absurdum*—considered women's suffrage? "Except in a few happy and highly civilized communities, [women] are strictly in a state of personal slavery." Mill says that the middle class will lead. Is that identity of interest? Will they be permitted? The whole people may vote, but only the majority will govern. Is the interest of majority and minority identical? Granted "self-interest," will it not oppress? And what is this great principle of "self-interest?" It is no novelty that "a man had rather do what he had rather do." But no man knows what another will do until he has done it. Then Macaulay, a Whig unwittingly reverting to Burke, lets fly a lethal shaft.

If there were a community consisting of two classes of man, one of which should be principally influenced by the one set of motives and the other by the other, government would clearly be necessary to restrain the class which was eager for plunder and careless of reputation: and yet the powers of government might be safely intrusted to the class which was chiefly actuated by the love of approbation. Now it might with no small plausibility be maintained that, in many countries, *there are two classes* which, in some degree, answer to this description: that the poor compose the class which government is established to restrain, and the people of some property the class to which the powers of government may without danger be confided. . . .

We do not assert all this. We only say that it was Mr. Mill's business to prove the contrary. . . . We are rather inclined to think that it would, on the whole, be for the interest of the majority to plunder the rich. If so, the Utilitarians will say, that the rich *ought* to be plundered. We deny the inference. For, in the first place, if the object of government be the greatest happiness of the greatest number, the intensity of the suffering which a measure inflicts must be taken into consideration, as well as the number of the sufferers. In the next place, we have to notice one most important distinction which Mr. Mill has altogether overlooked. Throughout his essay, he confounds the community with the species. He talks of the greatest happiness of the greatest number: but, when we examine his reasonings, we find that he thinks only of *the greatest number of a single generation*. . . . The greater the inequality of conditions, the stronger are the motives which impel the populace to spoliation. As for America, we appeal to the twentieth century.

They may as well be Utilitarians as jockeys or dandies. And, though quibbling about self-interest and motives, and objects of desire, and the greatest happiness of the greatest number, is but poor employment for a grown man, it certainly hurts the health less than hard drinking, and the fortune less than high play; it is not much more laughable than phrenology, and it is immeasurably more humane than cock-fighting.

Macaulay, after two further essays on the theme, rested from his work of detonating Benthamism. As Macaulay maliciously remarks, quoting Molière, "Hippocrate dira ce que lui plaira, mais le cocher est mort." Macaulay exaggerated. The great disciple, Mill, hesitates—decides to be magisterial, declines to refer to Macaulay by name, wraps him up in a fragment of Mackintosh.

> Sir James says, and [this is a master-stroke of the Style *putide Schmellfungus*] according to him, "the writer of a late criticism in the Edinburgh Review" says, that this "overthrows the whole fabric of Mr. Mill's political reasoning," [*i.e.*, that men do not always act in conformity with their true interest].
>
> I am not at all disposed to quibble with Sir James, about the meaning of the word "interest." It is very obvious, to anyone who has read Mr. Mill's Treatise, in what sense he uses it. He uses it, neither in the refined sense of a man's best interest, or in what is conducive to his happiness upon the whole; nor to signify every object which he desires, though that is a very intelligible meaning too. Mr. Mill uses it, on the rough and common acceptation, to denote the leading objects of human desire; Wealth, Power, Dignity, Ease; including escape from the contrary, Poverty, Impotence, Degradation, Toil.

And so the philosopher rode away, firing quotations from Berkeley, Hume, Blackstone and—Plato. Despite, however, all Macaulay's pyrotechnics, the practical consequences of the Benthamite campaign were more important than anything Macaulay had to show. Nay more, if dominie James Mill was not intellectually worth more than Macaulay, Bentham and the two Mills were worth more than Macaulay even if multiplied by three. Had it been true that the Benthamites achieved their success because of the dogmatic scholasticism for which Macaulay attacked them, it would have been a chastening thought. That dogmatism, however, was not of the "enthusiastic" variety, but a genuine attachment to the schematism necessary as an exploratory instrument of science—even of political science. Despite his contempt for this, Macaulay's own theorizing shows that when the rigidity of logical hypothesis is rejected, the pressure of personal prejudice, motivated by interest, comes into play.

James Mill hesitated. Perhaps he calculated. Anyhow he relented; in 1834 Macaulay became legal adviser to the Supreme Council of India; Mill did not obstruct and Macaulay was grateful. The essays on Mill, during Macaulay's life, were not republished. As for Mackintosh, he died.

Let us now turn to the famous essay itself, among others on Education, Liberty of the Press, Prison Discipline, about which there was this pother. It is brief, as befits an *Encyclopaedia Britannica* article—but it became the vade mecum of all good Utilitarians.

James Mill begins with an economic statement about which much more will be heard before many decades.

To obtain labour in the greatest possible quantity, we must raise to the greatest possible height the advantage attached to labour. It is impossible to attach to labour a greater degree of advantage than the whole of the product of labour. Why so? Because if you give more to one man than the produce of his labour, you can do it only by taking it away from the produce of some other man's labour. *The greatest possible happiness of society is, therefore, attained by insuring to every man the greatest possible quantity of the produce of his labour.*

How is this to be accomplished? for it is obvious that every man, who has not all the objects of his desire, has inducement to take them from any other man who is weaker than himself: and how is he to be prevented?

One mode is sufficiently obvious; and it does not appear that there is any other: The union of a certain number of men, to protect one another. . . .

The reason for which Government exists is, that one man, if stronger than another, will take from him whatever that other possesses and he desires.

In brief, government is the collaboration of the weak against the strong.* Mill goes on, from this good social contract doctrine, to prove, by a "chain of inference . . . strong to a most unusual degree," that Terror will be the grand instrument of a ruler or ruling group, constitutionally unchecked and confronted with opposition to its will. Despite the witticisms of Macaulay at the expense of Utilitarian pedantry, the experience of a century has shown Mill more right than the early Victorian optimists allowed for. Mill, however, makes an *experimentum crucis*, not without sardonic satisfaction.

An English Gentleman may be taken as a favourable specimen of civilization, of knowledge, of humanity, of all the qualities, in short, that make human nature estimable. The degree in which he desires to possess power over his fellow creatures, and the degree of oppression to which he finds motives for carrying the exercise of that power, will afford a standard from which, assuredly, there can be no appeal. Wherever the same motives exist, the same conduct, as that displayed by the English Gentleman, may be expected to follow, in all men not further advanced in human excellence than him. In the West Indies, before that vigilant attention of the English nation, which now, for thirty years, has imposed so great a check upon the masters of slaves, there was not a perfect absence of all check upon the dreadful propensities of power. But yet it is true, that these propensities led English Gentlemen, not only to

* *Cf.* pp. 44, 235.

deprive their slaves of property, and to make property of their fellow-creatures, but to treat them with a degree of cruelty, the very description of which froze the blood of their countrymen, who were placed in less unfavourable circumstances. The motives of this deplorable conduct are exactly those which we have described above, as arising out of the universal desire to render the actions of other men exactly conformable to our will.

The present British Royal Commission in Jamaica will please note.

A Monarchy or Aristocracy then must be restrained or it will encroach for its own interest upon others. Only a Democracy can be trusted to safeguard the interests [and here Jas. Mill oddly drops into Rousseau's fallacy*] of the whole community throughout the generations, *i.e.*, as he supposes, its own. But a direct democracy is today impracticable. What then is the remedy? "The divine principle" of representation.

In the grand discovery of modern times, the system of representation, the solution of all the difficulties, both speculative and practical, will perhaps be found. If it cannot, we seem to be forced upon the extraordinary conclusion that good Government is impossible.

How are the representatives to be checked? By frequent elections—not necessarily recall or annual elections, as the Chartists said, but frequent.† And would not the majority oppress the minority? The answer here deserves attention. The benefits of good government accruing to all might be expected to outbalance "the benefits of misrule peculiar to themselves," *i.e.*, the Majority. Not only have we a risk that must be taken on the greatest happiness principle, *but* the majority has a vested average interest in good government for *all*, since it itself is so nearly all, *i.e.*, *most.*

It is better, argued Mill, to be governed by the many which may occasionally be mistaken about its own interest—and he declines to refine on the phrase "true interest"—than by an oligarchy or privileged class which has a separatist interest, not identified with the mass of the community. He wins a resonant and quick victory over Aristocracy, as a form of government, by identifying it with those nobles and gentry whose names are in Burke's *Peerage* and in de Brett. He is more tender to those who figure in the columns of *Who's Who*. Mill rashly concedes

* *Cf.* p. 454.

† The demand of the British Chartist movement (1838–1858) was for (i) universal manhood suffrage; (ii) vote by ballot; (iii) payment of members of Parliament; (iv) members need not be property owners; (v) equal electoral districts; (vi) annual Parliaments. The first four points have been peacefully won; and for the last there is today no popular demand.

that an aristocracy, in the philosophic sense, "the wise and good in any class of man" do, to all general purposes, govern the rest. Who, briefly, are these "wise and good?" As Machiavelli ends his detached *Prince* with a passionate appeal for Italian national resurgence, so Mill ends with an appeal for the Middle Class:

> that intelligent and virtuous rank . . . to whom their [the poor's] children look up as models for their imitation, whose opinions they hear daily repeated, and account it their honour to adopt. There can be no doubt that the middle rank, which gives to science, to art, and to legislation itself, their most distinguished ornaments, the chief source of all that has exalted and refined human nature, is that portion of the community of which, if the basis of Representation were ever so far extended, the opinion would ultimately decide.

One recalls the argument of Hamilton in *The Federalist.**

James Mill took very seriously his science of government or political science—hence the crusading fury of his zeal against the deceiver Mackintosh. He had not the advantage of living in an age when a letter to the press recommending the removal of tariffs, or an article on foreign policy, by some best-selling writer of fiction, is in demand to the exclusion of those who may happen to have made a life study of these subjects. It is today patent that Miss X's music-hall sketches give her an especial influence in a democracy to move the electorate in the appropriate direction. The press and magazines are at the disposition, to sway opinion, of those who are eminently well known, it is immaterial for what. When James Mill outlined his scheme of representative government or sketched the future of education, in the days of the influence of the *Edinburgh* and the *Quarterly* magazines—looked forward to the guiding influence of the sober and reflective middle class—he did not contemplate these brisk developments. He was, indeed, a heavy fellow and, as Sir Leslie Stephen observes, it is not remarkable that his death was less lamented than that of the dissipated but amiable pillar of Church and State, Samuel Taylor Coleridge—who nevertheless took his German philosophy even too seriously.† Coleridge roundly damned those who demand "a French style . . . for those to comprehend who labour under the more pitiable asthma of a short-witted intellect." Both men tended to scold the Public. And, to put it briefly, James was bad-tempered.

* *Cf.* p. 314.
† *Cf.* p. 497.

2

JOHN STUART MILL (1806–1873), his son, was the chief sufferer. His education (which, nevertheless, in his *Autobiography*, he loyally defends as the best that could be done for an average sort of boy) has been happily compared to the refinements of the Spanish Inquisition. The unhappy child, in a household which held to the maxim that the mind is determined by the fit environmental stimulus, began Greek at the age of three under the watchful eye of James Mill, "one of the most impatient of men." At eight he records that he had completed all Herodotus, much of Diogenes Laertius' *Lives of the Philosophers* and Isocrates' *Ad Demonicum*. He had also read Plato's *Thœatetus*, "which last dialogue, I venture to think, would have been better omitted, as it was totally impossible I should understand it." "Of children's books, any more than of playthings, I had scarcely any, except an occasional gift from a relation or acquaintance." Aged eleven, the young Mill had begun "a History of the Roman Government, compiled from Livy and Dionysius."

The child was father to the man. At the age of twenty-three he withdrew from the Debating Society that he had been largely instrumental in founding. "I had enough of speech making." At the age of thirty-two he had already been an editor of the *London and Westminster Magazine*, and had resigned that post. In 1841, having completed his *System of Logic* he offered it to the publisher, Murray, but had the mortification of having it rejected; it was, however, published in 1843 and, oddly enough, came to be referred to, presumably in praise in the days before Green and Bradley, as "the Oxfordman's Bible." Until J. M. Keynes' *Treatise on Probability* it was to remain the major work on inductive logic. More immediately successful was the *Principles of Political Economy* (1848). At thirty-six, in the East India Company's offices and before long to become chief Examiner in his turn, he writes in his *Autobiography*, "From this time, what is worth relating of my life will come into a very small compass; for I have no further mental changes to tell of, but only, as I hope, a continued mental progress."

He had three sessions of Parliament, as Member for Westminster, still ahead of him. Having, however, firmly informed the party managers and electors that he did not propose to contribute to the funds of the former (although he did contribute to those of the unpopular pioneer, Bradlaugh) or to "undertake to give any of my time or labour to their local interests" or jobbing demands, it is not surprising that, in 1868, the said electors repented themselves of electing anyone so high-minded. What is perhaps surprising is that Mill was ever elected at all. Apparently, Mill, having told a large working-class audience that the British workers (although better than those abroad) were generally liars, this statement so startled the voters with delight that they put him in. In Parliament he was concerned with the Irish question and the condition of the peasantry; women's suffrage and suffrage for manual workers; the paying off of the National Debt before the coal supplies of Britain were exhausted; and—an admirable cause—the prosecution of Governor Eyre for his treatment by court martial of the disturbances in Jamaica.

It was, he tells us in his *Autobiography*, on mounting the steps of the Capitol at Rome, in 1855, that Mill decided to publish as a volume his famous essay *On Liberty* (1859), to be followed by the *Considerations on Representative Government* (1861) and by the writing of *The Subjection of Women*, only published (in 1869) after his parliamentary defeat. The first and last of these books, as well as the famous chapter "On the Probable Futurity of the Labouring Classes," in *Principles of Political Economy*, were, Mill assures us, written under the influence of Mrs. Helen Taylor, later Mill's wife. Although it has been customary, among Mill's admirers, to minimize this influence over him which he ascribes to Mrs. Taylor, I see no reason to doubt that this impression of an obviously able and intellectually integrated woman upon a highly susceptible and over-educated man was very great indeed.

The amazing education to which John Stuart Mill had been subjected by his father had two uncalculated effects. One was to produce—at the age of twenty—what Mill dignifies as "a crisis in my mental history." The other was to produce a conscience which was to affect his philosophy. Mill had indeed, by a precocity which his contemporaries confused with conceit, completely exhausted his nervous system. A cloud of melancholia descended upon him. He, who had hoped to be "a reformer of the world," asked himself gravely whether, could all the Benthamite changes to which he had been looking forward be effected as by a miracle, he would then be full of joy and happiness—the greatest number acclaiming with hallelujahs the greatest happiness according to the felicific calculus. "And an irrepressible self-consciousness distinctly answered, 'No!' At this my heart sank within me: the whole foundation on which my life was constructed fell down."

Mr. John Taylor was a dry-salter or druggist. His grandfather had lived in the next house to James Mill in Newington Green, London. John Stuart Mill rediscovered Mr. Taylor—and incidentally discovered

Mrs. Taylor—in 1830. Taylor was "a most upright, brave, and honourable man, of liberal opinions and good education, but without the intellectual and artistic tastes which would have made him a companion for her." Mrs. Helen Taylor, daughter of the lord of the manor of Birksgate, was such that "in thought and intellect, Shelley, so far as his powers were developed in his short life, was but a child compared with what she ultimately became." John Stuart was also an honourable man, and most high-minded. She was twenty-three and he was twenty-five, just recovering from Bentham. Mr. John Taylor obligingly took to the habit of dining out every Tuesday evening, and John Stuart dined with Mrs. Taylor. Later Mrs. Taylor lived alone in a cottage in the country with her daughter and occasionally she and Mr. Mill travelled together. Mill states that the relation was purely platonic and, since Mr. Mill was a man who would have despised a lie, the evidence may be taken to be convincing that this was in fact the case.

The psychological effects were as might have been anticipated. "Was the private life of Mill on the whole praiseworthy, or was much of his conduct in the highest degree reprehensible?" asks, in a biographical note, his step-granddaughter. If praiseworthiness is won by pain of good intentions, the answer is not in doubt. In his youthful writings—one easily forgets how youthful—Mill has a high-flown immaturity of sentiment. But Mill was never really young; nor, again, ever quite mature. All his life he was a middle-aged middle-class mid-Victorian. And, as time passes, he becomes almost oppressively noble. The romantic, intellectual, dissatisfied Helen made John Stuart Mill not only a feminist but the Marcus Aurelius of the nineteenth century. After twenty-one years (Taylor being dead) he married the lady. The Mill family (James also being dead) coolly disapproved. John Stuart chivalrously quarrelled with them.

Mill, we have said, developed a conscience; and this affects his philosophy. A conscience, and above all a virulent conscience (of which the utility was undemonstrable), was not explicitly allowed for by the Utilitarian philosophers. They were the dour book-keepers of pleasure—Scotsmen, suspicious of such intangibilities. It was, however, an inevitable product of their mood. Of James Mill, John Stuart writes,

> He would sometimes say, that if life were made what it might be, by good government and good education, it would be worth having: but he never spoke with anything like enthusiasm even of that possibility. He never varied in rating intellectual enjoyments above all others, even in value as pleasures, independently of their ulterior benefits. . . . For passionate emotions of all sorts, and for everything which has been seen or written in exaltation of them,

he professed the greatest contempt. He regarded them as a form of madness. "The intense" was with him a bye-word of scornful disapprobation.

This "rating of intellectual enjoyments above all," perhaps spontaneous with James Mill, was to have its effect upon John Stuart, who accepted it as almost axiomatic, and was to work havoc with the utilitarian hedonistic philosophy and with Jeremy Bentham's happy light-hearted theme that "quantity of pleasure being equal, push-pin is as good as poetry."

In his second phase, when militant discipleship of his father James had given way to melancholic reaction, John Stuart Mill writes almost with passion, if suppressed passion, of Bentham. It is to be suspected that Macaulay's sarcastic essay had left its marks on a sensitive mind.

> What Bentham's functional truths could do, there is no such good means of showing as by a review of his philosophy. . . . In many of the most natural and strongest feelings of human nature he had no sympathy; from many of its graver experiences he was altogether cut off; and the faculty by which one mind understands a mind different from itself, and throws itself into the feelings of that other mind, was denied him by his deficiency of Imagination. . . . A moralist on Bentham's principles . . . what will be his qualifications for regulating the nicer shades of human behaviour, or for laying down even the greater moralities as to those facts in human life which are liable to influence the depths of the character quite independently of any influence on worldly circumstances? . . . The moralities of these questions depend essentially on conditions which Bentham never so much as took into account; and when he happened to be in the right, it was always and necessarily, on wrong or insufficient grounds. . . .
>
> Nothing is more curious than the absence of recognition in any of his writings of the existence of conscience, as a thing distinct from philanthropy, from affection for God or man, and from self-interest in this world or in the next. . . . The feelings of moral approbation or disapprobation properly so called, either towards ourselves or our fellow-creatures, he seems unaware of the existence of; and neither the word self-respect, nor the idea to which that word is appropriated, occurs even once, so far as our recollection serves us, in his whole writings.

Actually Bentham had discussed the nature of conscience very fully, and had resolved it (as, for that matter, did the Thomist Schoolmen) into the principle of sympathy or antipathy *save* so far as guided by the monition (*synderesis*) of Reason. But John Stuart Mill, at this time, is under the influence of Thomas Carlyle. Jeremy Bentham was essentially, as has been said, an "original"—but an "original" in the sensationalist and indeed sensualist tradition of Franklin, Helvetius and Voltaire. Mid-Victorian John Stuart Mill, defending with his lips the eighteenth century which he oddly identified with his Scottish cobbling forebears, had so little sympathy with the background of that philosophy as even to omit to be shocked by it. Bentham, he admitted, advocated empiricism, but his own was "of one who has little experience." The implications of the Benthamite philosophy when (as Bentham in one passage hints) not practiced by those who are intellectuals by taste and training, the serious-minded Mill ignores. That is what makes St. Augustine, who knew both catholicity of experience and understanding of sin, so much more profound a philosopher than J. S. Mill.

Nevertheless, although Mill refers later to his Benthamite days as though to bachelor indiscretions, he does not hesitate to publish an epitome and defence of that philosophy, revised, in his *Utilitarianism*, as late as 1863. Here, however, we discover that there are, not only quantities, but also (*pace* Bentham) qualities of pleasure. Begging the question of higher and lower, Mill writes: "It may be questioned whether anyone who has remained equally susceptible to both classes of pleasure, ever knowingly and calmly preferred the lower." It is dubious whether Mill can be taken as an empirical authority on the lower pleasures. However, he appears to be asserting that no hungry man ever preferred the pleasure of a good meal to those of poetry; and to be hinting that no balanced judge could prefer the pleasures of power or even of speed to those of erudition or of solving elegantly a mathematical problem. Naturally no man deliberately prefers those pleasures which he at the moment accounts for himself the worse: that is not an issue worth discussing.

Mill dismisses Kant in nine lines; and claims Plato as a Utilitarian. The Golden Rule is adduced as the core of a Utilitarianism which despises a base Expediency. What has really happened is that the virile, tough and distinctive Aggression Philosophy or Power Philosophy of Hobbes, such as traces back to "Callicles" and forward to Nietzsche, has been transmuted by the tender mind of Mill into a philosophy of still more respectable lineage, but certainly not that of Hume and Bentham.

> It is noble to be capable of resigning entirely one's own portion of happiness or chances of it: but, after all, this self-sacrifice must be for some end. . . . I fully acknowledge that the readiness to make such a sacrifice is the highest virtue which can be found in man.

To what end, then? Not my pleasure; or even my happiness; or even the happiness of the greatest number; but the happiness or "good of the whole." Just as Bentham had learned, in penal reform, from Beccaria (1735–1794), so J. S. Mill had learned, in educational reform, from Pestalozzi (1746–1827). And the famous doctrine, derived from Hartley, of Association of Ideas, was to connect "by indissoluble association" my happiness and the general happiness; that of society "at large"; "the sum total of happiness"; the "general happiness" in "unity with our fellow-creatures"—disregarding my own "miserable individuality." Utility is becoming elastic to the point of evanescence.

Moral action, then, is not only a matter of duty or of the intuition of conscience, but of "consequences"—for the world through the ages and for its "happiness." It is not clear how this differs widely from the Catholic-Platonic assertion that it is action to the greater glory of God, of Whom the vision is beatific, which is the *summum bonum* or absolute good—nor might Mill have denied this, had he not been brought up by James Mill (himself brought up by Calvin's men), who held that religion—worshipping "the Omnipotent Author of Hell"—was "the greatest enemy of morality." Pascal, with odd lack of taste, J. S. Mill ranks below La Rochefoucauld and La Rochefoucauld below Montaigne. But Mill, with his statement that a being of higher faculties requires more to make him happy, is capable probably of more acute suffering, comes very near the doctrine of Pascal, of Man the Thinking Reed—quite quits hedonism—and then fails to attain either Pascal's insight or pathos. Complacently Mill concludes that "human nature is so constituted as to *desire nothing* which is not either a part of happiness or a means of happiness," and leaves it at that. Will is "produced" from desire, if persisting independently by habit—in the void as it were. Sardanapalus sadistically impaling his captives and Scott in Antarctica presumably alike "desire nothing," etc. It may be true, but the method of expression is surely bizarre and unilluminating. The actual differences between the decent and the indecent, that is, the beautiful and ugly, owing to the Benthamite concentration on useful means and consequences, remained unstressed in the formal philosophy.

The younger Mill, however, will be remembered primarily for two essays: those *On Liberty* and *Considerations on Representative Government.*

In *On Liberty*, while reviewing Bentham's and James Mill's thesis of the desirable identification of interest of rulers and ruled (overcoming the older supposition, of Locke and Paine, of their normal antagonism), in a democracy, J. S. Mill points out that there may be a need *to limit the power of the ruling people itself.*

> The "people" who exercise the power, are not the same people with those over whom it is exercised. . . . The will of the people, moreover, practically means, the will of the most numerous or most active *part* of the people; the majority, or those who succeed in making themselves accepted as the majority: the people, consequently, *may* desire to oppress a part of their number; and precautions are as much needed against this, as against any other abuse of power.

The discussion of this limitation of the power of government over individuals is the discussion of the field of Civil or Social Liberty.

Why should there be such a limitation? Is there room in, for example, a proletarian democracy, to speak of a "tyranny of the majority," including a tyranny of public opinion? And, in Mill's words, "how to make the fitting adjustment between individual independence and social control?"

Intolerance, Mill held very soundly, like sadism, is natural to mankind—especially to the more moral part of mankind. Although the morality of courtiers largely emanates from the class interests of an ascendant class, when there is one, where the majority, mass or proletariat becomes ascendant the same result may be anticipated.

> The majority have not yet learnt to feel the power of the government their power, or its opinions their opinions. When they do so, individual liberty will probably be as much exposed to invasion from the government, as it already is from public opinion.

Why should there be limitation? A citizen

> cannot rightfully be compelled to do or forbear because it will be better for him to do so, because it will make him happier, because, in the opinions of others, to do so would be wise, or even right. . . . Mankind are [*sic*] *greater gainers by suffering each other to live as seems good to themselves, than by compelling each to live as seems good to the rest.*

As a practical issue does not this conflict with Mill's own theory of Utility? Mill declares that he entirely denies the right of—not only the government, but—the people to control coercively the expression of opinion (as, for example, is done in all countries where only one party is permitted). "The power itself is illegitimate." There is, then, some test of legitimacy superior to the sovereign legislator. Is Mill not asserting here, as superior to the sovereign majority's view of the socially useful, some natural right or law? It is noteworthy that, in endeavouring (in his *Utilitarianism*) to reconcile the moral principle of Justice with Utility, he stresses the finality of Bentham's maxim, "everybody to count for one." That maxim, in effect, is one of natural right, transcending social Utility, and so admitted by Bentham. Mill, however, endeavours to rescue social Utility (as distinct from Bentham's final test, private Pleasure) by asserting that, only by this self-denying ordinance of the proletariat, will "mankind be the gainer."

It is his private, subjective opinion. He endeavours, however, to support it by reasons. The gain or progress of humanity depends upon initiative, and this must be the initiative of the individual which only flourishes under a régime of political and moral liberty. The liberty and even licence prevalent at the great periods of human mental efflorescence certainly seems to bear this out. As much as Priestley, J. S. Mill sees virtue in variety as such.* The relation of crime to genius has been discussed by sociologists, such as Durkheim, and it may be that mankind has to pay for its occasional geniuses by toleration of much crime. Mill, who for many years (under the joint influence of Coleridge and Carlyle) has been absorbing the German culture of the great age of Goethe, here frankly turns to his German authorities—to whom we shall revert†—for support.

Mill quotes Wilhelm von Humboldt:

> The end of man . . . is the highest and most harmonious development of his powers to a complete and consistent whole . . . the object towards which every human being must ceaselessly direct his efforts, and on which especially those who design to influence their fellowmen must ever keep their eyes, is the individuality of power and development [incidentally, a recipe, for all but Fortune's aristocrats, for misery and discontent].

How, then, shall an allocation be made between the provinces of governmental or social authority and individual liberty?

> The object [Mill writes] of this Essay is to assert one very simple principle, as entitled to govern absolutely the dealings of society with the individual in the way of compulsion and control. . . . That principle is, that the sole end for which mankind are warranted, individually or collectively, in interfering with the liberty of action of any of their number is self-protection.

Mill developed in this connection a distinction, anticipated by Kant, between self-regarding and other-regarding acts, which provoked a

* *Cf.* pp. 334, 420.

† *Cf.* p. 417.

controversy of which we shall hear more.* Mill also made two grave and important reservations: his theory of liberty, he explains, is meant to apply only to human beings in the maturity of their faculties; and not to "those backward states of society in which the human race itself may be considered as in its nonage." In his *Considerations on Representative Government* Mill develops this theme. Monarchy (despite the case of Switzerland) is more effective in uniting into a state petty, disconnected communities. It is more suited for a people that prefer conquest abroad or place-hunting at home to personal liberty. Also, secondly, Representative Government does not suit those who, on the contrary, obstinately abhor all government; or, from cowardice or want of public spirit, are unwilling to fulfil the conditions requisite for democratic government; or who, from local habit, distrust of the authorities and sympathy with the criminal, will not co-operate with such a government—like (observes Mill, of the East India Company) "the Hindoos, who will perjure themselves to screen the man who has robbed them, rather than take trouble or expose themselves to vindictiveness by giving evidence against him." Mill need not have referred only to Hindus: a corrupt police, anywhere in the world, is usually an adequate explanation.

However, J. S. Mill proceeds to an encomium on Englishmen, of questionable applicability but of some contemporary interest on both sides of the Atlantic.

> Not having the smallest sympathy with the passion for governing, while they are but too well acquainted with the motives of private interest from which that office is sought, they prefer that it should be performed by those to whom it comes without seeking, as a consequence of social position. . . . If we except the few families for connexions for whom official employment lies directly on the way, Englishmen's views of advancement in life take an altogether different direction—that of success in business, or in a profession.

Mill, however, is quite clear that representative majoritarian democracy, minimalist in its legislative tendencies, is the ideally best polity. A good despot is even worse than a bad despot because more conscientiously interfering. "*A good despot insists on doing them good*, by making them do their own business in a better way than they themselves know of."†

* *Cf.* p. 507.

† For the unconscious assumption of the "minimalist" attitude, *cf.* the ironically anti-Hellenic use of the word "politics"—"there's politics in it"—as broadly synonymous with "sharp practice," *i.e.*, not "straight *business*" competition, but some group *power*-pull, disconcerting to an honest, individualist shopkeeper.

An ideal polity will, Mill asserts, be a balanced one in which no sectional interest will prevail. He agrees with James Mill in his criticism of Burke's too facile laudation of a balanced constitution which actually was marked by heavy bias. True democracy, however, was representation of all; and *false democracy was representation of the majority only.* True, that the majority if it consulted its *real* interests would not abuse power—"but a king only now and then, and an oligarchy in no known instance [excellent though the record of some bureaucracies might be], have taken this exalted view of their self-interest: and why should we expect a loftier mode of thinking from the labouring classes?" The "real" issue in politics is that, not of "real" interests, but of "actual" or supposed interests.*

Just as his father had discovered the "divine" panacea of representative government, so the younger Mill found in proportional representation the remedy for its one defect. That defect is the risk of the extinction of the minority voice, or (more precisely) the risk of government by the mere majority (in the Congress) of a majority (in the country), which body might well be itself a minority. The form, however, of proportional representation, based on Hare's scheme, advocated by Mill is different from the customary. This scheme of "personal representation" would set up what have been called "crank" or "clique" constituencies, so many thousands of electors from anywhere in the country being entitled to elect a representative when he commended himself rather than the local representative. It would involve voting by national lists. This representation of "causes," Mill held, would both give a voice to minorities and a remedy for the situation in America, where "the highly cultivated members of the community . . . do not even offer themselves for Congress or the State Legislatures." Mill stated a problem—the gravest of all, that of minorities: it can scarcely be held that he propounded a remedy.

In *Considerations on Representative Government* Mill reverts to the Utilitarian theme that, so long as it remains true that men "prefer themselves to others, and those nearest them to those more remote," every man is the best guardian of his own interest. When this ceases to be the situation, Communism (St. Simonian style) becomes "*not only practicable, but the only defensible form of society.*" Under the contemporary suffrage and representation, Members of Parliament did not look at questions "with the eyes of a working man." That was as undesirable as that the manual worker interest should dominate

* *Cf.* pp. 451, 521.

Parliament without consideration of any other than proletarian interests. This suspicion of the domination of the morality of a country by some ascendant class, whatever that class might be, and the maxim that "each is the only safe guardian of his own rights and interest," is the basis of J. S. Mill's argument (in which he corrects the lapse from logic of Mill the Elder) in *The Subjection of Women* (1869). In this he carried on the work of Mary Wollstonecraft and reinforced that of Condorcet, Bentham and of the Americans, Emma Willard and Susan B. Anthony.

> Who doubts that there may be great goodness, and great happiness, and great affection, under the absolute government of a good man? Meanwhile, laws and institutions require to be adapted, not to good men, but to bad. Marriage is not an institution designed for a select few. . . . Even the commonest men reserve the violent, the sulky, the undisguisedly selfish side of their character for those who have no power to withstand it. The relation of superiors to dependents is the nursery of these vices of character, which, wherever else they exist, are an overflowing from that source.

Mill's pamphlet was immediately designed to promote the case for women's suffrage. It had, however, wider social aspects. Following Plato, he declined to "interfere on behalf of nature [by allocating a conventional lower status to women] for fear lest nature should not succeed in effecting its purpose." In his *Autobiography*, anticipating M. Léon Blum and in a fashion offensive to the prelates of Lambeth, he goes further and pays honour to the followers of St. Simon for "the boldness and freedom from prejudice with which they treated the subject of the family, the most important of any, and needing more fundamental alterations than remain to be made in any other great social institution, but on which scarcely any reformer has the courage to touch."

The same concern for the subjected sections of the community—those who historically have been at a disadvantage in the worldly competition of keen men to further their own interests of wealth and power—marks his chapter (also written, as was the *Subjection of Women*, under the influence of Mrs. Taylor), in the *Principles of Political Economy* (1848), "On the Probable Futurity of the Labouring Classes." Mill, in his *Autobiography* declares himself, by this time, on the one hand, a considered Socialist, although with qualifications, while, on the other, thanks to perusal of De Tocqueville's book on *Democracy in America,* remaining a democrat—subject to those reservations about minorities voiced in *On Representative Government.*

While we repudiated with the greatest energy that tyranny of society over the individual which most Socialistic systems are supposed to involve, we yet look forward to the time when society will no longer be divided into the idle [*i.e.*, hereditary rich] and the industrious; when the rule that they who do not work shall not eat, will be applied not to paupers only, but impartially to all.

In the *Political Economy* Mill makes an interesting comment on his own use, under protest, of the word "class." "So long as the great social evil exists of a non-labouring class, labourers also constitute a class, and may be spoken of, *though only provisionally,* in that character."

Mill, however, was right in describing his Socialism as strictly qualified. He praises Owen's work in initiating the Co-operative Movement; and admits that "Whatever, if left to spontaneous agency, can only be done by joint stock associations"—a line of argument interestingly anticipating that of Berle and Means, in their *The Modern Corporation and Private Property*—"will often be as well, and sometimes better done, as far as the actual work is concerned, by the state." Trade Unions he regards as doubtful organizations save when in competition with each other, but agreements on hours he admits should be enforced by law. However,

while I agree and sympathize with Socialists in this practical portion of their aims, I utterly dissent from the most conspicuous and vehement part of their teaching, their declamations against competition. . . . They forget that with the exception of competition among labourers, all other competition is for the benefit of the labourers, by cheapening the articles they consume; that competition even in the labour market is a source not of low but of high wages, wherever the competition *for* labour exceeds the competition *of* labour, as in America, in the colonies and in the skilled trades; and never could be a cause of low wages, save by the overstocking of the labour market through the too great number of the labourers' families; while, if the supply of labourers is excessive, not even Socialism can prevent their remuneration from being low.

Competition, for Mill, is not only an economic means to low prices for the consumer. It is a guaranty of liberty against bureaucracy. Proletarian Democracy alone is not an adequate safeguard.

Experience proves that the depositaries of power who are mere delegates of the people, that is of a majority, are quite as ready (when they think they can count on popular support) as any organs of oligarchy, to assume arbitrary power, and encroach unduly on the liberty of private life.

For the explanation of Mill's renewed attachment to this liberty we must look, not so much to Bentham as to Goethe and the Germans.* Mill's *On Liberty* marks the end of an epoch—the epoch of the "hard-boiled" individualist tradition that begins with Hobbes, if not with Machiavelli. It is "soft-shelled" and humanitarian, based not on faith in Christian Revelation (as was the Catholic humanitarianism) but on belief in Liberal Progress. A new collectivist tradition now enters into dominance. Against this Mill, although emotionally sympathetic, utters his intellectual warning.

The Utilitarians were moralists who spent their time discussing conduct. Bentham was an original. As John Stuart Mill tells us, Mr. Bentham "was a boy to the last." As to his father James, John Stuart feelingly remarks, "His temper was constitutionally irritable." The younger Mill himself had an education designed to perfect him as the Compleat Prig. Thanks perhaps to Mrs. Taylor, some if not all of that tendency was overcome. After having observed, with a Liberal complacency, uncorrected by real profundity, that the Tory was "the stupidest party," he called down upon himself the acid comment of Disraeli that he was "a political finishing mistress." It was the countercheck quarrelsome to Gladstone's praise of Mill as "the Saint of Rationalism." Nevertheless, Mill scarcely merited the obituary comment (so significant of how natural intolerance is to the natural human animal) of the "Evangelical" *Church Herald* (May 14, 1873): "His death is no loss to anybody, for he was a rank but amiable infidel, and a most dangerous person. The sooner those 'lights of thought,' who agree with him, go to the same place, the better it will be for both Church and State." His influence, not only in Anglo-Saxony, but on the Continent of Europe, in that heyday of Liberalism, was profound as, *e.g.*, the work of Theodor Gompertz, in the reinterpretation of Greek philosophy in the light of that of Mill, is witness—but, far more, the political and institutional changes (although here we must allow for the greater, because more congenial, influence of France) of the epoch, traceable to this thought as the Philosopher of Liberation.

Academically speaking, it is not of course necessary that a philosopher (who is usually the occupant of a paid post in order to teach young men how difficult it is to know what they have known all along) or even a *philosophe* should be a wise man—etymology or no etymology. Popularly, however, those who spend their lives on the theory of conduct are supposed in the end to have some observations on conduct to offer superior to those of common men. John Stuart Mill commands respect by the integrity of his character, if not by its charm—frank to

* *Cf.* p. 417.

say, he was a good deal of an old woman. Not above writing sixty lines to advise a young author on publishing, or penning a letter, with pleasing solemnity, to a fourteen-year-old on corporal punishment, he was stiff, self-conscious and self-righteous. His early aspiration was "to be a Girondist in an English Convention." For him it was a natural one—but he lacked the Girondin emotion. What is abundantly clear is that neither Mill, father or son, had learned from Bentham any secrets about morals that enabled them to live their own lives with that tolerable happiness about which they talked so much—far less to announce a discovery to others. What Macaulay had prophesied took place. Mill, indeed, declared his bankruptcy, even by his revisions of the sacred formulae. Not unnaturally the leadership of thought about man's social life passed into other hands.

The age of Leibnitz, with his federal world of immortal spiritual atoms moving in pre-established harmony, and of Alexander Pope had drawn to its close. That "Whatever is, is right" was to be given by Hegel a new meaning unexpected by Pope. The belief of the Enlightenment in cerebral Reason, and infinite Progress, wanes, sickening from the poison of a scepticism secreted by intellect itself. Confidence weakens in that

> Self-love, to urge, and Reason, to retrain,

of Pope's *Essay on Man*. Voltaire could afford to mock at Dr. Pangloss, but he spoke more profoundly than he knew. The Providence of the Economists who, after a century, still secured that

> God and Nature link'd the gen'ral frame,
> And bade Self-love and Social be the same [Pope],

was becoming overworked. The Benthamite optimistic exposition was wearing thin. To Malthus, with his inconvenient questions, succeeded Darwin and then Nietzsche. The dominion of Locke was challenged by Hegel. To Mill succeeded Marx.

READING

J. S. Mill: *On Liberty*, Chaps. I–III.

BIBLIOGRAPHICAL NOTE

James Mill: *An Essay on Government*.
*J. S. Mill: *Autobiography*.
J. S. Mill: *On Representative Government*.
*Bertrand Russell: *Freedom versus Organization*, 1814–1914, 1934.
Leslie Stephen: *The Utilitarians*, Vols. II and III, 1900.
G. M. Young: *Portrait of an Age*, 1936.

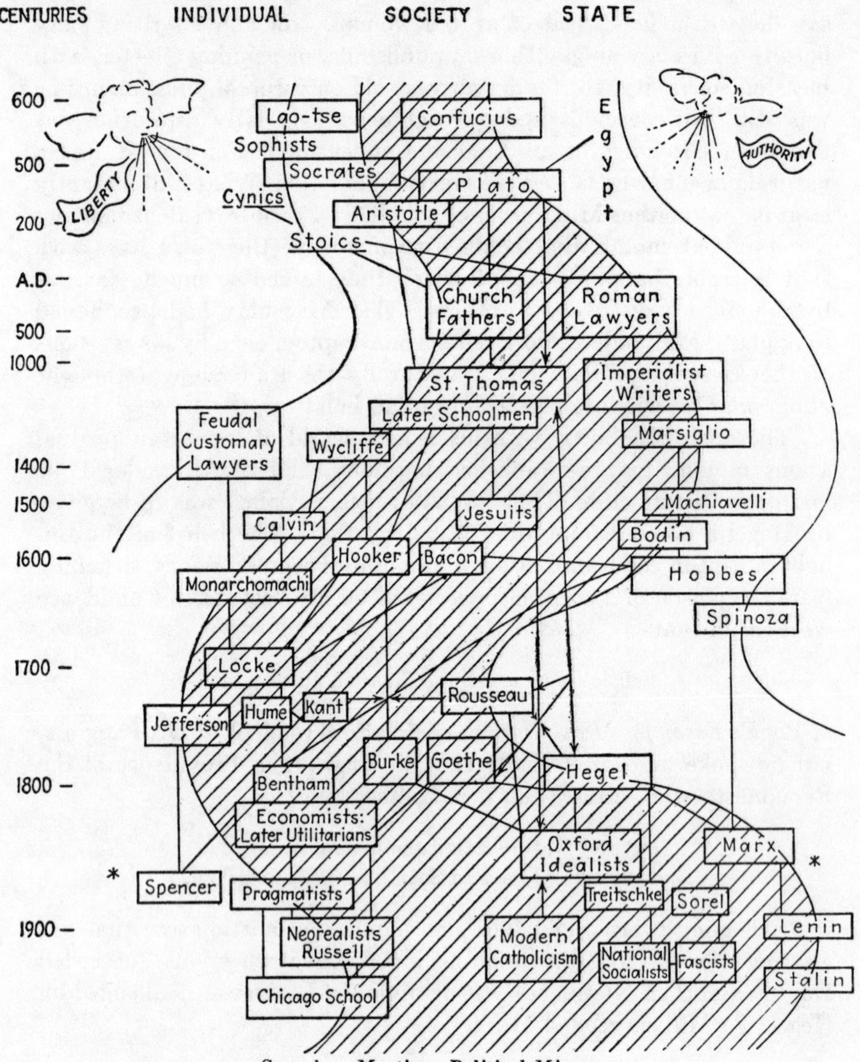

Speculum Mentis or Political Mirror.

*** Note the extremes meet. For reasons of convenience in drawing, this diagram is only approximately to scale.**

Chapter XIII

Individualists and Anarchists

1

JOHN STUART MILL marks the end of an epoch and is himself, although but partly consciously, transitional to a new age. Not all, however, were aware that the epoch was closing and that Cobden and the Manchester School—the politicians and economists who stood for one hundred per cent laissez-faire at home and Free Trade abroad—were not immortal.

In 1848, the editor of the *Economist* wrote about the Public Health Act, "suffering and evil are nature's admonitions; they cannot be got rid of; and the impatient attempts of benevolence to banish them from the world by legislation before it had learned their object and their end, have always been productive of more evil than good." It was in this spirit of economic orthodoxy that Gladstone's colleague, the great, religious and philanthropic politician, John Bright, maintained the "right" of children, of thirteen years and over, to work for longer than from 6.30 A.M. to 8.00 P.M.; and also argued against the placing of duties on slave-grown sugar imports.

The watchwords of the Manchester School were individual initiative: intelligent self-interest sanctioned (as said Paley and Whately) by God Himself; the natural and providential laws of economics; the right of a man to do what he will with his own; distrust of government; no interference with property; no government in business; and that the greatness of a nation depended on its industrial and commercial leaders, not its soldiers and politicians.

The mood persisted in the United States later than in Britain. It was directly connected with the Locke-Jefferson tradition. It was left for Mr. Justice Holmes to point out, to his colleagues of the Supreme Court of the United States, that their function was not to "enact M. Herbert Spencer's *Social Statics*."

Herbert Spencer (1820–1903) wings his solitary, individualistic flight across the scenes, after the rest of his breed have flown. His is the spirit of the classical economy—of Dupont de Nemours who declared that Natural Right is the right of a man to do that which is to his own advantage: "We are charged with our own preservation under penalty of suffering and death . . . the final degree of punishment decreed by this sovereign law is superior to every other interest and to every arbitrary law." It was on this basis that Spencer, in the days of and after Darwin, reconciled his individualism with his belief in a social organism and in sociology as a super-biology. To Herbert Spencer as exponent of political methodology and co-founder of sociology we shall return later.* Here we are only concerned with his political philosophy—begotten on the spirit of the classic economy by late Victorian Philistinism. "How, Mr. Spencer," asked George Eliot, "is it that there are no wrinkles on your forehead?" His reply was that he was never puzzled. His commentator's remark is that whenever he was confronted with a problem where solution was not obvious to him he would push it aside, and "abandon all conscious effort to solve it . . . no conscious effort, no weary drudgery or labour, nothing that education can ever supply; simply a succession of sudden inward flashes illuminating the whole of the darkened field."

Spencer was a self-educated man. In his case indeed the Almighty was relieved of a great responsibility. And he was precocious. A trained engineer at the age of seventeen, he was sub-editor of a journal called *The Pilot* at twenty-four. By the age of thirty he was editor of *The Economist*, and had published his *Social Statics*, in which he maintained the right of the law-abiding individual to "ignore" the state. His subsequent writings, in which he developed his Synthetic Philosophy, covered the fields of metaphysics and physics, biology, psychology and sociology. His broad biological knowledge and sudden inward flashes enabled him to detect the similarity between Mr. Gladstone, at once the Liberal leader (whom he respected) and the High Churchman (whom he detested) and an amphibian or frog, sometimes on dry land and sometimes sliding back into "the slimy waters of ecclesiasticism." Also he wrote his *Autobiography* in three volumes.

Frankly, the Bulwer Lyttons, who took him with them to Egypt, found him rather a bore. I cannot, however, agree with Mr. Keith Feiling that he was substantially without influence on his own times. Indeed no less a person than Somerset Maugham records his indebtedness. It is true that Spencer records, with horror, that the Cobden Club Prize of 1880 had been awarded to an essay referring to truth as

* *Cf.* p. 747.

being clouded over "by the *laissez-faire* fallacy!" Although the tide was running against him (and it would be grossly unfair to Spencer to conceal that he admitted this), his influence in Britain as a priest of Manchesterism and, still more, in America, was very far from inconsiderable.

The *Social Statics* (1850) of his earlier days—to which we shall revert—he declared later did not do justice to his more mature political thought. However, in the introduction to the articles republished as *The Man versus the State* (1884), Spencer stated that the views contained in this last were those he had held for twenty-four years unaltered. They may, therefore, be presumably taken as authoritative.

> Regulations have been made in yearly-growing numbers, restraining the citizen in directions where his actions were previously unchecked, and compelling actions which previously he might perform or not as he liked; and at the same time heavier public burdens, chiefly local, have further restricted his freedom, by lessening that portion of his earnings which he can spend as he pleases, and augmenting the portion taken from him to be spent as public agents please.

The Liberals had become Tories, if of a new type. Social legislation was pouring from the legislative mill—Bakehouse Regulation Act, Seed Supply (Ireland) Act, Cheap Trains Act—all of a kind with the bad, restrictive regulations of the Middle Ages against which Adam Smith had arisen in judgement. All, interferences with the law of supply and demand. "Everyone must see," observes Spencer in irony, "that the edicts issued by Henry VIII to prevent the lower classes from playing dice, cards, bowls, etc., were not more prompted by desire for popular welfare than were the Acts passed of late to check gambling."

Frankly, Spencer has no use for this legislation to protect the morals or—which is different—even to improve the condition of what he, the self-made man, refers to without inhibition as "the lower classes." Here he parts company with Mill. For Spencer there *are* lower classes, and these by Nature's law and Darwin's gospel—"good-for-nothings, who in one way or other live on the good-for-somethings." The notorious Jukeses—two hundred criminals from one "gutter-child," Margaret—are brought into the argument. Why there should be "gutter-children," and whether the two hundred came from the gutter or the child, disturbed the Blessed Thomas More but not Herbert Spencer.

Spencer is horrified that someone had even referred to the need for organizing pleasure as much as work. This social legislation has a momentum. Where will it end? Certainly in a rise in taxes . . . ultimately in slavery. For "all socialism involves slavery." See Rome, and its fall. "Increase of public burdens may end in forced cultivation under public control. . . . Liberties must be surrendered in proportion as their material welfares are cared for." "Surely," exclaims an objector, "you would not have this misery continue!" But this sentiment is moved by three ideas, all wrong: that all suffering ought to be prevented [it is not Nature's way]; that evils moved from one place are not moved into another; that the State is the appropriate instrument for reform. It is a delusion that an "ill-working humanity may be framed into well-working institutions."

There is more than a touch of belief in Original Sin in Spencer—as it were, economic original sin. But if man is salvable, the Collective Bureaucrat is not. "It is not to the State that we owe the multitudinous useful inventions from the spade to the telephone." The communal régime appropriate for the family of young, the Family Ethics, must be grown out of and repudiated in mature life, when to further the inferior individual is to degrade the species. No society "will be able to hold its own in the struggle with other societies, if it disadvantages its superior units that it may advantage its inferior units." There is a "discipline pitiless in the working out of good." Interfering benevolent social legislation penalizes the Poor Richards, the "widow who washes or sews from dawn to dark to feed her fatherless little ones," the thrifty, the hard-working self-helpers who are Nature's favourites. And the very people who use this humanitarian argument are quite unshocked by sending thousands to be slaughtered in a war.

For Spencer the forces of reaction are the forces of militarism—as a Sociologist he scientifically knows this. And the forces of progress are those of industry. Before we listen to the objections of men who talk of the oppressiveness of healthy industrial competition, let us know whether they will or will not recruit men to be slaughtered in a war or a class civil war. Malthus and Darwin are right: we must have some selective agencies. Which?

Will not, however, the majority take the bit between their teeth—make regulations, whatever sociologists may say, to suit their own immediate convenience? Spencer himself condemns a "political serfdom of the unrepresented." What about the sovereignty of Parliament?

There we come round again to the proposition that *the assumed divine right of parliaments, and the implied divine right of majorities, are superstitions.* While men have abandoned the old theory respecting the source of State-authority, they have retained a belief in that unlimited extent of State-authority which rightly accompanied the old theory, but does not rightly accompany the new one. Unrestricted power over subjects, rationally ascribed to the ruling man when he was held to be a deputy-god, is now ascribed to the ruling body, the deputy godhood of which nobody asserts. . . . The function of Liberalism in the past was that of putting a limit to the power of Kings. The function of true Liberalism in the future will be that of putting a limit to the power of Parliaments.

This sovereignty of the majority is the Great Political Superstition which leads to the Coming Slavery. It is not so in primitive societies: "the peaceful Arafuras" recognize the rights of property without there being any authority over them; there is "scrupulous regard for one another's claims among the Todos, Santals, Lepchas, Bodo, Chakmas, Jakuns, etc.," even among "the utterly uncivilized Wood-Veddahs." In Ashantee [far Ashantee] the attempt to change some customs, doubtless matrimonial, has caused a king's dethronement.

The Tory and the Socialist are yoke horses pulling towards this slavery—both militarists at heart. Now,

by the survival of the fittest, the militant type of society becomes characterized by profound faith in the governing power, joined with a loyalty causing submission to it in all matters whatever. And there must tend to be established among those who speculate about political affairs in a militant society, a theory giving form to the needful ideas and feelings; accompanied by assertions that the law-giver if not divine in nature is divinely directed, and that unlimited obedience to him is divinely ordered . . . in Russia, where that universality of State-regulation which characterizes the militant type of society has been carried furthest, we see this ambition pushed to its extreme. Says Mr. Wallace, quoting a passage from a play: "All men, even shopkeepers and cobblers, aim at becoming officers, and the man who has passed his whole life without official rank seems to be not a human being."

That, although not unanticipated by Plato, was not a false prophecy on Spencer's part. What, then, can make headway against this human tendency to fetish worship? Only the principles of an industrial civilization—peaceful if competitive (the next evolutionary stage on in the biological struggle). "In the absence of an agreement, the supremacy of a majority over a minority does not exist at all. . . . The real issue is whether the lives of citizens are more interfered with than they were; not the nature of the agency which interferes with them." There are indeed natural rights. And, although there was no Original Social Contract, common sense indicates that the limits of state action lie in agreement—*not* majority agreement, but the agreement of all, *i.e.*, the terms upon which men would *now* be prepared to enter upon civil society (not the same thing, as Locke showed long ago, as natural society) if a Social Contract were instantly proposed to them. Spencer, as a sociologist, knows that the Quakers are dying out. Therefore measures for defensive (not offensive) warfare, and for domestic security, including the enforcement of contracts, would win universal consent. So also, oddly enough, assent would be given to the thesis: that the will of the majority should prevail on "the use of the territory . . . the modes in which, and conditions under which, parts of the surface or sub-surface, may be utilized . . . the terms on which portions of it might be employed for raising food, for making means of communication, and for other purposes."

What then of utility? The utilitarians are at fault, as customarily expounded. Immediate utility is no adequate touchstone of legislation. There are, adds Spencer, with more wisdom than is his wont, natural laws. How can the ultimate rights of the people flow from a popular sovereign which this people has created, as Matthew Arnold seems foolishly to maintain?

> The changes of law now from time to time made after resistance, are similarly made in pursuance of current ideas concerning the requirements of justice: ideas which, instead of being derived from the law, are opposed to the law. For example, that recent Act which gives to a married woman a right of property in her own earnings, evidently originated in the consciousness that the natural connexion between labour expended and benefit enjoyed, is one which should be maintained in all cases. The reformed law did not create the right, but recognition of the right created the reformed law.

Might not then social legislation be dictated by a recognition of the "requirements of justice" and by an attempt to give expression to the natural rights of man based on his instinct for freedom to develop, for good health, and for adequate play? Spencer is at pains to insist that the Course of Evolution is not some external Fate—would be different if, *e.g.*, the philanthropic impulses were not there. What is required is the "uniting philanthropic energy with philosophic calm"—this presumably would lead to the maximum integration of personality with the minimum dissipation of force. What precise shape that philanthropy would take is not quite clear; but undoubtedly it would facilitate the survival of the fittest—that is, of those fittest to survive, or the success of the successful. Which, in itself, is a glittering prize. But to Mr. Hyndman's Social Democratic Federation notion of "agricultural and industrial *armies* under State-control," however immediately successful as a competitive instrument, Spencer took the strongest exception. "Be it or be it not true that Man is shapen in iniquity and conceived in sin, it is unquestionably true that Government is begotten of aggression [this is not Pope Gregory VII, but Herbert Spencer] and by aggression."

Herbert Spencer never contemplated the possibility that the extension of economic security might be the guaranty of day-by-day liberty. He could only see that the final political liberties were not worth sacrificing to subordinate economic securities. In his *Principles of Ethics*, Part IV (1891), Spencer provided a formula of just liberty which he had anticipated in *Social Statics*. "Every man is free to do that which he wills, provided that he infringes not the equal freedom of any other man." In the *Social Statics* Spencer had claimed this formula as an original discovery. Professor F. W. Maitland pointed out that Kant had said it a century earlier, and in the *Principles*, appendix, Spencer handsomely admits that "among the tracks of thought pursued by multitudinous minds in the course of ages, nearly all must have been entered upon, if not explored," although of course Kant was only an a-priori philosopher.

Nor could Spencer see that the law of supply and demand is no less interfered with by the graining and directing of supply, arbitrarily in certain societies, in accordance with the demands of the rich—whether the law tolerates the rich made such by creative gifts and by hard work only; or also by speculation and by confiscation; or even by straight brigandage and (as among moss-riders) honest theft—as it is by the encouragement of demand by man-made social arrangements. Concerning such minutiae of social "pull" the laws were apparently to be silent.

"*Administrative Nihilism*" was the name that the great scientist, Thomas Huxley (1825–1895), gave to Spencer's scheme. However, the criticism of Herbert Spencer's political theory is best left until we have reviewed the opposing collectivist movement which was receiving inspiration from Germany. It was to Germany that Herbert Spencer himself turned, with his appeal to the *Natur-recht* philosophers, as it had been to Germany that the younger Mill, as well as Coleridge and Carlyle, turned. Let us, then, view the development, first, of individualistic philosophy in that land of Luther and of the claim of the Protestant conscience.

2

Immanuel Kant (1724–1804), Scotsman by descent, son of a Königsberg saddler, is almost the first of a long line of philosophers of the chair. In the history of political theory, professional academics have hitherto been conspicuous by their absence. The great philosophers have been even soldiers, such as Descartes; men of the world, such as Hume; have, like Leibnitz, moved at courts. Kant scarcely wandered outside his own town, and after two applications for professorial rank had been refused, in 1770 settled down as Professor of Logic at Königsberg, with the reputation of a taste for astronomy and ethnology.

Twice he contemplated marriage but was unable to discover an appropriate formula of proposal. He contented himself with developing, in his anthropological lectures, the theory that the human baby must once have been very different since, had it howled in the jungle as loudly as it howled in Königsberg, it would assuredly have been devoured by wild animals. He also held that, in this rational universe, the other planets were probably inhabited. There was no reason to suppose, in these earlier days, that Dr. Kant would ever set either Thames or Pregel afire. He was a methodical man who, according to the poet Heine, took his afternoon "constitutional" so punctually that Königsberg citizens could set their clocks by him; practised breathing through the nose; and would place his handkerchief on the other side of the room in order to have perforce the exercise, when he desired to blow his nose, of walking across his room. A man of whimsical humours, Immanuel Kant was profoundly shocked by Hume, who had taken the lynch-pin of Cause out of the world, and left only Association—no *necessary* cause and effect; only *probable* association; no logic; no syllogistic reason; no rational universe; perhaps no God . . . although Hume, with customary bravura, had said that only a sceptic about truth could be a loyal member of the Church of England. Now Hume had rested his argument on Locke's thesis that knowledge is ultimately derived from the senses. "My question," says Kant, "is what we can hope to achieve with reason, when all the material and assistance of experience are taken away." That is the topic of the *Critique of Pure Reason* (1781).

Kant established to his own satisfaction the *a priori* moulding power of mind; but incidentally admitted that, although there was a Thing-in-itself (not only Berkeley's God on the other side of the veil, throwing upon the screen of mind the Universe itself as one great Fantasy), man could not know it. What then? Has not Kant himself shown that we cannot know God, how He exists, where He exists, perhaps if He exists? "They say," melancholically explained Kant to his friend, confidant and man-servant Lampe, "that, in my book, I have taken away God." "Do not trouble, Herr Professor," replied Lampe, "write another book and put him back again." Kant's mother had been a religious rigorist of the German Pietist persuasion. Never had her son doubted these values or that there was a moral order of the universe. Dr. Kant took up his pen. There was a Practical, a Moral Judgement. In his *Critique of the Practical Reason* he showed God as the Author of the Moral Universe, nay as the guarantor that there was that universe. God must be because a moral world must be: and the moral world must be because God was. Briefly, Kant returns to the Protestant moral sense. Man *knows* that justice is good; and the world is worthless to him unless his value is realized—at least in the long, long run. We are not far from St. Thomas' doctrine of the implanted promise of immortality and divine justice.

The moral sense is then the key word, conscience: its categorical imperative, duty. What application has this to Politics? For one thing, a categorical imperative to build a League of Nations, and without delay. To this theme we shall revert.* For another, a basic, *a priori* theory of Liberty and Right. Kant must go carefully here. He is a salaried German professor, *i.e.*, a civil servant of the Prussian Government. The *Critique of Pure Reason*, scandalous to the orthodox, was published under the great Frederick. His nephew was of a pettier mould. And, categorical imperative or no categorical imperative, Frederick William II was King of Prussia. "If everything you say has to be true, it is yet not your duty to tell the whole truth in public," writes Kant on a revealing slip of paper—but also "To deny one's inner convictions is mean." Not until Rousseau's *Social Contract* had come by the mail-coach to Königsberg and, for once, the afternoon "constitutional" had been interrupted, had Kant ever been interested in politics. Cursed fate that he, metaphysician and humanist, had this categorical urge to write on these impassioned issues of politics and religion.

It is a fashionable belief today, much encouraged by journalists, that lucidity is the test of a great mind. The history of great minds unfortunately does not bear the thesis out. They have preferred accuracy. Kant, who scarcely achieved correct grammar, certainly cannot be accused of lucidity. In a pamphlet on *Principles of Political Right* (1793), marvellously contorted in style and written against Hobbes, all the machinery of the *a priori* metaphysical steam hammer is used to show that resistance to the Head of the State, who is above the law, is the worst of crimes. It conduces to Anarchy, with all its abominations. Indeed if those who had led the revolutions in Britain,

* *Cf*. p. 700.

Switzerland and so forth had only failed, they would have been regarded as great political criminals. So much for the demolition of one Dr. Achenwall, who had seemed to maintain the opposite—and not much here with which Hobbes would disagree.

What then? There are, Kant says, certain rights, founded on rational principles, which the Head of the State *ought* to respect. Such rights are: liberty as a man and equality as a subject, *i.e.*, equality before the law. "Right in general may be defined as the limitation of the freedom of any individual to the extent of its agreement with the freedom of all other individuals, in so far as this is possible by a universal law." There is no right where a violation is involved of this principle of impartiality. A pyramidical society built with the hierarchy of *ability* is right and proper: a nobility, exercising power, with status determined by *birth*, violates the principle of right. If, of course, the ruler does not in fact respect these rights, at least we have the satisfaction of knowing that the ruler is doing what is "not done."

What of progress? For one thing, this will be aided by the Liberty of the Press which Kant, as a bold pioneer out there in East Prussia, thinks the ruler ought to respect. But there is another guaranty. It is sometimes asserted that no one has expressed a belief in automatic Progress. This, however, is precisely what Kant, in *The Principle of Progress*, does express.

> *Fata volentem ducunt, nolentem trahunt.** Under the Nature of things, Human Nature is also to be taken into account; and as in human nature there is always a living respect for Right and Duty, I neither can nor will regard it as so sunk in evil that the practical moral Reason could ultimately fail to triumph over this evil, even after many of its attempts have failed.

Briefly, for Kant the Moral Reason is a substance, a presiding entity, otherwise called Providence. No wonder, therefore, that rebellion is superfluous.

What matters, for Kant, is Duty, *not* Happiness. It is the opposite thesis to that of Locke and his followers. Happiness is the lax, chaotic, experimental principle, not at all logical, like Duty. It is interesting in this connection to observe how Kant treats social or civil Liberty.

> No one has a right to compel me to be happy in the peculiar way in which he may think of the well-being of other men; but everyone is entitled to seek his own happiness in the way that seems to him best, if it does not infringe the liberty of others in striving after a similar end for themselves when their

* "The Fates lead the willing, drag the resisting."

Liberty is capable of consisting with the Right of Liberty in all others according to possible universal laws. . . . Such a Government would be the greatest conceivable despotism.

This strangely involved, anti-utilitarian formula is not to be taken as reactionary. It is a covert attack upon Benevolent Despotism—and, incidentally, upon Catholicism and Platonism, both of which claimed to know, better than the individual, how each man should avoid that true unhappiness and slavery which is sin. When a Government decides to ensure not Justice but Happiness for its people, it is on the road to Despotism—a thesis not without relevance to contemporary Moscow, Berlin and Rome.

Kant argues that each man, exercising his own Protestant spiritual freedom—and Kant is, even unwittingly, the man who gave Protestantism a belated philosophy—must make the discovery of what is sin for himself, guided by rational maxims and the intuitive light of conscience. Intimately connected with this is Kant's famous maxim that *each man must be treated* (being an immortal, free soul, having value because of that freedom of will) *as an end in himself and not as a means*. No wonder Kant proceeds to a denunciation, bitter for him, of war and of the spending of money on arms. His doctrine is the antithesis of the Catholic one of the Social Organism.

Wilhelm von Humboldt describes Kant's political writings as "on the whole, not very important." Bertrand Russell has gone farther and has described him as "a mere misfortune." There is, however, one brief pamphlet, not less obscure in diction than most of Kant's writings, of which every word requires to be weighed. The place to discuss this profound little study is in a work on methodology. Shortly, however, the argument is again one of inevitable development. Again we are told that Nature—which is a *sobriquet* for Bishop Bossuet's God—has "designs" in history. But the point of the argument is that the social order (as indeed Hobbes said) comes out of men's egoistic natures. Even without their conscious collaboration or any formal compacts (and Kant restates a doctrine of a rational, tacit contract) men have to discover, if life is to be tolerable, a *modus vivendi* in civil society through government. Their very natures goad them on. But—and this is the contribution—this original egoistic nature is not merely nasty and brutish. On the contrary, it is precisely man's claim, of infinite value, to Liberty that is the original motive force which constructs Authority as that sanction of Law which regulates just Liberty.

The means which Nature employs to bring about the development of all the capacities implanted in men, is *their mutual Antagonism in society,* but only so far as this antagonism becomes at length the cause of an Order among them that is regulated by Law.

Kant here comes as near as any writer to insight into the essential relation of Liberty and Authority. It is a theme developed later, at great length, by Professor Rudolf von Ihering in his *Law as a Means to an End* (1877).

Kant's views on happiness so far colour his political theory as to demand comment. Not happiness but duty, ordered by the categorical imperative of conscience and delineated by reason, is the true guide for individual conduct. It must be remembered that the whole background of the German thought of this period, from Leibnitz on through Wolff, is mathematical and abstract. This and Protestantism are the dominant influences.

Reason prescribes to men so to behave as they could suppose it would be good if all behaved in the same fashion—*ceteris paribus* (but Kant did not add *ceteris paribus*).* No privilege in morals, no indulgence. What, however, is the final object of the performance of duty—what object for society? Moral progress, is Kant's answer, thanks to life in accordance with reason. Admit that we have eternity before us in which immortal souls will have the justice done them which they lacked in their lifetime, what yet is the content of this justice and moral progress? Is it not, for example, the development of benevolence and the enjoyment of it? The answer is that, the enlargement of human happiness apart, Kant visualizes, as the end of progress, the development of human powers as such, of the creative rational powers, and especially of the rational respect for justice. However removed from the manners of the ape, this may seem an arid and cheerless prospect; but of justice Kant says, "*If justice perishes it is of no value any longer that man live on the earth.*" It is an heroic affirmation of the importance in civilization of values.

Injustice, however, still lived on the earth. There was Kant—but there was also Frederick William II. In 1794 the King of Prussia issued his decree. The great formalist philosopher was accused of desecrating the dogmas of Scripture. What now was Kant's "duty"? He collapsed—promised to write and speak no more on religion. The Delphic Oracle of conscience had given forth an uncertain sound—should *all* deny the truth that was in them? or, again, should *all* resist their lawful sov-

* "Other things being equal."

ereign? It was poor Archbishop Cranmer's old problem. A fortunate but irrational accident solved the high moral dilemma, most informally. Frederick William died; and Kant lived to fight again and write the *Contest of the Faculties*. The social battle of liberty and authority had reproduced itself—but conveniently, *inside* the mind of Kant, as between its faculties. Kant, after all, was a critical idealist.

Wilhelm von Humboldt (1767–1835) was the especial source of inspiration, as we have said, of John Stuart Mill in his third phase. Like Kant, von Humboldt had read his Rousseau and had been profoundly influenced by the romantic individualism of the author of *Émile*. The important line, however, of spiritual inheritance is to Mill through von Humboldt from his friend, the poet, Wolfgang von Goethe (1749–1832). The school, growing up at the end of the age of Lessing and Winckelmann, in its wider circle includes Novalis with his cult of "the beautiful soul" and comes to terms with the Christian religion through a revived mysticism. In England, in its more strictly classical form, it finds expression in Matthew Arnold and his group and even in Walter Pater with his famous injunction "to burn always with this hard, gem-like flame."

The great Goethe himself was a pacifist who yet recognized in Napoleon a world-spirit; a poet who felt that some new Cervantes was needed to write some new *Don Quixote* ridiculing the duellings about honour of the nations; an administrator who frankly preferred order to liberty with disorder. It was, after all, always possible to retire to one's estate and "cultivate one's garden" under tyranny (but not under mass violence), although Goethe was philosopher anarchist to the point of objecting to growth of regulation, at least for creative minds.

Goethe's thought was developed against the background of Benevolent Despotism—and of the French Revolution. Frankly, he preferred the despotism to the popular revolution, provided the despotism were enlightened. As Voltaire had said, rather be governed by one lion than by "a hundred subaltern tigers." Thomas Carlyle, we shall see, was Goethe's, perhaps wrong-headed, disciple. The Goethean attitude tends to develop as a belief that "politics" is relatively unimportant; as a belief that there are more important things "beyond politics"; as mysticism or even as that poor bungle, "art for art's sake." So far as this will bear examination it is a view close to that of St. Thomas, that the Catholic Church is unconcerned about forms of secular government, provided that the Church might live its own [corporate] life in its own way. The Goethean view is based upon a profound cynicism concerning the slogans for which men fight—"justice," "liberty," "nationality," "democracy"; upon a magnificent indifference to how they earn their bread and still more their butter; upon a belief that one could be tolerant of any civil regime that did not poke its secular dirty fingers into the development of a creative civilization; and upon a contempt for fools who indulged in the otiose sport of making themselves objectionable to the men of blood and the government. It could appreciate Schiller's apostrophe of Wallenstein as the hero; but, for the mass, it was best for them to recognize that they could not draw the bow of Ulysses and there was much to be said for Bishop Berkeley's doctrine of passive obedience, the little flaccid brother of non-violent resistance.

The outlook is through and through aristocratic—concerned with freedom for the creator, the genius, the world-controller, but not troubling its head about the mass, Mr. Aldous Huxley's "betas" and "gammas." It has not confronted the Catholic issue, as St. Thomas had, of the ordering of the corporate life and of the objective, actual relations between spiritual and temporal, eternal and secular, the few concerned with ideal vocation and the many concerned with food and drink. It had a "good view" of human nature and hoped for the best. When disappointed, philosophic anarchism tended to change its tune, as we shall see. In Goethe's case, however, the combination of individualism and tradition, individualism enriched into personality by the nourish-milk of tradition in culture—the recognition of a Grand Tradition along with Faustian quest—is so profound as to save Goethe from this fate. Although riding a Teutonic horse of Imagination—*furor teutonicus*—restive under the rein, Goethe maintained Reason, the Reason of Hellene and Schoolman, Humanist and Scientist, still as charioteer. Another generation, and the charioteer is thrown.

The Prussian nobleman, ambassador, minister of Public Instruction, von Humboldt, shares with the French nobleman, Mirabeau, a horror of "*la fureur de gouverner, la plus funeste maladie des gouvernements modernes*." With Goethe, and after the style of the English Lord Shaftesbury, the stress is on the civilized cultivation of the personality. The emphasis in this philosophy has shifted from the abstract reason to the creative individual. There is a tendency to stress the meaning of chance, and a reaction against the French influence and its doctrine of rational progress. There is an immensely significant beginning of a reaction, following Rousseau, against systematic reason or the understanding; but still the development of personality is to take place in accordance with "the eternal and commendable dictate of reason."

Von Humboldt writes to a feminine friend:

> In the events of the world and the events which whole states experience, the intrinsically important thing remains that which relates to the activity, the intellect and the feelings of individuals. Man is the centre everywhere and each human being remains in the end solitary.

Wilhelm von Humboldt is in many ways the rural solitary, interested in birds, engaging in politics in despite of himself. His admiration is for what Kant would have called the "self-dependent" peasant farmer. The bureaucrats of Berlin were upstart intruders. What matters is that individuals should learn, through their own choice, experience and discipline, how to live. So far as social aid was required, that of village and family was less injurious than that of the state. *The provision of security, and this alone, is the business of the state.* Von Humboldt's views on the end of man in the integration of a personality of developed powers was quoted by J. S. Mill and has already been cited here.* Happiness, in the Benthamite sense, this nobleman rejects, as the end of social action, in favour of a doctrine, semi-Kantian but far more Shaftesburian and aesthetic. He writes to Madam de Staël: "*L'homme n'est pas fait pour être précisément heureux, mais pour remplir l'existence telle que le sort l'a lui donnée.*"† In his *Ideas to Determine the Limits of State Activity* (1792, but discreetly not published in full until 1851), he writes:

> The happiness for which man is plainly destined, is no other than that which his own energies enable him to secure; and the very nature of such a self-dependent position furnishes him means whereby to discipline his intellect and cultivate his character. . . . This individual vigour, then, and manifold diversity, combine themselves in originality; and hence, that on which the consummate grandeur of our nature ultimately depends,—that towards which every human being must ceaselessly direct his efforts, and on which especially those who design to influence their fellow men must ever keep their eyes, is the individuality of Power and Development. . . . The evil results of a too extended solicitude on the part of the State, are still more strikingly manifested in the suppression of all active energy, and necessary deterioration of the moral character. . . . Any State interference in private affairs, not directly implying violence done to individual rights, should be absolutely condemned.

* *Cf.* p. 397.

† "Man is not made to be precisely happy, but to fulfil such an existence as his lot has given him." On this aesthetic judgment, *vide* Hume's *Treatise*.

Although von Humboldt is right in saying that state measures cannot always meet individual cases, it cannot be said that the recent flight of the Soviet aviators over the North Pole demonstrates that a regime of state solicitude necessarily destroys active energy, although it may, of course, liquidate unwanted variety.

This "rich variety" was the foundation stone of the political structure of von Humboldt and his followers. Unlike Hume he was not prepared to welcome a strong, authoritarian government, inculcating certain habits. And, unlike Hume, individualists of the type of von Humboldt regard the business of constitution-making with indifference, as mechanical. They would assert that their concern is with culture, not constitution-mongery. They would have approved of Aldous Huxley's "Savage," that "world-controller" *manqué* in *Brave New World* (1932), although of course a savage of a very cultivated order.

The influence of German Classical thought of the Goethe circle (deeply permeated indeed by Rousseauite Romanticism and specifically German non-classical influences) crossed, not only the Channel, but the Atlantic. Here it found an individualistic Protestantism of the eighteenth century, that was profoundly suspicious of the State but that had lost its early religious grip, awaiting refertilization. German immigrants were bringing their ideas, although more especially after 1848. Ralph Waldo Emerson (who, like Schopenhauer, was looking as far afield as India for inspiration) was listening for sounds of the Over-soul.

3

HENRY THOREAU (1817–1862) was another of the bird-loving brethren. Son of the local pencil-maker in Concord, Harvard student, he took a room in the Emerson house until he decided, in 1845, to build a hut at Walden, fifteen feet by ten, with a borrowed axe and at a total cost of $28.12. Thoreau—flitting through the woods at nightfall, with a ledge inside his hat for botanical specimens; taking the reluctant Hawthorne down to the swamp's edge to look at the flora; daring to ask the fundamental question: "Why community?"

Thoreau had little patience even with the mild utopian (and not unsuccessful) experiment of Brook Farm. "I had rather keep bachelor's hall in hell than go to board in heaven." "Doing good," reforming others, was a foul thing. The aristocrat Jefferson had, like the aristocrat von Humboldt, praised the rural life. Henry Thoreau still found it feasible to practice it self-sufficiently. At other times Thoreau was writer or township schoolmaster. Wilhelm von Humboldt had been minister of public instruction. It is interesting to note how many of these near-anarchists are educators—trying to form a theory of politics on the deeper basis of a theory of education.

Not that Henry Thoreau produces anything, in his *Essays*, very systematic. Disliking reformers, he yet found a hero in John Brown, the Slavery Abolitionist. Henry Thoreau, like Herbert Spencer, aspired to ignore the State. He was fastidious about paying taxes (others had a habit, being New Englanders and sympathetic, of paying them for him); he disapproved of too much that governments spend their money on. "Men," said William Penn, the Quaker, "must either be governed by God or they must be ruled by tyrants." The implicit belief, however, in that remark, in a natural "candle of reason," was not entirely appreciated by the whimsical Thoreau.

> *That government is best which governs not at all;* and when men are prepared for it, that will be the kind of government which they will have. . . . *A government in which the majority rule in all cases cannot be based on justice, even as far as men understand it.* . . . I think we should be men first, and subjects afterward. It is not desirable to cultivate a respect for law, so much as for the right. . . . If a thousand men were not to pay their tax-bills this year, that would not be a violent bloody measure, as it would be to pay them, and enable the State to commit violence and shed innocent blood. . . . Under a government which imprisons any unjustly, the true place for a just man is also a prison. . . . Let your life be a counterfriction to stop the machine.

So Thoreau wrote in his essay on *Civil Disobedience* (1840). He adds, in a style reminiscent of Kant: "The character inherent in the American people has done all that has been accomplished; and it would have done somewhat more, if the government had not sometimes got in its way."

Thoreau returned to the thought and feeling of Rousseau, in his first phase of praise of the simple life.* "This world is a place of business," complains Thoreau, "there is no Sabbath." But Henry Thoreau was equally capable of praise of Thomas Carlyle. He is markworthy as an expression of the grand New England spirit, with its stress on personal liberty. There is a radical challenge in the phrase, "I feel that any connection with and obligation to society are still very slight and transient . . . The community has no bribe that will tempt a wise man." But it cannot be said that Thoreau has attained intellectual coherence. The statement, even today, has a certain vogue, "What is called politics is comparatively something so superficial and inhuman,

* *Cf.* p. 447.

that, practically, I have never fairly recognized that it concerns me at all." It is periodically echoed by literary critics. But it is not a wise saying, save in the one sense that civilization matters more than nation or class or party. Plato had better ideas.

The stately Emerson, friend of the Boston Brahmins, in his essay on Politics went to the extent of agreeing with his protégé Thoreau that "we live in a very low state of the world, and pay unwilling tribute to governments founded on force . . . with the appearance of the wise man, the State expires."

> Not the less does nature continue to fill the heart of youth with suggestions of this enthusiasm, and there are new men,—if indeed I can speak in the plural number,—more exactly, I will say, I have just been conversing with one man, to whom no weight of adverse experience will make it for a moment appear impossible, that thousands of human beings might exercise towards each other the grandest and simplest sentiments, as well as a knot of friends, or a pair of lovers.

4

Count Leo Tolstoi (1828–1910) lived in a different world from the schoolmaster of Concord. It was, however, also an agricultural world and one strongly impregnated with religion and the sense of sin. As Puritan Independency and Quakerism were in the air of America so Nihilism was (as we shall see*) in the air of the Russian Empire. In both countries the decay of conventional religion was leading to a re-examination of the basis of Christianity. Tolstoi, like Thoreau, was led by his meditations to a violent conviction of the iniquity of war, a distrust of the military state and an objection to the payment of taxes for these purposes. With this, moreover, for Tolstoi, as for Rousseau, was conjoined a reaction against an over-cultivated courtly civilization. Further, of learned exposition to the effect that Tolstoi's cure for social evils was founded upon, and limited by, his acquaintance with the Russian *mir* (village community) Thoreau's like theme is sufficient refutation.

Not that the Russian is not dominant in Tolstoi. There is in him a strongly masochistic vein, appearing in *The Kreutzer Sonata;* in *Resurrection;* and in his correspondence. (It shows in his countryman Dostoievski.) It affects his attitude—utterly un-Greek and un-Humanist—to civilization. The criticism of the Greek ideal must include consideration of the great Russian who maltreated his wife and returned to primitive Christianity.

* *Cf.* p. 427.

In his book *What Must We Do Then?* (1885) Tolstoi begins with a macabre description of the evils of contemporary society, peculiarly Russian. The life of the drunken prostitute, the penniless, consumptive laundry-maid is described. One could admire the imaginative human sympathy displayed, could one rid one's mind of a certain sense of zest in the description.

> "I want to help my father by my labor," says a common un-learned man. "I want also to marry; but instead, I am taken and sent to Kazan, to be a soldier for six years. I leave the military service. I want to plough the ground, and earn food for my family; but I am not allowed to plough for one hundred versts around me, unless I pay money, which I have not got, and pay it to those men who do not understand how to plough, and who require for the land so much money, that I must give them all my labour to procure it: however, I still manage to save something, and I want to give my savings to my children; but a police sergeant comes to me, and takes from me all I have saved for taxes; I earn a little more, and am again deprived of it. All my activity is under the influence of state demands; and it appears to me that the bettering of my position, and that of my brethren, will follow our liberation from the demands of the state." But he is told, such reasoning is the result of his ignorance.

It is the *Ancien Régime*. What is its defence? The economists discuss supply and demand, but never ask the fundamental question: Why the State? They recognize the influence of the oppressor as a natural condition of the life of a people.

> So-called science supports this superstition with all its power, and with the utmost zeal. This superstition resembles exactly the religious one, and consists in affirming, that, besides the duties of man to man, there are still more important duties towards an imaginary being, which theologians call God, and political science the State.

The state is then a system for raising taxes to protect property. But this property system is largely built up because some men free themselves from the labour, *the manual labour*, proper to all, and impose it on others. They are only entitled to do this if these, the few, regard themselves as beings of a different clay or at least having a special function; or if all men recognize this especial task as socially useful. But neither is true: there is no evidence of this special function. Ask the working man if he recognizes the utility of the priest, artist, royalty owner, shareholder, hereditary rich man, or civil servant. Let us have the simple life *au* Rousseau (*first* phase) and primitive communism which shall yet be so primitive as to be free and anarchist.

What is it, then, that confirms the theory that state activity is useful to men? Only the fact that those men who perform it, firmly believe it to be useful, and that it has been always in existence; but so have always been not only useless institutions, but very pernicious ones, like slavery, prostitution, and wars. . . . The lie is the same, because the men who justify themselves are in the same false position. The lie consists in the fact that, before beginning to reason about the advantages conferred on the people by men who have freed themselves from labor, certain men, Pharaohs, priests, or we ourselves,—educated people,—assume this position, and only afterwards excogitate the justification for it. . . .

Comte's positive philosophy and its outcome, the doctrine that mankind is an organism; Darwin's doctrine of the struggle for existence, directing life and its conclusion, the teaching of diversity of human races, the now so popular anthropology, biology, and sociology,—all have the same aim. These sciences have become favorites because they all serve for the justification of the existing fact of some men being able to free themselves from the human duty of labor, and to consume other men's labor.

Tolstoi, convinced of the sinfulness of his present life, renounced the title (although not always the manner) of a count, divested himself of his estate, being ultimately persuaded to make it over to his wife as guardian for the children—women's rights were "astounding nonsense": what mattered was the simple life; no competition for careers; and large families—and lived, so far as a count in Russia could, the life of the unwashed peasant, near to the soil.

What then was to happen to science, art and education? In each case their object was the benefit of the *moujik*. But with the peasant and worker they had—being so grand—lost all touch. These no longer understood. "Should we satisfy their want of knowledge by giving them spectrum analysis?" What is needed, remarks the world's greatest novelist in remorse about his fame, is proletarian art and science.

Food is, indeed, necessary, but perhaps what I offer is not food at all. This very thing has happened with our science and art. And to us it seems that when we add to a Greek word the termination *logy*, and call this science, it will be science indeed; and if we call an indecency, like the dancing of naked women, by the Greek word "choreography," and term it art, it will be art indeed.

But, however much we may say this, the business which we are about, in counting up the insects, and chemically analyzing the contents of the Milky Way, in painting water-nymphs and historical pictures, in writing novels, and in composing symphonies, this, our business, will not become science or art until it is willingly accepted by those for whom it is being done.

As for engineering developments, these might be well enough, but "owing to some unlucky chance, recognized, too, by men of science, this progress has not as yet ameliorated, but it has rather deteriorated, the condition of working men."

It is possible, and even justifiable, to dismiss Tolstoi's attitude to advance in civilization through science as (with Rousseau's, in his earlier phase*) frankly reactionary. Tolstoi, however, it will be observed, unlike Kant, is interested in happiness. But his trust, like that of those who lived in the great, still rural Republic of the West, is still in an agricultural happiness, discovered in pursuing the vocation of serving other people. And manual work. Before we dismiss this theory of culture which includes manual work in the regimen of the complete life, it is well to recall the like belief of those pioneers of civilization and beautiful buildings, beautiful music, beautiful painting, the Benedictine communists, with their prudent Rule.†

Prince Peter Kropotkin (1842–1921), the junior contemporary of Count Tolstoi, is more definitely connected with the explicitly political movements of the time. In Switzerland, in 1872, he came into touch with the Anarchist movement of Count Michael Bakunin; sacrificed a scientific career; was imprisoned; lived in England; and returned to his now Bolshevist homeland to die in the bitter distresses of those first Revolutionary years.

It is not perhaps merely accidental that so many of the leaders of philosophic anarchism have been noblemen. Possibly an aristocratic upbringing especially inclines a man, otherwise radical, to view the prejudices of vested interests, not with fear or ferocity and a sense of the need for collective attack, but with undisturbed contempt.

Kropotkin retained his technical interests. Much of his best known book, *Fields, Factories and Workshops* (1898), consists of an exposition of technological discoveries, especially in food and agriculture, and the possibilities they hold in store for lessening the servile and merely mechanical labour of human beings. The elaboration of machinery may indeed lead to such division of labour as to reduce human beings to automata. Here Kropotkin, as humanist, challenges Adam Smith. This division of labour must go no farther. There must be a reintegration especially between hand and brain—*éducation intégrale.* More sanely than Tolstoi, Kropotkin states the case, in education and in adult-life, for manual training and an admixture of manual work;

* *Cf.* p. 446.

† *Cf.* p. 143.

for a departure from the Free Trade principles of national division of labour and international exploitation of finance; and for a return of the worker to the countryside.

Again the theme is education. The Moscow Technical Institute, which is more satisfactory than President White's liberal scheme at Cornell University,

perfectly well proved the possibility of combining a scientific education of a very high standard with the education which is necessary for becoming an excellent skilled labourer. . . . Under the pretext of division of labour, we have sharply separated the brain worker from the manual worker. . . . The parents either stupidly paralyse the passion [for invention], or do not know how to utilize it. Most of them despise manual work and prefer sending their children to the study of Roman history, or of Franklin's teachings about saving money, to seeing them at a work which is good for the "lower classes only." They thus do their best to render subsequent learning the more difficult.

Kropotkin is concerned, however, not only with a theory of education, but with one of psychology and of society. If all took their due share in production, the hours of labour could be greatly shortened; the standard of living raised—and this without drudgery, but by the development in communities, garden-factories, of the co-operative spirit. Men suffer from mental cowardice. What is required are

factories and workshops into which men, women and children will not be driven by hunger, but will be attracted by the desire of finding an activity suited to their tastes, and where, aided by the motor and the machine, they will choose the branch of activity which best suits their inclinations.

Let these factories and workshops be erected, not for making profits by selling shoddy or useless and noxious things to enslaved Africans, but to satisfy the unsatisfied needs of millions of Europeans. And again, you will be struck to see with what facility and in how short a time your needs of dress and of thousands of articles of luxury can be satisfied, when production is carried on for satisfying real needs rather than for satisfying shareholders by high profits or for pouring gold into the pockets of promoters and bogus directors. . . . Communist individualism is not a war of each against all; it is an opportunity for a full expansion of man's faculties, the superior development of whatever is original in him, the greatest fruitfulness of intelligence and will [*Cf.* von Humboldt and J. S. Mill, as also R. Owen].

It is noteworthy that Kropotkin also, towards the end, reverts to a line of Goethe's. "*Greift nur hinein in's volle Menschenleben*"—"Do but grasp full human life." It shows a different but a profounder insight than that of Spencer.

5

Count Michael Bakunin (1814–1876), influential in forming Kropotkin's views, yet wearing his anarchism with a difference, has little in common with the pacifist Tolstoi, and Thoreau, and much with the Russian Nihilists. In the case of Tolstoi one finds an emphatic repudiation of violence. Kropotkin is hesitant. The new society, co-operative, using the full results of technology, not so dissimilar from that visualized by the Count de St. Simon, might require for its inauguration a pressure against oppressors amounting to violence. Bakunin, inspired by the 1848 risings in Europe (and perhaps, it has been suggested, by dislike of his mother . . .), with bitter experience of the Russia of the Czardom, having been condemned to death both by Saxons and (for inciting the Czechs) by Austrians, and having tasted Siberian exile, is clear that oppression would require the purgation of force.

Michael Alexandrovich Bakunin, however, Russian, aristocratic, erratic, discontinuous, always in debt, was not only—he was indeed not at all—the organizer of force, although he intrigued in conspiracy. His greatest practical achievement, except in terms of personal inspiration, was so to alarm Marx about the possibility of a revolt of non-German Socialists against Marx's own stern patriarchate, that Marx preferred to kill his own child, the First Socialist International, by transferring the General Council (1872) to New York, rather than endure the humiliation of seeing it fall into the hands of Bakunin, as foster-parent. The euphemistically named "League of Peace and Freedom" (1867), to stir men to arms against war and tyranny, in which Bakunin was the leading spirit, was rather a secularistic than a socialistic organization. He is the exponent of a theory—when that theory can be disentangled from his obsessions about God, explicable but reminiscent of the preceding century—profound in its implications as an antidote to Plato. Bakunin is the father of Anarchism.

In his best known book, *God and the State* (posthumously published —an incomplete manuscript) he remarks, typically enough:

> I have wandered from my subject, because anger gets hold of me whenever I think of the base and criminal means which [governments] employ to keep the nations in perpetual slavery, undoubtedly that they may be the better able to fleece them. Of what consequence are the crimes of all the Tropmanns in the world compared with this crime of treason against humanity committed daily, in broad day, over the whole surface of the civilized world, by those who dare to call themselves the guardians and the fathers of the people? I return to the myth of original sin.

Bakunin is much preoccupied with Original Sin—but in a novel manner. The Anti-God zeal which consumed the recent rulers of Russia finds its explanation in his writings. He regarded a church as a temperance reformer might a gin-shop. It is obvious that, for Bakunin, God is very like the Czar. Thus he is able to explain quite simply how the Czar is like God, a tyrant.

The materialists, Bakunin alleges, start with matter and there is an evolution steadily upwards to humanity: an ascent of man. The idealists, he asserts, begin with God or the Idea; then by a *salto mortale* God makes matter and then the matter (it is the Hegelian philosophy Bakunin is sketching) is impregnated with divine mind: but God who fell down into matter takes several millennia to recover consciousness. And even when man has the divine grace in him, he is still a miserable worm compared with the Omnipotent; and most of his kind (although a few may "find salvation") are damned to hell. Now this religion, says Bakunin, is designed to humiliate humanity, and menaces liberty. Bakunin, as much as Rousseau or Tolstoi, is a romantic about the simple life and an irrationalist. Specifically Bakunin praises, against sophistication, "the solid, barbarian elements." Instinctive Nature plus Benevolence plus Courage—that is the prescription.

Bakunin points out, in passing, [and probably rightly] the intimate connection between much so-called idealism and cruelty. The basis of all advance is the power to think—eating the Tree of Knowledge or Science—and the desire to rebel—Liberty. Religion represses both. Against religion—but also be it noted, against Marx—Bakunin declares himself a man without a dogma. "I cleave to no system. I am a seeker." This did not prevent him from expressing very odd sentiments about the moral importance, for an anarchist, of *voluntarily conforming* to [the right] public opinion and a strange hankering admiration of the Jesuits. His excuse must be that the other great sentimental romantic, Rousseau, had the same tendencies.

Having flayed, in the spirit of Paine, priests and kings Bakunin, the irrationalist, passes on to a third and fresher Tolstoiian assault—against the pontiffs of science itself. What he has to say is highly important. Apparently he feels that a free man is not abbreviated in his liberty by admitting the authority of "natural laws." They are indeed (why not God also?) "inherent in us."

As to the pressure upon individuals of "Public Opinion"—that "Public Opinion" or Herd Feeling of which J. S. Mill walked in fear, and of which the final, violent expression is lynch-law—apparently public opinion would be improved, granted only the social condition of "equality, the supreme condition of liberty and humanity." Then it would be possible "to make *all needs really solidary,* and cause the material and social interests of each to conform to the human duties of each." Solidary, instinctive anarchism . . . There was, however, a real danger, not in "science," but in men of science assuming the technological prerogative of direction, being a new priesthood and commissarate; as Comte suggested—yes, and for that matter, in Marx assuming it . . .

> The Church will no longer call itself Church; it will call itself School. . . . The State will no longer call itself Monarchy; it will call itself Republic: but it will be none the less the State—that is, a tutelage officially and regularly established by a minority of competent men, men of virtuous genius or talent, who will watch and guide the conduct of this great, incorrigible, and terrible child, the people. . . . We accept all natural authorities and all influences of fact, but none of right. . . . *Of all despotisms that of the doctrinaires or inspired religionists is the worst.* They are so jealous of the glory of their God and of the triumph of their idea that they have no heart left for the liberty or the dignity or even the suffering of living men, of real men. . . . The government of science and of men of science, even be they positivists, disciples of Auguste Comte, or, a few, disciples of the *doctrinaire* school of German Communism, cannot fail to be impotent, ridiculous, inhuman, cruel, oppressive, exploiting, maleficent. We may say of men of science, *as such,* what I have said of theologians and metaphysicians: they have neither sense nor heart for individual and living beings.

Bakunin pursues the elaboration of his doctrine in his thesis on *Federalism, Socialism and Anti-theologism,* submitted to the Central Committee of the League of Peace and Liberty, in 1867, and in his *Historical Sophisms of the Doctrinaire School of German Communists* (1872; significantly still unpublished). He has the merit of being one of the first to point out the dangers of a *political* theology—one of the first after Burke!

In his argument, however, against the priests of science, Bakunin is guilty of ambiguity. He apparently believes that economic and social equality will harmonize—all ambition and will to power forgotten—the divergent interests of human beings. He admits, however, explicitly that human beings will *not* be equal in intelligence or knowledge. Why should not then the man who knows more, the more conscious worker for human well-being, guide the man who knows less? In effect, Bakunin admits that human ambition and love of exercising authority will play their part—even with men of science, as with the Jesuits of Paraguay—and that, as Mill said, no man can be trusted not to abuse irresponsible power, least of all a priesthood, least of all a soviet of savants, an omniscient, intolerant priesthood of science.

Behind the screens of noble abstractions, Bakunin detected at work a new species of sinister interests, vampires.

> What I preach then is, to a certain extent, the revolt of life against science, or rather against the government of science, not to destroy science—*that would be high treason to humanity—but to remand it to its place* so that it can never leave it again. Until now all human history has been only a perpetual and *bloody immolation of millions of poor human beings in honour of some pitiless abstraction*—God, country, power of State, national honor, historic rights, judicial rights, political liberty, public welfare . . . devouring abstractions, *the vampires of history*, ever nourished upon human blood. . . . By a judicious criticism which [natural science, as distinct from metaphysics] can and finally will be forced to pass upon itself, it would understand, on the contrary, that it is only a means for the realization of a much higher object—that of the complete humanization of the *real* situation of the *real* individuals who are born, who live, and who die, on earth.

If Michael Bakunin had written nothing else but these words, for their wisdom the great Anarchist would deserve a place in history.

Bakunin has direct political influence in Russia and in Spain to this day. His federalist theories agreed with the federal nationalism of such writers as Pi y Margal, whose *Nationalities* merits attention. His proletarian theory inspires the theory of proletarian evolution of Anselmo Lorenzo. In the uplands of Spain in 1937 small village communities, run on Kropotkinite co-operative principles, were to be found as curiosities. But Spanish and, especially, Catalan Anarchism became a force by fusion with Syndicalism, to which we shall return.* Contemplating Spanish Anarchism and Communism, the Spanish Anarchist Minister of Justice of 1937, Garcia Oliver, said to the writer: "We co-operate now; but the problem for the politics of the future is —Liberty or Authority?"

We return to the query of Lao-tze at the beginning of the ages of history: "Why are the people so restless? Because there is so much government."

It is significant that the same American publishing house, Emma Goldman's, which published Bakunin, published the writings, somewhat different in their political progeny, of Max Stirner and of Friedrich Nietzsche. To these, in a different context, we shall return; as we shall to the Pragmatist exponents of liberal humanism and to the

* *Cf.* p. 653.

philosophic humanism of Earl Russell (Bertrand Russell).* It is, however, impossible to appreciate these philosophies until we have studied that great Collectivist Movement—confronting the classical individualism of Milton, Locke, Jefferson, Paine and the Mills—which culminated in Michael Bakunin's revolutionary colleague but philosophical and personal enemy, Karl Marx.

BIBLIOGRAPHICAL NOTE

Michael Bakunin: *God and the State.*
Van Wyck Brooks: *The Flowering of New England,* 1936.
W. Hastie: *Political Philosophy of Kant,* 1891.
*P. Kropotkin: *Fields, Factories and Workshops,* 1898.
*Herbert Spencer: *The Man versus the State,* 1884.
H. D. Thoreau: *Essays.*

* *Cf.* p. 756.